the AMAZING SPIDER-MAN

Writer: **J. MICHAEL STRACZYNSKI**
Pencils: **JOHN ROMITA JR.**
Inks: **SCOTT HANNA**
Colors: **DAN KEMP** & **AVALON STUDIOS**
Letters: **RS** & **COMICRAFT'S WES ABBOTT**
& **JIMMY BETANCOURT**
Cover Art: **J. SCOTT CAMPBELL** & **TIM TOWNSEND**
(Issues #30-35), **KAARE ANDREWS** (Issues #37-38),
JASON PEARSON (Issues #39-42) and
JOHN ROMITA JR. (Issues #43-45)
Assistant Editor: **JOHN MIESEGAES**
Editor: **AXEL ALONSO**

Collection Editor: **JENNIFER GRÜNWALD**
Editorial Assistant: **ALEX STARBUCK**
Assistant Editors: **CORY LEVINE** & **JOHN DENNING**
Editor, Special Projects: **MARK D. BEAZLEY**
Senior Editor, Special Projects: **JEFF YOUNGQUIST**
Senior Vice President of Sales: **DAVID GABRIEL**

Editor in Chief: **JOE QUESADA**
Publisher: **DAN BUCKLEY**
Executive Producer: **ALAN FINE**

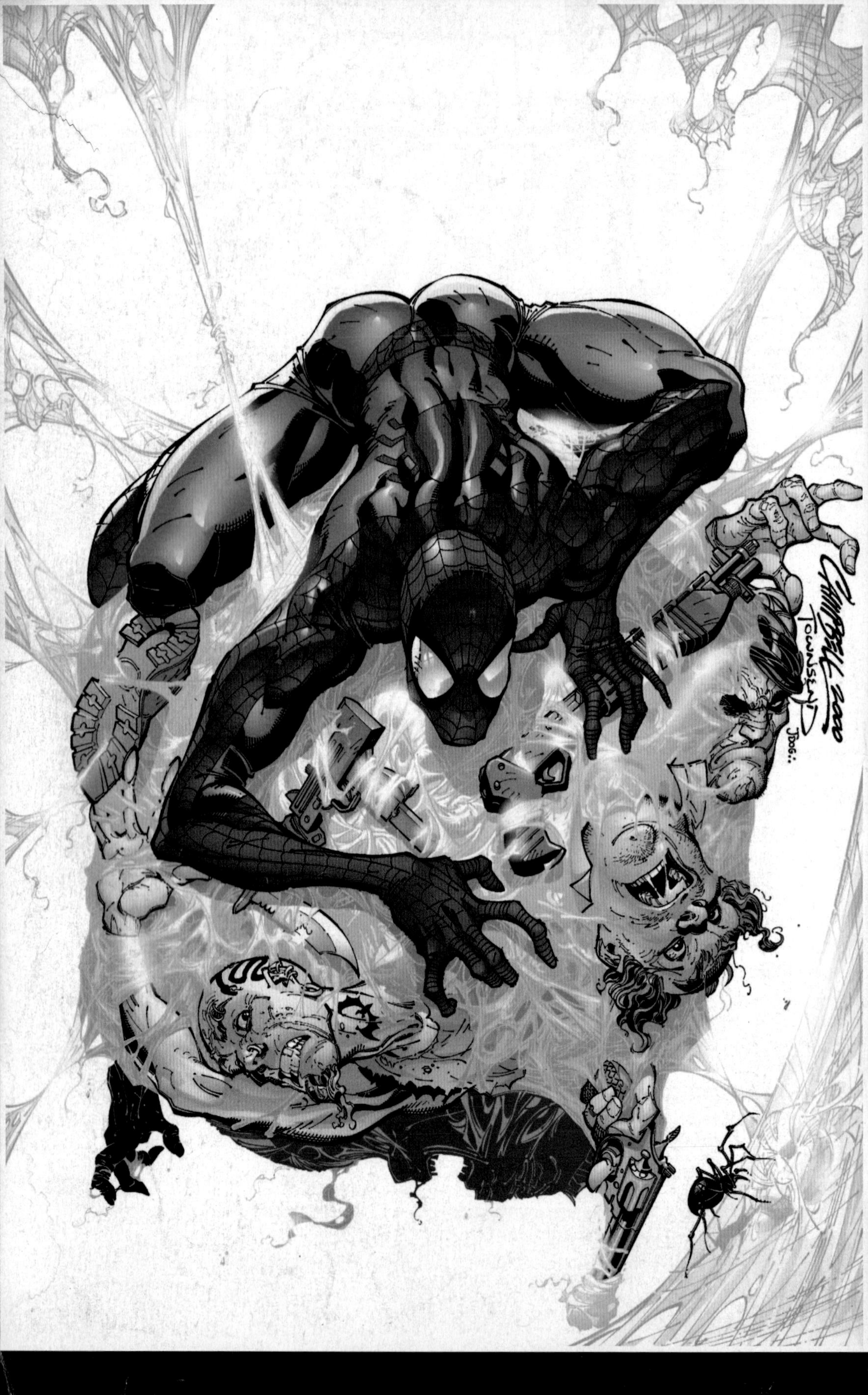

AMAZING SPIDER-MAN #30

AT A DEMONSTRATION ON RADIATION, HIGH SCHOOL STUDENT PETER PARKER WAS BITTEN BY AN IRRADIATED SPIDER FROM WHICH HE GAINED THE ARACHNID'S INCREDIBLE ABILITIES. WHEN A BURGLAR KILLED HIS BELOVED UNCLE BEN, A GRIEF-STRICKEN PETER VOWED TO USE HIS GREAT POWERS IN THE SERVICE OF HIS FELLOW MAN, BECAUSE HE LEARNED AN INVALUABLE LESSON: WITH GREAT POWER THERE MUST ALSO COME GREAT RESPONSIBILITY.

STAN LEE PRESENTS: THE AMAZING SPIDER-MAN

RING RING

CLICK

HI, THIS IS PETER. I'M STILL SETTLING INTO MY NEW DIGS, SO I'M EITHER WORKING, OUT FORAGING FOR FOOD, OR TRAPPED UNDER DEBRIS. LEAVE A MESSAGE AND I'LL GET BACK TO YOU WHEN THE DUST CLEARS.

BEEEEEP

PETER, THIS IS YOUR AUNT MAY. I KNOW YOU'RE GOING THROUGH A LOT RIGHT NOW, WITH MARY JANE LEAVING, AND THE MOVE, AND... WELL, I JUST WANTED TO SEE IF YOU WERE OKAY.

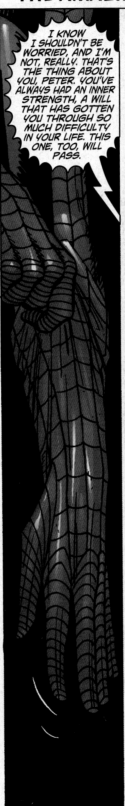

I KNOW I SHOULDN'T BE WORRIED, AND I'M NOT, REALLY. THAT'S THE THING ABOUT YOU, PETER. YOU'VE ALWAYS HAD AN INNER STRENGTH, A WILL THAT HAS GOTTEN YOU THROUGH SO MUCH DIFFICULTY IN YOUR LIFE. THIS ONE, TOO, WILL PASS.

MEANWHILE, IF YOU NEED TO TALK, YOU KNOW WHERE TO FIND ME.

GOOD NIGHT, PETER. I'LL TALK TO YOU IN THE MORNING.

BEEEEEP

SHE'S A GOOD WOMAN. I SOMETIMES THINK THERE ISN'T A SONAR IN EXISTENCE THAT CAN SOUND OUT THE DEPTH OF HER COMPASSION.

BUT RIGHT NOW, THAT ISN'T WHAT I NEED. WHAT I NEED...

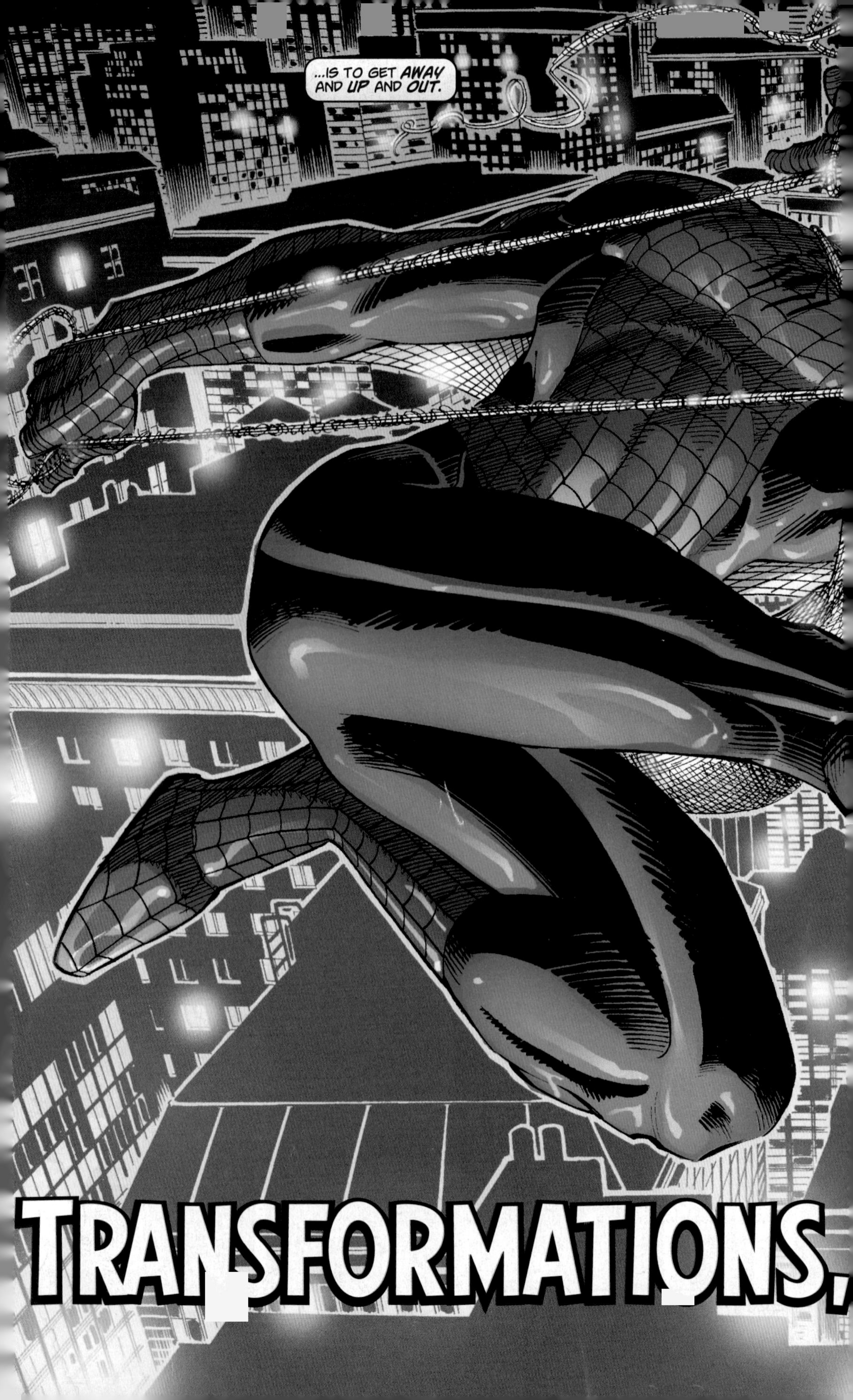
...IS TO GET AWAY AND UP AND OUT.
TRANSFORMATIONS,

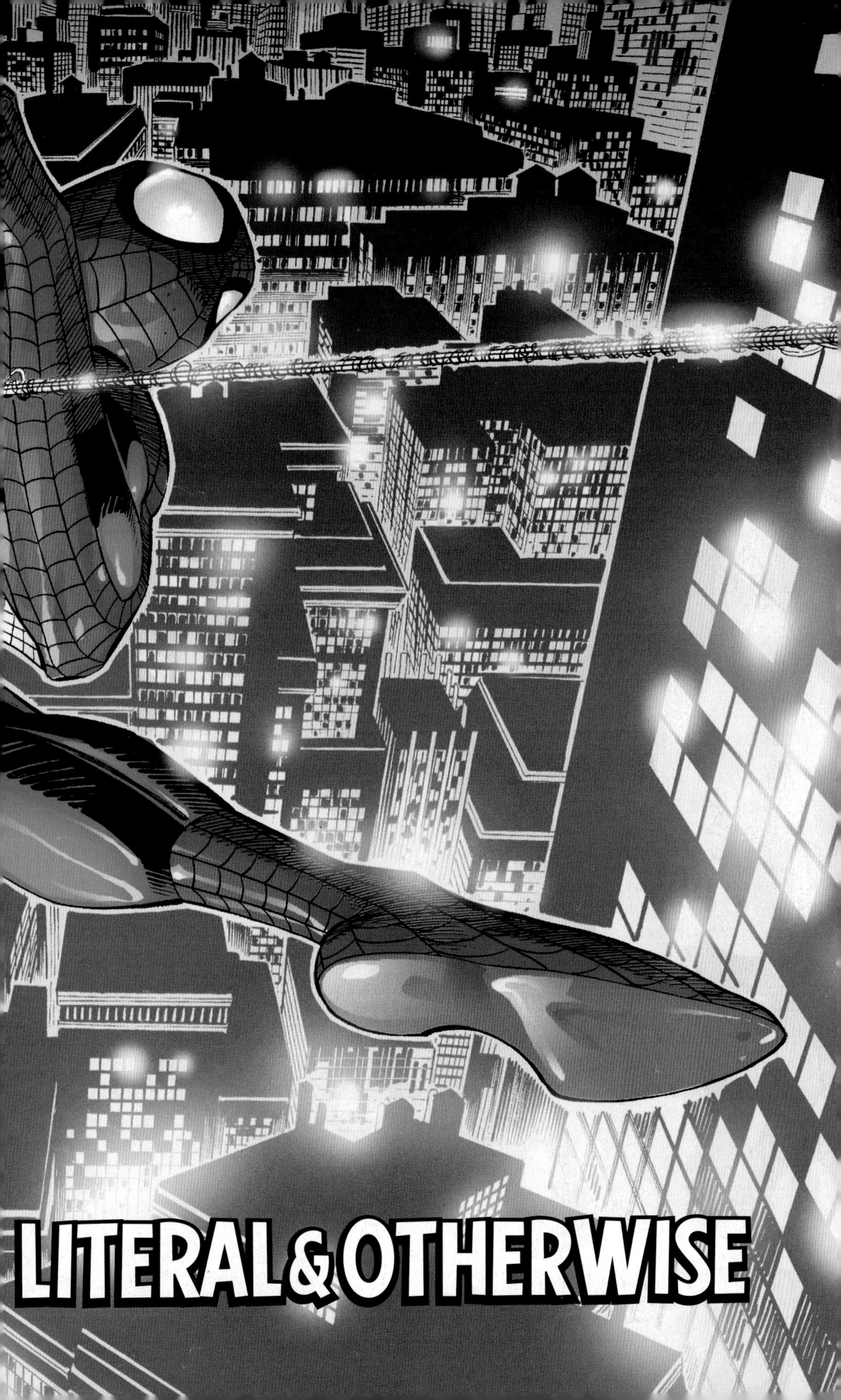
LITERAL & OTHERWISE

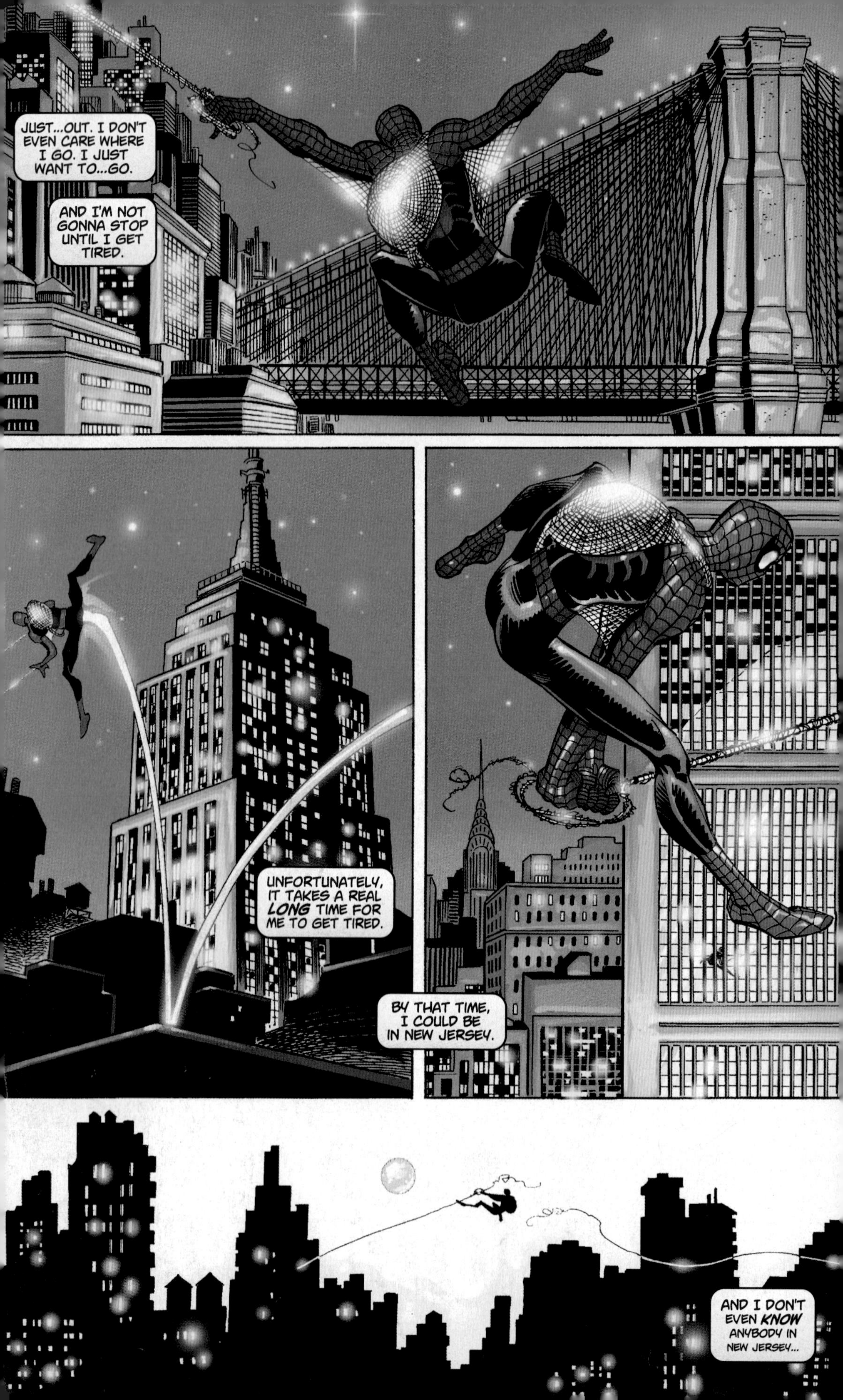
JUST...OUT. I DON'T EVEN CARE WHERE I GO. I JUST WANT TO...GO.
AND I'M NOT GONNA STOP UNTIL I GET TIRED.
UNFORTUNATELY, IT TAKES A REAL LONG TIME FOR ME TO GET TIRED.
BY THAT TIME, I COULD BE IN NEW JERSEY.
AND I DON'T EVEN KNOW ANYBODY IN NEW JERSEY...

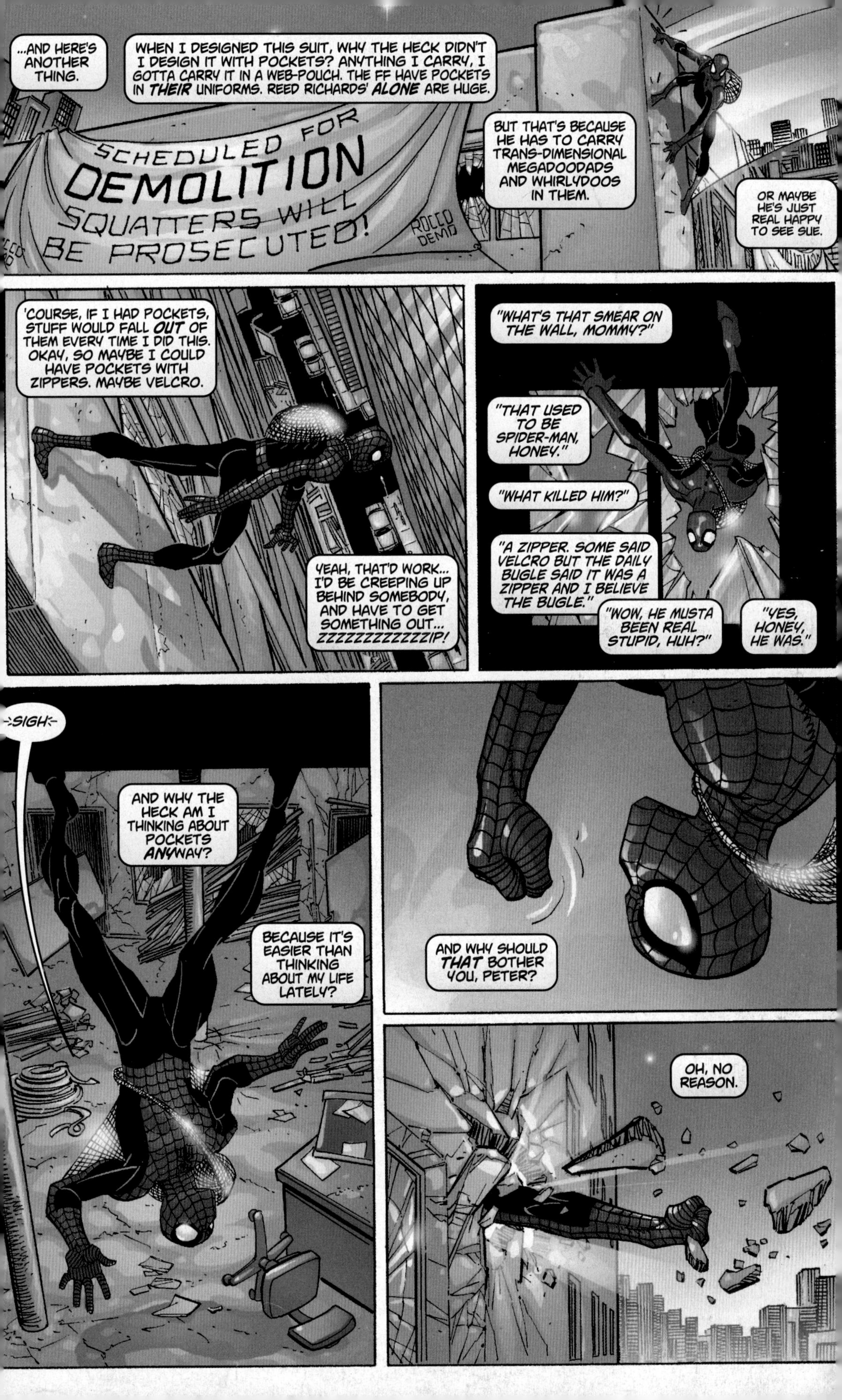
...AND HERE'S ANOTHER THING.
WHEN I DESIGNED THIS SUIT, WHY THE HECK DIDN'T I DESIGN IT WITH POCKETS? ANYTHING I CARRY, I GOTTA CARRY IT IN A WEB-POUCH. THE FF HAVE POCKETS IN ***THEIR*** UNIFORMS. REED RICHARDS' ***ALONE*** ARE HUGE.
SCHEDULED FOR DEMOLITION SQUATTERS WILL BE PROSECUTED!
ROCCO DEMO
BUT THAT'S BECAUSE HE HAS TO CARRY TRANS-DIMENSIONAL MEGADOODADS AND WHIRLYDOOS IN THEM.
OR MAYBE HE'S JUST REAL HAPPY TO SEE SUE.
'COURSE, IF I HAD POCKETS, STUFF WOULD FALL ***OUT*** OF THEM EVERY TIME I DID THIS. OKAY, SO MAYBE I COULD HAVE POCKETS WITH ZIPPERS. MAYBE VELCRO.
YEAH, THAT'D WORK... I'D BE CREEPING UP BEHIND SOMEBODY, AND HAVE TO GET SOMETHING OUT... ZZZZZZZZZZZZZIP!
"WHAT'S THAT SMEAR ON THE WALL, MOMMY?"
"THAT USED TO BE SPIDER-MAN, HONEY."
"WHAT KILLED HIM?"
"A ZIPPER. SOME SAID VELCRO BUT THE DAILY BUGLE SAID IT WAS A ZIPPER AND I BELIEVE THE BUGLE."
"WOW, HE MUSTA BEEN REAL STUPID, HUH?"
"YES, HONEY, HE WAS."
-SIGH-
AND WHY THE HECK AM I THINKING ABOUT POCKETS ***ANY***WAY?
BECAUSE IT'S EASIER THAN THINKING ABOUT MY LIFE LATELY?
AND WHY SHOULD ***THAT*** BOTHER YOU, PETER?
OH, NO REASON.

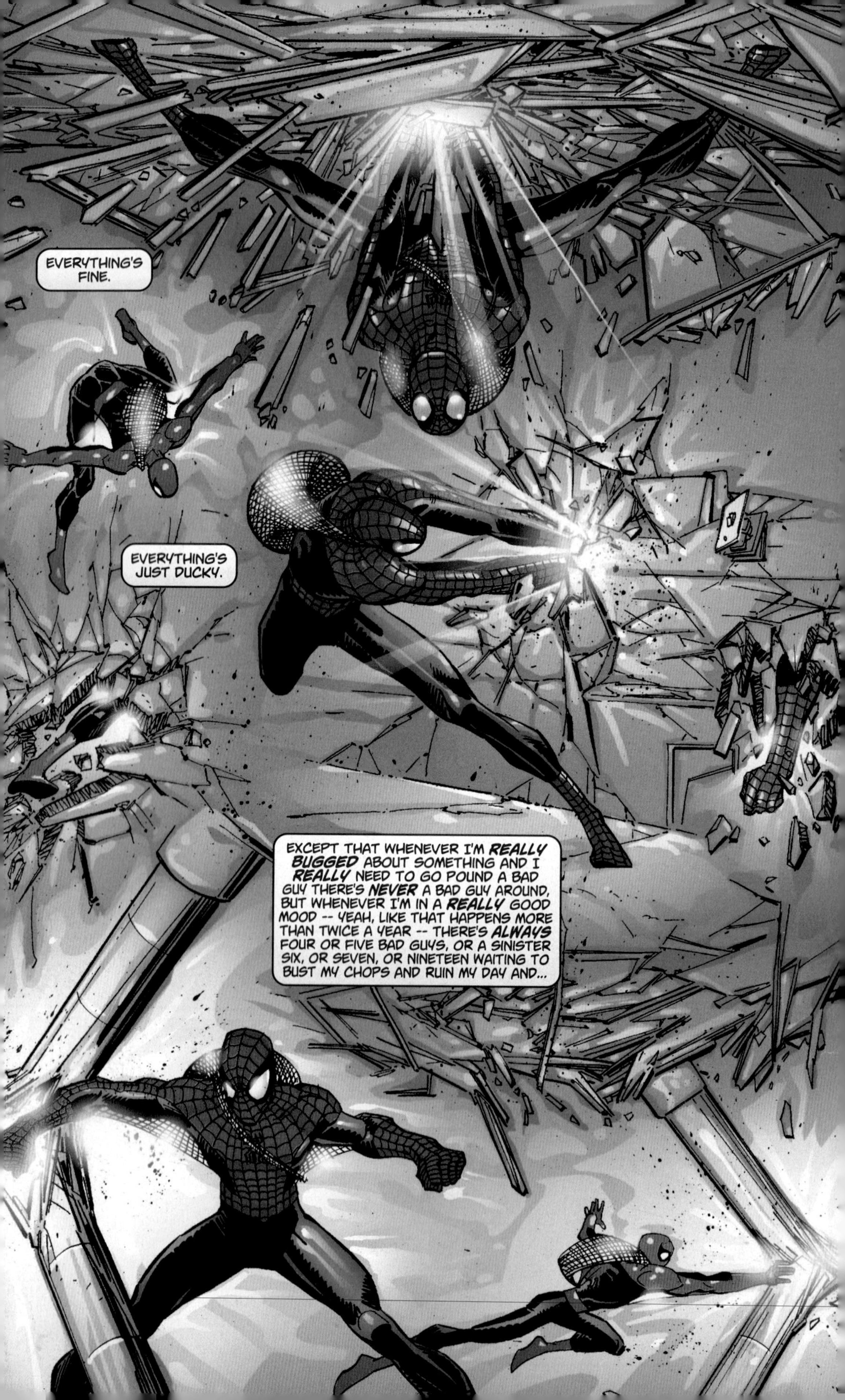
EVERYTHING'S FINE.
EVERYTHING'S JUST DUCKY.
EXCEPT THAT WHENEVER I'M REALLY BUGGED ABOUT SOMETHING AND I REALLY NEED TO GO POUND A BAD GUY THERE'S NEVER A BAD GUY AROUND, BUT WHENEVER I'M IN A REALLY GOOD MOOD -- YEAH, LIKE THAT HAPPENS MORE THAN TWICE A YEAR -- THERE'S ALWAYS FOUR OR FIVE BAD GUYS, OR A SINISTER SIX, OR SEVEN, OR NINETEEN WAITING TO BUST MY CHOPS AND RUIN MY DAY AND...

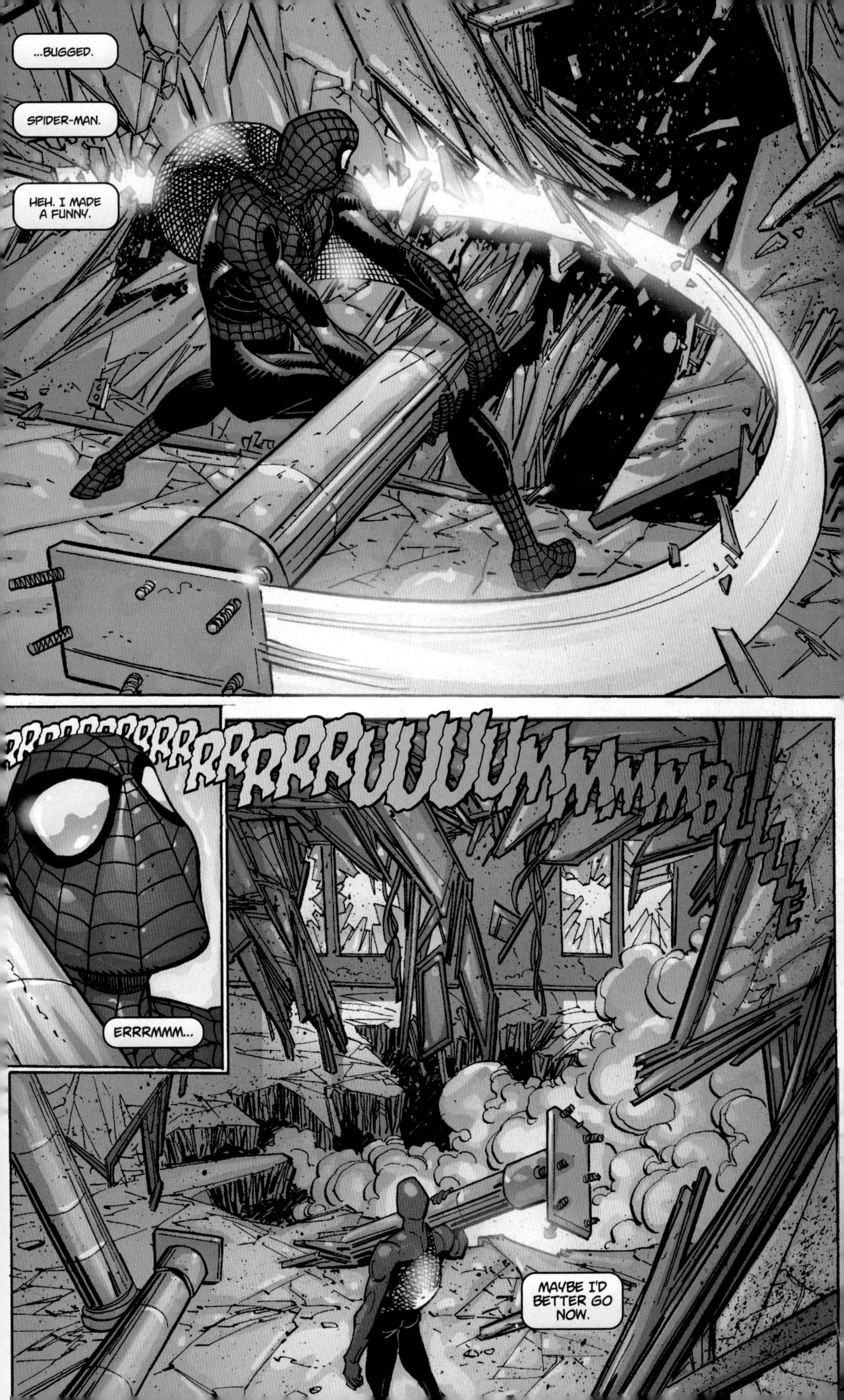

...BUGGED.
SPIDER-MAN.
HEH. I MADE A FUNNY.
RRRRRRRRRRRRRRRRRUUUUMMMMBLLLE
ERRRMMM...
MAYBE I'D BETTER GO NOW.

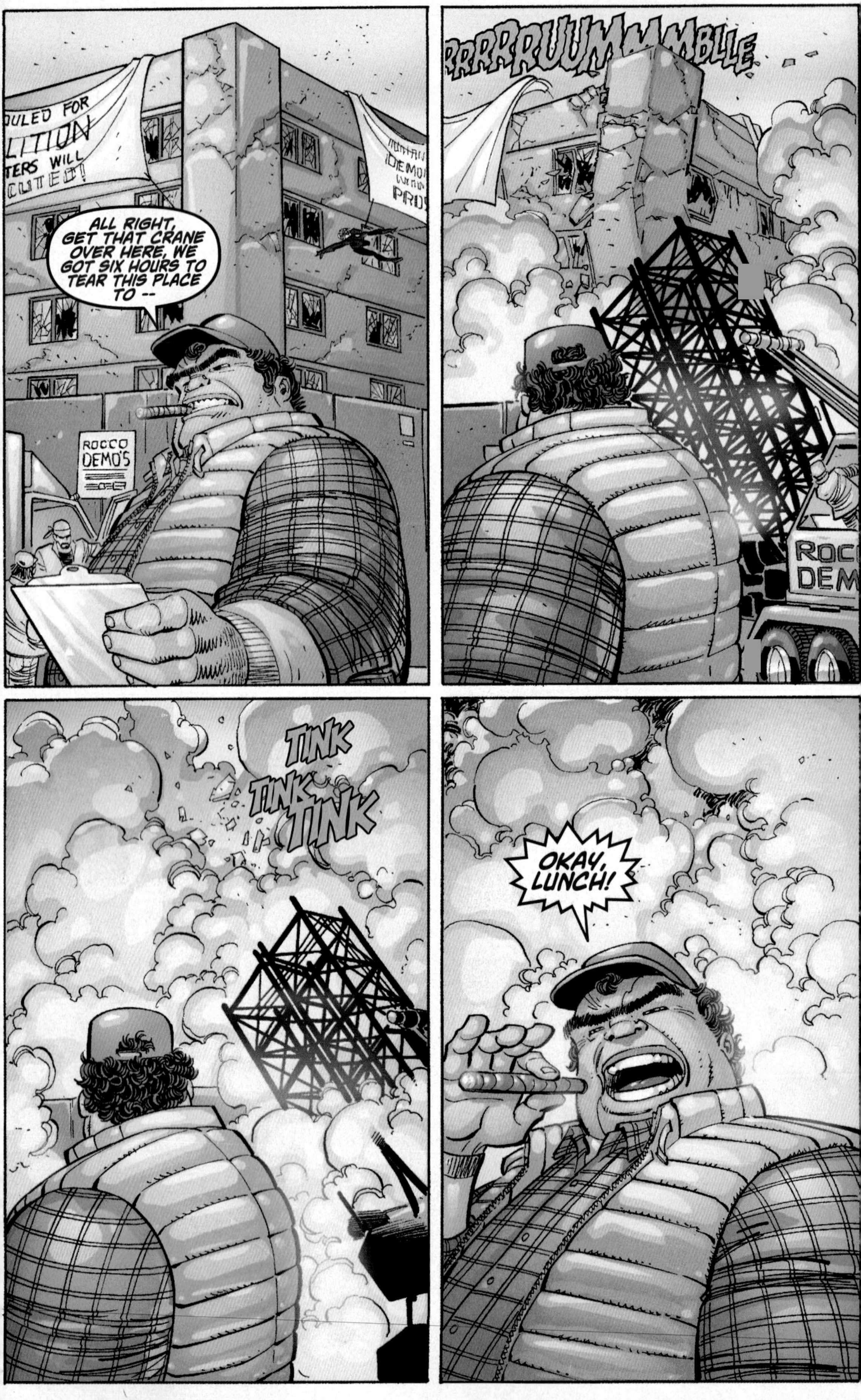

ALL RIGHT, GET THAT CRANE OVER HERE, WE GOT SIX HOURS TO TEAR THIS PLACE TO --
ROCCO DEMO'S
RRRRRUUMMMBLLE
ROCC DEM
TINK
TINK TINK
OKAY, LUNCH!

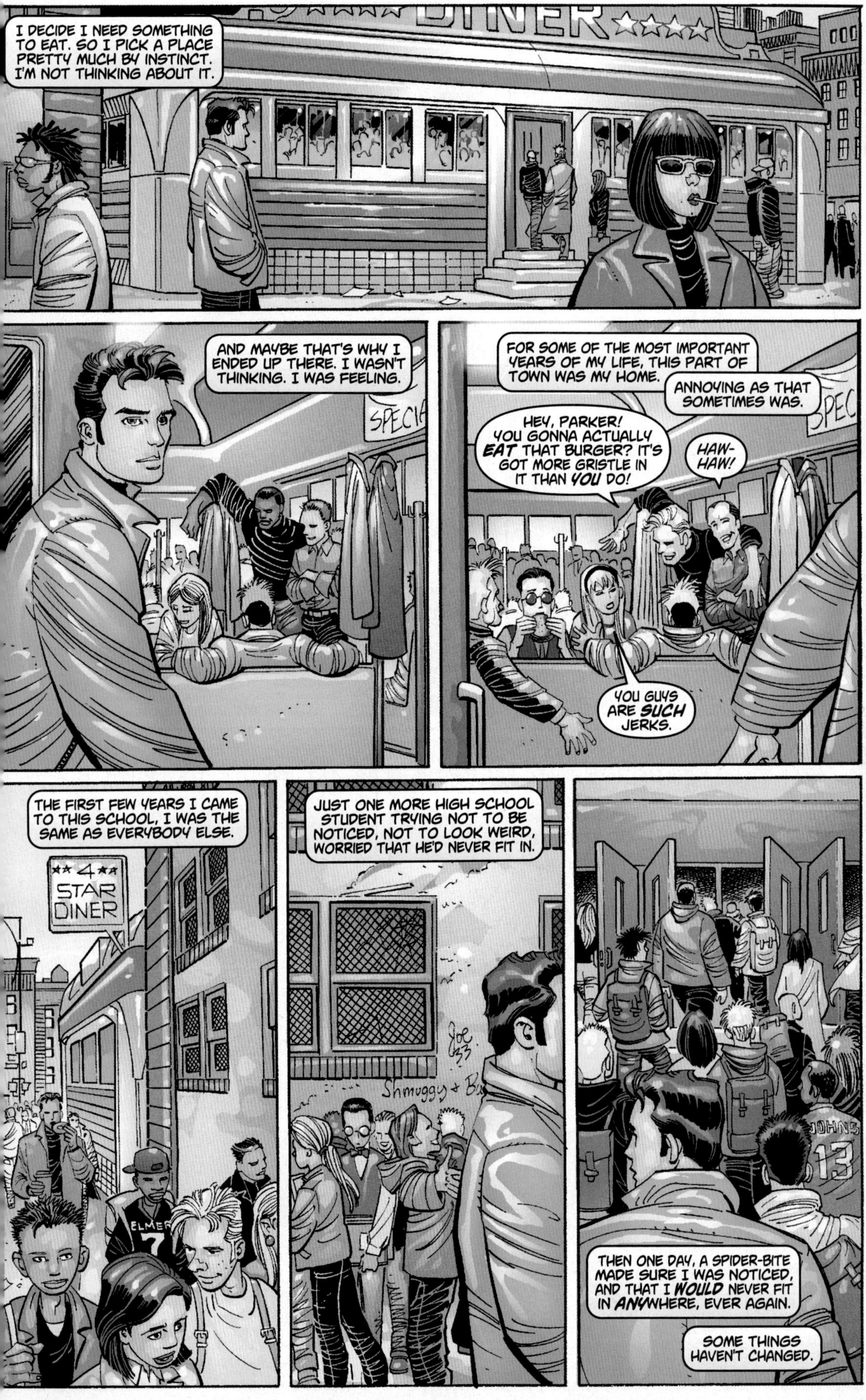

★★★★ DINER ★★★★
I DECIDE I NEED SOMETHING TO EAT. SO I PICK A PLACE PRETTY MUCH BY INSTINCT. I'M NOT THINKING ABOUT IT.
AND MAYBE THAT'S WHY I ENDED UP THERE. I WASN'T THINKING. I WAS FEELING.
FOR SOME OF THE MOST IMPORTANT YEARS OF MY LIFE, THIS PART OF TOWN WAS MY HOME.
ANNOYING AS THAT SOMETIMES WAS.
HEY, PARKER! YOU GONNA ACTUALLY EAT THAT BURGER? IT'S GOT MORE GRISTLE IN IT THAN YOU DO!
HAW-HAW!
YOU GUYS ARE SUCH JERKS.
THE FIRST FEW YEARS I CAME TO THIS SCHOOL, I WAS THE SAME AS EVERYBODY ELSE.
★★ 4 ★★ STAR DINER
ELMER 7
JUST ONE MORE HIGH SCHOOL STUDENT TRYING NOT TO BE NOTICED, NOT TO LOOK WEIRD, WORRIED THAT HE'D NEVER FIT IN.
JOHNS 13
THEN ONE DAY, A SPIDER-BITE MADE SURE I WAS NOTICED, AND THAT I WOULD NEVER FIT IN ANYWHERE, EVER AGAIN.
SOME THINGS HAVEN'T CHANGED.

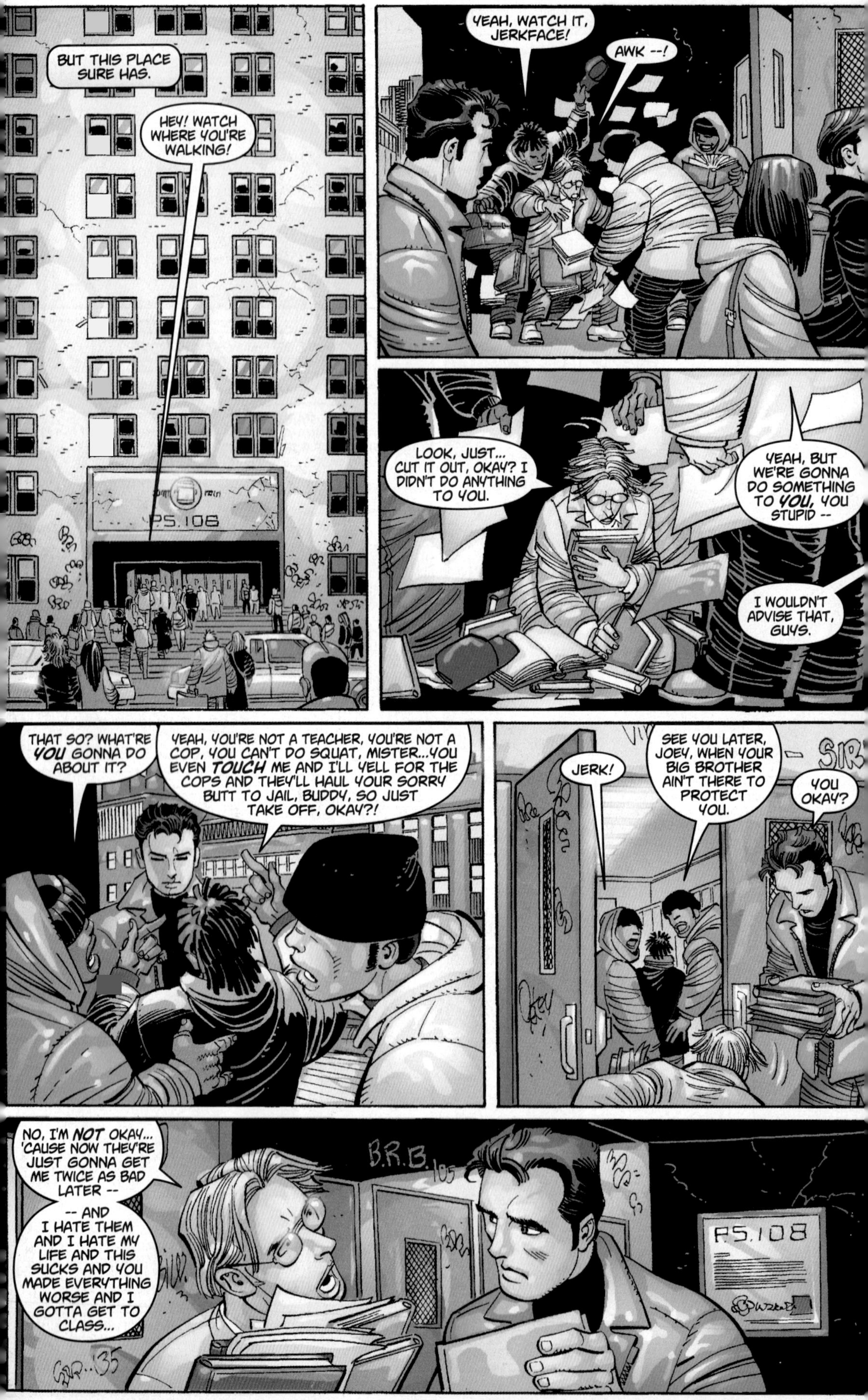
BUT THIS PLACE SURE HAS.
HEY! WATCH WHERE YOU'RE WALKING!
P.S. 108
YEAH, WATCH IT, JERKFACE!
AWK --!
LOOK, JUST... CUT IT OUT, OKAY? I DIDN'T DO ANYTHING TO YOU.
YEAH, BUT WE'RE GONNA DO SOMETHING TO *YOU,* YOU STUPID --
I WOULDN'T ADVISE THAT, GUYS.
THAT SO? WHAT'RE *YOU* GONNA DO ABOUT IT?
YEAH, YOU'RE NOT A TEACHER, YOU'RE NOT A COP, YOU CAN'T DO SQUAT, MISTER...YOU EVEN *TOUCH* ME AND I'LL YELL FOR THE COPS AND THEY'LL HAUL YOUR SORRY BUTT TO JAIL, BUDDY, SO JUST TAKE OFF, OKAY?!
JERK!
SEE YOU LATER, JOEY, WHEN YOUR BIG BROTHER AIN'T THERE TO PROTECT YOU.
YOU OKAY?
NO, I'M *NOT* OKAY... 'CAUSE NOW THEY'RE JUST GONNA GET ME TWICE AS BAD LATER --
-- AND I HATE THEM AND I HATE MY LIFE AND THIS SUCKS AND YOU MADE EVERYTHING WORSE AND I GOTTA GET TO CLASS...
B.R.B.
P.S. 108

I... I MEAN... I'M SORRY, I --

I SAW WHAT HAPPENED THERE, BUDDY.

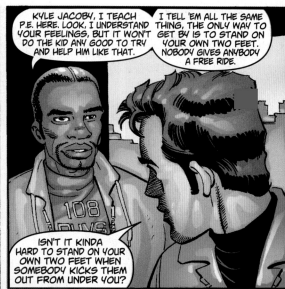

KYLE JACOBY, I TEACH P.E. HERE. LOOK, I UNDERSTAND YOUR FEELINGS, BUT IT WON'T DO THE KID ANY GOOD TO TRY AND HELP HIM LIKE THAT.

I TELL 'EM ALL THE SAME THING, THE ONLY WAY TO GET BY IS TO STAND ON YOUR OWN TWO FEET. NOBODY GIVES ANYBODY A FREE RIDE.

ISN'T IT KINDA HARD TO STAND ON YOUR OWN TWO FEET WHEN SOMEBODY KICKS THEM OUT FROM UNDER YOU?

BUDDY, THERE'S ALWAYS SOMEBODY TRYING TO KICK YOUR FEET OUT FROM UNDER YOU. YOU JUST GOTTA KICK FIRST. JOEY'S GOTTA LEARN THAT FOR HIMSELF.

EVOLVE OR DIE, YOU KNOW?

ESPECIALLY IN A DUMP LIKE THIS. IT WAS QUITE A PLACE ONCE. BUT THINGS CHANGE, YOU KNOW?

HE'S RIGHT. SOME THINGS CHANGE.

BUT SOME THINGS NEVER CHANGE.

UNLESS SOMEBODY MAKES THEM CHANGE.

NOW, I'M NOT SAYING I'M THE KIND OF GUY WHO CARRIES A GRUDGE. FAR BE IT FOR ME TO *EVER* CARRY A GRUDGE.

BUT I FIGURE, YOU HANG OUT LONG ENOUGH, YOU WATCH SOME PEOPLE, OH, I DUNNO, RANDOMLY...AND SONOVAGUN, AN OPPORTUNITY PRESENTS ITSELF FOR THE UNIVERSE TO BALANCE THINGS OUT.

AS SOMEBODY ONCE SAID, CHANCE FAVORS THE PREPARED MIND.

C'MON MAN, WE AIN'T GOT ALL DAY.

JUST A SEC, I ALMOST GOT IT --

UUUHHHHH...

BOO.

AAAAAGGGGHHHHH!

SLOW DOWN! I CAN'T KEEP UP! AWK!

JEEZ, MAN, I WET 'EM, SLOW DOWN...

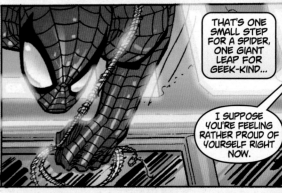

THAT'S ONE SMALL STEP FOR A SPIDER, ONE GIANT LEAP FOR GEEK-KIND...

I SUPPOSE YOU'RE FEELING RATHER PROUD OF YOURSELF RIGHT NOW.

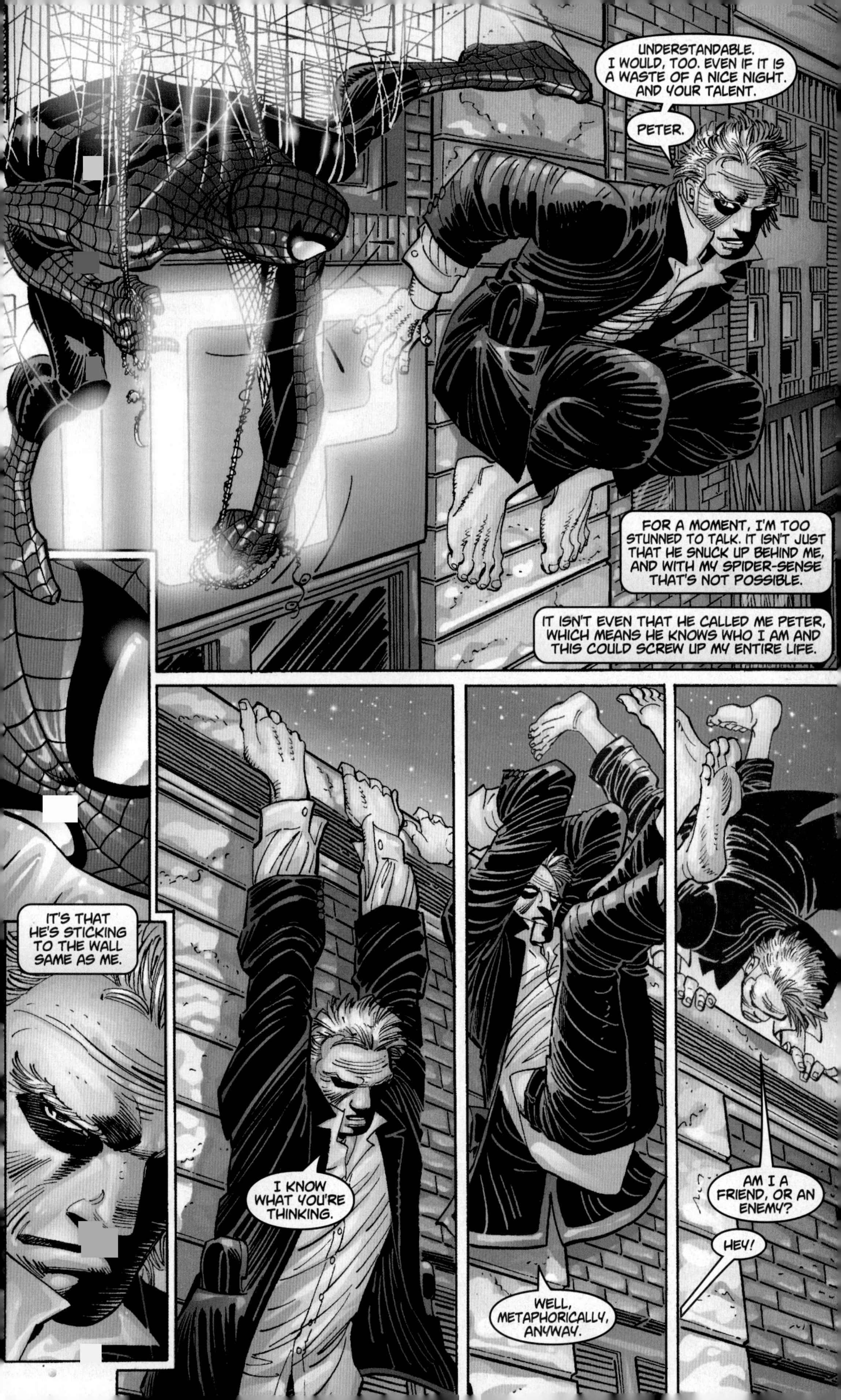

UNDERSTANDABLE. I WOULD, TOO. EVEN IF IT IS A WASTE OF A NICE NIGHT. AND YOUR TALENT.
PETER.
FOR A MOMENT, I'M TOO STUNNED TO TALK. IT ISN'T JUST THAT HE SNUCK UP BEHIND ME, AND WITH MY SPIDER-SENSE THAT'S NOT POSSIBLE.
IT ISN'T EVEN THAT HE CALLED ME PETER, WHICH MEANS HE KNOWS WHO I AM AND THIS COULD SCREW UP MY ENTIRE LIFE.
IT'S THAT HE'S STICKING TO THE WALL SAME AS ME.
I KNOW WHAT YOU'RE THINKING.
WELL, METAPHORICALLY, ANYWAY.
AM I A FRIEND, OR AN ENEMY?
HEY!

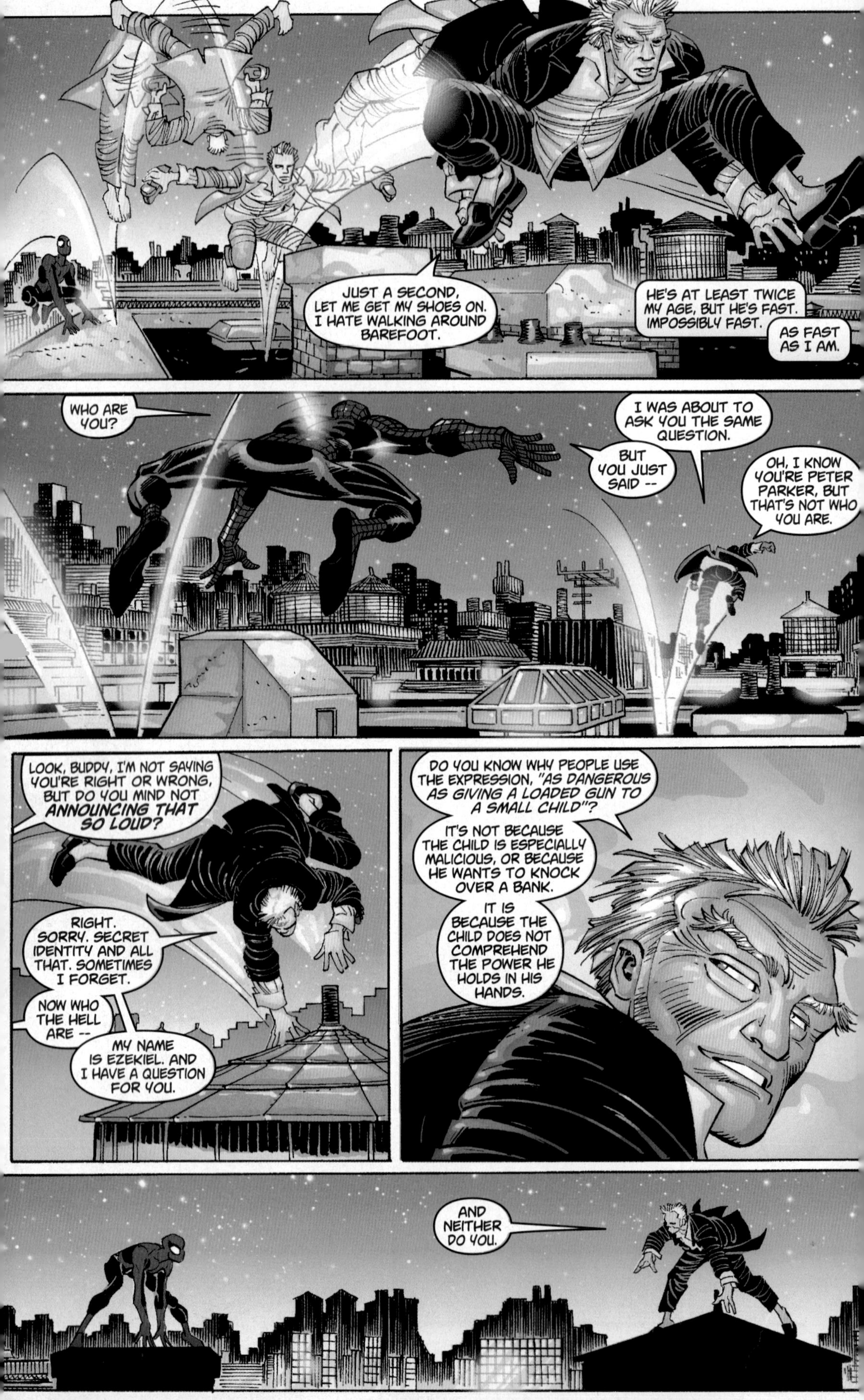

JUST A SECOND, LET ME GET MY SHOES ON. I HATE WALKING AROUND BAREFOOT.
HE'S AT LEAST TWICE MY AGE, BUT HE'S FAST. IMPOSSIBLY FAST.
AS FAST AS I AM.
WHO ARE YOU?
I WAS ABOUT TO ASK YOU THE SAME QUESTION.
BUT YOU JUST SAID --
OH, I KNOW YOU'RE PETER PARKER, BUT THAT'S NOT WHO YOU ARE.
LOOK, BUDDY, I'M NOT SAYING YOU'RE RIGHT OR WRONG, BUT DO YOU MIND NOT ANNOUNCING THAT SO LOUD?
RIGHT. SORRY. SECRET IDENTITY AND ALL THAT. SOMETIMES I FORGET.
NOW WHO THE HELL ARE --
MY NAME IS EZEKIEL. AND I HAVE A QUESTION FOR YOU.
DO YOU KNOW WHY PEOPLE USE THE EXPRESSION, "AS DANGEROUS AS GIVING A LOADED GUN TO A SMALL CHILD"?
IT'S NOT BECAUSE THE CHILD IS ESPECIALLY MALICIOUS, OR BECAUSE HE WANTS TO KNOCK OVER A BANK.
IT IS BECAUSE THE CHILD DOES NOT COMPREHEND THE POWER HE HOLDS IN HIS HANDS.
AND NEITHER DO YOU.

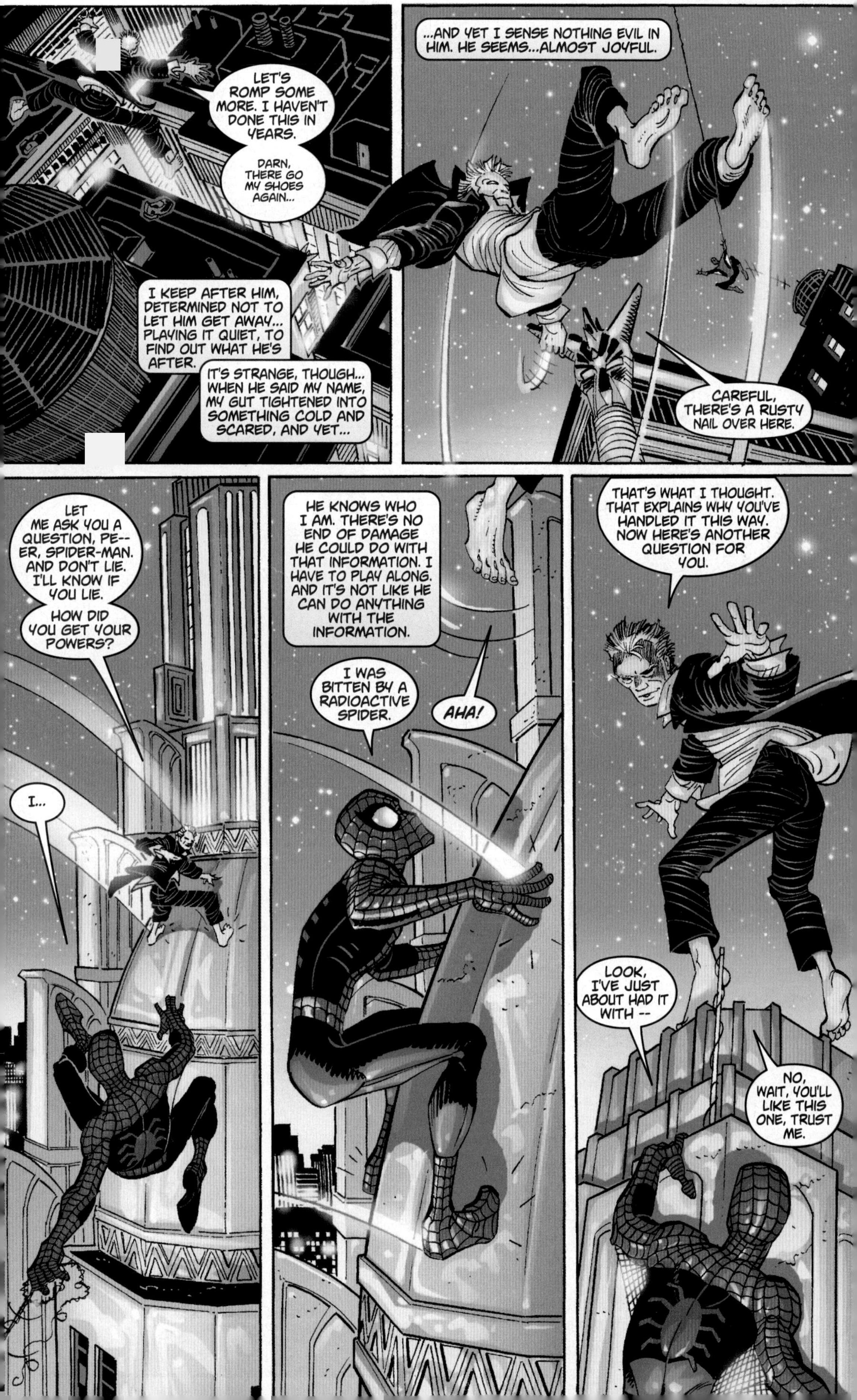
LET'S ROMP SOME MORE. I HAVEN'T DONE THIS IN YEARS.
DARN, THERE GO MY SHOES AGAIN...
I KEEP AFTER HIM, DETERMINED NOT TO LET HIM GET AWAY... PLAYING IT QUIET, TO FIND OUT WHAT HE'S AFTER.
IT'S STRANGE, THOUGH... WHEN HE SAID MY NAME, MY GUT TIGHTENED INTO SOMETHING COLD AND SCARED, AND YET...
...AND YET I SENSE NOTHING EVIL IN HIM. HE SEEMS...ALMOST JOYFUL.
CAREFUL, THERE'S A RUSTY NAIL OVER HERE.
LET ME ASK YOU A QUESTION, PE-- ER, SPIDER-MAN. AND DON'T LIE. I'LL KNOW IF YOU LIE.
HOW DID YOU GET YOUR POWERS?
I...
HE KNOWS WHO I AM. THERE'S NO END OF DAMAGE HE COULD DO WITH THAT INFORMATION. I HAVE TO PLAY ALONG. AND IT'S NOT LIKE HE CAN DO ANYTHING WITH THE INFORMATION.
I WAS BITTEN BY A RADIOACTIVE SPIDER.
AHA!
THAT'S WHAT I THOUGHT. THAT EXPLAINS WHY YOU'VE HANDLED IT THIS WAY. NOW HERE'S ANOTHER QUESTION FOR YOU.
LOOK, I'VE JUST ABOUT HAD IT WITH --
NO, WAIT, YOU'LL LIKE THIS ONE, TRUST ME.

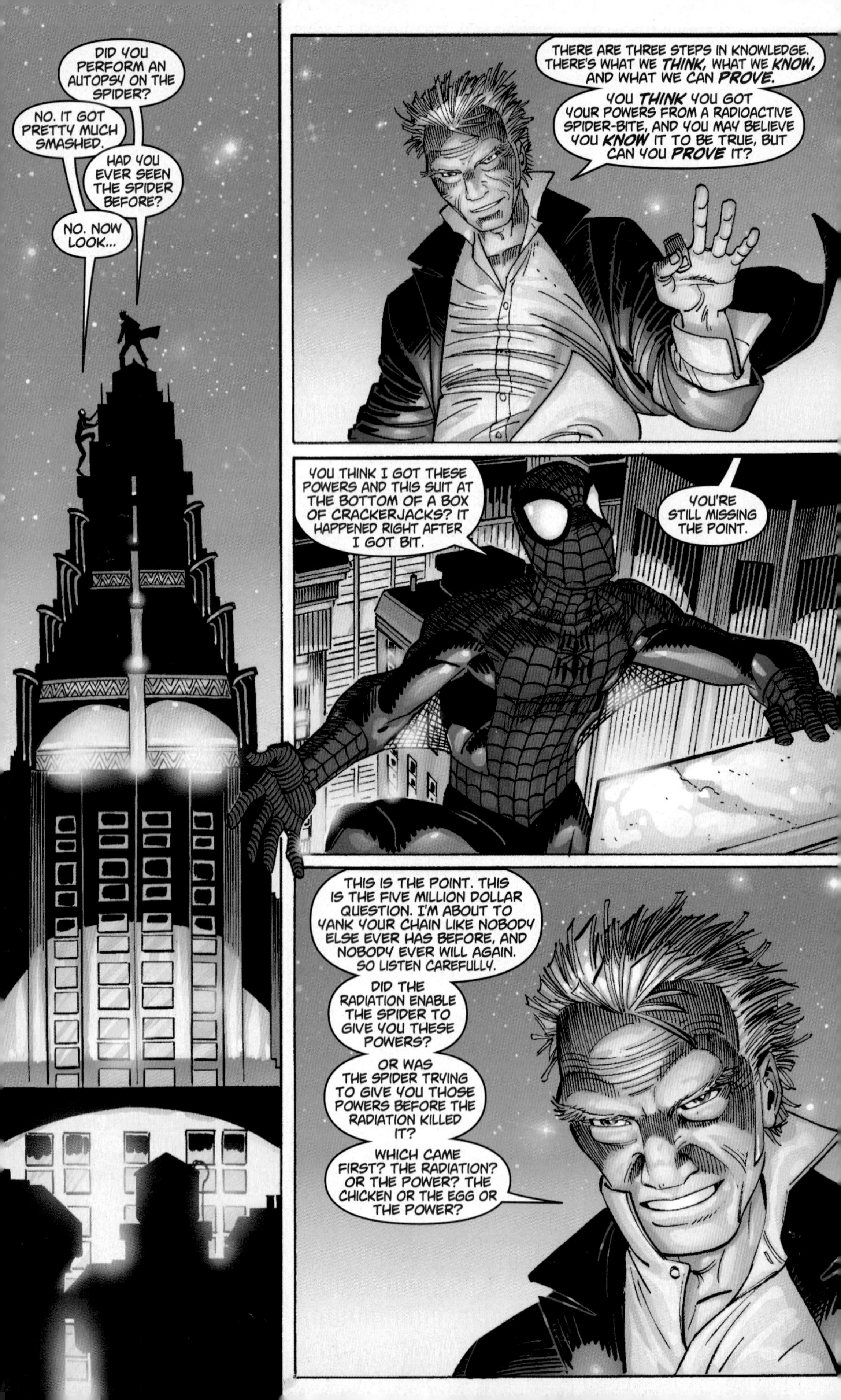

DID YOU PERFORM AN AUTOPSY ON THE SPIDER?
NO. IT GOT PRETTY MUCH SMASHED.
HAD YOU EVER SEEN THE SPIDER BEFORE?
NO. NOW LOOK...
THERE ARE THREE STEPS IN KNOWLEDGE. THERE'S WHAT WE THINK, WHAT WE KNOW, AND WHAT WE CAN PROVE.
YOU THINK YOU GOT YOUR POWERS FROM A RADIOACTIVE SPIDER-BITE, AND YOU MAY BELIEVE YOU KNOW IT TO BE TRUE, BUT CAN YOU PROVE IT?
YOU THINK I GOT THESE POWERS AND THIS SUIT AT THE BOTTOM OF A BOX OF CRACKERJACKS? IT HAPPENED RIGHT AFTER I GOT BIT.
YOU'RE STILL MISSING THE POINT.
THIS IS THE POINT. THIS IS THE FIVE MILLION DOLLAR QUESTION. I'M ABOUT TO YANK YOUR CHAIN LIKE NOBODY ELSE EVER HAS BEFORE, AND NOBODY EVER WILL AGAIN. SO LISTEN CAREFULLY.
DID THE RADIATION ENABLE THE SPIDER TO GIVE YOU THESE POWERS?
OR WAS THE SPIDER TRYING TO GIVE YOU THOSE POWERS BEFORE THE RADIATION KILLED IT?
WHICH CAME FIRST? THE RADIATION? OR THE POWER? THE CHICKEN OR THE EGG OR THE POWER?

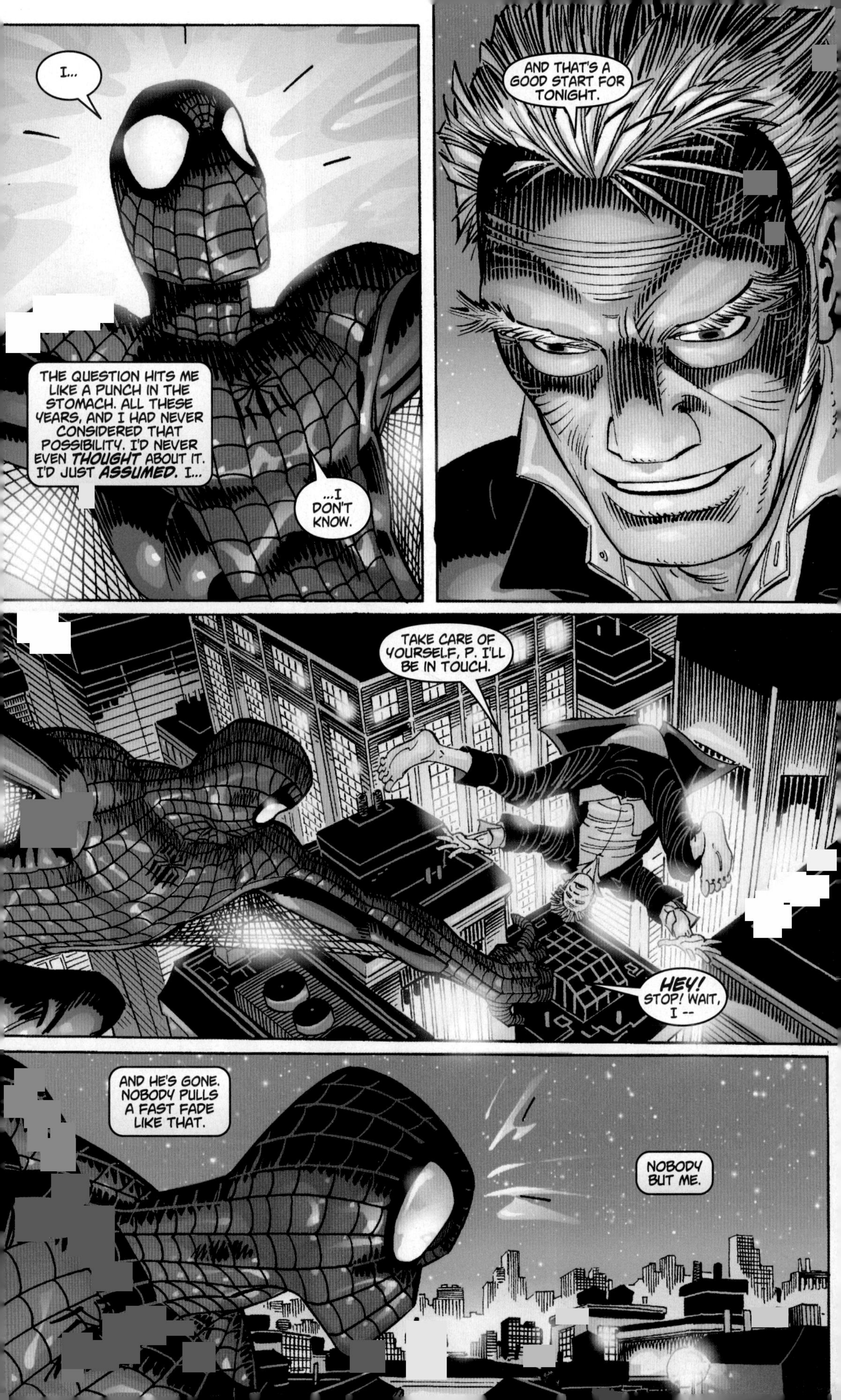
I...
THE QUESTION HITS ME LIKE A PUNCH IN THE STOMACH. ALL THESE YEARS, AND I HAD NEVER CONSIDERED THAT POSSIBILITY. I'D NEVER EVEN THOUGHT ABOUT IT. I'D JUST ASSUMED. I...
...I DON'T KNOW.
AND THAT'S A GOOD START FOR TONIGHT.
TAKE CARE OF YOURSELF, P. I'LL BE IN TOUCH.
HEY! STOP! WAIT, I --
AND HE'S GONE. NOBODY PULLS A FAST FADE LIKE THAT.
NOBODY BUT ME.

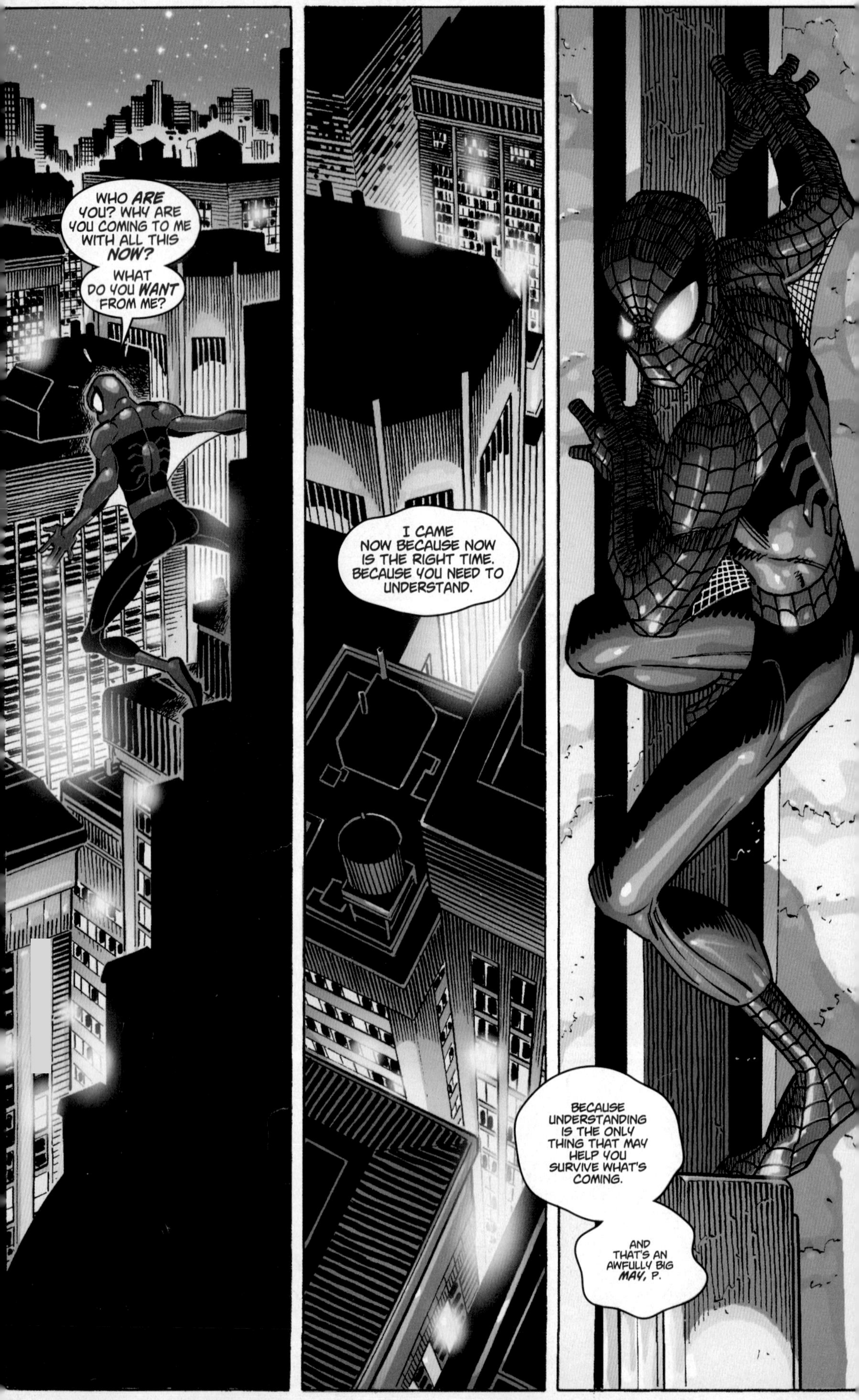
WHO *ARE* YOU? WHY ARE YOU COMING TO ME WITH ALL THIS *NOW?*
WHAT DO YOU *WANT* FROM ME?
I CAME NOW BECAUSE NOW IS THE RIGHT TIME. BECAUSE YOU NEED TO UNDERSTAND.
BECAUSE UNDERSTANDING IS THE ONLY THING THAT MAY HELP YOU SURVIVE WHAT'S COMING.
AND THAT'S AN AWFULLY BIG *MAY,* P.

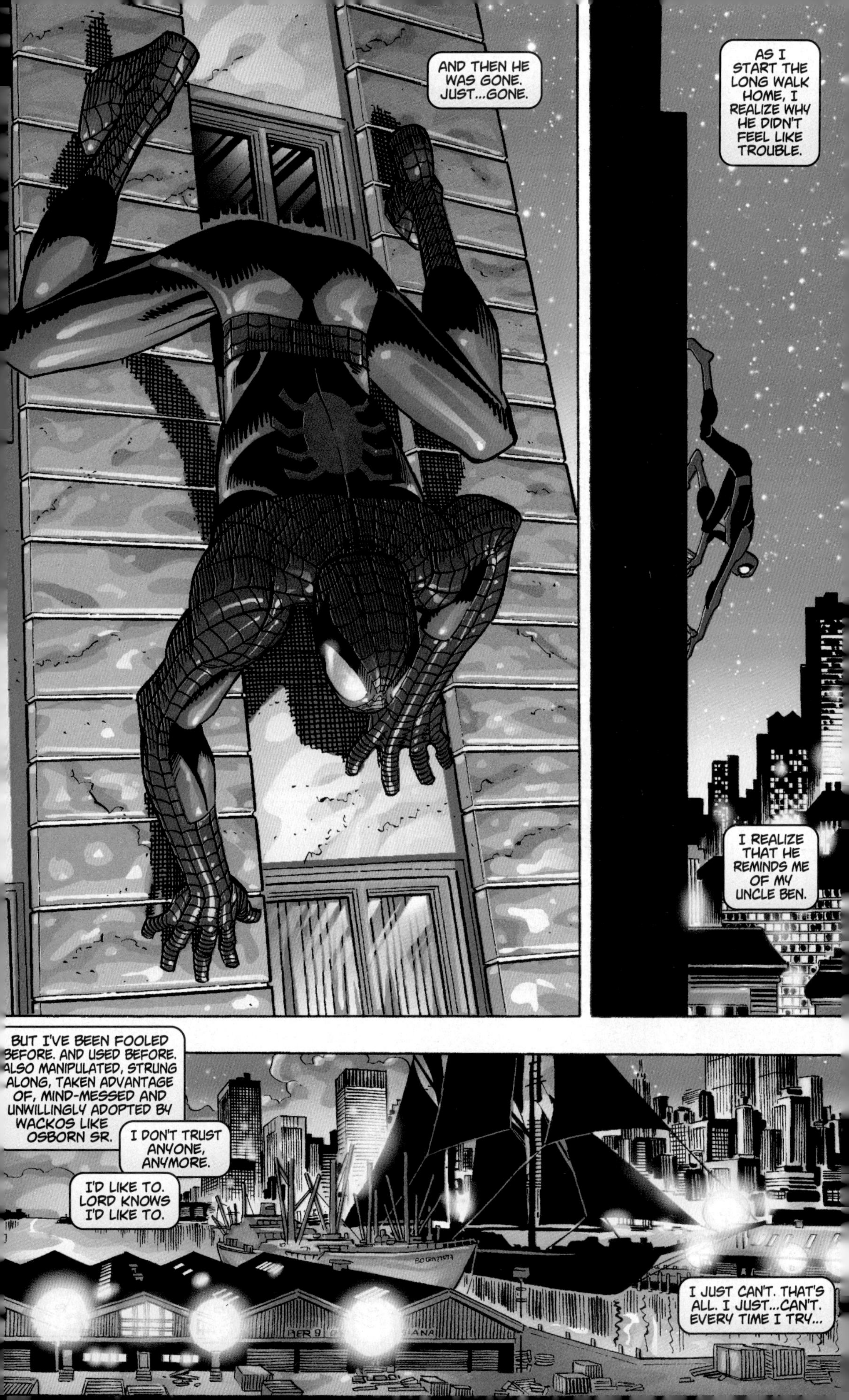
AND THEN HE WAS GONE. JUST...GONE.
AS I START THE LONG WALK HOME, I REALIZE WHY HE DIDN'T FEEL LIKE TROUBLE.
I REALIZE THAT HE REMINDS ME OF MY UNCLE BEN.
BUT I'VE BEEN FOOLED BEFORE. AND USED BEFORE. ALSO MANIPULATED, STRUNG ALONG, TAKEN ADVANTAGE OF, MIND-MESSED AND UNWILLINGLY ADOPTED BY WACKOS LIKE OSBORN SR.
I DON'T TRUST ANYONE, ANYMORE.
I'D LIKE TO. LORD KNOWS I'D LIKE TO.
I JUST CAN'T. THAT'S ALL. I JUST...CAN'T. EVERY TIME I TRY...

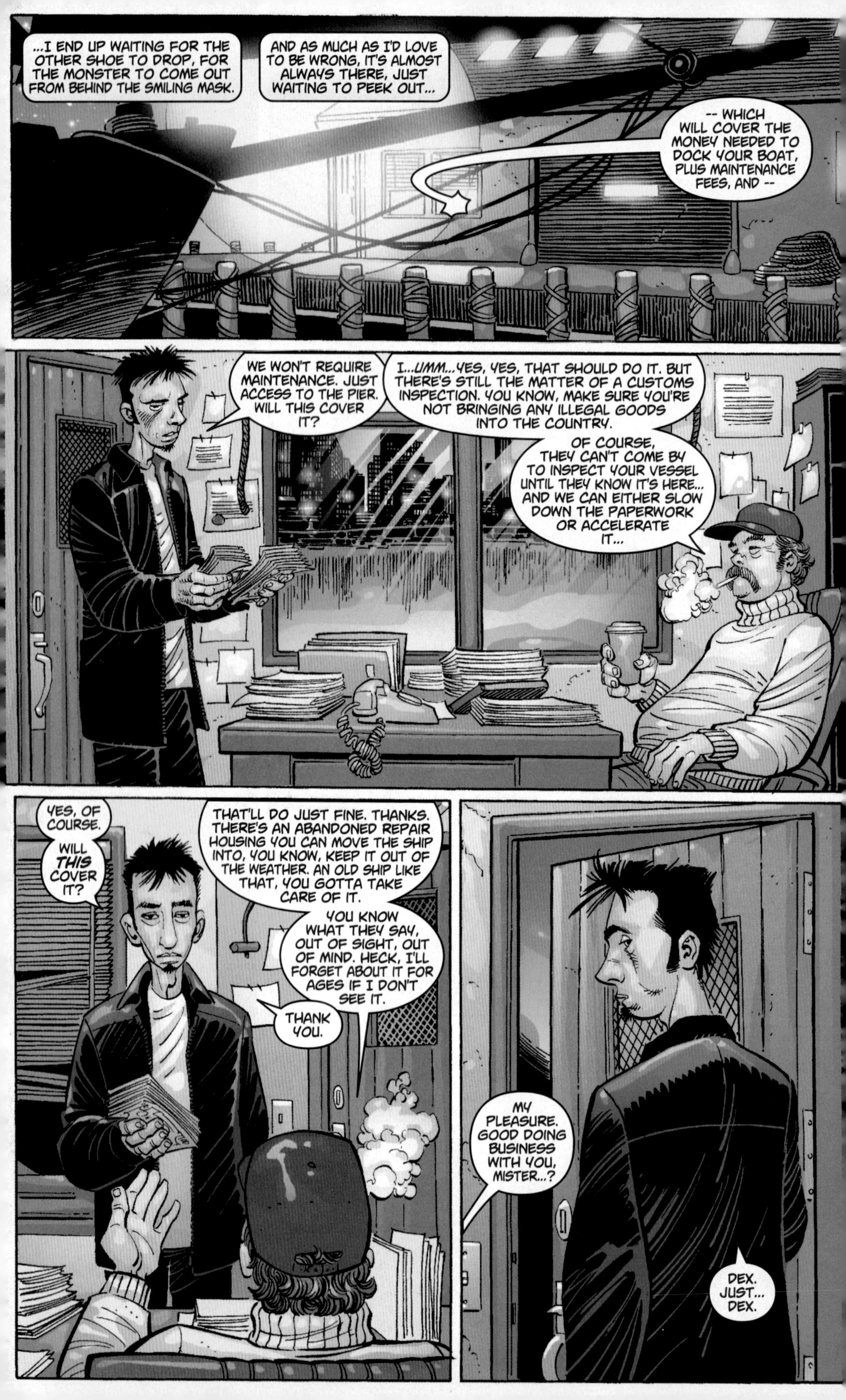
...I END UP WAITING FOR THE OTHER SHOE TO DROP, FOR THE MONSTER TO COME OUT FROM BEHIND THE SMILING MASK.
AND AS MUCH AS I'D LOVE TO BE WRONG, IT'S ALMOST ALWAYS THERE, JUST WAITING TO PEEK OUT...
-- WHICH WILL COVER THE MONEY NEEDED TO DOCK YOUR BOAT, PLUS MAINTENANCE FEES, AND --
WE WON'T REQUIRE MAINTENANCE. JUST ACCESS TO THE PIER. WILL THIS COVER IT?
I...*UMM*...YES, YES, THAT SHOULD DO IT. BUT THERE'S STILL THE MATTER OF A CUSTOMS INSPECTION. YOU KNOW, MAKE SURE YOU'RE NOT BRINGING ANY ILLEGAL GOODS INTO THE COUNTRY.
OF COURSE, THEY CAN'T COME BY TO INSPECT YOUR VESSEL UNTIL THEY KNOW IT'S HERE... AND WE CAN EITHER SLOW DOWN THE PAPERWORK OR ACCELERATE IT...
YES, OF COURSE.
WILL *THIS* COVER IT?
THAT'LL DO JUST FINE. THANKS. THERE'S AN ABANDONED REPAIR HOUSING YOU CAN MOVE THE SHIP INTO, YOU KNOW, KEEP IT OUT OF THE WEATHER. AN OLD SHIP LIKE THAT, YOU GOTTA TAKE CARE OF IT.
YOU KNOW WHAT THEY SAY, OUT OF SIGHT, OUT OF MIND. HECK, I'LL FORGET ABOUT IT FOR AGES IF I DON'T SEE IT.
THANK YOU.
MY PLEASURE. GOOD DOING BUSINESS WITH YOU, MISTER...?
DEX. JUST... DEX.

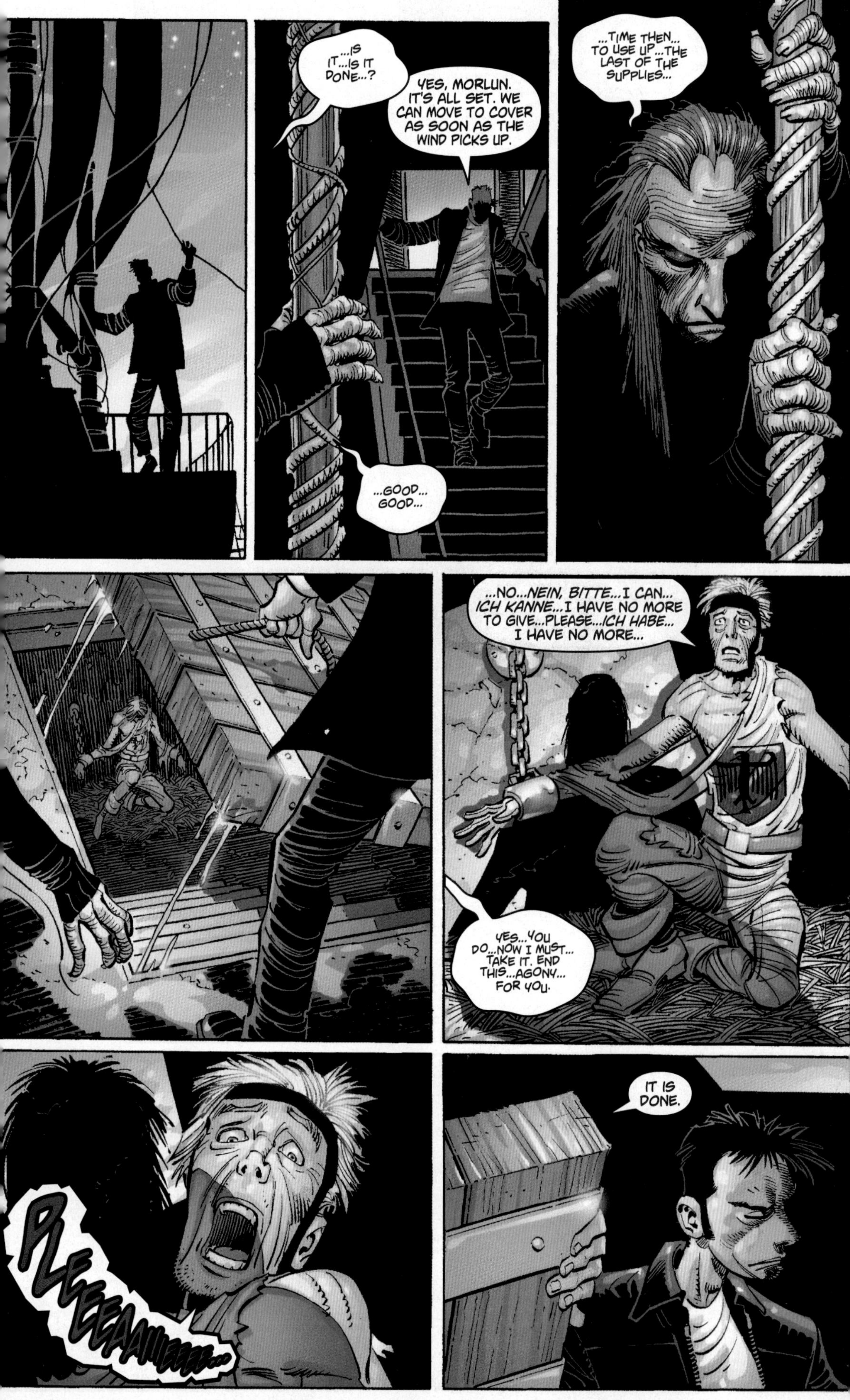
...IS IT...IS IT DONE...?
YES, MORLUN. IT'S ALL SET. WE CAN MOVE TO COVER AS SOON AS THE WIND PICKS UP.
...GOOD... GOOD...
...TIME THEN... TO USE UP...THE LAST OF THE SUPPLIES...
...NO...NEIN, BITTE...I CAN... ICH KANNE...I HAVE NO MORE TO GIVE...PLEASE...ICH HABE... I HAVE NO MORE...
YES...YOU DO...NOW I MUST... TAKE IT. END THIS...AGONY... FOR YOU.
PLEEEAAAIIIIEEEE...
IT IS DONE.

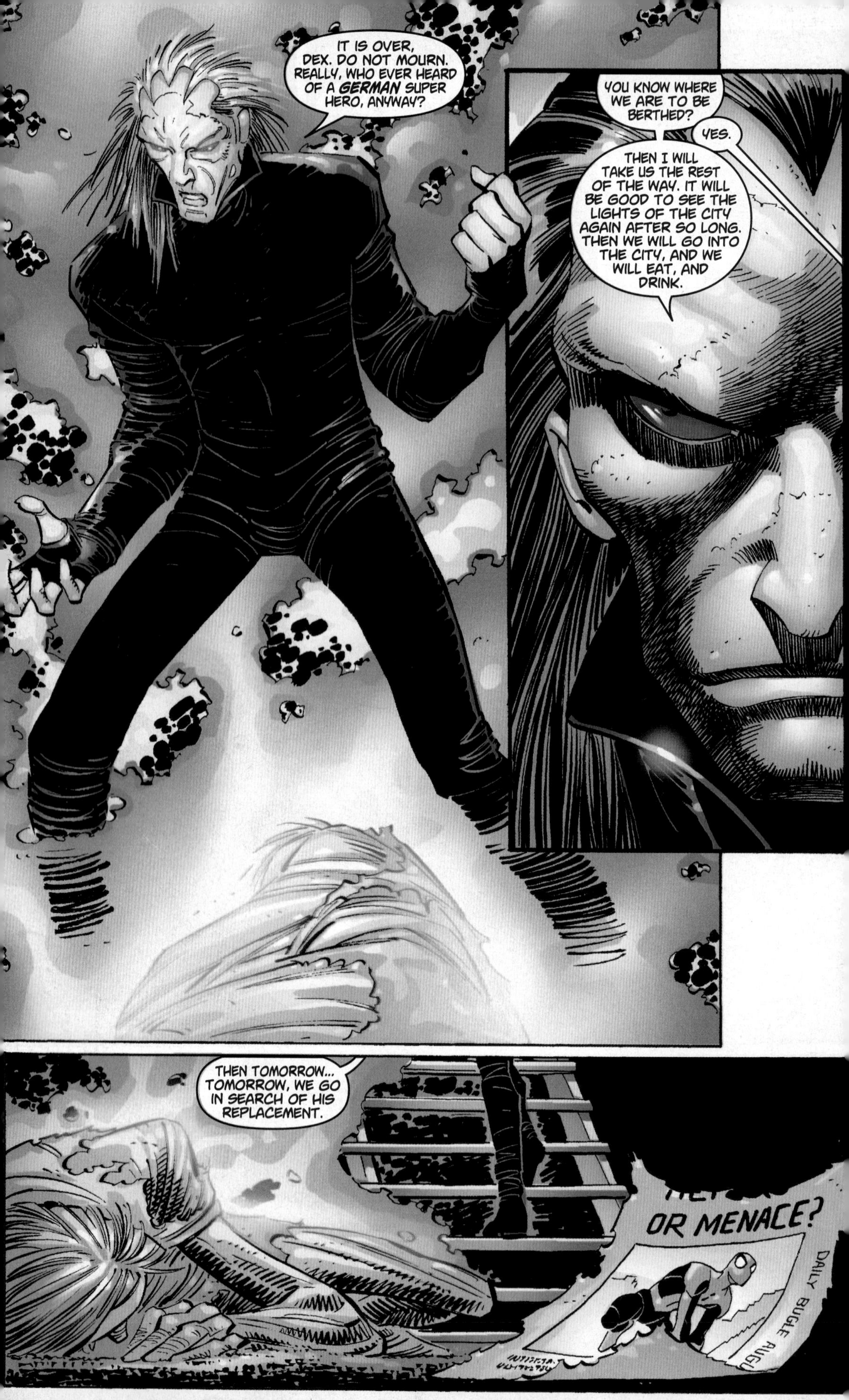

IT IS OVER, DEX. DO NOT MOURN. REALLY, WHO EVER HEARD OF A GERMAN SUPER HERO, ANYWAY?
YOU KNOW WHERE WE ARE TO BE BERTHED?
YES.
THEN I WILL TAKE US THE REST OF THE WAY. IT WILL BE GOOD TO SEE THE LIGHTS OF THE CITY AGAIN AFTER SO LONG. THEN WE WILL GO INTO THE CITY, AND WE WILL EAT, AND DRINK.
THEN TOMORROW... TOMORROW, WE GO IN SEARCH OF HIS REPLACEMENT.
OR MENACE?
DAILY BUGLE

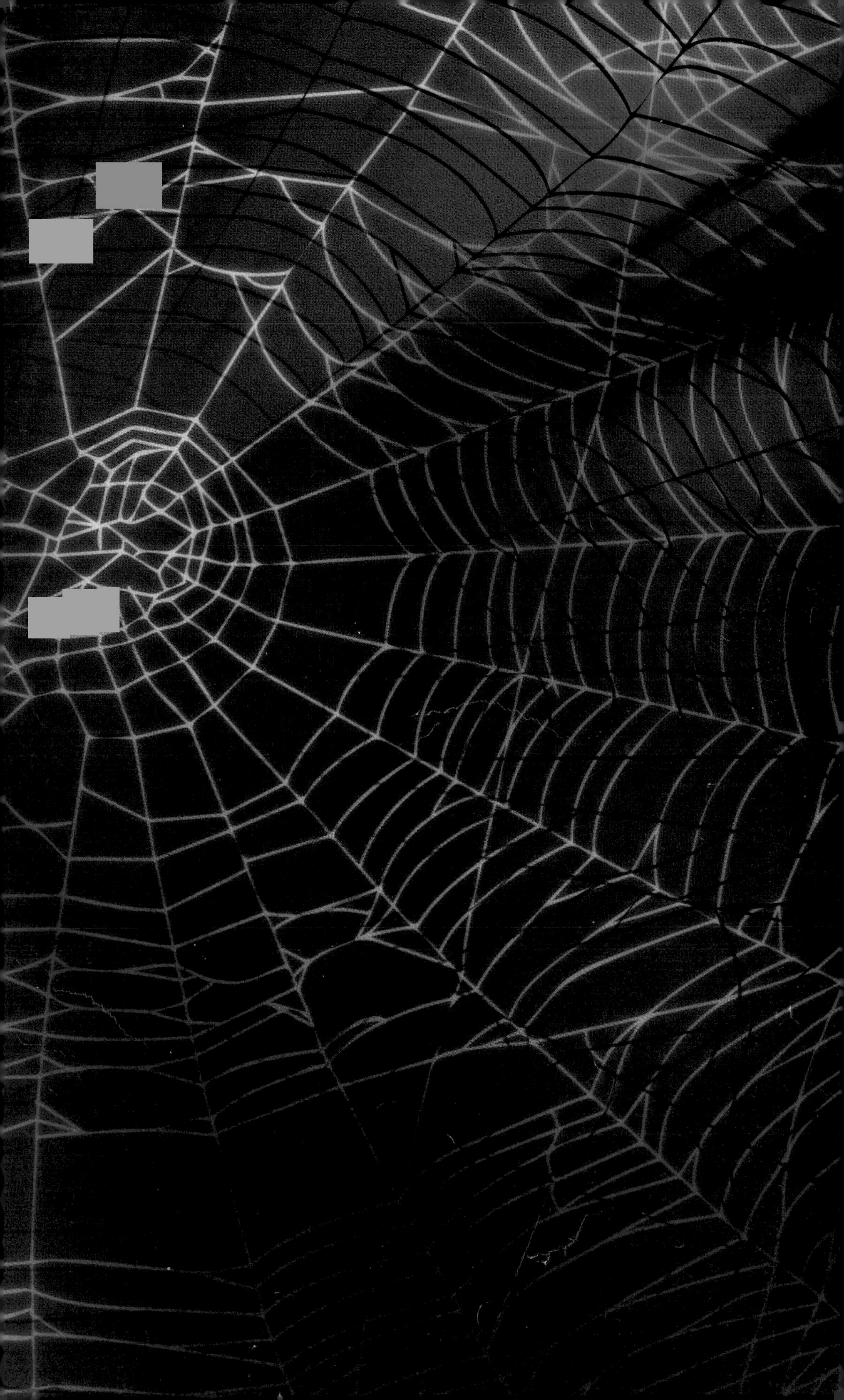

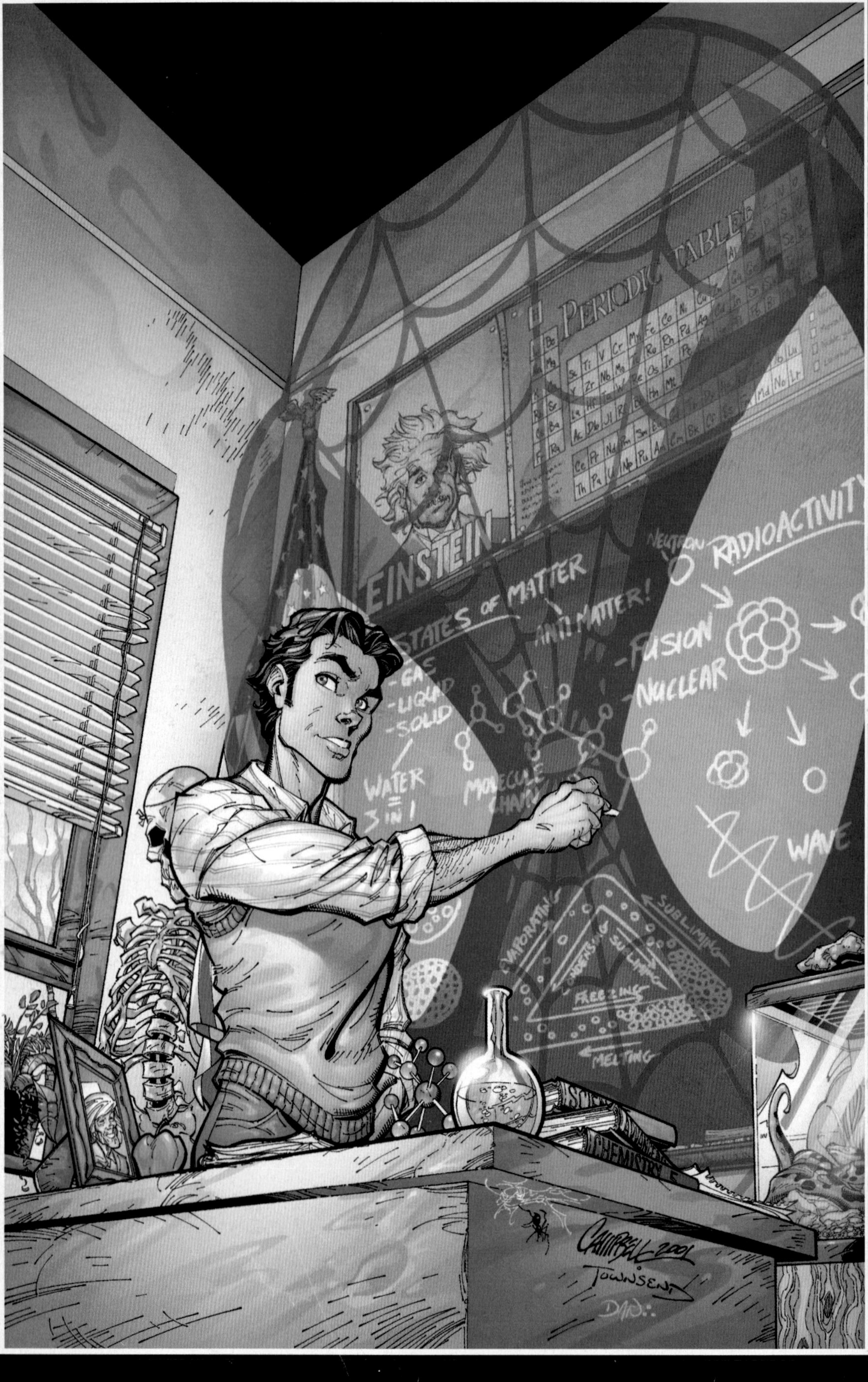
PERIODIC TABLE
EINSTEIN
STATES OF MATTER
ANTI MATTER!
-FUSION
-NUCLEAR
RADIOACTIVITY
-LIQUID
-SOLID
WATER = 3 IN 1
WAVE
SUBLIMING
FREEZING
MELTING
CHEMISTRY
CAMPBELL 2001
TOWNSEND

AMAZING SPIDER-MAN #31

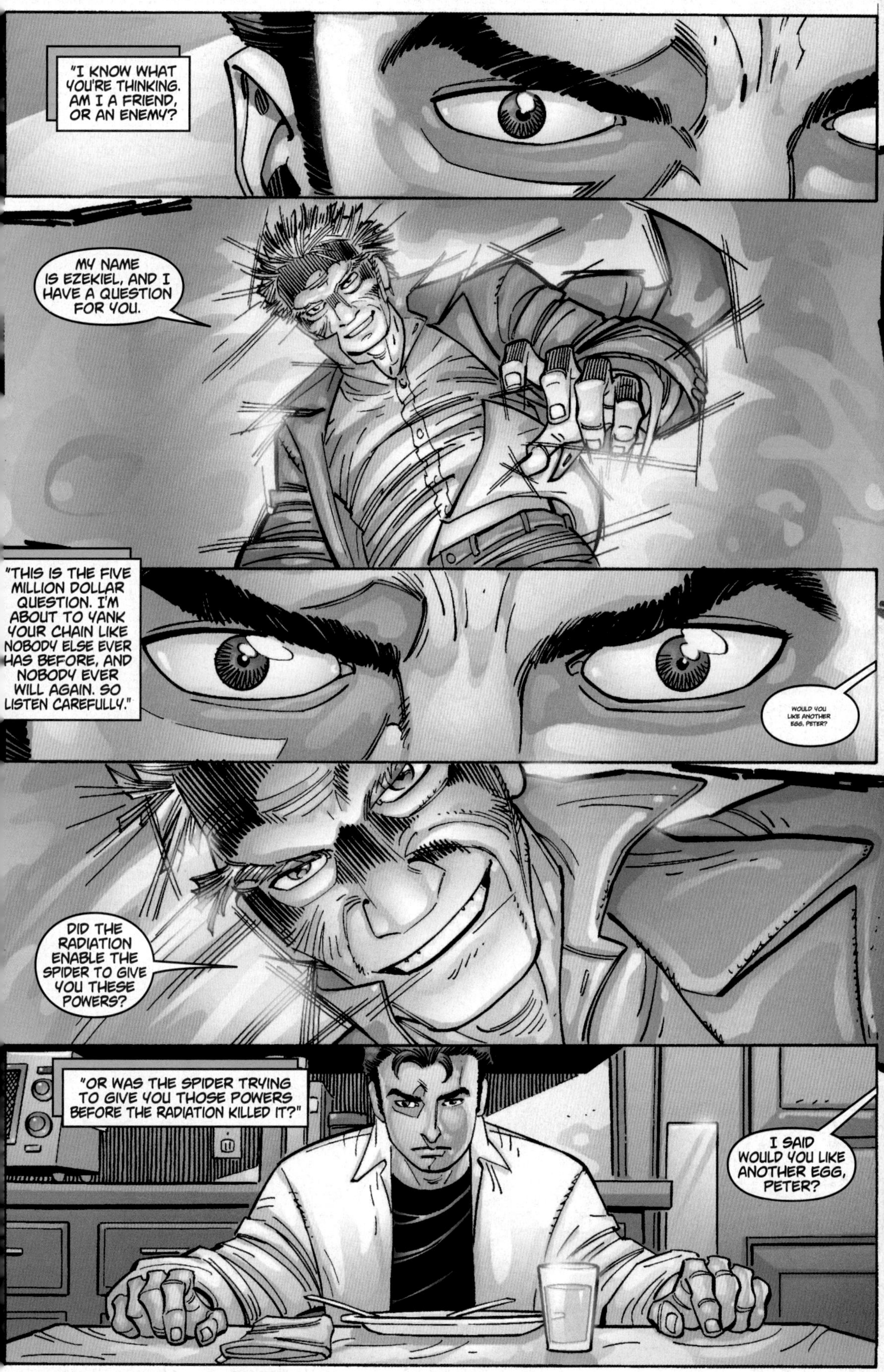
"I KNOW WHAT YOU'RE THINKING. AM I A FRIEND, OR AN ENEMY?
MY NAME IS EZEKIEL, AND I HAVE A QUESTION FOR YOU.
"THIS IS THE FIVE MILLION DOLLAR QUESTION. I'M ABOUT TO YANK YOUR CHAIN LIKE NOBODY ELSE EVER HAS BEFORE, AND NOBODY EVER WILL AGAIN. SO LISTEN CAREFULLY."
WOULD YOU LIKE ANOTHER EGG, PETER?
DID THE RADIATION ENABLE THE SPIDER TO GIVE YOU THESE POWERS?
"OR WAS THE SPIDER TRYING TO GIVE YOU THOSE POWERS BEFORE THE RADIATION KILLED IT?"
I SAID WOULD YOU LIKE ANOTHER EGG, PETER?

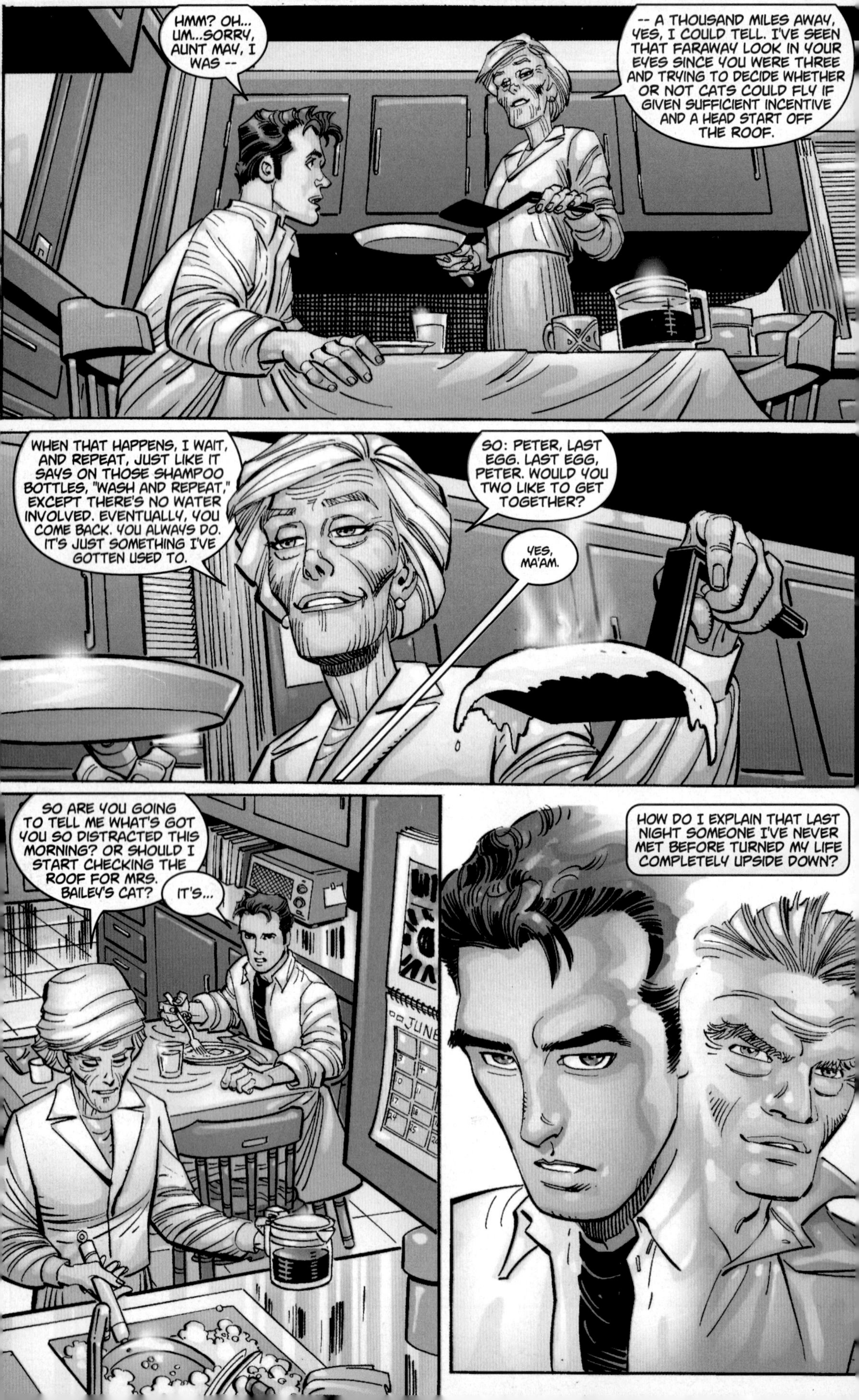
HMM? OH... UM...SORRY, AUNT MAY, I WAS --
-- A THOUSAND MILES AWAY, YES, I COULD TELL. I'VE SEEN THAT FARAWAY LOOK IN YOUR EYES SINCE YOU WERE THREE AND TRYING TO DECIDE WHETHER OR NOT CATS COULD FLY IF GIVEN SUFFICIENT INCENTIVE AND A HEAD START OFF THE ROOF.
WHEN THAT HAPPENS, I WAIT, AND REPEAT, JUST LIKE IT SAYS ON THOSE SHAMPOO BOTTLES, "WASH AND REPEAT," EXCEPT THERE'S NO WATER INVOLVED. EVENTUALLY, YOU COME BACK. YOU ALWAYS DO. IT'S JUST SOMETHING I'VE GOTTEN USED TO.
SO: PETER, LAST EGG. LAST EGG, PETER. WOULD YOU TWO LIKE TO GET TOGETHER?
YES, MA'AM.
SO ARE YOU GOING TO TELL ME WHAT'S GOT YOU SO DISTRACTED THIS MORNING? OR SHOULD I START CHECKING THE ROOF FOR MRS. BAILEY'S CAT?
IT'S...
HOW DO I EXPLAIN THAT LAST NIGHT SOMEONE I'VE NEVER MET BEFORE TURNED MY LIFE COMPLETELY UPSIDE DOWN?

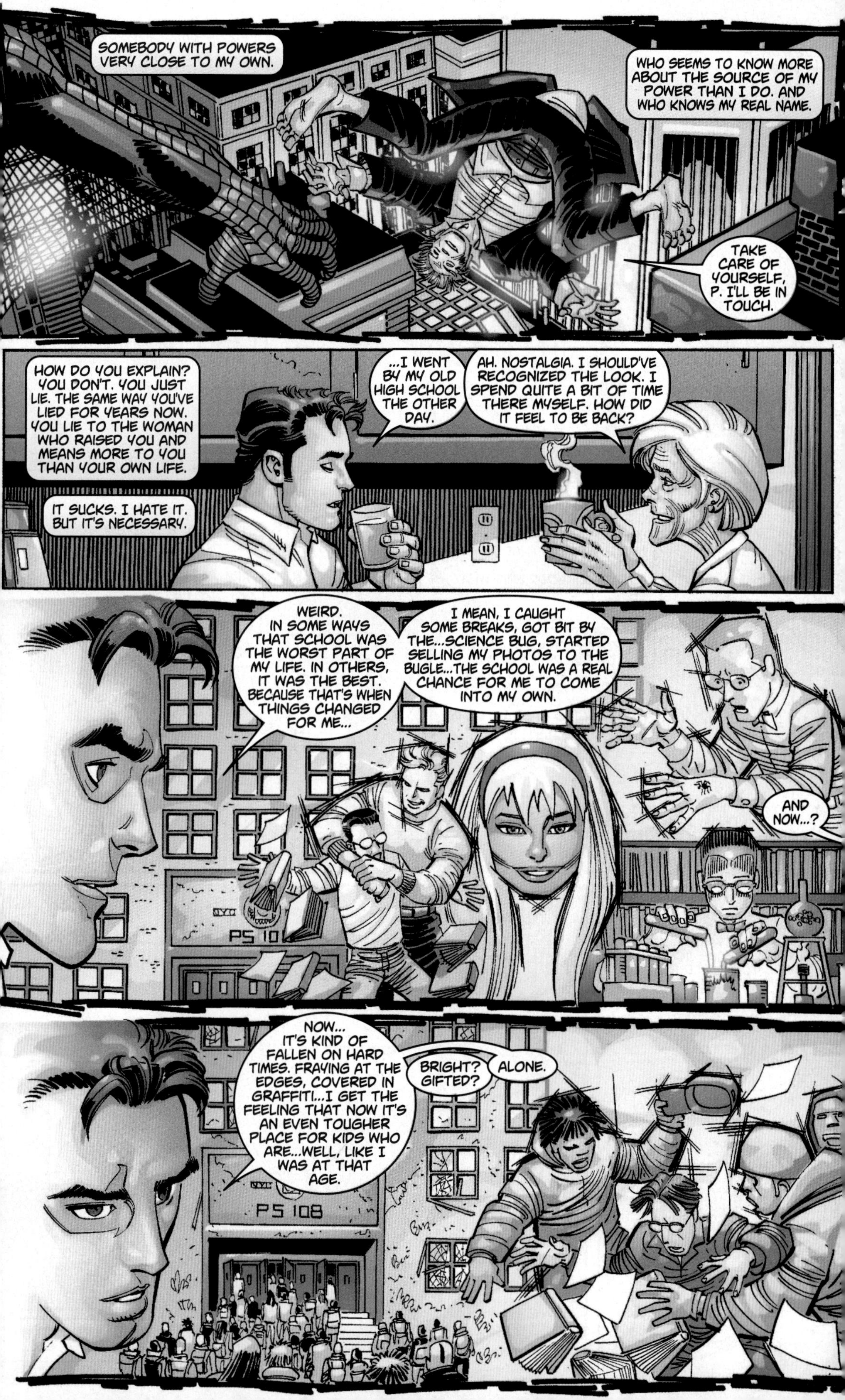

SOMEBODY WITH POWERS VERY CLOSE TO MY OWN.
WHO SEEMS TO KNOW MORE ABOUT THE SOURCE OF MY POWER THAN I DO. AND WHO KNOWS MY REAL NAME.
TAKE CARE OF YOURSELF, P. I'LL BE IN TOUCH.
HOW DO YOU EXPLAIN? YOU DON'T. YOU JUST LIE. THE SAME WAY YOU'VE LIED FOR YEARS NOW. YOU LIE TO THE WOMAN WHO RAISED YOU AND MEANS MORE TO YOU THAN YOUR OWN LIFE.
IT SUCKS. I HATE IT. BUT IT'S NECESSARY.
...I WENT BY MY OLD HIGH SCHOOL THE OTHER DAY.
AH. NOSTALGIA. I SHOULD'VE RECOGNIZED THE LOOK. I SPEND QUITE A BIT OF TIME THERE MYSELF. HOW DID IT FEEL TO BE BACK?
WEIRD. IN SOME WAYS THAT SCHOOL WAS THE WORST PART OF MY LIFE. IN OTHERS, IT WAS THE BEST. BECAUSE THAT'S WHEN THINGS CHANGED FOR ME...
I MEAN, I CAUGHT SOME BREAKS, GOT BIT BY THE...SCIENCE BUG, STARTED SELLING MY PHOTOS TO THE BUGLE...THE SCHOOL WAS A REAL CHANCE FOR ME TO COME INTO MY OWN.
AND NOW...?
NOW... IT'S KIND OF FALLEN ON HARD TIMES. FRAYING AT THE EDGES, COVERED IN GRAFFITI...I GET THE FEELING THAT NOW IT'S AN EVEN TOUGHER PLACE FOR KIDS WHO ARE...WELL, LIKE I WAS AT THAT AGE.
BRIGHT? GIFTED?
ALONE.
PS 108

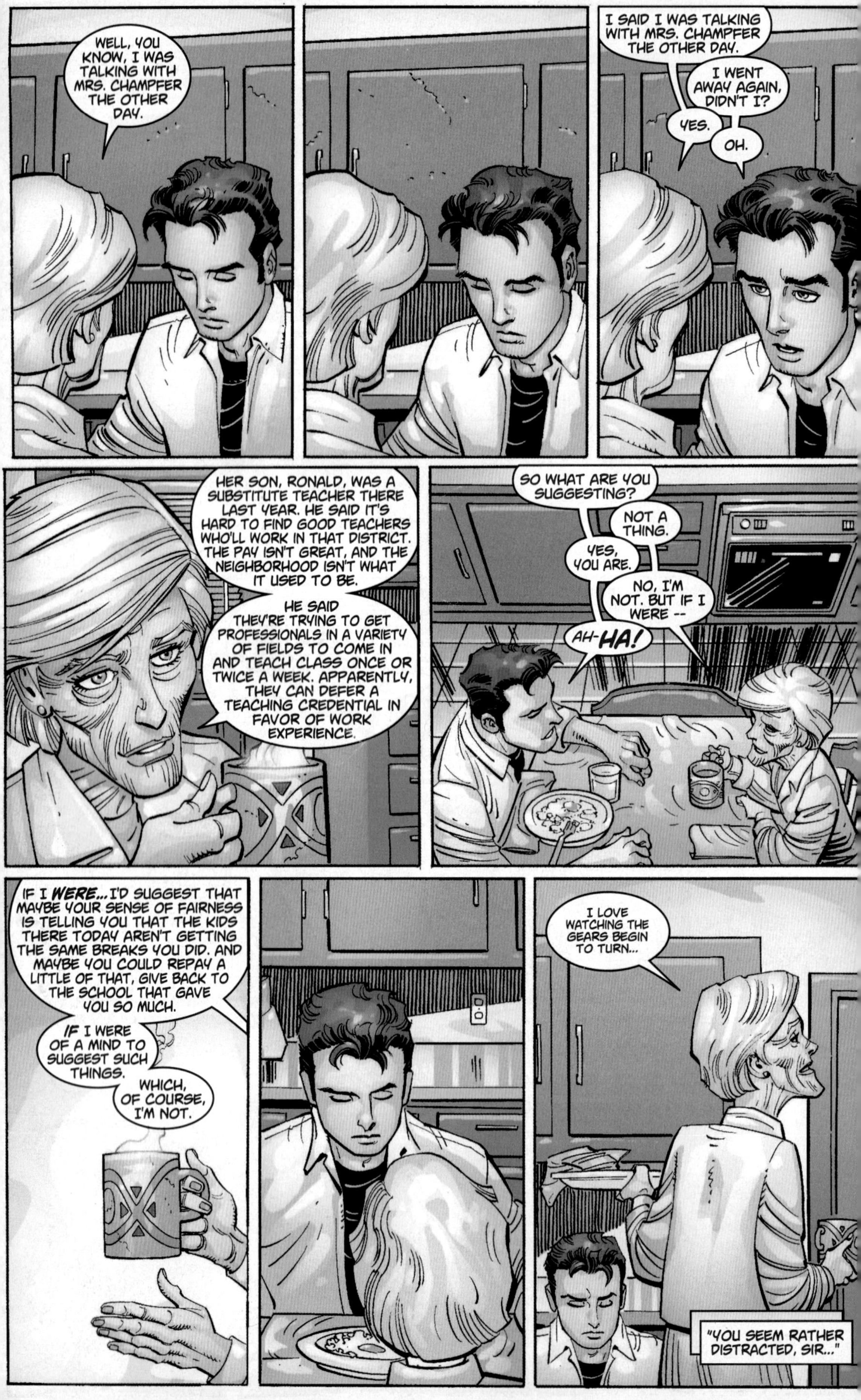

WELL, YOU KNOW, I WAS TALKING WITH MRS. CHAMPFER THE OTHER DAY.
I SAID I WAS TALKING WITH MRS. CHAMPFER THE OTHER DAY.
I WENT AWAY AGAIN, DIDN'T I?
YES.
OH.
HER SON, RONALD, WAS A SUBSTITUTE TEACHER THERE LAST YEAR. HE SAID IT'S HARD TO FIND GOOD TEACHERS WHO'LL WORK IN THAT DISTRICT. THE PAY ISN'T GREAT, AND THE NEIGHBORHOOD ISN'T WHAT IT USED TO BE.
HE SAID THEY'RE TRYING TO GET PROFESSIONALS IN A VARIETY OF FIELDS TO COME IN AND TEACH CLASS ONCE OR TWICE A WEEK. APPARENTLY, THEY CAN DEFER A TEACHING CREDENTIAL IN FAVOR OF WORK EXPERIENCE.
SO WHAT ARE YOU SUGGESTING?
NOT A THING.
YES, YOU ARE.
NO, I'M NOT. BUT IF I WERE --
AH-HA!
IF I WERE... I'D SUGGEST THAT MAYBE YOUR SENSE OF FAIRNESS IS TELLING YOU THAT THE KIDS THERE TODAY AREN'T GETTING THE SAME BREAKS YOU DID. AND MAYBE YOU COULD REPAY A LITTLE OF THAT, GIVE BACK TO THE SCHOOL THAT GAVE YOU SO MUCH.
IF I WERE OF A MIND TO SUGGEST SUCH THINGS.
WHICH, OF COURSE, I'M NOT.
I LOVE WATCHING THE GEARS BEGIN TO TURN...
"YOU SEEM RATHER DISTRACTED, SIR..."

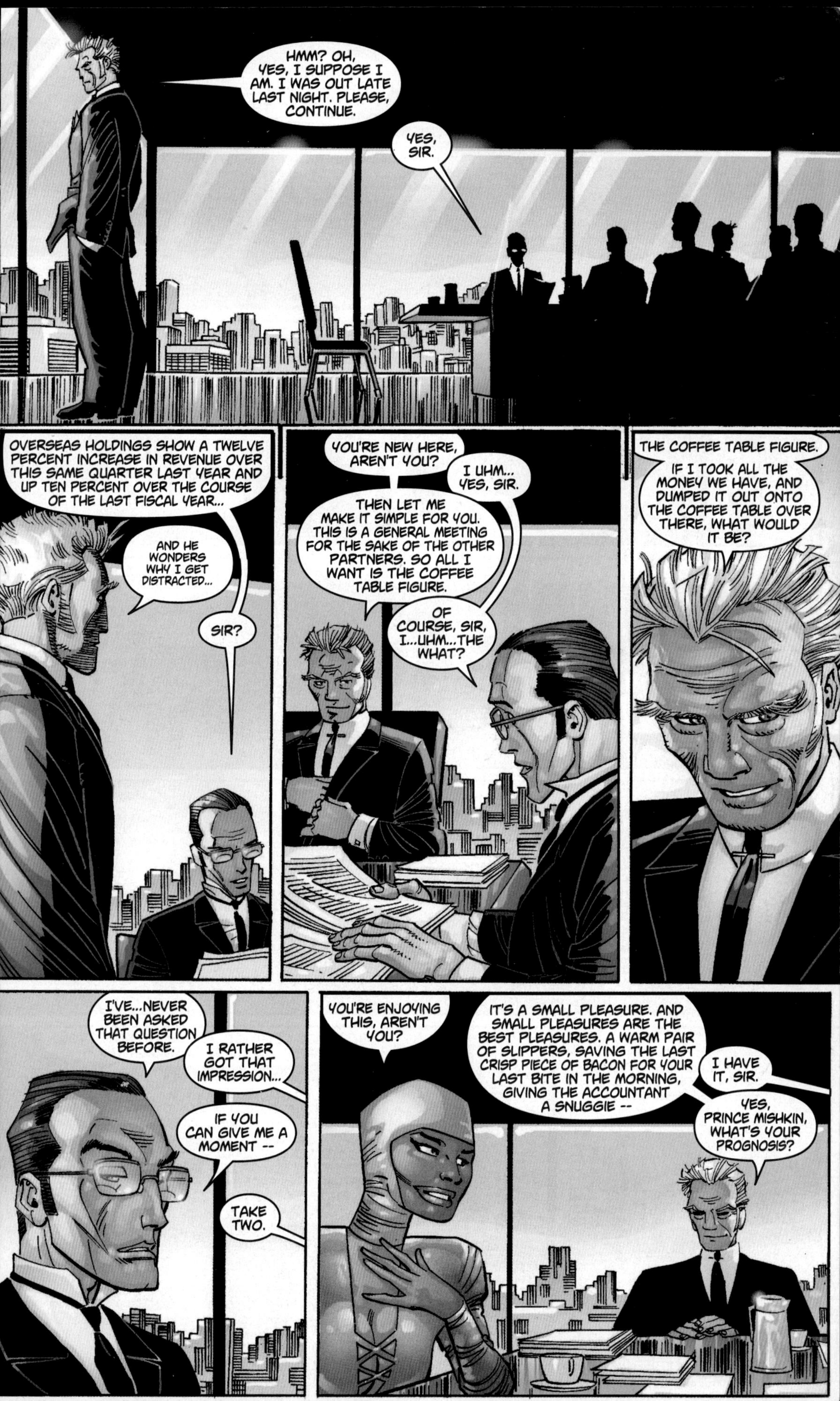
HMM? OH, YES, I SUPPOSE I AM. I WAS OUT LATE LAST NIGHT. PLEASE, CONTINUE.
YES, SIR.
OVERSEAS HOLDINGS SHOW A TWELVE PERCENT INCREASE IN REVENUE OVER THIS SAME QUARTER LAST YEAR AND UP TEN PERCENT OVER THE COURSE OF THE LAST FISCAL YEAR...
AND HE WONDERS WHY I GET DISTRACTED...
SIR?
YOU'RE NEW HERE, AREN'T YOU?
I UHM... YES, SIR.
THEN LET ME MAKE IT SIMPLE FOR YOU. THIS IS A GENERAL MEETING FOR THE SAKE OF THE OTHER PARTNERS. SO ALL I WANT IS THE COFFEE TABLE FIGURE.
OF COURSE, SIR, I...UHM...THE WHAT?
THE COFFEE TABLE FIGURE.
IF I TOOK ALL THE MONEY WE HAVE, AND DUMPED IT OUT ONTO THE COFFEE TABLE OVER THERE, WHAT WOULD IT BE?
I'VE...NEVER BEEN ASKED THAT QUESTION BEFORE.
I RATHER GOT THAT IMPRESSION...
IF YOU CAN GIVE ME A MOMENT --
TAKE TWO.
YOU'RE ENJOYING THIS, AREN'T YOU?
IT'S A SMALL PLEASURE. AND SMALL PLEASURES ARE THE BEST PLEASURES. A WARM PAIR OF SLIPPERS, SAVING THE LAST CRISP PIECE OF BACON FOR YOUR LAST BITE IN THE MORNING, GIVING THE ACCOUNTANT A SNUGGIE --
I HAVE IT, SIR.
YES, PRINCE MISHKIN, WHAT'S YOUR PROGNOSIS?

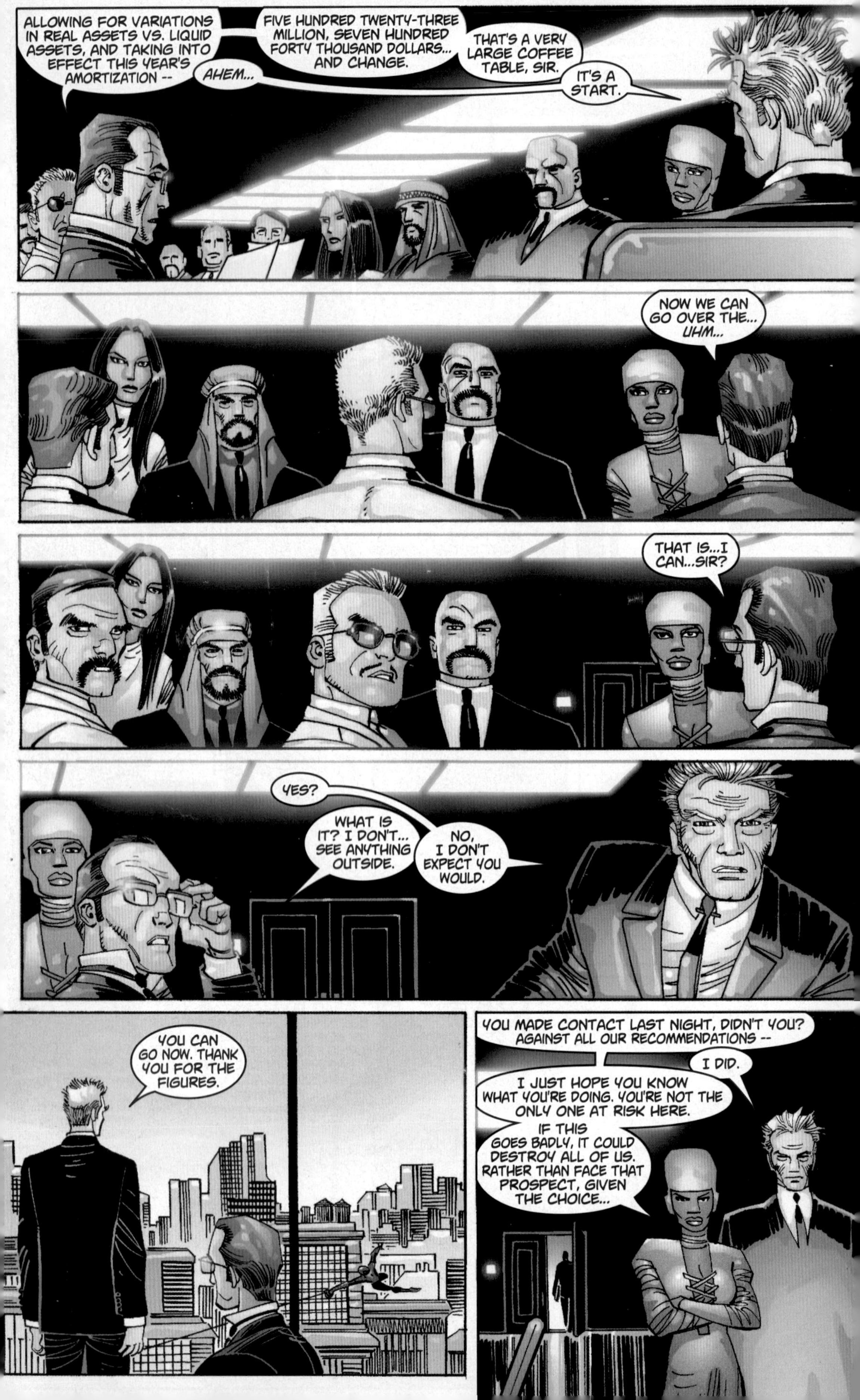
ALLOWING FOR VARIATIONS IN REAL ASSETS VS. LIQUID ASSETS, AND TAKING INTO EFFECT THIS YEAR'S AMORTIZATION --
AHEM...
FIVE HUNDRED TWENTY-THREE MILLION, SEVEN HUNDRED FORTY THOUSAND DOLLARS... AND CHANGE.
THAT'S A VERY LARGE COFFEE TABLE, SIR.
IT'S A START.
NOW WE CAN GO OVER THE... UHM...
THAT IS...I CAN...SIR?
YES?
WHAT IS IT? I DON'T... SEE ANYTHING OUTSIDE.
NO, I DON'T EXPECT YOU WOULD.
YOU CAN GO NOW. THANK YOU FOR THE FIGURES.
YOU MADE CONTACT LAST NIGHT, DIDN'T YOU? AGAINST ALL OUR RECOMMENDATIONS --
I DID.
I JUST HOPE YOU KNOW WHAT YOU'RE DOING. YOU'RE NOT THE ONLY ONE AT RISK HERE.
IF THIS GOES BADLY, IT COULD DESTROY ALL OF US. RATHER THAN FACE THAT PROSPECT, GIVEN THE CHOICE...

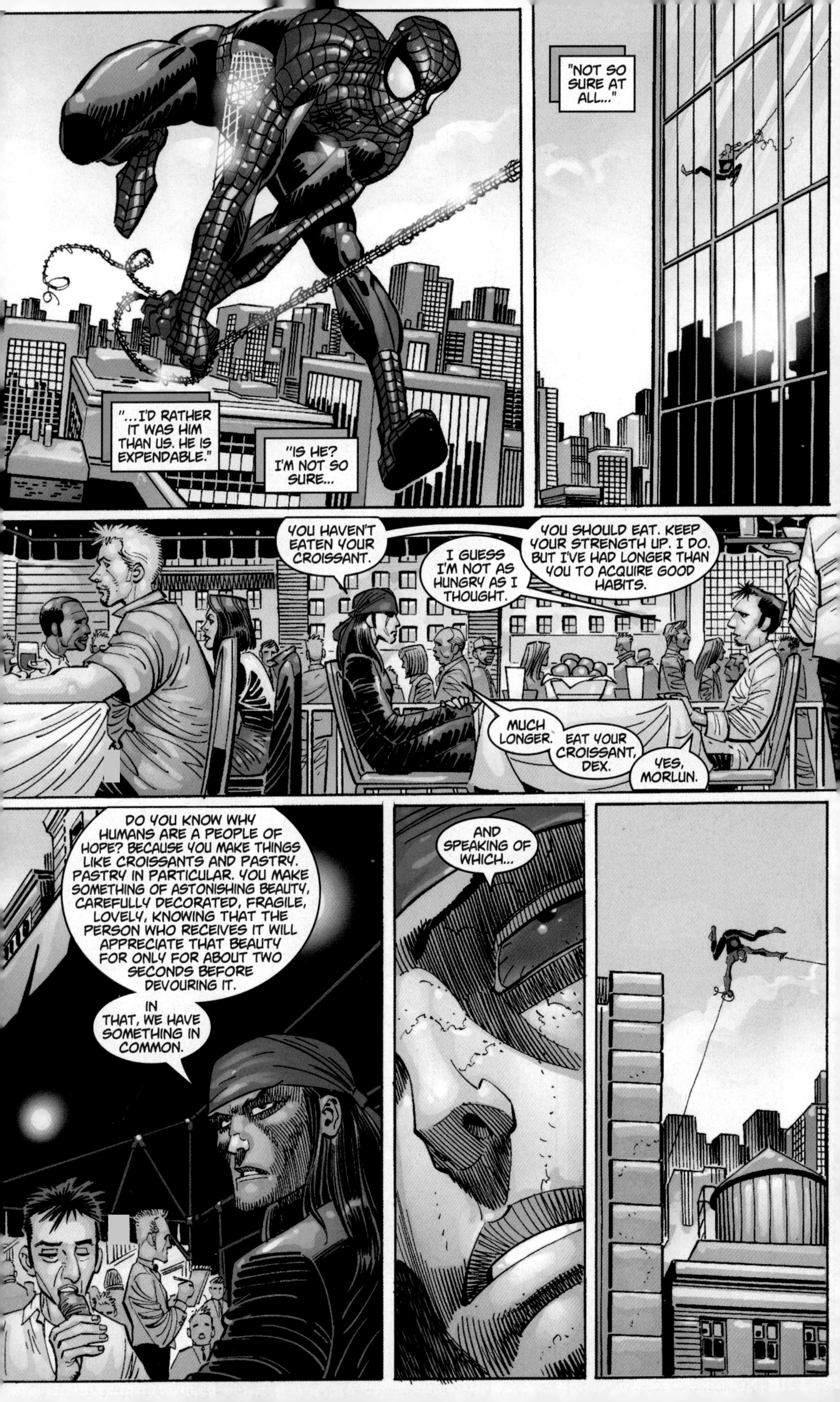

"...I'D RATHER IT WAS HIM THAN US. HE IS EXPENDABLE."
"IS HE? I'M NOT SO SURE...
"NOT SO SURE AT ALL..."
YOU HAVEN'T EATEN YOUR CROISSANT.
I GUESS I'M NOT AS HUNGRY AS I THOUGHT.
YOU SHOULD EAT. KEEP YOUR STRENGTH UP. I DO. BUT I'VE HAD LONGER THAN YOU TO ACQUIRE GOOD HABITS.
MUCH LONGER.
EAT YOUR CROISSANT, DEX.
YES, MORLUN.
DO YOU KNOW WHY HUMANS ARE A PEOPLE OF HOPE? BECAUSE YOU MAKE THINGS LIKE CROISSANTS AND PASTRY. PASTRY IN PARTICULAR. YOU MAKE SOMETHING OF ASTONISHING BEAUTY, CAREFULLY DECORATED, FRAGILE, LOVELY, KNOWING THAT THE PERSON WHO RECEIVES IT WILL APPRECIATE THAT BEAUTY FOR ONLY FOR ABOUT TWO SECONDS BEFORE DEVOURING IT.
IN THAT, WE HAVE SOMETHING IN COMMON.
AND SPEAKING OF WHICH...

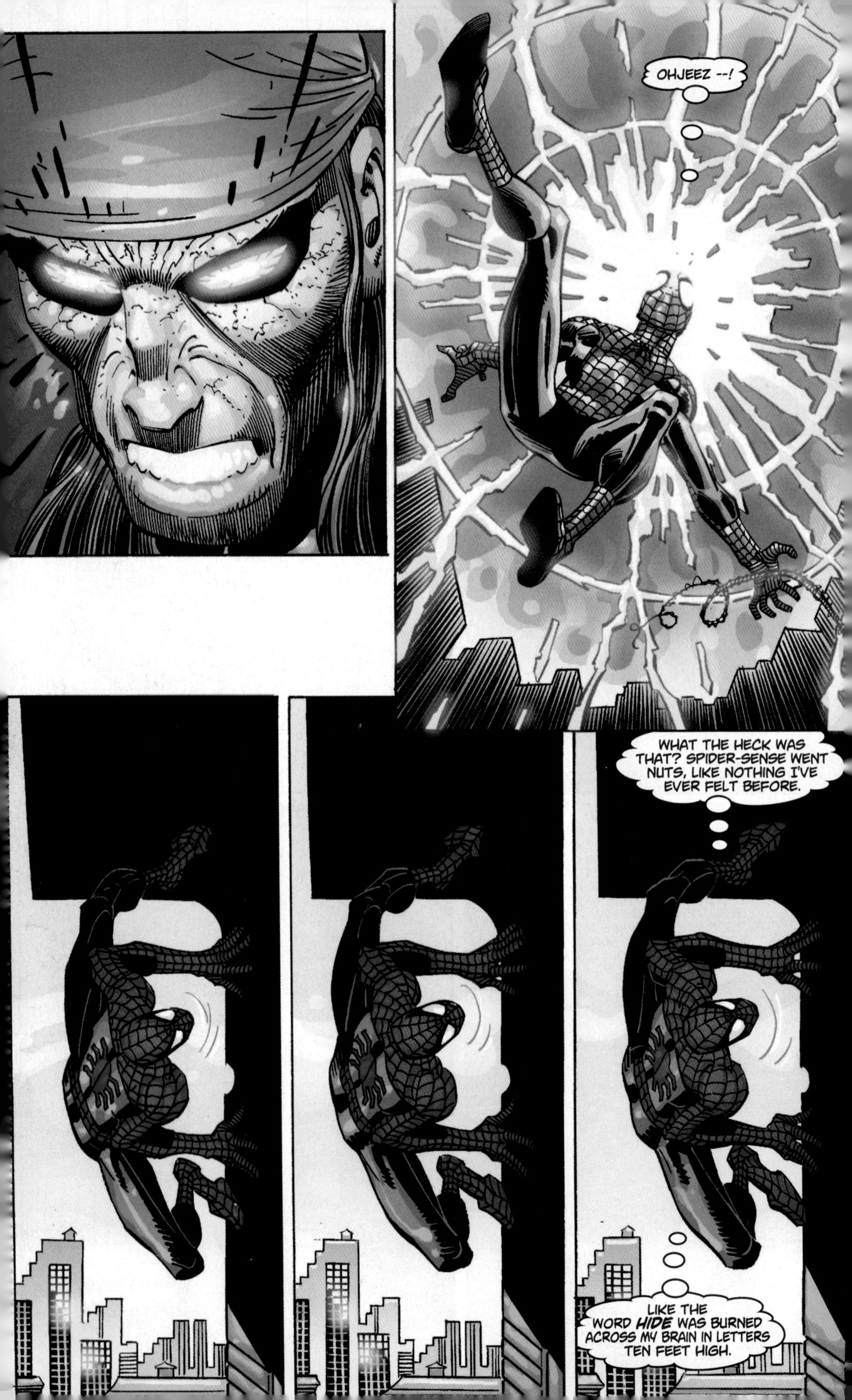
OHJEEZ --!
WHAT THE HECK WAS THAT? SPIDER-SENSE WENT NUTS, LIKE NOTHING I'VE EVER FELT BEFORE.
LIKE THE WORD HIDE WAS BURNED ACROSS MY BRAIN IN LETTERS TEN FEET HIGH.

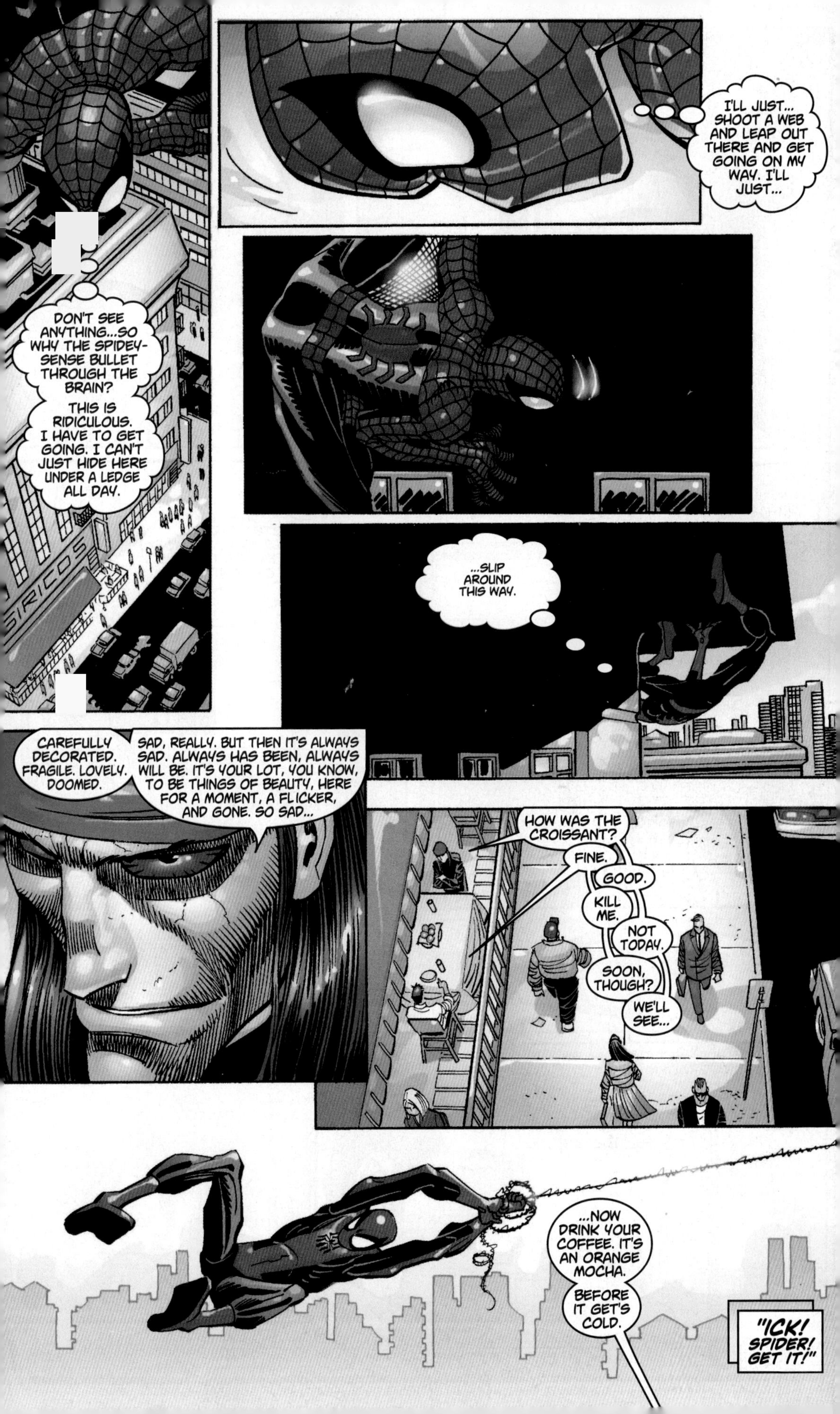
DON'T SEE ANYTHING...SO WHY THE SPIDEY-SENSE BULLET THROUGH THE BRAIN?
THIS IS RIDICULOUS. I HAVE TO GET GOING. I CAN'T JUST HIDE HERE UNDER A LEDGE ALL DAY.
SIRICOS
I'LL JUST... SHOOT A WEB AND LEAP OUT THERE AND GET GOING ON MY WAY. I'LL JUST...
...SLIP AROUND THIS WAY.
CAREFULLY DECORATED. FRAGILE. LOVELY. DOOMED.
SAD, REALLY. BUT THEN IT'S ALWAYS SAD. ALWAYS HAS BEEN, ALWAYS WILL BE. IT'S YOUR LOT, YOU KNOW, TO BE THINGS OF BEAUTY, HERE FOR A MOMENT, A FLICKER, AND GONE. SO SAD...
HOW WAS THE CROISSANT?
FINE.
GOOD.
KILL ME.
NOT TODAY.
SOON, THOUGH?
WE'LL SEE...
...NOW DRINK YOUR COFFEE. IT'S AN ORANGE MOCHA.
BEFORE IT GET'S COLD.
"ICK! SPIDER! GET IT!"

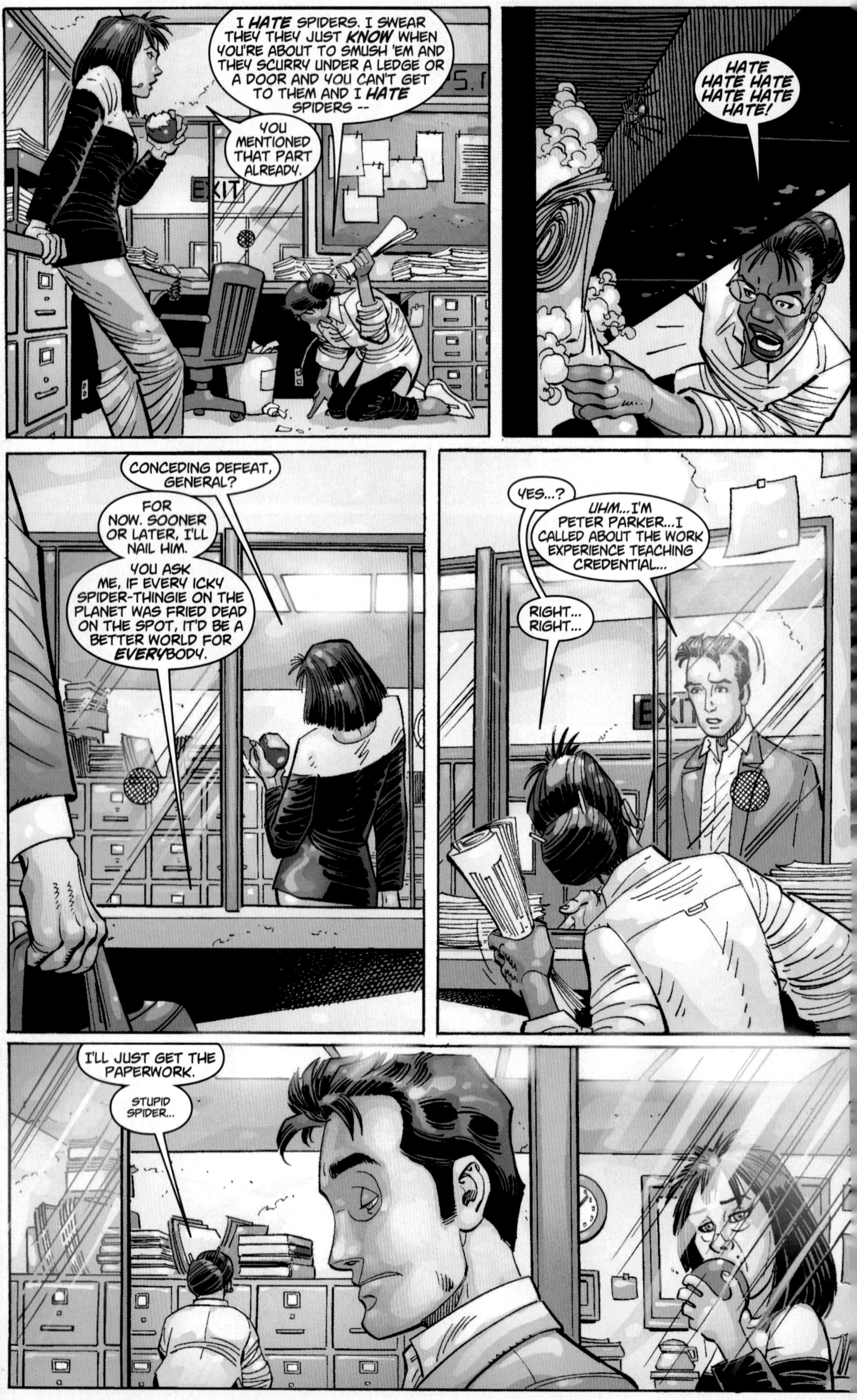
I HATE SPIDERS. I SWEAR THEY THEY JUST KNOW WHEN YOU'RE ABOUT TO SMUSH 'EM AND THEY SCURRY UNDER A LEDGE OR A DOOR AND YOU CAN'T GET TO THEM AND I HATE SPIDERS --
YOU MENTIONED THAT PART ALREADY.
EXIT
HATE HATE HATE HATE HATE HATE!
CONCEDING DEFEAT, GENERAL?
FOR NOW. SOONER OR LATER, I'LL NAIL HIM.
YOU ASK ME, IF EVERY ICKY SPIDER-THINGIE ON THE PLANET WAS FRIED DEAD ON THE SPOT, IT'D BE A BETTER WORLD FOR EVERYBODY.
YES...?
UHM... I'M PETER PARKER... I CALLED ABOUT THE WORK EXPERIENCE TEACHING CREDENTIAL...
RIGHT... RIGHT...
I'LL JUST GET THE PAPERWORK.
STUPID SPIDER...

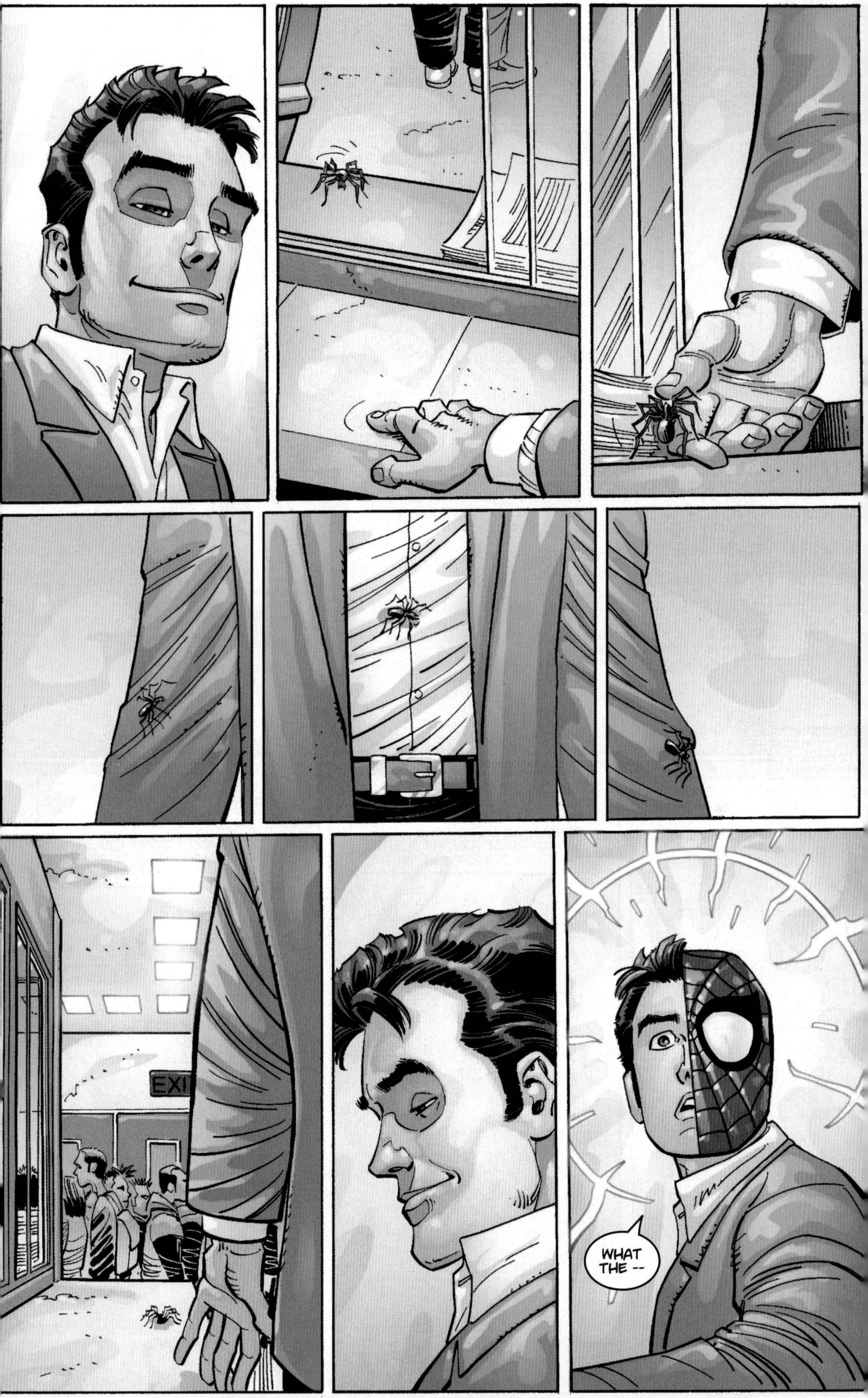
EXIT
WHAT THE --

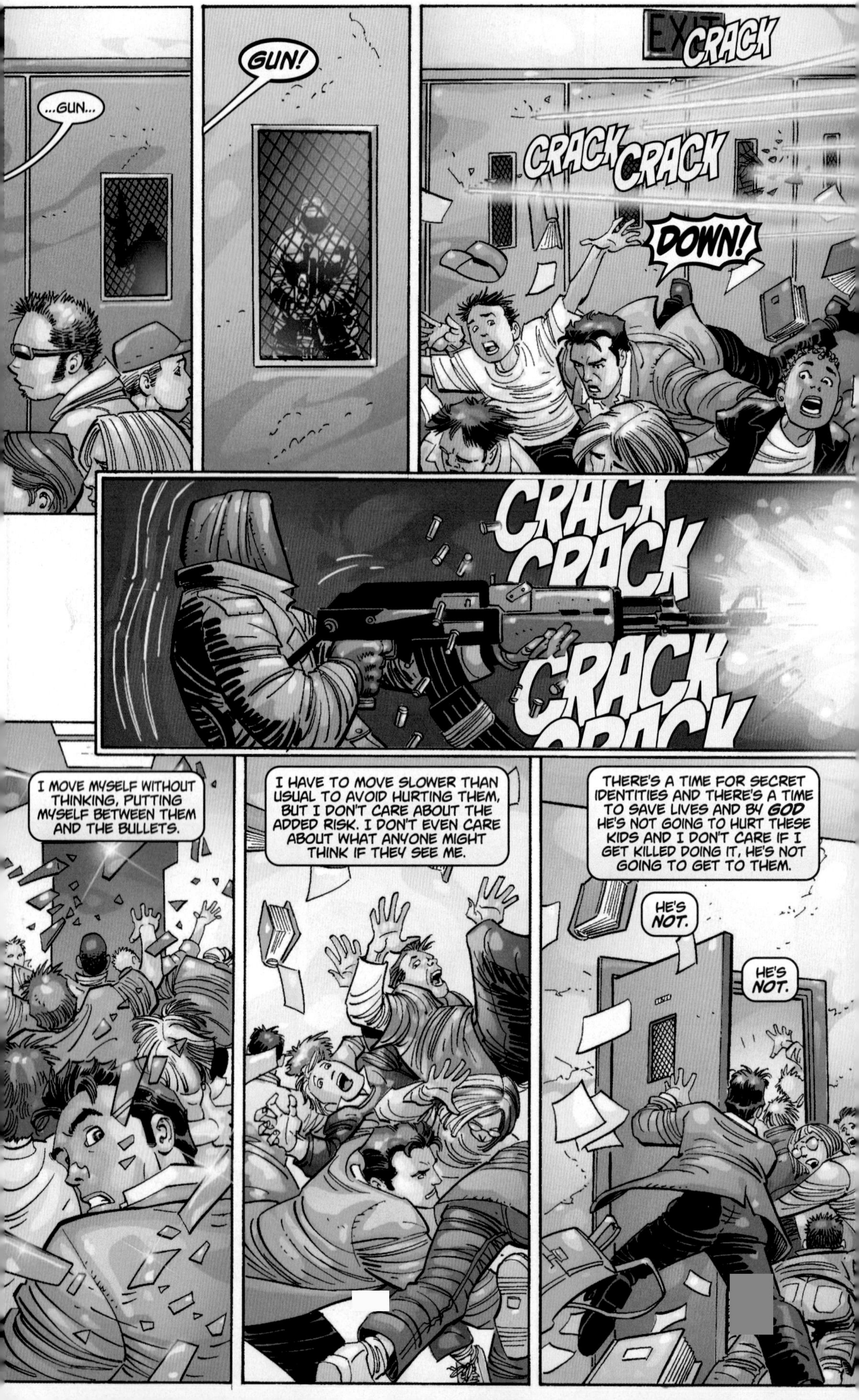

...GUN...
GUN!
CRACK
CRACK CRACK
DOWN!
CRACK
CRACK
CRACK
I MOVE MYSELF WITHOUT THINKING, PUTTING MYSELF BETWEEN THEM AND THE BULLETS.
I HAVE TO MOVE SLOWER THAN USUAL TO AVOID HURTING THEM, BUT I DON'T CARE ABOUT THE ADDED RISK. I DON'T EVEN CARE ABOUT WHAT ANYONE MIGHT THINK IF THEY SEE ME.
THERE'S A TIME FOR SECRET IDENTITIES AND THERE'S A TIME TO SAVE LIVES AND BY GOD HE'S NOT GOING TO HURT THESE KIDS AND I DON'T CARE IF I GET KILLED DOING IT, HE'S NOT GOING TO GET TO THEM.
HE'S NOT.
HE'S NOT.

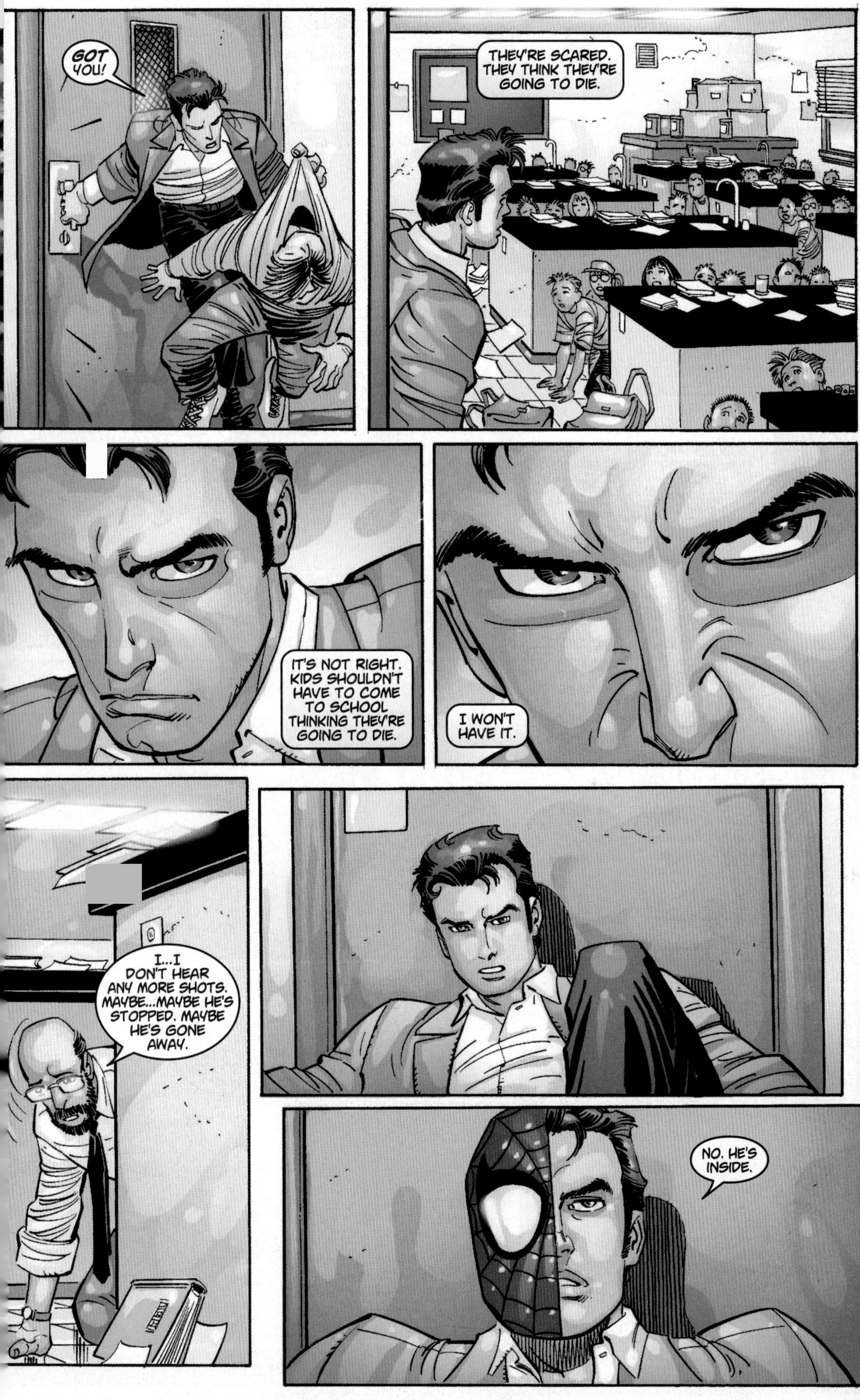
GOT YOU!
THEY'RE SCARED. THEY THINK THEY'RE GOING TO DIE.
IT'S NOT RIGHT. KIDS SHOULDN'T HAVE TO COME TO SCHOOL THINKING THEY'RE GOING TO DIE.
I WON'T HAVE IT.
I...I DON'T HEAR ANY MORE SHOTS. MAYBE...MAYBE HE'S STOPPED. MAYBE HE'S GONE AWAY.
NO. HE'S INSIDE.

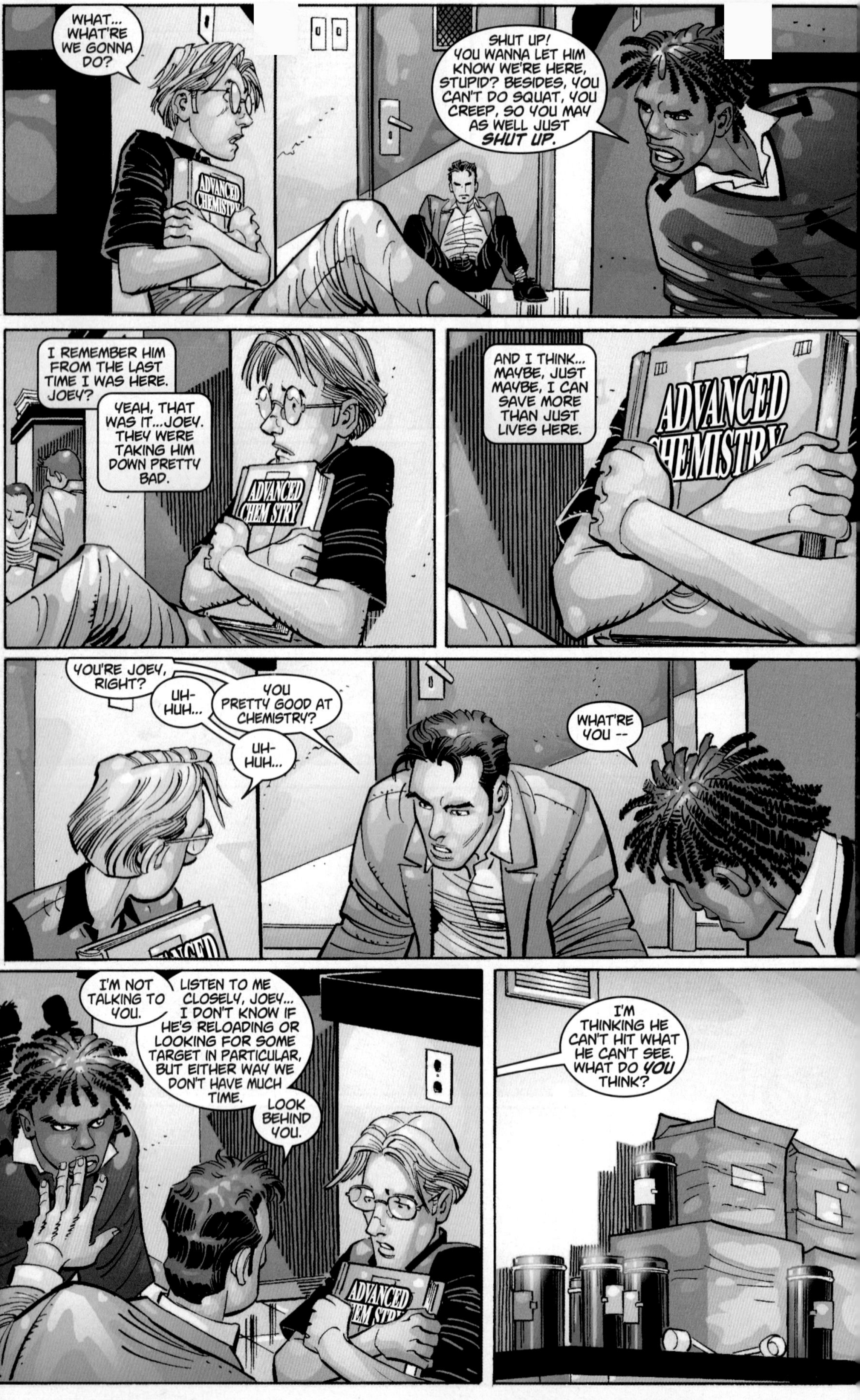
WHAT... WHAT'RE WE GONNA DO?
SHUT UP! YOU WANNA LET HIM KNOW WE'RE HERE, STUPID? BESIDES, YOU CAN'T DO SQUAT, YOU CREEP, SO YOU MAY AS WELL JUST SHUT UP.
ADVANCED CHEMISTRY
I REMEMBER HIM FROM THE LAST TIME I WAS HERE. JOEY?
YEAH, THAT WAS IT...JOEY. THEY WERE TAKING HIM DOWN PRETTY BAD.
ADVANCED CHEMISTRY
AND I THINK... MAYBE, JUST MAYBE, I CAN SAVE MORE THAN JUST LIVES HERE.
ADVANCED CHEMISTRY
YOU'RE JOEY, RIGHT?
UH-HUH...
YOU PRETTY GOOD AT CHEMISTRY?
UH-HUH...
WHAT'RE YOU --
I'M NOT TALKING TO YOU.
LISTEN TO ME CLOSELY, JOEY... I DON'T KNOW IF HE'S RELOADING OR LOOKING FOR SOME TARGET IN PARTICULAR, BUT EITHER WAY WE DON'T HAVE MUCH TIME.
LOOK BEHIND YOU.
I'M THINKING HE CAN'T HIT WHAT HE CAN'T SEE. WHAT DO YOU THINK?

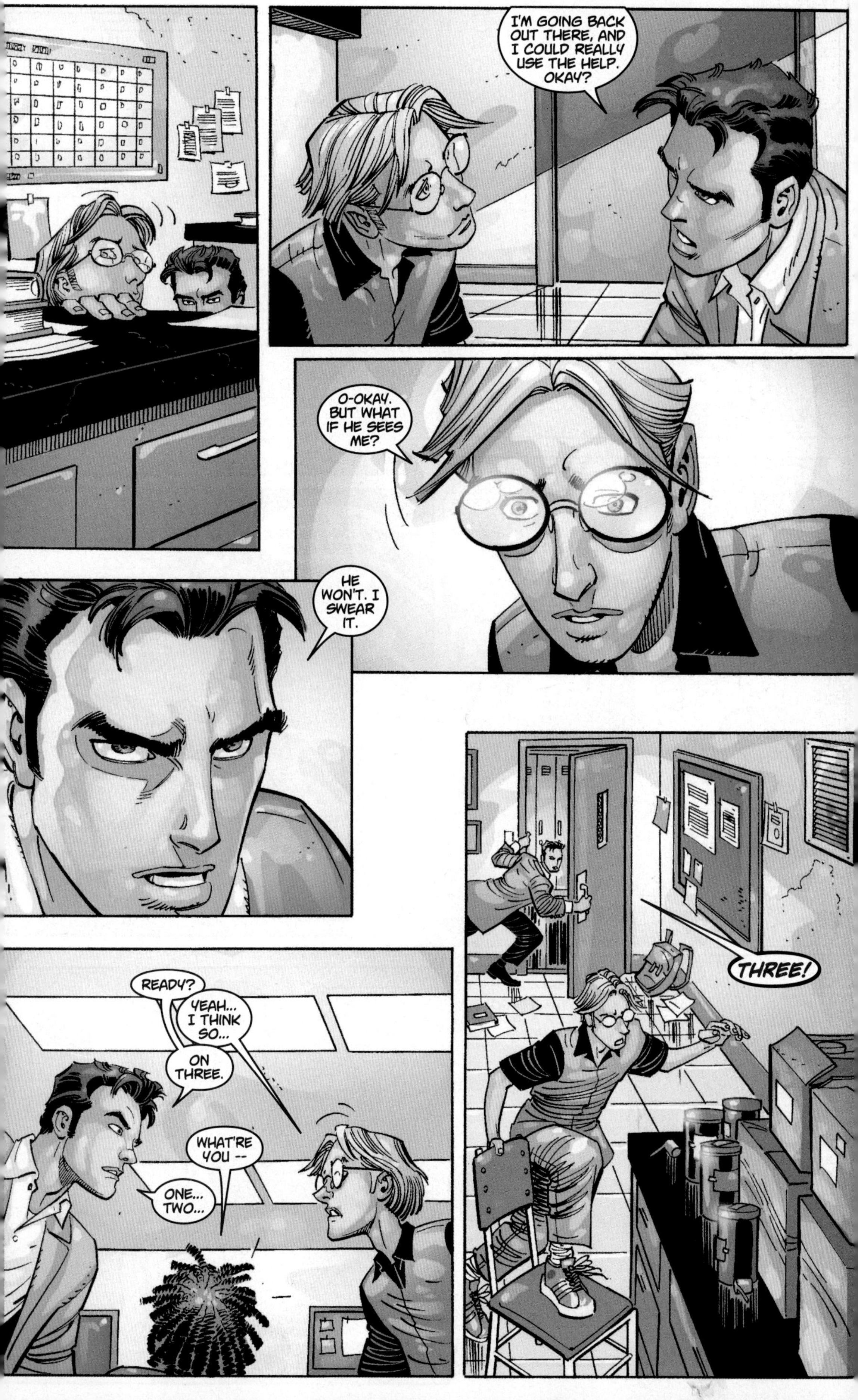
I'M GOING BACK OUT THERE, AND I COULD REALLY USE THE HELP. OKAY?
O-OKAY. BUT WHAT IF HE SEES ME?
HE WON'T. I SWEAR IT.
READY?
YEAH... I THINK SO...
ON THREE.
WHAT'RE YOU --
ONE... TWO...
THREE!

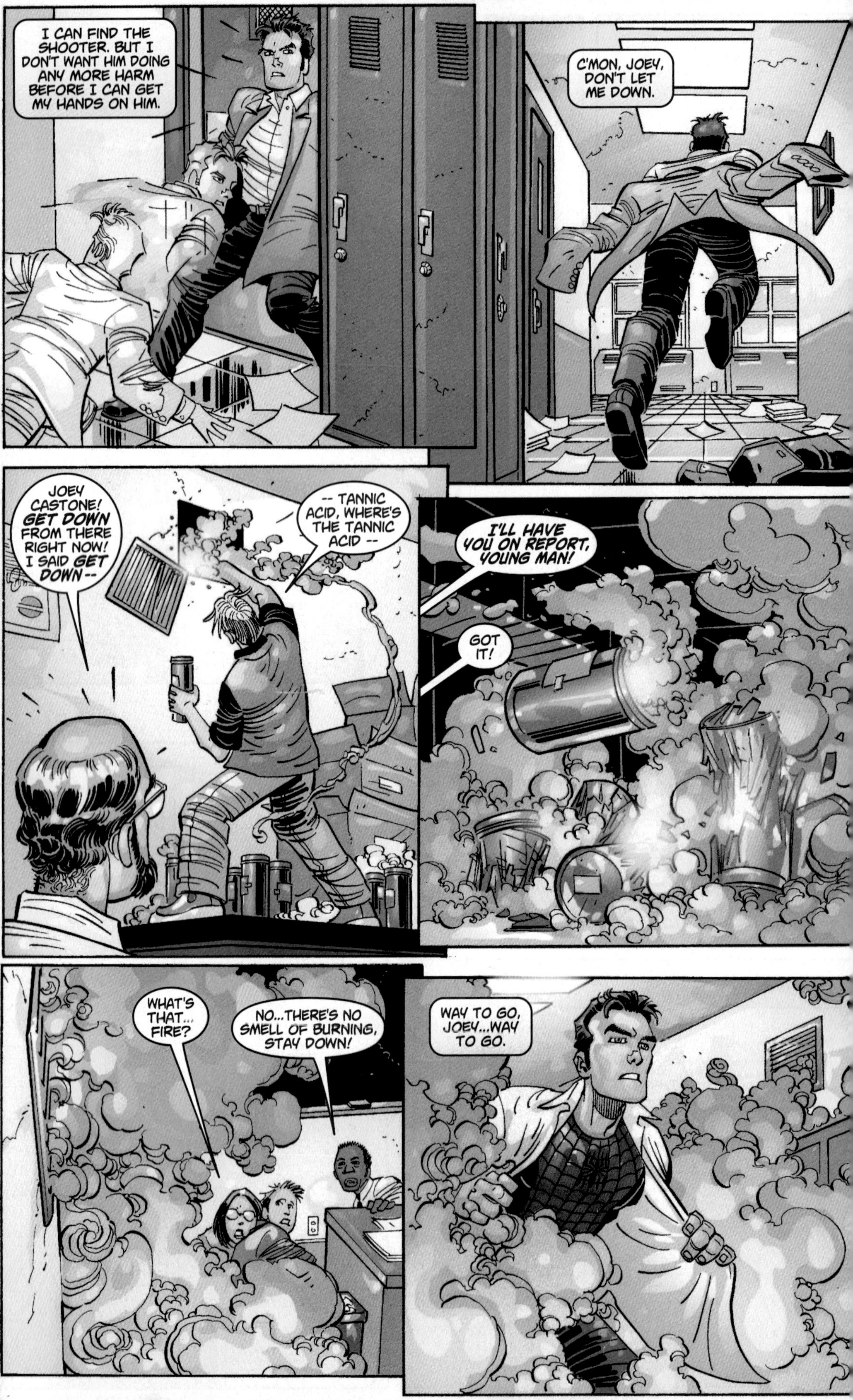

I CAN FIND THE SHOOTER. BUT I DON'T WANT HIM DOING ANY MORE HARM BEFORE I CAN GET MY HANDS ON HIM.
C'MON, JOEY, DON'T LET ME DOWN.
JOEY CASTONE! **GET DOWN** FROM THERE RIGHT NOW! I SAID **GET DOWN**--
-- TANNIC ACID, WHERE'S THE TANNIC ACID --
I'LL HAVE YOU ON REPORT, YOUNG MAN!
GOT IT!
WHAT'S THAT... FIRE?
NO...THERE'S NO SMELL OF BURNING, STAY DOWN!
WAY TO GO, JOEY...WAY TO GO.

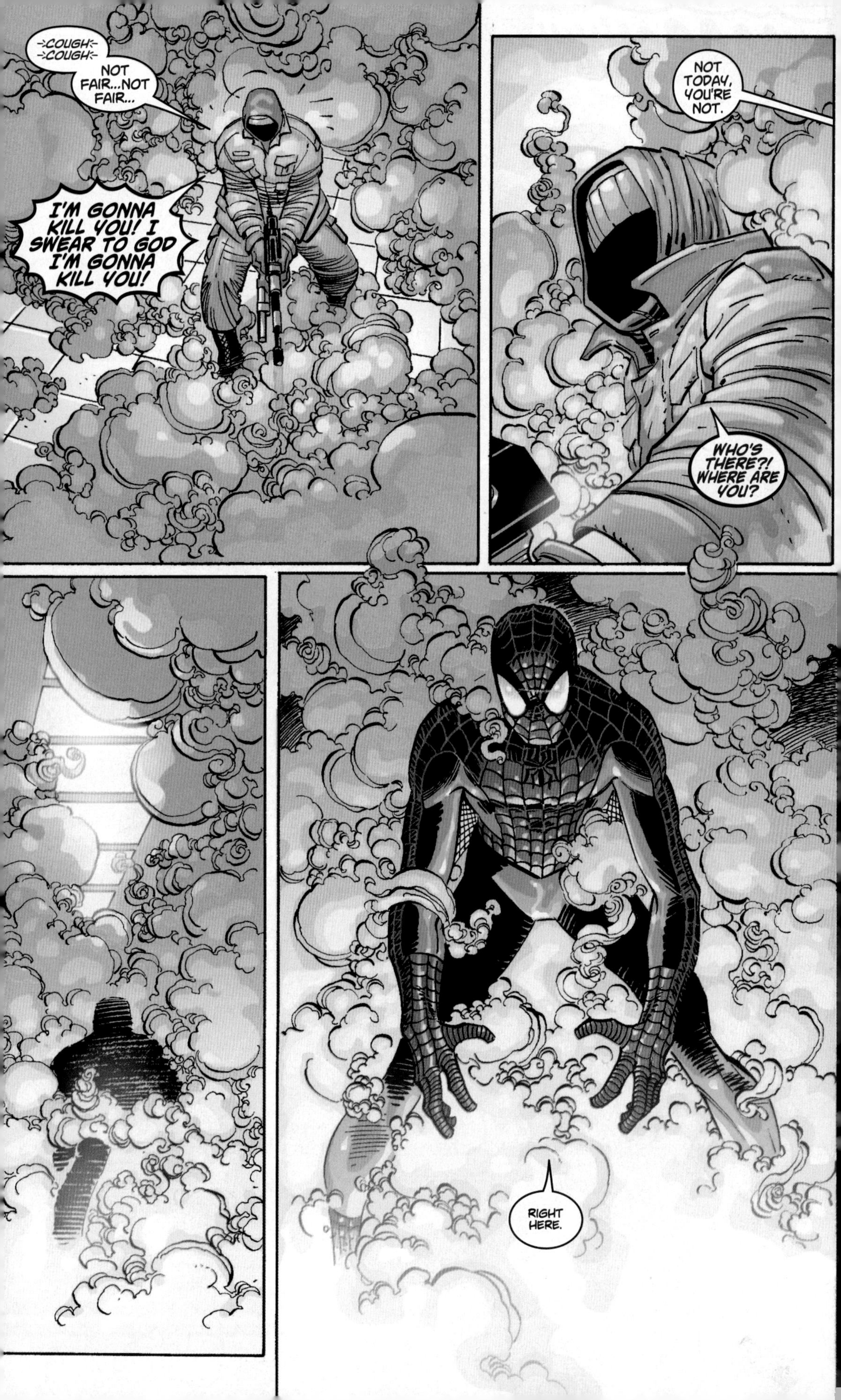

-COUGH-
-COUGH-
NOT FAIR...NOT FAIR...
I'M GONNA KILL YOU! I SWEAR TO GOD I'M GONNA KILL YOU!
NOT TODAY, YOU'RE NOT.
WHO'S THERE?! WHERE ARE YOU?
RIGHT HERE.

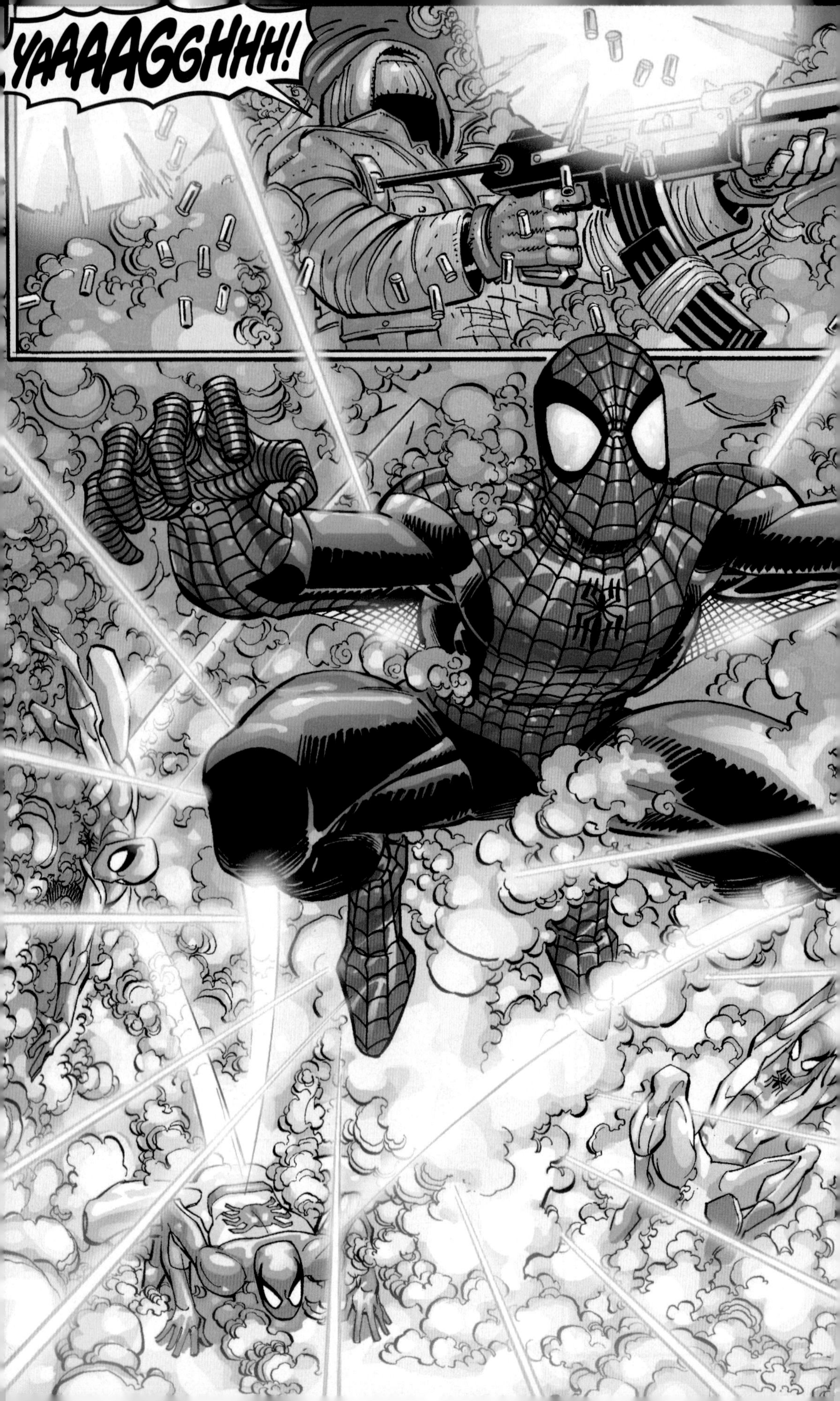
YAAAAGGHHH!

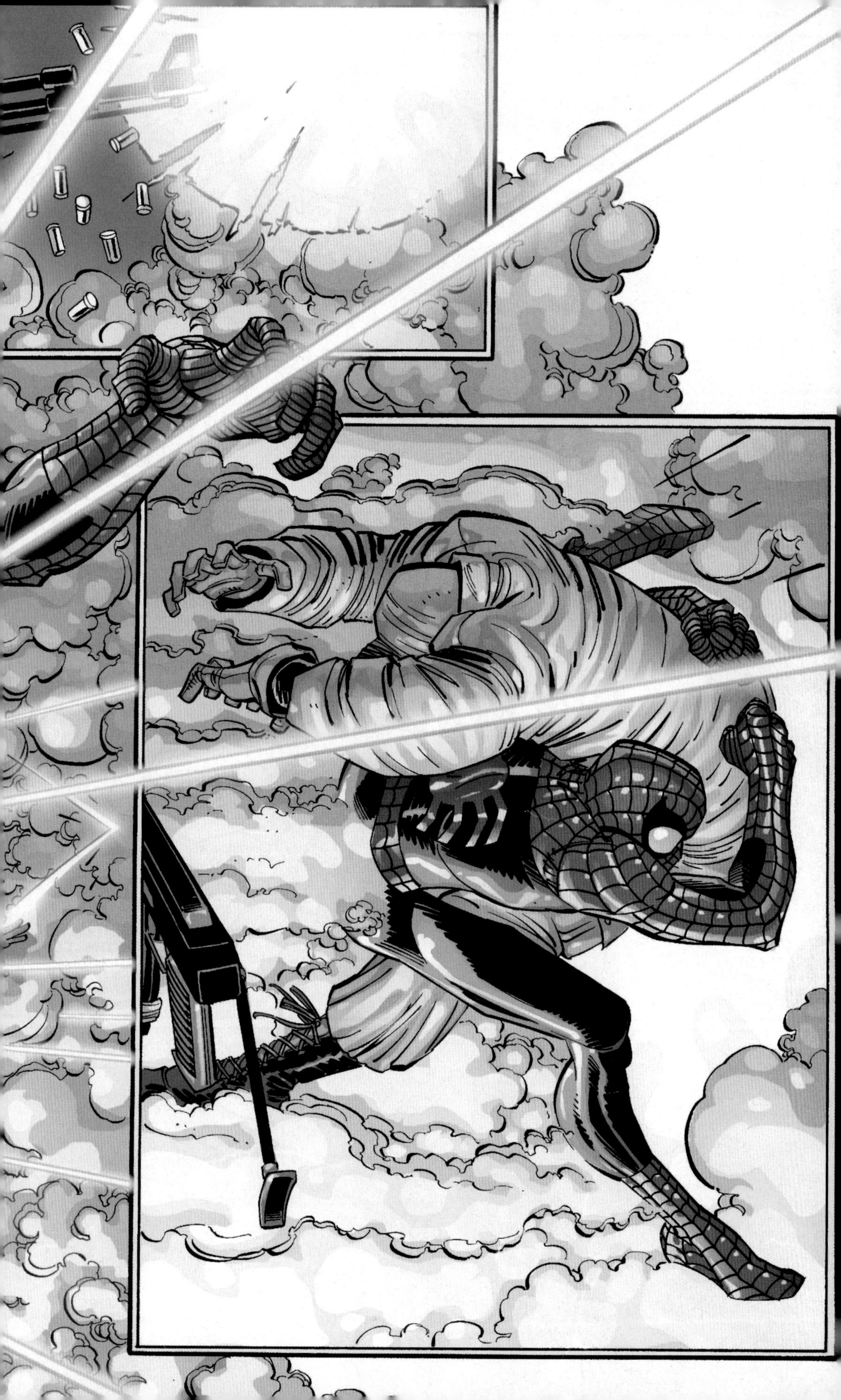

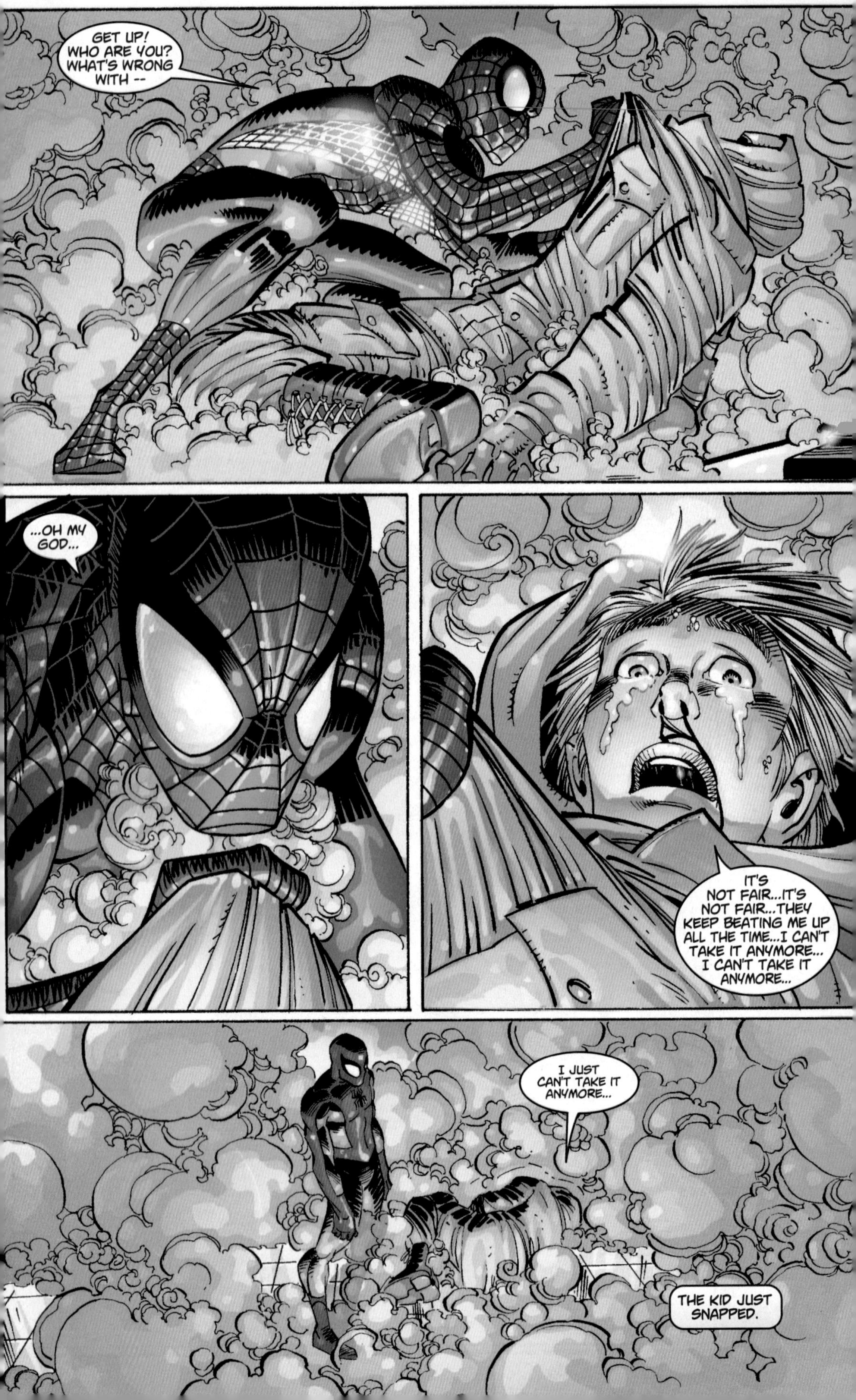
GET UP! WHO ARE YOU? WHAT'S WRONG WITH --
...OH MY GOD...
IT'S NOT FAIR...IT'S NOT FAIR...THEY KEEP BEATING ME UP ALL THE TIME...I CAN'T TAKE IT ANYMORE... I CAN'T TAKE IT ANYMORE...
I JUST CAN'T TAKE IT ANYMORE...
THE KID JUST SNAPPED.

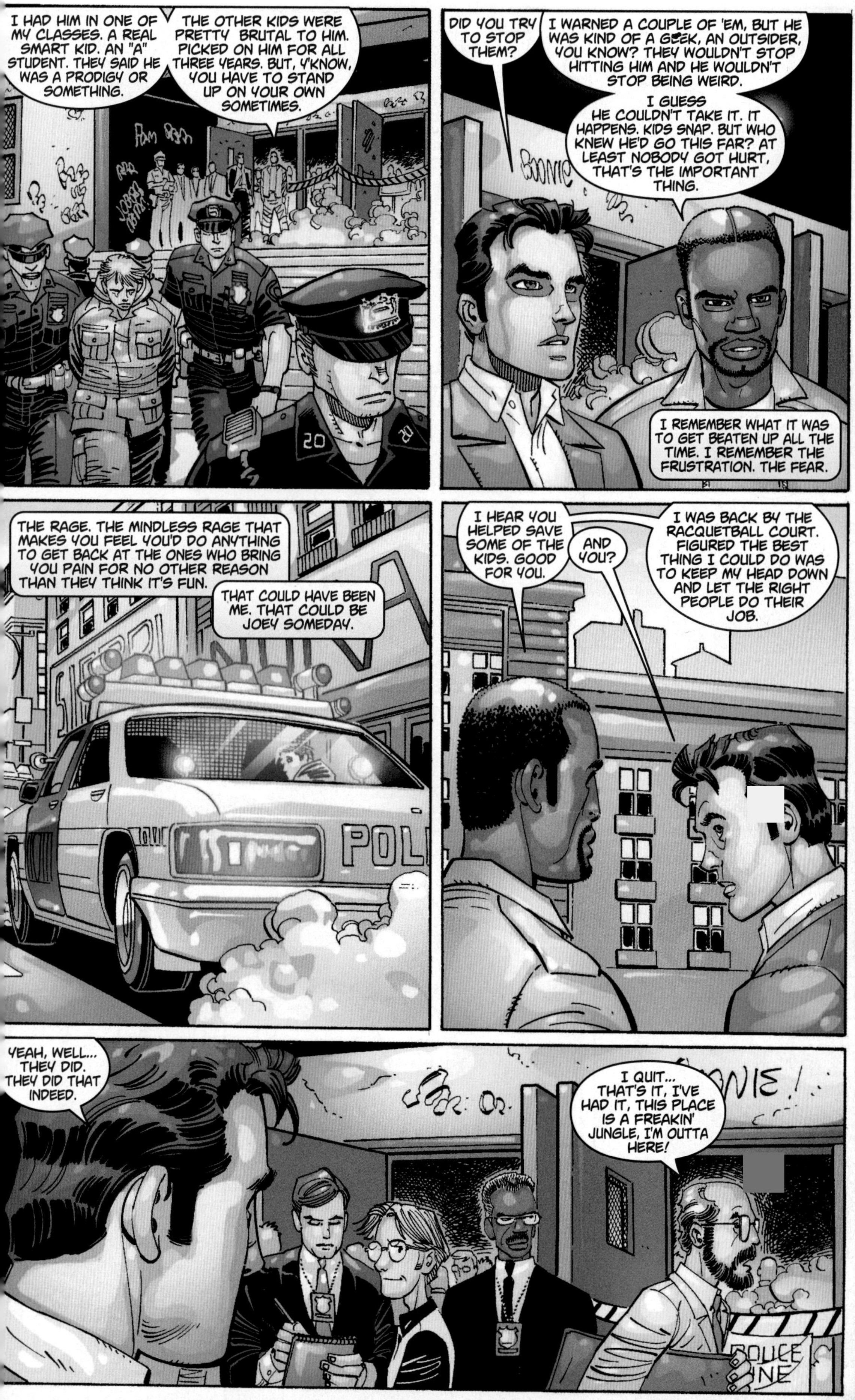
I HAD HIM IN ONE OF MY CLASSES. A REAL SMART KID. AN "A" STUDENT. THEY SAID HE WAS A PRODIGY OR SOMETHING.
THE OTHER KIDS WERE PRETTY BRUTAL TO HIM. PICKED ON HIM FOR ALL THREE YEARS. BUT, Y'KNOW, YOU HAVE TO STAND UP ON YOUR OWN SOMETIMES.
DID YOU TRY TO STOP THEM?
I WARNED A COUPLE OF 'EM, BUT HE WAS KIND OF A GEEK, AN OUTSIDER, YOU KNOW? THEY WOULDN'T STOP HITTING HIM AND HE WOULDN'T STOP BEING WEIRD.
I GUESS HE COULDN'T TAKE IT. IT HAPPENS. KIDS SNAP. BUT WHO KNEW HE'D GO THIS FAR? AT LEAST NOBODY GOT HURT, THAT'S THE IMPORTANT THING.
I REMEMBER WHAT IT WAS TO GET BEATEN UP ALL THE TIME. I REMEMBER THE FRUSTRATION. THE FEAR.
THE RAGE. THE MINDLESS RAGE THAT MAKES YOU FEEL YOU'D DO ANYTHING TO GET BACK AT THE ONES WHO BRING YOU PAIN FOR NO OTHER REASON THAN THEY THINK IT'S FUN.
THAT COULD HAVE BEEN ME. THAT COULD BE JOEY SOMEDAY.
POLI
I HEAR YOU HELPED SAVE SOME OF THE KIDS. GOOD FOR YOU.
AND YOU?
I WAS BACK BY THE RACQUETBALL COURT. FIGURED THE BEST THING I COULD DO WAS TO KEEP MY HEAD DOWN AND LET THE RIGHT PEOPLE DO THEIR JOB.
YEAH, WELL... THEY DID. THEY DID THAT INDEED.
I QUIT... THAT'S IT, I'VE HAD IT, THIS PLACE IS A FREAKIN' JUNGLE, I'M OUTTA HERE!

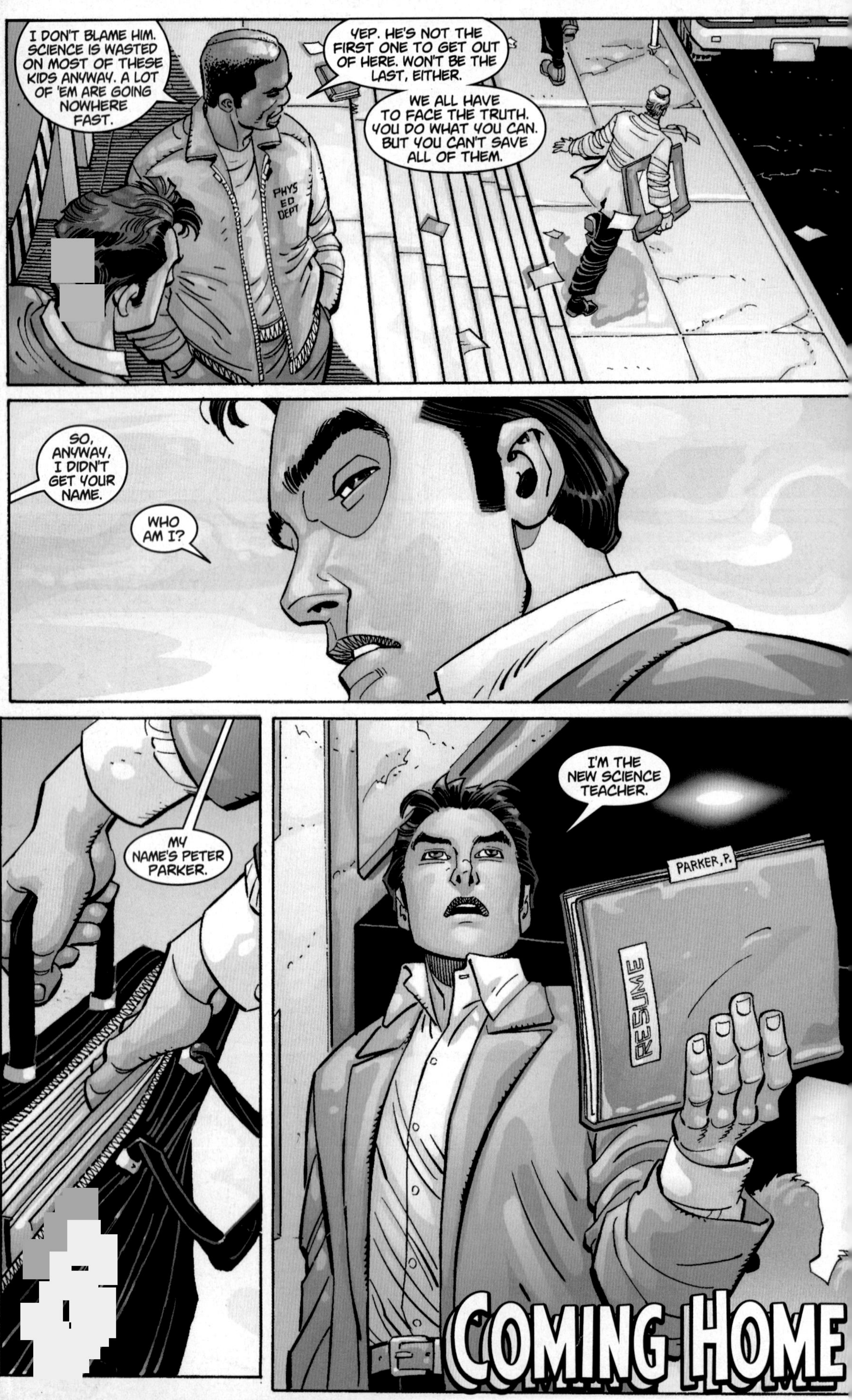
I DON'T BLAME HIM. SCIENCE IS WASTED ON MOST OF THESE KIDS ANYWAY. A LOT OF 'EM ARE GOING NOWHERE FAST.
YEP. HE'S NOT THE FIRST ONE TO GET OUT OF HERE. WON'T BE THE LAST, EITHER.
WE ALL HAVE TO FACE THE TRUTH. YOU DO WHAT YOU CAN. BUT YOU CAN'T SAVE ALL OF THEM.
PHYS ED DEPT
SO, ANYWAY, I DIDN'T GET YOUR NAME.
WHO AM I?
MY NAME'S PETER PARKER.
I'M THE NEW SCIENCE TEACHER.
PARKER, P.
RESUME
COMING HOME

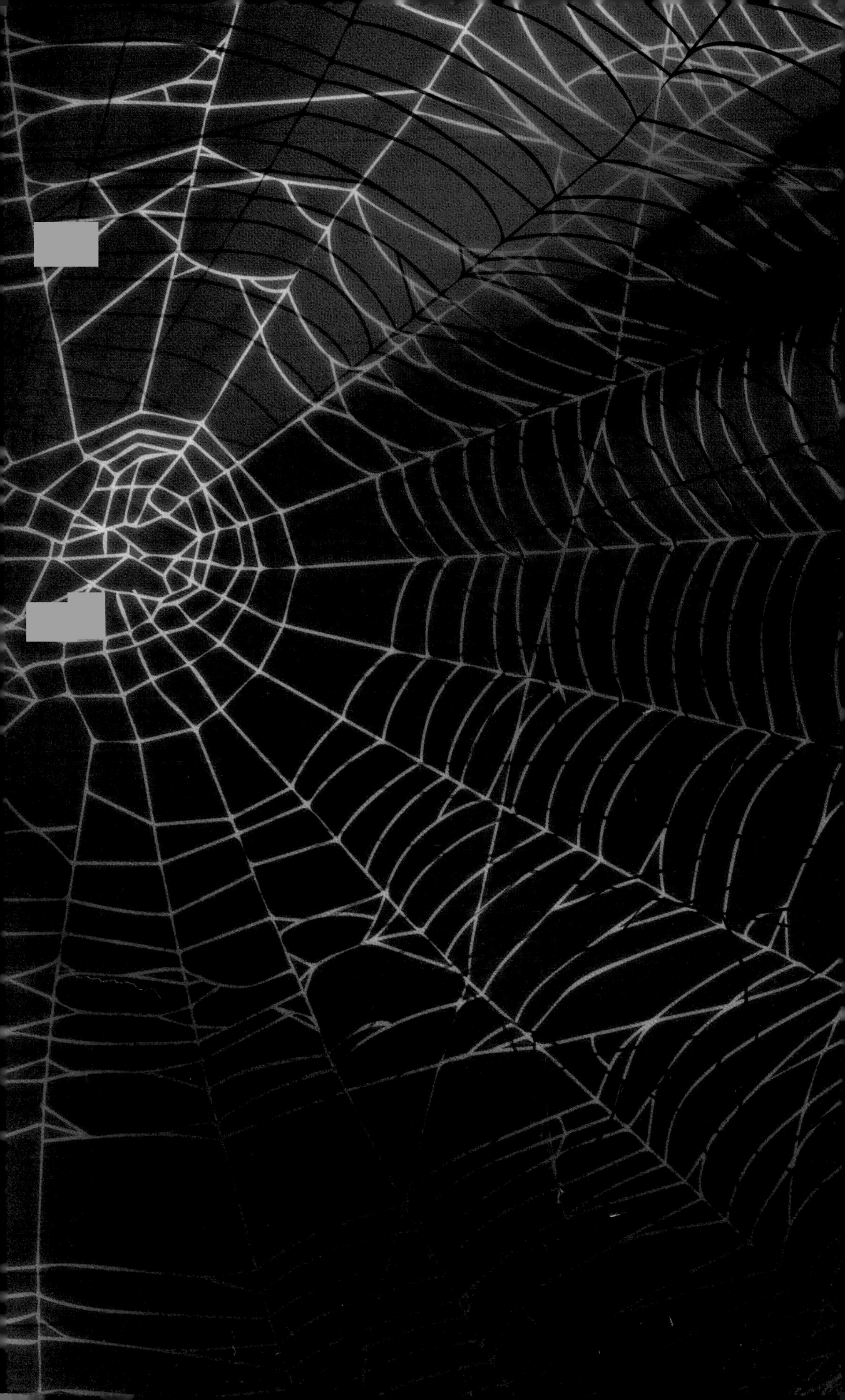

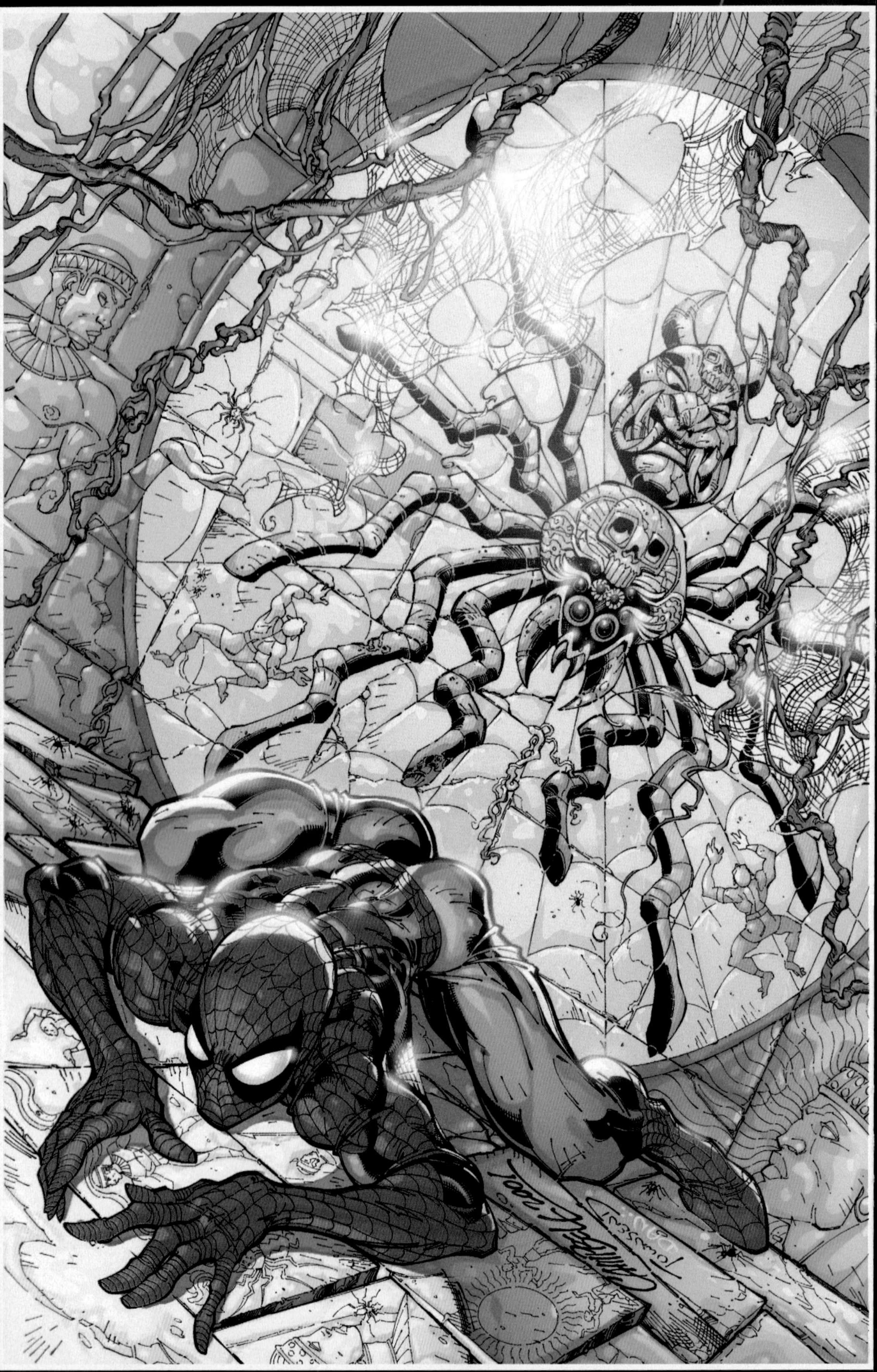

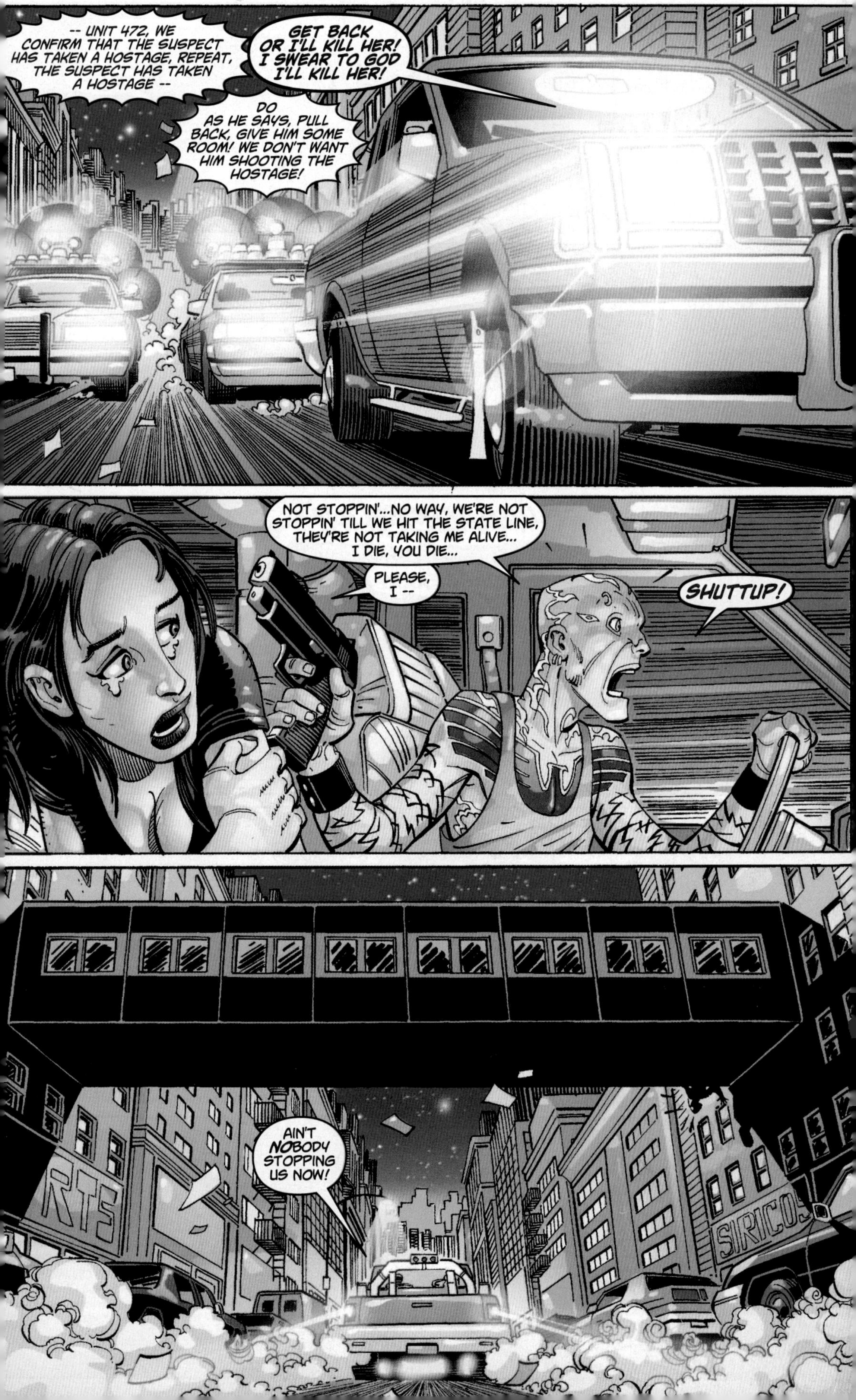

-- UNIT 472, WE CONFIRM THAT THE SUSPECT HAS TAKEN A HOSTAGE, REPEAT, THE SUSPECT HAS TAKEN A HOSTAGE --
GET BACK OR I'LL KILL HER! I SWEAR TO GOD I'LL KILL HER!
DO AS HE SAYS, PULL BACK, GIVE HIM SOME ROOM! WE DON'T WANT HIM SHOOTING THE HOSTAGE!
NOT STOPPIN'...NO WAY, WE'RE NOT STOPPIN' TILL WE HIT THE STATE LINE, THEY'RE NOT TAKING ME ALIVE... I DIE, YOU DIE...
PLEASE, I --
SHUTTUP!
AIN'T NOBODY STOPPING US NOW!
SIRICO

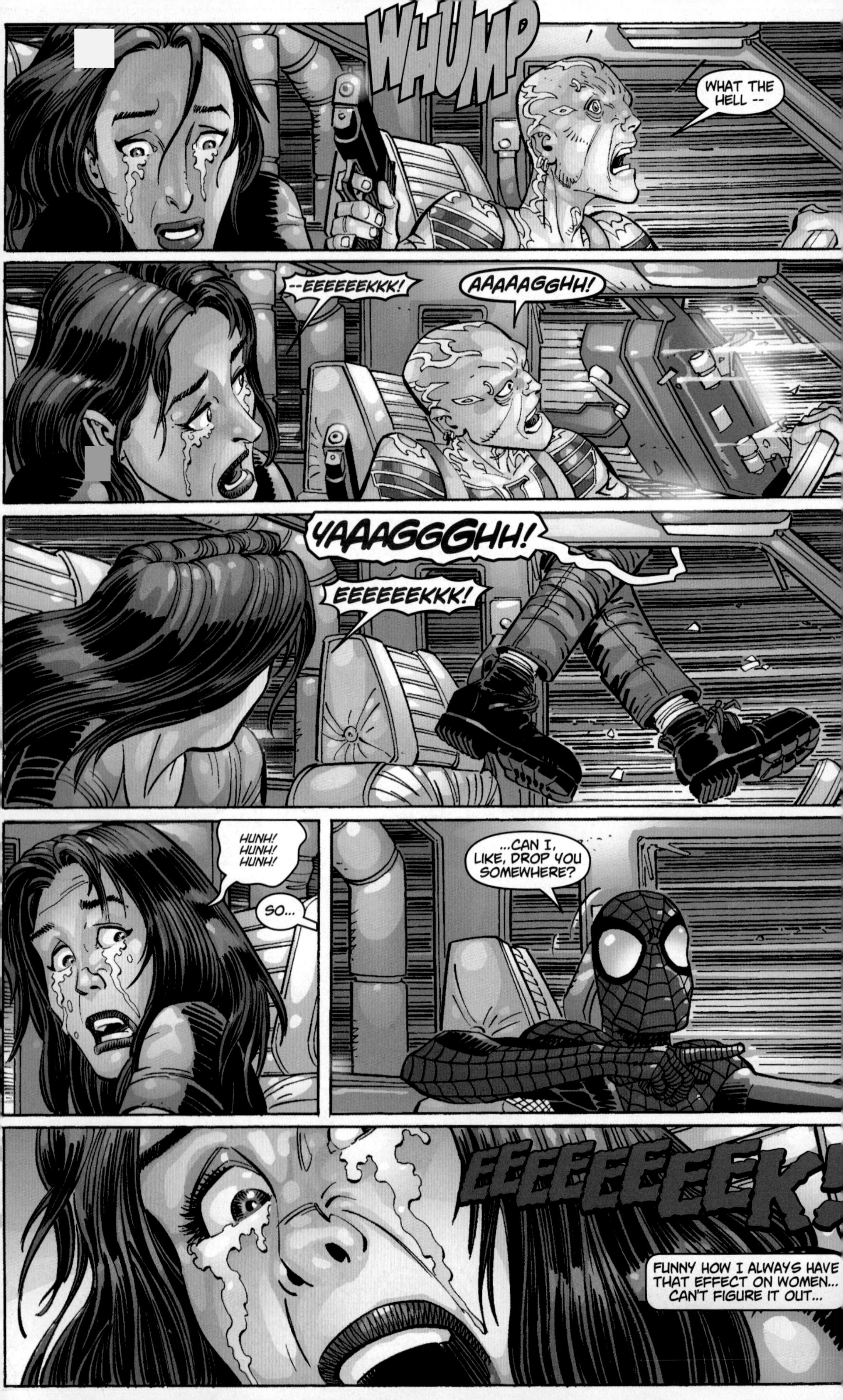
WHUMP
WHAT THE HELL --
--EEEEEEKKK!
AAAAAGGHH!
YAAAGGGHH!
EEEEEEKKK!
HUNH! HUNH! HUNH!
SO...
...CAN I, LIKE, DROP YOU SOMEWHERE?
EEEEEEEEK!
FUNNY HOW I ALWAYS HAVE THAT EFFECT ON WOMEN... CAN'T FIGURE IT OUT...

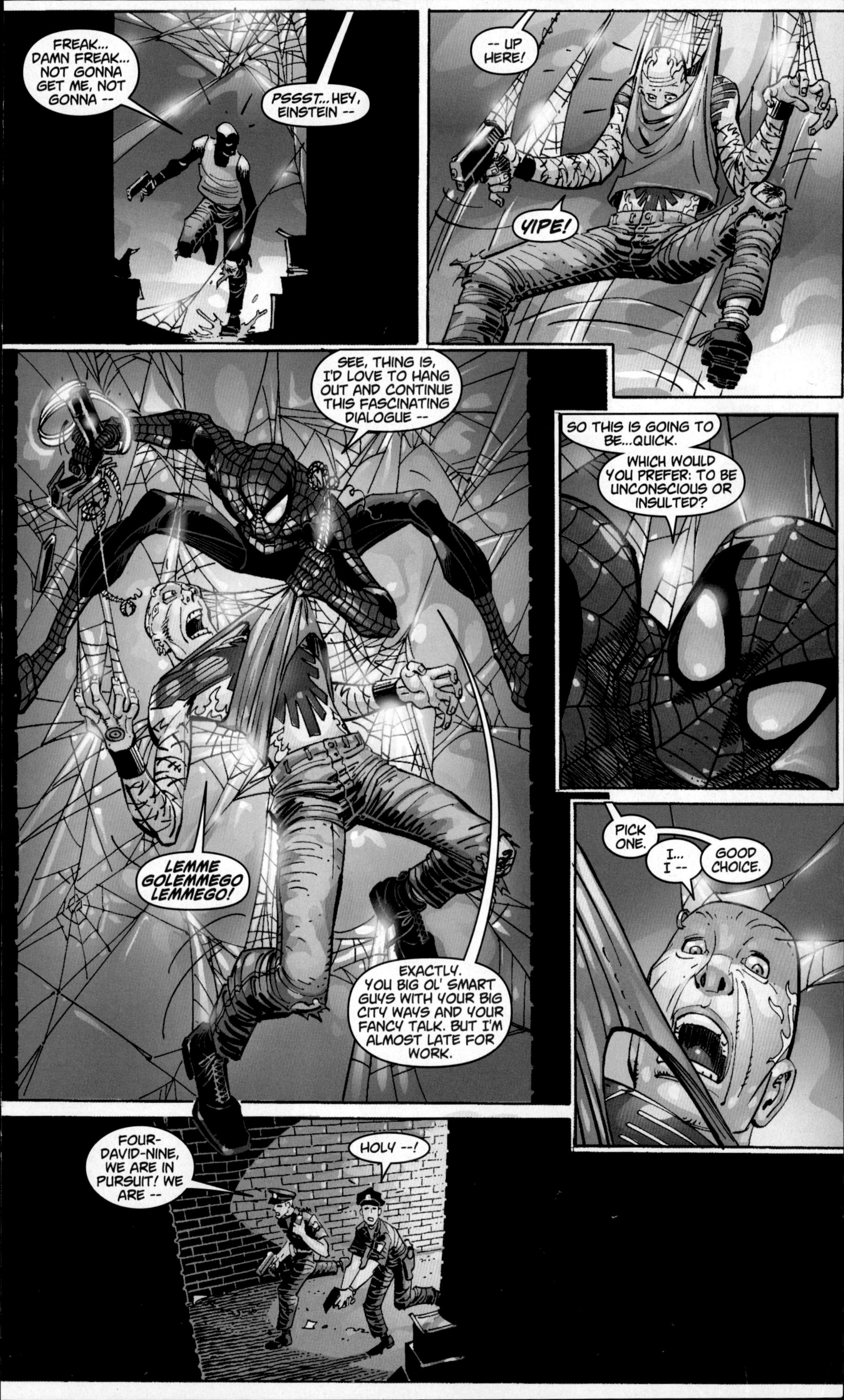
FREAK... DAMN FREAK... NOT GONNA GET ME, NOT GONNA --
PSSST... HEY, EINSTEIN --
-- UP HERE!
YIPE!
SEE, THING IS, I'D LOVE TO HANG OUT AND CONTINUE THIS FASCINATING DIALOGUE --
LEMME GOLEMMEGO LEMMEGO!
EXACTLY. YOU BIG OL' SMART GUYS WITH YOUR BIG CITY WAYS AND YOUR FANCY TALK. BUT I'M ALMOST LATE FOR WORK.
SO THIS IS GOING TO BE...QUICK.
WHICH WOULD YOU PREFER: TO BE UNCONSCIOUS OR INSULTED?
PICK ONE.
I... I --
GOOD CHOICE.
FOUR-DAVID-NINE, WE ARE IN PURSUIT! WE ARE --
HOLY --!

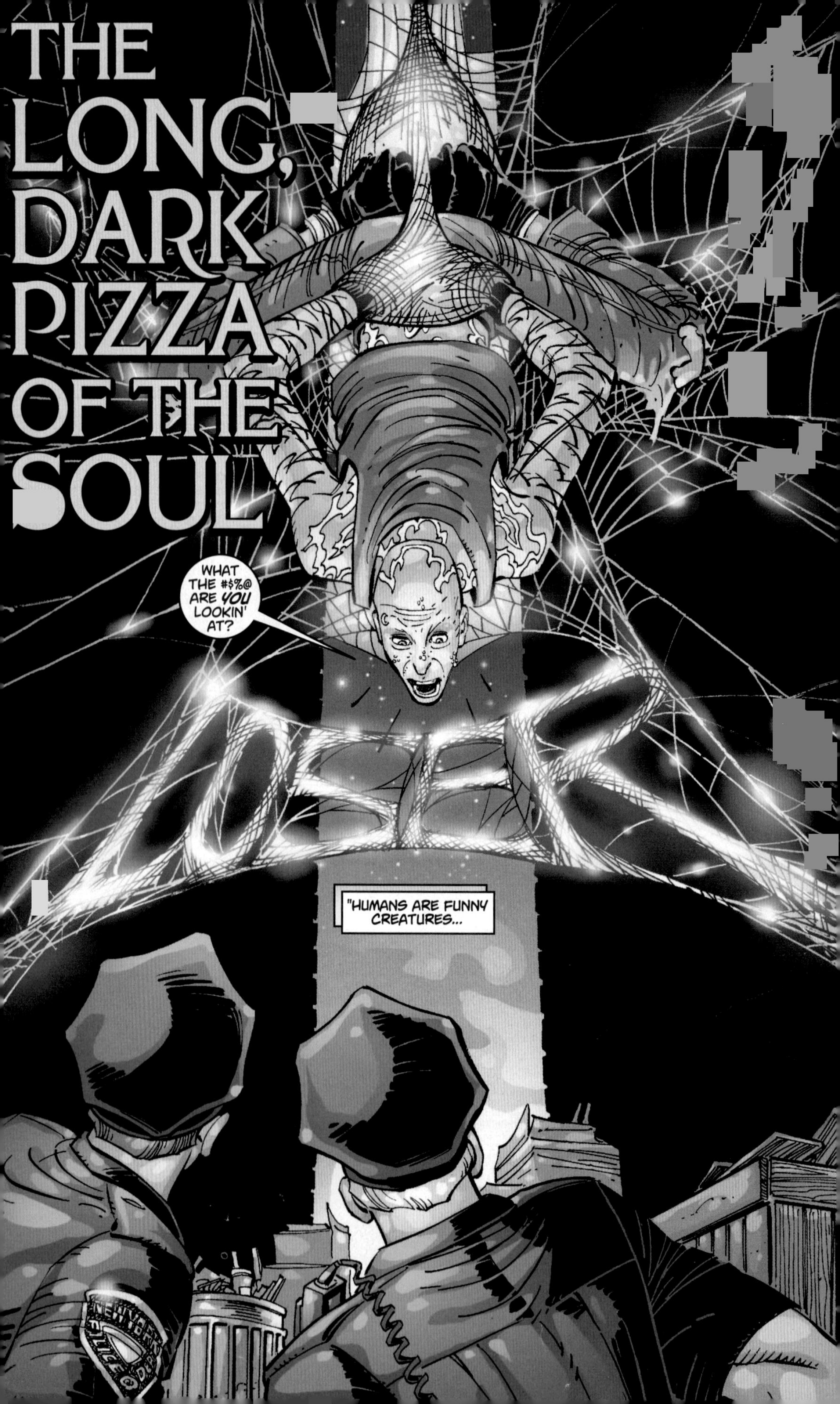
THE LONG, DARK PIZZA OF THE SOUL
WHAT THE #$%@ ARE YOU LOOKIN' AT?
"HUMANS ARE FUNNY CREATURES...

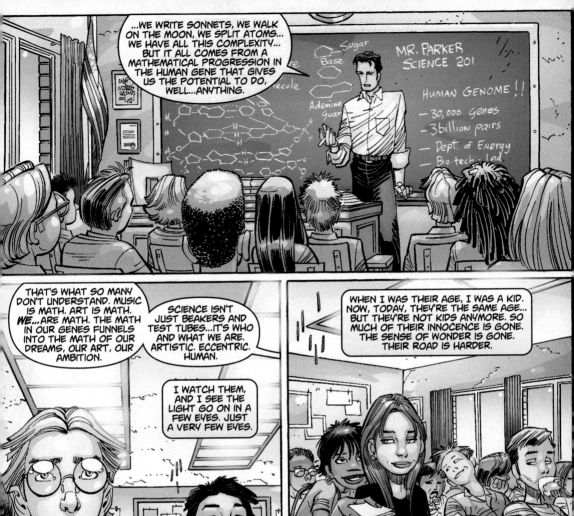

...WE WRITE SONNETS, WE WALK ON THE MOON, WE SPLIT ATOMS... WE HAVE ALL THIS COMPLEXITY... BUT IT ALL COMES FROM A MATHEMATICAL PROGRESSION IN THE HUMAN GENE THAT GIVES US THE POTENTIAL TO DO, WELL...ANYTHING.

Sugar

Base

Adenine Guan

MR. PARKER
SCIENCE 201

HUMAN GENOME!!
- 30,000 Genes
- 3 billion pairs
- Dept. of Energy
- Bio-tech. Ind

THAT'S WHAT SO MANY DON'T UNDERSTAND. MUSIC IS MATH. ART IS MATH. WE...ARE MATH. THE MATH IN OUR GENES FUNNELS INTO THE MATH OF OUR DREAMS, OUR ART, OUR AMBITION.

SCIENCE ISN'T JUST BEAKERS AND TEST TUBES...IT'S WHO AND WHAT WE ARE. ARTISTIC. ECCENTRIC. HUMAN.

I WATCH THEM, AND I SEE THE LIGHT GO ON IN A FEW EYES. JUST A VERY FEW EYES.

WHEN I WAS THEIR AGE, I WAS A KID. NOW, TODAY, THEY'RE THE SAME AGE... BUT THEY'RE NOT KIDS ANYMORE. SO MUCH OF THEIR INNOCENCE IS GONE. THE SENSE OF WONDER IS GONE. THEIR ROAD IS HARDER.

SO I'LL JUST WORK THAT MUCH HARDER TO GET THROUGH. I KNOW I CAN DO IT. I HAVE TO DO IT.

SOMEHOW.

-- SO THE FUNNY THING IS... AND YOU'RE GONNA LOVE THIS...IT ALL STARTED WITH SCIENTISTS MESSING AROUND WITH THE LOVE LIVES OF FRUIT FLIES...

RRIINNNNGG

AND READ CHAPTER TWELVE FOR TOMORROW!

WAS PRETTY COOL --

SO LAME, GIVE ME A BREAK --

THE PART ABOUT THE MATH OF ART, I NEVER THOUGHT --

YOU WANNA COME OVER, MY DAD'S AWAY, WE CAN GET LOADED --

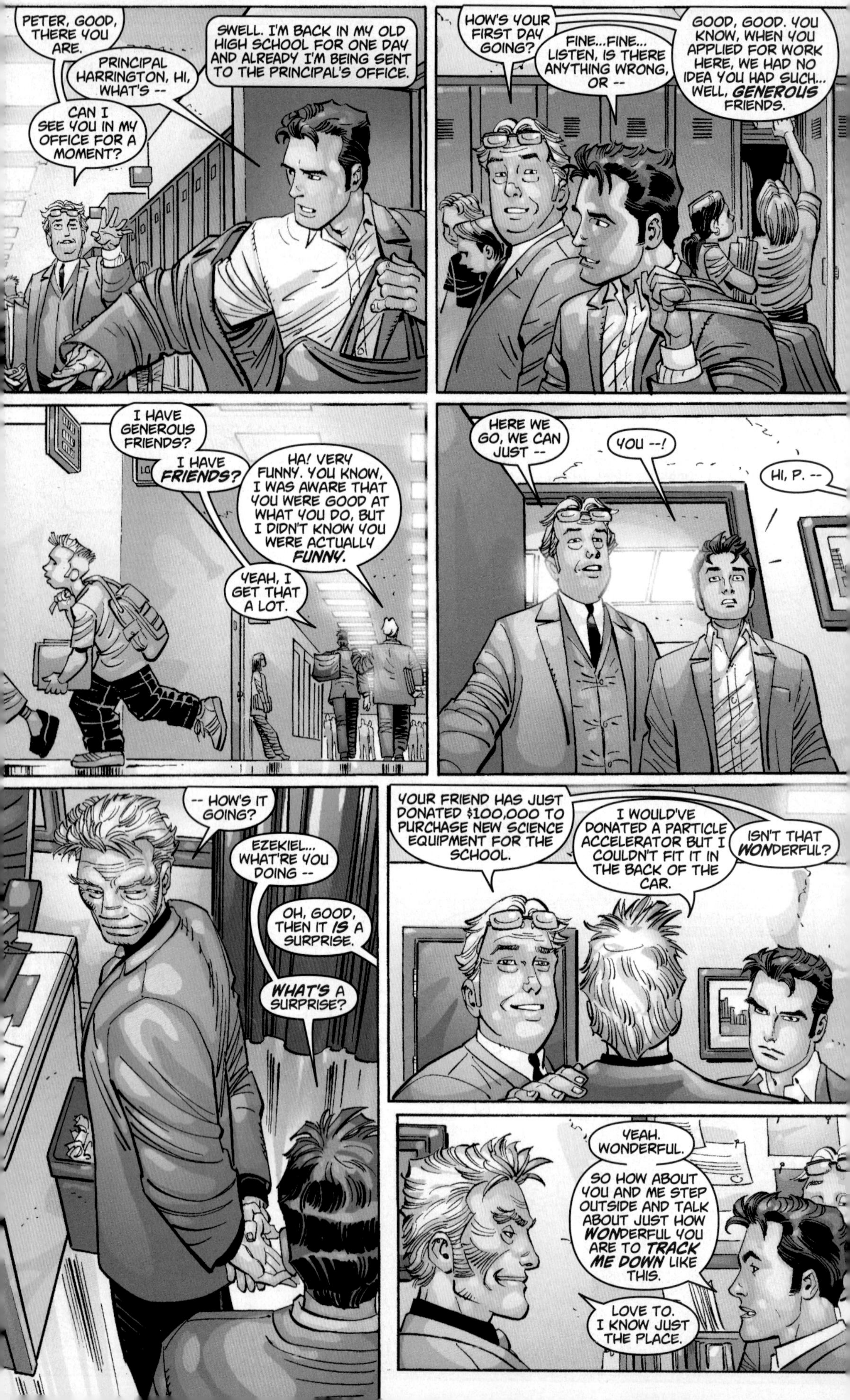
PETER, GOOD, THERE YOU ARE.
PRINCIPAL HARRINGTON, HI, WHAT'S --
CAN I SEE YOU IN MY OFFICE FOR A MOMENT?
SWELL. I'M BACK IN MY OLD HIGH SCHOOL FOR ONE DAY AND ALREADY I'M BEING SENT TO THE PRINCIPAL'S OFFICE.
HOW'S YOUR FIRST DAY GOING?
FINE...FINE... LISTEN, IS THERE ANYTHING WRONG, OR --
GOOD, GOOD. YOU KNOW, WHEN YOU APPLIED FOR WORK HERE, WE HAD NO IDEA YOU HAD SUCH... WELL, GENEROUS FRIENDS.
I HAVE GENEROUS FRIENDS?
I HAVE FRIENDS?
HA! VERY FUNNY. YOU KNOW, I WAS AWARE THAT YOU WERE GOOD AT WHAT YOU DO, BUT I DIDN'T KNOW YOU WERE ACTUALLY FUNNY.
YEAH, I GET THAT A LOT.
HERE WE GO, WE CAN JUST --
YOU --!
HI, P. --
-- HOW'S IT GOING?
EZEKIEL... WHAT'RE YOU DOING --
OH, GOOD, THEN IT IS A SURPRISE.
WHAT'S A SURPRISE?
YOUR FRIEND HAS JUST DONATED $100,000 TO PURCHASE NEW SCIENCE EQUIPMENT FOR THE SCHOOL.
I WOULD'VE DONATED A PARTICLE ACCELERATOR BUT I COULDN'T FIT IT IN THE BACK OF THE CAR.
ISN'T THAT WONDERFUL?
YEAH. WONDERFUL.
SO HOW ABOUT YOU AND ME STEP OUTSIDE AND TALK ABOUT JUST HOW WONDERFUL YOU ARE TO TRACK ME DOWN LIKE THIS.
LOVE TO. I KNOW JUST THE PLACE.

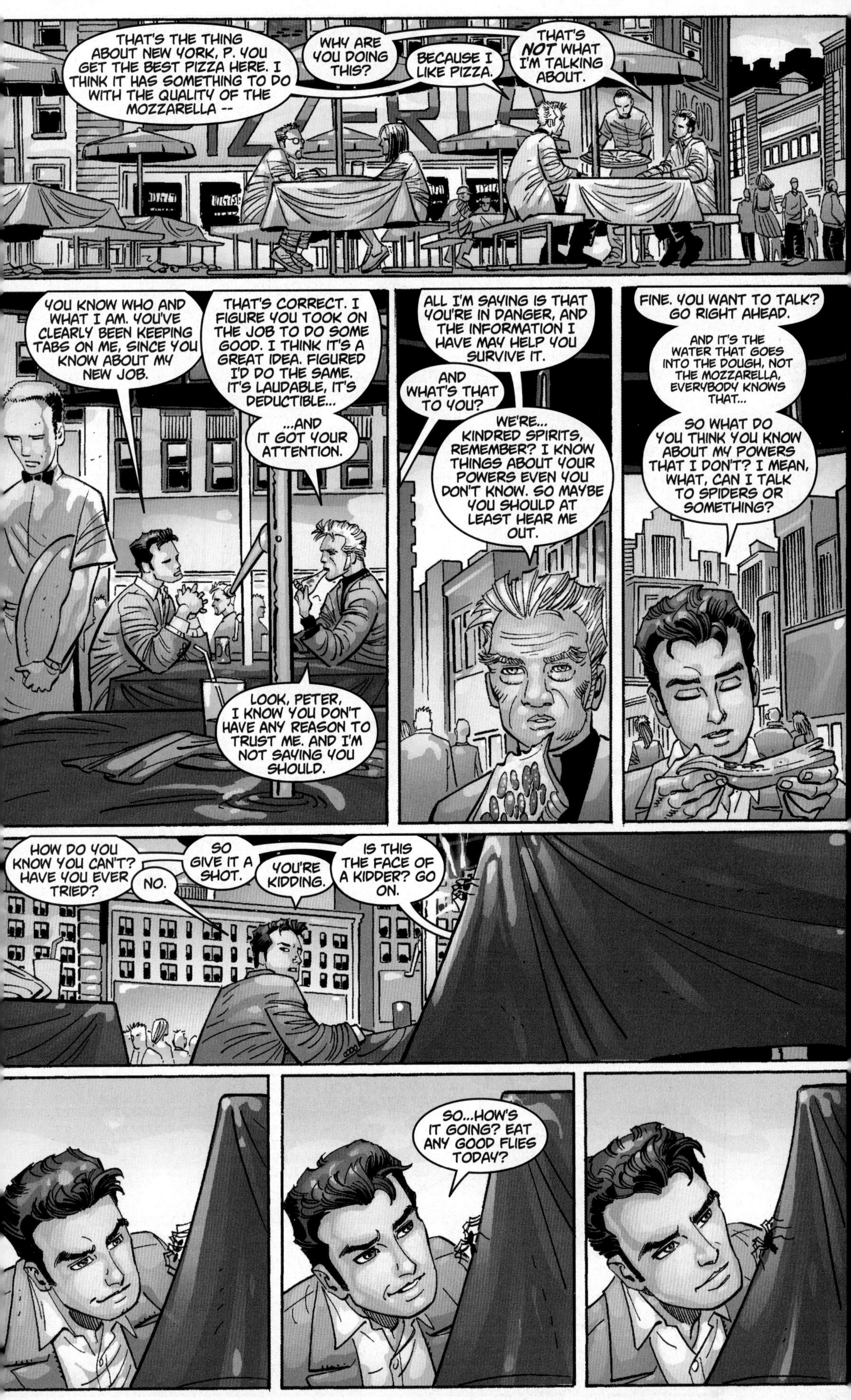
THAT'S THE THING ABOUT NEW YORK, P. YOU GET THE BEST PIZZA HERE. I THINK IT HAS SOMETHING TO DO WITH THE QUALITY OF THE MOZZARELLA --
WHY ARE YOU DOING THIS?
BECAUSE I LIKE PIZZA.
THAT'S NOT WHAT I'M TALKING ABOUT.
YOU KNOW WHO AND WHAT I AM. YOU'VE CLEARLY BEEN KEEPING TABS ON ME, SINCE YOU KNOW ABOUT MY NEW JOB.
THAT'S CORRECT. I FIGURE YOU TOOK ON THE JOB TO DO SOME GOOD. I THINK IT'S A GREAT IDEA. FIGURED I'D DO THE SAME. IT'S LAUDABLE, IT'S DEDUCTIBLE...
...AND IT GOT YOUR ATTENTION.
LOOK, PETER, I KNOW YOU DON'T HAVE ANY REASON TO TRUST ME. AND I'M NOT SAYING YOU SHOULD.
ALL I'M SAYING IS THAT YOU'RE IN DANGER, AND THE INFORMATION I HAVE MAY HELP YOU SURVIVE IT.
AND WHAT'S THAT TO YOU?
WE'RE... KINDRED SPIRITS, REMEMBER? I KNOW THINGS ABOUT YOUR POWERS EVEN YOU DON'T KNOW. SO MAYBE YOU SHOULD AT LEAST HEAR ME OUT.
FINE. YOU WANT TO TALK? GO RIGHT AHEAD.
AND IT'S THE WATER THAT GOES INTO THE DOUGH, NOT THE MOZZARELLA, EVERYBODY KNOWS THAT...
SO WHAT DO YOU THINK YOU KNOW ABOUT MY POWERS THAT I DON'T? I MEAN, WHAT, CAN I TALK TO SPIDERS OR SOMETHING?
HOW DO YOU KNOW YOU CAN'T? HAVE YOU EVER TRIED?
NO.
SO GIVE IT A SHOT.
YOU'RE KIDDING.
IS THIS THE FACE OF A KIDDER? GO ON.
SO...HOW'S IT GOING? EAT ANY GOOD FLIES TODAY?

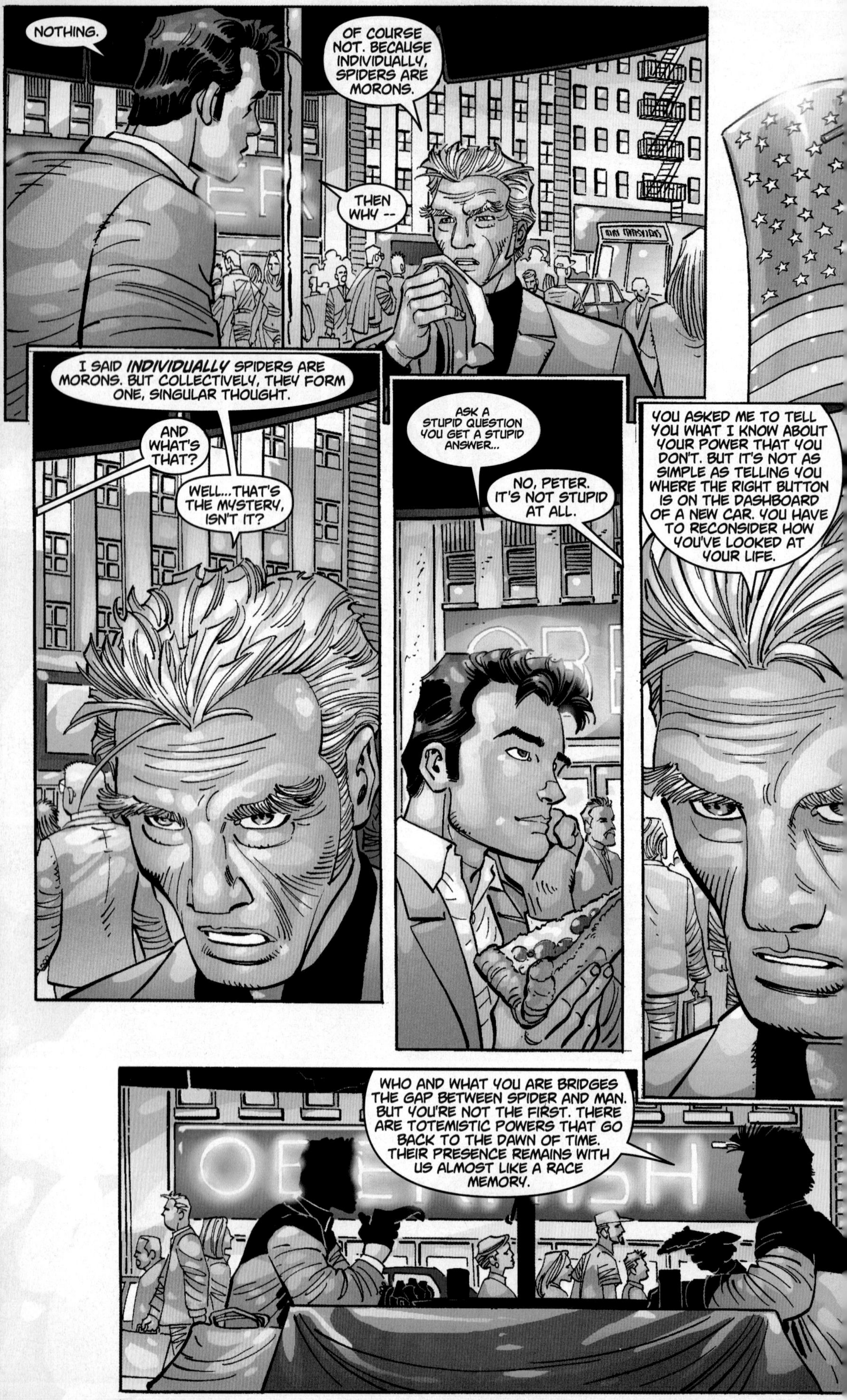
NOTHING.
OF COURSE NOT. BECAUSE INDIVIDUALLY, SPIDERS ARE MORONS.
THEN WHY --
I SAID *INDIVIDUALLY* SPIDERS ARE MORONS. BUT COLLECTIVELY, THEY FORM ONE, SINGULAR THOUGHT.
AND WHAT'S THAT?
WELL...THAT'S THE MYSTERY, ISN'T IT?
ASK A STUPID QUESTION YOU GET A STUPID ANSWER...
NO, PETER. IT'S NOT STUPID AT ALL.
YOU ASKED ME TO TELL YOU WHAT I KNOW ABOUT YOUR POWER THAT YOU DON'T. BUT IT'S NOT AS SIMPLE AS TELLING YOU WHERE THE RIGHT BUTTON IS ON THE DASHBOARD OF A NEW CAR. YOU HAVE TO RECONSIDER HOW YOU'VE LOOKED AT YOUR LIFE.
WHO AND WHAT YOU ARE BRIDGES THE GAP BETWEEN SPIDER AND MAN. BUT YOU'RE NOT THE FIRST. THERE ARE TOTEMISTIC POWERS THAT GO BACK TO THE DAWN OF TIME. THEIR PRESENCE REMAINS WITH US ALMOST LIKE A RACE MEMORY.

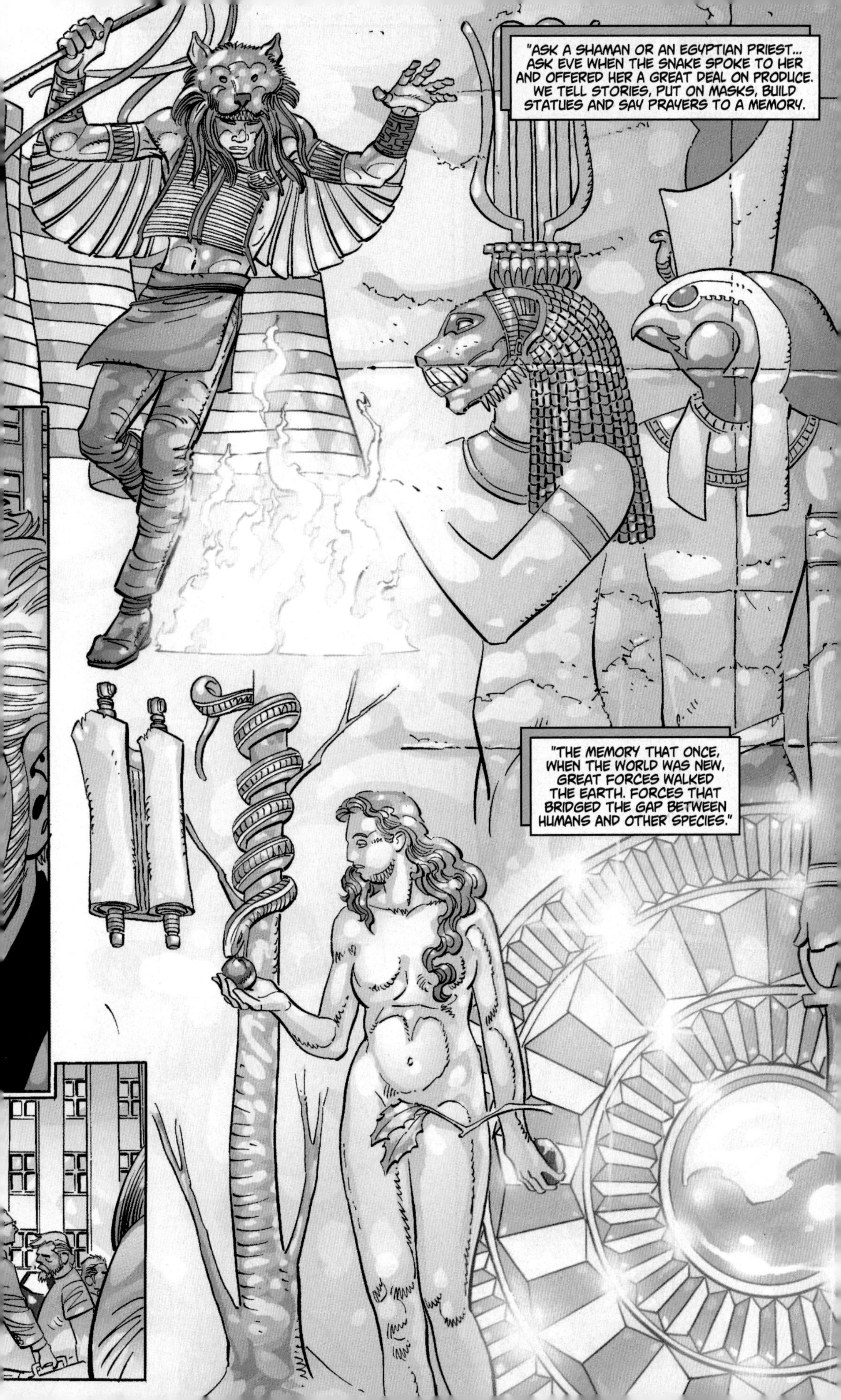
"ASK A SHAMAN OR AN EGYPTIAN PRIEST... ASK EVE WHEN THE SNAKE SPOKE TO HER AND OFFERED HER A GREAT DEAL ON PRODUCE. WE TELL STORIES, PUT ON MASKS, BUILD STATUES AND SAY PRAYERS TO A MEMORY.
"THE MEMORY THAT ONCE, WHEN THE WORLD WAS NEW, GREAT FORCES WALKED THE EARTH. FORCES THAT BRIDGED THE GAP BETWEEN HUMANS AND OTHER SPECIES."

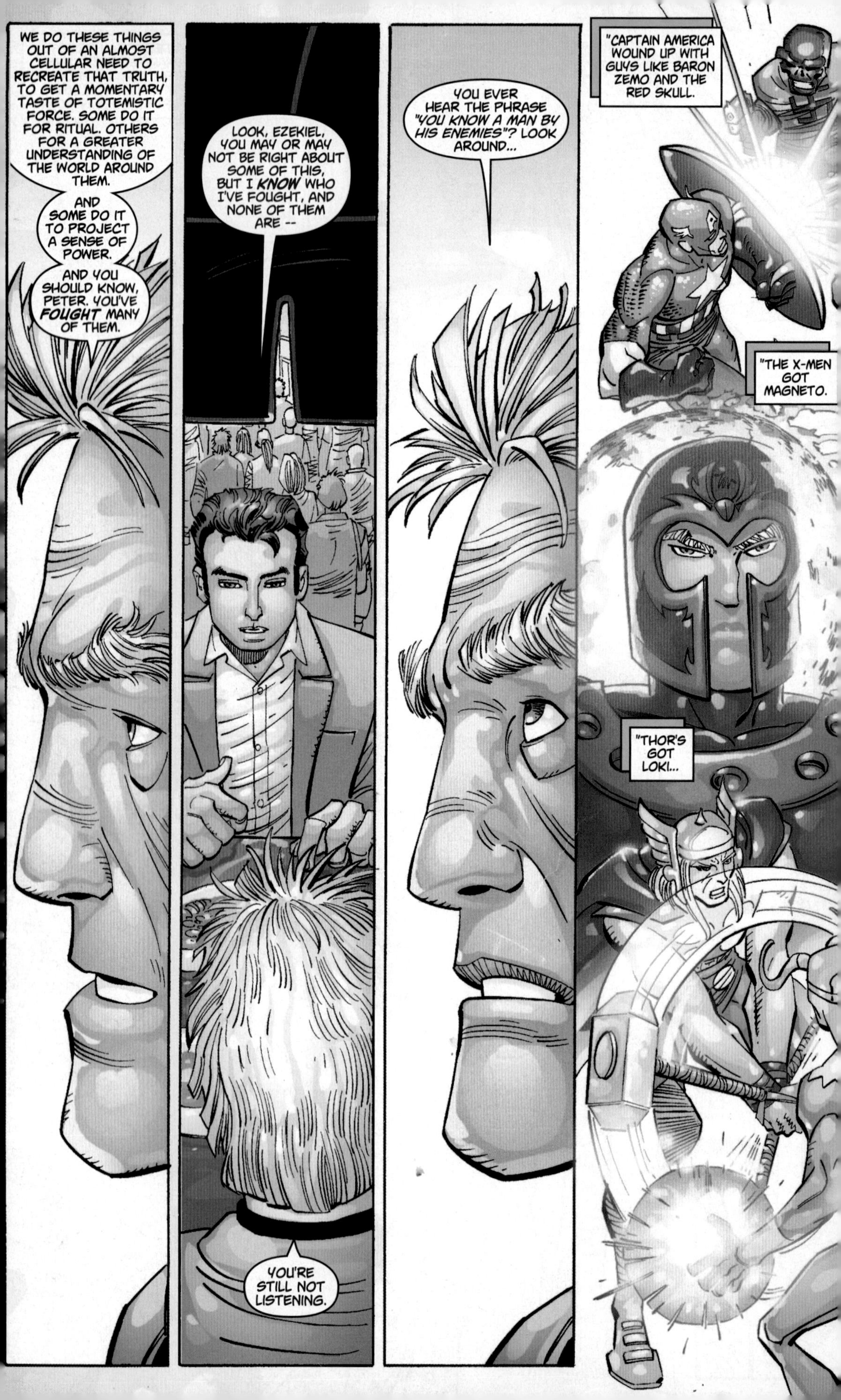

WE DO THESE THINGS OUT OF AN ALMOST CELLULAR NEED TO RECREATE THAT TRUTH, TO GET A MOMENTARY TASTE OF TOTEMISTIC FORCE. SOME DO IT FOR RITUAL. OTHERS FOR A GREATER UNDERSTANDING OF THE WORLD AROUND THEM.
AND SOME DO IT TO PROJECT A SENSE OF POWER.
AND YOU SHOULD KNOW, PETER. YOU'VE *FOUGHT* MANY OF THEM.
LOOK, EZEKIEL, YOU MAY OR MAY NOT BE RIGHT ABOUT SOME OF THIS, BUT I *KNOW* WHO I'VE FOUGHT, AND NONE OF THEM ARE --
YOU'RE STILL NOT LISTENING.
YOU EVER HEAR THE PHRASE *"YOU KNOW A MAN BY HIS ENEMIES"*? LOOK AROUND...
"CAPTAIN AMERICA WOUND UP WITH GUYS LIKE BARON ZEMO AND THE RED SKULL.
"THE X-MEN GOT MAGNETO.
"THOR'S GOT LOKI...

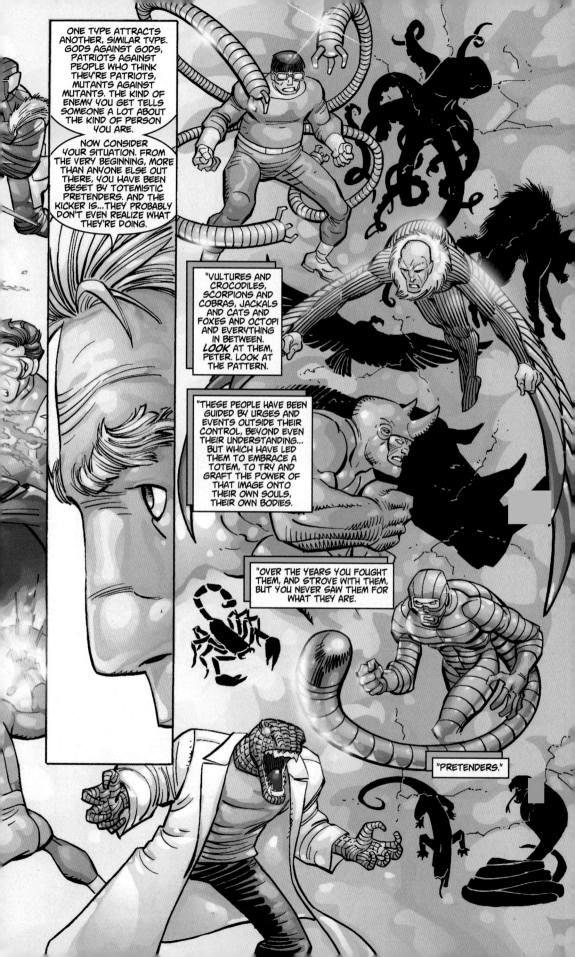

ONE TYPE ATTRACTS ANOTHER, SIMILAR TYPE. GODS AGAINST GODS, PATRIOTS AGAINST PEOPLE WHO THINK THEY'RE PATRIOTS, MUTANTS AGAINST MUTANTS. THE KIND OF ENEMY YOU GET TELLS SOMEONE A LOT ABOUT THE KIND OF PERSON YOU ARE.

NOW CONSIDER YOUR SITUATION. FROM THE VERY BEGINNING, MORE THAN ANYONE ELSE OUT THERE, YOU HAVE BEEN BESET BY TOTEMISTIC PRETENDERS. AND THE KICKER IS...THEY PROBABLY DON'T EVEN REALIZE WHAT THEY'RE DOING.

"VULTURES AND CROCODILES, SCORPIONS AND COBRAS, JACKALS AND CATS AND FOXES AND OCTOPI AND EVERYTHING IN BETWEEN. *LOOK* AT THEM, PETER. LOOK AT THE PATTERN.

"THESE PEOPLE HAVE BEEN GUIDED BY URGES AND EVENTS OUTSIDE THEIR CONTROL, BEYOND EVEN THEIR UNDERSTANDING... BUT WHICH HAVE LED THEM TO EMBRACE A TOTEM, TO TRY AND GRAFT THE POWER OF THAT IMAGE ONTO THEIR OWN SOULS, THEIR OWN BODIES.

"OVER THE YEARS YOU FOUGHT THEM, AND STROVE WITH THEM, BUT YOU NEVER SAW THEM FOR WHAT THEY ARE.

"PRETENDERS."

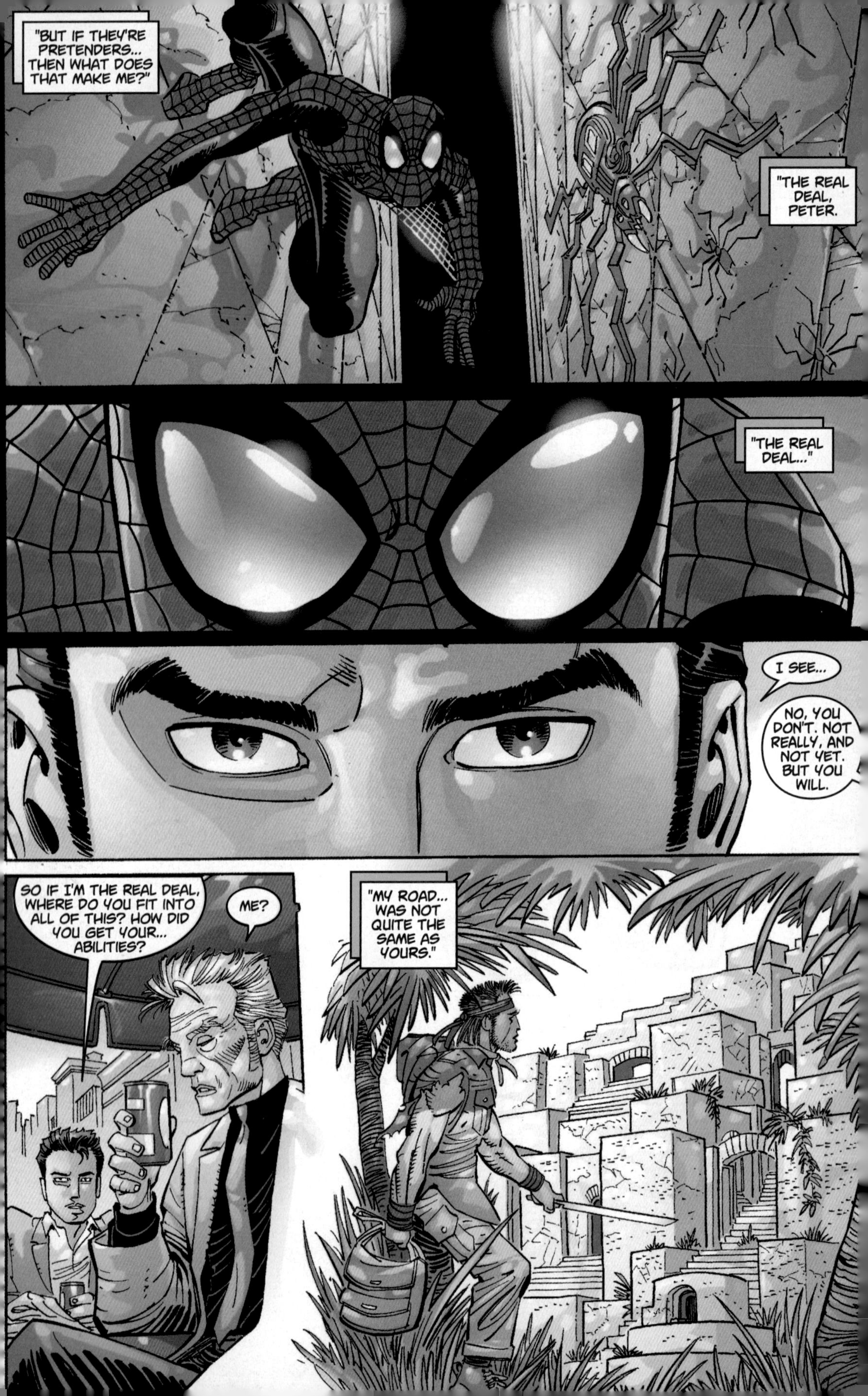
"BUT IF THEY'RE PRETENDERS... THEN WHAT DOES THAT MAKE ME?"
"THE REAL DEAL, PETER.
"THE REAL DEAL..."
I SEE...
NO, YOU DON'T. NOT REALLY, AND NOT YET. BUT YOU WILL.
SO IF I'M THE REAL DEAL, WHERE DO YOU FIT INTO ALL OF THIS? HOW DID YOU GET YOUR... ABILITIES?
ME?
"MY ROAD... WAS NOT QUITE THE SAME AS YOURS."

"IT WAS NOT AS...PURE AS YOURS.

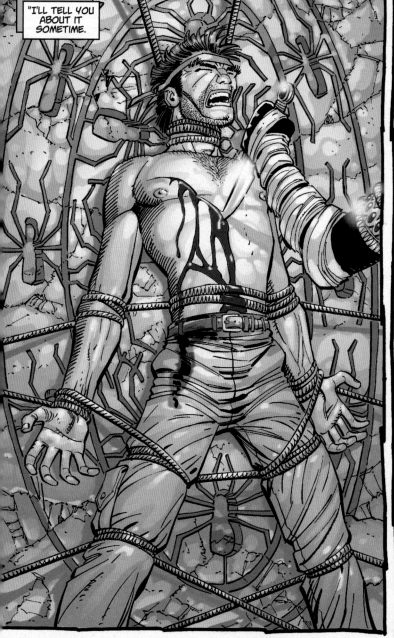

"I'LL TELL YOU ABOUT IT SOMETIME.

"I'M SURE YOU'LL GET A KICK OUT OF IT."

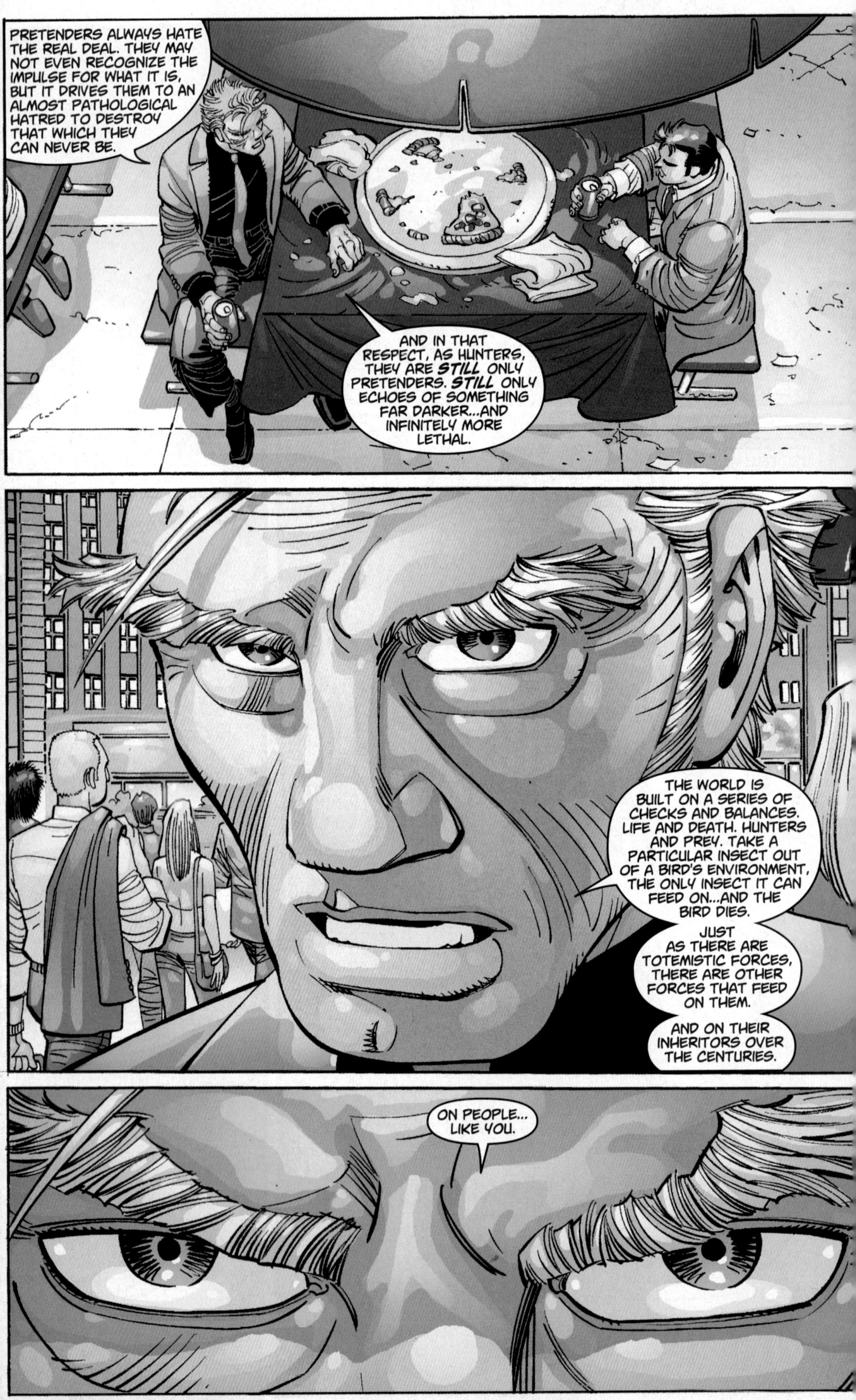
PRETENDERS ALWAYS HATE THE REAL DEAL. THEY MAY NOT EVEN RECOGNIZE THE IMPULSE FOR WHAT IT IS, BUT IT DRIVES THEM TO AN ALMOST PATHOLOGICAL HATRED TO DESTROY THAT WHICH THEY CAN NEVER BE.
AND IN THAT RESPECT, AS HUNTERS, THEY ARE *STILL* ONLY PRETENDERS. *STILL* ONLY ECHOES OF SOMETHING FAR DARKER...AND INFINITELY MORE LETHAL.
THE WORLD IS BUILT ON A SERIES OF CHECKS AND BALANCES. LIFE AND DEATH. HUNTERS AND PREY. TAKE A PARTICULAR INSECT OUT OF A BIRD'S ENVIRONMENT, THE ONLY INSECT IT CAN FEED ON...AND THE BIRD DIES.
JUST AS THERE ARE TOTEMISTIC FORCES, THERE ARE OTHER FORCES THAT FEED ON THEM.
AND ON THEIR INHERITORS OVER THE CENTURIES.
ON PEOPLE... LIKE YOU.

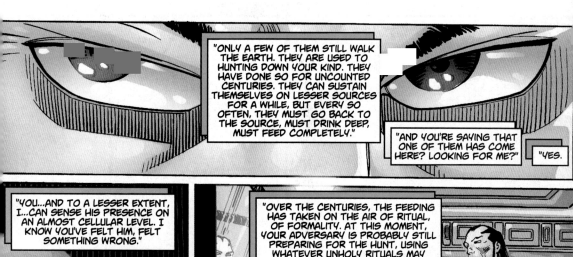

"ONLY A FEW OF THEM STILL WALK THE EARTH. THEY ARE USED TO HUNTING DOWN YOUR KIND. THEY HAVE DONE SO FOR UNCOUNTED CENTURIES. THEY CAN SUSTAIN THEMSELVES ON LESSER SOURCES FOR A WHILE, BUT EVERY SO OFTEN, THEY MUST GO BACK TO THE SOURCE, MUST DRINK DEEP, MUST FEED COMPLETELY."

"AND YOU'RE SAYING THAT ONE OF THEM HAS COME HERE? LOOKING FOR ME?"

"YES.

"YOU...AND TO A LESSER EXTENT, I...CAN SENSE HIS PRESENCE ON AN ALMOST CELLULAR LEVEL. I KNOW YOU'VE FELT HIM, FELT SOMETHING WRONG."

"SO WHY HASN'T HE COME AFTER ME?"

HMMM... I DON'T KNOW...

"OVER THE CENTURIES, THE FEEDING HAS TAKEN ON THE AIR OF RITUAL, OF FORMALITY. AT THIS MOMENT, YOUR ADVERSARY IS PROBABLY STILL PREPARING FOR THE HUNT, USING WHATEVER UNHOLY RITUALS MAY BE APPROPRIATE."

...DO YOU THINK THIS MAKES MY BUTT LOOK FAT?

NO, MORLUN.

SO HOW DOES THIS GUY --

MY PEOPLE BELIEVE HIS NAME IS MORLUN.

HOW DOES THIS MORLUN KNOW I'M THE ONE HE WANTS?

PETER...*YOU DRESS LIKE A SPIDER.* THIS WAS NOT YOUR BEST MOVE. I MEAN, YOU PUT THE SOURCE OF YOUR POWER *RIGHT THERE* ON YOUR CHEST.

OKAY --

WHAT IF CAPTAIN AMERICA CALLED HIMSELF SUPER-SERUM MAN, OR THE HULK WAS GAMMA-RAY MAN, OR --

ALL RIGHT, ALL RIGHT, JEEZ...

I WAS FIFTEEN YEARS OLD, CUT ME A LITTLE SLACK, HERE.

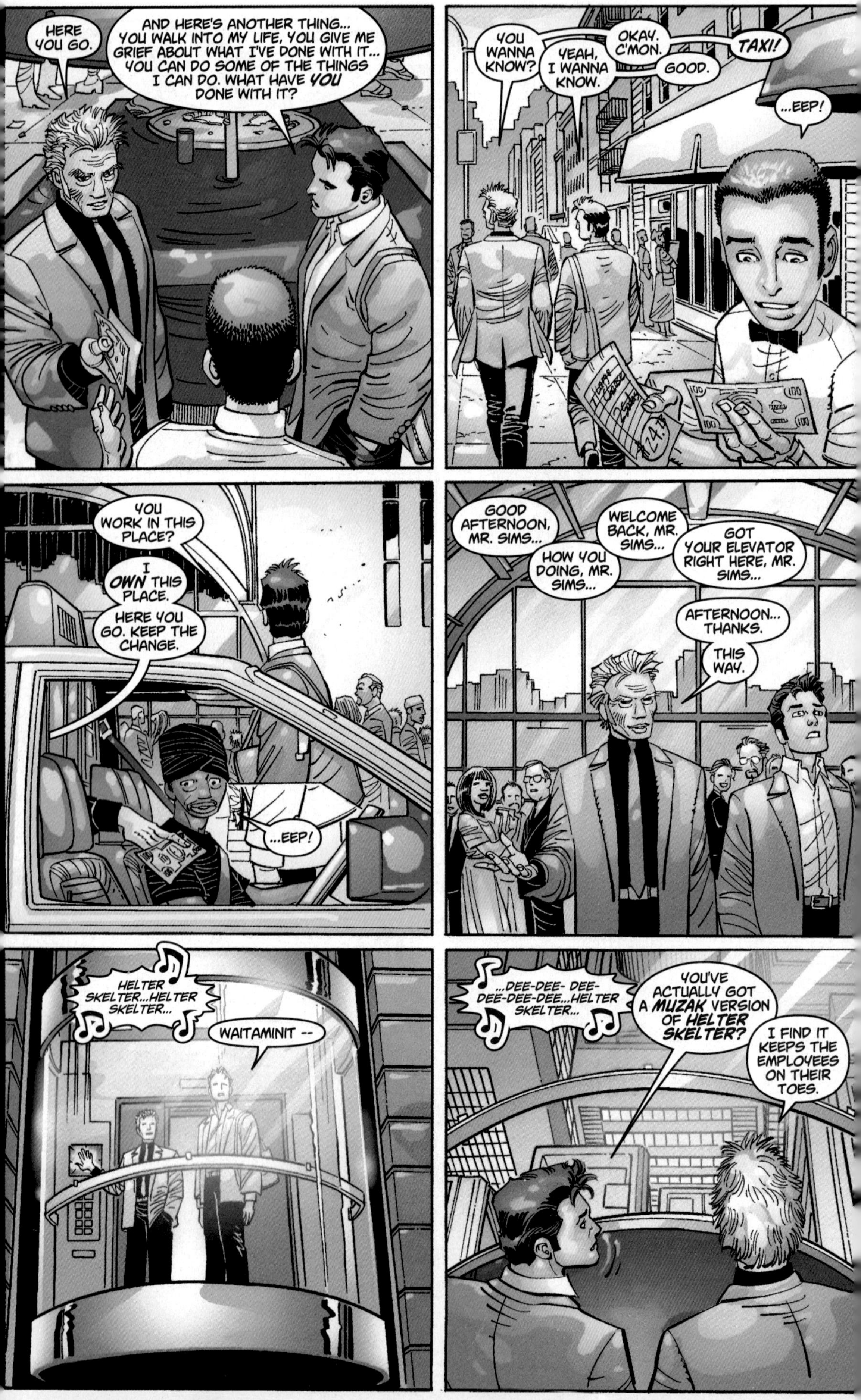
HERE YOU GO.
AND HERE'S ANOTHER THING... YOU WALK INTO MY LIFE, YOU GIVE ME GRIEF ABOUT WHAT I'VE DONE WITH IT... YOU CAN DO SOME OF THE THINGS I CAN DO. WHAT HAVE YOU DONE WITH IT?
YOU WANNA KNOW?
YEAH, I WANNA KNOW.
OKAY. C'MON.
GOOD.
TAXI!
...EEP!
YOU WORK IN THIS PLACE?
I OWN THIS PLACE.
HERE YOU GO. KEEP THE CHANGE.
...EEP!
GOOD AFTERNOON, MR. SIMS...
HOW YOU DOING, MR. SIMS...
WELCOME BACK, MR. SIMS...
GOT YOUR ELEVATOR RIGHT HERE, MR. SIMS...
AFTERNOON... THANKS.
THIS WAY.
HELTER SKELTER...HELTER SKELTER...
WAITAMINIT --
...DEE-DEE- DEE-DEE-DEE-DEE...HELTER SKELTER...
YOU'VE ACTUALLY GOT A MUZAK VERSION OF HELTER SKELTER?
I FIND IT KEEPS THE EMPLOYEES ON THEIR TOES.

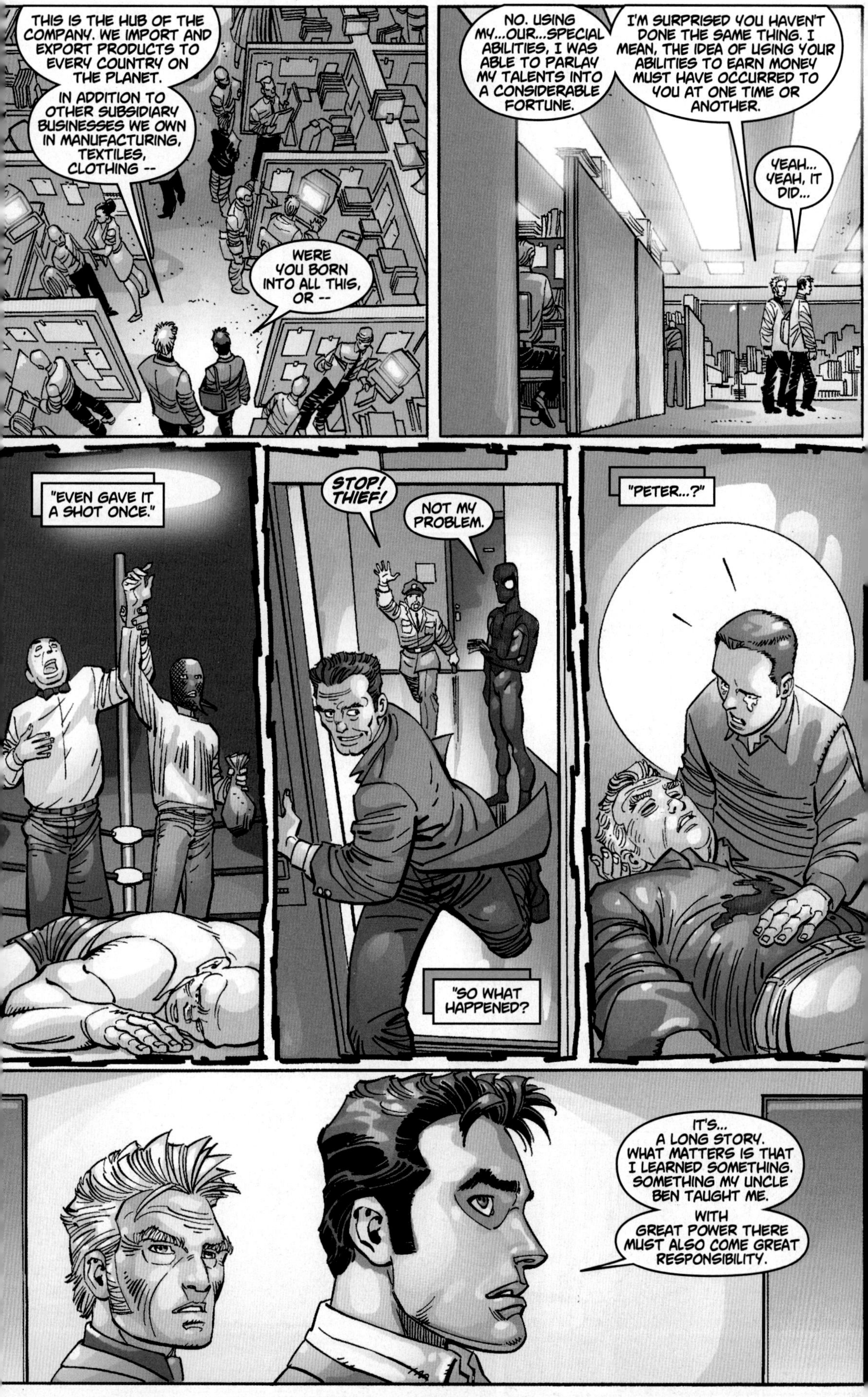
THIS IS THE HUB OF THE COMPANY. WE IMPORT AND EXPORT PRODUCTS TO EVERY COUNTRY ON THE PLANET.
IN ADDITION TO OTHER SUBSIDIARY BUSINESSES WE OWN IN MANUFACTURING, TEXTILES, CLOTHING --
WERE YOU BORN INTO ALL THIS, OR --
NO. USING MY...OUR...SPECIAL ABILITIES, I WAS ABLE TO PARLAY MY TALENTS INTO A CONSIDERABLE FORTUNE.
I'M SURPRISED YOU HAVEN'T DONE THE SAME THING. I MEAN, THE IDEA OF USING YOUR ABILITIES TO EARN MONEY MUST HAVE OCCURRED TO YOU AT ONE TIME OR ANOTHER.
YEAH... YEAH, IT DID...
"EVEN GAVE IT A SHOT ONCE."
STOP! THIEF!
NOT MY PROBLEM.
"SO WHAT HAPPENED?
"PETER...?"
IT'S... A LONG STORY. WHAT MATTERS IS THAT I LEARNED SOMETHING. SOMETHING MY UNCLE BEN TAUGHT ME.
WITH GREAT POWER THERE MUST ALSO COME GREAT RESPONSIBILITY.

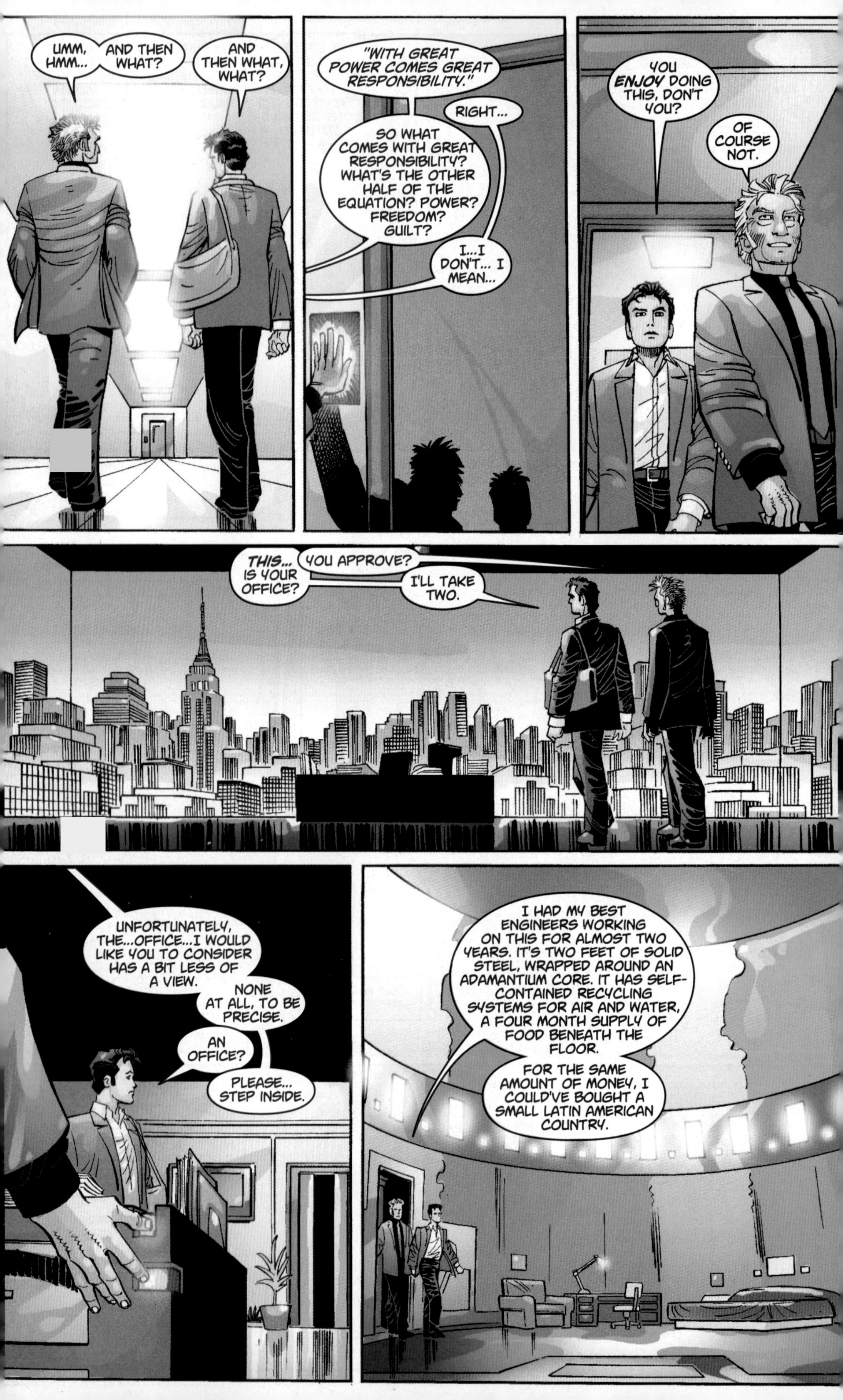
UMM, HMM...
AND THEN WHAT?
AND THEN WHAT, WHAT?
"WITH GREAT POWER COMES GREAT RESPONSIBILITY."
RIGHT...
SO WHAT COMES WITH GREAT RESPONSIBILITY? WHAT'S THE OTHER HALF OF THE EQUATION? POWER? FREEDOM? GUILT?
I...I DON'T... I MEAN...
YOU ENJOY DOING THIS, DON'T YOU?
OF COURSE NOT.
THIS... IS YOUR OFFICE?
YOU APPROVE?
I'LL TAKE TWO.
UNFORTUNATELY, THE...OFFICE...I WOULD LIKE YOU TO CONSIDER HAS A BIT LESS OF A VIEW.
NONE AT ALL, TO BE PRECISE.
AN OFFICE?
PLEASE... STEP INSIDE.
I HAD MY BEST ENGINEERS WORKING ON THIS FOR ALMOST TWO YEARS. IT'S TWO FEET OF SOLID STEEL, WRAPPED AROUND AN ADAMANTIUM CORE. IT HAS SELF-CONTAINED RECYCLING SYSTEMS FOR AIR AND WATER, A FOUR MONTH SUPPLY OF FOOD BENEATH THE FLOOR.
FOR THE SAME AMOUNT OF MONEY, I COULD'VE BOUGHT A SMALL LATIN AMERICAN COUNTRY.

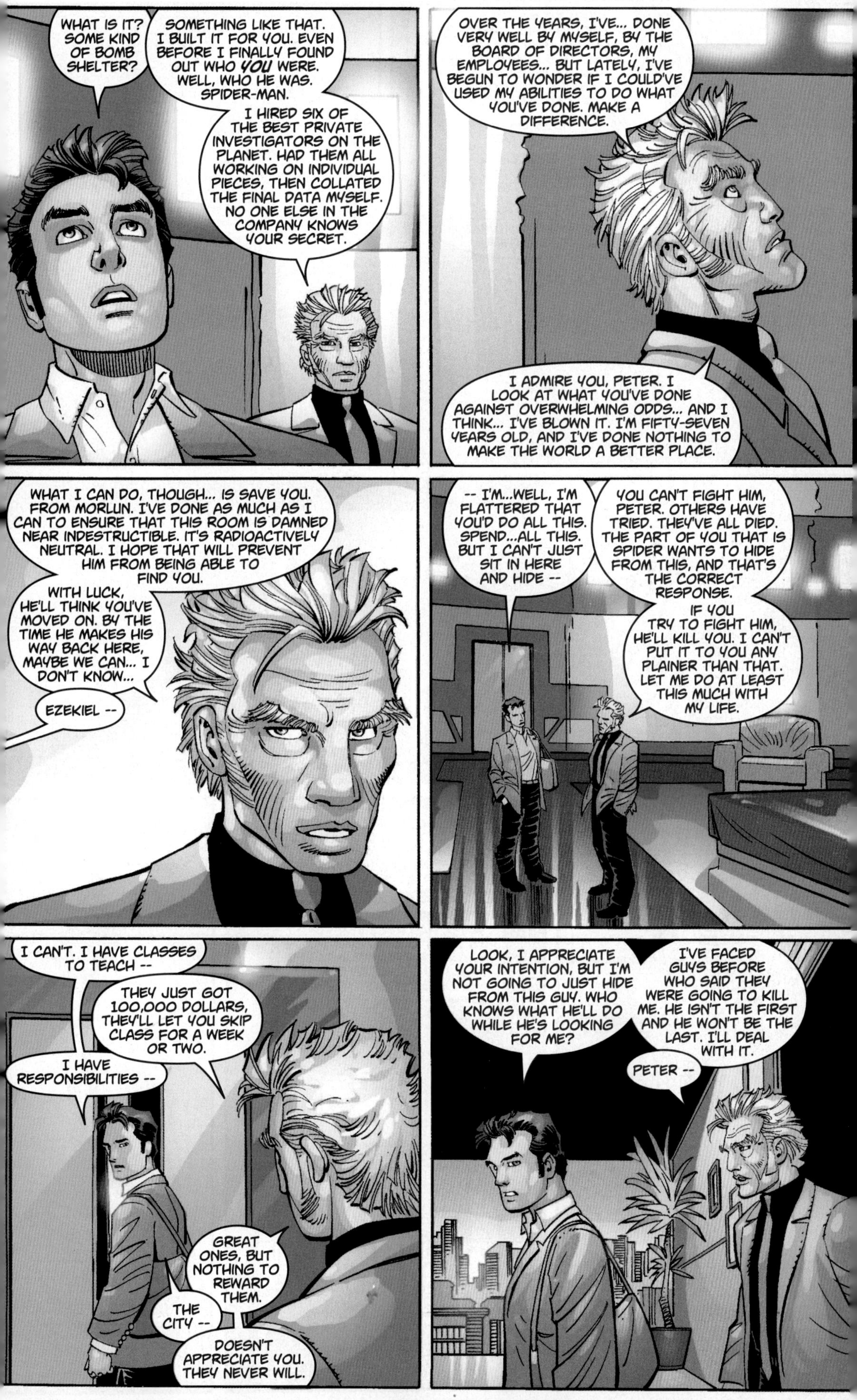
WHAT IS IT? SOME KIND OF BOMB SHELTER?
SOMETHING LIKE THAT. I BUILT IT FOR YOU. EVEN BEFORE I FINALLY FOUND OUT WHO *YOU* WERE. WELL, WHO HE WAS. SPIDER-MAN.
I HIRED SIX OF THE BEST PRIVATE INVESTIGATORS ON THE PLANET. HAD THEM ALL WORKING ON INDIVIDUAL PIECES, THEN COLLATED THE FINAL DATA MYSELF. NO ONE ELSE IN THE COMPANY KNOWS YOUR SECRET.
OVER THE YEARS, I'VE... DONE VERY WELL BY MYSELF, BY THE BOARD OF DIRECTORS, MY EMPLOYEES... BUT LATELY, I'VE BEGUN TO WONDER IF I COULD'VE USED MY ABILITIES TO DO WHAT YOU'VE DONE. MAKE A DIFFERENCE.
I ADMIRE YOU, PETER. I LOOK AT WHAT YOU'VE DONE AGAINST OVERWHELMING ODDS... AND I THINK... I'VE BLOWN IT. I'M FIFTY-SEVEN YEARS OLD, AND I'VE DONE NOTHING TO MAKE THE WORLD A BETTER PLACE.
WHAT I CAN DO, THOUGH... IS SAVE YOU. FROM MORLUN. I'VE DONE AS MUCH AS I CAN TO ENSURE THAT THIS ROOM IS DAMNED NEAR INDESTRUCTIBLE. IT'S RADIOACTIVELY NEUTRAL. I HOPE THAT WILL PREVENT HIM FROM BEING ABLE TO FIND YOU.
WITH LUCK, HE'LL THINK YOU'VE MOVED ON. BY THE TIME HE MAKES HIS WAY BACK HERE, MAYBE WE CAN... I DON'T KNOW...
EZEKIEL --
-- I'M...WELL, I'M FLATTERED THAT YOU'D DO ALL THIS. SPEND...ALL THIS. BUT I CAN'T JUST SIT IN HERE AND HIDE --
YOU CAN'T FIGHT HIM, PETER. OTHERS HAVE TRIED. THEY'VE ALL DIED. THE PART OF YOU THAT IS SPIDER WANTS TO HIDE FROM THIS, AND THAT'S THE CORRECT RESPONSE.
IF YOU TRY TO FIGHT HIM, HE'LL KILL YOU. I CAN'T PUT IT TO YOU ANY PLAINER THAN THAT. LET ME DO AT LEAST THIS MUCH WITH MY LIFE.
I CAN'T. I HAVE CLASSES TO TEACH --
THEY JUST GOT 100,000 DOLLARS, THEY'LL LET YOU SKIP CLASS FOR A WEEK OR TWO.
I HAVE RESPONSIBILITIES --
GREAT ONES, BUT NOTHING TO REWARD THEM.
THE CITY --
DOESN'T APPRECIATE YOU. THEY NEVER WILL.
LOOK, I APPRECIATE YOUR INTENTION, BUT I'M NOT GOING TO JUST HIDE FROM THIS GUY. WHO KNOWS WHAT HE'LL DO WHILE HE'S LOOKING FOR ME?
I'VE FACED GUYS BEFORE WHO SAID THEY WERE GOING TO KILL ME. HE ISN'T THE FIRST AND HE WON'T BE THE LAST. I'LL DEAL WITH IT.
PETER --

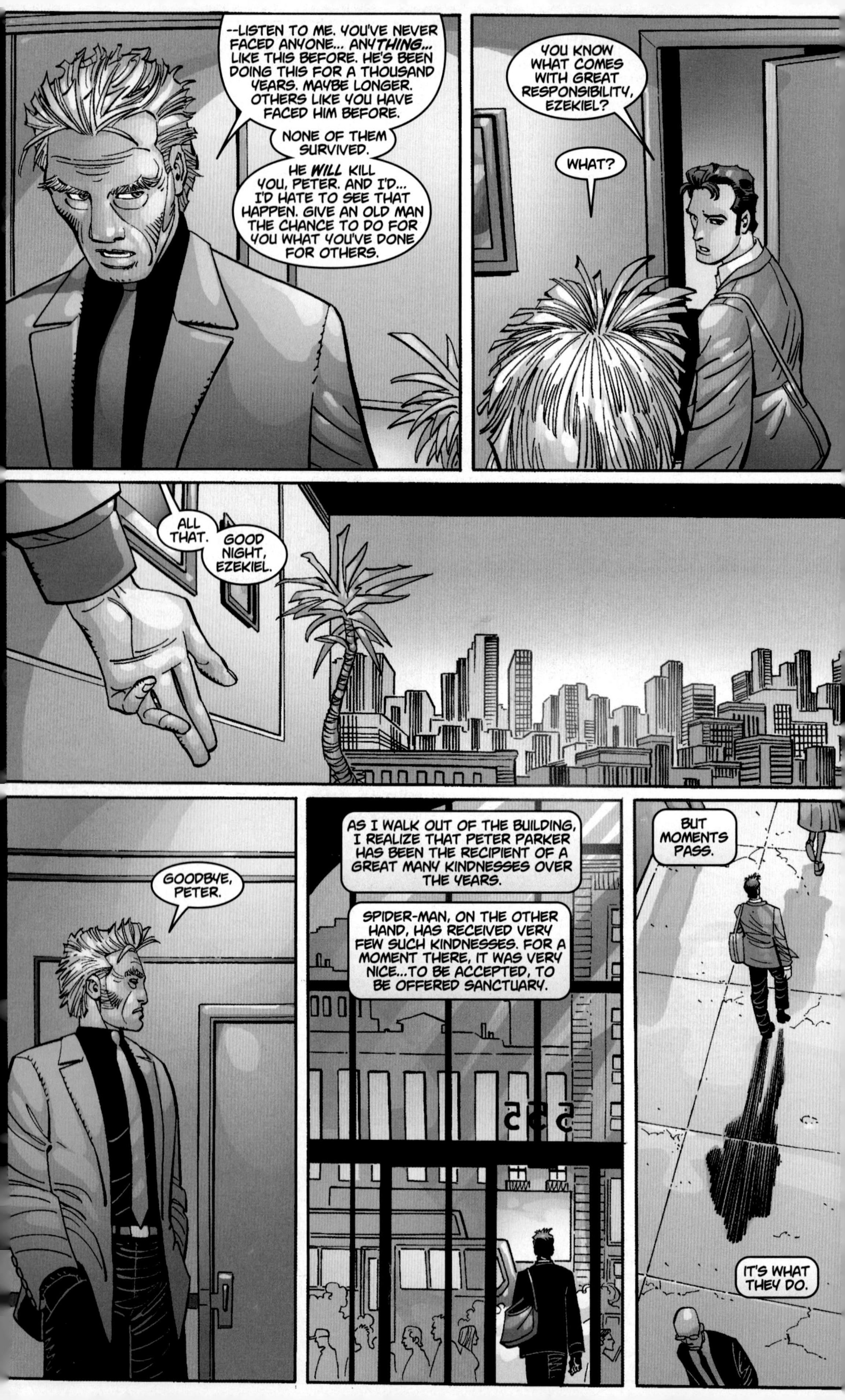
--LISTEN TO ME. YOU'VE NEVER FACED ANYONE... ANYTHING... LIKE THIS BEFORE. HE'S BEEN DOING THIS FOR A THOUSAND YEARS. MAYBE LONGER. OTHERS LIKE YOU HAVE FACED HIM BEFORE.
NONE OF THEM SURVIVED.
HE WILL KILL YOU, PETER. AND I'D... I'D HATE TO SEE THAT HAPPEN. GIVE AN OLD MAN THE CHANCE TO DO FOR YOU WHAT YOU'VE DONE FOR OTHERS.
YOU KNOW WHAT COMES WITH GREAT RESPONSIBILITY, EZEKIEL?
WHAT?
ALL THAT.
GOOD NIGHT, EZEKIEL.
GOODBYE, PETER.
AS I WALK OUT OF THE BUILDING, I REALIZE THAT PETER PARKER HAS BEEN THE RECIPIENT OF A GREAT MANY KINDNESSES OVER THE YEARS.
SPIDER-MAN, ON THE OTHER HAND, HAS RECEIVED VERY FEW SUCH KINDNESSES. FOR A MOMENT THERE, IT WAS VERY NICE...TO BE ACCEPTED, TO BE OFFERED SANCTUARY.
BUT MOMENTS PASS.
IT'S WHAT THEY DO.

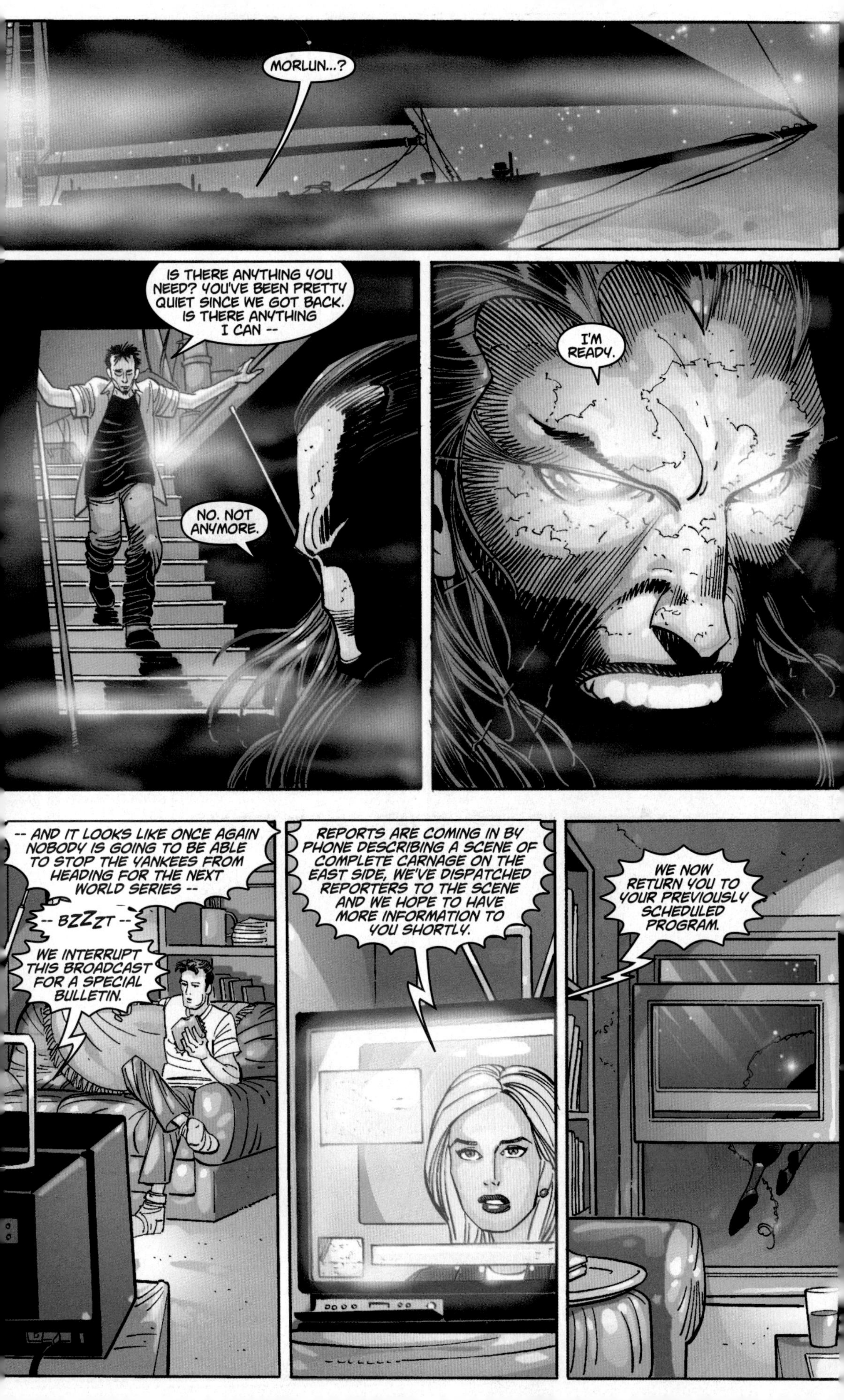
MORLUN...?
IS THERE ANYTHING YOU NEED? YOU'VE BEEN PRETTY QUIET SINCE WE GOT BACK. IS THERE ANYTHING I CAN --
NO. NOT ANYMORE.
I'M READY.
-- AND IT LOOKS LIKE ONCE AGAIN NOBODY IS GOING TO BE ABLE TO STOP THE YANKEES FROM HEADING FOR THE NEXT WORLD SERIES --
-- BZZZT --
WE INTERRUPT THIS BROADCAST FOR A SPECIAL BULLETIN.
REPORTS ARE COMING IN BY PHONE DESCRIBING A SCENE OF COMPLETE CARNAGE ON THE EAST SIDE, WE'VE DISPATCHED REPORTERS TO THE SCENE AND WE HOPE TO HAVE MORE INFORMATION TO YOU SHORTLY.
WE NOW RETURN YOU TO YOUR PREVIOUSLY SCHEDULED PROGRAM.

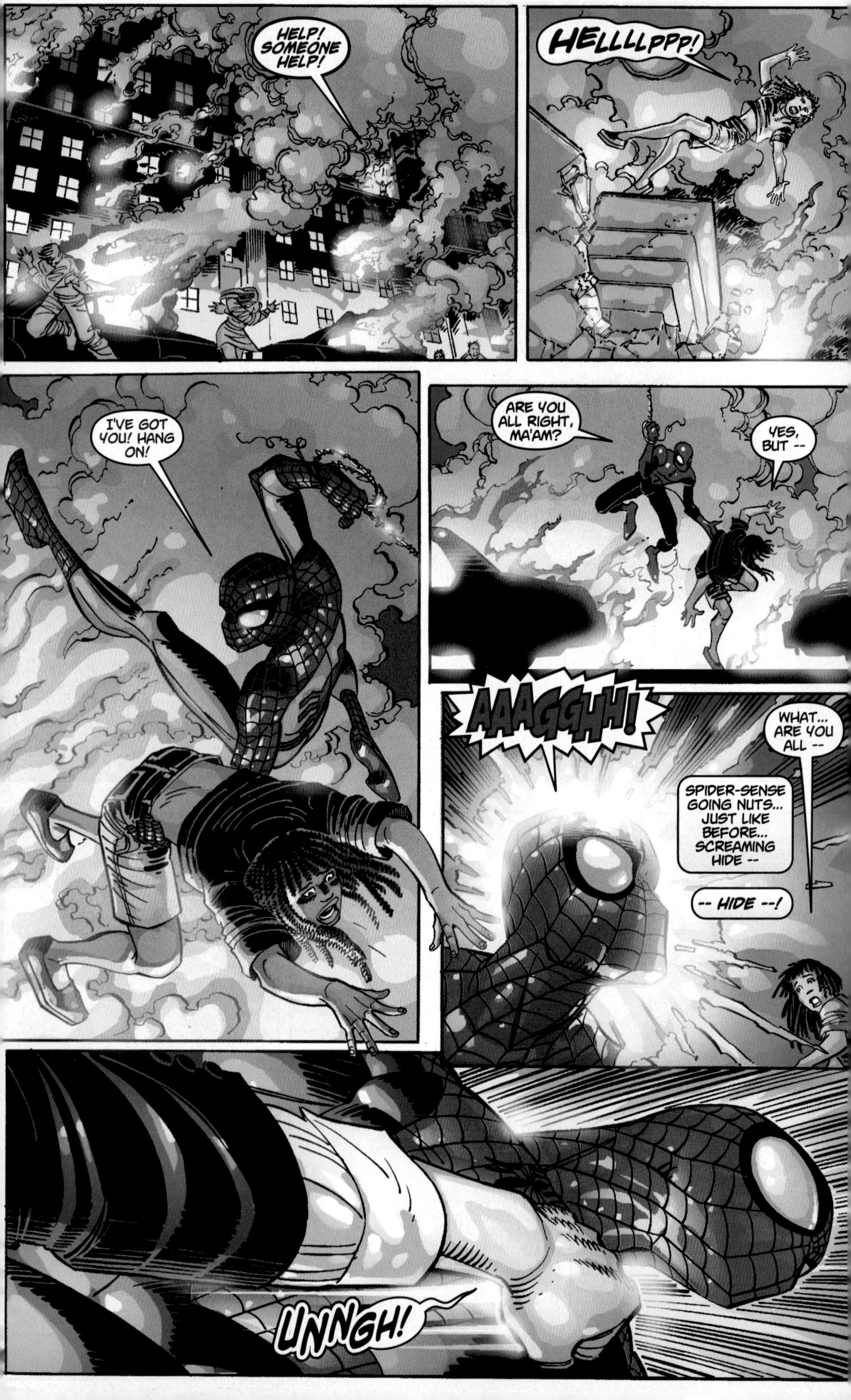
HELP! SOMEONE HELP!
HELLLLPPP!
I'VE GOT YOU! HANG ON!
ARE YOU ALL RIGHT, MA'AM?
YES, BUT --
AAAGGHH!
WHAT... ARE YOU ALL --
SPIDER-SENSE GOING NUTS... JUST LIKE BEFORE... SCREAMING HIDE --
-- HIDE --!
UNNGH!

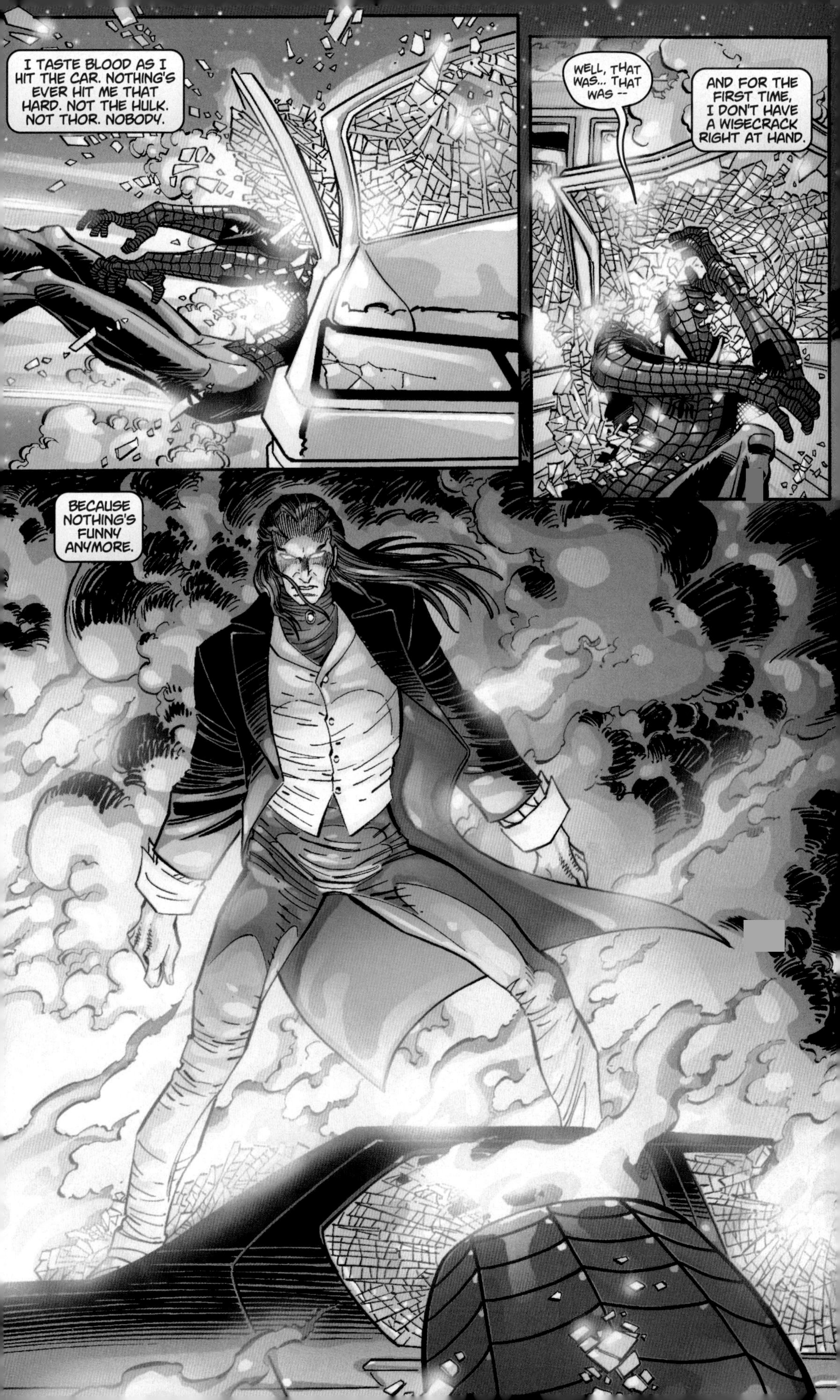
I TASTE BLOOD AS I HIT THE CAR. NOTHING'S EVER HIT ME THAT HARD. NOT THE HULK. NOT THOR. NOBODY.
WELL, THAT WAS... THAT WAS --
AND FOR THE FIRST TIME, I DON'T HAVE A WISECRACK RIGHT AT HAND.
BECAUSE NOTHING'S FUNNY ANYMORE.

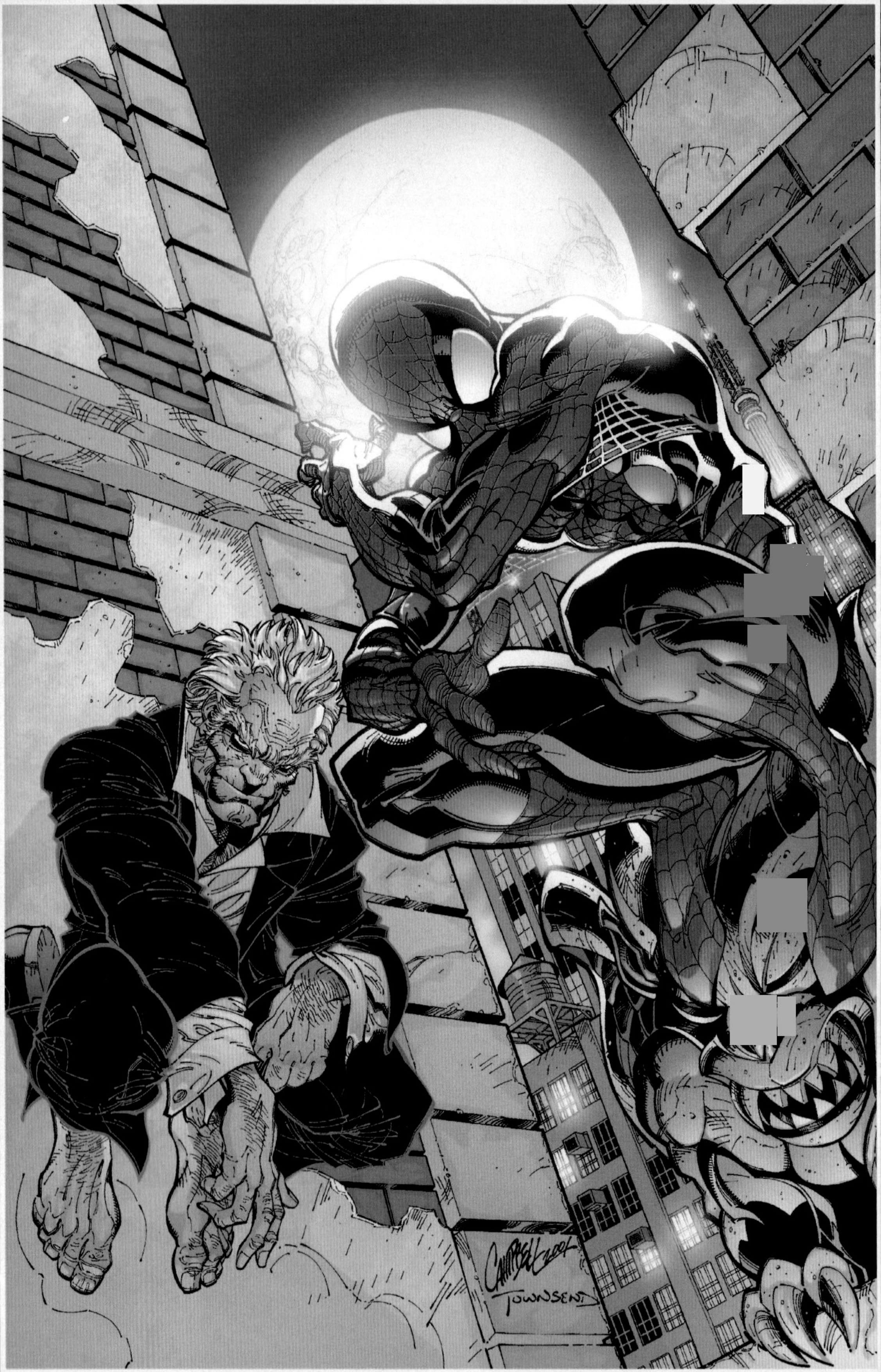
TOWNSEND

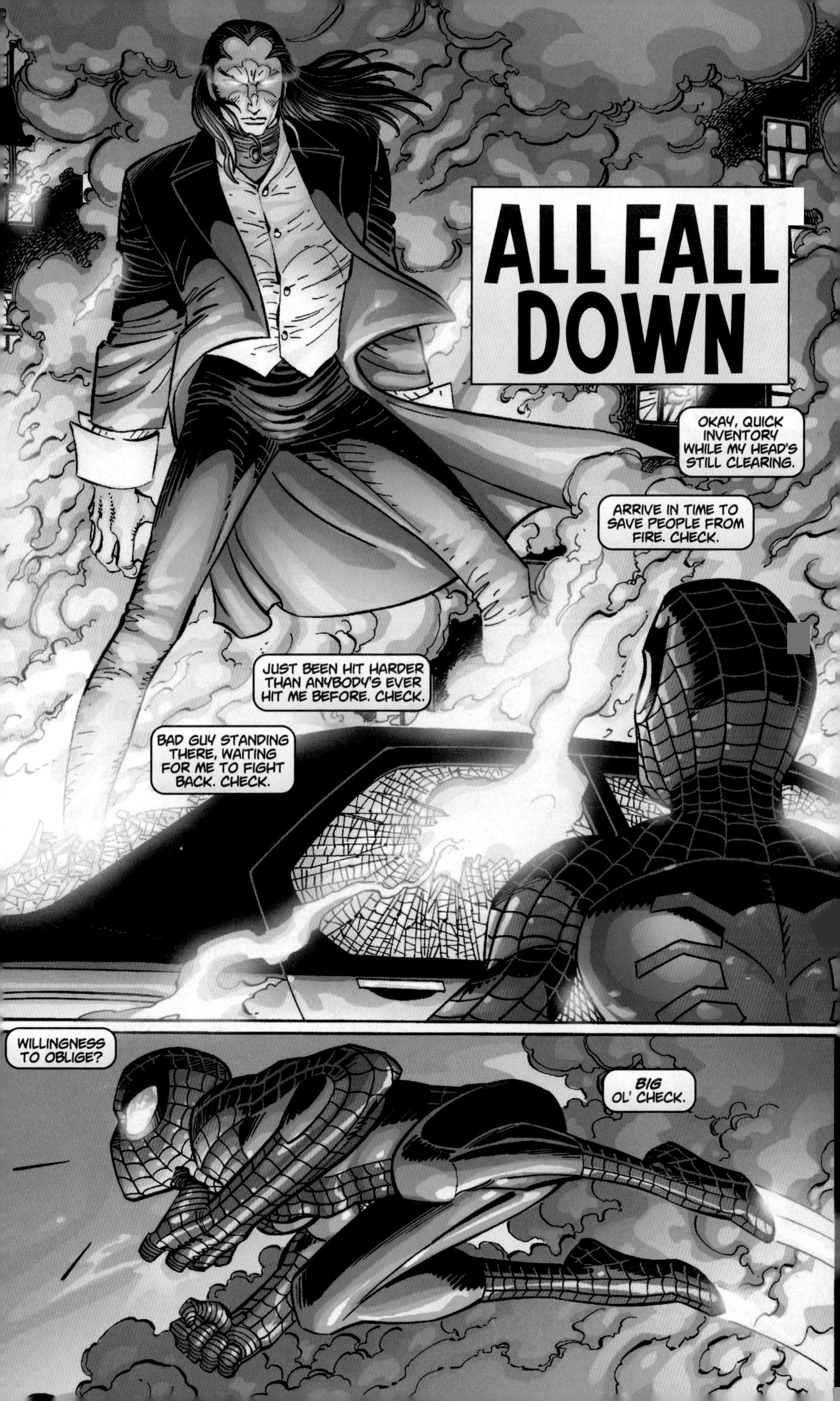

ALL FALL DOWN
OKAY, QUICK INVENTORY WHILE MY HEAD'S STILL CLEARING.
ARRIVE IN TIME TO SAVE PEOPLE FROM FIRE. CHECK.
JUST BEEN HIT HARDER THAN ANYBODY'S EVER HIT ME BEFORE. CHECK.
BAD GUY STANDING THERE, WAITING FOR ME TO FIGHT BACK. CHECK.
WILLINGNESS TO OBLIGE?
BIG OL' CHECK.

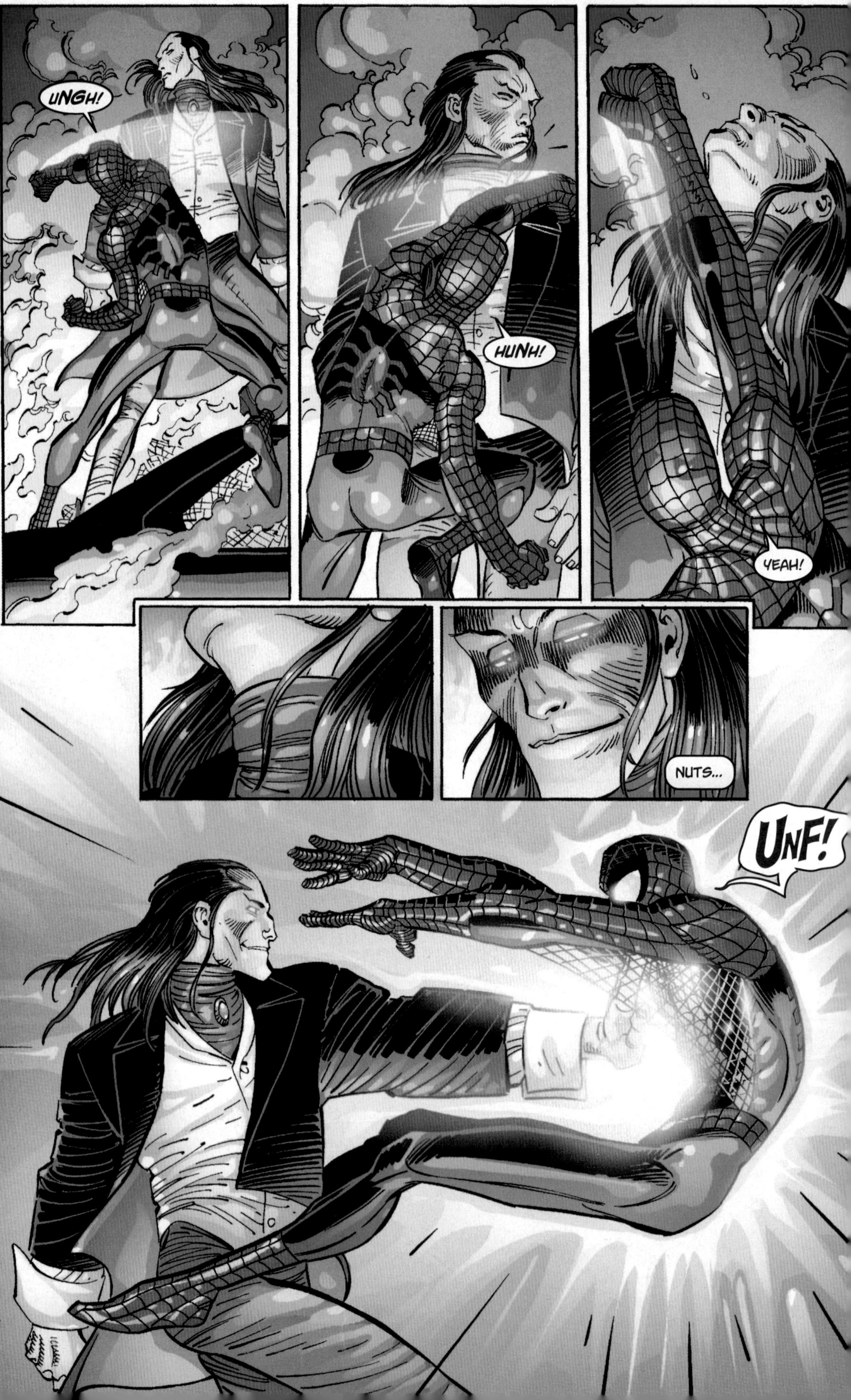
UNGH!
HUNH!
YEAH!
NUTS...
UNF!

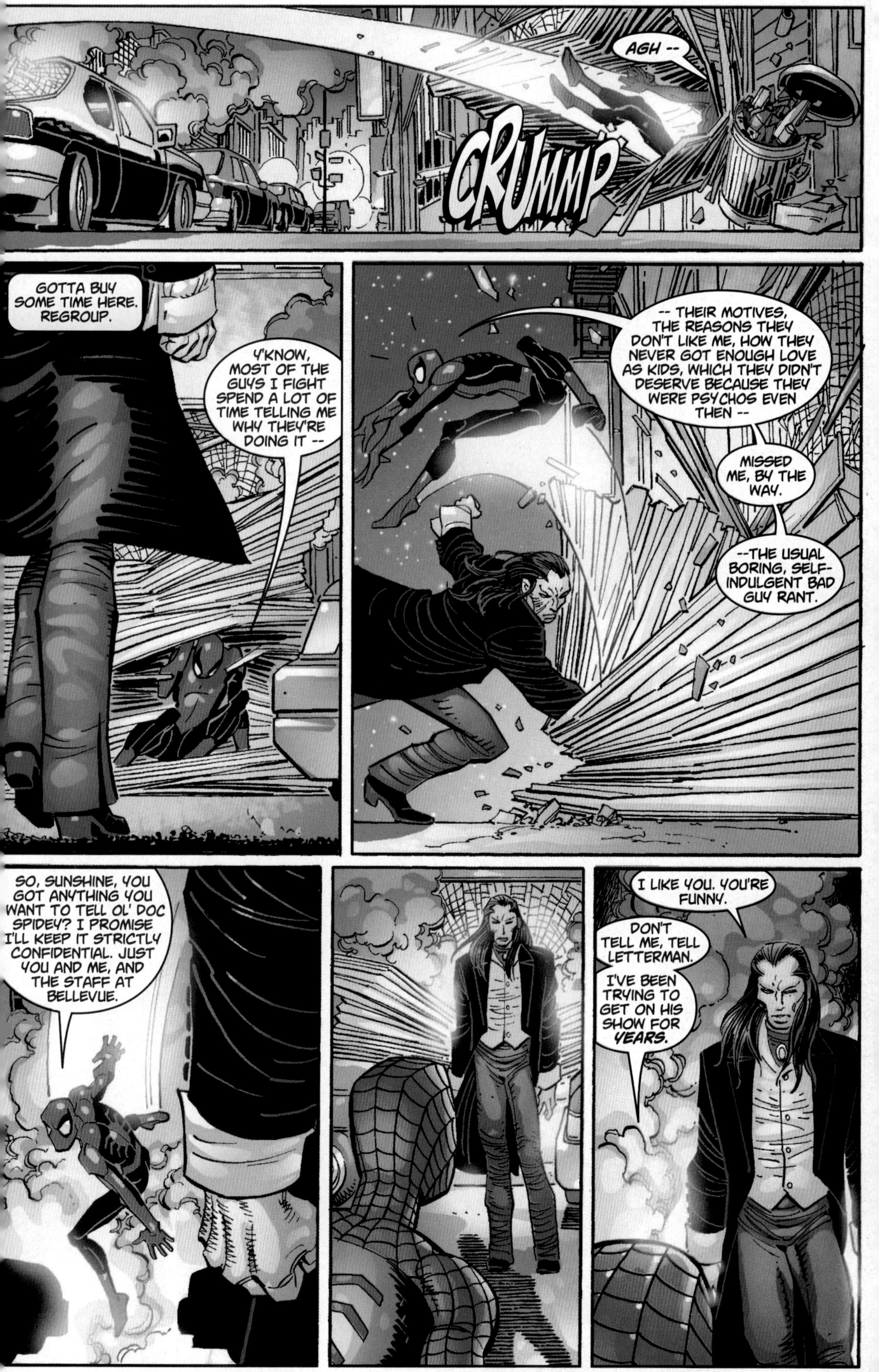
AGH --
CRUMMP
GOTTA BUY SOME TIME HERE. REGROUP.
Y'KNOW, MOST OF THE GUYS I FIGHT SPEND A LOT OF TIME TELLING ME WHY THEY'RE DOING IT --
-- THEIR MOTIVES, THE REASONS THEY DON'T LIKE ME, HOW THEY NEVER GOT ENOUGH LOVE AS KIDS, WHICH THEY DIDN'T DESERVE BECAUSE THEY WERE PSYCHOS EVEN THEN --
MISSED ME, BY THE WAY.
--THE USUAL BORING, SELF-INDULGENT BAD GUY RANT.
SO, SUNSHINE, YOU GOT ANYTHING YOU WANT TO TELL OL' DOC SPIDEY? I PROMISE I'LL KEEP IT STRICTLY CONFIDENTIAL. JUST YOU AND ME, AND THE STAFF AT BELLEVUE.
I LIKE YOU. YOU'RE FUNNY.
DON'T TELL ME, TELL LETTERMAN.
I'VE BEEN TRYING TO GET ON HIS SHOW FOR YEARS.

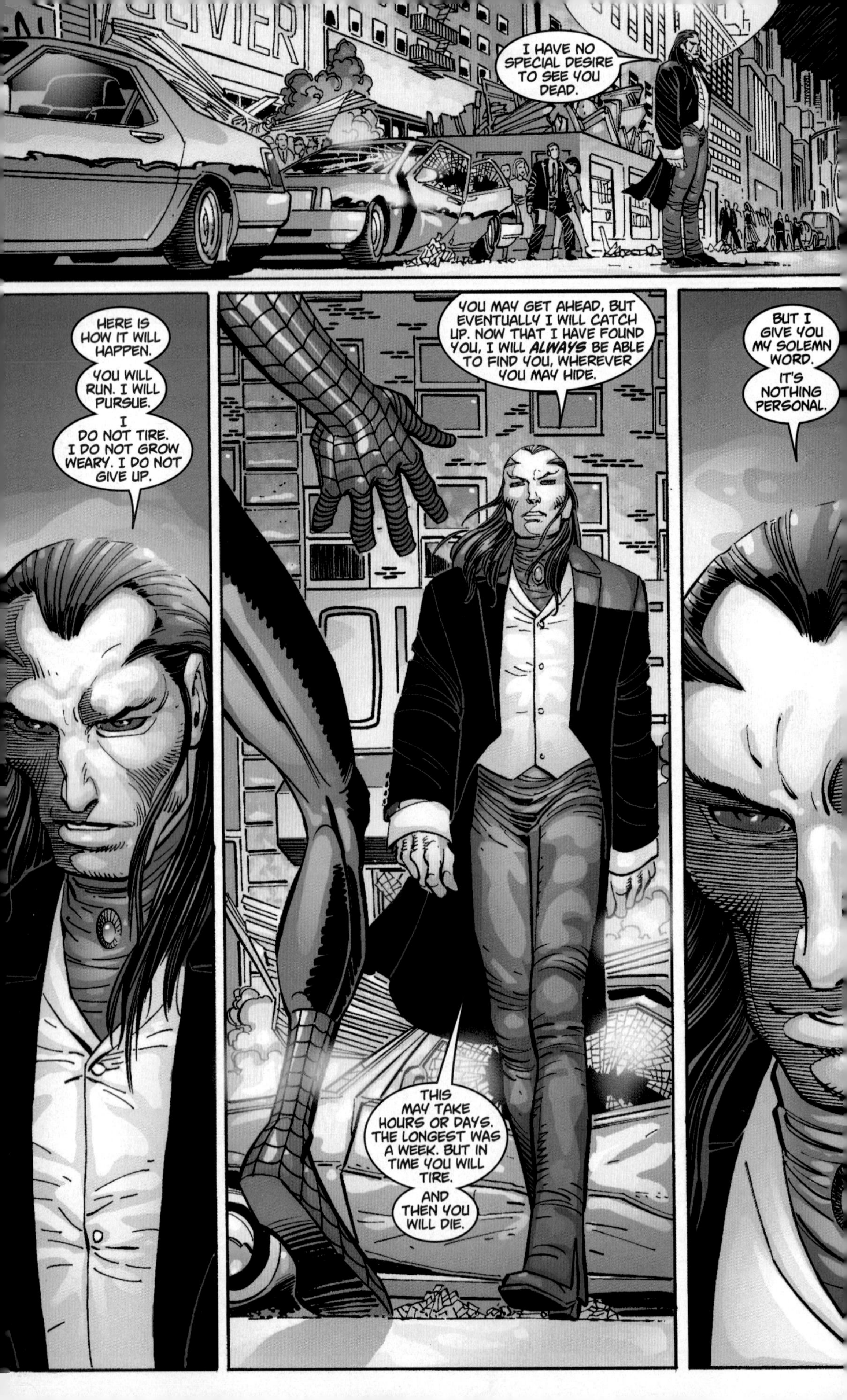
OLIVIERI
I HAVE NO SPECIAL DESIRE TO SEE YOU DEAD.
HERE IS HOW IT WILL HAPPEN.
YOU WILL RUN. I WILL PURSUE.
I DO NOT TIRE. I DO NOT GROW WEARY. I DO NOT GIVE UP.
YOU MAY GET AHEAD, BUT EVENTUALLY I WILL CATCH UP. NOW THAT I HAVE FOUND YOU, I WILL ALWAYS BE ABLE TO FIND YOU, WHEREVER YOU MAY HIDE.
THIS MAY TAKE HOURS OR DAYS. THE LONGEST WAS A WEEK. BUT IN TIME YOU WILL TIRE.
AND THEN YOU WILL DIE.
BUT I GIVE YOU MY SOLEMN WORD.
IT'S NOTHING PERSONAL.

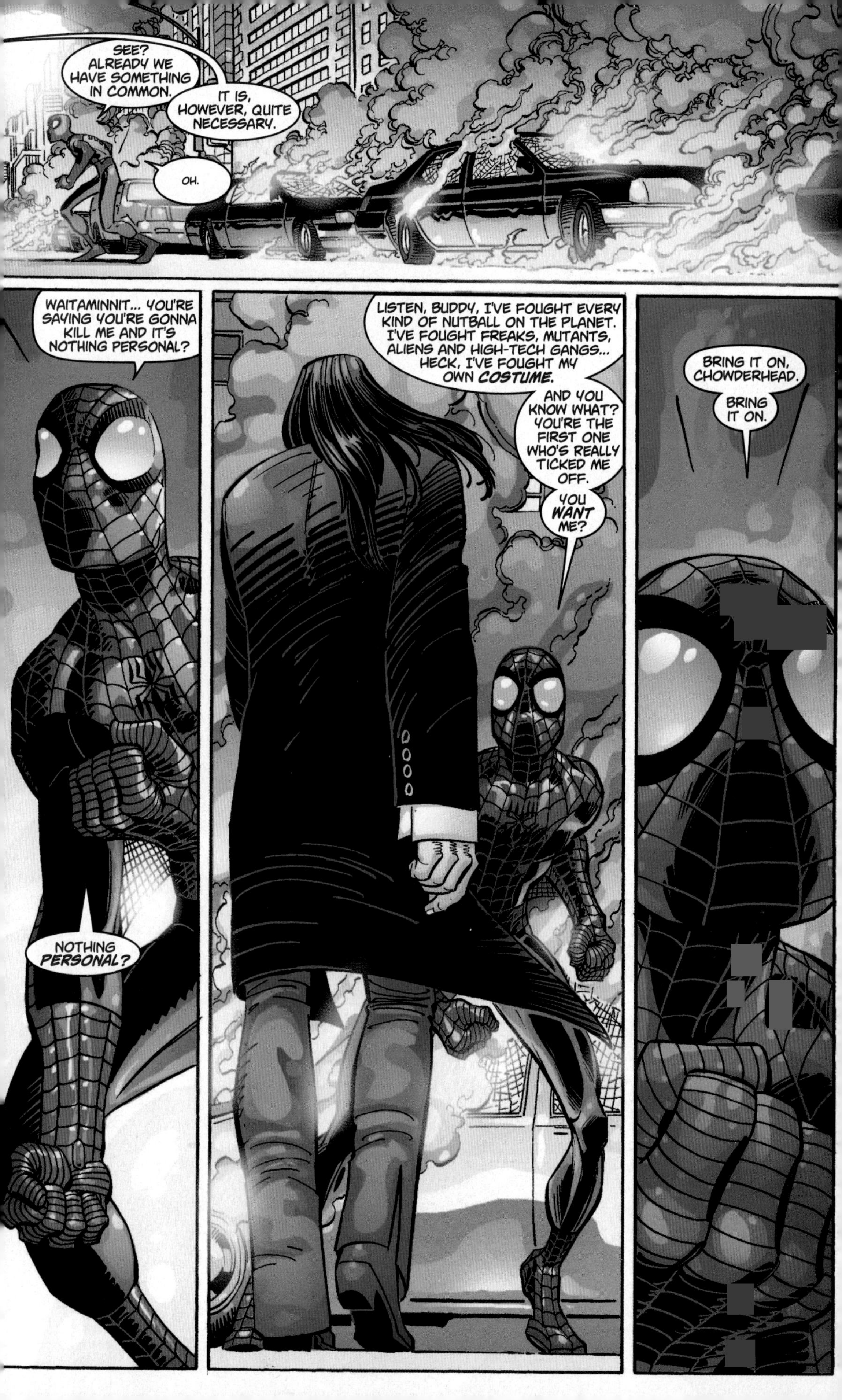
SEE? ALREADY WE HAVE SOMETHING IN COMMON.
IT IS, HOWEVER, QUITE NECESSARY.
OH.
WAITAMINNIT... YOU'RE SAYING YOU'RE GONNA KILL ME AND IT'S NOTHING PERSONAL?
NOTHING PERSONAL?
LISTEN, BUDDY, I'VE FOUGHT EVERY KIND OF NUTBALL ON THE PLANET. I'VE FOUGHT FREAKS, MUTANTS, ALIENS AND HIGH-TECH GANGS... HECK, I'VE FOUGHT MY OWN COSTUME.
AND YOU KNOW WHAT? YOU'RE THE FIRST ONE WHO'S REALLY TICKED ME OFF.
YOU WANT ME?
BRING IT ON, CHOWDERHEAD.
BRING IT ON.

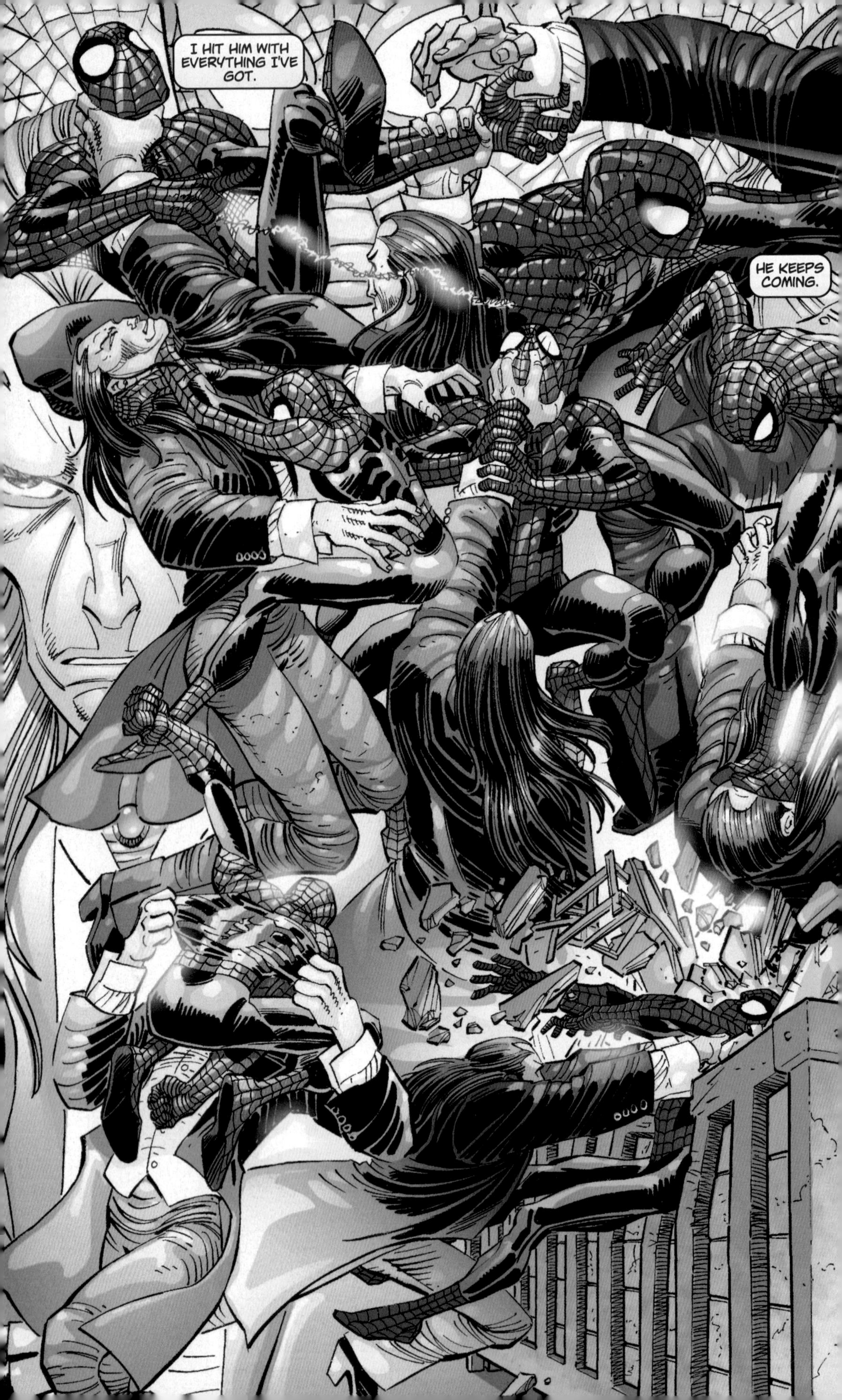
I HIT HIM WITH EVERYTHING I'VE GOT.
HE KEEPS COMING.

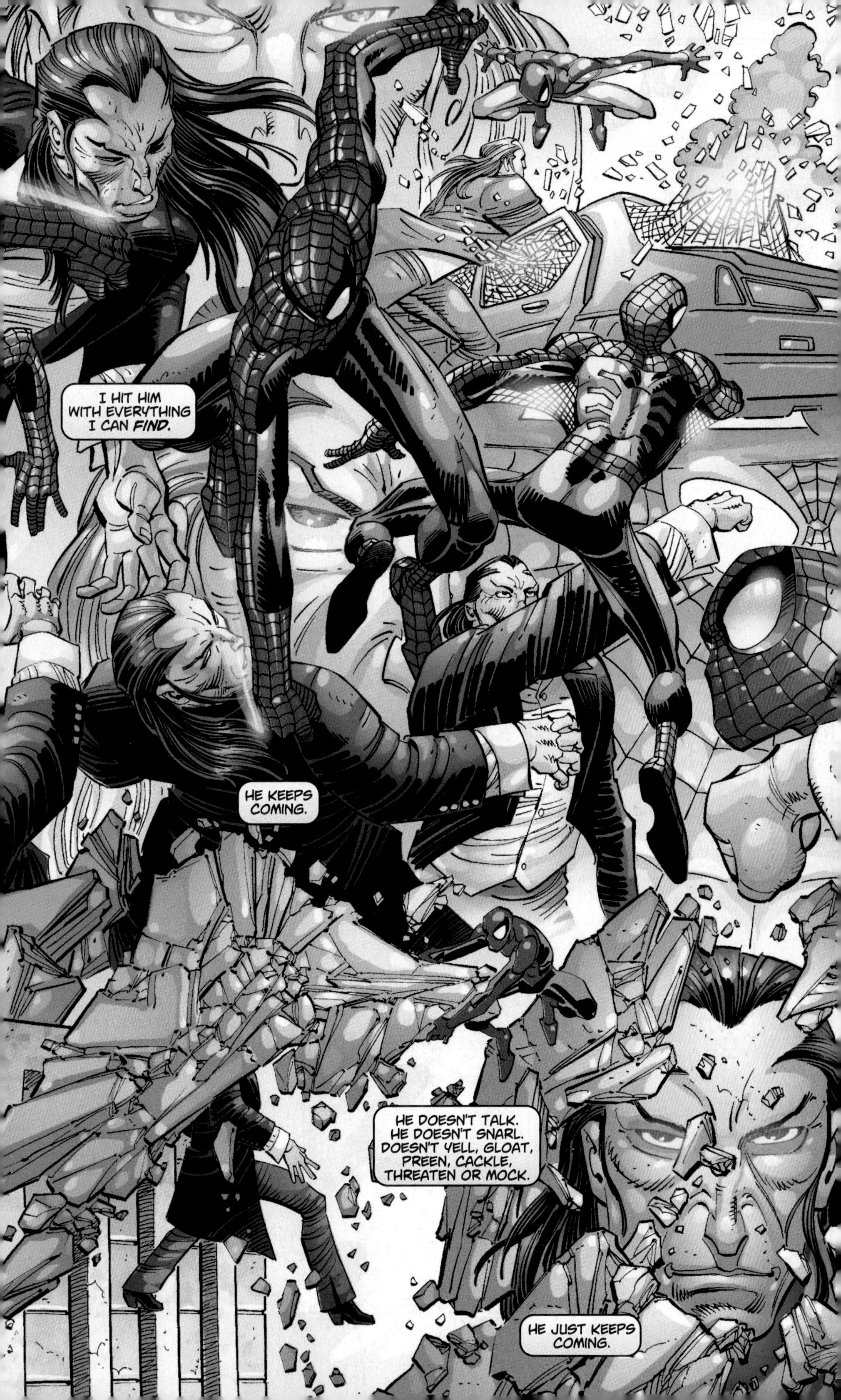

I HIT HIM WITH EVERYTHING I CAN *FIND*.
HE KEEPS COMING.
HE DOESN'T TALK. HE DOESN'T SNARL. DOESN'T YELL, GLOAT, PREEN, CACKLE, THREATEN OR MOCK.
HE JUST KEEPS COMING.

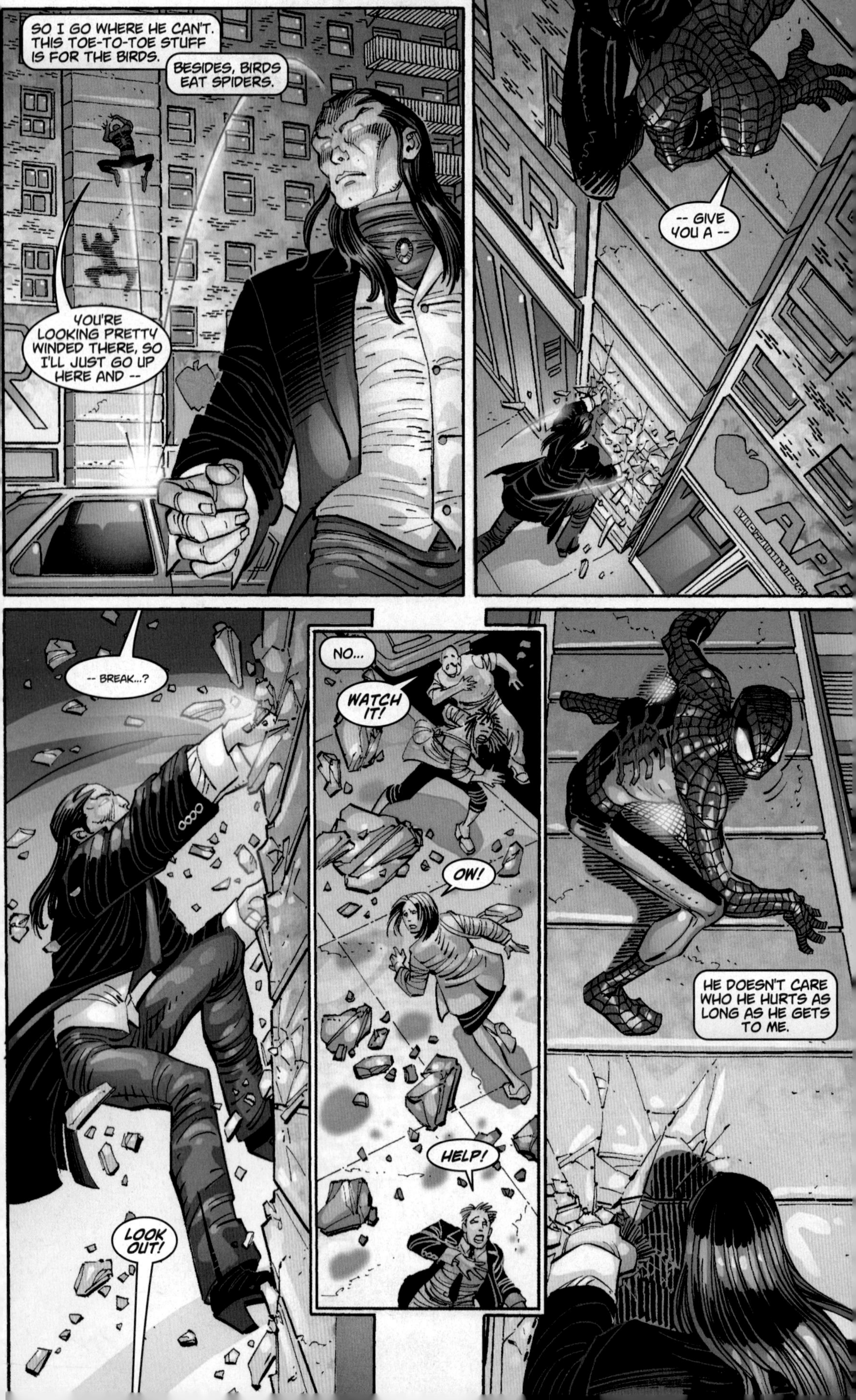
SO I GO WHERE HE CAN'T. THIS TOE-TO-TOE STUFF IS FOR THE BIRDS.
BESIDES, BIRDS EAT SPIDERS.
YOU'RE LOOKING PRETTY WINDED THERE, SO I'LL JUST GO UP HERE AND --
-- GIVE YOU A --
-- BREAK...?
NO...
WATCH IT!
OW!
HELP!
LOOK OUT!
HE DOESN'T CARE WHO HE HURTS AS LONG AS HE GETS TO ME.

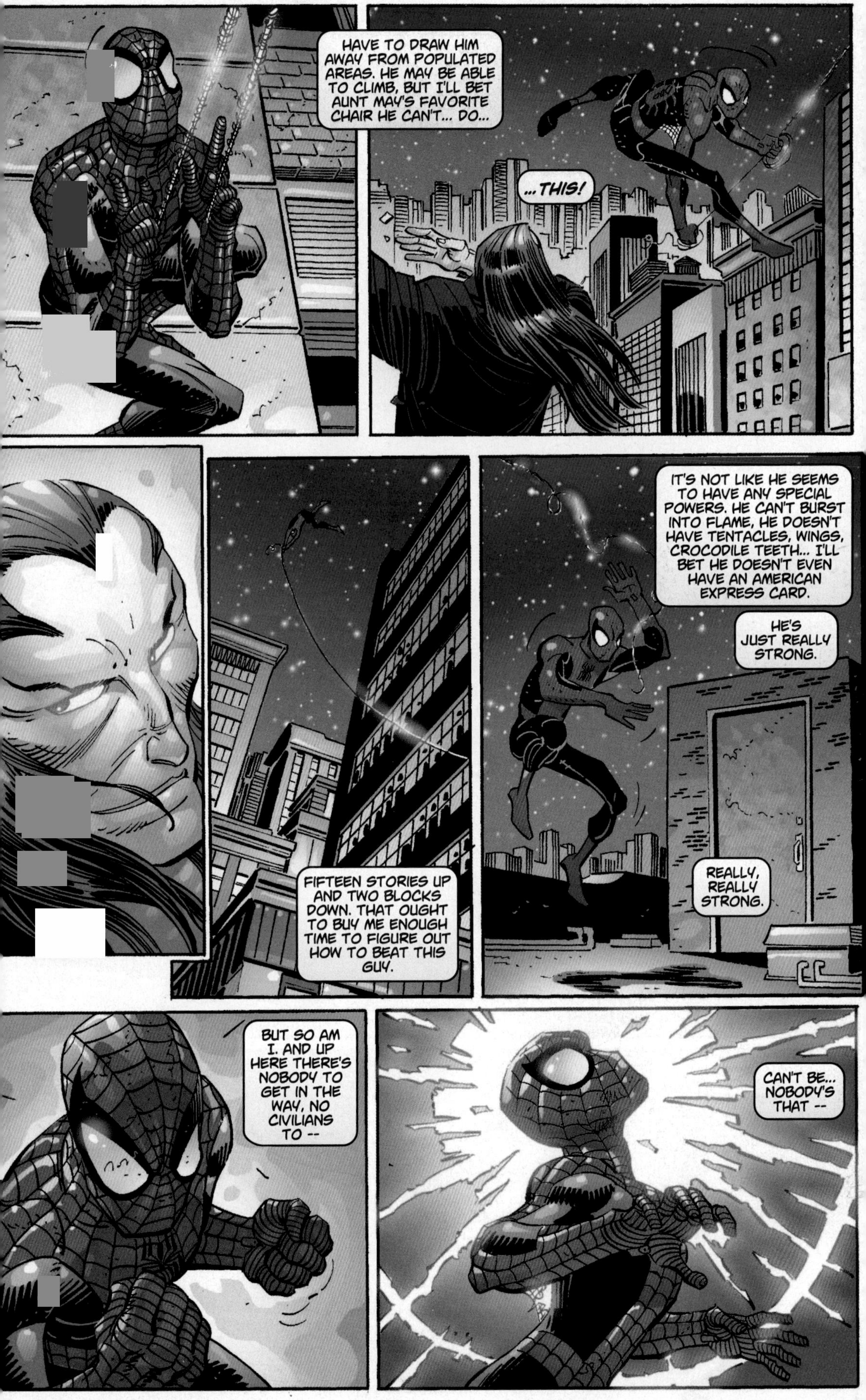

HAVE TO DRAW HIM AWAY FROM POPULATED AREAS. HE MAY BE ABLE TO CLIMB, BUT I'LL BET AUNT MAY'S FAVORITE CHAIR HE CAN'T... DO...
...THIS!
FIFTEEN STORIES UP AND TWO BLOCKS DOWN. THAT OUGHT TO BUY ME ENOUGH TIME TO FIGURE OUT HOW TO BEAT THIS GUY.
IT'S NOT LIKE HE SEEMS TO HAVE ANY SPECIAL POWERS. HE CAN'T BURST INTO FLAME, HE DOESN'T HAVE TENTACLES, WINGS, CROCODILE TEETH... I'LL BET HE DOESN'T EVEN HAVE AN AMERICAN EXPRESS CARD.
HE'S JUST REALLY STRONG.
REALLY, REALLY STRONG.
BUT SO AM I. AND UP HERE THERE'S NOBODY TO GET IN THE WAY, NO CIVILIANS TO --
CAN'T BE... NOBODY'S THAT --

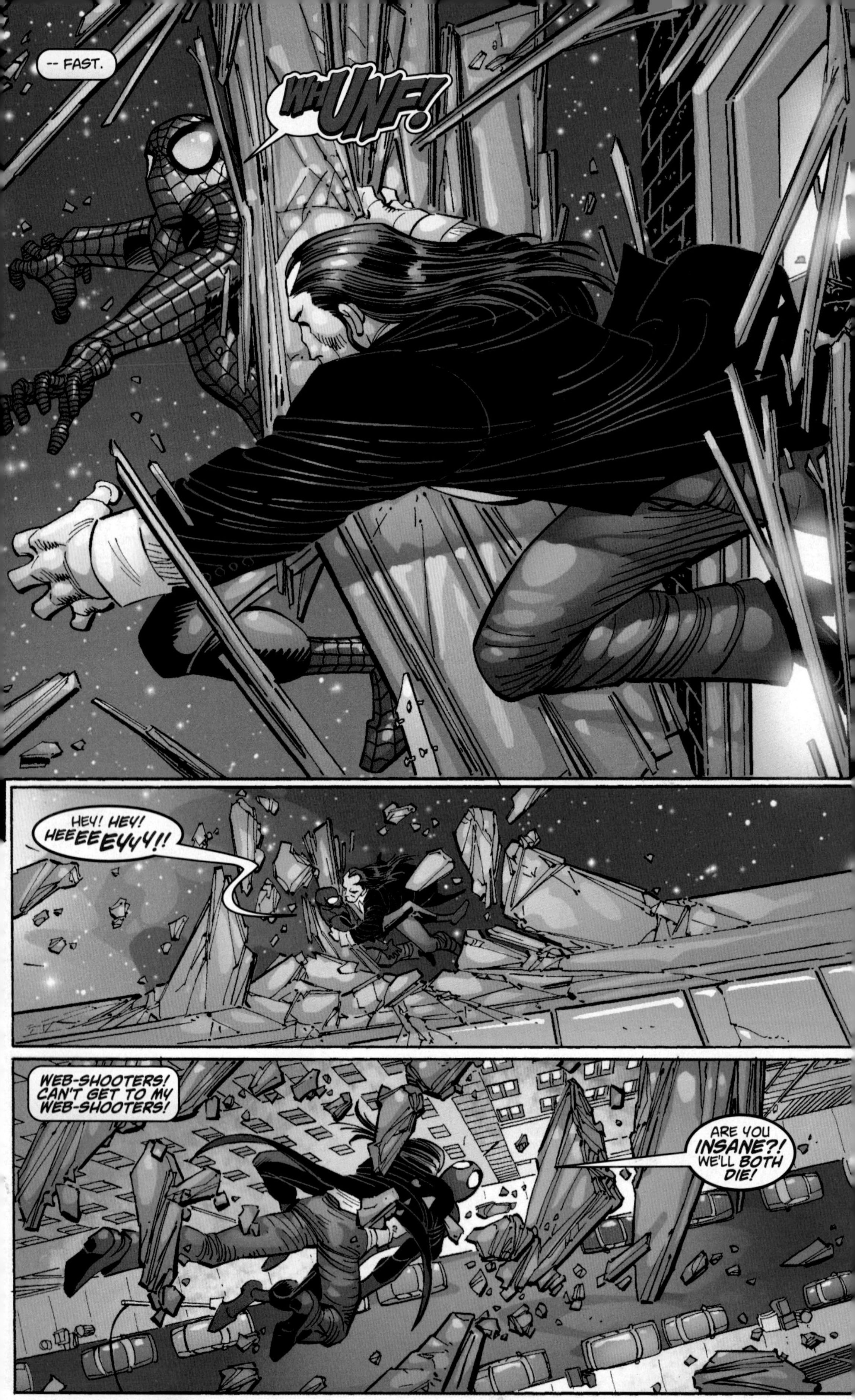
-- FAST.
WHUNF!
HEY! HEY! HEEEEEEYYY!!
WEB-SHOOTERS! CAN'T GET TO MY WEB-SHOOTERS!
ARE YOU INSANE?! WE'LL BOTH DIE!

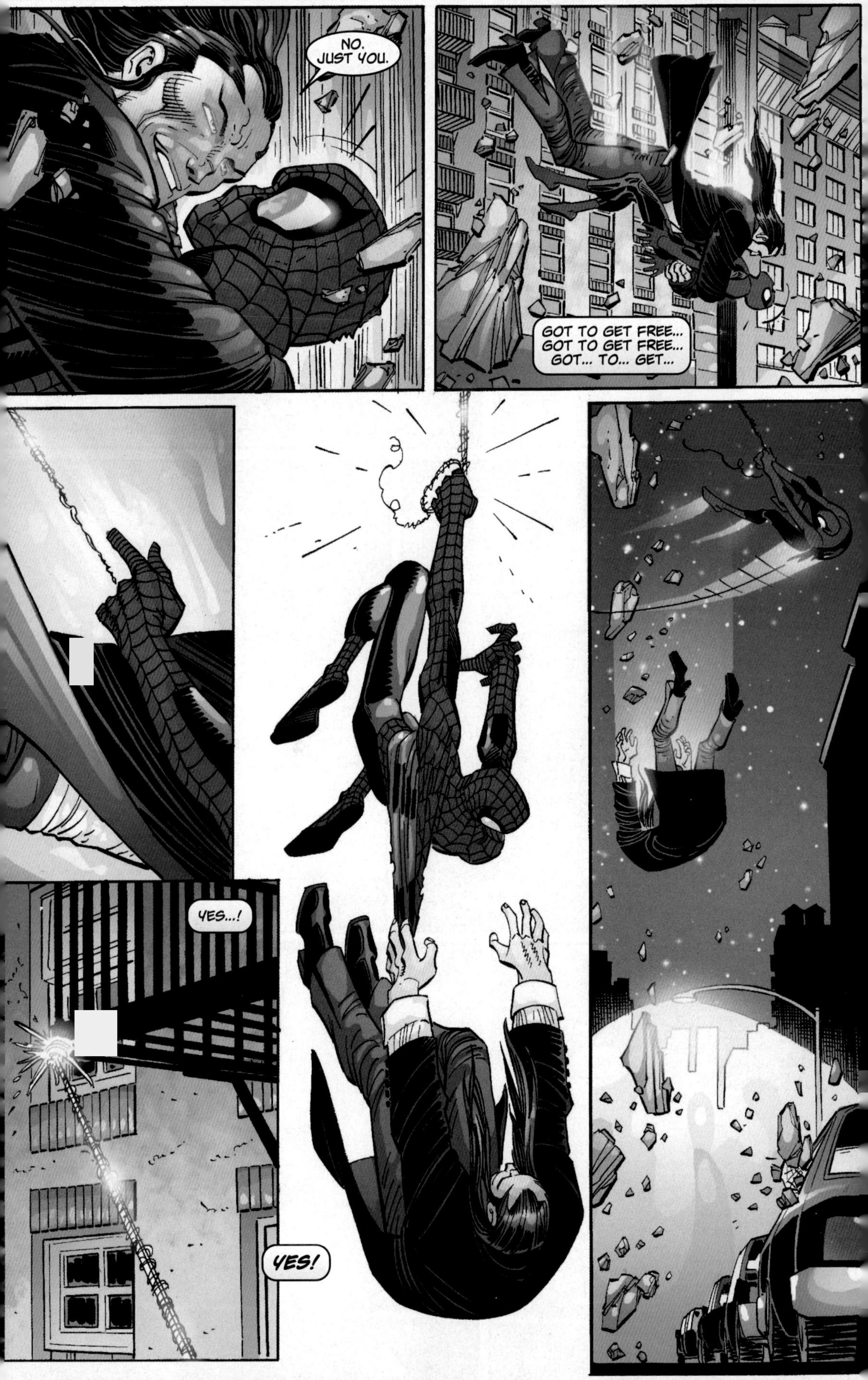
NO. JUST YOU.
GOT TO GET FREE... GOT TO GET FREE... GOT... TO... GET...
YES...!
YES!

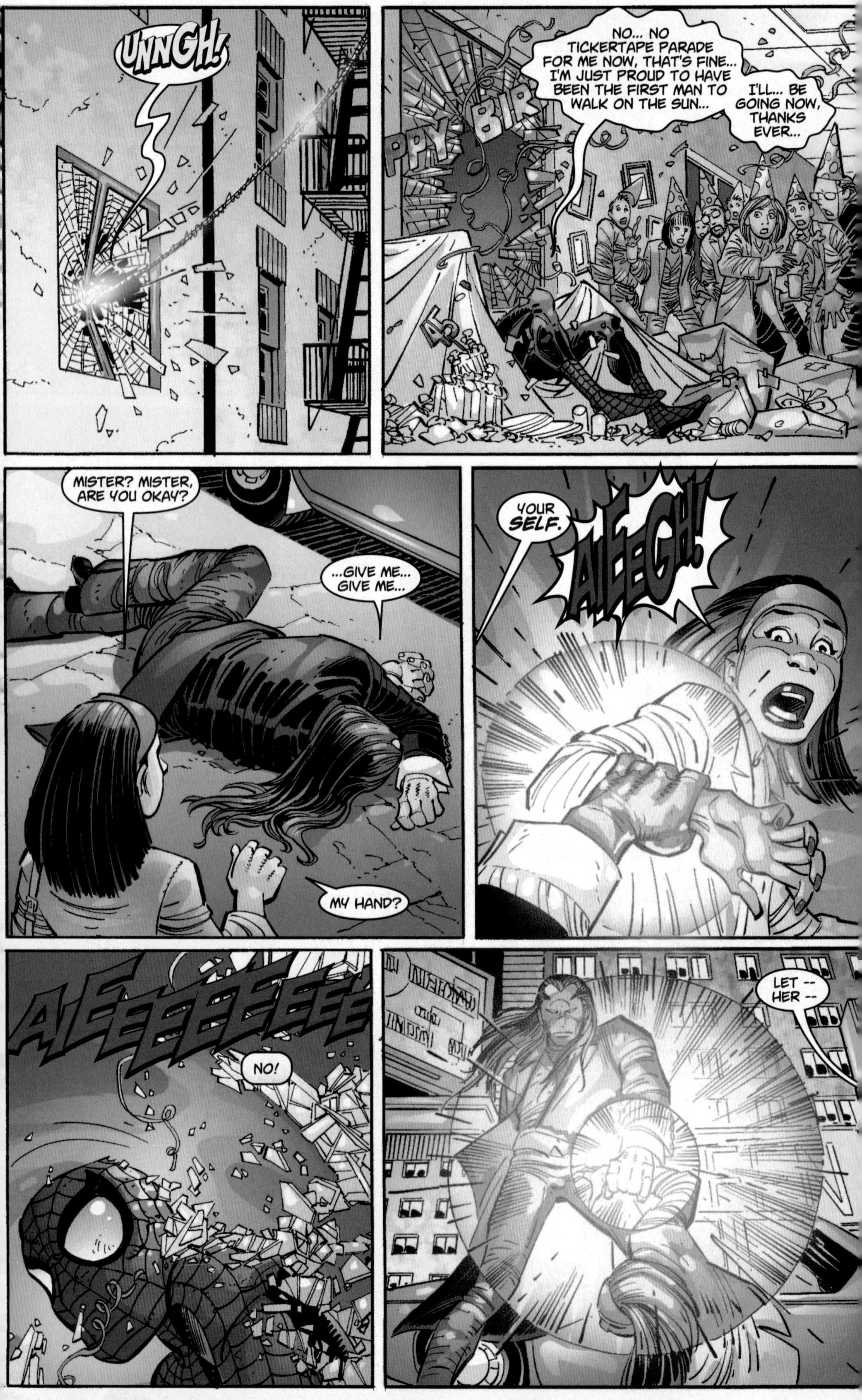
UNNGH!
NO... NO TICKERTAPE PARADE FOR ME NOW, THAT'S FINE... I'M JUST PROUD TO HAVE BEEN THE FIRST MAN TO WALK ON THE SUN...
I'LL... BE GOING NOW, THANKS EVER...
MISTER? MISTER, ARE YOU OKAY?
...GIVE ME... GIVE ME...
MY HAND?
YOUR SELF.
AIEEGH!
AIEEEEEEEE
NO!
LET -- HER --

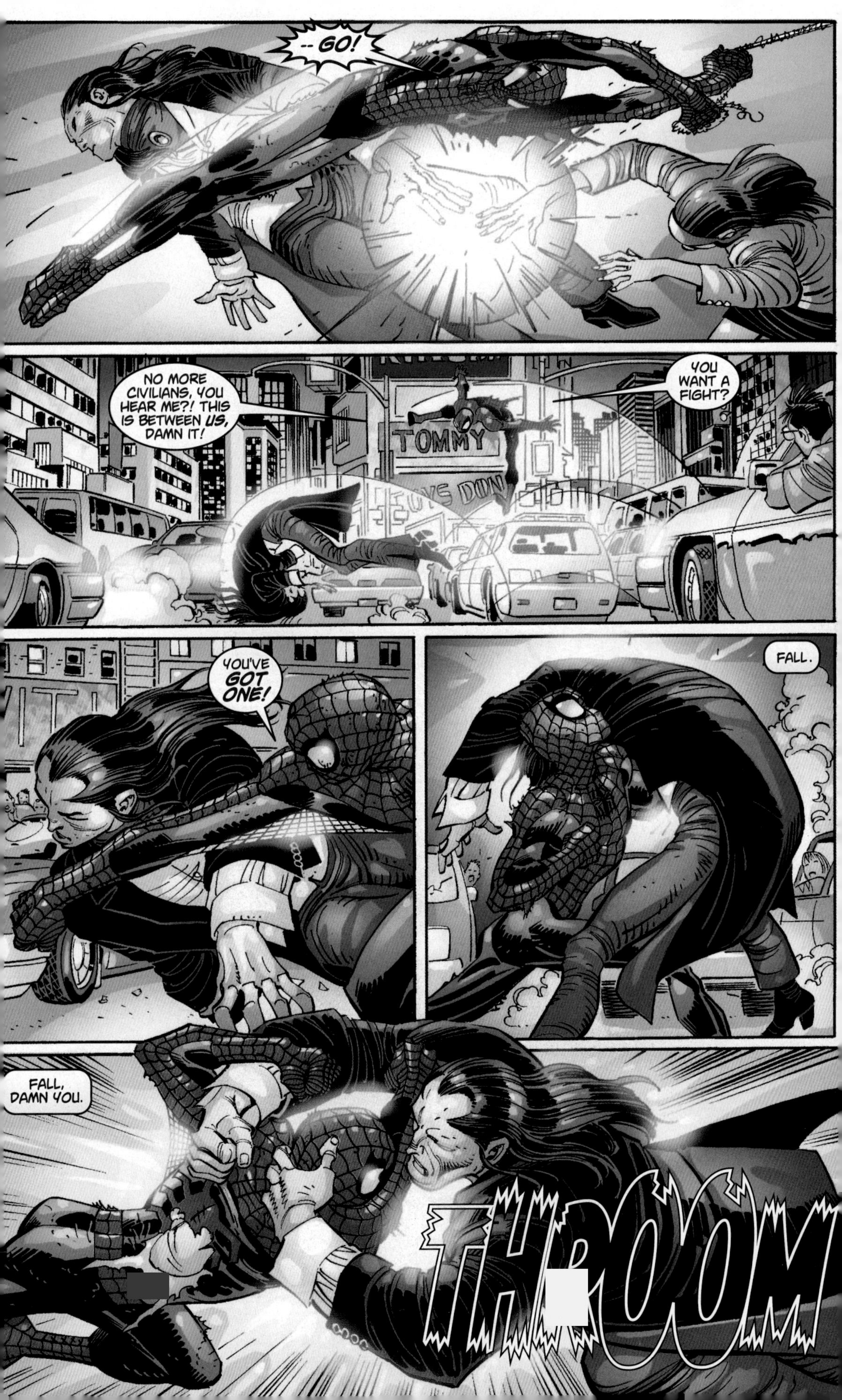
-- GO!
NO MORE CIVILIANS, YOU HEAR ME?! THIS IS BETWEEN US, DAMN IT!
YOU WANT A FIGHT?
TOMMY
YOU'VE GOT ONE!
FALL.
FALL, DAMN YOU.
THROOM

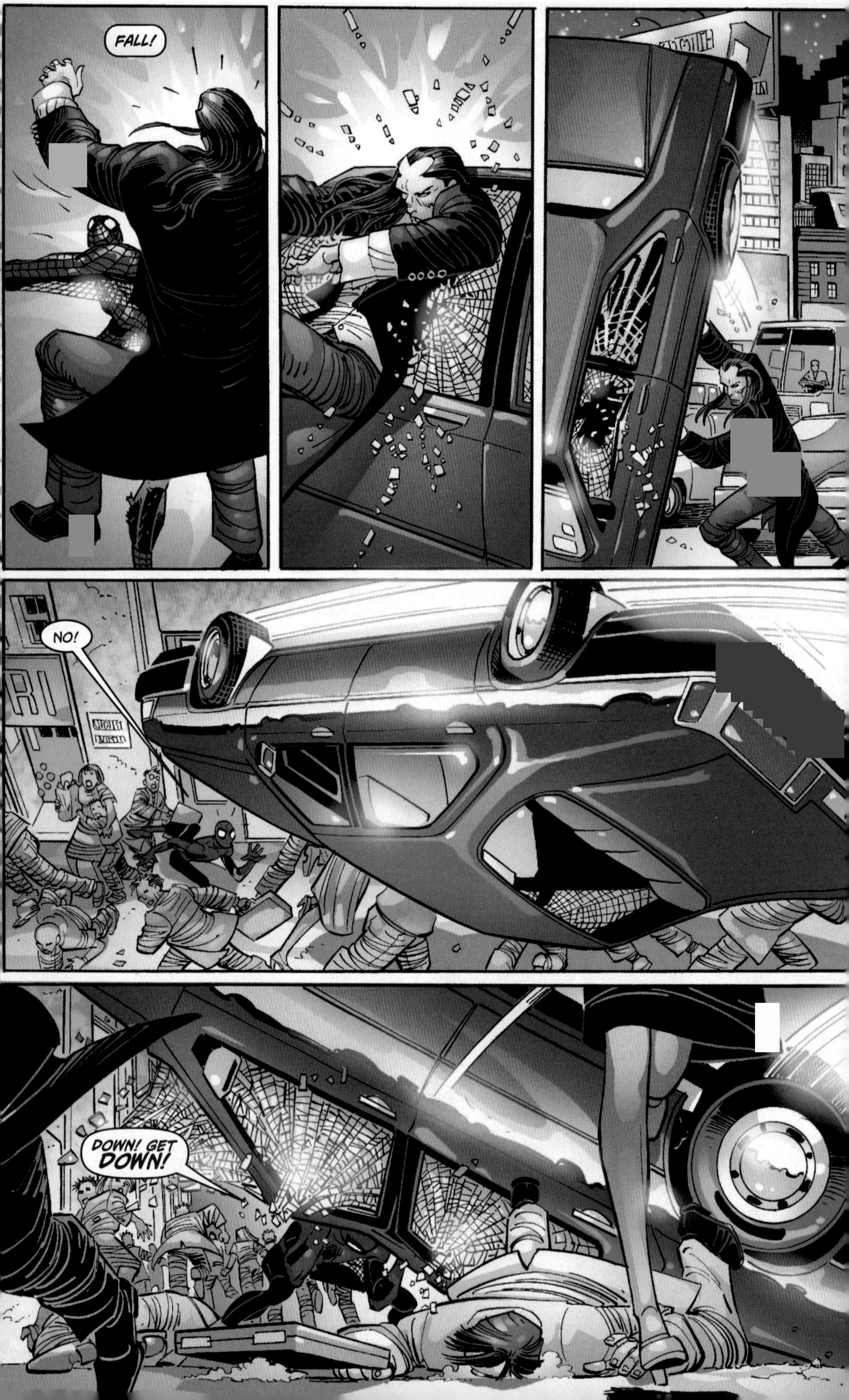
FALL!
NO!
DOWN! GET DOWN!

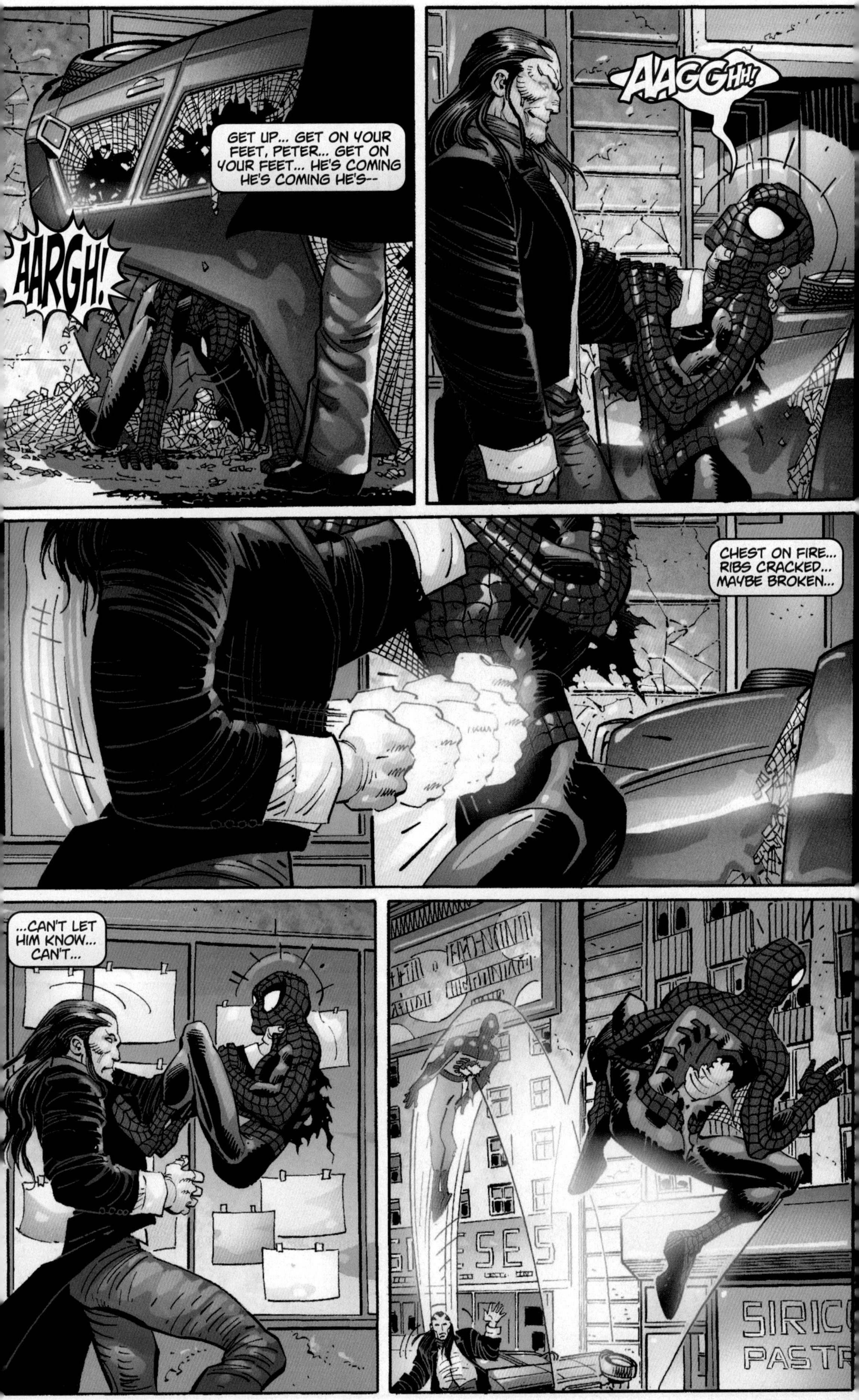
GET UP... GET ON YOUR FEET, PETER... GET ON YOUR FEET... HE'S COMING HE'S COMING HE'S--
AARGH!
AAGGHH!
CHEST ON FIRE... RIBS CRACKED... MAYBE BROKEN...
...CAN'T LET HIM KNOW... CAN'T...
SIRIC
PASTR

GOT TO PUT SOME ROOM BETWEEN US... DRAW HIM AWAY FROM THE CIVILIANS AGAIN.

HE KEEPS COMING... SILENT, SO SILENT. I FIND MYSELF ALMOST WISHING HE WOULD TAUNT ME... THAT HE'D SAY SOMETHING, ANYTHING...BECAUSE VANITY IS A WEAKNESS AND RIGHT NOW --

-- I DON'T SEE ANY OTHER WEAKNESSES.

MY ONLY CHANCE FOR NOW IS TO STAY AHEAD OF HIM AS MUCH AS I CAN.

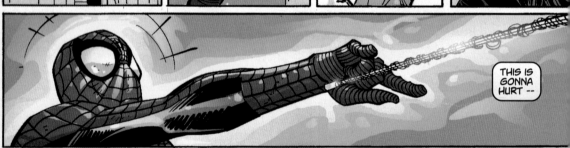

THIS IS GONNA HURT --

-- REAL --

...BAD...

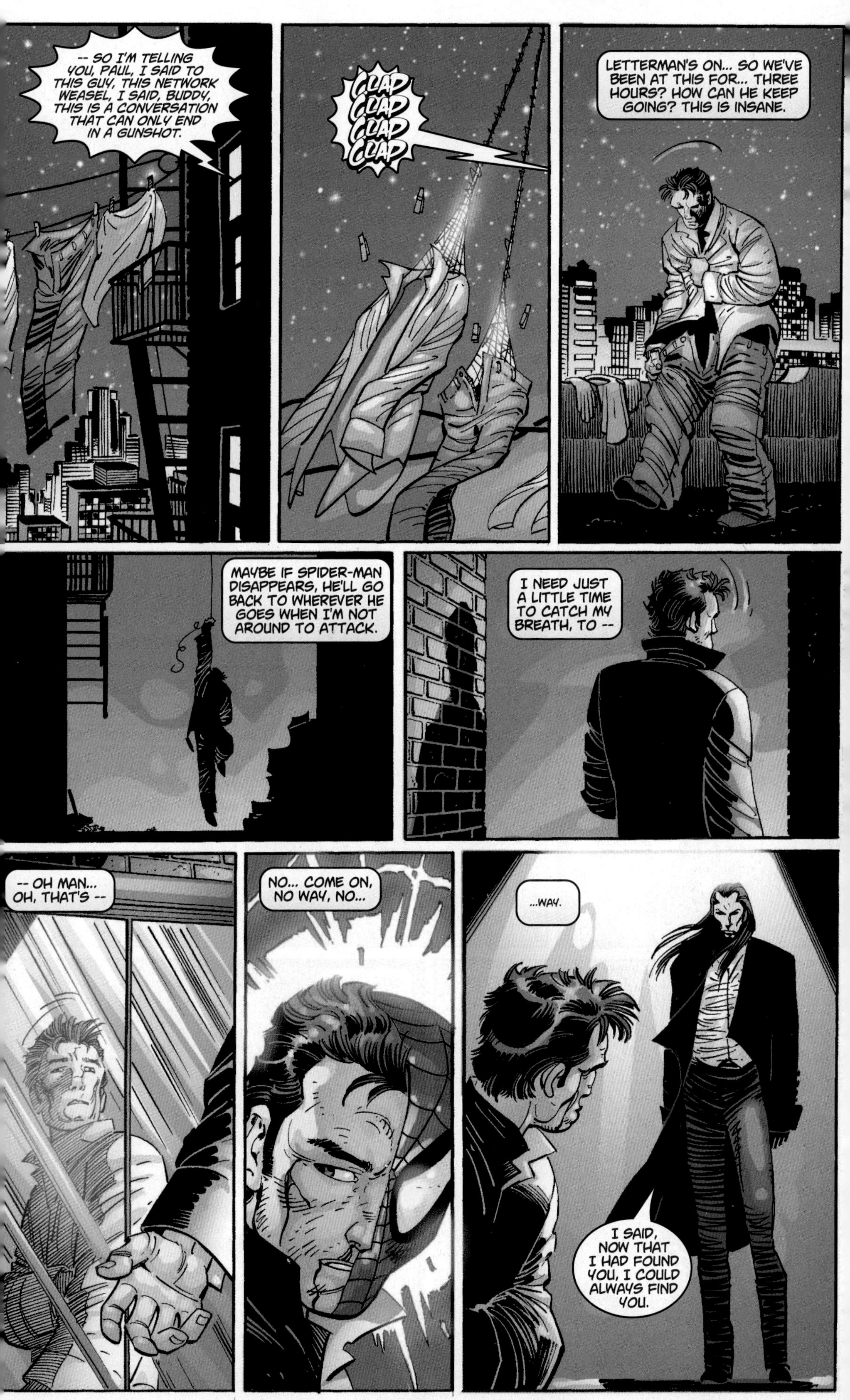
-- SO I'M TELLING YOU, PAUL, I SAID TO THIS GUY, THIS NETWORK WEASEL, I SAID, BUDDY, THIS IS A CONVERSATION THAT CAN ONLY END IN A GUNSHOT.
CLAP CLAP CLAP CLAP
LETTERMAN'S ON... SO WE'VE BEEN AT THIS FOR... THREE HOURS? HOW CAN HE KEEP GOING? THIS IS INSANE.
MAYBE IF SPIDER-MAN DISAPPEARS, HE'LL GO BACK TO WHEREVER HE GOES WHEN I'M NOT AROUND TO ATTACK.
I NEED JUST A LITTLE TIME TO CATCH MY BREATH, TO --
-- OH MAN... OH, THAT'S --
NO... COME ON, NO WAY, NO...
...WAY.
I SAID, NOW THAT I HAD FOUND YOU, I COULD ALWAYS FIND YOU.

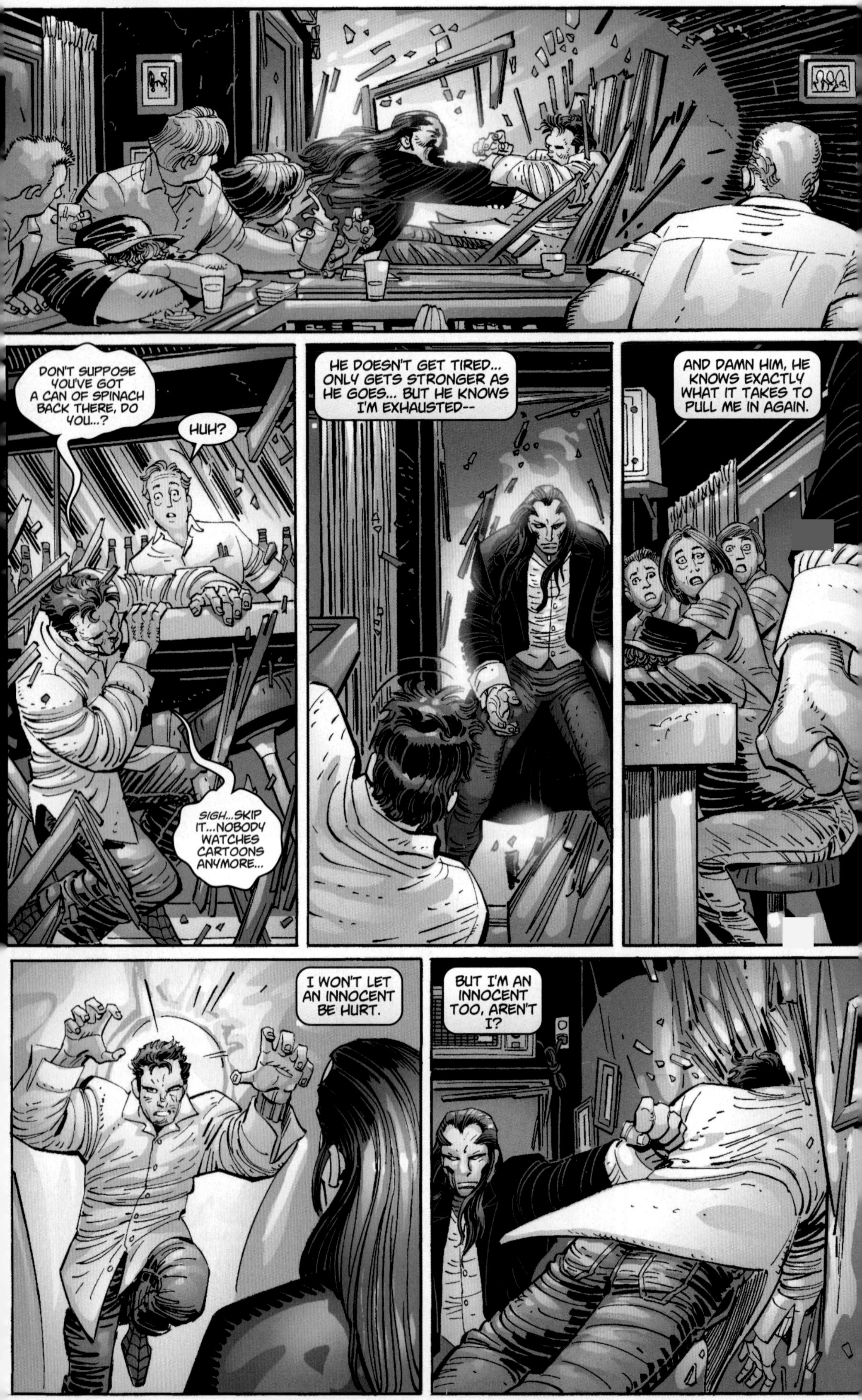

DON'T SUPPOSE YOU'VE GOT A CAN OF SPINACH BACK THERE, DO YOU...?
HUH?
SIGH...SKIP IT...NOBODY WATCHES CARTOONS ANYMORE...
HE DOESN'T GET TIRED... ONLY GETS STRONGER AS HE GOES... BUT HE KNOWS I'M EXHAUSTED--
AND DAMN HIM, HE KNOWS EXACTLY WHAT IT TAKES TO PULL ME IN AGAIN.
I WON'T LET AN INNOCENT BE HURT.
BUT I'M AN INNOCENT TOO, AREN'T I?

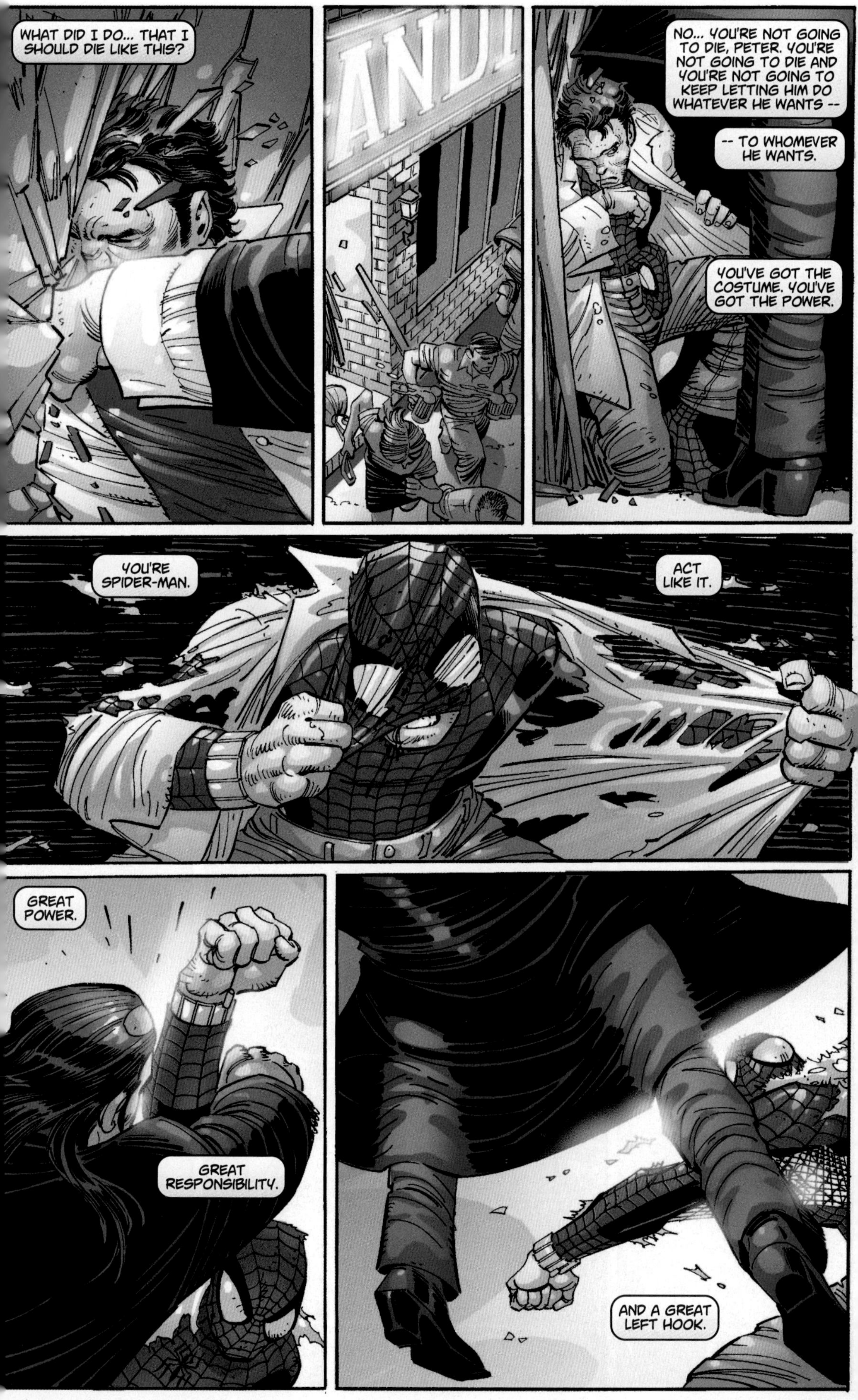
WHAT DID I DO... THAT I SHOULD DIE LIKE THIS?
NO... YOU'RE NOT GOING TO DIE, PETER. YOU'RE NOT GOING TO DIE AND YOU'RE NOT GOING TO KEEP LETTING HIM DO WHATEVER HE WANTS --
-- TO WHOMEVER HE WANTS.
YOU'VE GOT THE COSTUME. YOU'VE GOT THE POWER.
YOU'RE SPIDER-MAN.
ACT LIKE IT.
GREAT POWER.
GREAT RESPONSIBILITY.
AND A GREAT LEFT HOOK.

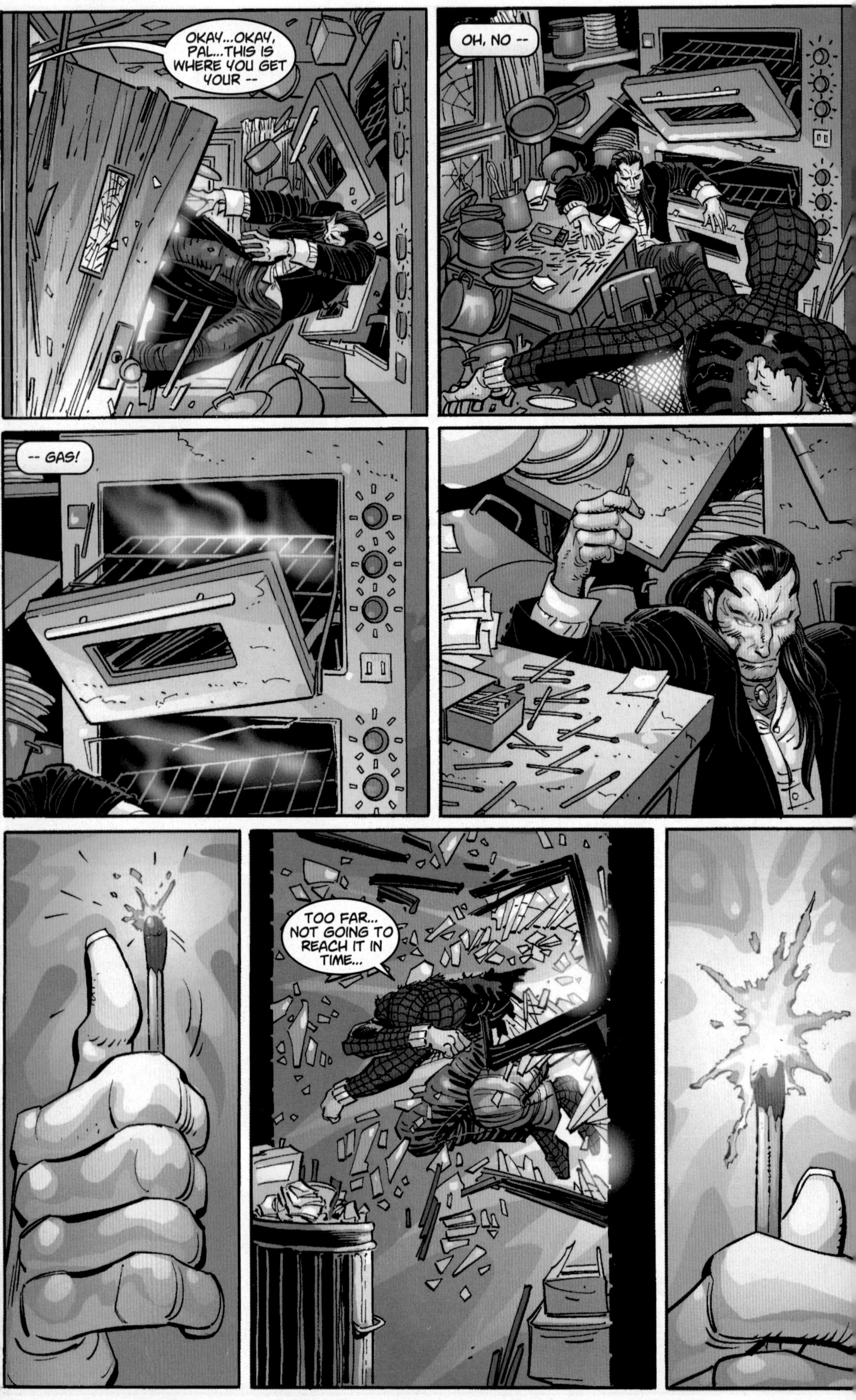
OKAY...OKAY, PAL...THIS IS WHERE YOU GET YOUR --
OH, NO --
-- GAS!
TOO FAR... NOT GOING TO REACH IT IN TIME...

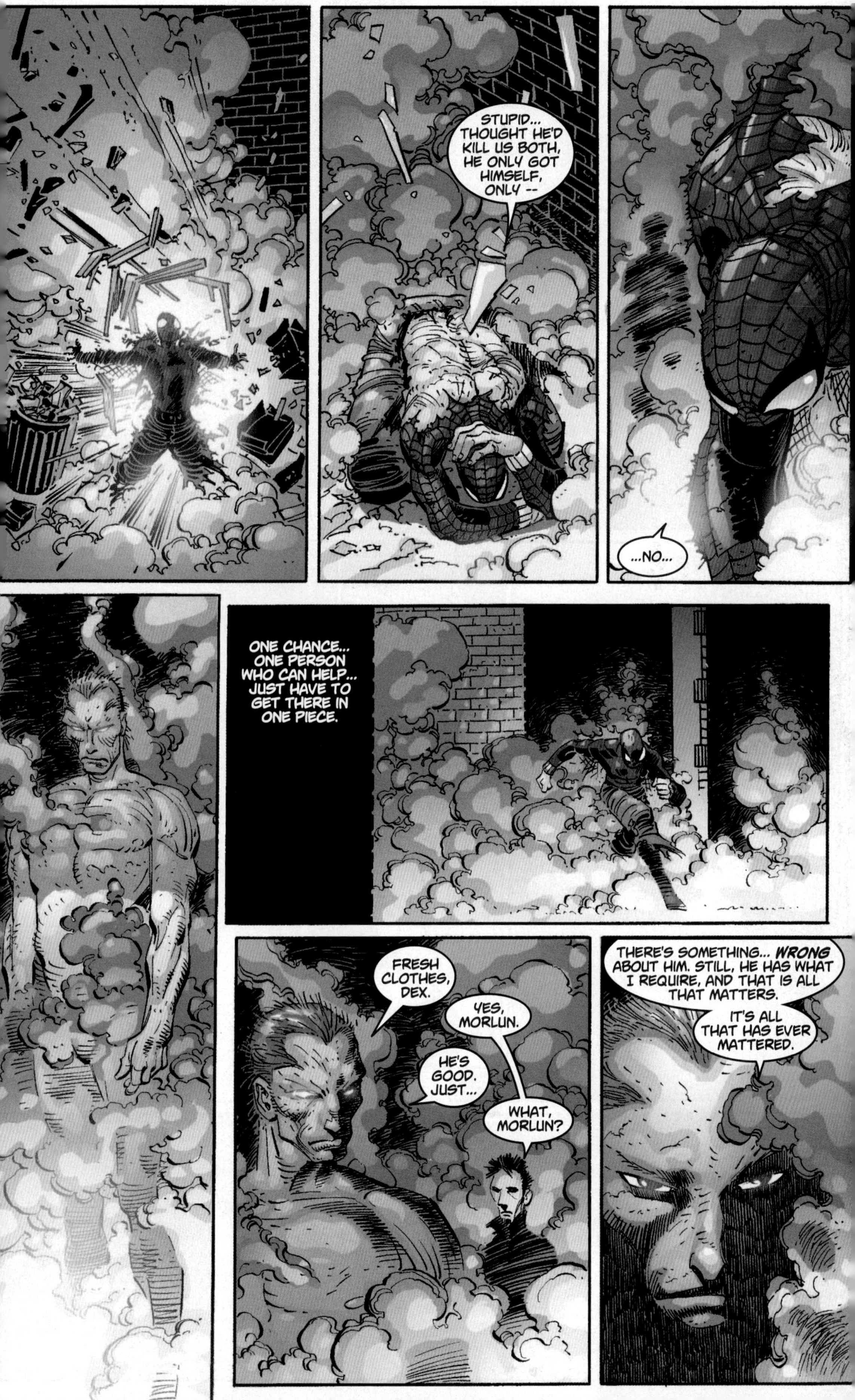
STUPID... THOUGHT HE'D KILL US BOTH, HE ONLY GOT HIMSELF, ONLY --
...NO...
ONE CHANCE... ONE PERSON WHO CAN HELP... JUST HAVE TO GET THERE IN ONE PIECE.
FRESH CLOTHES, DEX.
YES, MORLUN.
HE'S GOOD. JUST...
WHAT, MORLUN?
THERE'S SOMETHING... WRONG ABOUT HIM. STILL, HE HAS WHAT I REQUIRE, AND THAT IS ALL THAT MATTERS.
IT'S ALL THAT HAS EVER MATTERED.

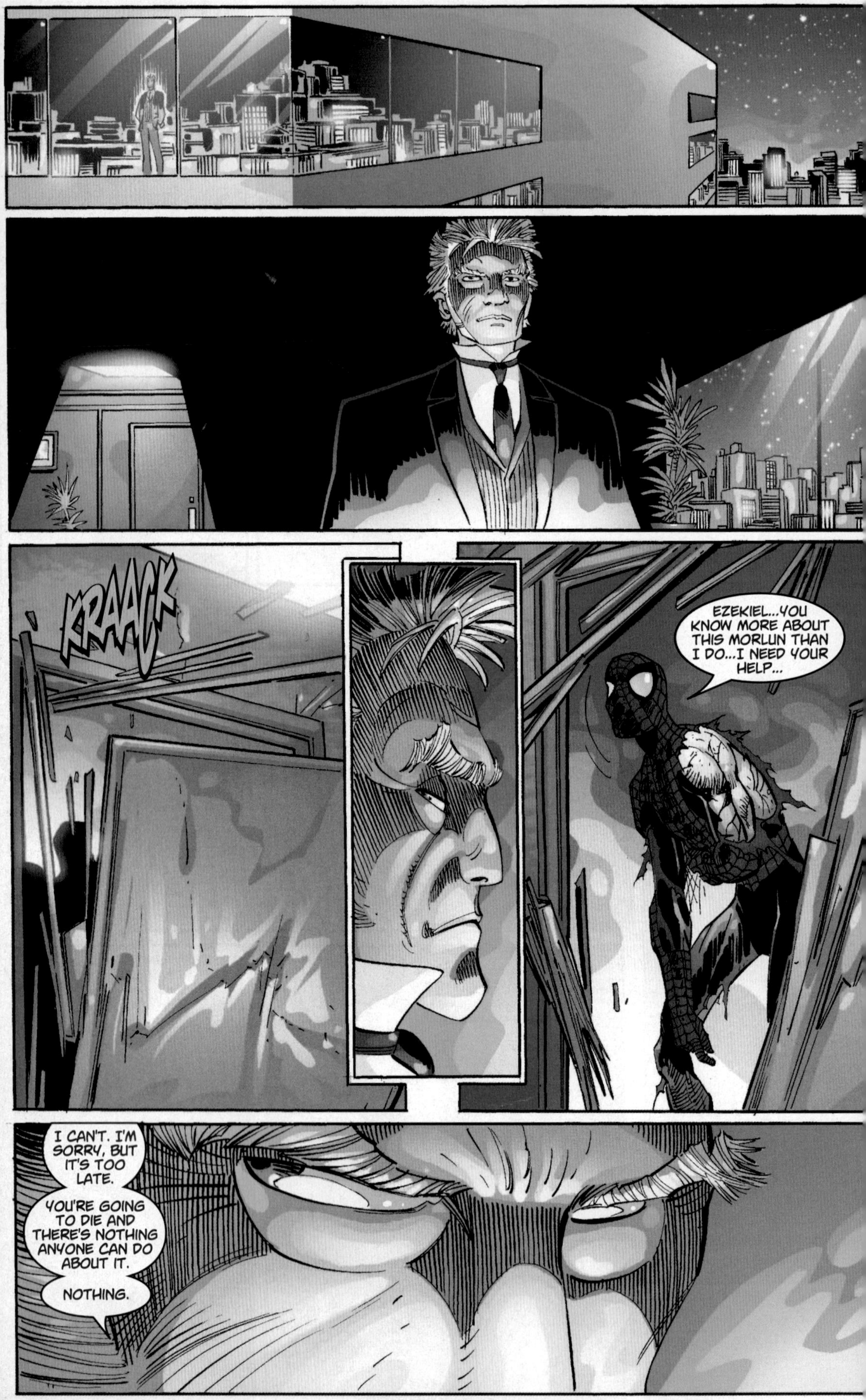
KRAACK
EZEKIEL...YOU KNOW MORE ABOUT THIS MORLUN THAN I DO...I NEED YOUR HELP...
I CAN'T. I'M SORRY, BUT IT'S TOO LATE.
YOU'RE GOING TO DIE AND THERE'S NOTHING ANYONE CAN DO ABOUT IT.
NOTHING.

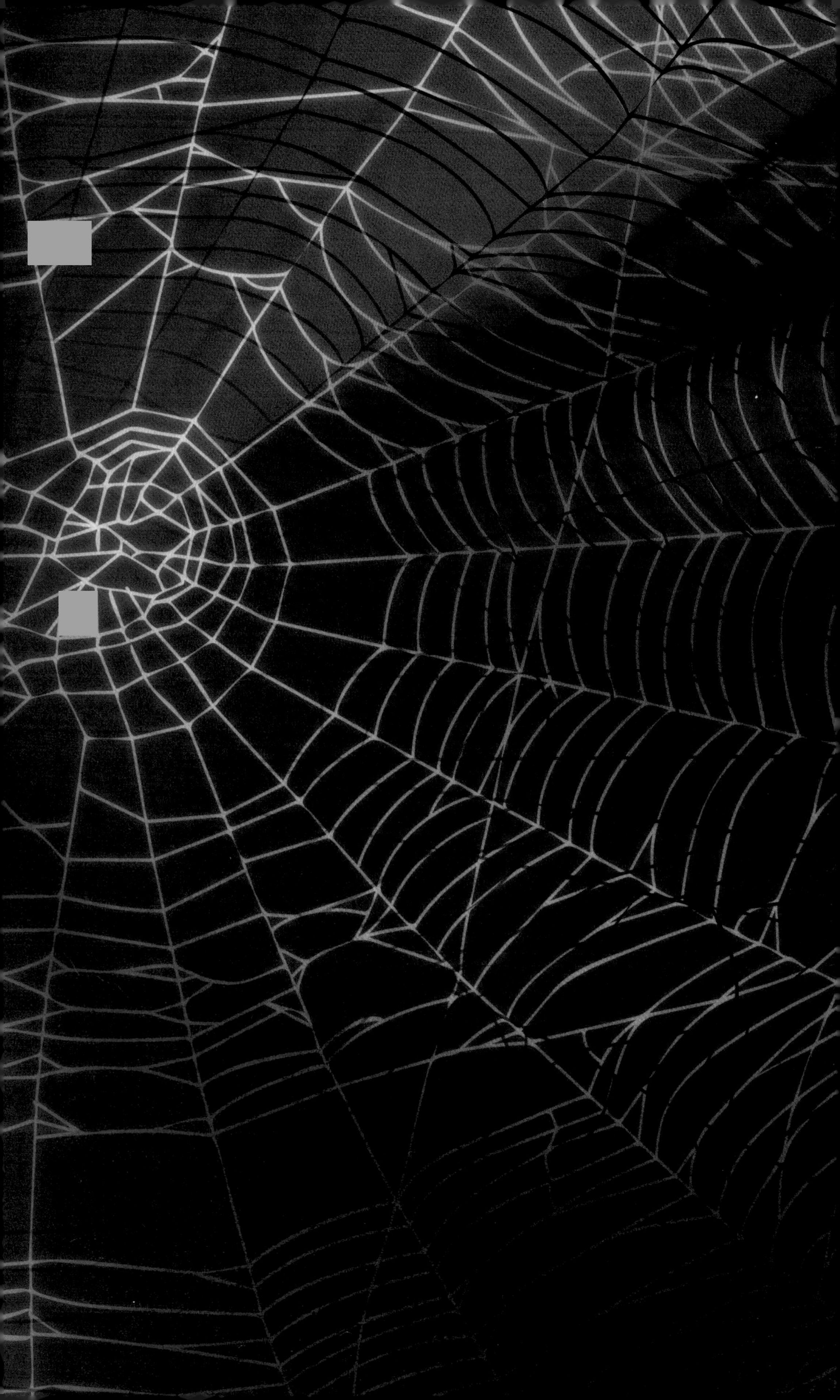

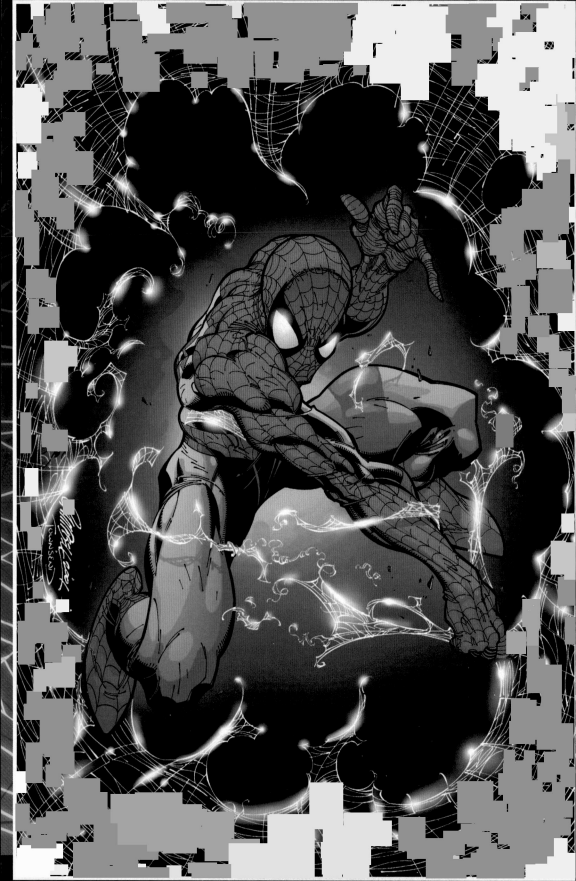

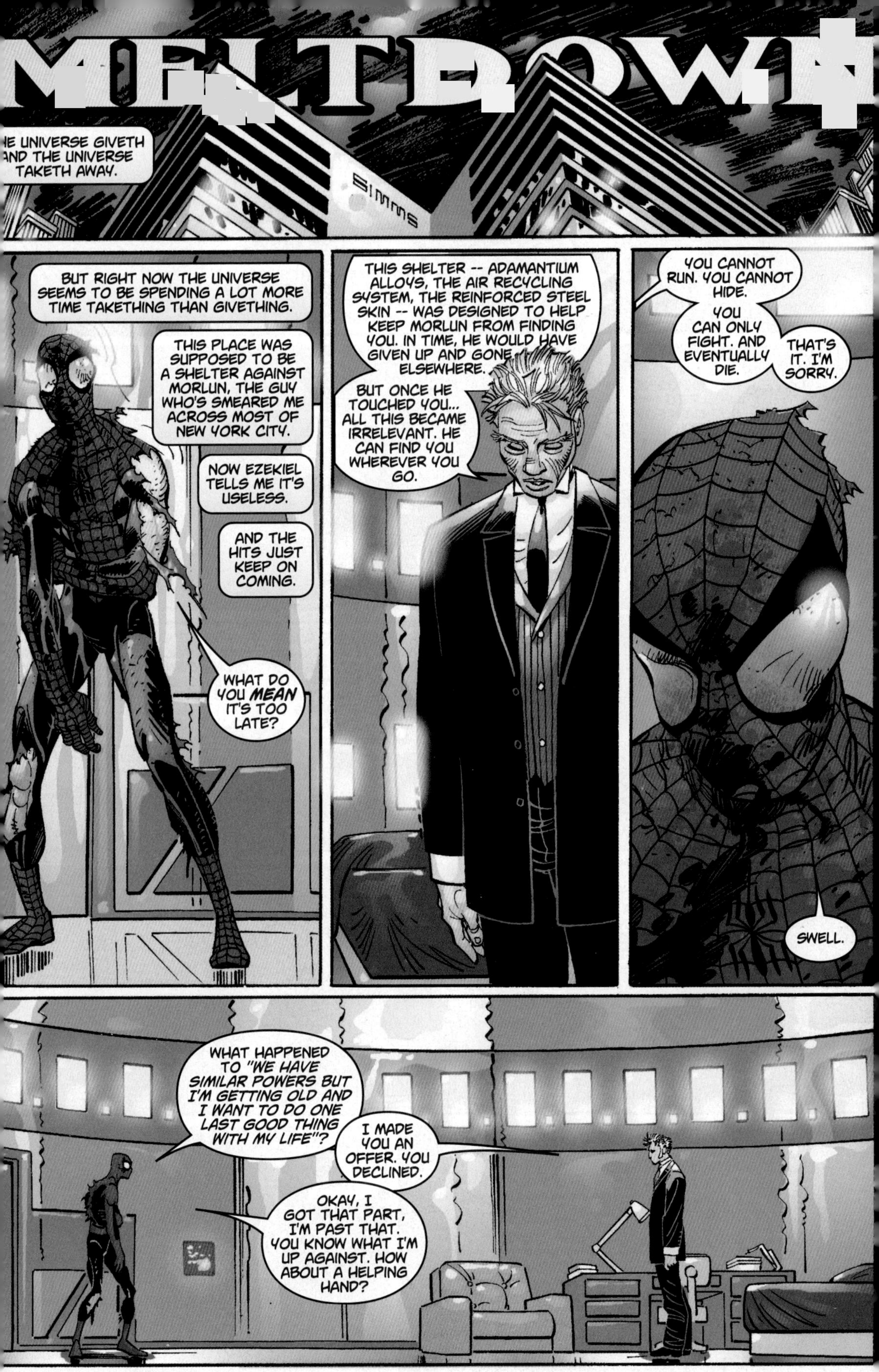
MELTDOWN
HE UNIVERSE GIVETH AND THE UNIVERSE TAKETH AWAY.
BUT RIGHT NOW THE UNIVERSE SEEMS TO BE SPENDING A LOT MORE TIME TAKETHING THAN GIVETHING.
THIS PLACE WAS SUPPOSED TO BE A SHELTER AGAINST MORLUN, THE GUY WHO'S SMEARED ME ACROSS MOST OF NEW YORK CITY.
NOW EZEKIEL TELLS ME IT'S USELESS.
AND THE HITS JUST KEEP ON COMING.
WHAT DO YOU MEAN IT'S TOO LATE?
THIS SHELTER -- ADAMANTIUM ALLOYS, THE AIR RECYCLING SYSTEM, THE REINFORCED STEEL SKIN -- WAS DESIGNED TO HELP KEEP MORLUN FROM FINDING YOU. IN TIME, HE WOULD HAVE GIVEN UP AND GONE ELSEWHERE.
BUT ONCE HE TOUCHED YOU... ALL THIS BECAME IRRELEVANT. HE CAN FIND YOU WHEREVER YOU GO.
YOU CANNOT RUN. YOU CANNOT HIDE.
YOU CAN ONLY FIGHT. AND EVENTUALLY DIE.
THAT'S IT. I'M SORRY.
SWELL.
WHAT HAPPENED TO "WE HAVE SIMILAR POWERS BUT I'M GETTING OLD AND I WANT TO DO ONE LAST GOOD THING WITH MY LIFE"?
I MADE YOU AN OFFER. YOU DECLINED.
OKAY, I GOT THAT PART, I'M PAST THAT. YOU KNOW WHAT I'M UP AGAINST. HOW ABOUT A HELPING HAND?

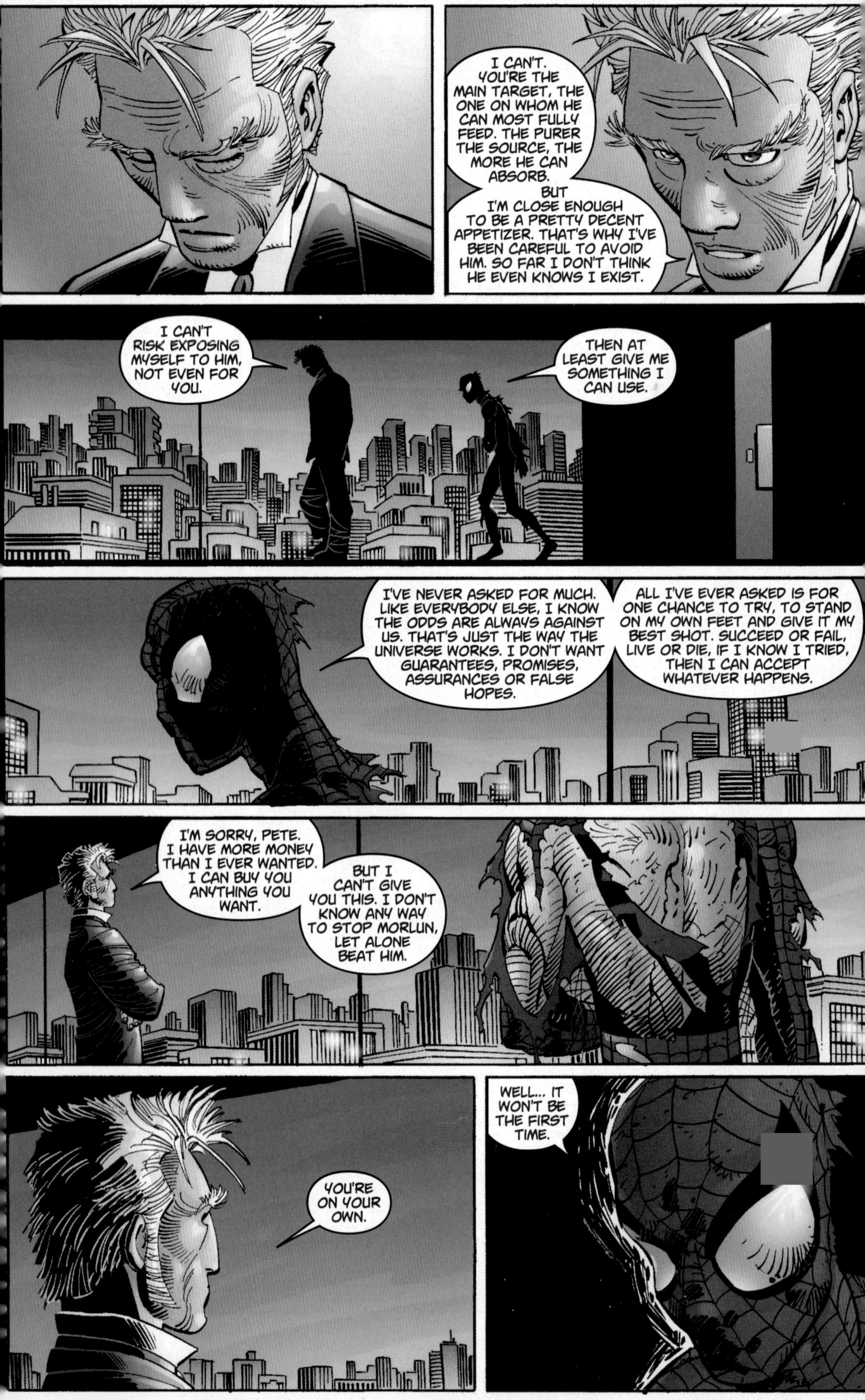
I CAN'T. YOU'RE THE MAIN TARGET, THE ONE ON WHOM HE CAN MOST FULLY FEED. THE PURER THE SOURCE, THE MORE HE CAN ABSORB.
BUT I'M CLOSE ENOUGH TO BE A PRETTY DECENT APPETIZER. THAT'S WHY I'VE BEEN CAREFUL TO AVOID HIM. SO FAR I DON'T THINK HE EVEN KNOWS I EXIST.
I CAN'T RISK EXPOSING MYSELF TO HIM, NOT EVEN FOR YOU.
THEN AT LEAST GIVE ME SOMETHING I CAN USE.
I'VE NEVER ASKED FOR MUCH. LIKE EVERYBODY ELSE, I KNOW THE ODDS ARE ALWAYS AGAINST US. THAT'S JUST THE WAY THE UNIVERSE WORKS. I DON'T WANT GUARANTEES, PROMISES, ASSURANCES OR FALSE HOPES.
ALL I'VE EVER ASKED IS FOR ONE CHANCE TO TRY, TO STAND ON MY OWN FEET AND GIVE IT MY BEST SHOT. SUCCEED OR FAIL, LIVE OR DIE, IF I KNOW I TRIED, THEN I CAN ACCEPT WHATEVER HAPPENS.
I'M SORRY, PETE. I HAVE MORE MONEY THAN I EVER WANTED. I CAN BUY YOU ANYTHING YOU WANT.
BUT I CAN'T GIVE YOU THIS. I DON'T KNOW ANY WAY TO STOP MORLUN, LET ALONE BEAT HIM.
YOU'RE ON YOUR OWN.
WELL... IT WON'T BE THE FIRST TIME.

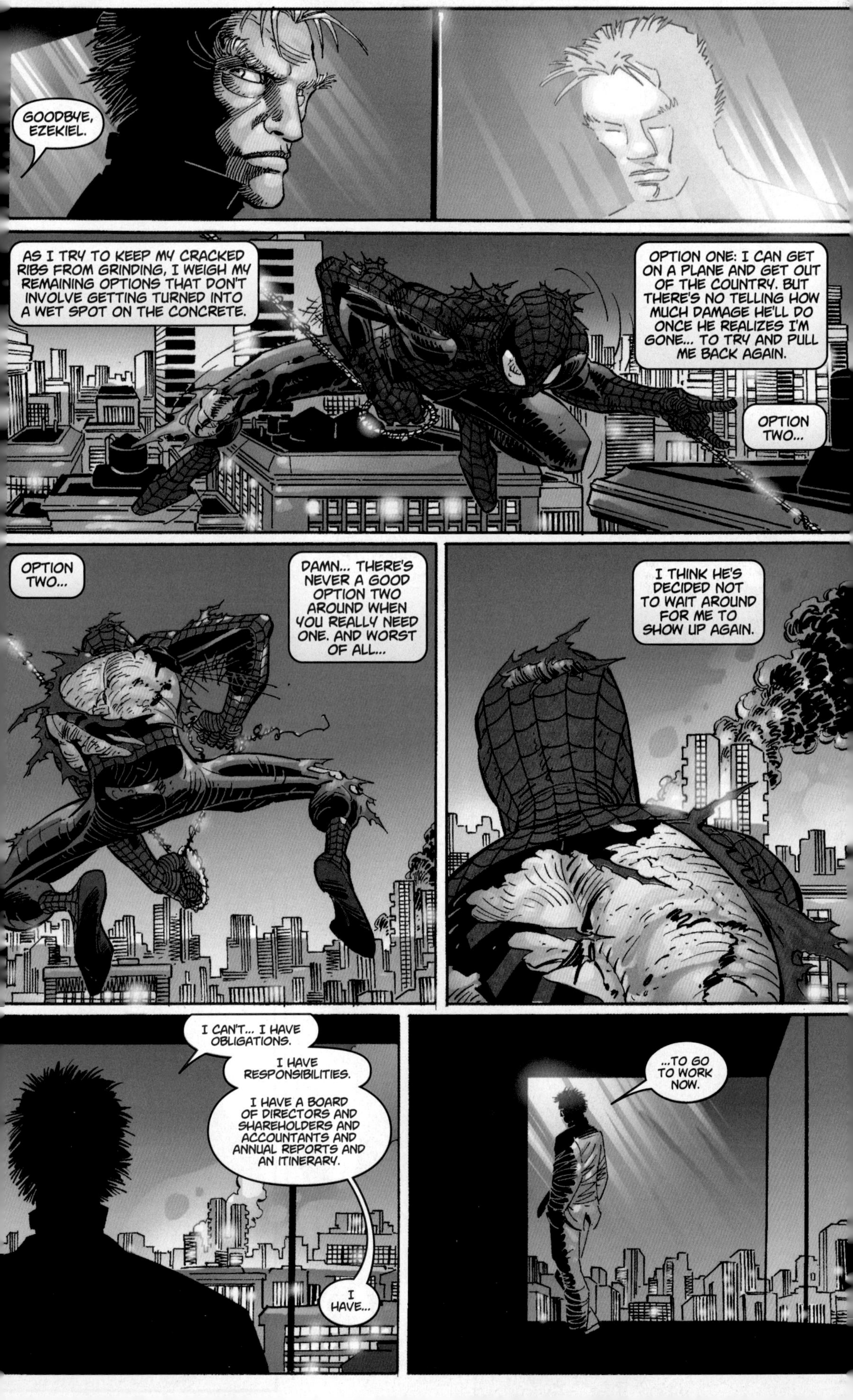
GOODBYE, EZEKIEL.
AS I TRY TO KEEP MY CRACKED RIBS FROM GRINDING, I WEIGH MY REMAINING OPTIONS THAT DON'T INVOLVE GETTING TURNED INTO A WET SPOT ON THE CONCRETE.
OPTION ONE: I CAN GET ON A PLANE AND GET OUT OF THE COUNTRY. BUT THERE'S NO TELLING HOW MUCH DAMAGE HE'LL DO ONCE HE REALIZES I'M GONE... TO TRY AND PULL ME BACK AGAIN.
OPTION TWO...
OPTION TWO...
DAMN... THERE'S NEVER A GOOD OPTION TWO AROUND WHEN YOU REALLY NEED ONE. AND WORST OF ALL...
I THINK HE'S DECIDED NOT TO WAIT AROUND FOR ME TO SHOW UP AGAIN.
I CAN'T... I HAVE OBLIGATIONS.
I HAVE RESPONSIBILITIES.
I HAVE A BOARD OF DIRECTORS AND SHAREHOLDERS AND ACCOUNTANTS AND ANNUAL REPORTS AND AN ITINERARY.
I HAVE...
...TO GO TO WORK NOW.

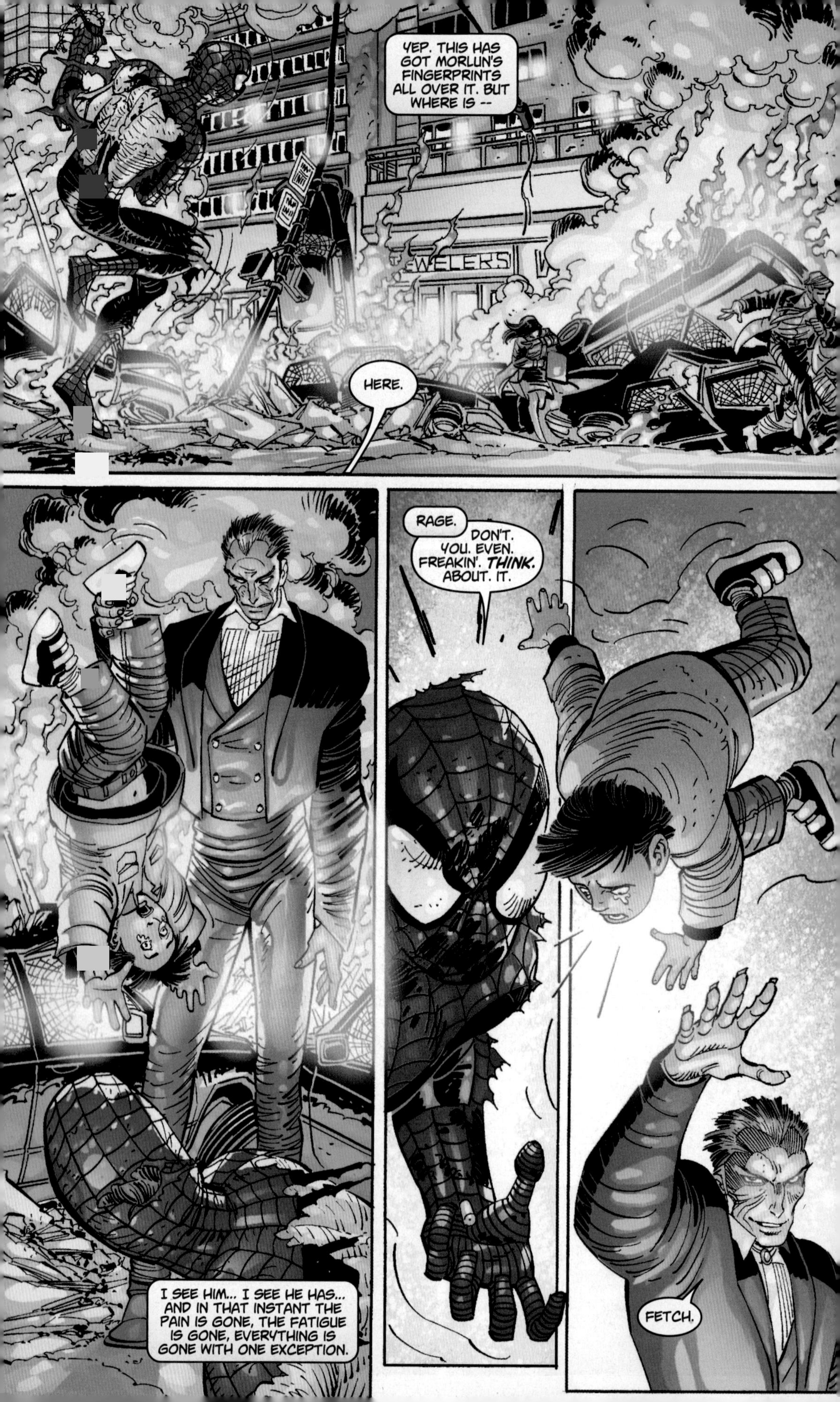
YEP. THIS HAS GOT MORLUN'S FINGERPRINTS ALL OVER IT. BUT WHERE IS --
HERE.
I SEE HIM... I SEE HE HAS... AND IN THAT INSTANT THE PAIN IS GONE, THE FATIGUE IS GONE, EVERYTHING IS GONE WITH ONE EXCEPTION.
RAGE.
DON'T. YOU. EVEN. FREAKIN'. THINK. ABOUT. IT.
FETCH.

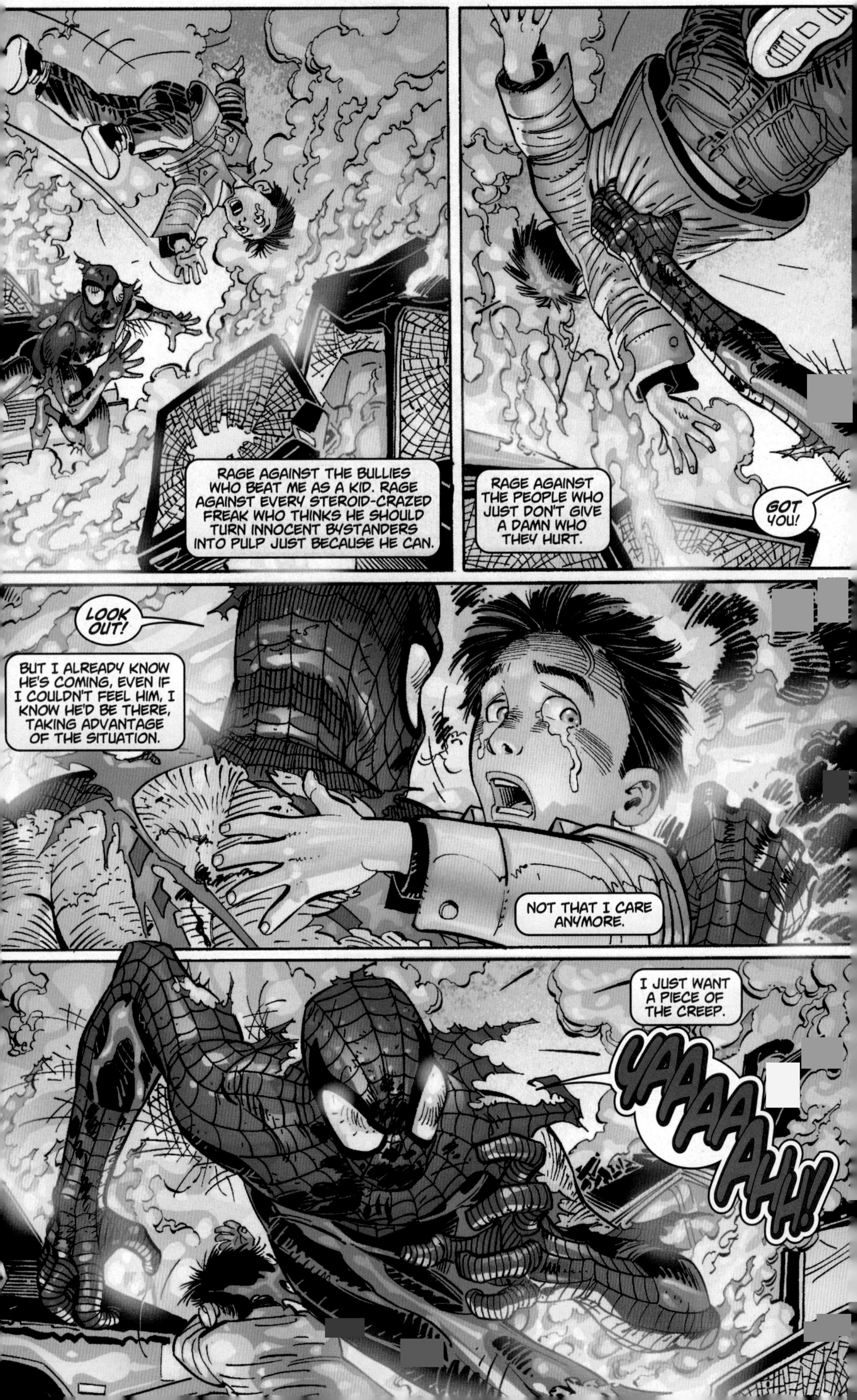
RAGE AGAINST THE BULLIES WHO BEAT ME AS A KID. RAGE AGAINST EVERY STEROID-CRAZED FREAK WHO THINKS HE SHOULD TURN INNOCENT BYSTANDERS INTO PULP JUST BECAUSE HE CAN.
RAGE AGAINST THE PEOPLE WHO JUST DON'T GIVE A DAMN WHO THEY HURT.
GOT YOU!
LOOK OUT!
BUT I ALREADY KNOW HE'S COMING, EVEN IF I COULDN'T FEEL HIM, I KNOW HE'D BE THERE, TAKING ADVANTAGE OF THE SITUATION.
NOT THAT I CARE ANYMORE.
I JUST WANT A PIECE OF THE CREEP.
YAAAAAHH!!

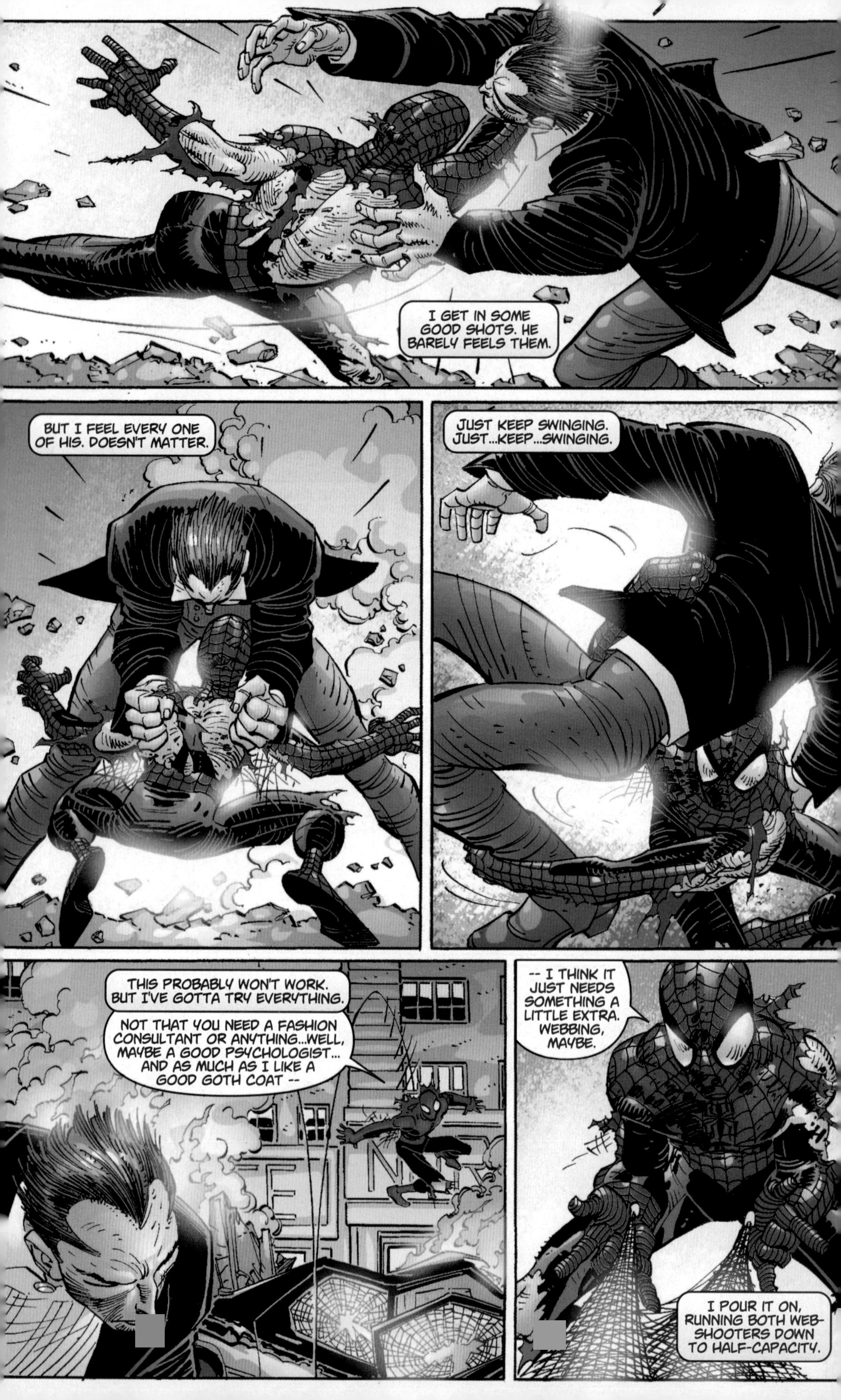
I GET IN SOME GOOD SHOTS. HE BARELY FEELS THEM.
BUT I FEEL EVERY ONE OF HIS. DOESN'T MATTER.
JUST KEEP SWINGING. JUST...KEEP...SWINGING.
THIS PROBABLY WON'T WORK. BUT I'VE GOTTA TRY EVERYTHING.
NOT THAT YOU NEED A FASHION CONSULTANT OR ANYTHING...WELL, MAYBE A GOOD PSYCHOLOGIST... AND AS MUCH AS I LIKE A GOOD GOTH COAT --
-- I THINK IT JUST NEEDS SOMETHING A LITTLE EXTRA. WEBBING, MAYBE.
I POUR IT ON, RUNNING BOTH WEB-SHOOTERS DOWN TO HALF-CAPACITY.

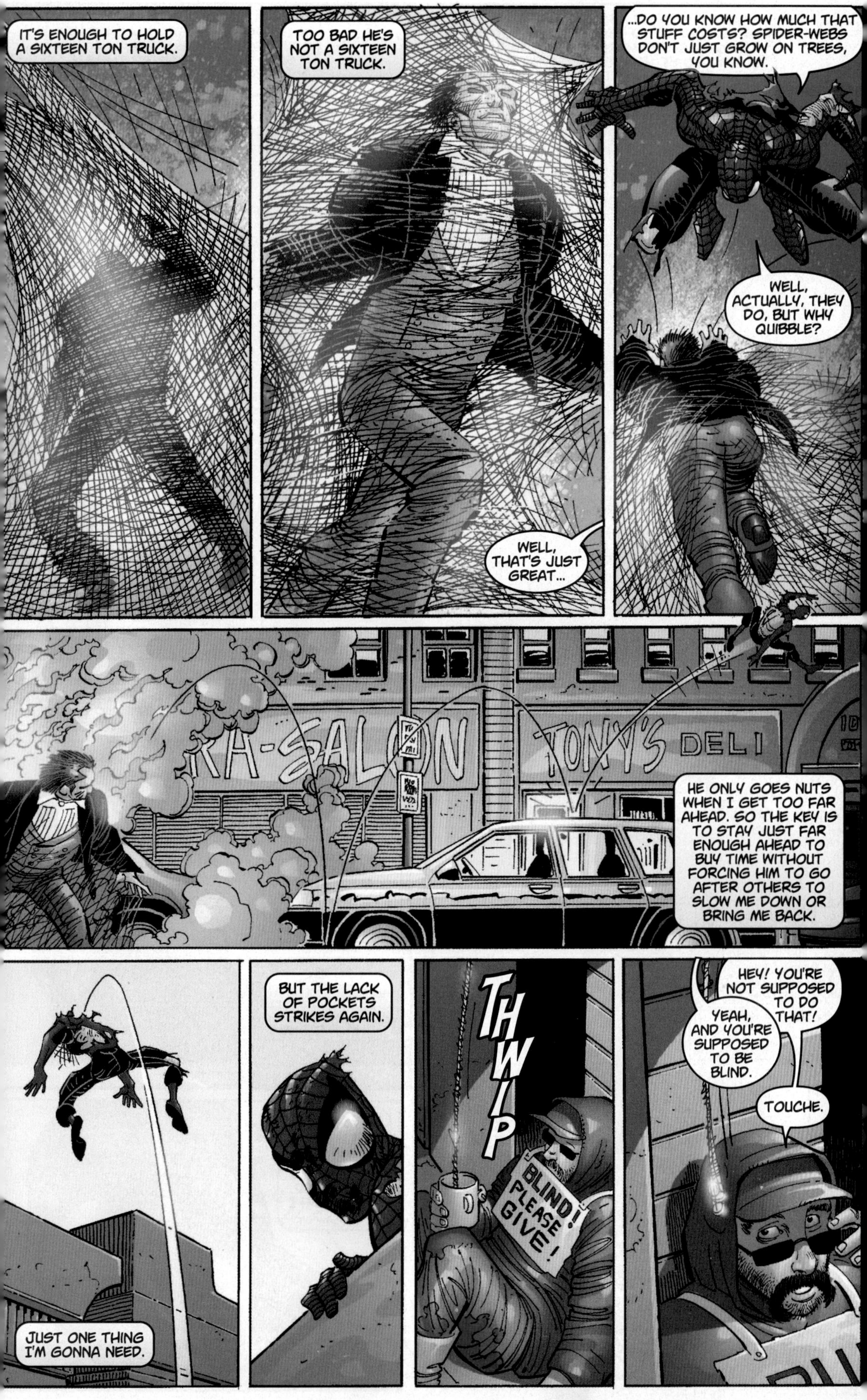
IT'S ENOUGH TO HOLD A SIXTEEN TON TRUCK.
TOO BAD HE'S NOT A SIXTEEN TON TRUCK.
WELL, THAT'S JUST GREAT...
...DO YOU KNOW HOW MUCH THAT STUFF COSTS? SPIDER-WEBS DON'T JUST GROW ON TREES, YOU KNOW.
WELL, ACTUALLY, THEY DO, BUT WHY QUIBBLE?
RA-SALON
TONY'S DELI
HE ONLY GOES NUTS WHEN I GET TOO FAR AHEAD. SO THE KEY IS TO STAY JUST FAR ENOUGH AHEAD TO BUY TIME WITHOUT FORCING HIM TO GO AFTER OTHERS TO SLOW ME DOWN OR BRING ME BACK.
JUST ONE THING I'M GONNA NEED.
BUT THE LACK OF POCKETS STRIKES AGAIN.
THWIP
BLIND! PLEASE GIVE!
HEY! YOU'RE NOT SUPPOSED TO DO THAT!
YEAH, AND YOU'RE SUPPOSED TO BE BLIND.
TOUCHE.

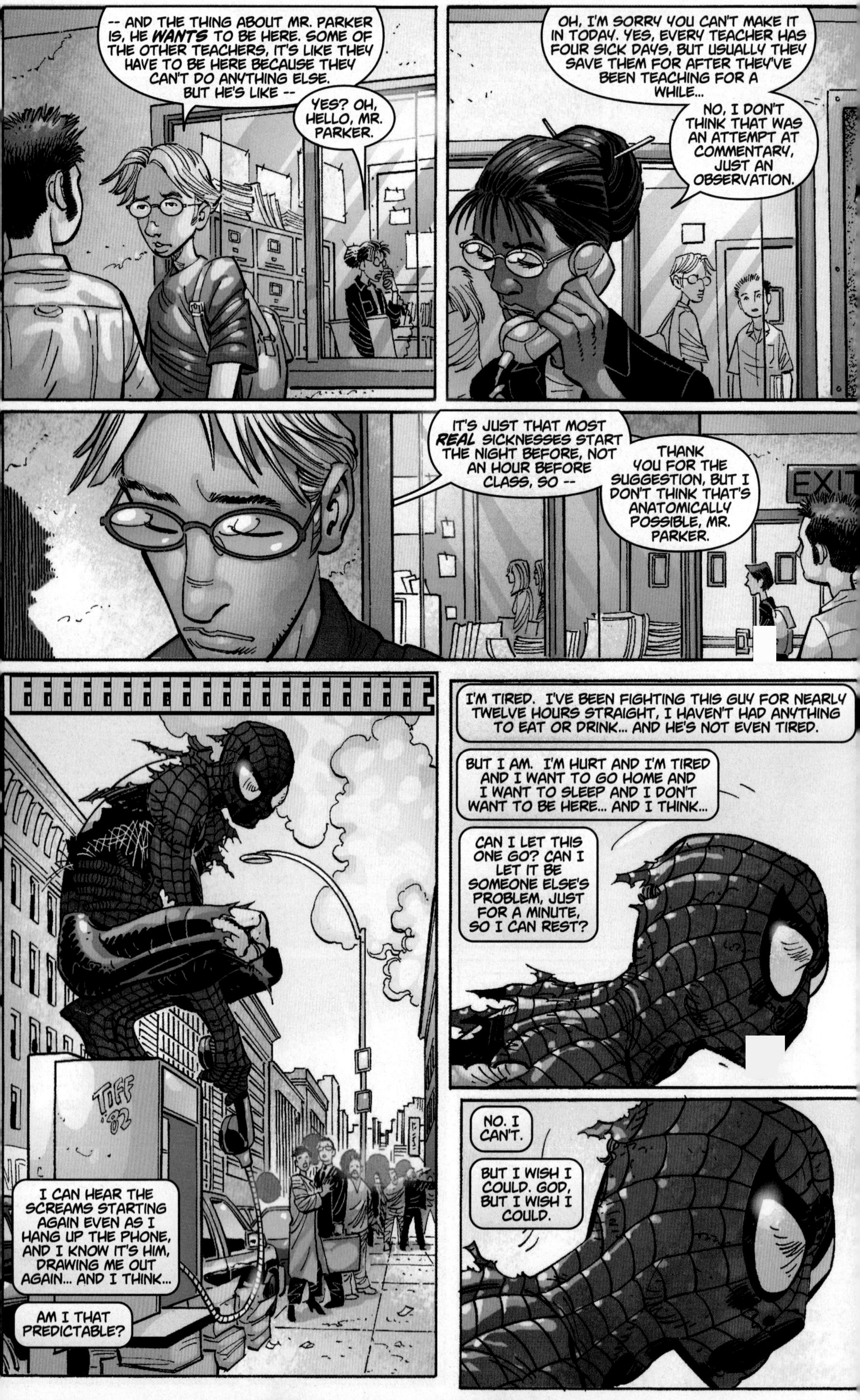
-- AND THE THING ABOUT MR. PARKER IS, HE WANTS TO BE HERE. SOME OF THE OTHER TEACHERS, IT'S LIKE THEY HAVE TO BE HERE BECAUSE THEY CAN'T DO ANYTHING ELSE. BUT HE'S LIKE --
YES? OH, HELLO, MR. PARKER.
OH, I'M SORRY YOU CAN'T MAKE IT IN TODAY. YES, EVERY TEACHER HAS FOUR SICK DAYS, BUT USUALLY THEY SAVE THEM FOR AFTER THEY'VE BEEN TEACHING FOR A WHILE...
NO, I DON'T THINK THAT WAS AN ATTEMPT AT COMMENTARY, JUST AN OBSERVATION.
IT'S JUST THAT MOST REAL SICKNESSES START THE NIGHT BEFORE, NOT AN HOUR BEFORE CLASS, SO --
THANK YOU FOR THE SUGGESTION, BUT I DON'T THINK THAT'S ANATOMICALLY POSSIBLE, MR. PARKER.
EXIT
EEEEEEEEEEEEEEEEEEEEEEE
TOFF '82
I CAN HEAR THE SCREAMS STARTING AGAIN EVEN AS I HANG UP THE PHONE, AND I KNOW IT'S HIM, DRAWING ME OUT AGAIN... AND I THINK...
AM I THAT PREDICTABLE?
I'M TIRED. I'VE BEEN FIGHTING THIS GUY FOR NEARLY TWELVE HOURS STRAIGHT, I HAVEN'T HAD ANYTHING TO EAT OR DRINK... AND HE'S NOT EVEN TIRED.
BUT I AM. I'M HURT AND I'M TIRED AND I WANT TO GO HOME AND I WANT TO SLEEP AND I DON'T WANT TO BE HERE... AND I THINK...
CAN I LET THIS ONE GO? CAN I LET IT BE SOMEONE ELSE'S PROBLEM, JUST FOR A MINUTE, SO I CAN REST?
NO. I CAN'T.
BUT I WISH I COULD. GOD, BUT I WISH I COULD.

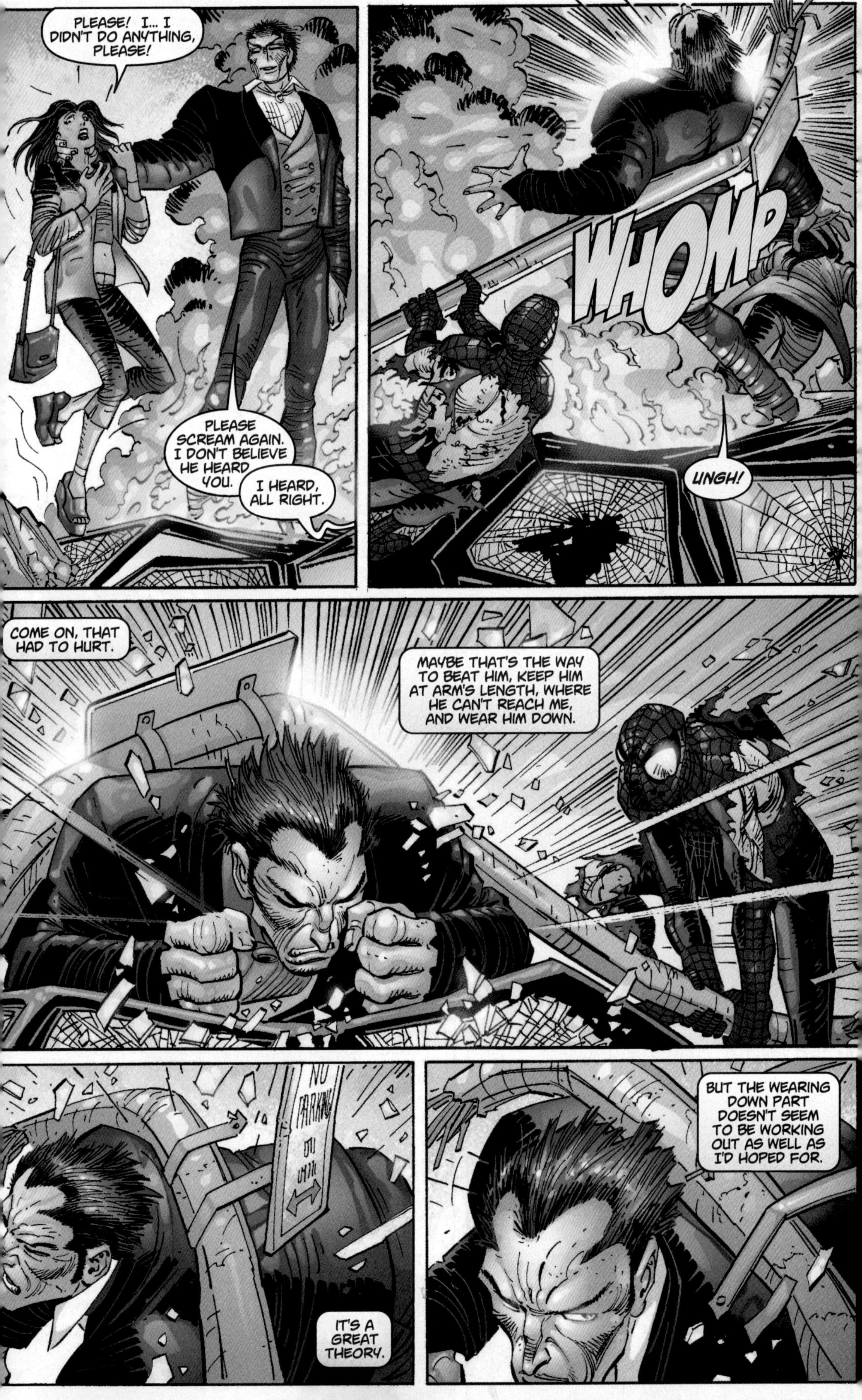
PLEASE! I... I DIDN'T DO ANYTHING, PLEASE!
PLEASE SCREAM AGAIN. I DON'T BELIEVE HE HEARD YOU.
I HEARD, ALL RIGHT.
WHOMP
UNGH!
COME ON, THAT HAD TO HURT.
MAYBE THAT'S THE WAY TO BEAT HIM, KEEP HIM AT ARM'S LENGTH, WHERE HE CAN'T REACH ME, AND WEAR HIM DOWN.
NO PARKING
IT'S A GREAT THEORY.
BUT THE WEARING DOWN PART DOESN'T SEEM TO BE WORKING OUT AS WELL AS I'D HOPED FOR.

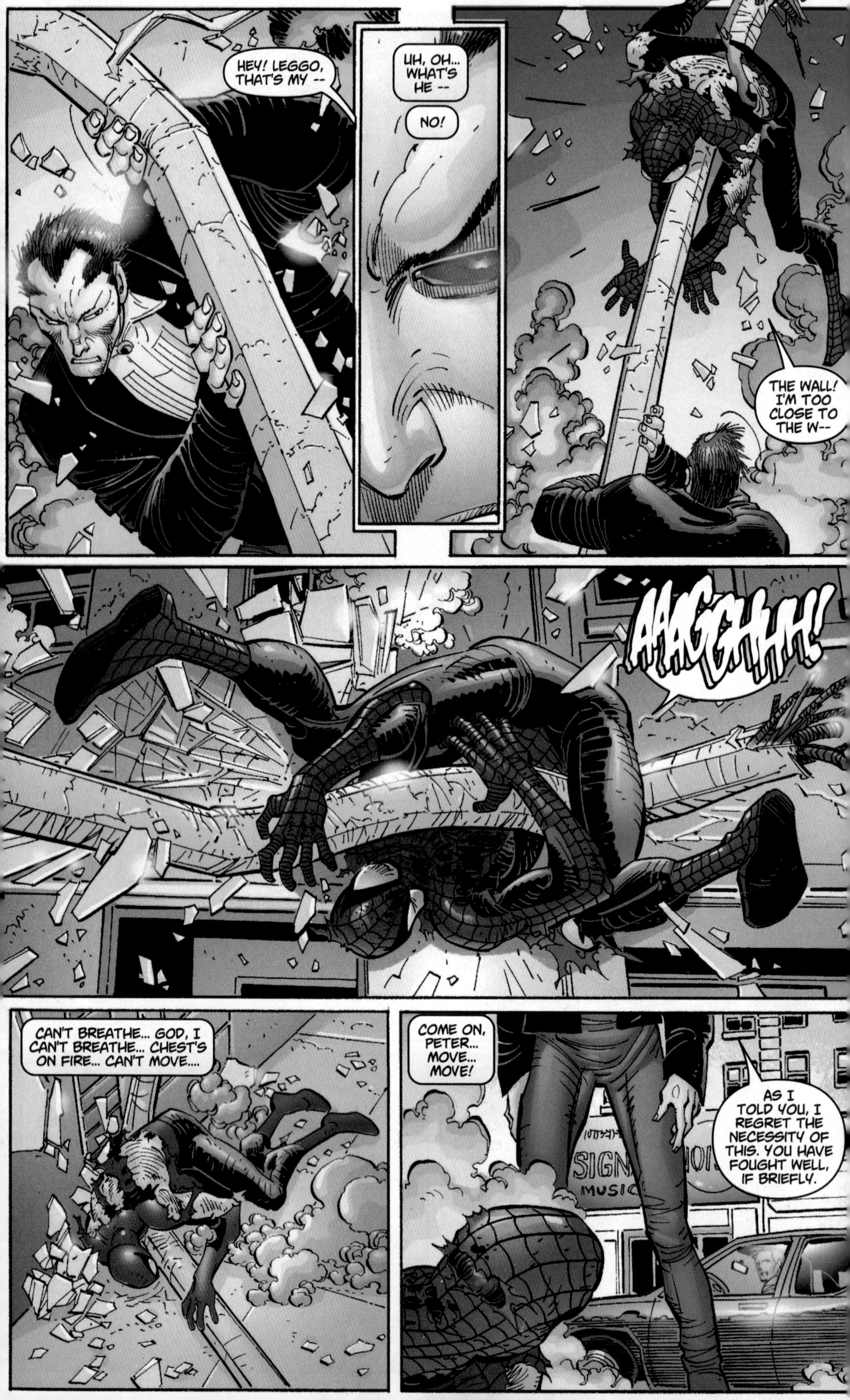

HEY! LEGGO, THAT'S MY --
UH, OH... WHAT'S HE --
NO!
THE WALL! I'M TOO CLOSE TO THE W--
AAAGHHH!
CAN'T BREATHE... GOD, I CAN'T BREATHE... CHEST'S ON FIRE... CAN'T MOVE....
COME ON, PETER... MOVE... MOVE!
AS I TOLD YOU, I REGRET THE NECESSITY OF THIS. YOU HAVE FOUGHT WELL, IF BRIEFLY.
MUSIC

BRIEFLY? *BRIEFLY?!* BRIEFLY MY DEAR AUNT FANNY.

...SCREW...

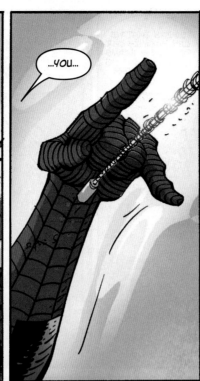

...YOU...

GOT IT!

AGH! AGGHH...

*AGGH*H...

YOU SEEM RATHER DISTRACTED, SIR.

HMM? OH, SORRY. NOTHING. YOU WERE SAYING --

I WAS SAYING THAT WE CAN MAXIMIZE OUR REVENUE STREAMS BY CONSOLIDATING THE OFFSHORE ACCOUNTS.

FURTHER, IF WE EXPAND THE FACILITIES AT MAZATLAN USING A LINE OF CREDIT INSTEAD OF SPENDING REAL MONIES, WE CAN USE THE CAPITAL TO...

NOT MUCH MONEY LEFT...

...I COULD TRY CALLING THE FF, BUT IF THEY'RE NOT IN TOWN... AND WHY THE HECK AREN'T MORE SUPER HEROES IN THE PHONE BOOK ANYWAY...

...DON'T BLACK OUT, DON'T BLACK OUT, YOU CAN'T AFFORD THAT...

THINK.

RING... RING... RING...

C'MON, ANSWER --

RING... CLICK

HI --

MJ? MJ, IT'S ME, IT'S --

phone

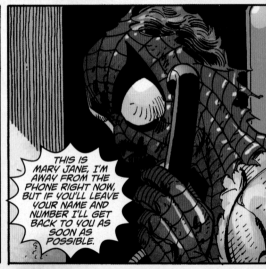

THIS IS MARY JANE, I'M AWAY FROM THE PHONE RIGHT NOW, BUT IF YOU'LL LEAVE YOUR NAME AND NUMBER I'LL GET BACK TO YOU AS SOON AS POSSIBLE.

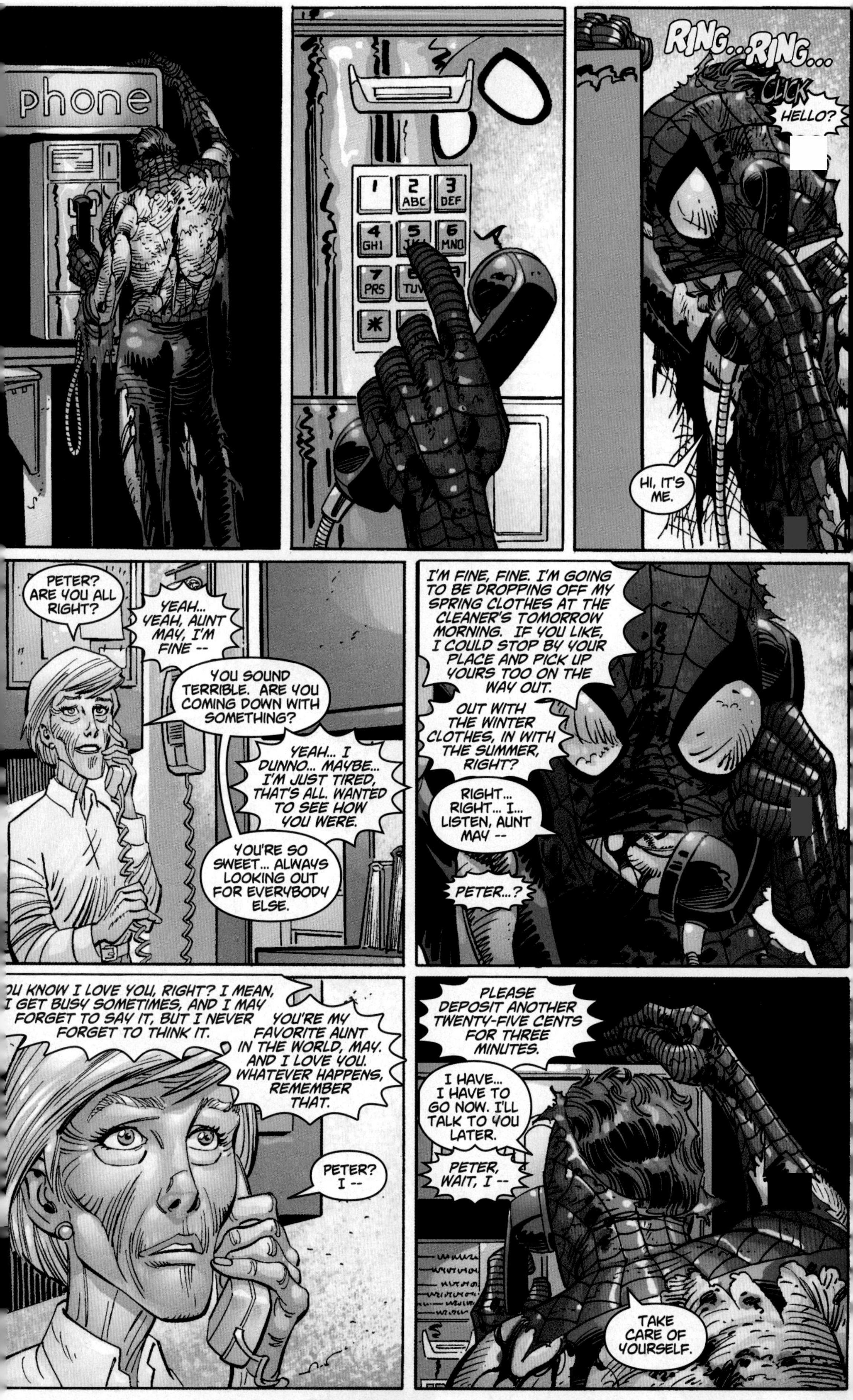
phone
1
2 ABC
3 DEF
4 GHI
6 MNO
7 PRS
RING...RING...
CLICK
HELLO?
HI, IT'S ME.
PETER? ARE YOU ALL RIGHT?
YEAH... YEAH, AUNT MAY, I'M FINE --
YOU SOUND TERRIBLE. ARE YOU COMING DOWN WITH SOMETHING?
YEAH... I DUNNO... MAYBE... I'M JUST TIRED, THAT'S ALL. WANTED TO SEE HOW YOU WERE.
YOU'RE SO SWEET... ALWAYS LOOKING OUT FOR EVERYBODY ELSE.
I'M FINE, FINE. I'M GOING TO BE DROPPING OFF MY SPRING CLOTHES AT THE CLEANER'S TOMORROW MORNING. IF YOU LIKE, I COULD STOP BY YOUR PLACE AND PICK UP YOURS TOO ON THE WAY OUT.
OUT WITH THE WINTER CLOTHES, IN WITH THE SUMMER, RIGHT?
RIGHT... RIGHT... I... LISTEN, AUNT MAY --
PETER...?
OU KNOW I LOVE YOU, RIGHT? I MEAN, I GET BUSY SOMETIMES, AND I MAY FORGET TO SAY IT, BUT I NEVER FORGET TO THINK IT.
YOU'RE MY FAVORITE AUNT IN THE WORLD, MAY. AND I LOVE YOU. WHATEVER HAPPENS, REMEMBER THAT.
PETER? I --
PLEASE DEPOSIT ANOTHER TWENTY-FIVE CENTS FOR THREE MINUTES.
I HAVE... I HAVE TO GO NOW. I'LL TALK TO YOU LATER.
PETER, WAIT, I --
TAKE CARE OF YOURSELF.

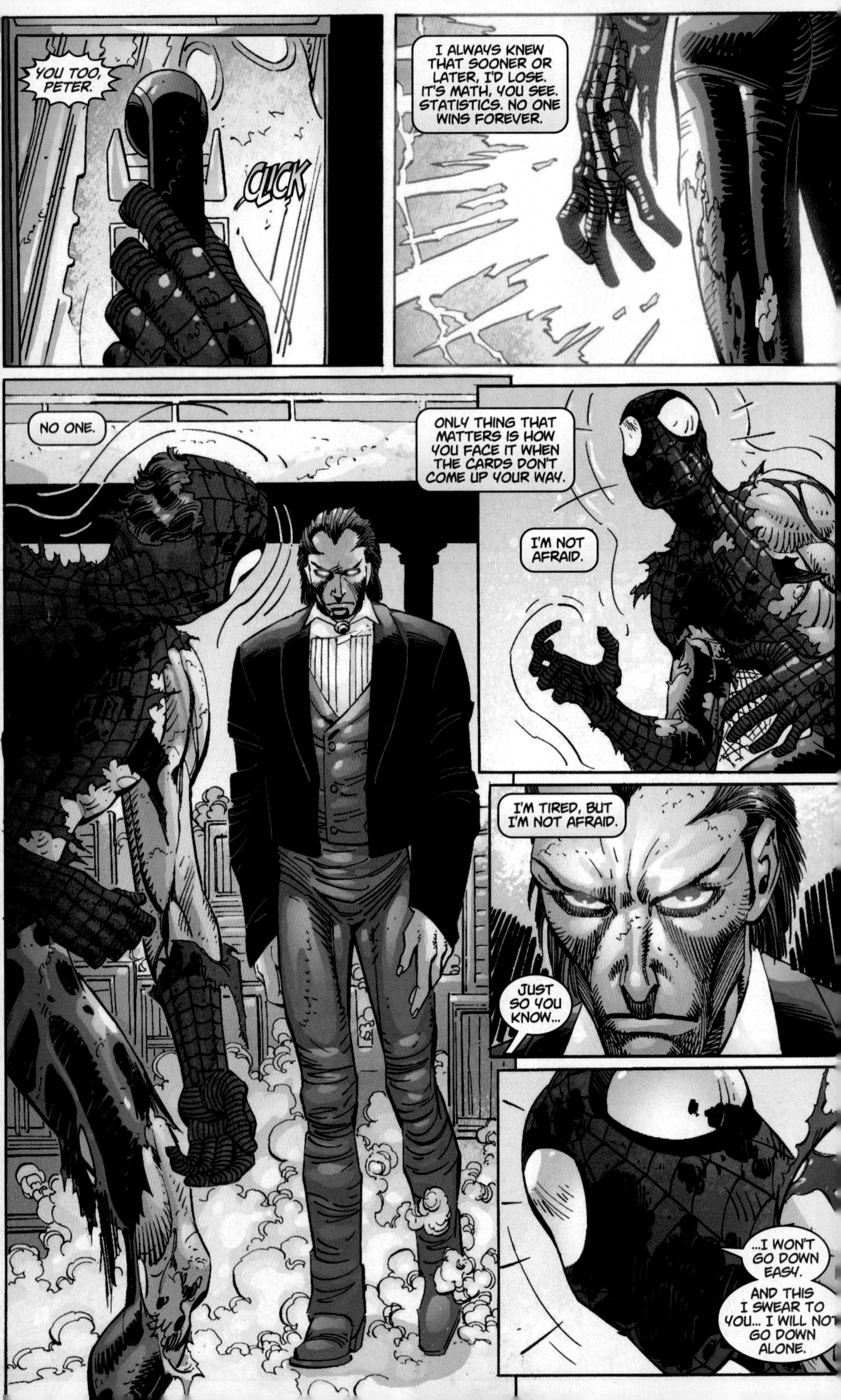
YOU TOO, PETER.
CLICK
I ALWAYS KNEW THAT SOONER OR LATER, I'D LOSE. IT'S MATH, YOU SEE. STATISTICS. NO ONE WINS FOREVER.
NO ONE.
ONLY THING THAT MATTERS IS HOW YOU FACE IT WHEN THE CARDS DON'T COME UP YOUR WAY.
I'M NOT AFRAID.
I'M TIRED, BUT I'M NOT AFRAID.
JUST SO YOU KNOW...
...I WON'T GO DOWN EASY.
AND THIS I SWEAR TO YOU... I WILL NOT GO DOWN ALONE.

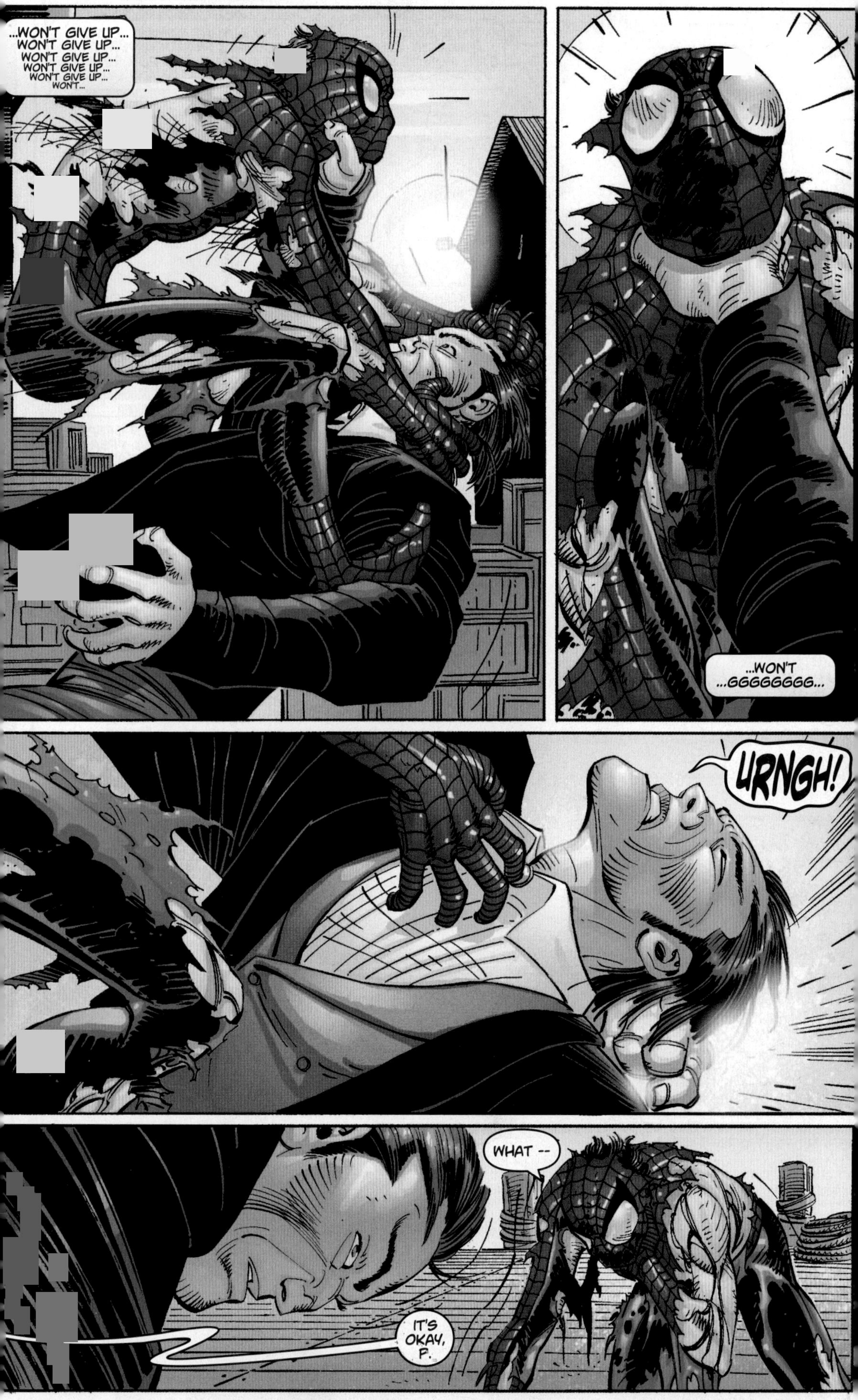
...WON'T GIVE UP... WON'T GIVE UP... WON'T GIVE UP... WON'T GIVE UP... WON'T GIVE UP... WON'T...
...WON'T ...GGGGGGGG...
URNGH!
WHAT --
IT'S OKAY, F.

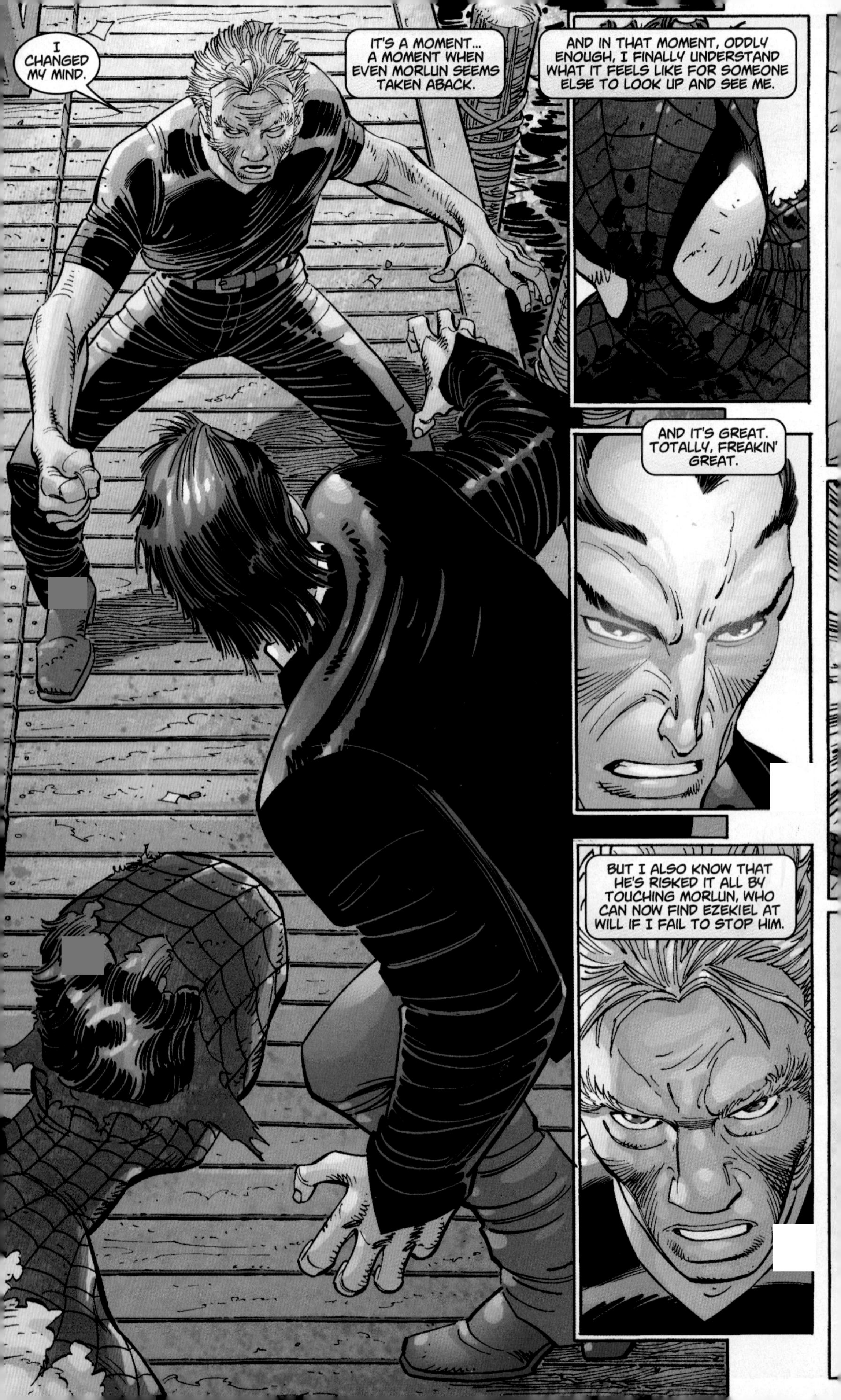
I CHANGED MY MIND.
IT'S A MOMENT... A MOMENT WHEN EVEN MORLUN SEEMS TAKEN ABACK.
AND IN THAT MOMENT, ODDLY ENOUGH, I FINALLY UNDERSTAND WHAT IT FEELS LIKE FOR SOMEONE ELSE TO LOOK UP AND SEE ME.
AND IT'S GREAT. TOTALLY, FREAKIN' GREAT.
BUT I ALSO KNOW THAT HE'S RISKED IT ALL BY TOUCHING MORLUN, WHO CAN NOW FIND EZEKIEL AT WILL IF I FAIL TO STOP HIM.

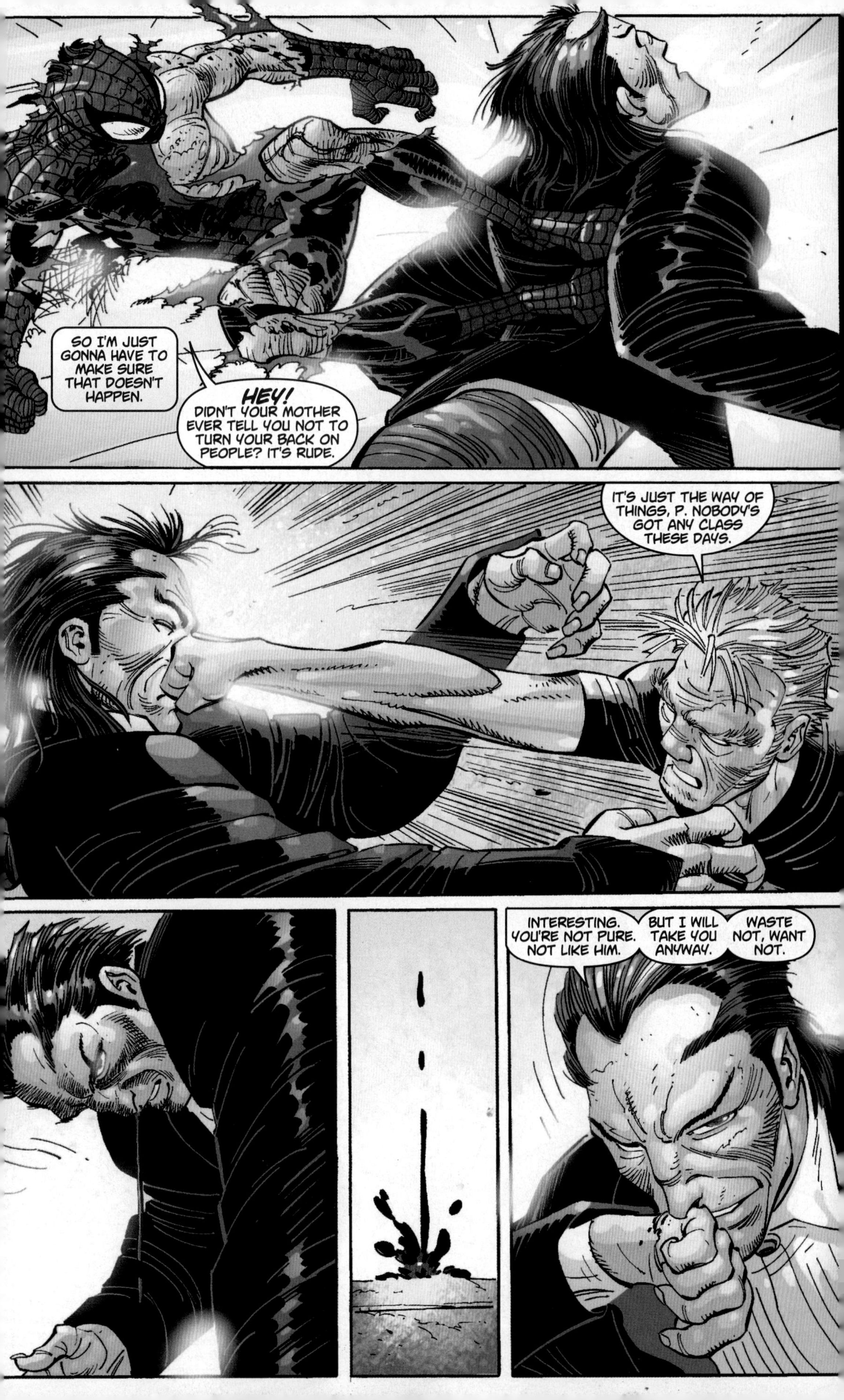
SO I'M JUST GONNA HAVE TO MAKE SURE THAT DOESN'T HAPPEN.
HEY! DIDN'T YOUR MOTHER EVER TELL YOU NOT TO TURN YOUR BACK ON PEOPLE? IT'S RUDE.
IT'S JUST THE WAY OF THINGS, P. NOBODY'S GOT ANY CLASS THESE DAYS.
INTERESTING. YOU'RE NOT PURE. NOT LIKE HIM.
BUT I WILL TAKE YOU ANYWAY.
WASTE NOT, WANT NOT.

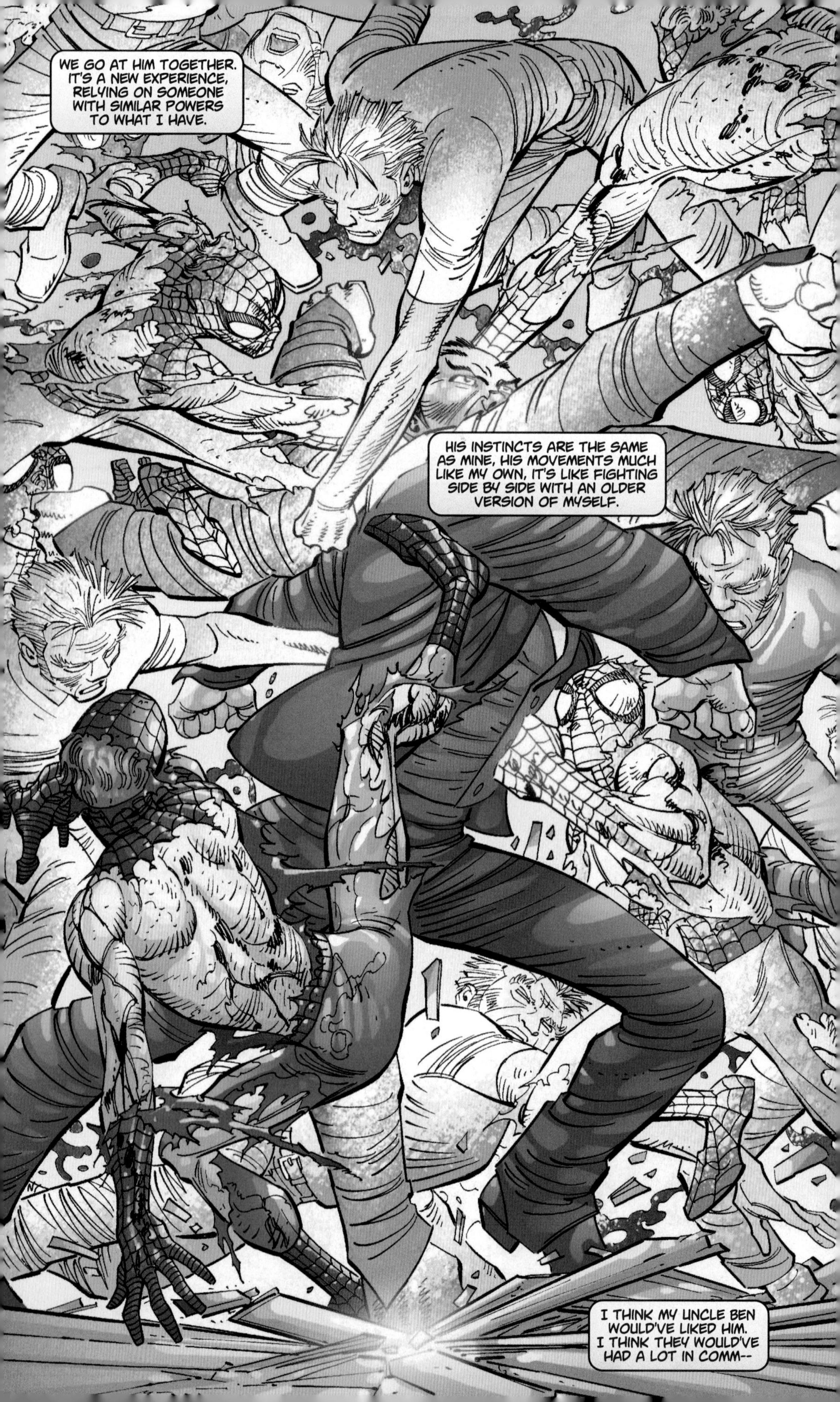
WE GO AT HIM TOGETHER. IT'S A NEW EXPERIENCE, RELYING ON SOMEONE WITH SIMILAR POWERS TO WHAT I HAVE.
HIS INSTINCTS ARE THE SAME AS MINE, HIS MOVEMENTS MUCH LIKE MY OWN, IT'S LIKE FIGHTING SIDE BY SIDE WITH AN OLDER VERSION OF MYSELF.
I THINK MY UNCLE BEN WOULD'VE LIKED HIM. I THINK THEY WOULD'VE HAD A LOT IN COMM--

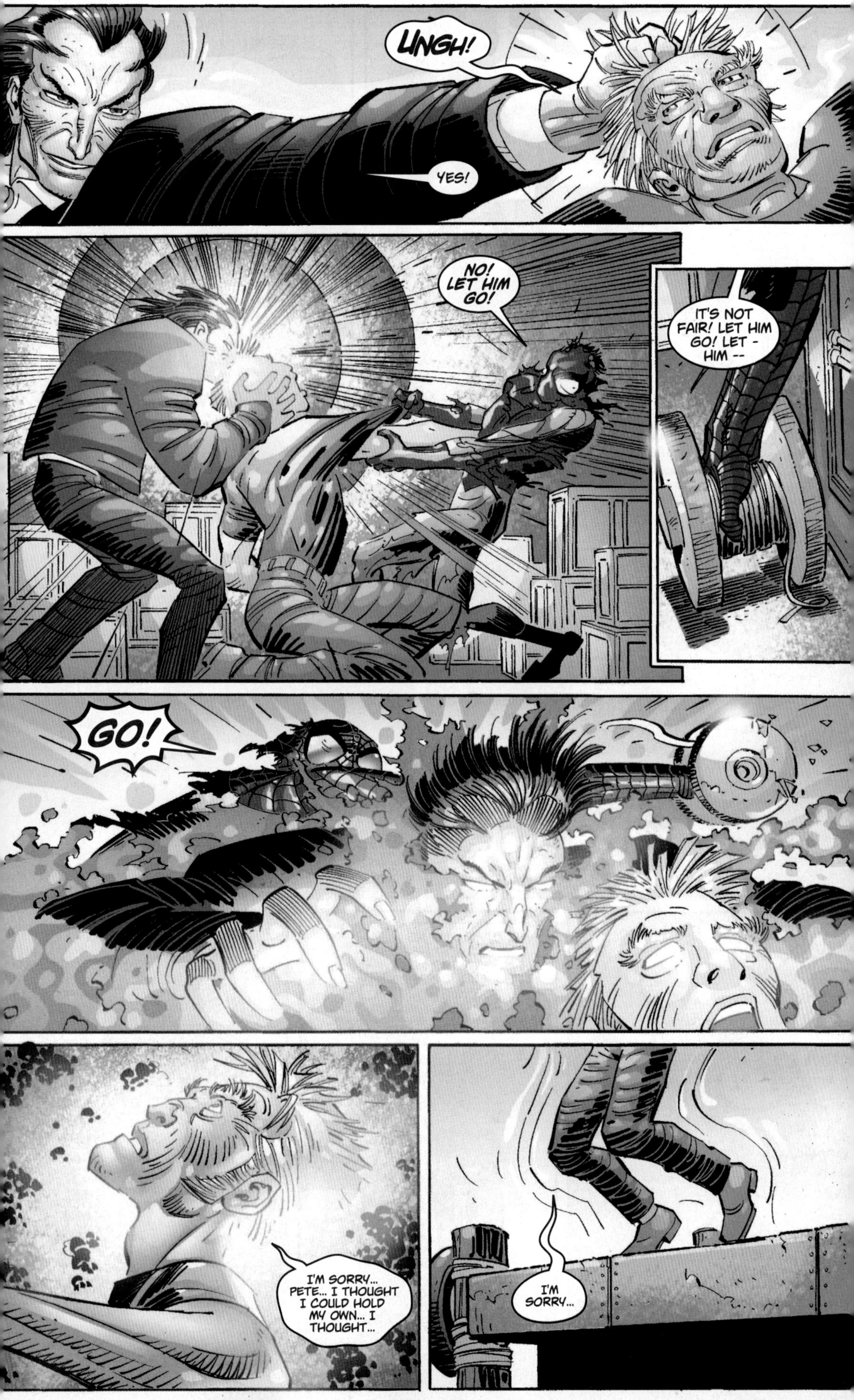
UNGH!
YES!
NO! LET HIM GO!
IT'S NOT FAIR! LET HIM GO! LET - HIM --
GO!
I'M SORRY... PETE... I THOUGHT I COULD HOLD MY OWN... I THOUGHT...
I'M SORRY...

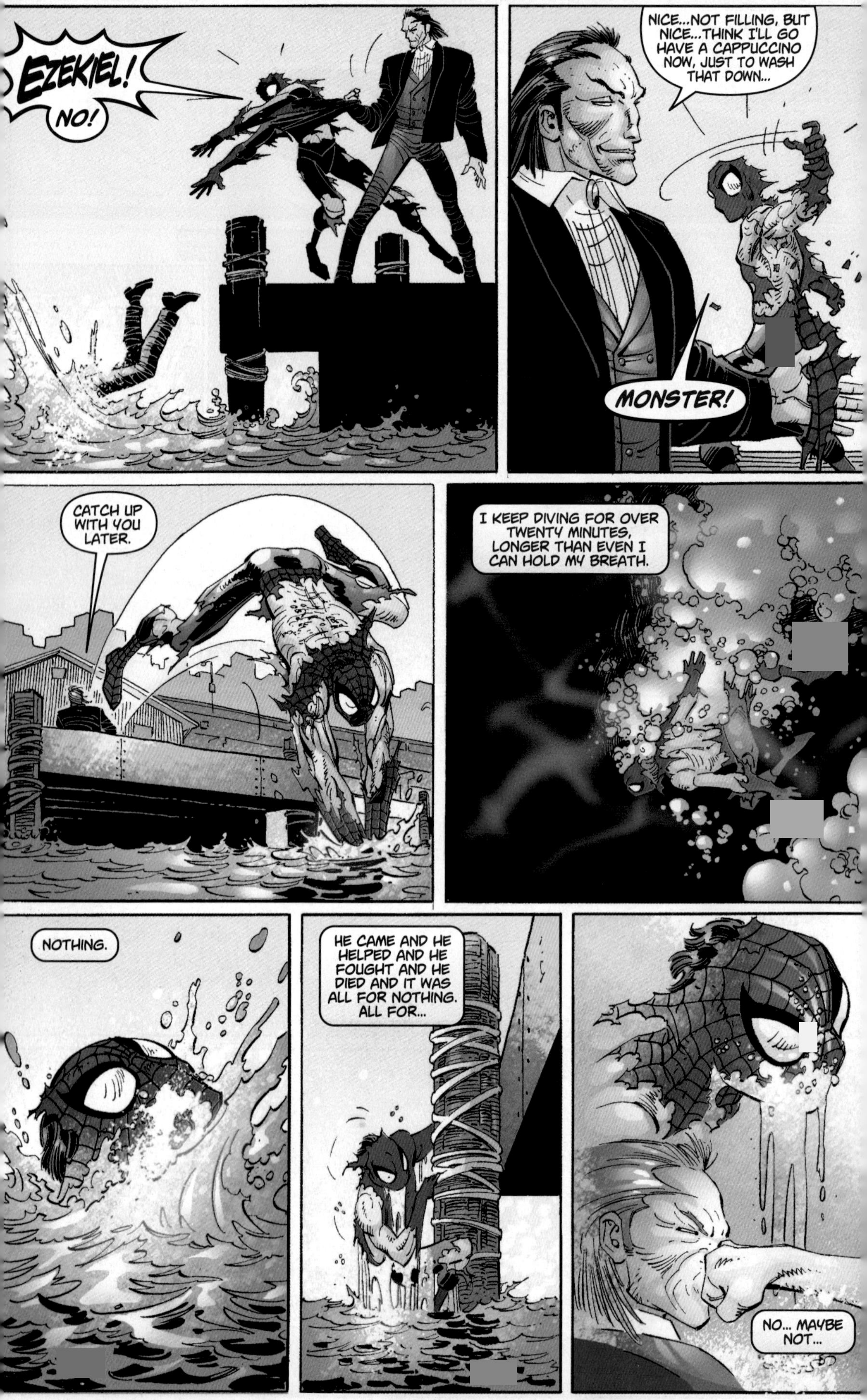
EZEKIEL! NO!
NICE...NOT FILLING, BUT NICE...THINK I'LL GO HAVE A CAPPUCCINO NOW, JUST TO WASH THAT DOWN...
MONSTER!
CATCH UP WITH YOU LATER.
I KEEP DIVING FOR OVER TWENTY MINUTES, LONGER THAN EVEN I CAN HOLD MY BREATH.
NOTHING.
HE CAME AND HE HELPED AND HE FOUGHT AND HE DIED AND IT WAS ALL FOR NOTHING. ALL FOR...
NO... MAYBE NOT...

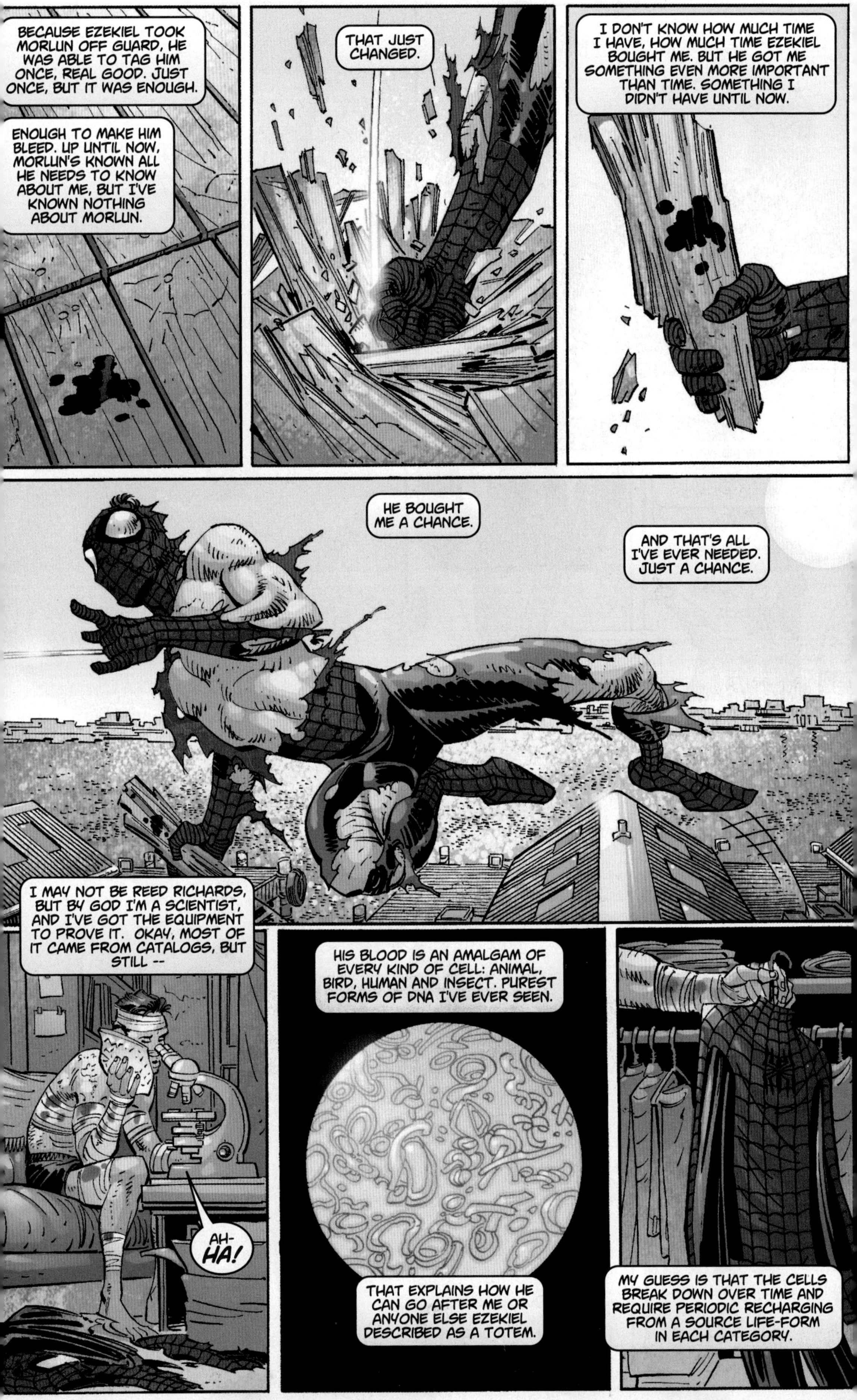

BECAUSE EZEKIEL TOOK MORLUN OFF GUARD, HE WAS ABLE TO TAG HIM ONCE, REAL GOOD. JUST ONCE, BUT IT WAS ENOUGH.
ENOUGH TO MAKE HIM BLEED. UP UNTIL NOW, MORLUN'S KNOWN ALL HE NEEDS TO KNOW ABOUT ME, BUT I'VE KNOWN NOTHING ABOUT MORLUN.
THAT JUST CHANGED.
I DON'T KNOW HOW MUCH TIME I HAVE, HOW MUCH TIME EZEKIEL BOUGHT ME. BUT HE GOT ME SOMETHING EVEN MORE IMPORTANT THAN TIME. SOMETHING I DIDN'T HAVE UNTIL NOW.
HE BOUGHT ME A CHANCE.
AND THAT'S ALL I'VE EVER NEEDED. JUST A CHANCE.
I MAY NOT BE REED RICHARDS, BUT BY GOD I'M A SCIENTIST, AND I'VE GOT THE EQUIPMENT TO PROVE IT. OKAY, MOST OF IT CAME FROM CATALOGS, BUT STILL --
AH-HA!
HIS BLOOD IS AN AMALGAM OF EVERY KIND OF CELL: ANIMAL, BIRD, HUMAN AND INSECT. PUREST FORMS OF DNA I'VE EVER SEEN.
THAT EXPLAINS HOW HE CAN GO AFTER ME OR ANYONE ELSE EZEKIEL DESCRIBED AS A TOTEM.
MY GUESS IS THAT THE CELLS BREAK DOWN OVER TIME AND REQUIRE PERIODIC RECHARGING FROM A SOURCE LIFE-FORM IN EACH CATEGORY.

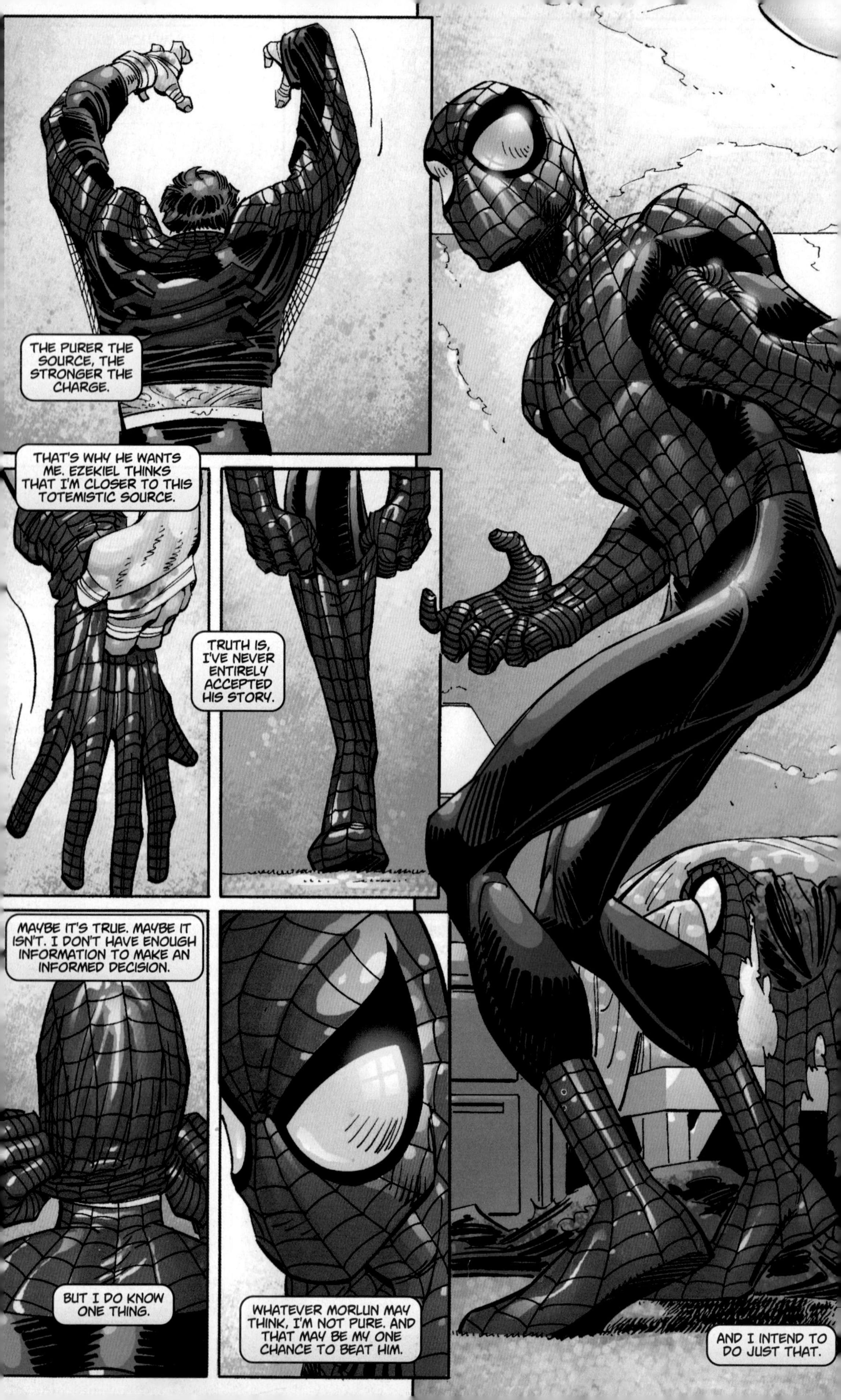
THE PURER THE SOURCE, THE STRONGER THE CHARGE.
THAT'S WHY HE WANTS ME. EZEKIEL THINKS THAT I'M CLOSER TO THIS TOTEMISTIC SOURCE.
TRUTH IS, I'VE NEVER ENTIRELY ACCEPTED HIS STORY.
MAYBE IT'S TRUE. MAYBE IT ISN'T. I DON'T HAVE ENOUGH INFORMATION TO MAKE AN INFORMED DECISION.
BUT I DO KNOW ONE THING.
WHATEVER MORLUN MAY THINK, I'M NOT PURE. AND THAT MAY BE MY ONE CHANCE TO BEAT HIM.
AND I INTEND TO DO JUST THAT.

SOUTHERN NEW YORK NUCLEAR POWER PLANT.

-- SO HE SAYS TO ME, "HOW CAN YOU WATCH THAT BABYLON 5 CRAP? I MEAN, IT TAKES FIVE YEARS TO PAY OFF SOMETHING YOU SEE IN YEAR ONE!" AND I SAID, "THAT'S EXACTLY IT!"

THAT'S GREAT, I --

OH, JEEZ...THAT'S THE REACTOR ALERT!

THIS IS THE PLANT SUPERVISOR...YOU ARE INSTRUCTED TO EVACUATE IMMEDIATELY...I REPEAT...EVACUATE THE FACILITIES AT ONCE...

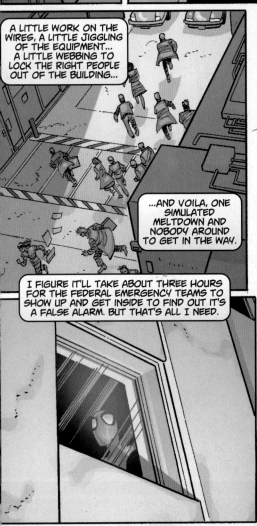

A LITTLE WORK ON THE WIRES, A LITTLE JIGGLING OF THE EQUIPMENT... A LITTLE WEBBING TO LOCK THE RIGHT PEOPLE OUT OF THE BUILDING...

...AND VOILA, ONE SIMULATED MELTDOWN AND NOBODY AROUND TO GET IN THE WAY.

I FIGURE IT'LL TAKE ABOUT THREE HOURS FOR THE FEDERAL EMERGENCY TEAMS TO SHOW UP AND GET INSIDE TO FIND OUT IT'S A FALSE ALARM. BUT THAT'S ALL I NEED.

WE'RE GONNA DANCE, YOU AND I, MORLUN. AND THIS IS GONNA END, RIGHT HERE, RIGHT NOW, FOREVER.

BECAUSE I'VE REACHED MY OWN CRITICAL MASS.

AND I'M TAKING YOU WITH ME.

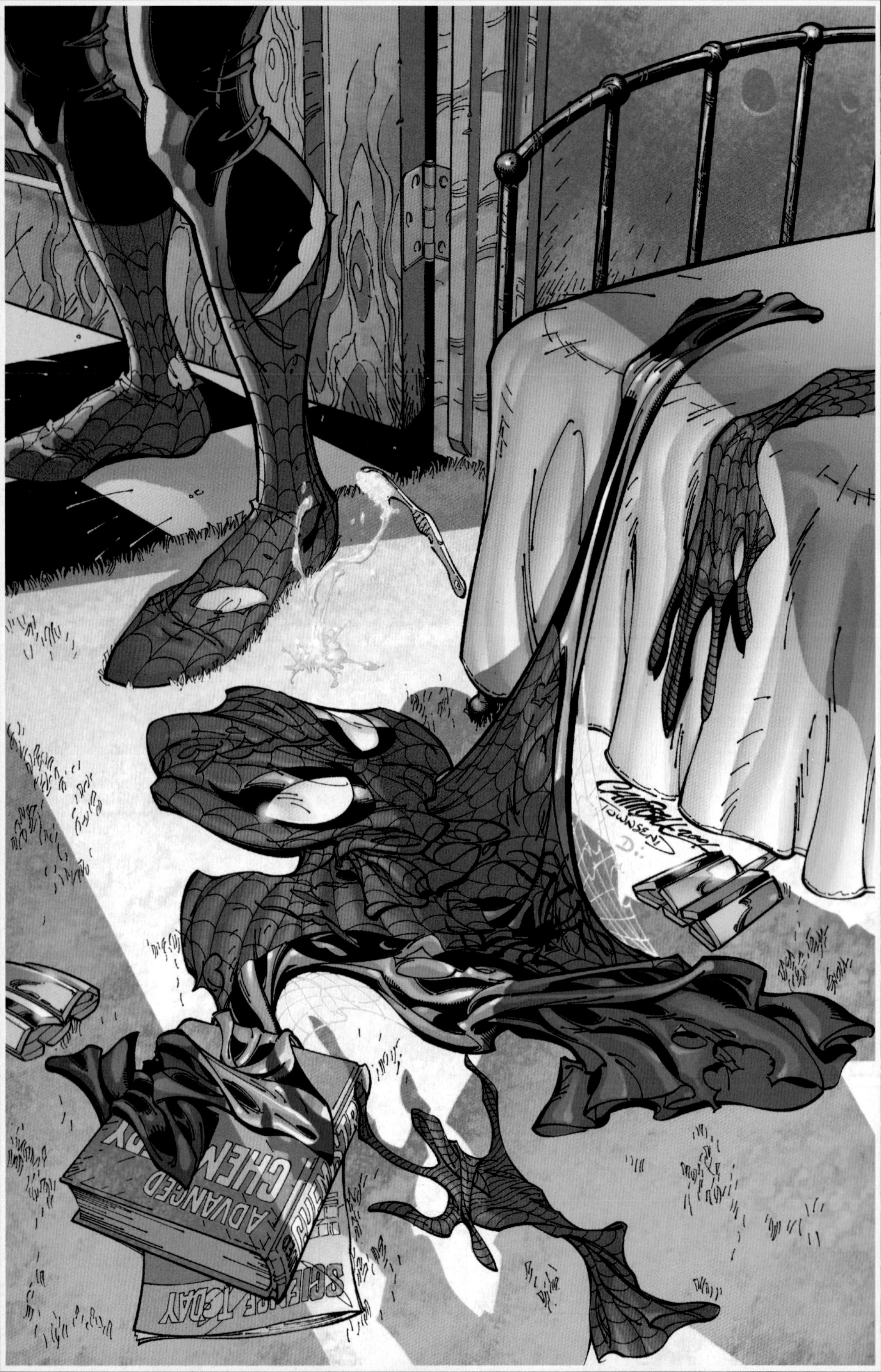
ADVANCED
SCIENCE TODAY

I CAN FEEL MORLUN APPROACHING. ALMOST HERE.

COMING OUT

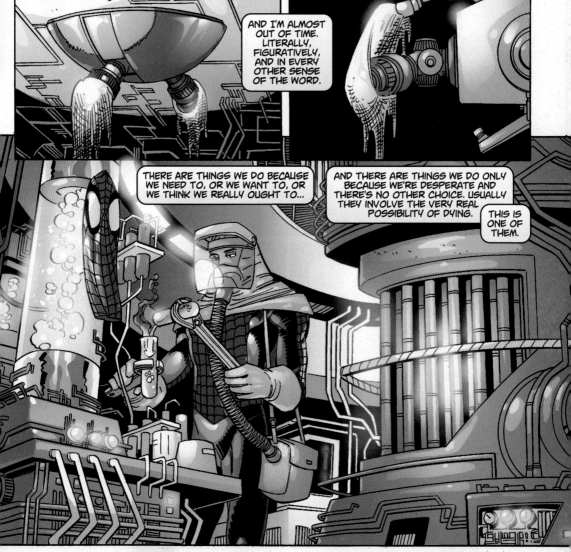

AND I'M ALMOST OUT OF TIME. LITERALLY, FIGURATIVELY, AND IN EVERY OTHER SENSE OF THE WORD.

THERE ARE THINGS WE DO BECAUSE WE NEED TO, OR WE WANT TO, OR WE THINK WE REALLY OUGHT TO...

AND THERE ARE THINGS WE DO ONLY BECAUSE WE'RE DESPERATE AND THERE'S NO OTHER CHOICE. USUALLY THEY INVOLVE THE VERY REAL POSSIBILITY OF DYING.

THIS IS ONE OF THEM.

I CAN'T KID MYSELF. THIS COULD KILL ME EVERY BIT AS EFFECTIVELY AS MORLUN.

IF IT DOES, THEN AT LEAST I'LL DENY HIM THE PLEASURE OF FEEDING OFF THE SPIDER IN ME.

HEY! STOP!

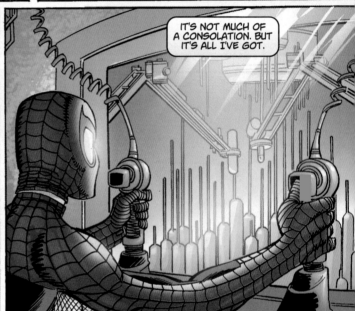

IT'S NOT MUCH OF A CONSOLATION. BUT IT'S ALL I'VE GOT.

HE'S INSIDE. WAIT FOR ME HERE.

TIME TO END THIS.

YES, MORLUN.

ORGANIC FLUID SUSPENSION COMPOUND. CHECK. BUFFERING COMPOUND. CHECK. ACCEPTABLE RADIATION LEVELS...

UNKNOWN. WHAT I CAN CONTROL IS THE AMOUNT OF FLUID I INJECT. TOO LITTLE AND IT WON'T HAVE ANY EFFECT. ASSUMING IT HAS ANY EFFECT AT ALL.

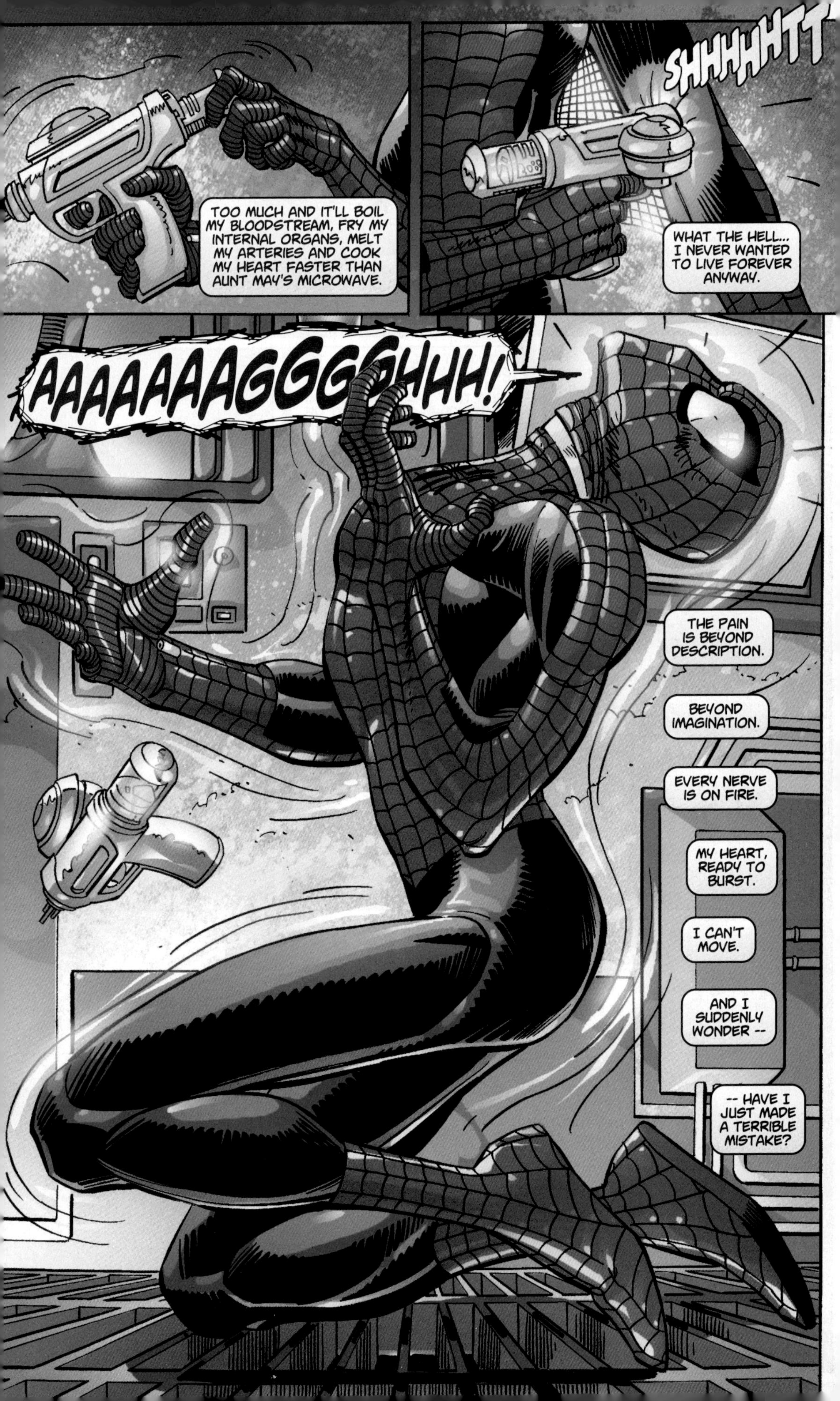
TOO MUCH AND IT'LL BOIL MY BLOODSTREAM, FRY MY INTERNAL ORGANS, MELT MY ARTERIES AND COOK MY HEART FASTER THAN AUNT MAY'S MICROWAVE.
SHHHHHTT
WHAT THE HELL... I NEVER WANTED TO LIVE FOREVER ANYWAY.
AAAAAAAGGGGHHH!
THE PAIN IS BEYOND DESCRIPTION.
BEYOND IMAGINATION.
EVERY NERVE IS ON FIRE.
MY HEART, READY TO BURST.
I CAN'T MOVE.
AND I SUDDENLY WONDER --
-- HAVE I JUST MADE A TERRIBLE MISTAKE?

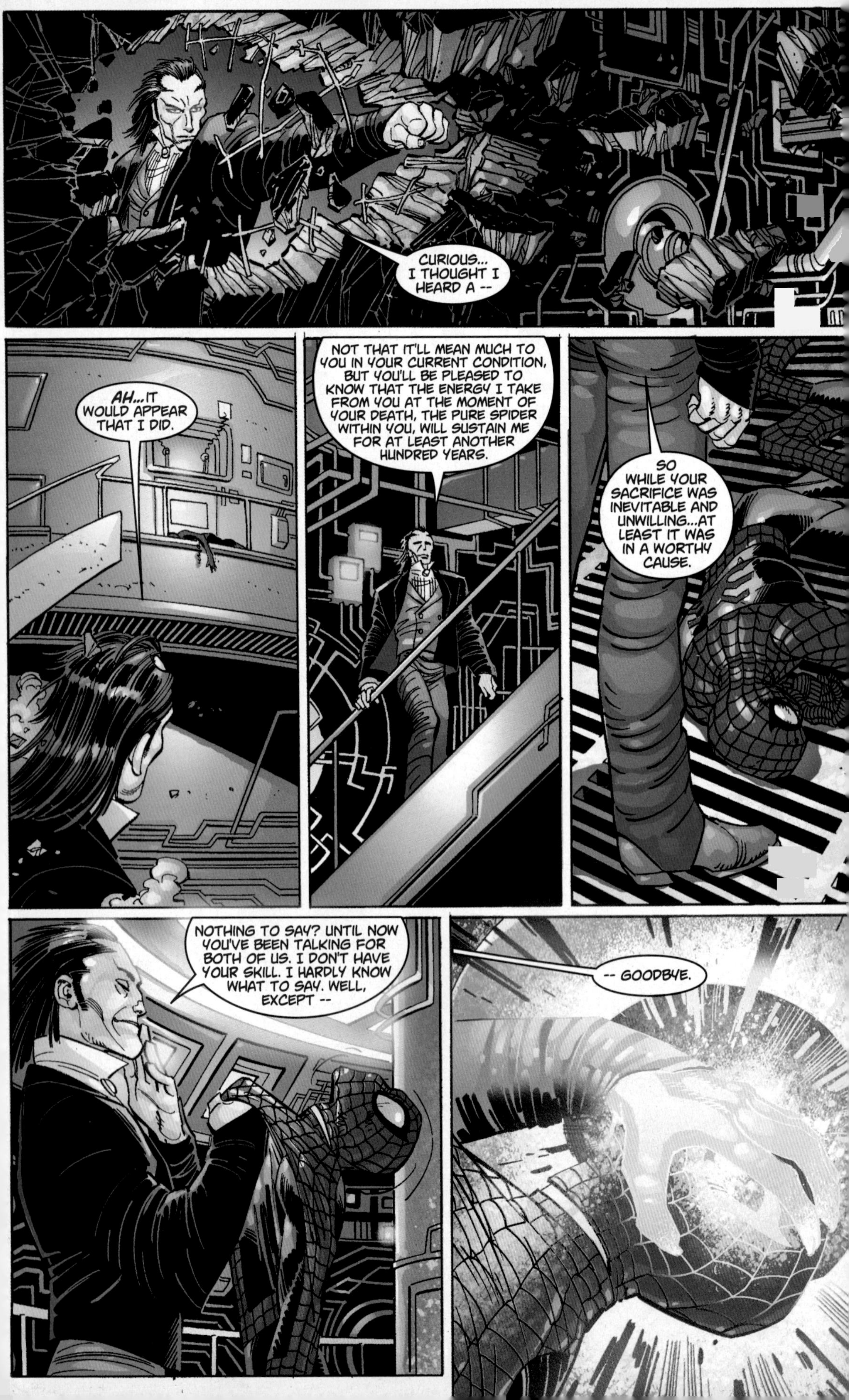
CURIOUS... I THOUGHT I HEARD A --
AH...IT WOULD APPEAR THAT I DID.
NOT THAT IT'LL MEAN MUCH TO YOU IN YOUR CURRENT CONDITION, BUT YOU'LL BE PLEASED TO KNOW THAT THE ENERGY I TAKE FROM YOU AT THE MOMENT OF YOUR DEATH, THE PURE SPIDER WITHIN YOU, WILL SUSTAIN ME FOR AT LEAST ANOTHER HUNDRED YEARS.
SO WHILE YOUR SACRIFICE WAS INEVITABLE AND UNWILLING...AT LEAST IT WAS IN A WORTHY CAUSE.
NOTHING TO SAY? UNTIL NOW YOU'VE BEEN TALKING FOR BOTH OF US. I DON'T HAVE YOUR SKILL. I HARDLY KNOW WHAT TO SAY. WELL, EXCEPT --
-- GOODBYE.

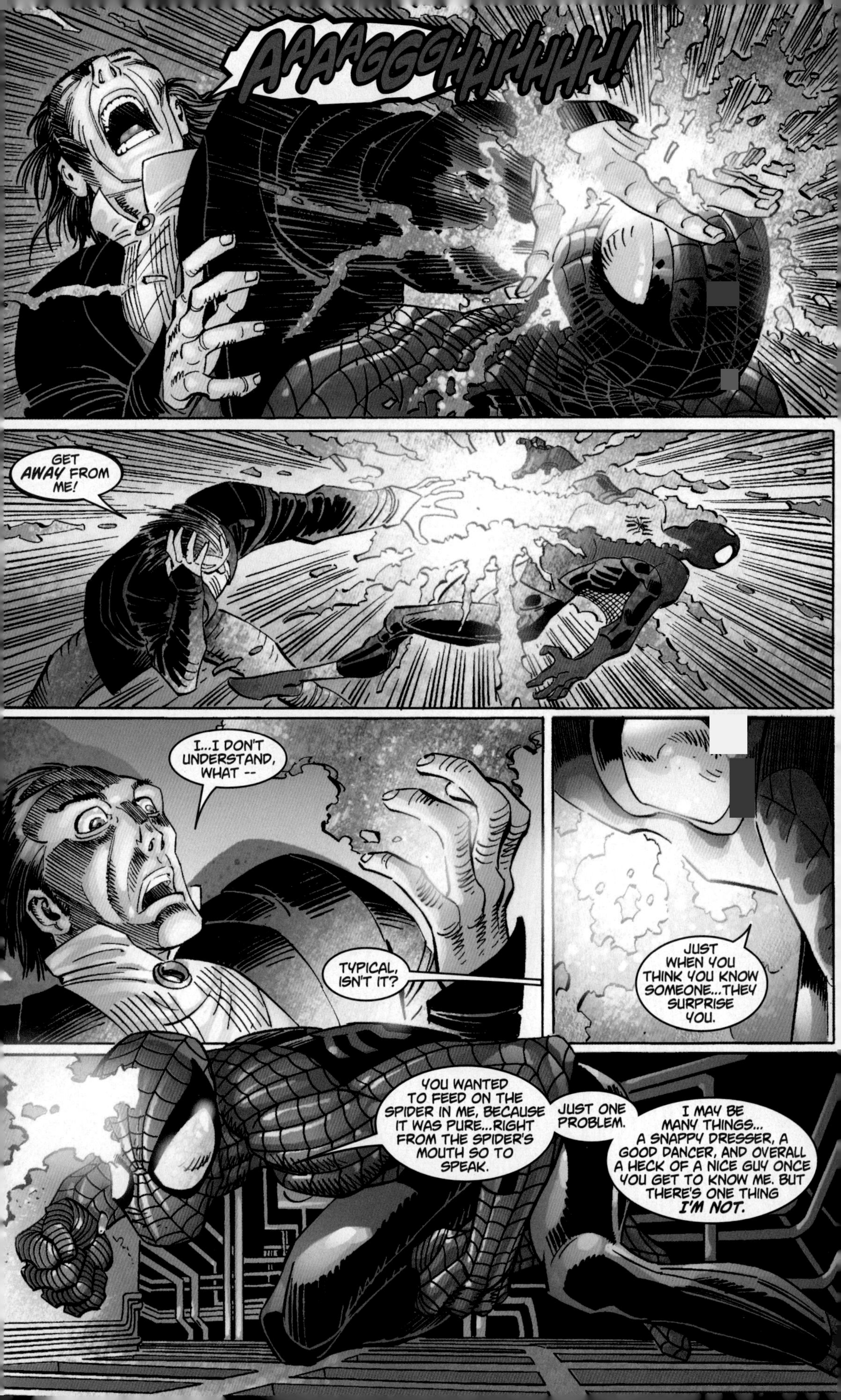
AAAAGGGHHHHHH!
GET AWAY FROM ME!
I...I DON'T UNDERSTAND, WHAT --
TYPICAL, ISN'T IT?
JUST WHEN YOU THINK YOU KNOW SOMEONE...THEY SURPRISE YOU.
YOU WANTED TO FEED ON THE SPIDER IN ME, BECAUSE IT WAS PURE...RIGHT FROM THE SPIDER'S MOUTH SO TO SPEAK.
JUST ONE PROBLEM.
I MAY BE MANY THINGS... A SNAPPY DRESSER, A GOOD DANCER, AND OVERALL A HECK OF A NICE GUY ONCE YOU GET TO KNOW ME. BUT THERE'S ONE THING I'M NOT.

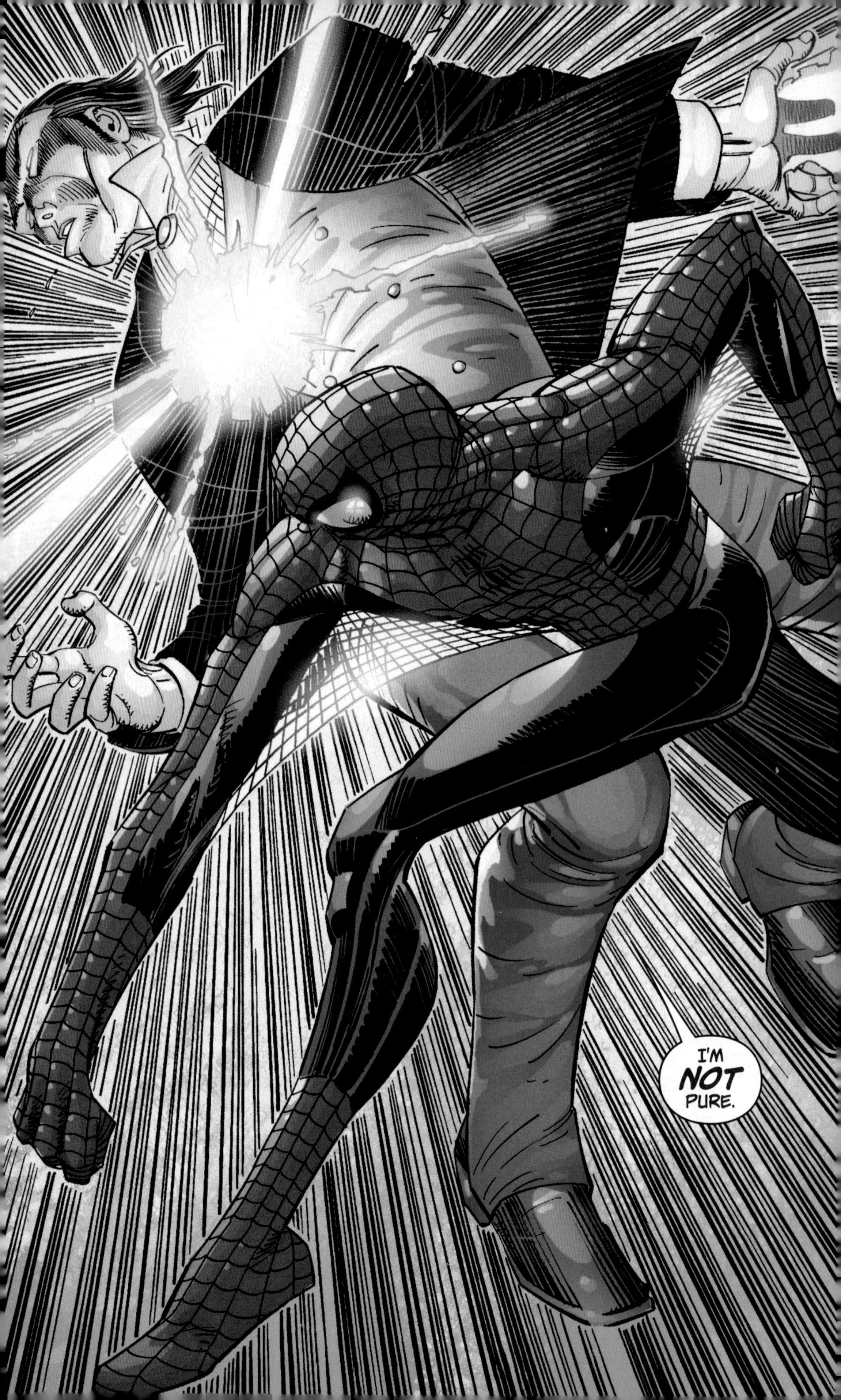
I'M NOT PURE.

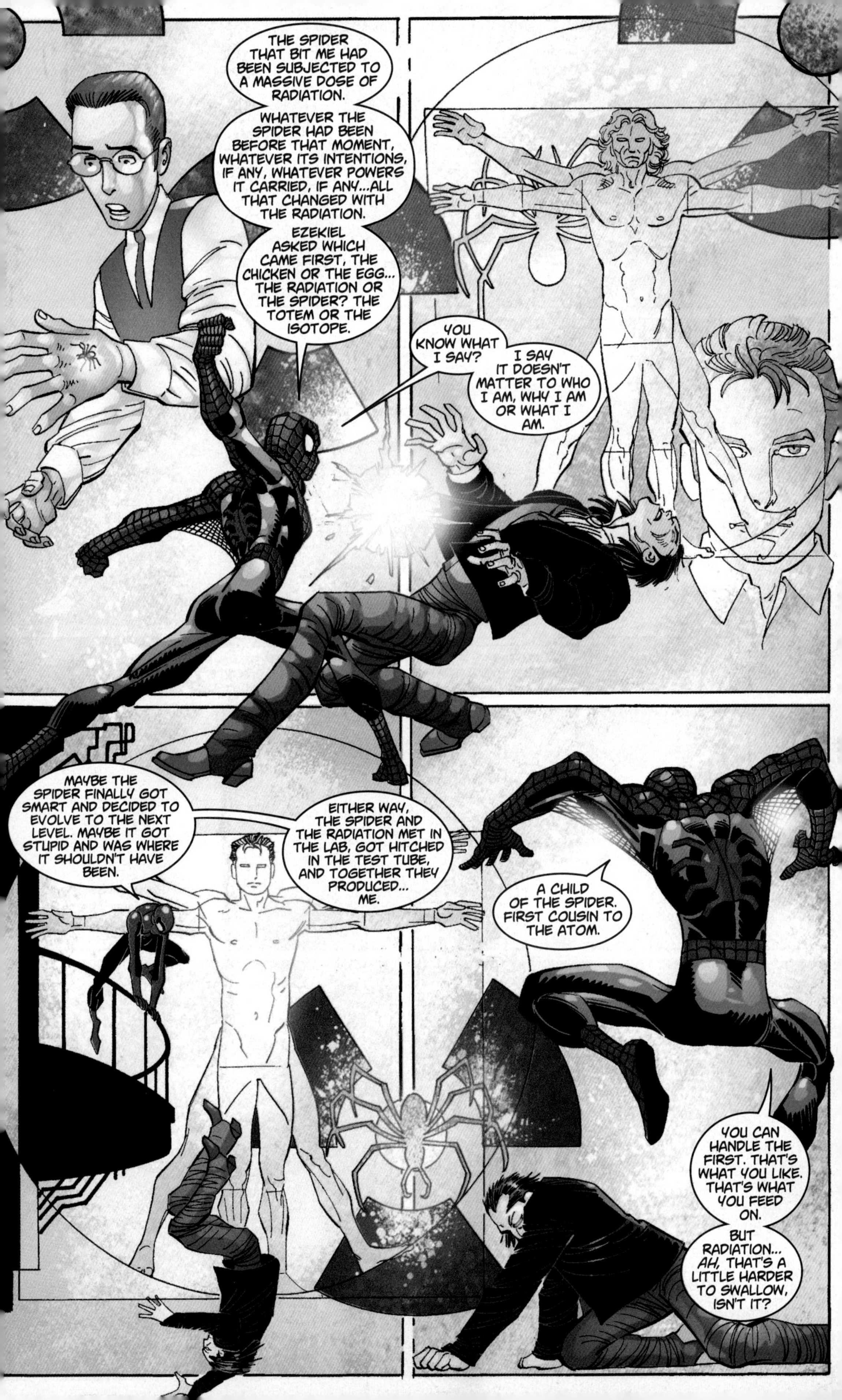
THE SPIDER THAT BIT ME HAD BEEN SUBJECTED TO A MASSIVE DOSE OF RADIATION.
WHATEVER THE SPIDER HAD BEEN BEFORE THAT MOMENT, WHATEVER ITS INTENTIONS, IF ANY, WHATEVER POWERS IT CARRIED, IF ANY...ALL THAT CHANGED WITH THE RADIATION.
EZEKIEL ASKED WHICH CAME FIRST, THE CHICKEN OR THE EGG... THE RADIATION OR THE SPIDER? THE TOTEM OR THE ISOTOPE.
YOU KNOW WHAT I SAY?
I SAY IT DOESN'T MATTER TO WHO I AM, WHY I AM OR WHAT I AM.
MAYBE THE SPIDER FINALLY GOT SMART AND DECIDED TO EVOLVE TO THE NEXT LEVEL. MAYBE IT GOT STUPID AND WAS WHERE IT SHOULDN'T HAVE BEEN.
EITHER WAY, THE SPIDER AND THE RADIATION MET IN THE LAB, GOT HITCHED IN THE TEST TUBE, AND TOGETHER THEY PRODUCED... ME.
A CHILD OF THE SPIDER. FIRST COUSIN TO THE ATOM.
YOU CAN HANDLE THE FIRST. THAT'S WHAT YOU LIKE. THAT'S WHAT YOU FEED ON.
BUT RADIATION... AH, THAT'S A LITTLE HARDER TO SWALLOW, ISN'T IT?

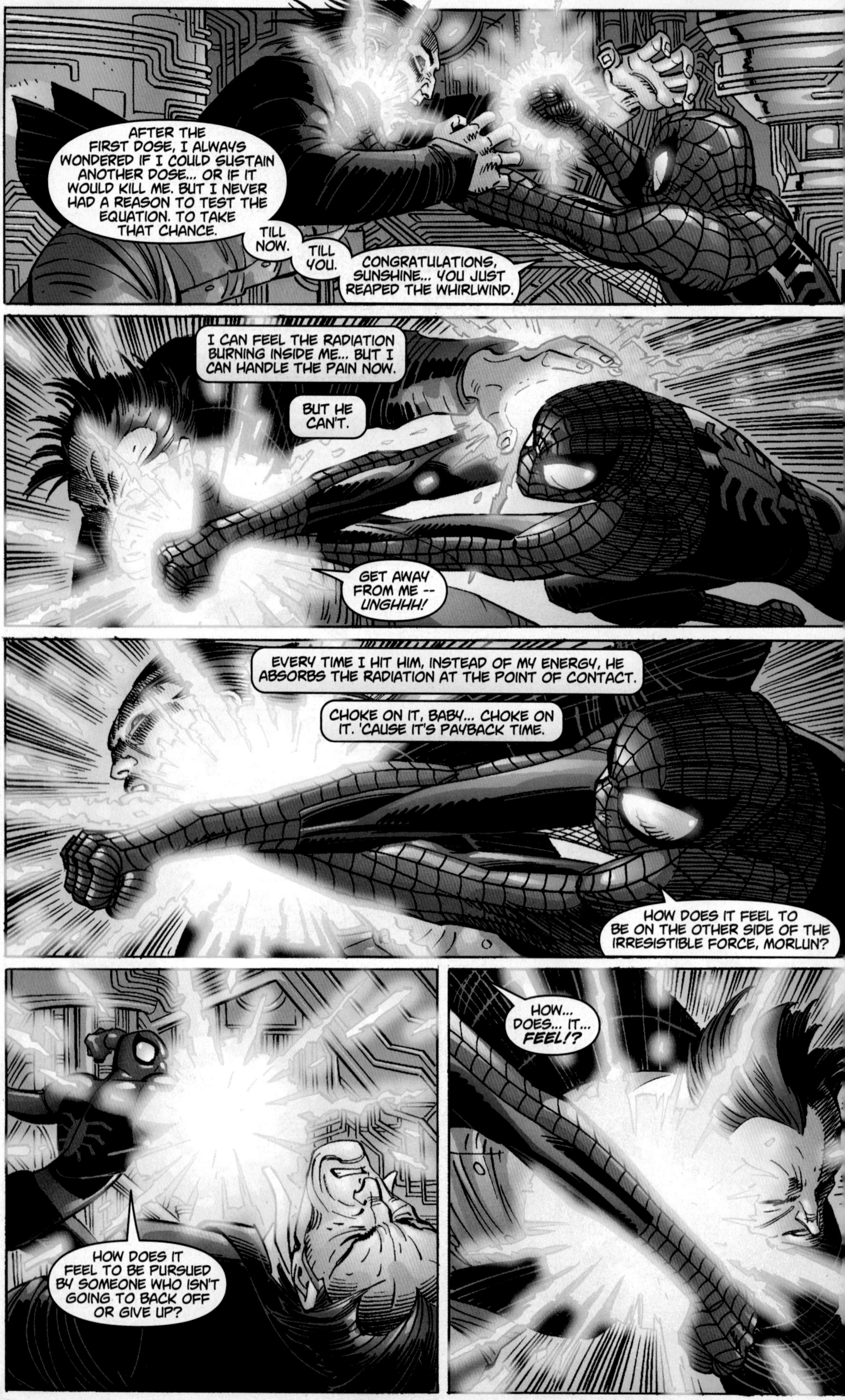

AFTER THE FIRST DOSE, I ALWAYS WONDERED IF I COULD SUSTAIN ANOTHER DOSE... OR IF IT WOULD KILL ME. BUT I NEVER HAD A REASON TO TEST THE EQUATION. TO TAKE THAT CHANCE.
TILL NOW.
TILL YOU.
CONGRATULATIONS, SUNSHINE... YOU JUST REAPED THE WHIRLWIND.
I CAN FEEL THE RADIATION BURNING INSIDE ME... BUT I CAN HANDLE THE PAIN NOW.
BUT HE CAN'T.
GET AWAY FROM ME -- *UNGHHH!*
EVERY TIME I HIT HIM, INSTEAD OF MY ENERGY, HE ABSORBS THE RADIATION AT THE POINT OF CONTACT.
CHOKE ON IT, BABY... CHOKE ON IT. 'CAUSE IT'S PAYBACK TIME.
HOW DOES IT FEEL TO BE ON THE OTHER SIDE OF THE IRRESISTIBLE FORCE, MORLUN?
HOW DOES IT FEEL TO BE PURSUED BY SOMEONE WHO ISN'T GOING TO BACK OFF OR GIVE UP?
HOW... DOES... IT... ***FEEL!?***

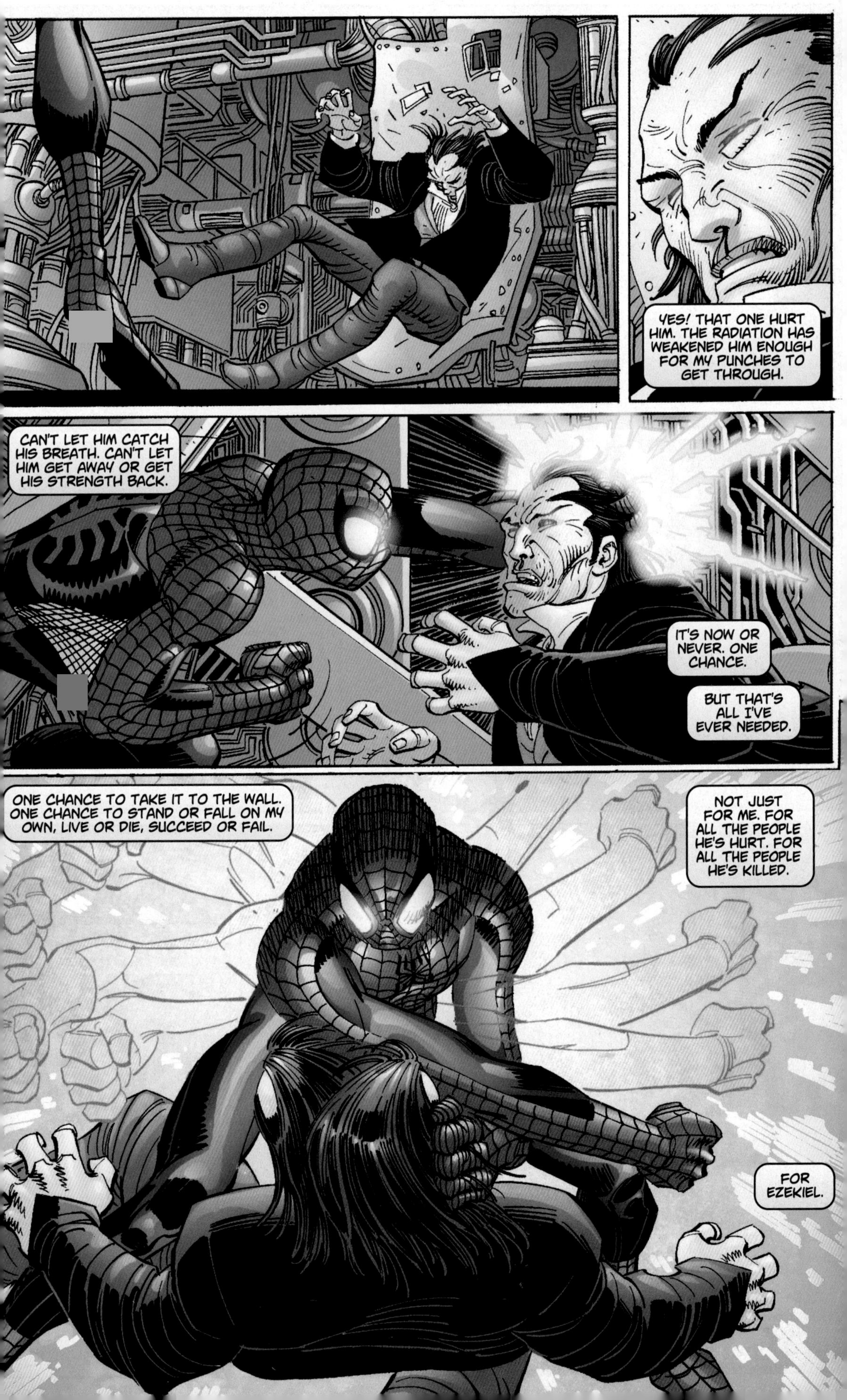

YES! THAT ONE HURT HIM. THE RADIATION HAS WEAKENED HIM ENOUGH FOR MY PUNCHES TO GET THROUGH.
CAN'T LET HIM CATCH HIS BREATH. CAN'T LET HIM GET AWAY OR GET HIS STRENGTH BACK.
IT'S NOW OR NEVER. ONE CHANCE.
BUT THAT'S ALL I'VE EVER NEEDED.
ONE CHANCE TO TAKE IT TO THE WALL. ONE CHANCE TO STAND OR FALL ON MY OWN, LIVE OR DIE, SUCCEED OR FAIL.
NOT JUST FOR ME. FOR ALL THE PEOPLE HE'S HURT. FOR ALL THE PEOPLE HE'S KILLED.
FOR EZEKIEL.

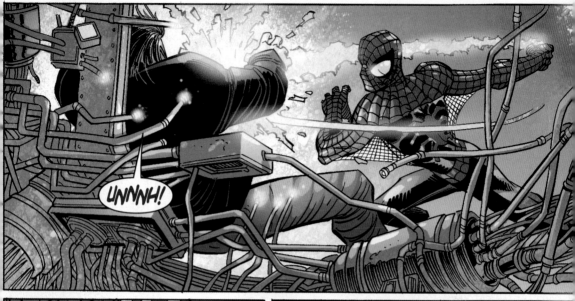

UNNNH!

PLEASE... NO MORE... I GIVE YOU MY WORD, I WILL LEAVE... I WILL NEVER RETURN --

-- JUST LET ME LIVE, I BEG YOU.

... holy ...

PLEASE...

I CAN'T LET HIM GO... I CAN'T LET HIM GET HIS STRENGTH BACK... I STOPPED HIM ONCE, I DON'T KNOW IF I CAN DO IT AGAIN.

EVEN IF HE DOESN'T COME AFTER ME, HE'LL COME AFTER SOMEBODY ELSE.

HE'S VULNERABLE. HE CAN BE HURT. HE CAN BE KILLED. I STOP HIM RIGHT HERE, RIGHT NOW, OR HE GOES BACK TO KILLING.

GOD IN HEAVEN, PETER... HOW FAR ARE YOU PREPARED TO GO?

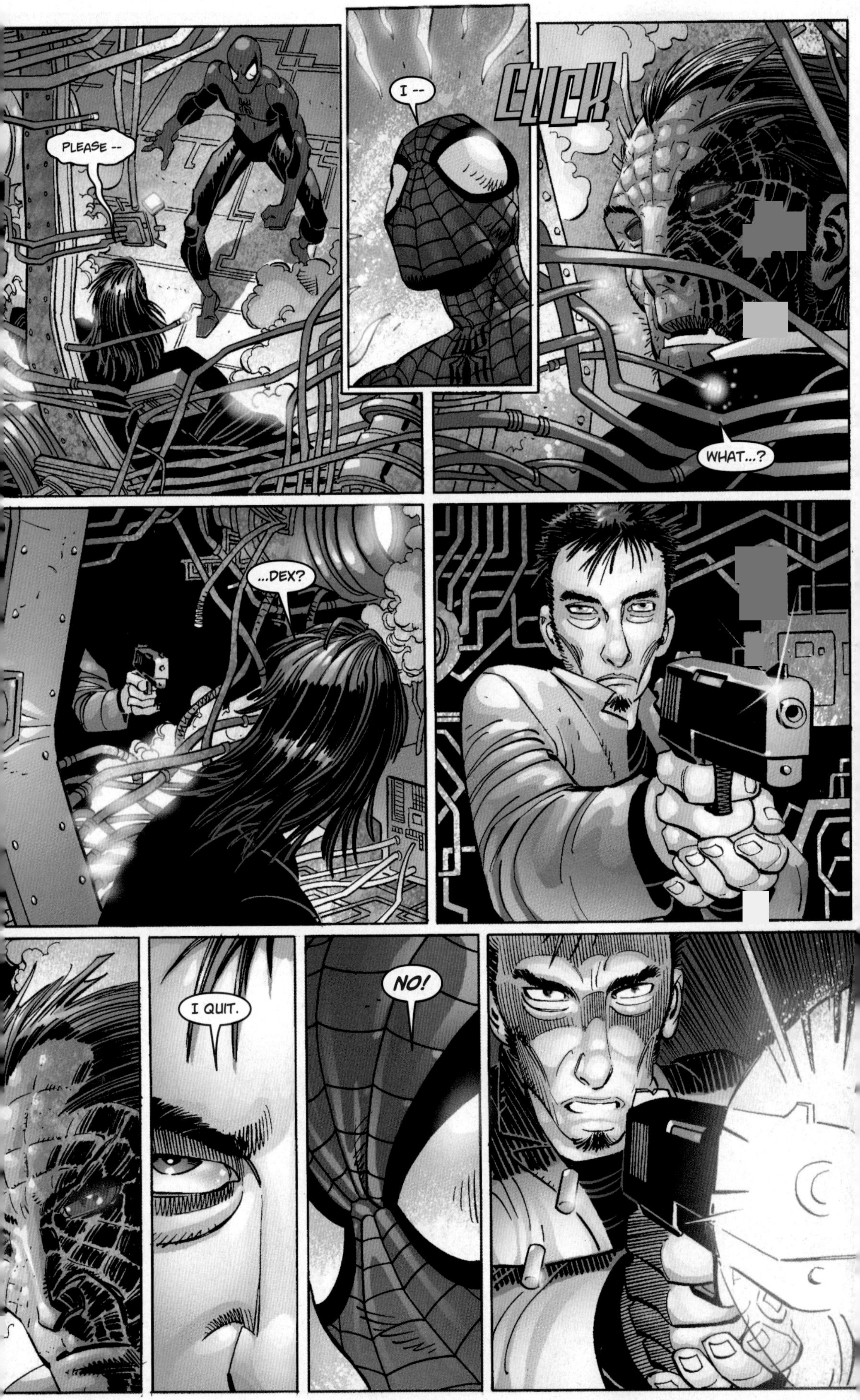
PLEASE --
I --
CLICK
WHAT...?
...DEX?
I QUIT.
NO!

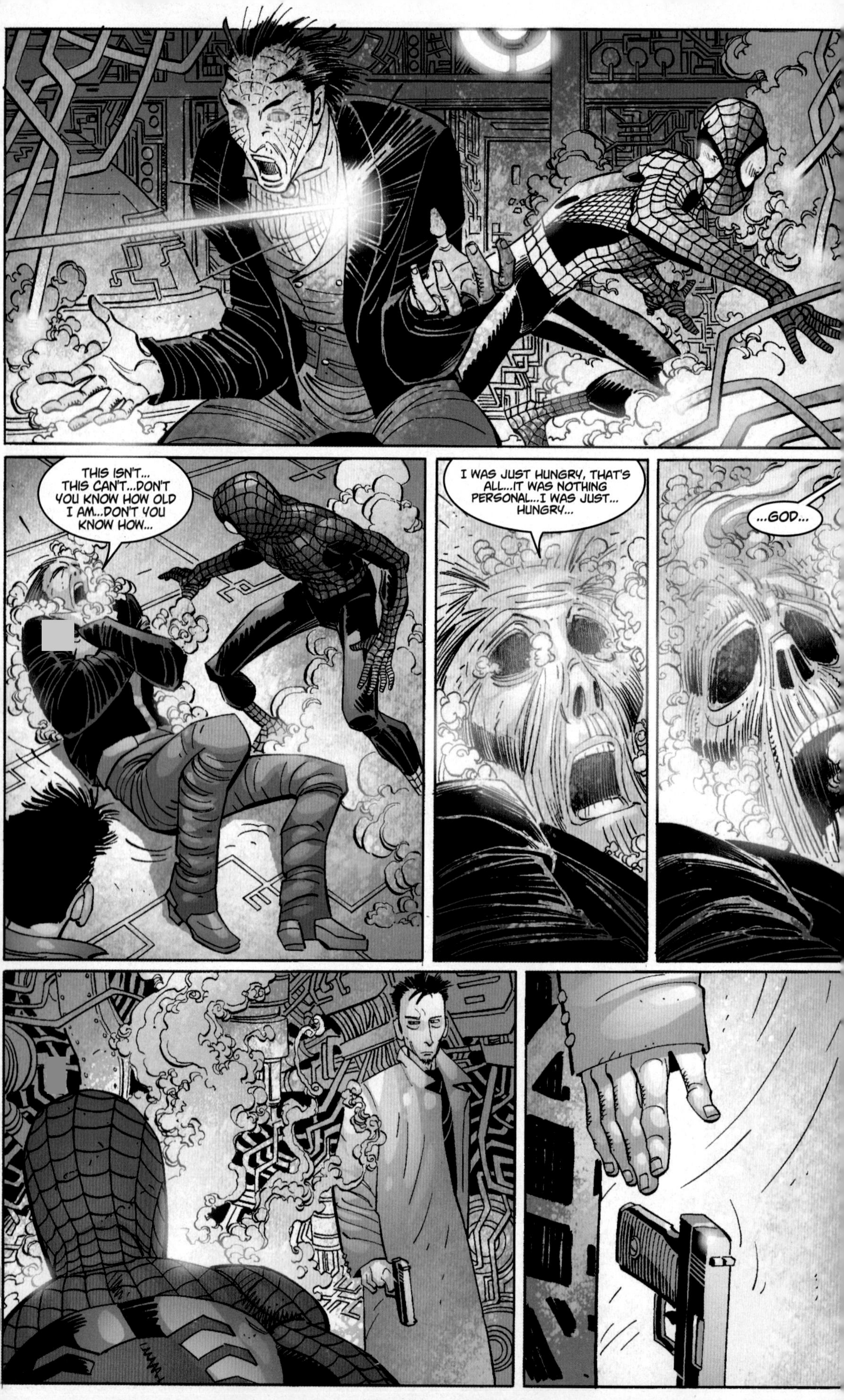
THIS ISN'T... THIS CAN'T...DON'T YOU KNOW HOW OLD I AM...DON'T YOU KNOW HOW...
I WAS JUST HUNGRY, THAT'S ALL...IT WAS NOTHING PERSONAL...I WAS JUST... HUNGRY...
...GOD...

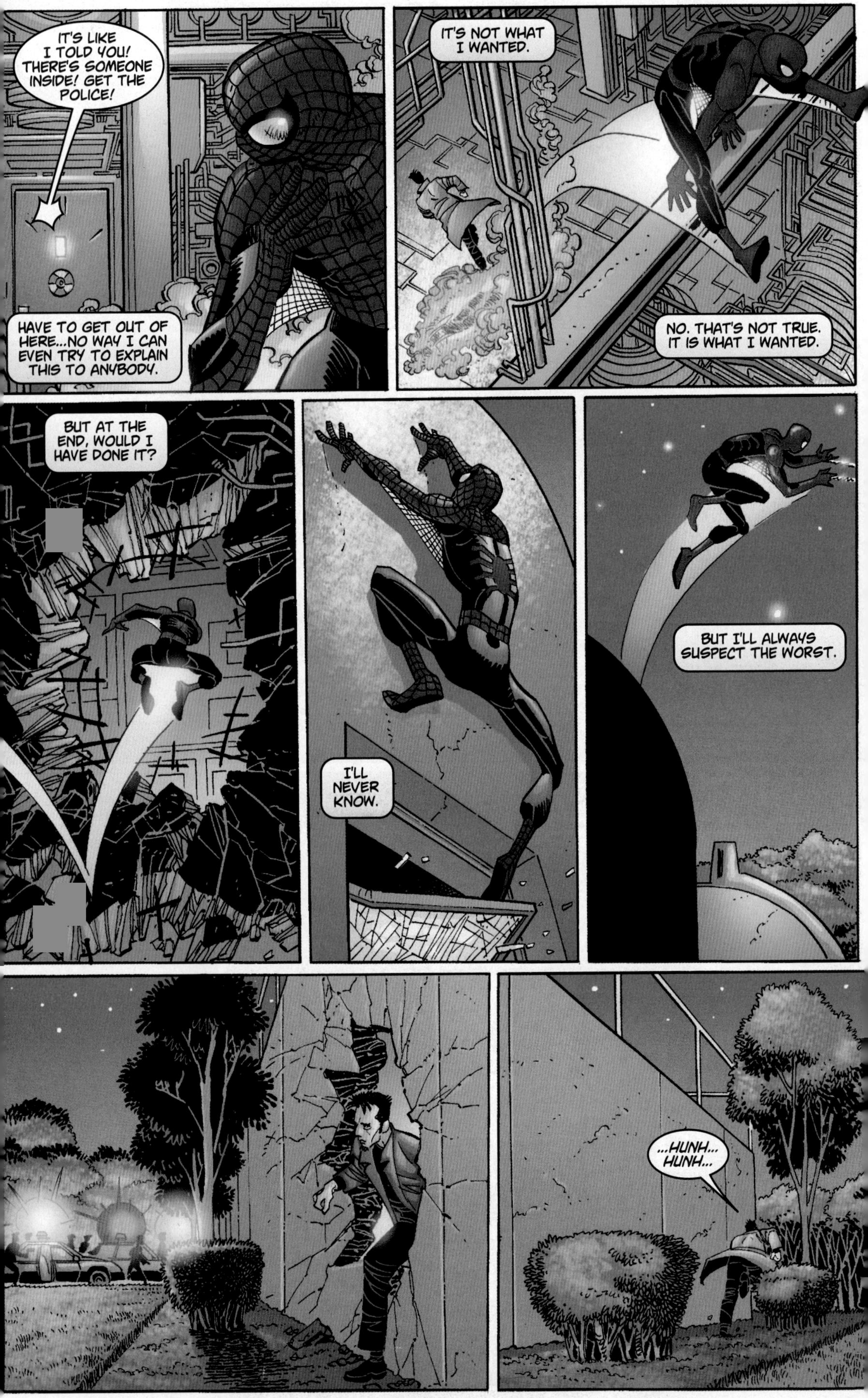

IT'S LIKE I TOLD YOU! THERE'S SOMEONE INSIDE! GET THE POLICE!
HAVE TO GET OUT OF HERE...NO WAY I CAN EVEN TRY TO EXPLAIN THIS TO ANYBODY.
IT'S NOT WHAT I WANTED.
NO. THAT'S NOT TRUE. IT IS WHAT I WANTED.
BUT AT THE END, WOULD I HAVE DONE IT?
I'LL NEVER KNOW.
BUT I'LL ALWAYS SUSPECT THE WORST.
...HUNH... HUNH...

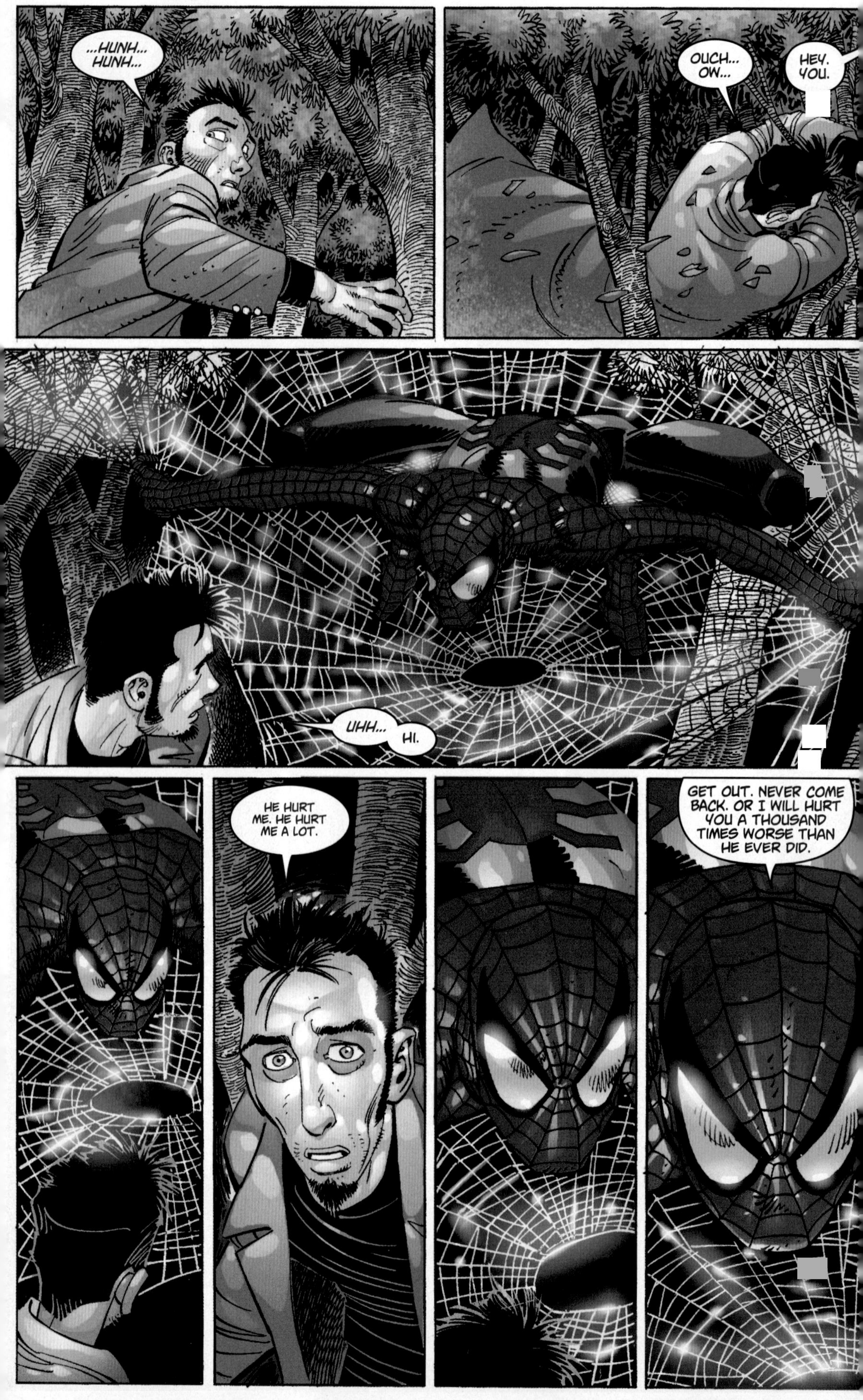
...HUNH... HUNH...
OUCH... OW...
HEY. YOU.
UHH...
HI.
HE HURT ME. HE HURT ME A LOT.
GET OUT. NEVER COME BACK. OR I WILL HURT YOU A THOUSAND TIMES WORSE THAN HE EVER DID.

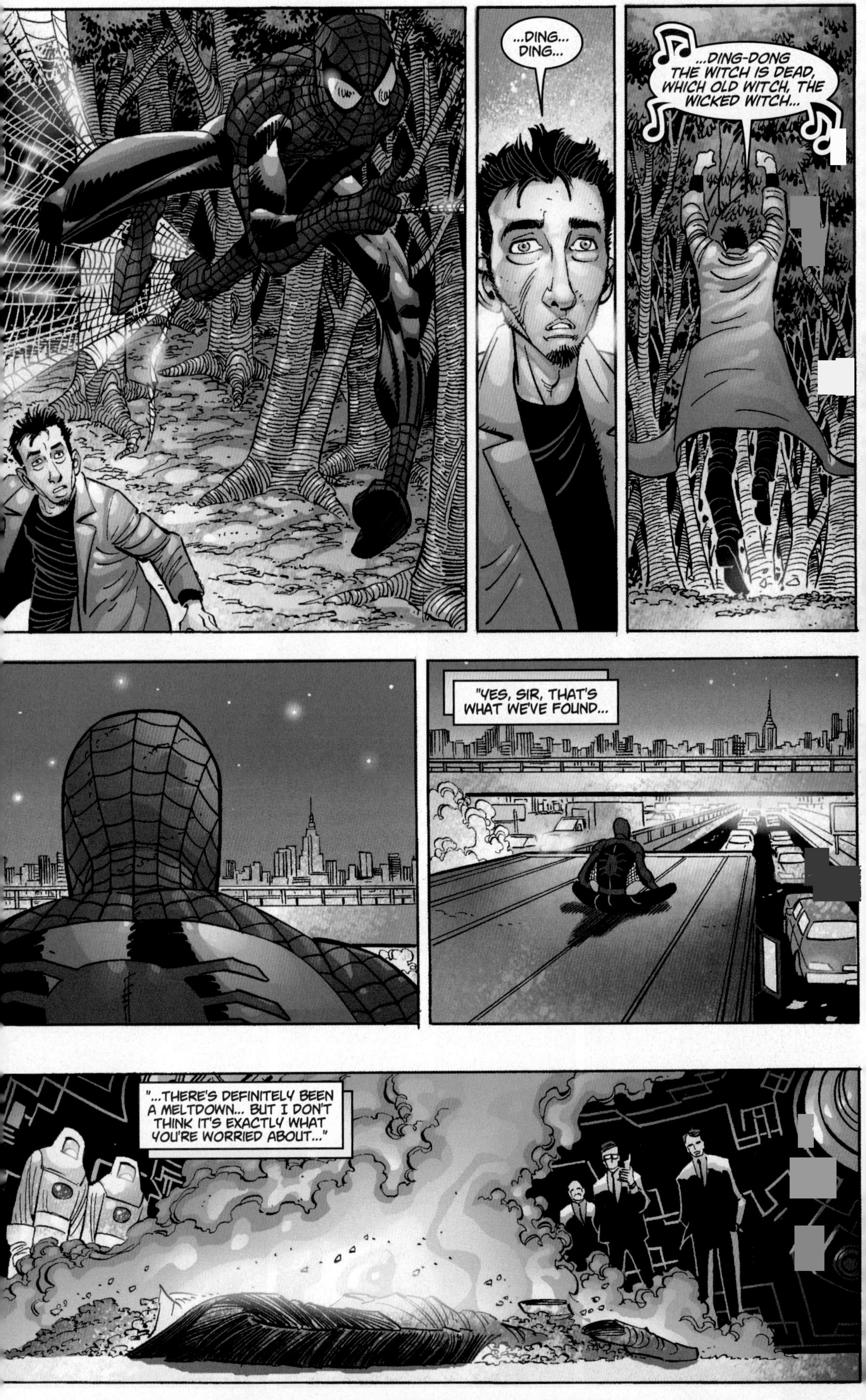
...DING... DING...
...DING-DONG THE WITCH IS DEAD, WHICH OLD WITCH, THE WICKED WITCH...
"YES, SIR, THAT'S WHAT WE'VE FOUND...
"...THERE'S DEFINITELY BEEN A MELTDOWN... BUT I DON'T THINK IT'S EXACTLY WHAT YOU'RE WORRIED ABOUT..."

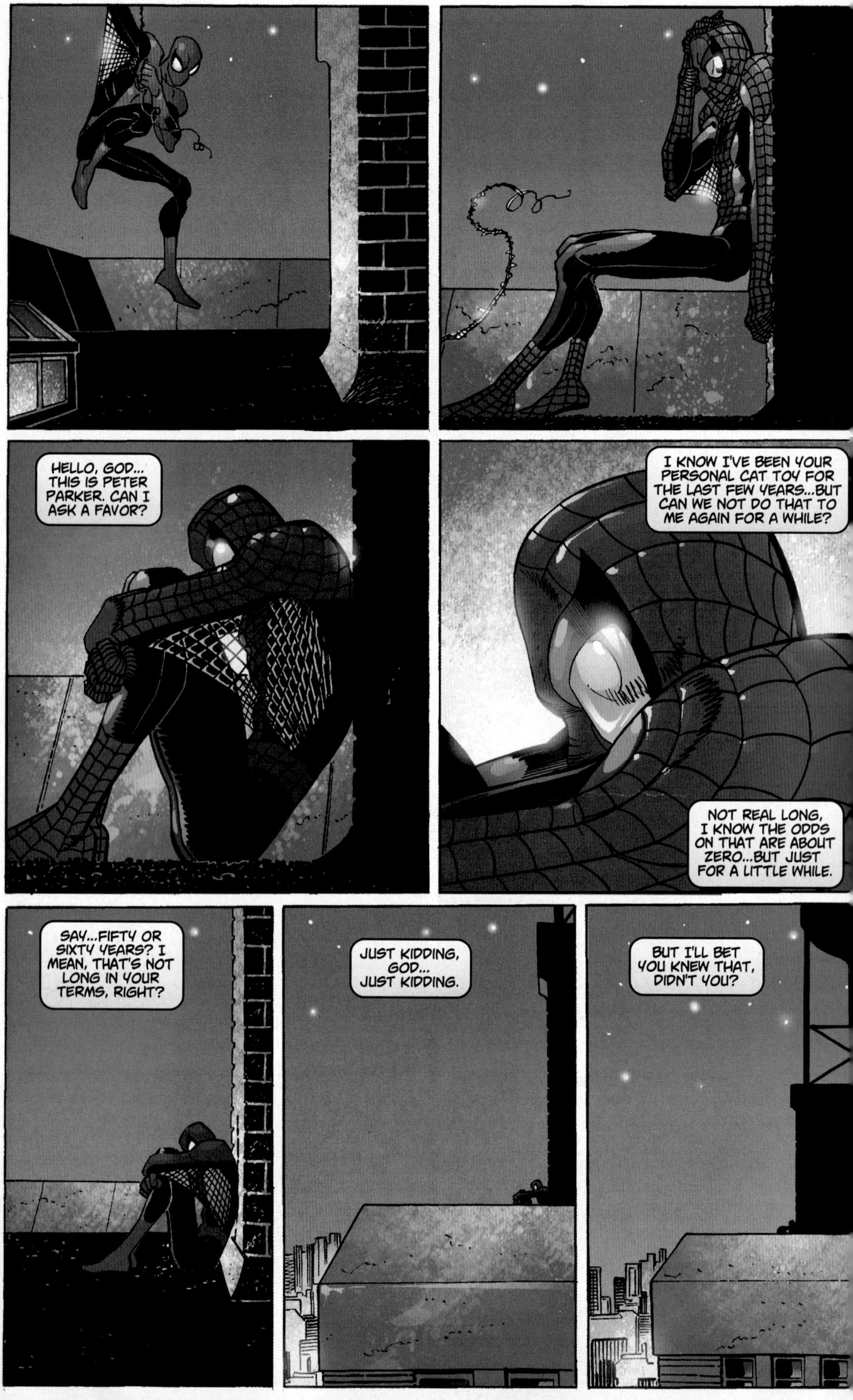

HELLO, GOD... THIS IS PETER PARKER. CAN I ASK A FAVOR?
I KNOW I'VE BEEN YOUR PERSONAL CAT TOY FOR THE LAST FEW YEARS...BUT CAN WE NOT DO THAT TO ME AGAIN FOR A WHILE?
NOT REAL LONG, I KNOW THE ODDS ON THAT ARE ABOUT ZERO...BUT JUST FOR A LITTLE WHILE.
SAY...FIFTY OR SIXTY YEARS? I MEAN, THAT'S NOT LONG IN YOUR TERMS, RIGHT?
JUST KIDDING, GOD... JUST KIDDING.
BUT I'LL BET YOU KNEW THAT, DIDN'T YOU?

SIMMS

WHEN MY KNEES STOP SHAKING, I GO TO CHECK ON EZEKIEL'S PLACE. I FIGURE SOMEBODY HAS TO TELL THEM HE'S GONE. TELL THEM HE STOOD UP, ANTED IN, AND WENT DOWN SWINGING.

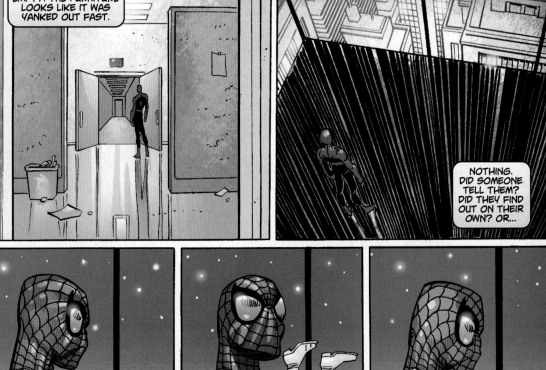

BUT THE PLACE IS EMPTY. THE FURNITURE LOOKS LIKE IT WAS YANKED OUT FAST.

NOTHING. DID SOMEONE TELL THEM? DID THEY FIND OUT ON THEIR OWN? OR...

ARE YOU OUT THERE, EZEKIEL? DID YOU LAND ON YOUR FEET?

DO I NOT HAVE TO CARRY ONE MORE DEATH ON MY CONSCIENCE?

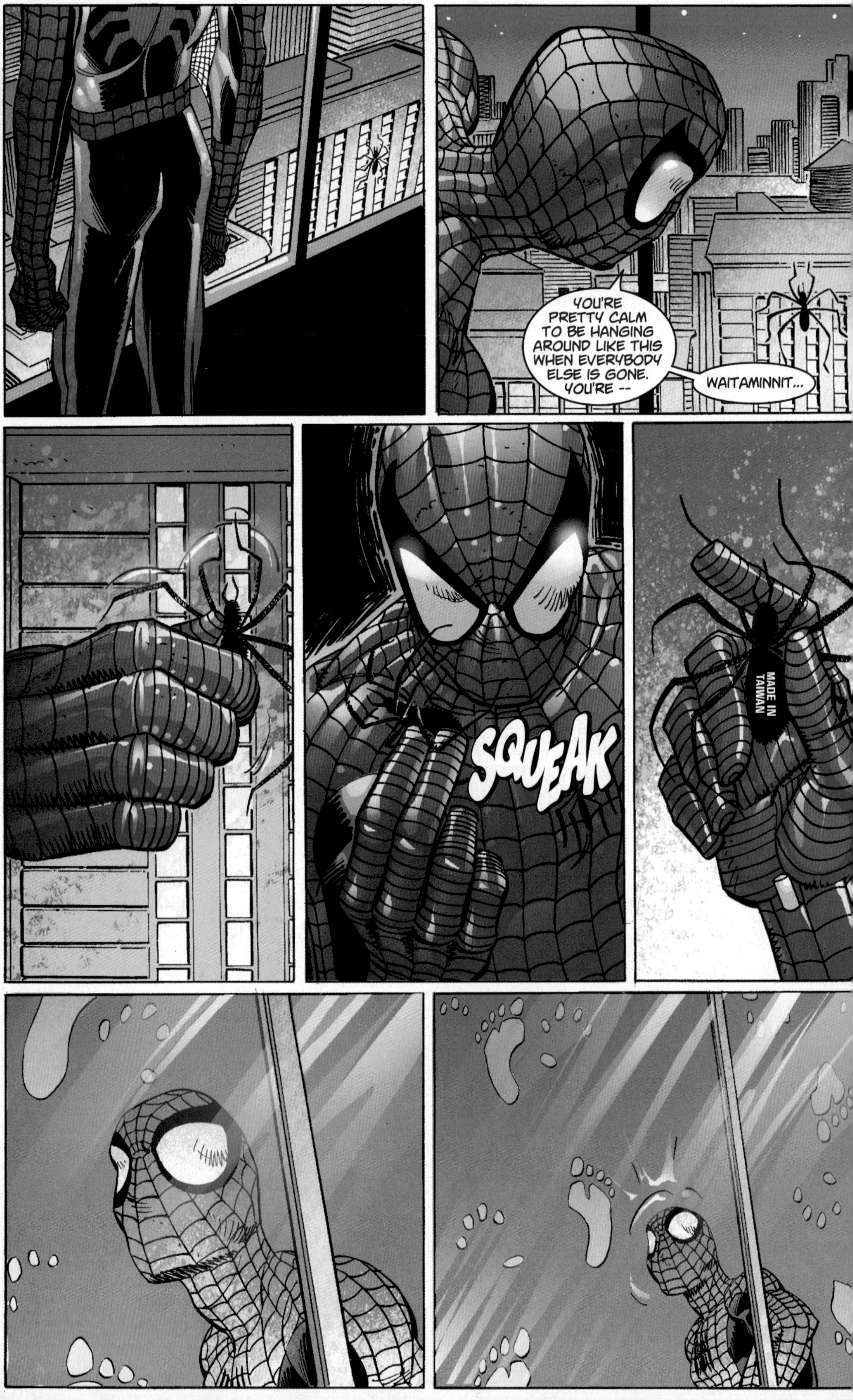
YOU'RE PRETTY CALM TO BE HANGING AROUND LIKE THIS WHEN EVERYBODY ELSE IS GONE. YOU'RE --
WAITAMINNIT...
SQUEAK
MADE IN TAIWAN

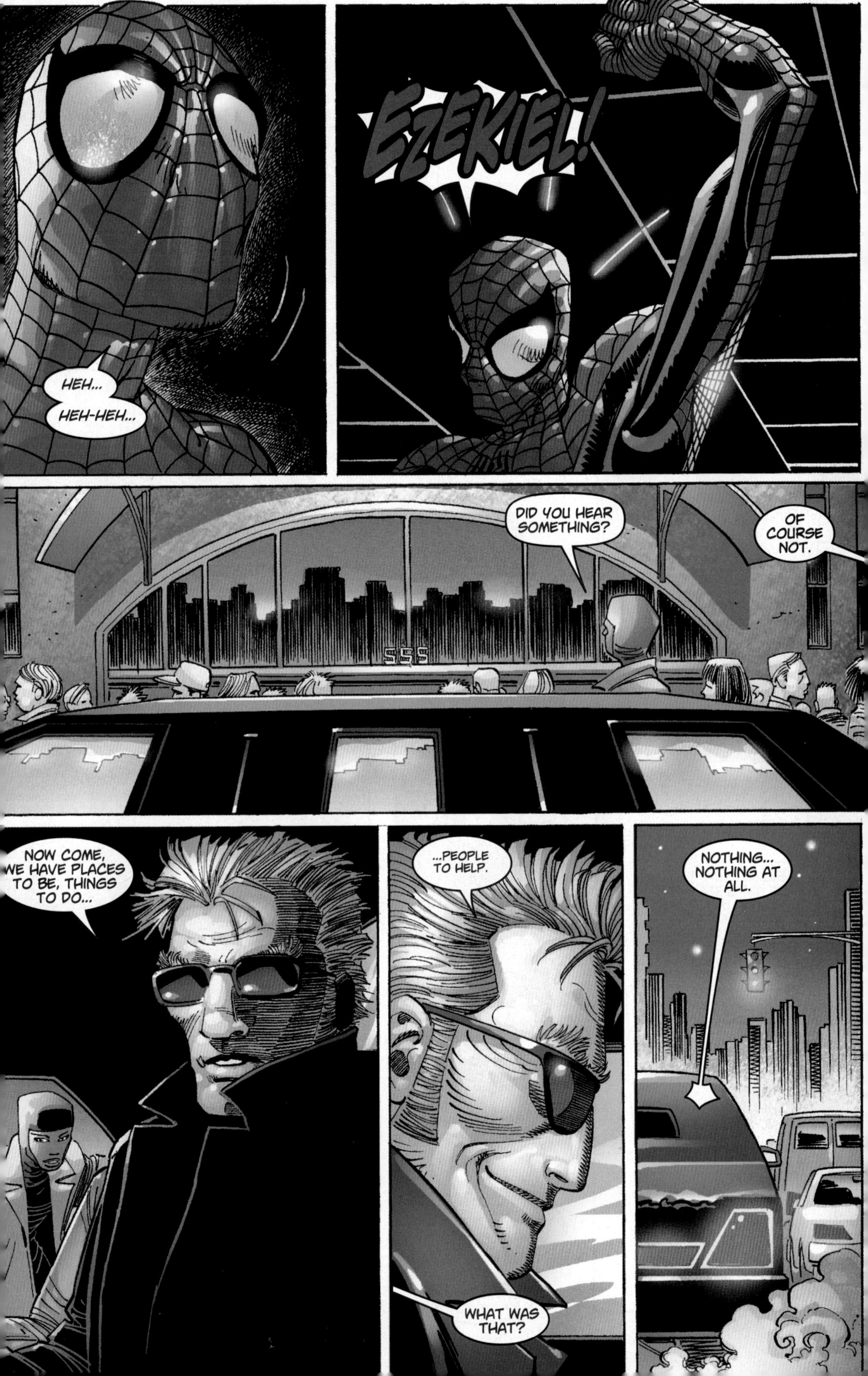
HEH...
HEH-HEH...
EZEKIEL!
DID YOU HEAR SOMETHING?
OF COURSE NOT.
NOW COME, WE HAVE PLACES TO BE, THINGS TO DO...
...PEOPLE TO HELP.
WHAT WAS THAT?
NOTHING... NOTHING AT ALL.

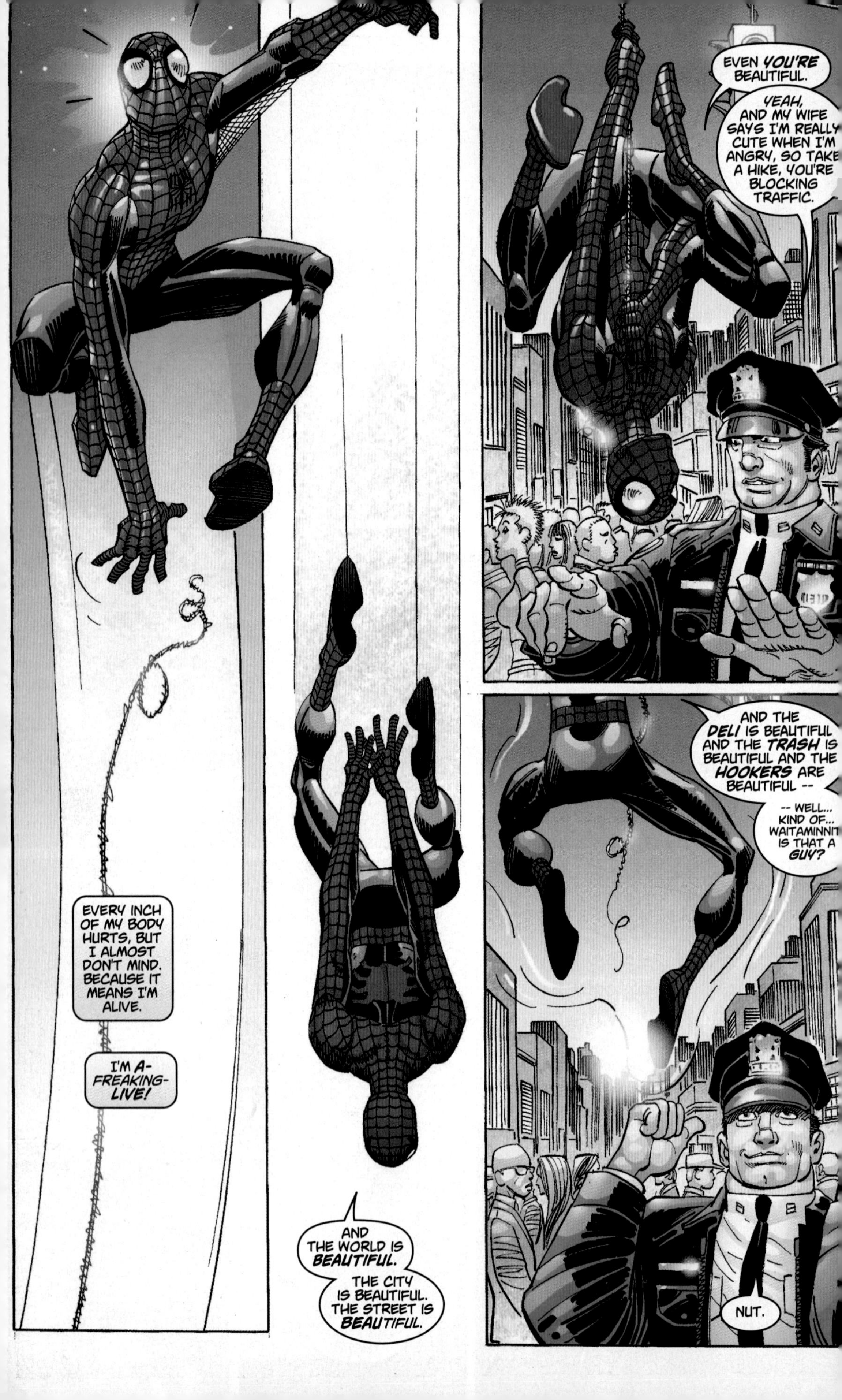
EVERY INCH OF MY BODY HURTS, BUT I ALMOST DON'T MIND. BECAUSE IT MEANS I'M ALIVE.
I'M A-FREAKING-LIVE!
AND THE WORLD IS BEAUTIFUL.
THE CITY IS BEAUTIFUL. THE STREET IS BEAUTIFUL.
EVEN YOU'RE BEAUTIFUL.
YEAH, AND MY WIFE SAYS I'M REALLY CUTE WHEN I'M ANGRY, SO TAKE A HIKE, YOU'RE BLOCKING TRAFFIC.
AND THE DELI IS BEAUTIFUL AND THE TRASH IS BEAUTIFUL AND THE HOOKERS ARE BEAUTIFUL --
-- WELL... KIND OF... WAITAMINNIT IS THAT A GUY?
NUT.

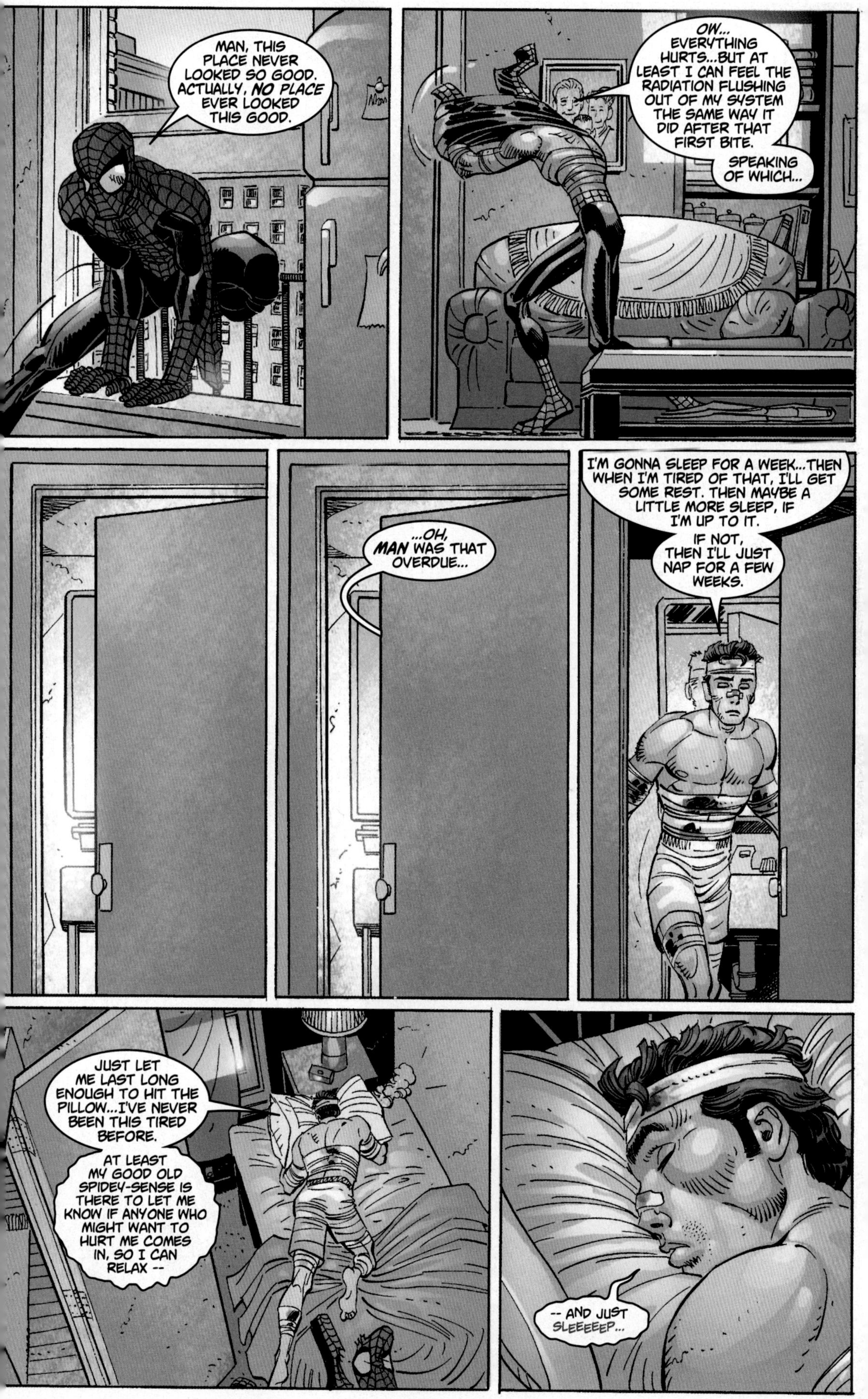

MAN, THIS PLACE NEVER LOOKED SO GOOD. ACTUALLY, NO PLACE EVER LOOKED THIS GOOD.
OW... EVERYTHING HURTS...BUT AT LEAST I CAN FEEL THE RADIATION FLUSHING OUT OF MY SYSTEM THE SAME WAY IT DID AFTER THAT FIRST BITE.
SPEAKING OF WHICH...
...OH, MAN WAS THAT OVERDUE...
I'M GONNA SLEEP FOR A WEEK...THEN WHEN I'M TIRED OF THAT, I'LL GET SOME REST. THEN MAYBE A LITTLE MORE SLEEP, IF I'M UP TO IT.
IF NOT, THEN I'LL JUST NAP FOR A FEW WEEKS.
JUST LET ME LAST LONG ENOUGH TO HIT THE PILLOW...I'VE NEVER BEEN THIS TIRED BEFORE.
AT LEAST MY GOOD OLD SPIDEY-SENSE IS THERE TO LET ME KNOW IF ANYONE WHO MIGHT WANT TO HURT ME COMES IN, SO I CAN RELAX --
-- AND JUST SLEEEEEP...

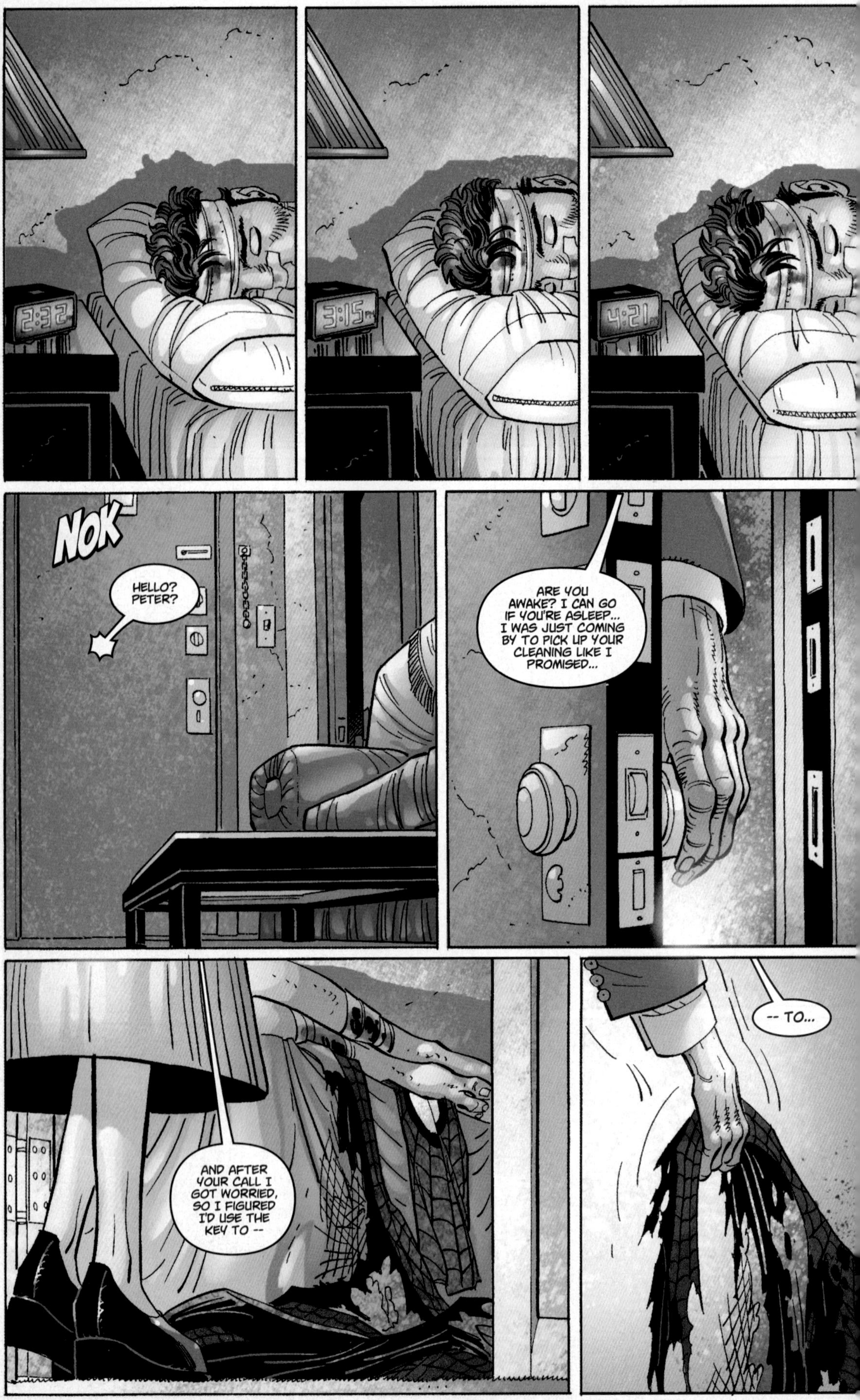

2:32
3:15
4:21
NOK
HELLO? PETER?
ARE YOU AWAKE? I CAN GO IF YOU'RE ASLEEP... I WAS JUST COMING BY TO PICK UP YOUR CLEANING LIKE I PROMISED...
AND AFTER YOUR CALL I GOT WORRIED, SO I FIGURED I'D USE THE KEY TO --
-- TO...

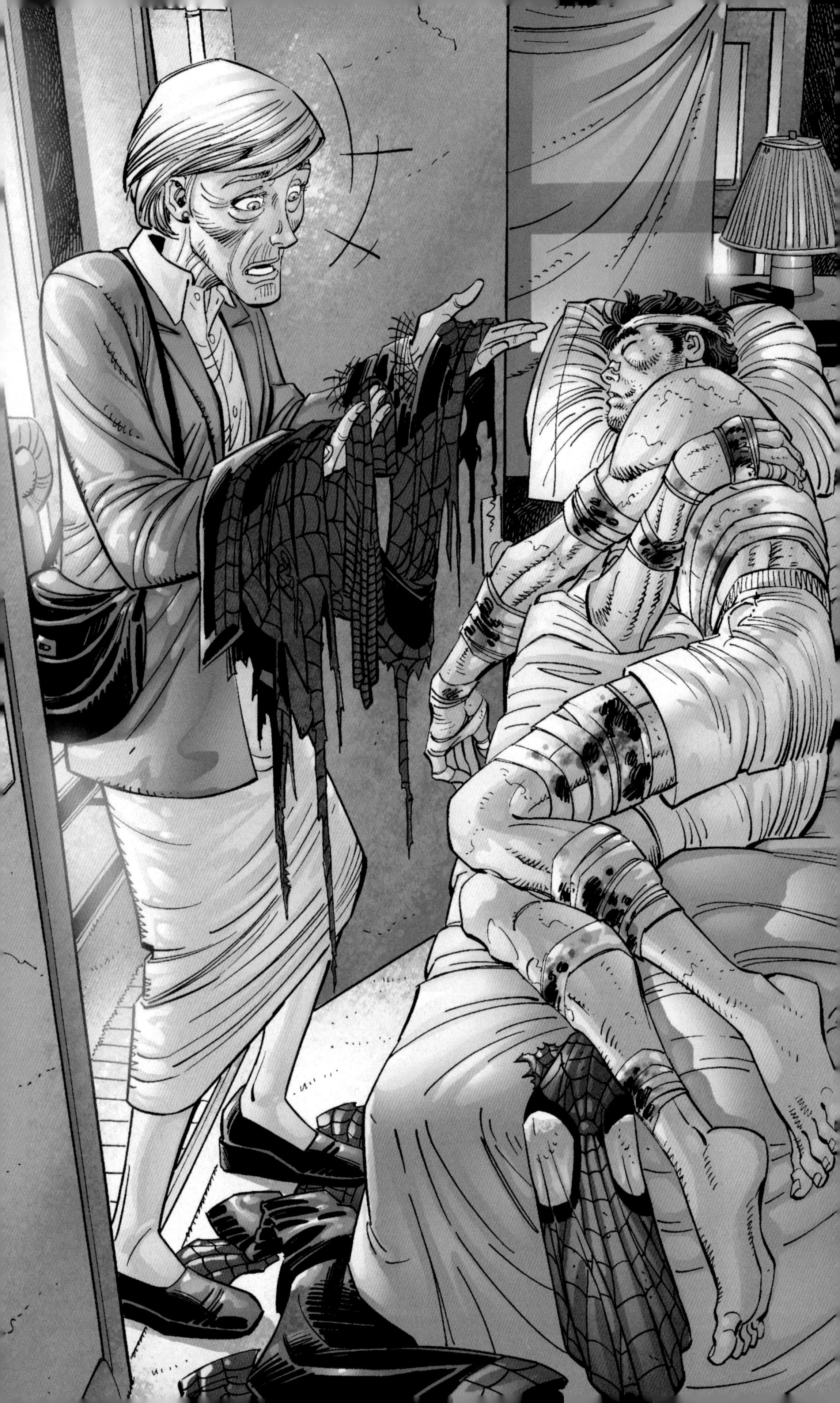

MARVEL® COMICS

the AMAZING SPIDER-MAN®

36

We interrupt our regularly
scheduled program to bring you
the following Special Bulletin.

LONGITUDE: 74 DEGREES,
0 MINUTES, 23 SECONDS WEST.
LATITUDE: 40 DEGREES,
42 MINUTES, 51 SECONDS NORTH.

FOLLOW THE SOUND
OF SIRENS...

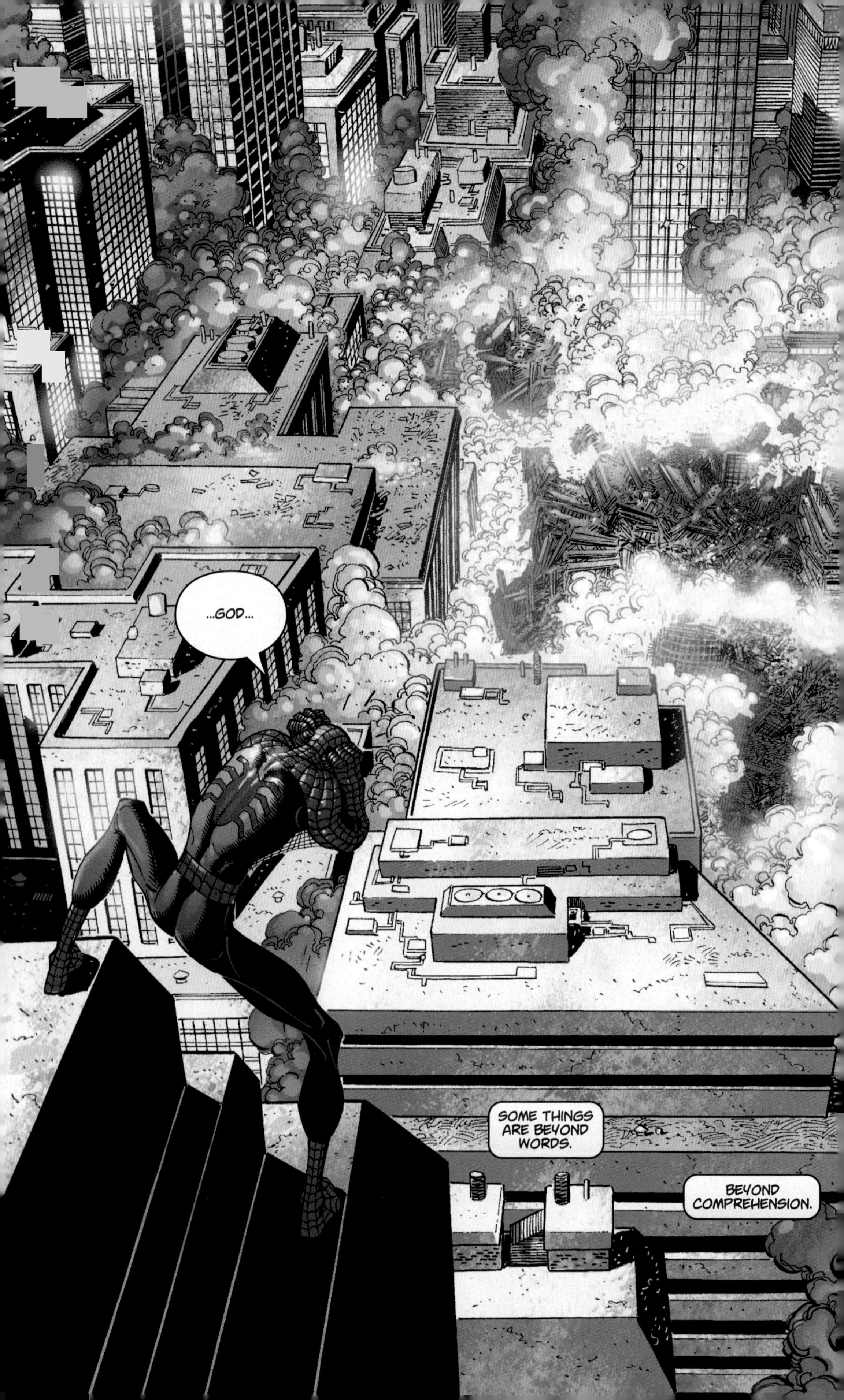
...GOD...
SOME THINGS ARE BEYOND WORDS.
BEYOND COMPREHENSION.

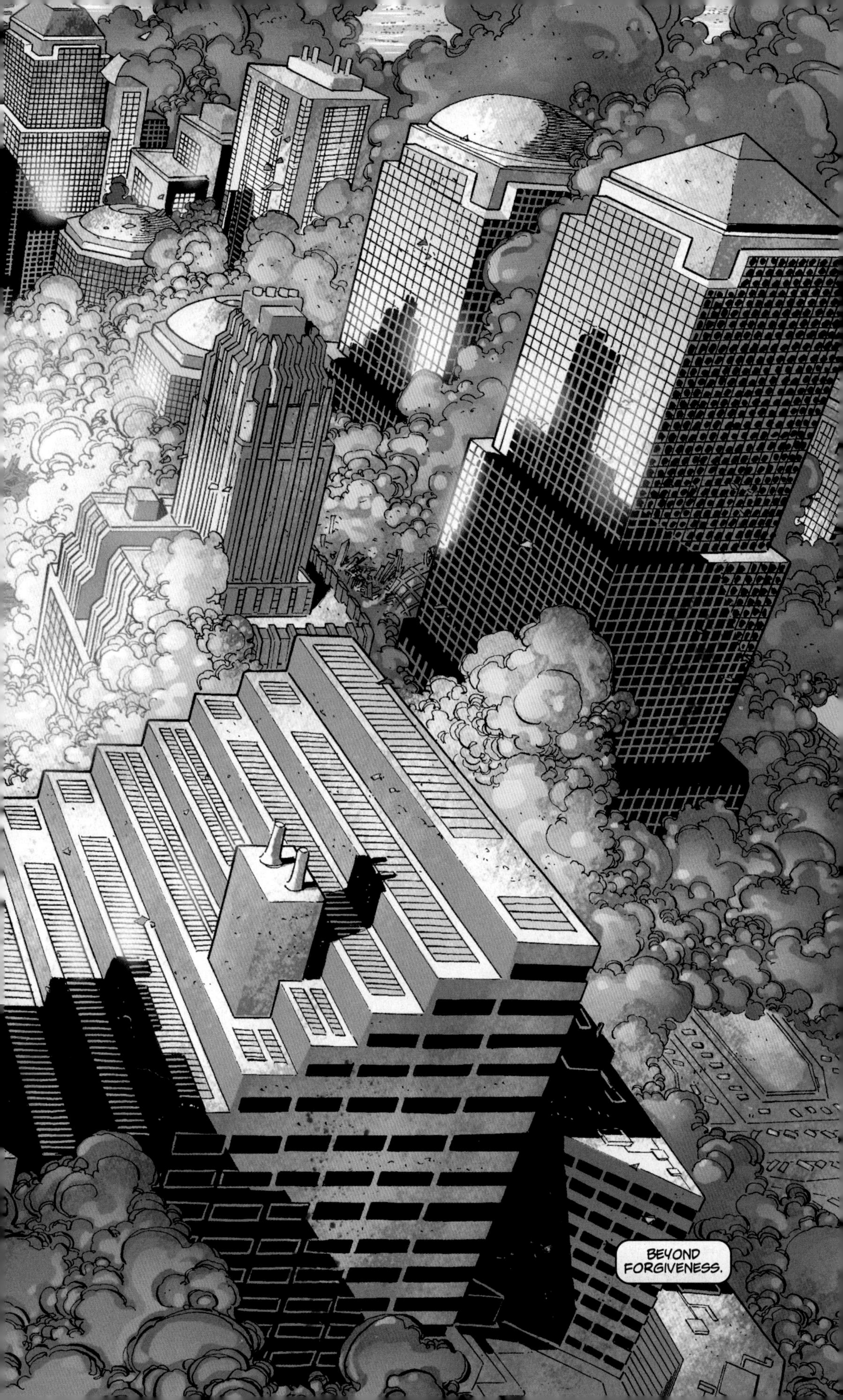
BEYOND FORGIVENESS.

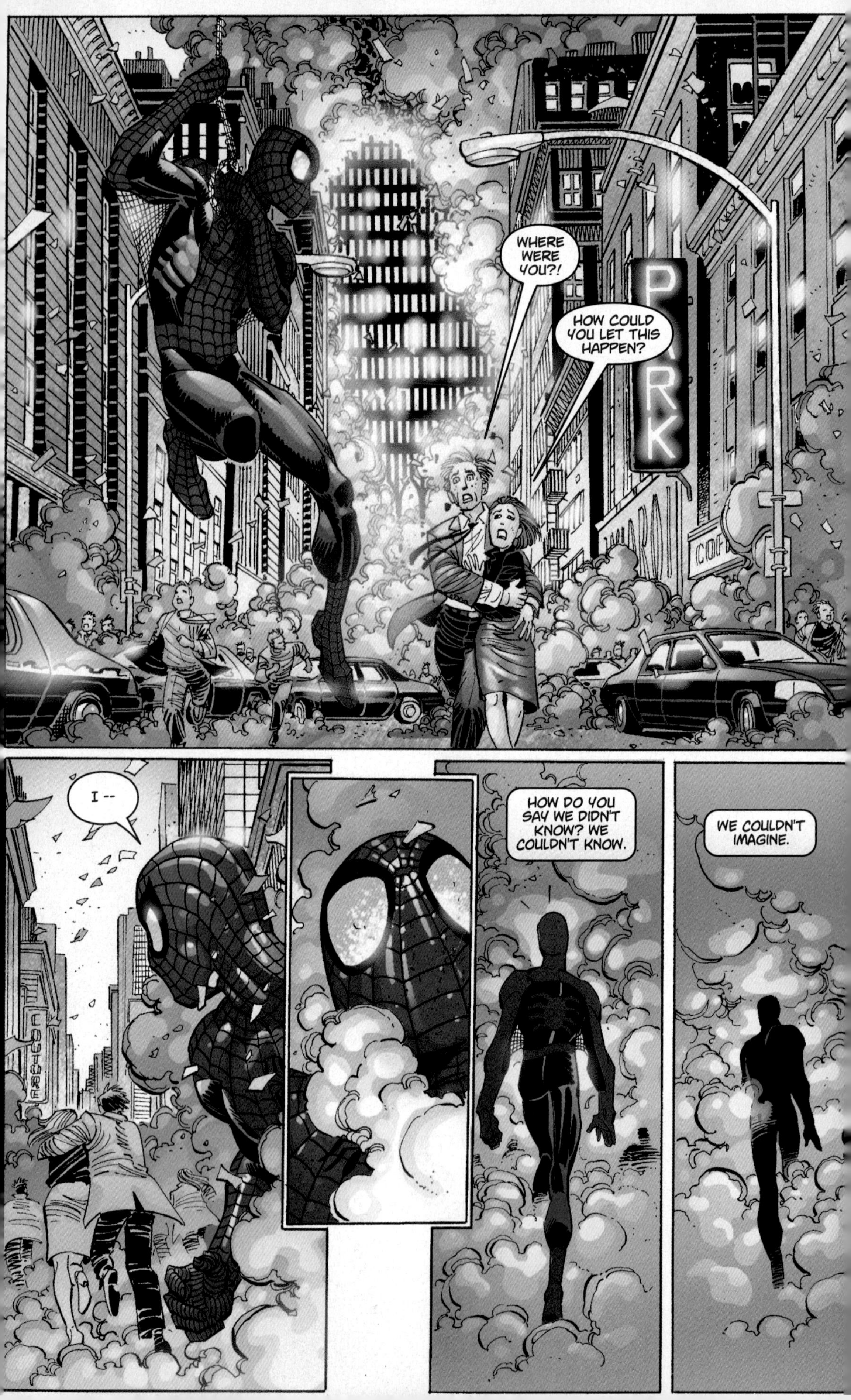
PARK
WHERE WERE YOU?!
HOW COULD YOU LET THIS HAPPEN?
I --
HOW DO YOU SAY WE DIDN'T KNOW? WE COULDN'T KNOW.
WE COULDN'T IMAGINE.

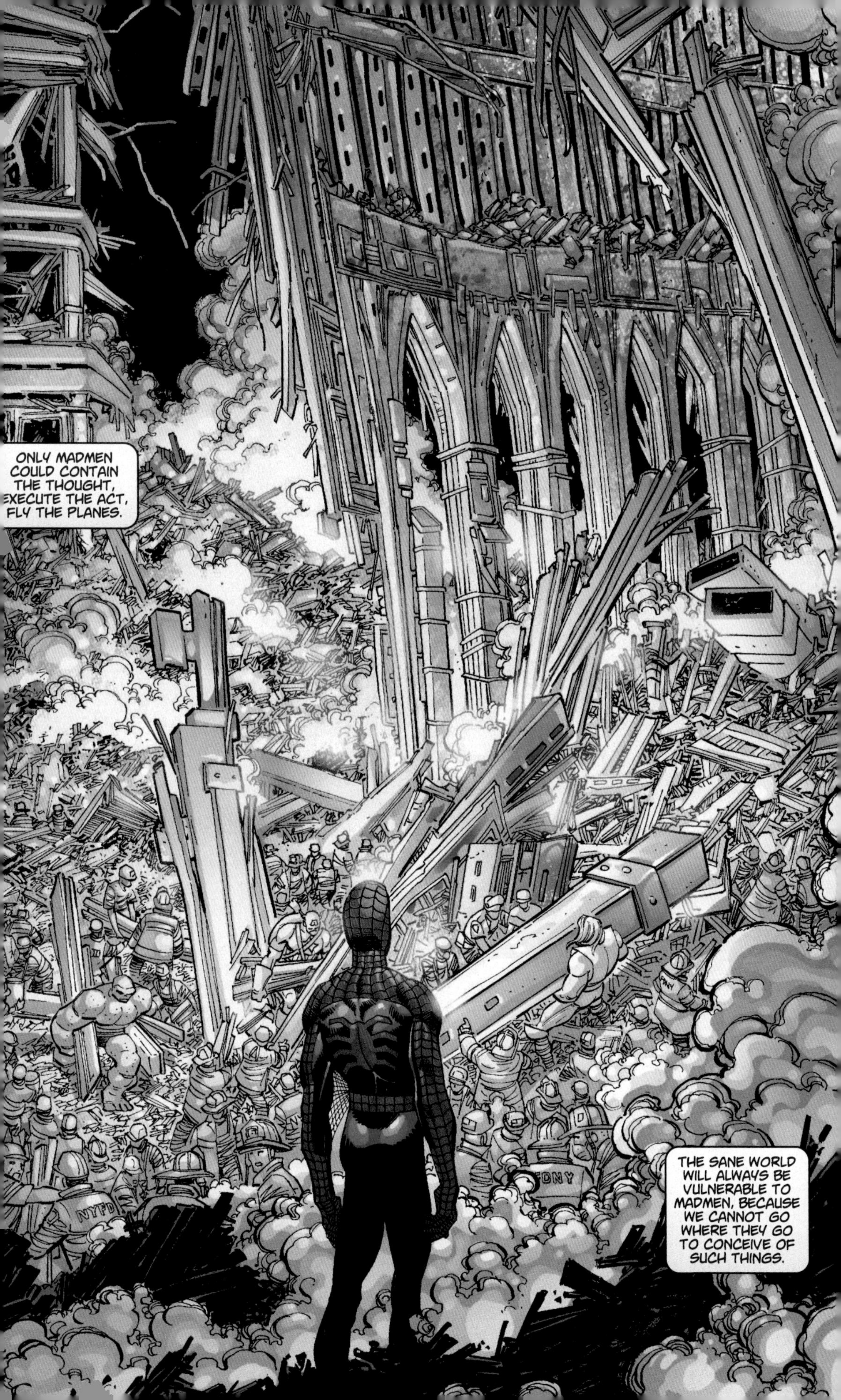
ONLY MADMEN COULD CONTAIN THE THOUGHT, EXECUTE THE ACT, FLY THE PLANES.
NYPD
FDNY
THE SANE WORLD WILL ALWAYS BE VULNERABLE TO MADMEN, BECAUSE WE CANNOT GO WHERE THEY GO TO CONCEIVE OF SUCH THINGS.

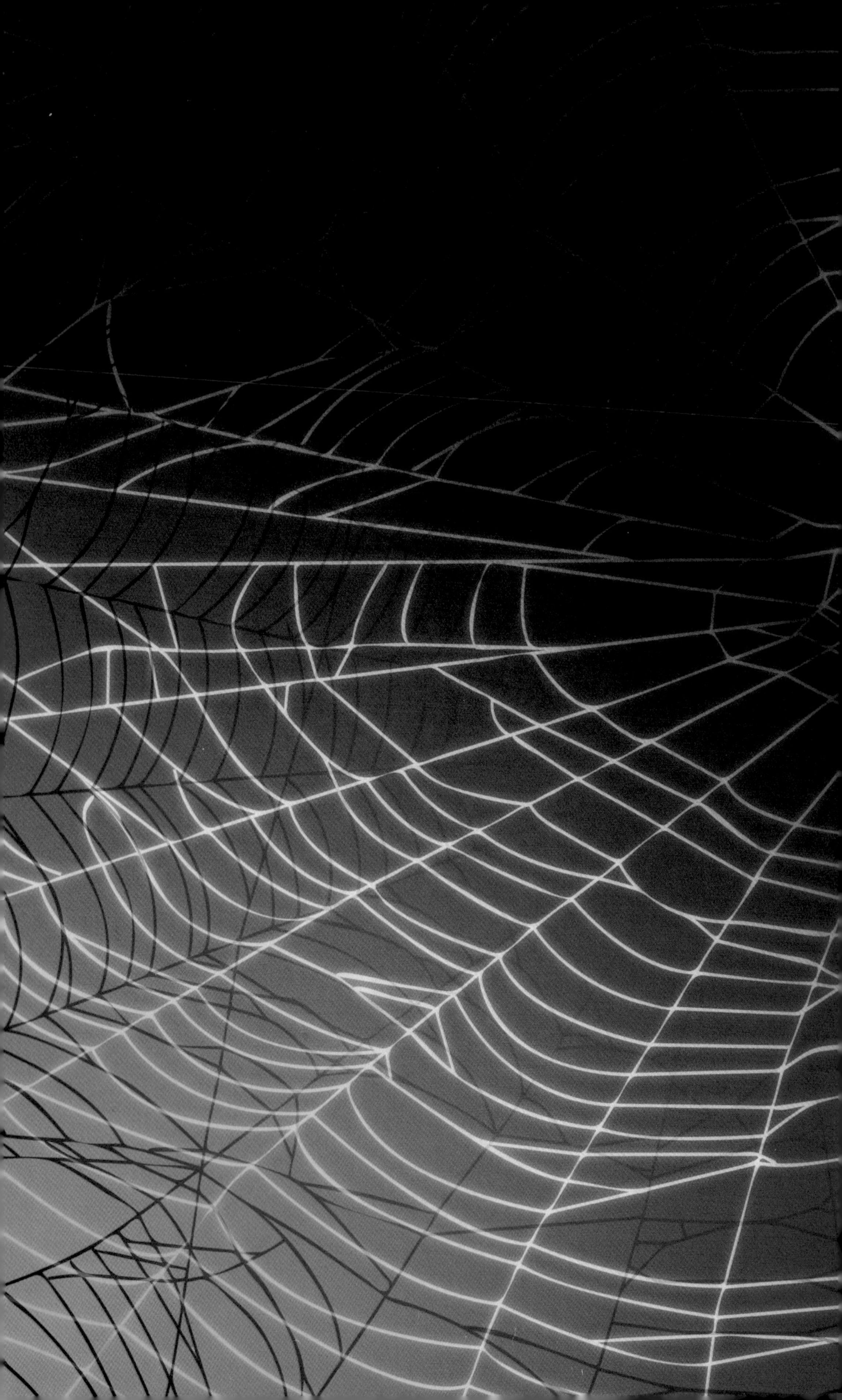

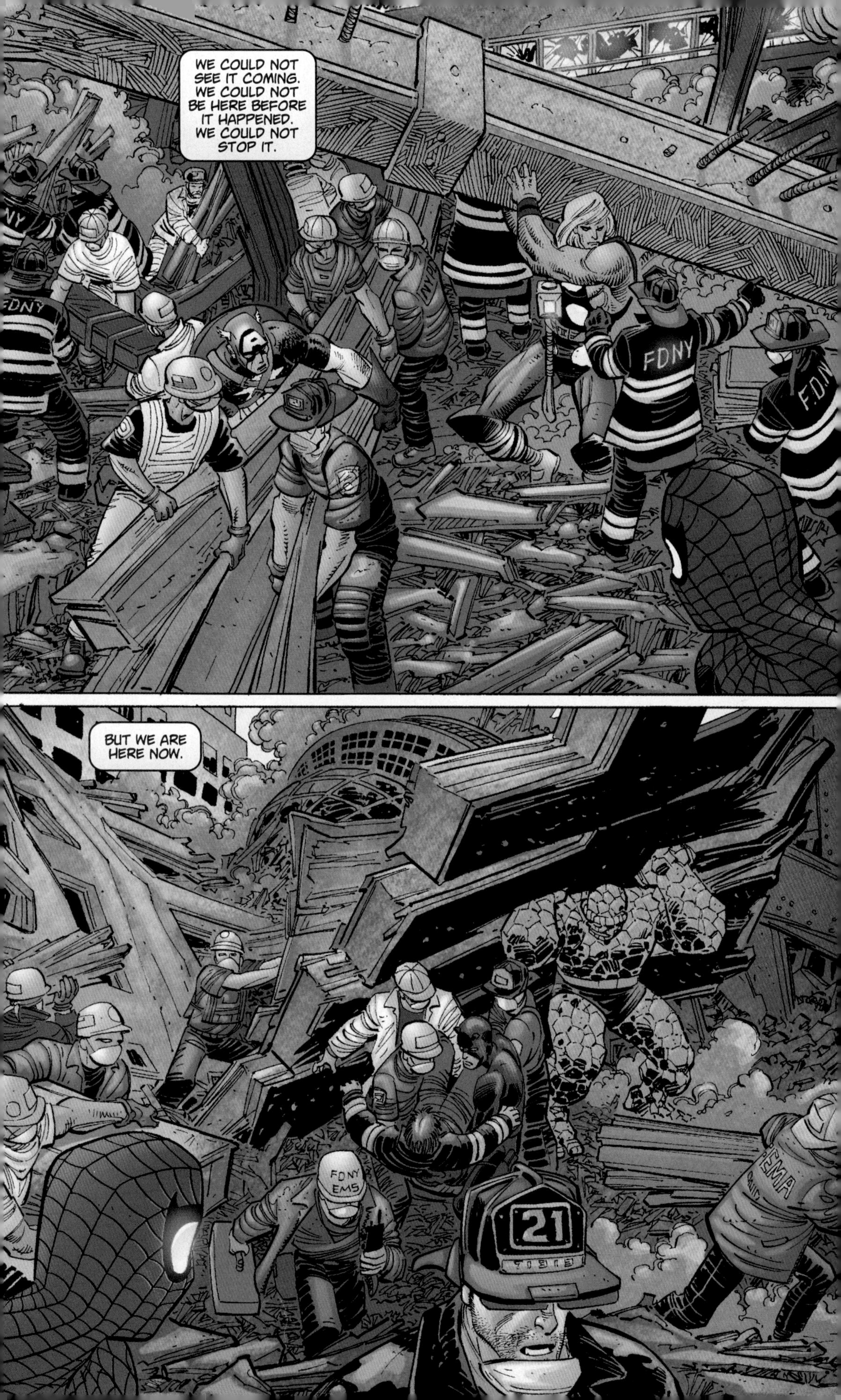
WE COULD NOT SEE IT COMING. WE COULD NOT BE HERE BEFORE IT HAPPENED. WE COULD NOT STOP IT.
BUT WE ARE HERE NOW.

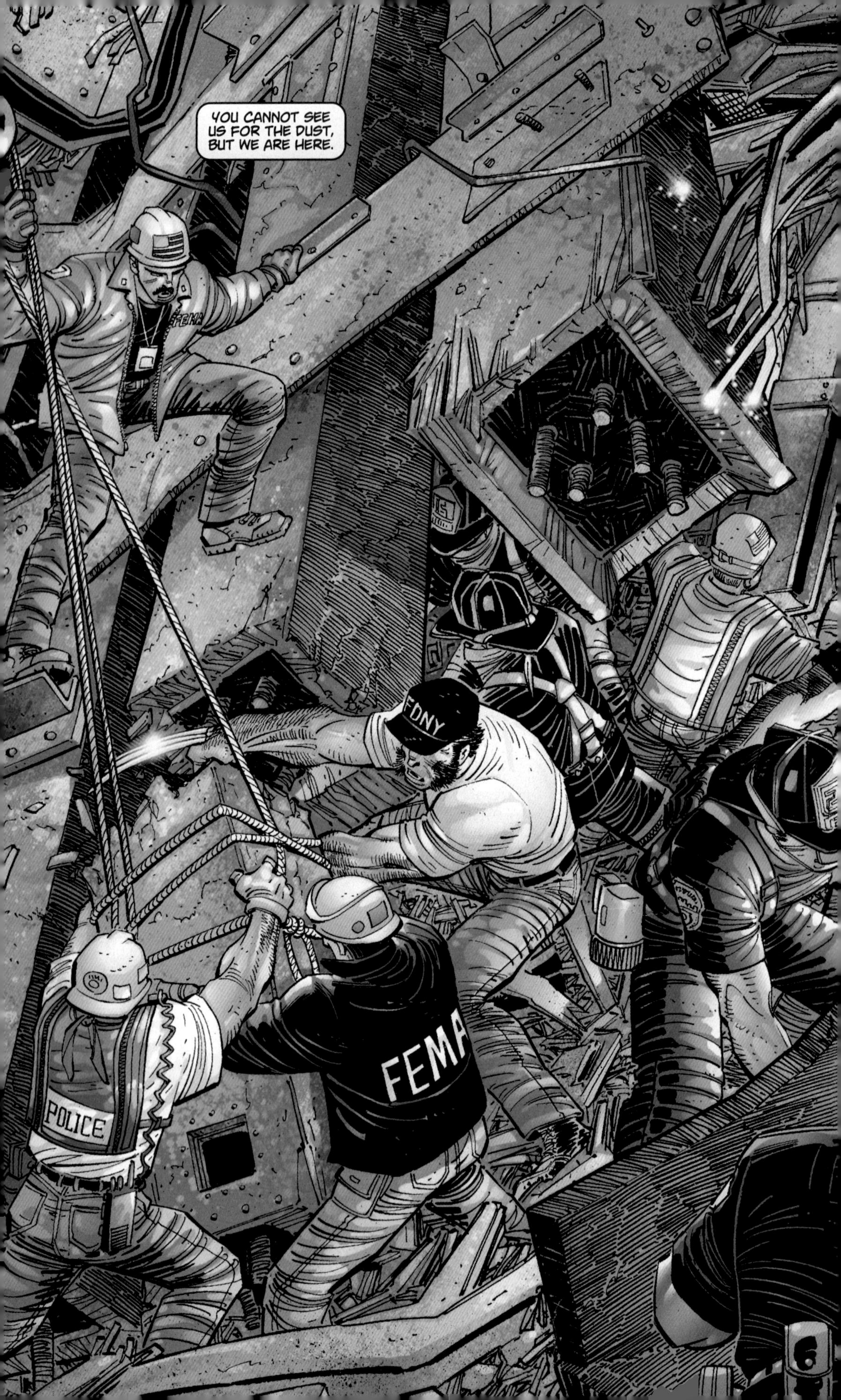

YOU CANNOT SEE US FOR THE DUST, BUT WE ARE HERE.
FDNY
FEMA
POLICE

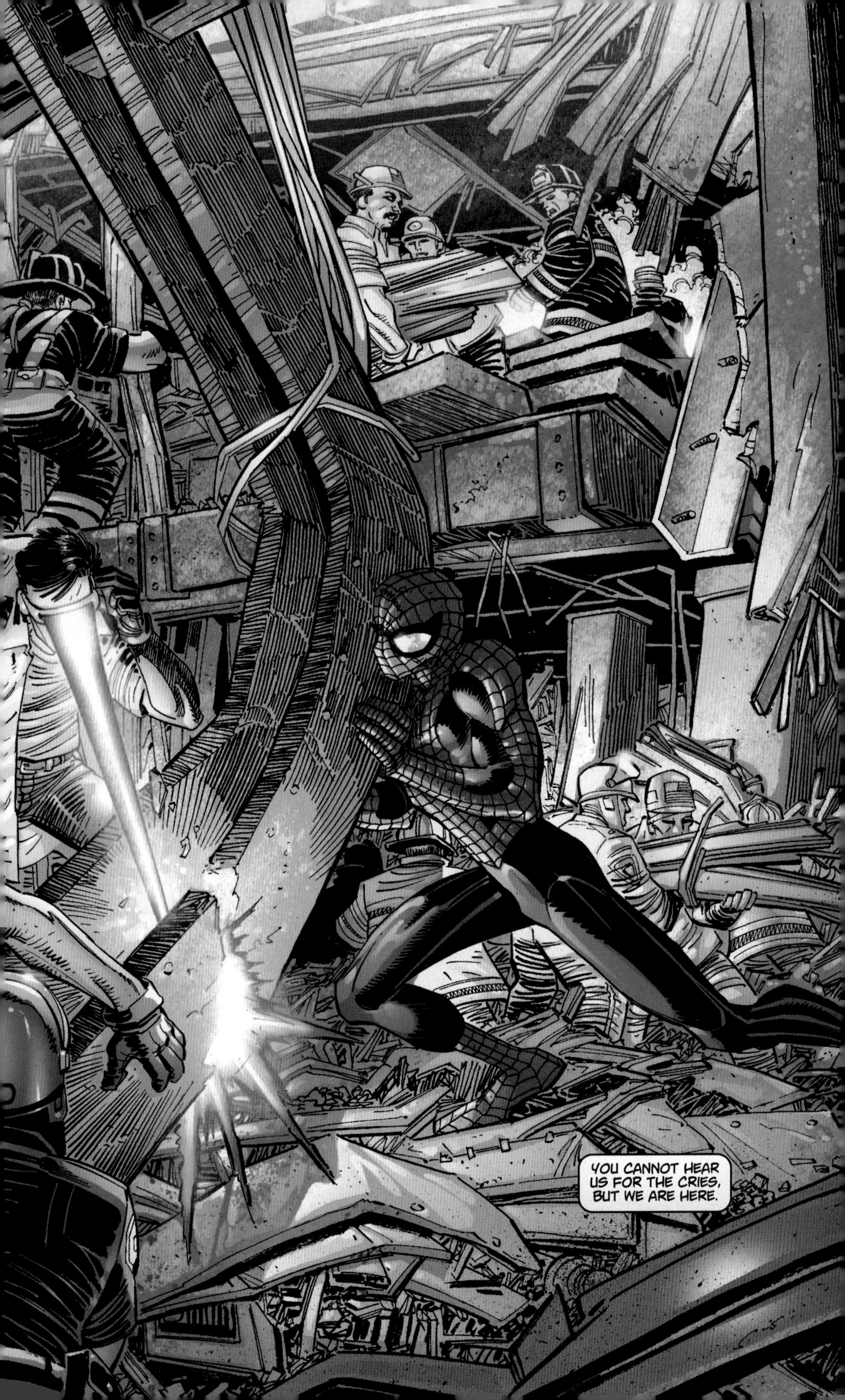
YOU CANNOT HEAR US FOR THE CRIES, BUT WE ARE HERE.

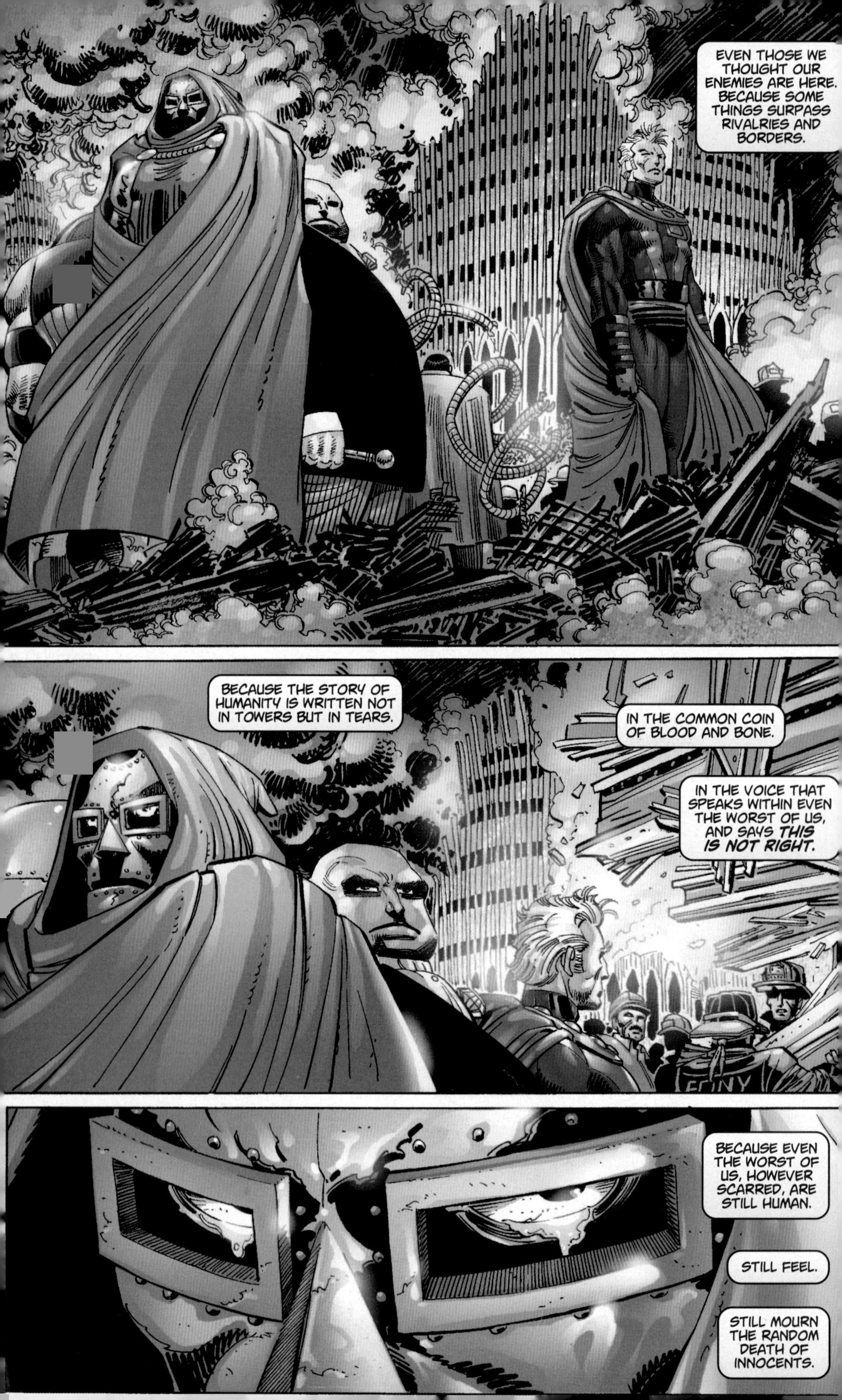
EVEN THOSE WE THOUGHT OUR ENEMIES ARE HERE. BECAUSE SOME THINGS SURPASS RIVALRIES AND BORDERS.
BECAUSE THE STORY OF HUMANITY IS WRITTEN NOT IN TOWERS BUT IN TEARS.
IN THE COMMON COIN OF BLOOD AND BONE.
IN THE VOICE THAT SPEAKS WITHIN EVEN THE WORST OF US, AND SAYS *THIS IS NOT RIGHT*.
BECAUSE EVEN THE WORST OF US, HOWEVER SCARRED, ARE STILL HUMAN.
STILL FEEL.
STILL MOURN THE RANDOM DEATH OF INNOCENTS.

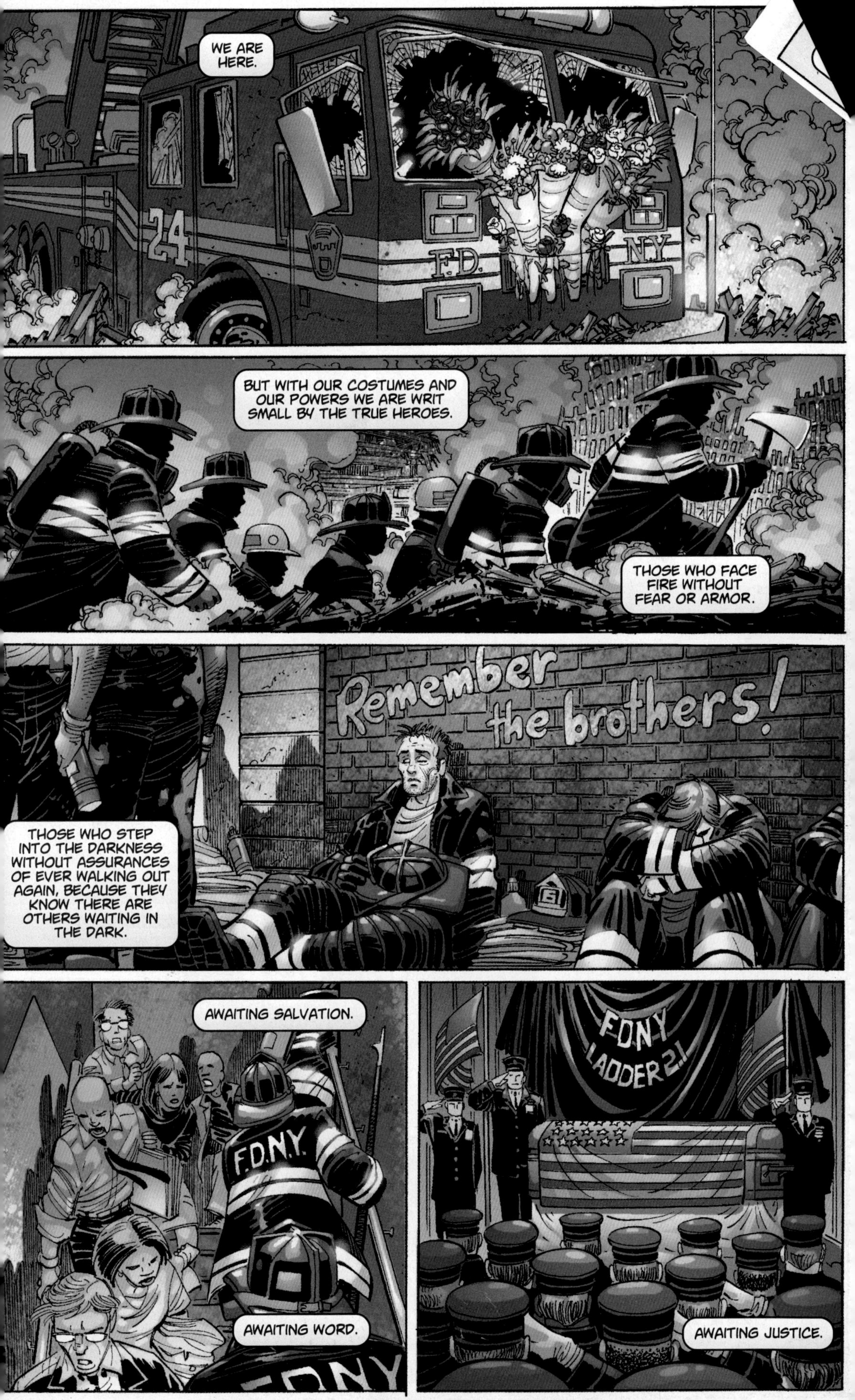
WE ARE HERE.
24
F.D.
N.Y.
BUT WITH OUR COSTUMES AND OUR POWERS WE ARE WRIT SMALL BY THE TRUE HEROES.
THOSE WHO FACE FIRE WITHOUT FEAR OR ARMOR.
Remember the brothers!
THOSE WHO STEP INTO THE DARKNESS WITHOUT ASSURANCES OF EVER WALKING OUT AGAIN, BECAUSE THEY KNOW THERE ARE OTHERS WAITING IN THE DARK.
AWAITING SALVATION.
F.D.N.Y.
AWAITING WORD.
FDNY
LADDER 21
AWAITING JUSTICE.

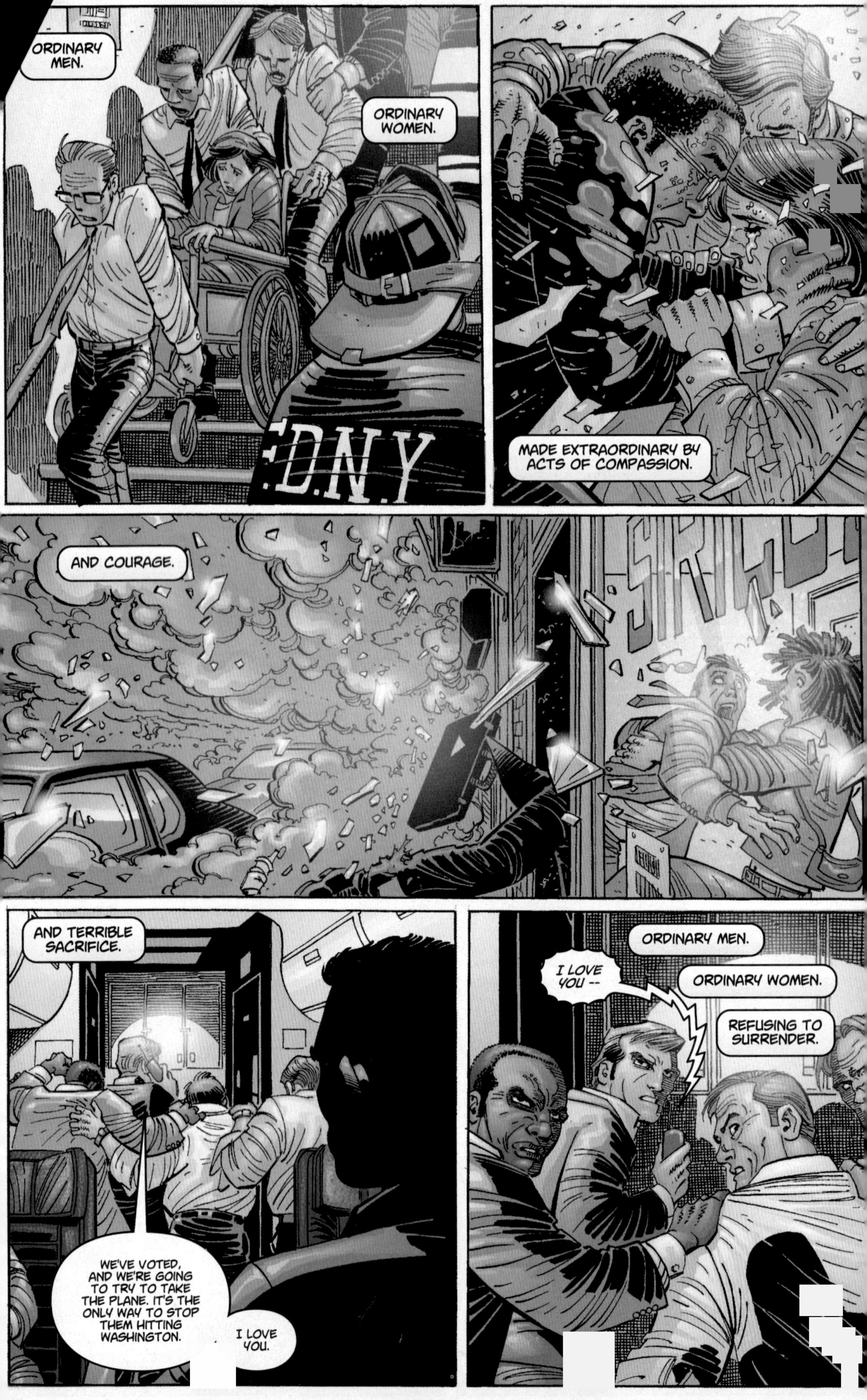
ORDINARY MEN.
ORDINARY WOMEN.
F.D.N.Y
MADE EXTRAORDINARY BY ACTS OF COMPASSION.
AND COURAGE.
AND TERRIBLE SACRIFICE.
WE'VE VOTED, AND WE'RE GOING TO TRY TO TAKE THE PLANE. IT'S THE ONLY WAY TO STOP THEM HITTING WASHINGTON.
I LOVE YOU.
ORDINARY MEN.
I LOVE YOU --
ORDINARY WOMEN.
REFUSING TO SURRENDER.

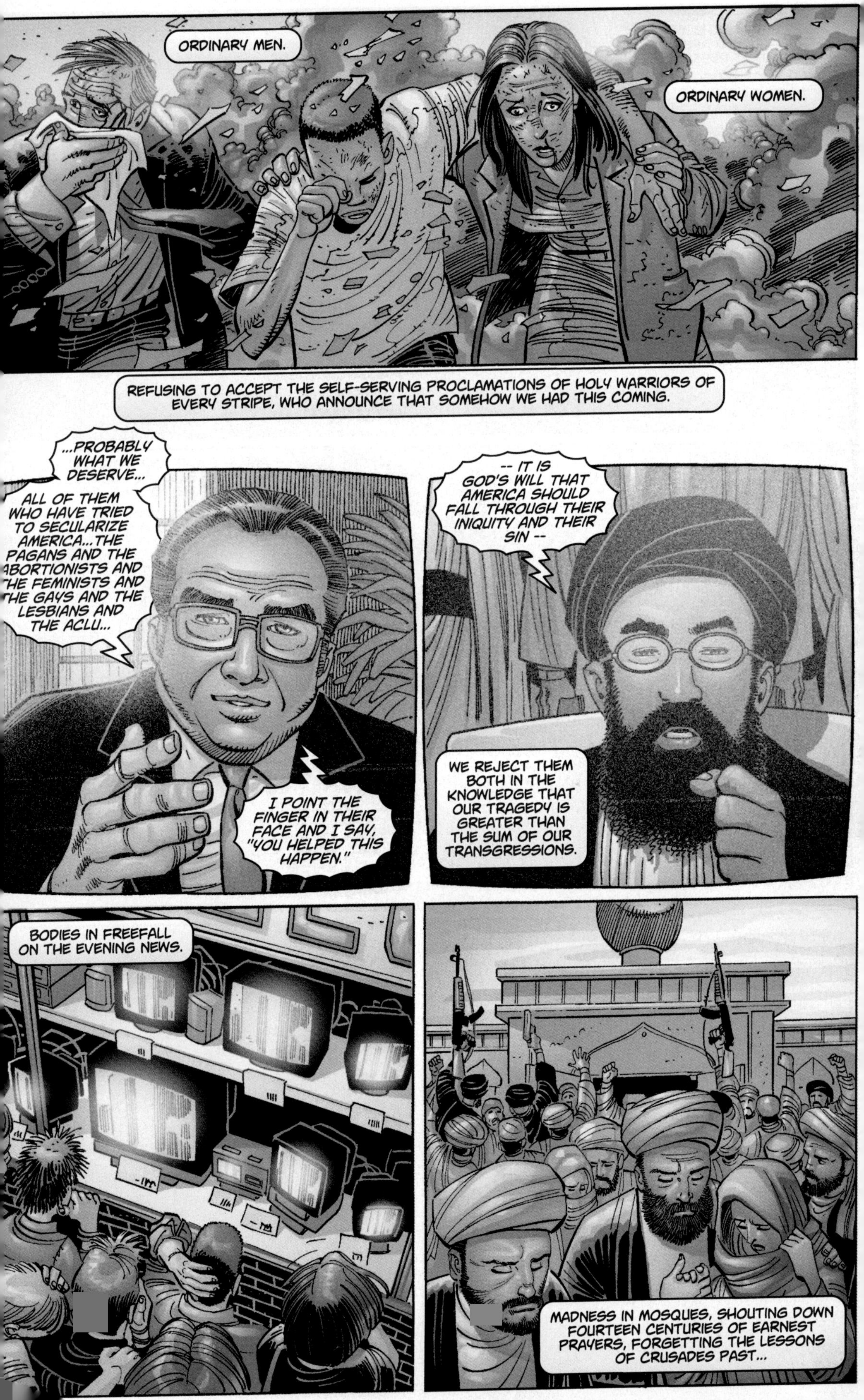
ORDINARY MEN.
ORDINARY WOMEN.
REFUSING TO ACCEPT THE SELF-SERVING PROCLAMATIONS OF HOLY WARRIORS OF EVERY STRIPE, WHO ANNOUNCE THAT SOMEHOW WE HAD THIS COMING.
...PROBABLY WHAT WE DESERVE...
ALL OF THEM WHO HAVE TRIED TO SECULARIZE AMERICA...THE PAGANS AND THE ABORTIONISTS AND THE FEMINISTS AND THE GAYS AND THE LESBIANS AND THE ACLU...
I POINT THE FINGER IN THEIR FACE AND I SAY, "YOU HELPED THIS HAPPEN."
-- IT IS GOD'S WILL THAT AMERICA SHOULD FALL THROUGH THEIR INIQUITY AND THEIR SIN --
WE REJECT THEM BOTH IN THE KNOWLEDGE THAT OUR TRAGEDY IS GREATER THAN THE SUM OF OUR TRANSGRESSIONS.
BODIES IN FREEFALL ON THE EVENING NEWS.
MADNESS IN MOSQUES, SHOUTING DOWN FOURTEEN CENTURIES OF EARNEST PRAYERS, FORGETTING THE LESSONS OF CRUSADES PAST...

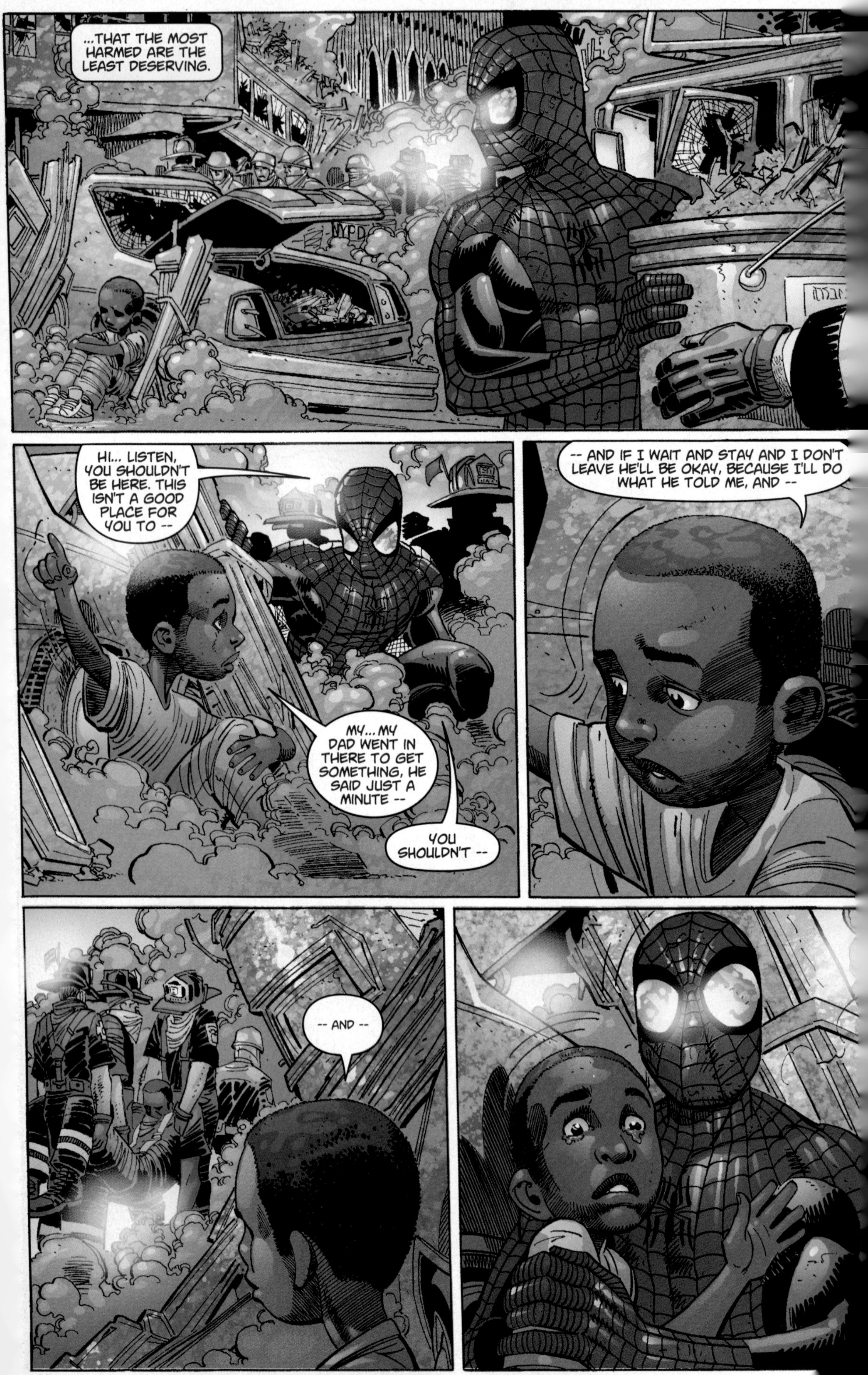
...THAT THE MOST HARMED ARE THE LEAST DESERVING.
NYPD
HI... LISTEN, YOU SHOULDN'T BE HERE. THIS ISN'T A GOOD PLACE FOR YOU TO --
MY... MY DAD WENT IN THERE TO GET SOMETHING, HE SAID JUST A MINUTE --
YOU SHOULDN'T --
-- AND IF I WAIT AND STAY AND I DON'T LEAVE HE'LL BE OKAY, BECAUSE I'LL DO WHAT HE TOLD ME, AND --
-- AND --

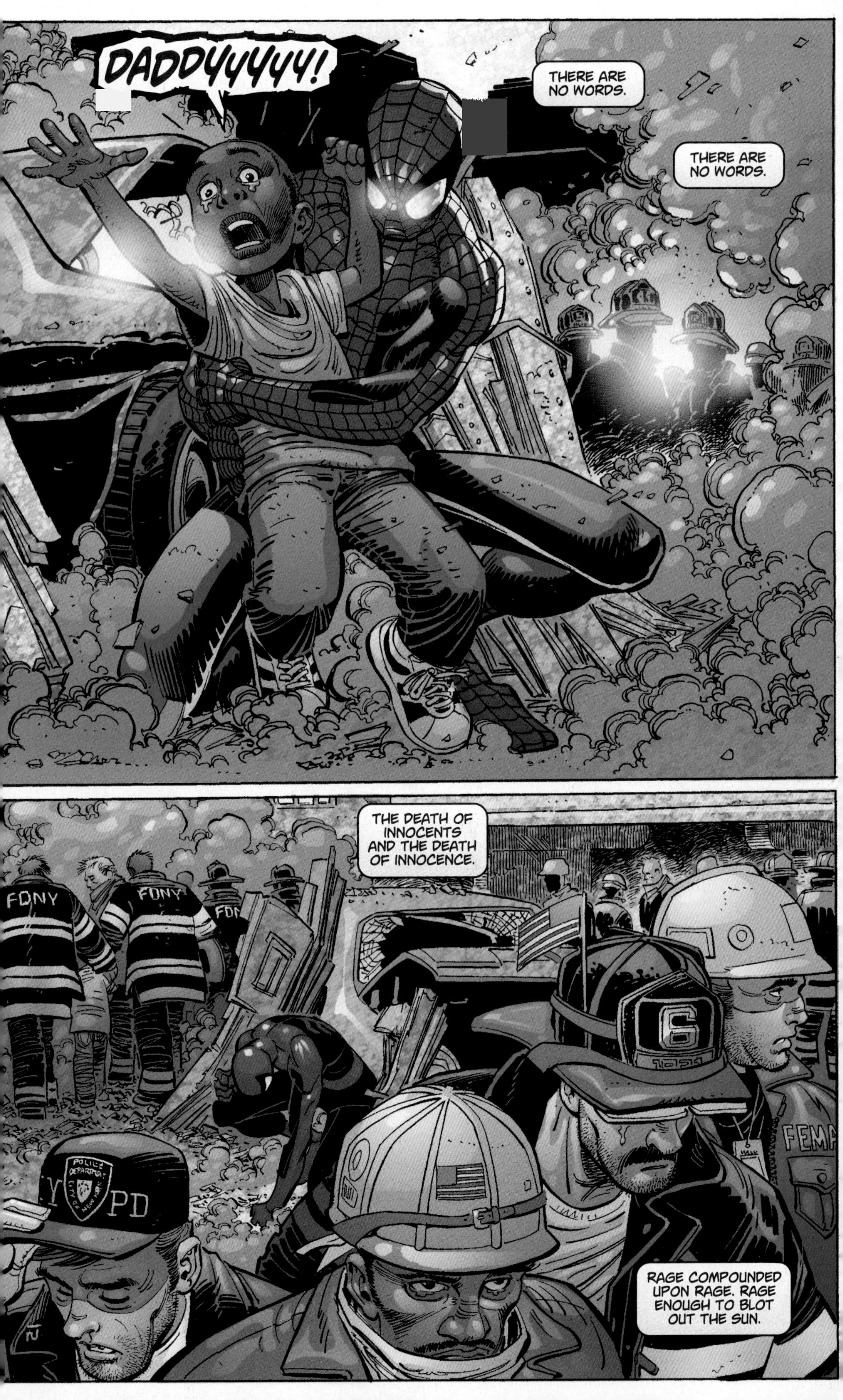
DADDYYYYY!
THERE ARE NO WORDS.
THERE ARE NO WORDS.
THE DEATH OF INNOCENTS AND THE DEATH OF INNOCENCE.
FDNY
FDNY
6
POLICE DEPARTMENT
PD
FEMA
RAGE COMPOUNDED UPON RAGE. RAGE ENOUGH TO BLOT OUT THE SUN.

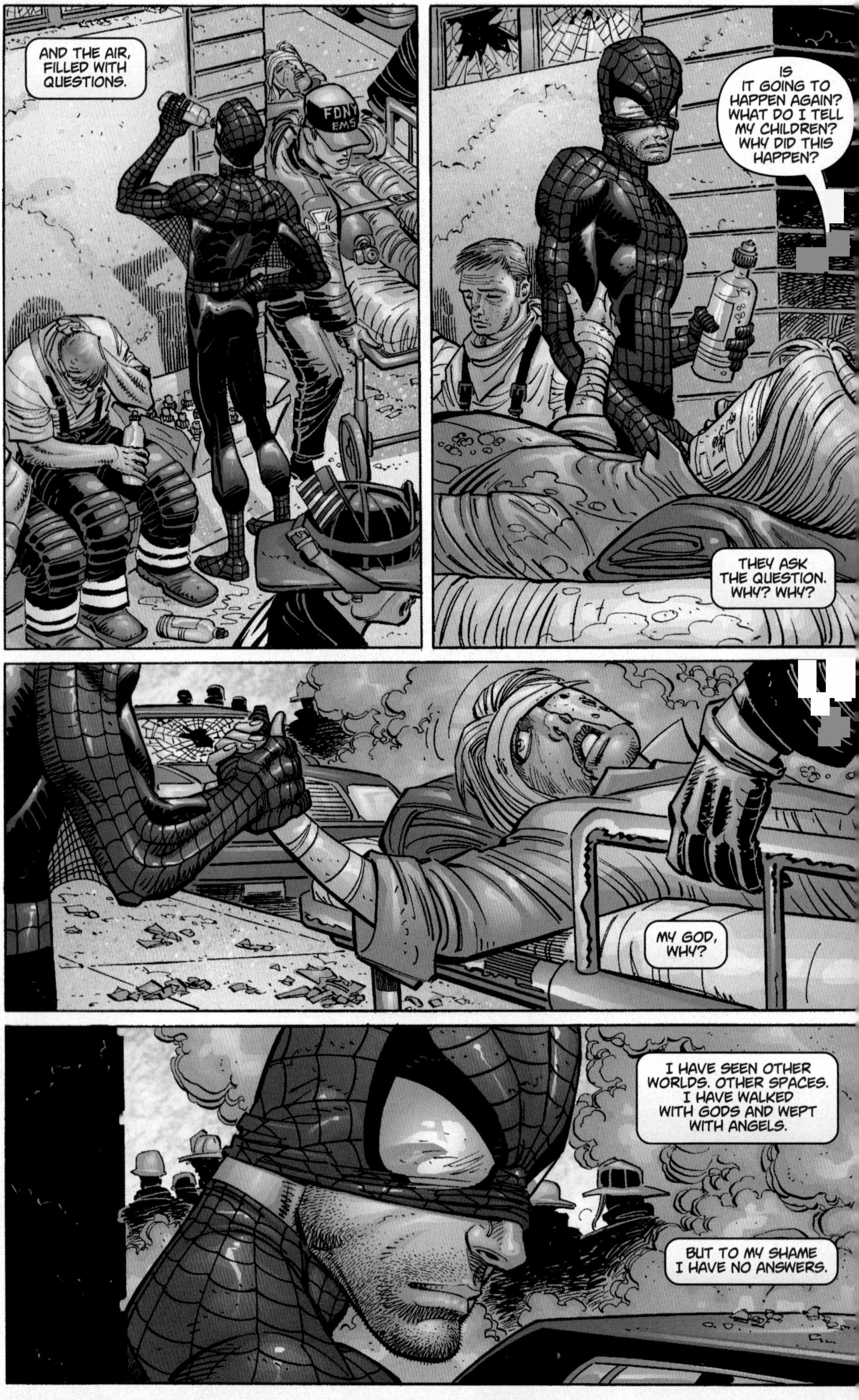
AND THE AIR, FILLED WITH QUESTIONS.
FDNY EMS
IS IT GOING TO HAPPEN AGAIN? WHAT DO I TELL MY CHILDREN? WHY DID THIS HAPPEN?
THEY ASK THE QUESTION. WHY? WHY?
MY GOD, WHY?
I HAVE SEEN OTHER WORLDS. OTHER SPACES. I HAVE WALKED WITH GODS AND WEPT WITH ANGELS.
BUT TO MY SHAME I HAVE NO ANSWERS.

HE'S THE ONLY ONE WHO COULD KNOW. BECAUSE HE'S BEEN HERE BEFORE.

I WISH I HAD NOT LIVED TO SEE THIS ONCE.

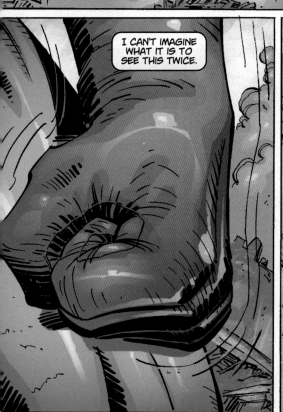

I CAN'T IMAGINE WHAT IT IS TO SEE THIS TWICE.

I JUST CAN'T IMAGINE.

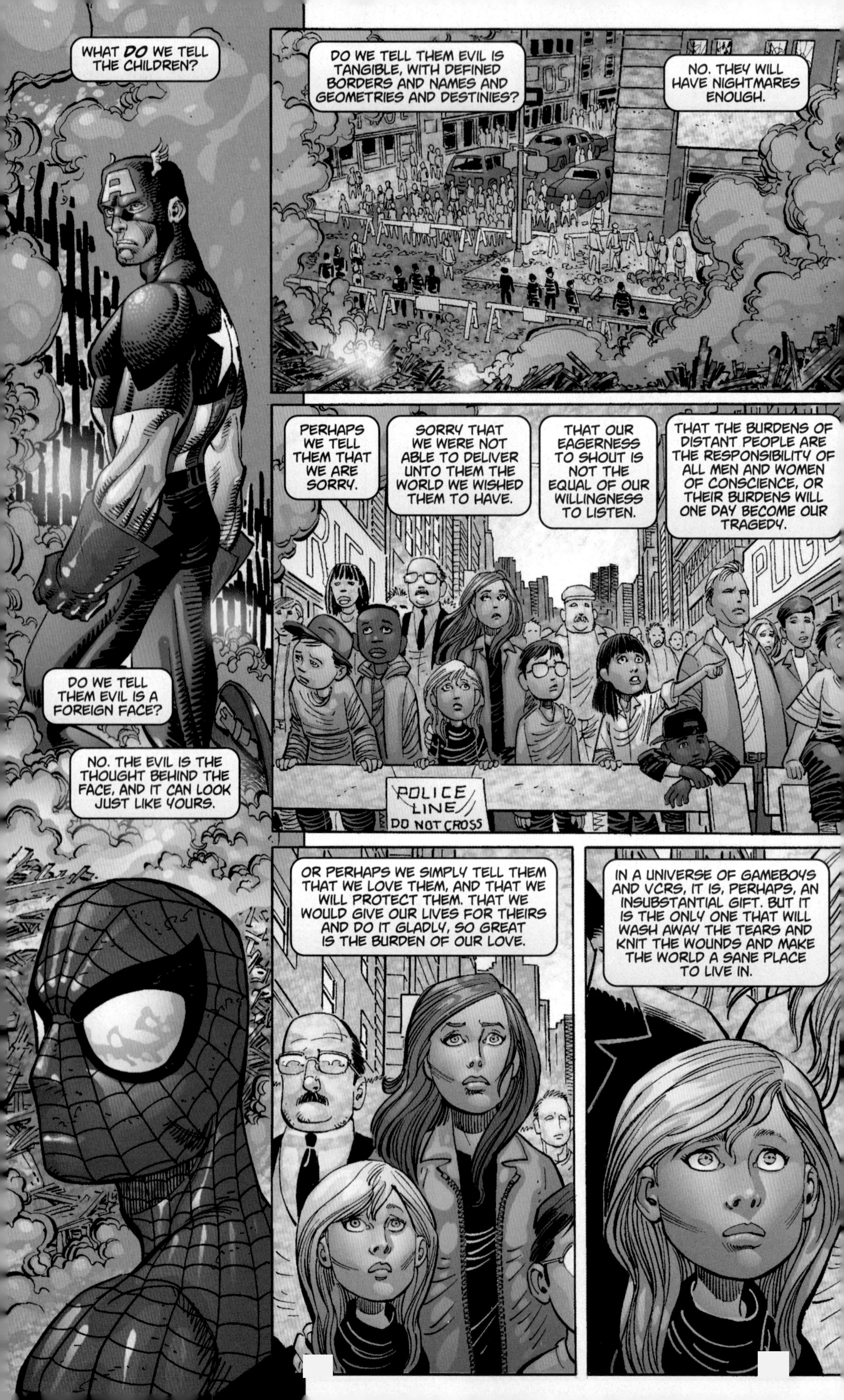

WHAT DO WE TELL THE CHILDREN?
DO WE TELL THEM EVIL IS TANGIBLE, WITH DEFINED BORDERS AND NAMES AND GEOMETRIES AND DESTINIES?
NO. THEY WILL HAVE NIGHTMARES ENOUGH.
DO WE TELL THEM EVIL IS A FOREIGN FACE?
NO. THE EVIL IS THE THOUGHT BEHIND THE FACE, AND IT CAN LOOK JUST LIKE YOURS.
PERHAPS WE TELL THEM THAT WE ARE SORRY.
SORRY THAT WE WERE NOT ABLE TO DELIVER UNTO THEM THE WORLD WE WISHED THEM TO HAVE.
THAT OUR EAGERNESS TO SHOUT IS NOT THE EQUAL OF OUR WILLINGNESS TO LISTEN.
THAT THE BURDENS OF DISTANT PEOPLE ARE THE RESPONSIBILITY OF ALL MEN AND WOMEN OF CONSCIENCE, OR THEIR BURDENS WILL ONE DAY BECOME OUR TRAGEDY.
POLICE LINE DO NOT CROSS
OR PERHAPS WE SIMPLY TELL THEM THAT WE LOVE THEM, AND THAT WE WILL PROTECT THEM. THAT WE WOULD GIVE OUR LIVES FOR THEIRS AND DO IT GLADLY, SO GREAT IS THE BURDEN OF OUR LOVE.
IN A UNIVERSE OF GAMEBOYS AND VCRS, IT IS, PERHAPS, AN INSUBSTANTIAL GIFT. BUT IT IS THE ONLY ONE THAT WILL WASH AWAY THE TEARS AND KNIT THE WOUNDS AND MAKE THE WORLD A SANE PLACE TO LIVE IN.

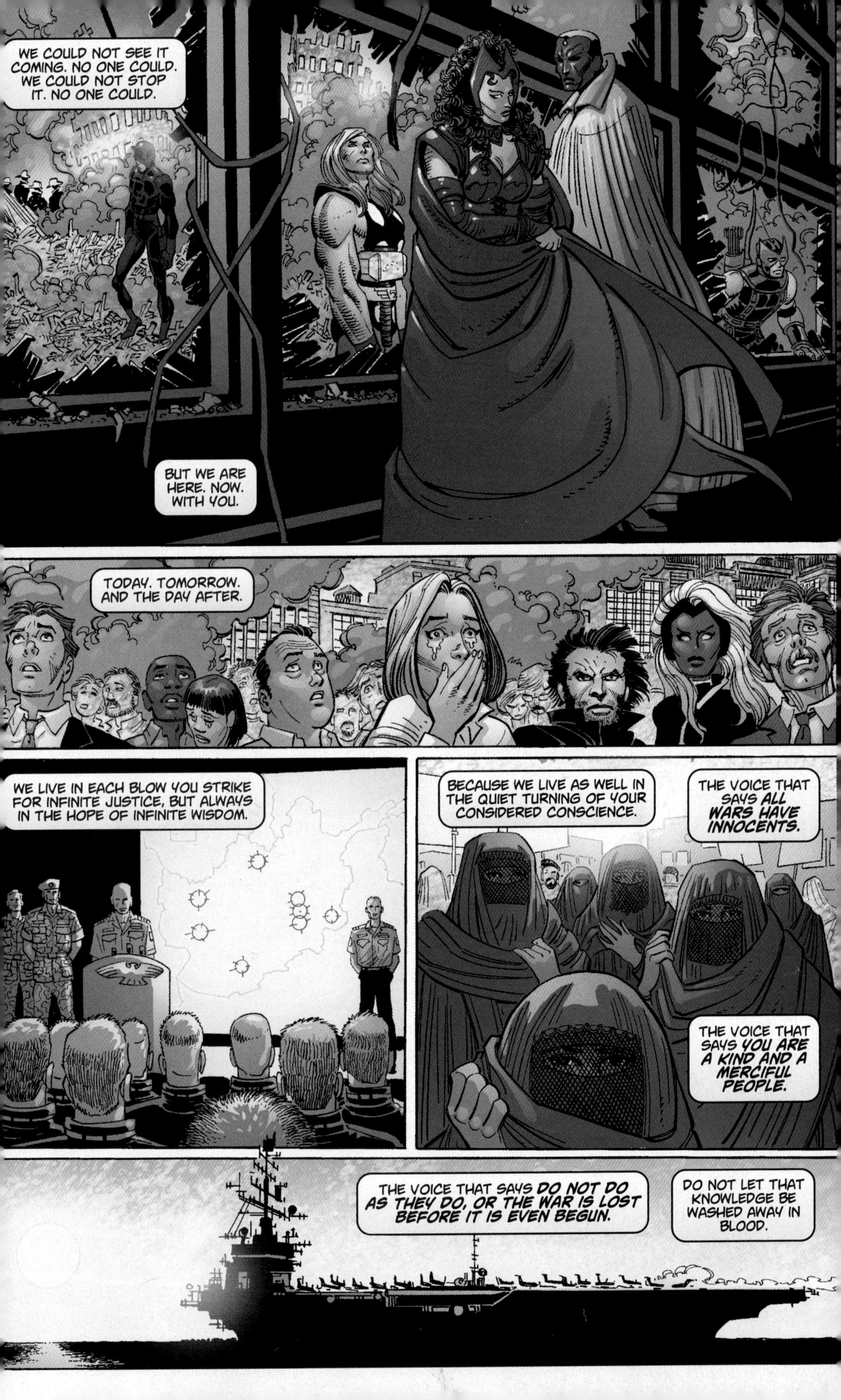

WE COULD NOT SEE IT COMING. NO ONE COULD. WE COULD NOT STOP IT. NO ONE COULD.
BUT WE ARE HERE. NOW. WITH YOU.
TODAY. TOMORROW. AND THE DAY AFTER.
WE LIVE IN EACH BLOW YOU STRIKE FOR INFINITE JUSTICE, BUT ALWAYS IN THE HOPE OF INFINITE WISDOM.
BECAUSE WE LIVE AS WELL IN THE QUIET TURNING OF YOUR CONSIDERED CONSCIENCE.
THE VOICE THAT SAYS *ALL WARS HAVE INNOCENTS.*
THE VOICE THAT SAYS *YOU ARE A KIND AND A MERCIFUL PEOPLE.*
THE VOICE THAT SAYS *DO NOT DO AS THEY DO, OR THE WAR IS LOST BEFORE IT IS EVEN BEGUN.*
DO NOT LET THAT KNOWLEDGE BE WASHED AWAY IN BLOOD.

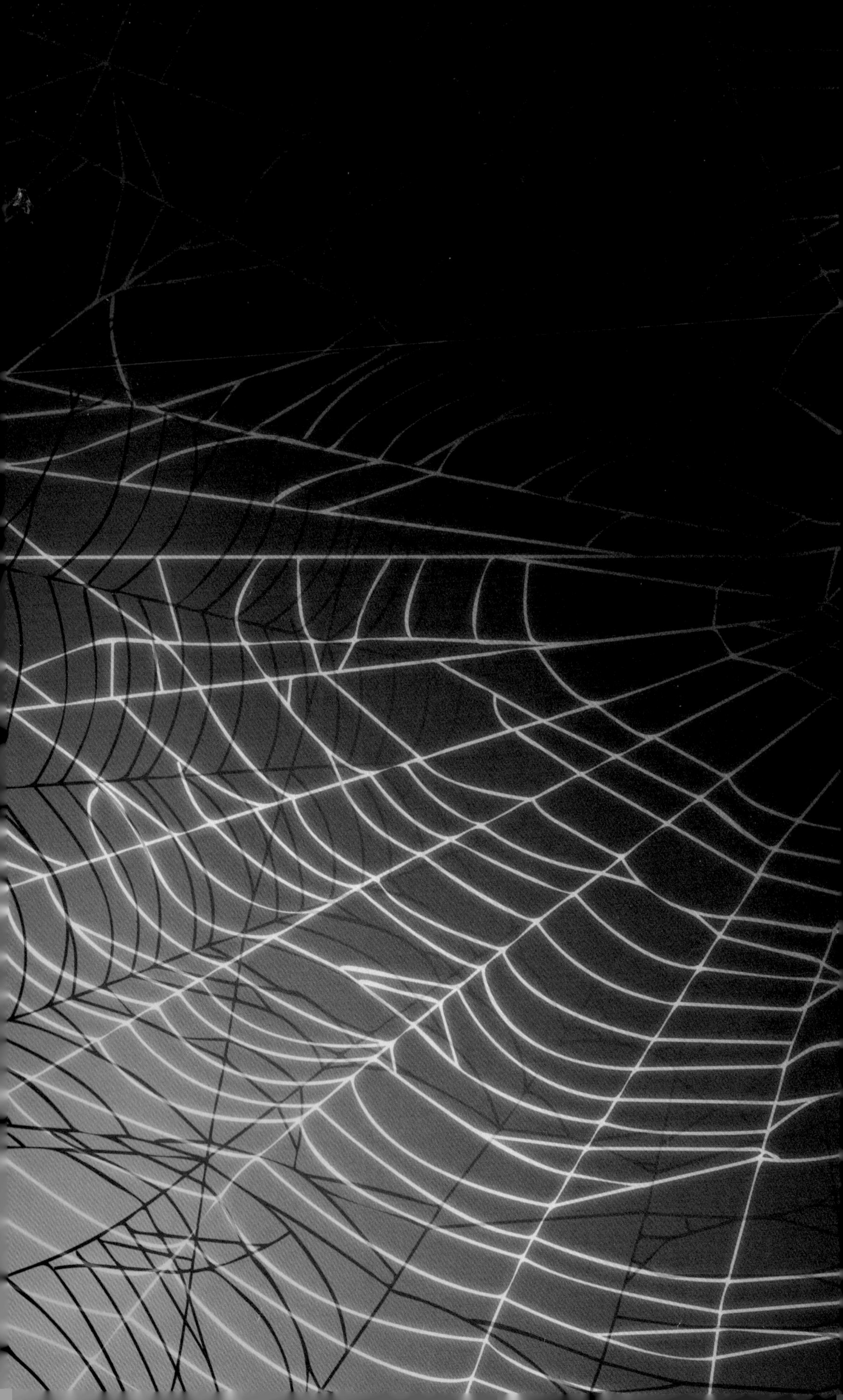

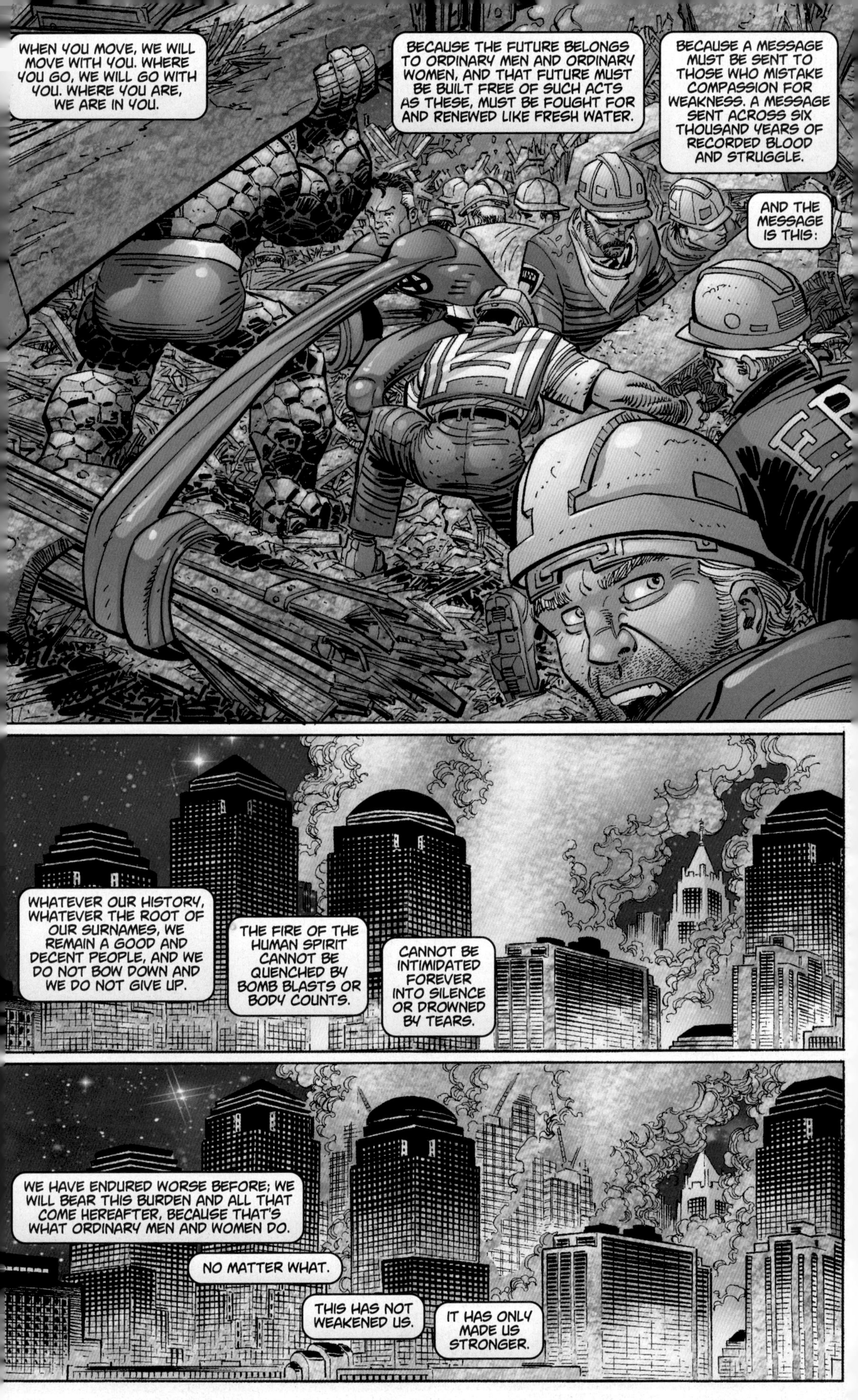
WHEN YOU MOVE, WE WILL MOVE WITH YOU. WHERE YOU GO, WE WILL GO WITH YOU. WHERE YOU ARE, WE ARE IN YOU.
BECAUSE THE FUTURE BELONGS TO ORDINARY MEN AND ORDINARY WOMEN, AND THAT FUTURE MUST BE BUILT FREE OF SUCH ACTS AS THESE, MUST BE FOUGHT FOR AND RENEWED LIKE FRESH WATER.
BECAUSE A MESSAGE MUST BE SENT TO THOSE WHO MISTAKE COMPASSION FOR WEAKNESS. A MESSAGE SENT ACROSS SIX THOUSAND YEARS OF RECORDED BLOOD AND STRUGGLE.
AND THE MESSAGE IS THIS:
WHATEVER OUR HISTORY, WHATEVER THE ROOT OF OUR SURNAMES, WE REMAIN A GOOD AND DECENT PEOPLE, AND WE DO NOT BOW DOWN AND WE DO NOT GIVE UP.
THE FIRE OF THE HUMAN SPIRIT CANNOT BE QUENCHED BY BOMB BLASTS OR BODY COUNTS.
CANNOT BE INTIMIDATED FOREVER INTO SILENCE OR DROWNED BY TEARS.
WE HAVE ENDURED WORSE BEFORE; WE WILL BEAR THIS BURDEN AND ALL THAT COME HEREAFTER, BECAUSE THAT'S WHAT ORDINARY MEN AND WOMEN DO.
NO MATTER WHAT.
THIS HAS NOT WEAKENED US.
IT HAS ONLY MADE US STRONGER.

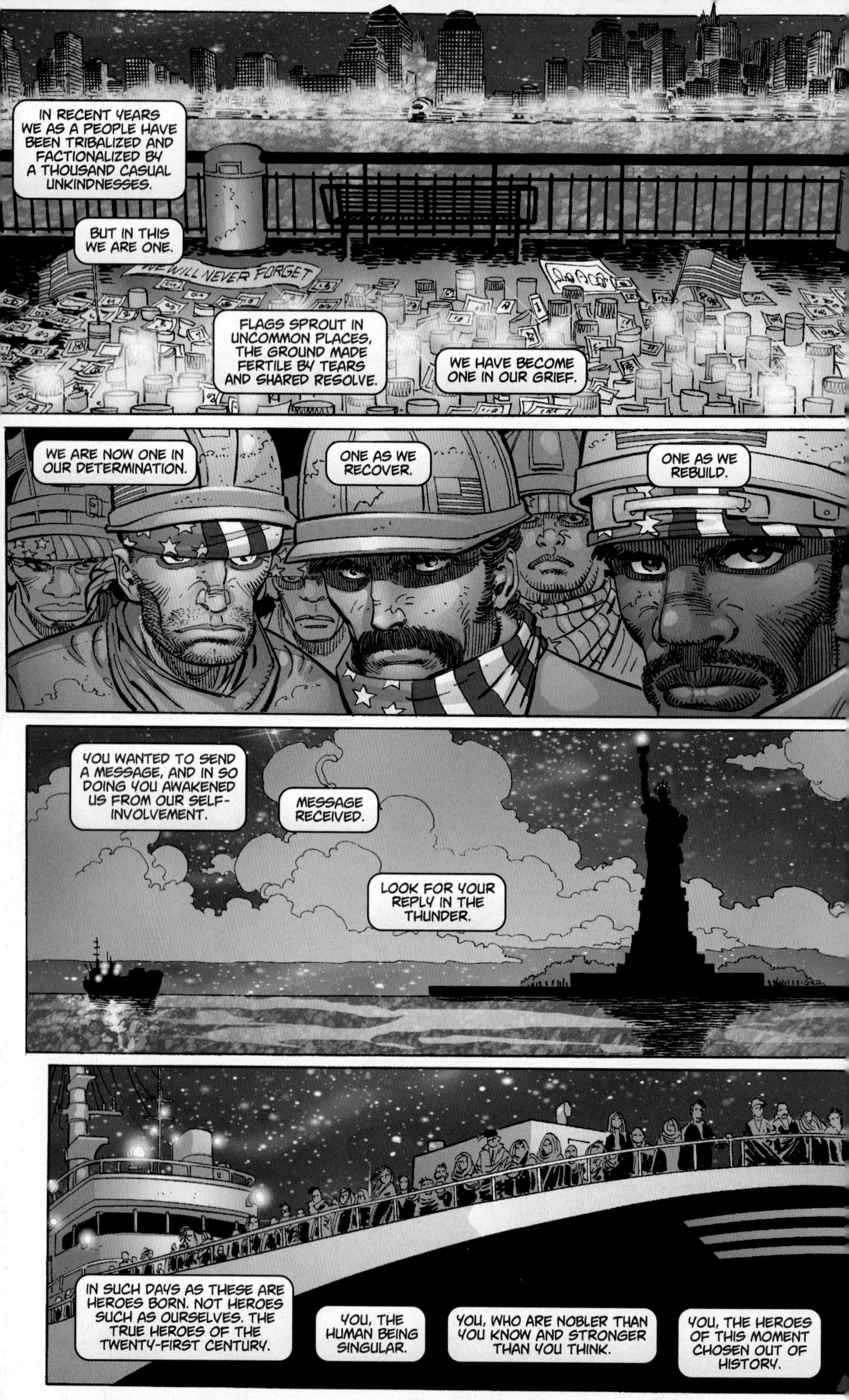
IN RECENT YEARS WE AS A PEOPLE HAVE BEEN TRIBALIZED AND FACTIONALIZED BY A THOUSAND CASUAL UNKINDNESSES.
BUT IN THIS WE ARE ONE.
WE WILL NEVER FORGET
FLAGS SPROUT IN UNCOMMON PLACES, THE GROUND MADE FERTILE BY TEARS AND SHARED RESOLVE.
WE HAVE BECOME ONE IN OUR GRIEF.
WE ARE NOW ONE IN OUR DETERMINATION.
ONE AS WE RECOVER.
ONE AS WE REBUILD.
YOU WANTED TO SEND A MESSAGE, AND IN SO DOING YOU AWAKENED US FROM OUR SELF-INVOLVEMENT.
MESSAGE RECEIVED.
LOOK FOR YOUR REPLY IN THE THUNDER.
IN SUCH DAYS AS THESE ARE HEROES BORN. NOT HEROES SUCH AS OURSELVES. THE TRUE HEROES OF THE TWENTY-FIRST CENTURY.
YOU, THE HUMAN BEING SINGULAR.
YOU, WHO ARE NOBLER THAN YOU KNOW AND STRONGER THAN YOU THINK.
YOU, THE HEROES OF THIS MOMENT CHOSEN OUT OF HISTORY.

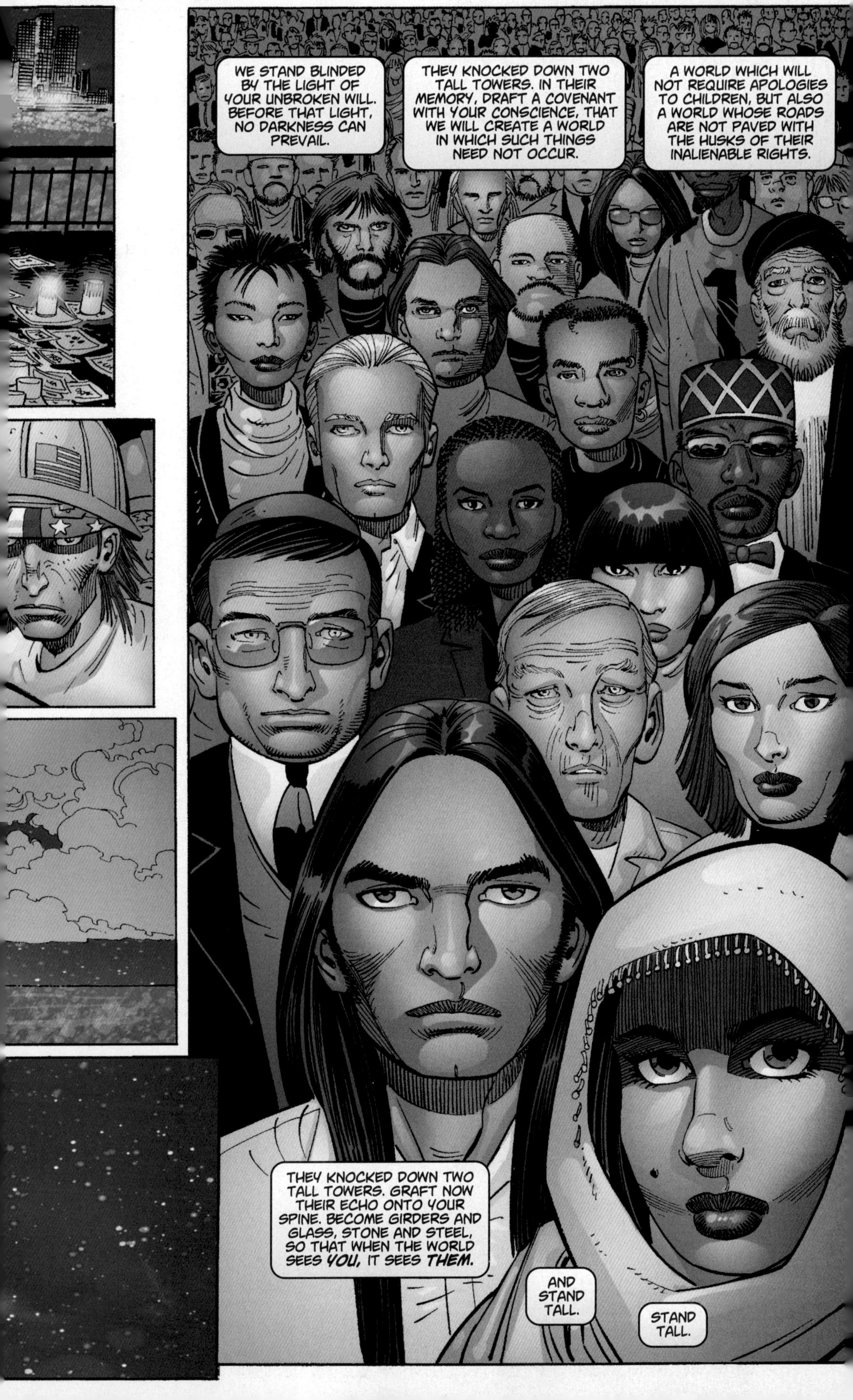
WE STAND BLINDED BY THE LIGHT OF YOUR UNBROKEN WILL. BEFORE THAT LIGHT, NO DARKNESS CAN PREVAIL.
THEY KNOCKED DOWN TWO TALL TOWERS. IN THEIR MEMORY, DRAFT A COVENANT WITH YOUR CONSCIENCE, THAT WE WILL CREATE A WORLD IN WHICH SUCH THINGS NEED NOT OCCUR.
A WORLD WHICH WILL NOT REQUIRE APOLOGIES TO CHILDREN, BUT ALSO A WORLD WHOSE ROADS ARE NOT PAVED WITH THE HUSKS OF THEIR INALIENABLE RIGHTS.
THEY KNOCKED DOWN TWO TALL TOWERS. GRAFT NOW THEIR ECHO ONTO YOUR SPINE. BECOME GIRDERS AND GLASS, STONE AND STEEL, SO THAT WHEN THE WORLD SEES *YOU,* IT SEES *THEM.*
AND STAND TALL.
STAND TALL.

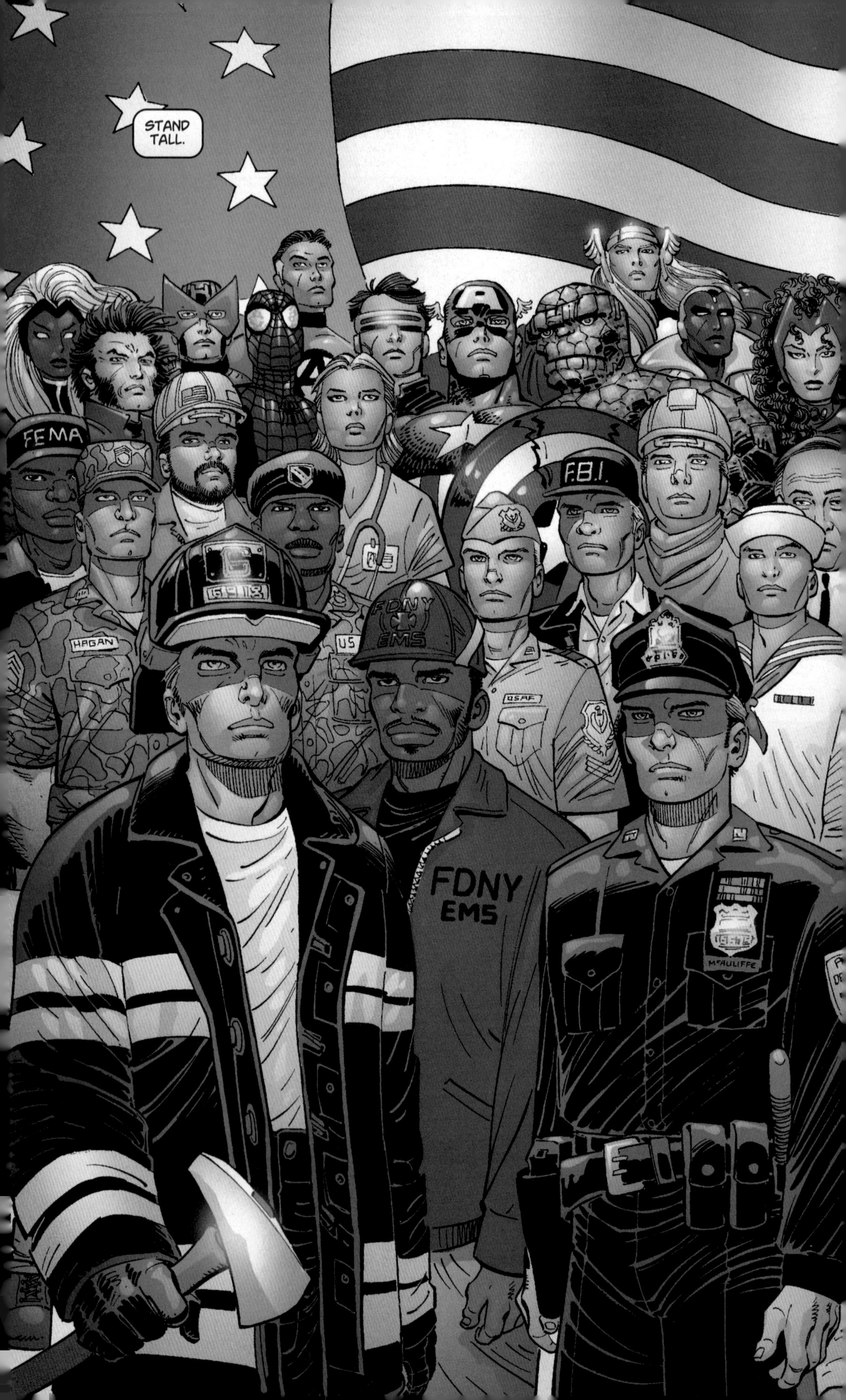
STAND TALL.
FEMA
F.B.I.
HAGAN
US
FDNY EMS
USAF
FDNY EMS
McAULIFFE

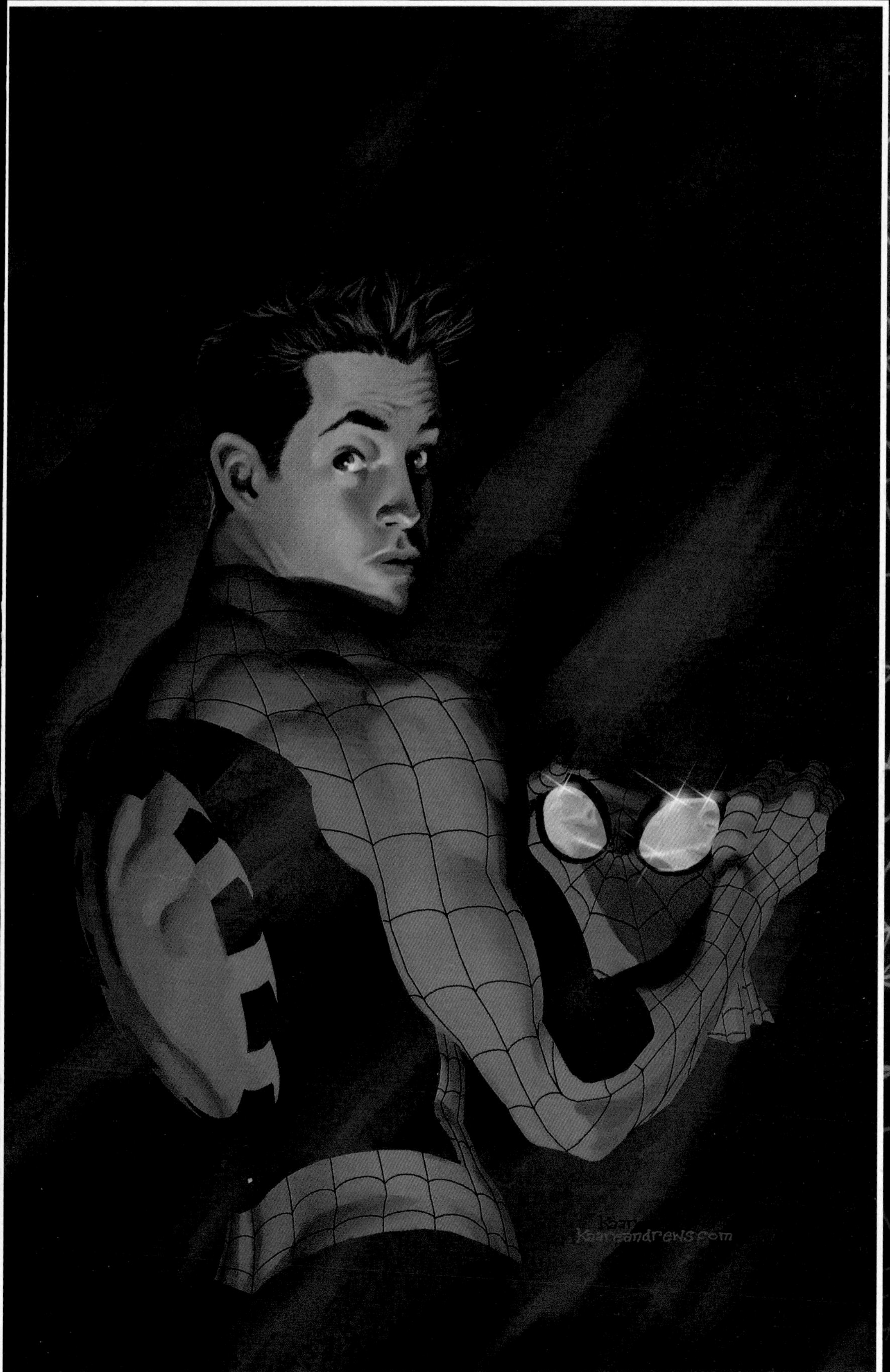
kaareandrews.com

AMAZING SPIDER-MAN #37

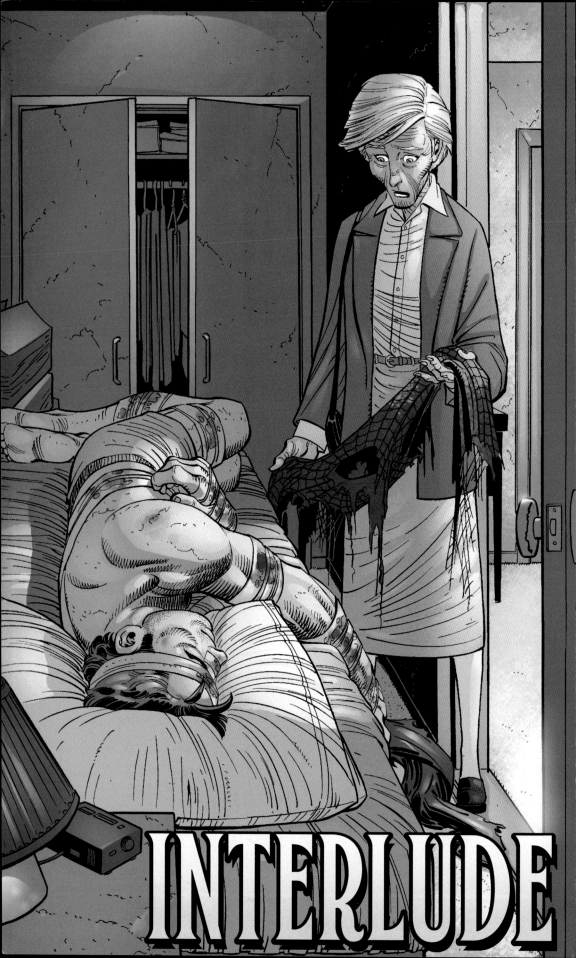

INTERLUDE

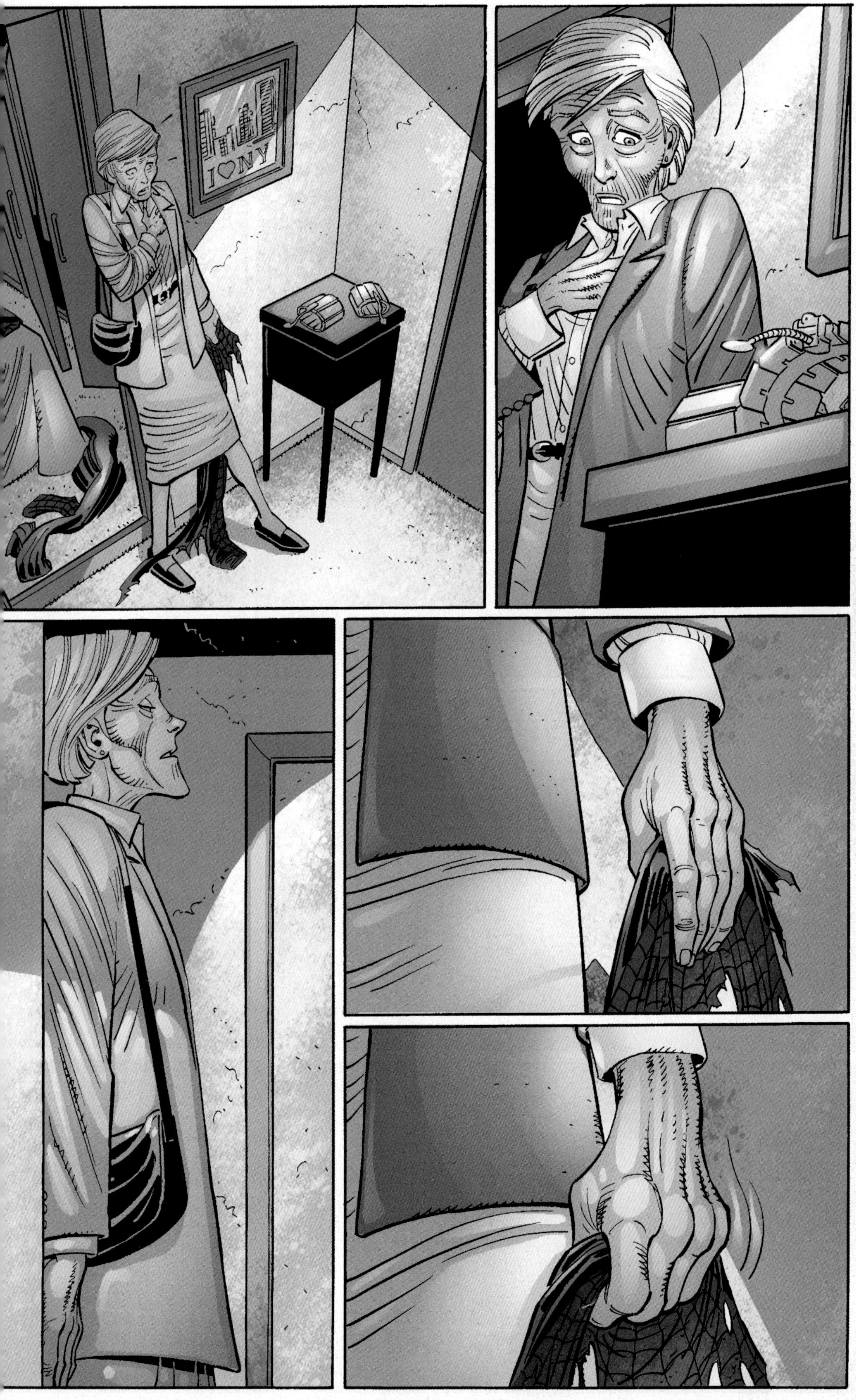
I ♥ NY

...SNORF... HURMF...

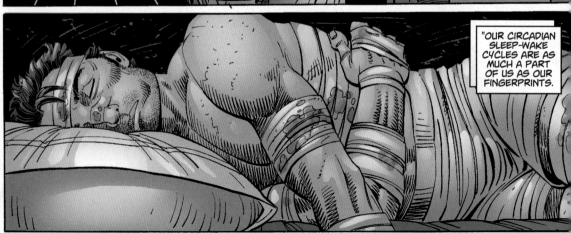

"OUR CIRCADIAN SLEEP-WAKE CYCLES ARE AS MUCH A PART OF US AS OUR FINGERPRINTS.

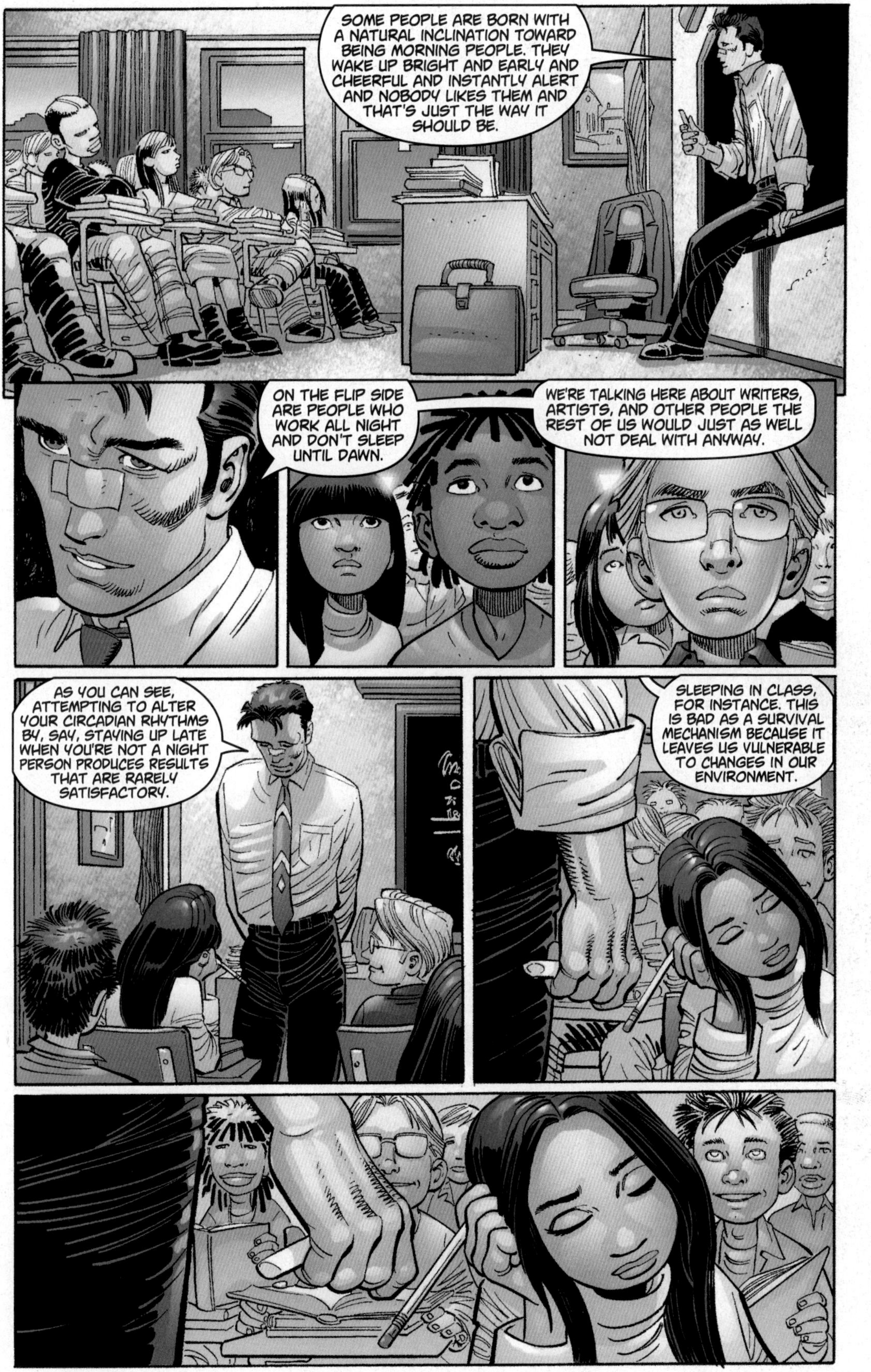

SOME PEOPLE ARE BORN WITH A NATURAL INCLINATION TOWARD BEING MORNING PEOPLE. THEY WAKE UP BRIGHT AND EARLY AND CHEERFUL AND INSTANTLY ALERT AND NOBODY LIKES THEM AND THAT'S JUST THE WAY IT SHOULD BE.
ON THE FLIP SIDE ARE PEOPLE WHO WORK ALL NIGHT AND DON'T SLEEP UNTIL DAWN.
WE'RE TALKING HERE ABOUT WRITERS, ARTISTS, AND OTHER PEOPLE THE REST OF US WOULD JUST AS WELL NOT DEAL WITH ANYWAY.
AS YOU CAN SEE, ATTEMPTING TO ALTER YOUR CIRCADIAN RHYTHMS BY, SAY, STAYING UP LATE WHEN YOU'RE NOT A NIGHT PERSON PRODUCES RESULTS THAT ARE RARELY SATISFACTORY.
SLEEPING IN CLASS, FOR INSTANCE. THIS IS BAD AS A SURVIVAL MECHANISM BECAUSE IT LEAVES US VULNERABLE TO CHANGES IN OUR ENVIRONMENT.

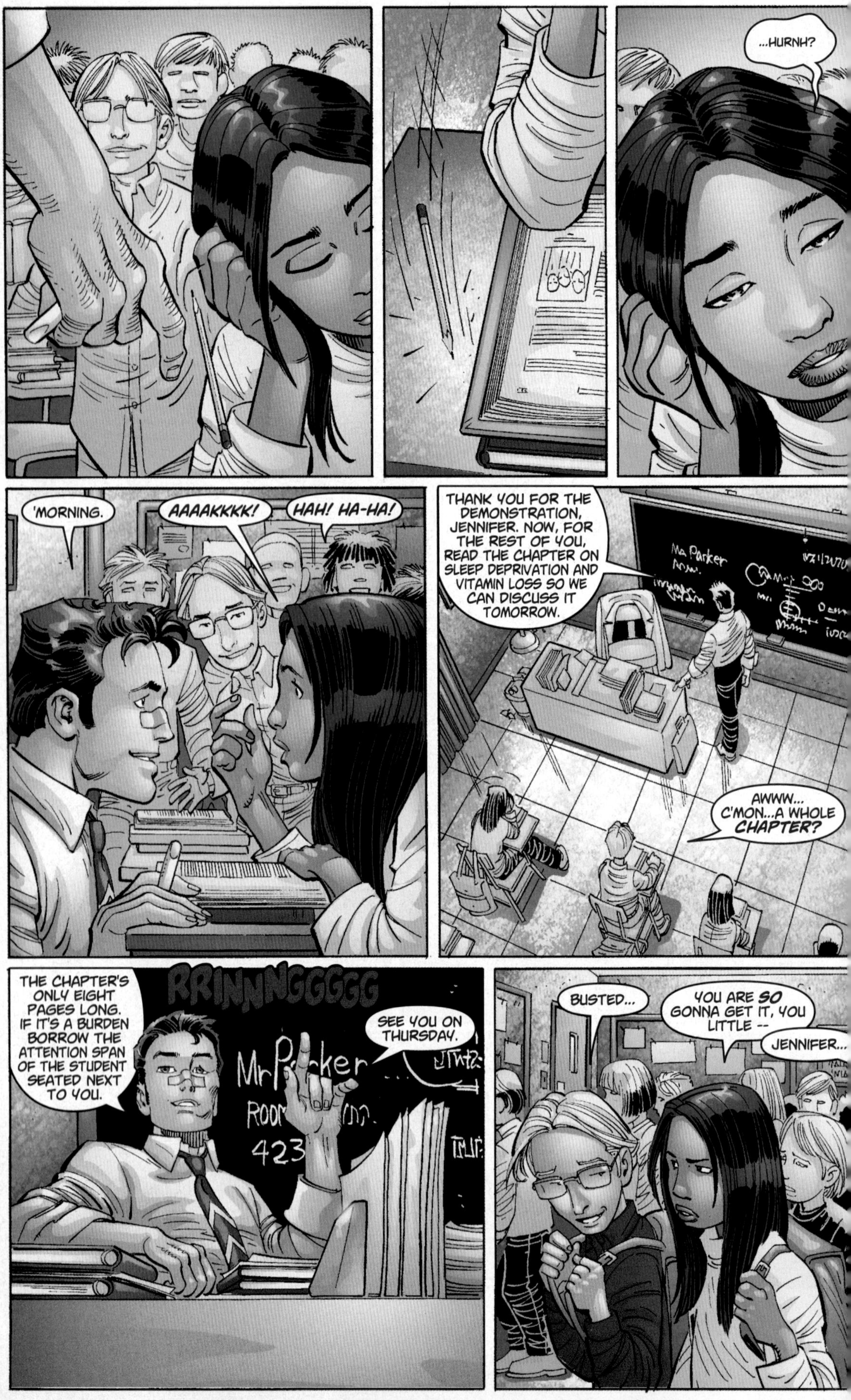

...HURNH?
'MORNING.
AAAAKKKK!
HAH! HA-HA!
THANK YOU FOR THE DEMONSTRATION, JENNIFER. NOW, FOR THE REST OF YOU, READ THE CHAPTER ON SLEEP DEPRIVATION AND VITAMIN LOSS SO WE CAN DISCUSS IT TOMORROW.
AWWW... C'MON...A WHOLE CHAPTER?
RRINNNGGGGG
THE CHAPTER'S ONLY EIGHT PAGES LONG. IF IT'S A BURDEN BORROW THE ATTENTION SPAN OF THE STUDENT SEATED NEXT TO YOU.
SEE YOU ON THURSDAY.
Mr Parker
ROOM
423
BUSTED...
YOU ARE SO GONNA GET IT, YOU LITTLE --
JENNIFER...

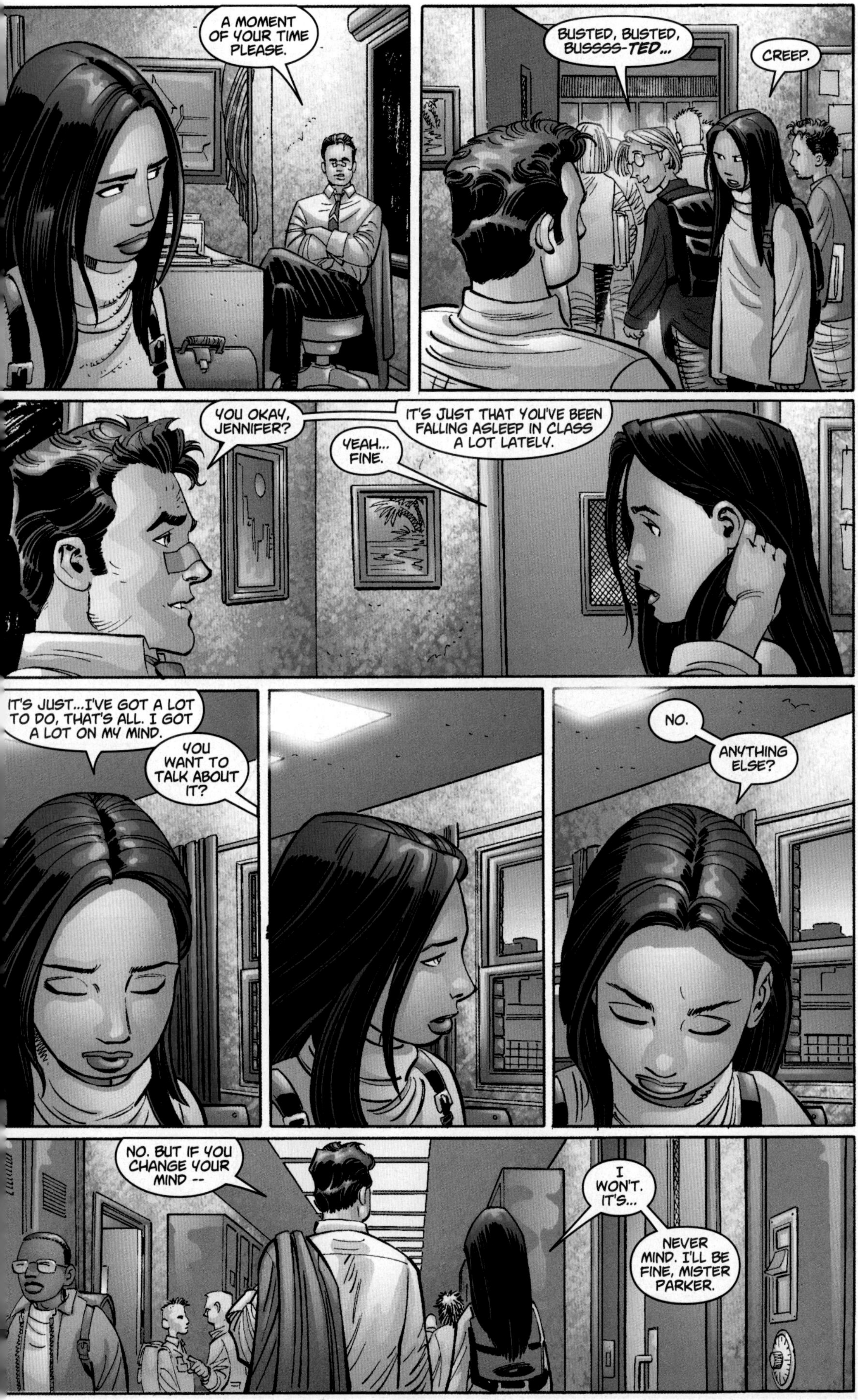
A MOMENT OF YOUR TIME PLEASE.
BUSTED, BUSTED, BUSSSS-TED...
CREEP.
YOU OKAY, JENNIFER?
YEAH... FINE.
IT'S JUST THAT YOU'VE BEEN FALLING ASLEEP IN CLASS A LOT LATELY.
IT'S JUST...I'VE GOT A LOT TO DO, THAT'S ALL. I GOT A LOT ON MY MIND.
YOU WANT TO TALK ABOUT IT?
NO.
ANYTHING ELSE?
NO. BUT IF YOU CHANGE YOUR MIND --
I WON'T. IT'S...
NEVER MIND. I'LL BE FINE, MISTER PARKER.

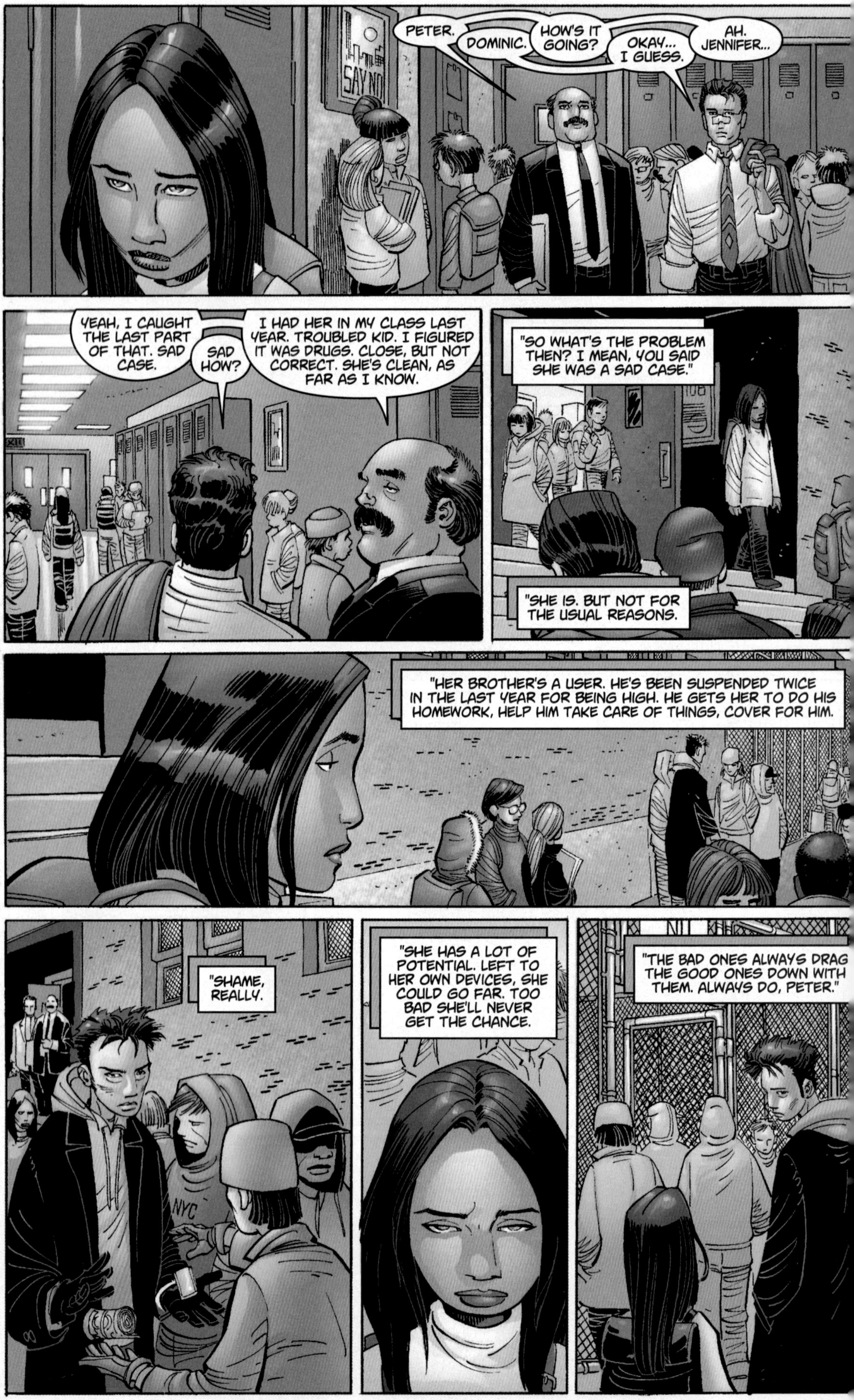

PETER.
DOMINIC.
HOW'S IT GOING?
OKAY... I GUESS.
AH. JENNIFER...
SAY NO
YEAH, I CAUGHT THE LAST PART OF THAT. SAD CASE.
SAD HOW?
I HAD HER IN MY CLASS LAST YEAR. TROUBLED KID. I FIGURED IT WAS DRUGS. CLOSE, BUT NOT CORRECT. SHE'S CLEAN, AS FAR AS I KNOW.
"SO WHAT'S THE PROBLEM THEN? I MEAN, YOU SAID SHE WAS A SAD CASE."
"SHE IS. BUT NOT FOR THE USUAL REASONS.
"HER BROTHER'S A USER. HE'S BEEN SUSPENDED TWICE IN THE LAST YEAR FOR BEING HIGH. HE GETS HER TO DO HIS HOMEWORK, HELP HIM TAKE CARE OF THINGS, COVER FOR HIM.
"SHAME, REALLY.
NYC
"SHE HAS A LOT OF POTENTIAL. LEFT TO HER OWN DEVICES, SHE COULD GO FAR. TOO BAD SHE'LL NEVER GET THE CHANCE.
"THE BAD ONES ALWAYS DRAG THE GOOD ONES DOWN WITH THEM. ALWAYS DO, PETER."

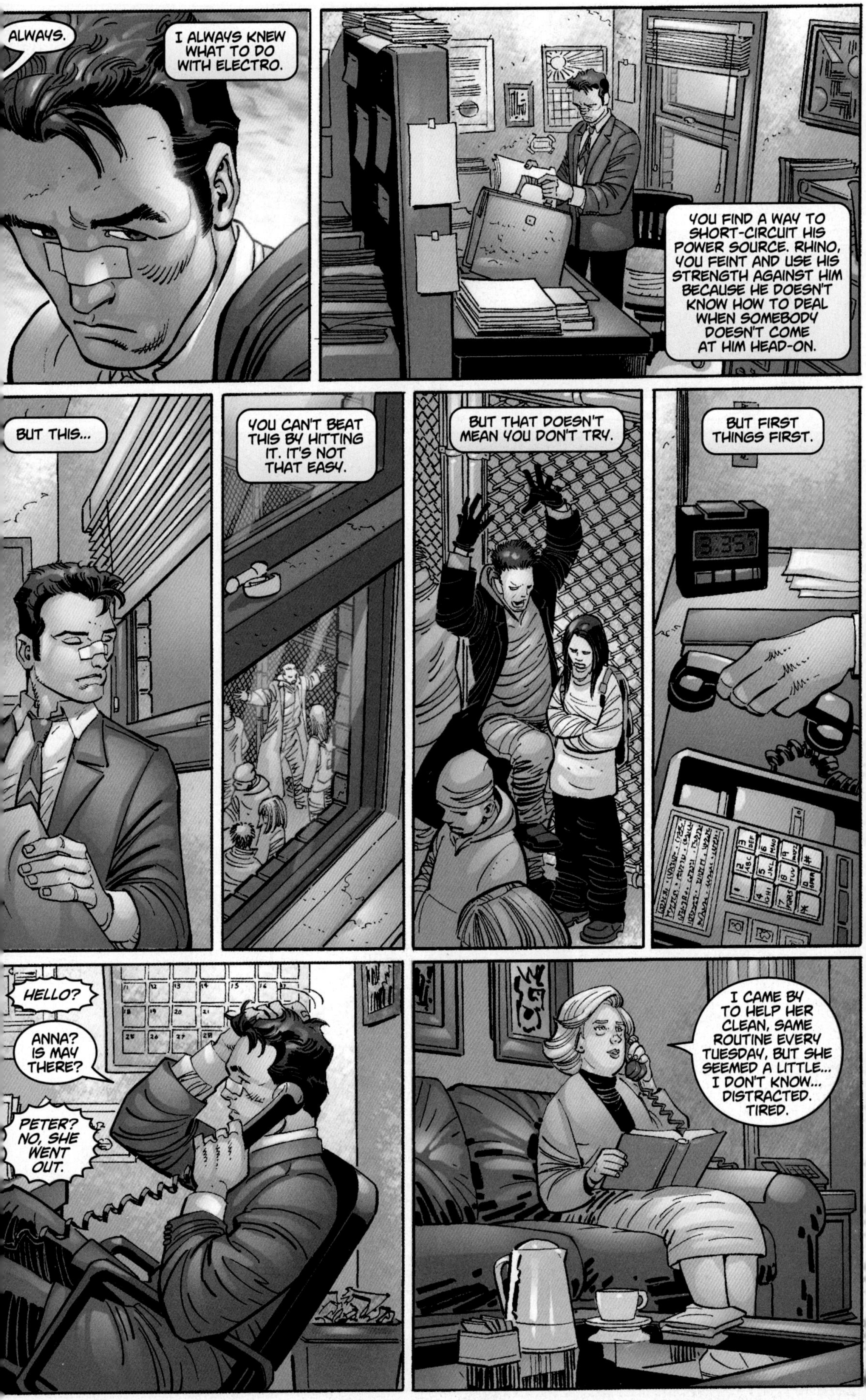
ALWAYS.
I ALWAYS KNEW WHAT TO DO WITH ELECTRO.
YOU FIND A WAY TO SHORT-CIRCUIT HIS POWER SOURCE. RHINO, YOU FEINT AND USE HIS STRENGTH AGAINST HIM BECAUSE HE DOESN'T KNOW HOW TO DEAL WHEN SOMEBODY DOESN'T COME AT HIM HEAD-ON.
BUT THIS...
YOU CAN'T BEAT THIS BY HITTING IT. IT'S NOT THAT EASY.
BUT THAT DOESN'T MEAN YOU DON'T TRY.
BUT FIRST THINGS FIRST.
HELLO?
ANNA? IS MAY THERE?
PETER? NO, SHE WENT OUT.
I CAME BY TO HELP HER CLEAN, SAME ROUTINE EVERY TUESDAY, BUT SHE SEEMED A LITTLE... I DON'T KNOW... DISTRACTED. TIRED.

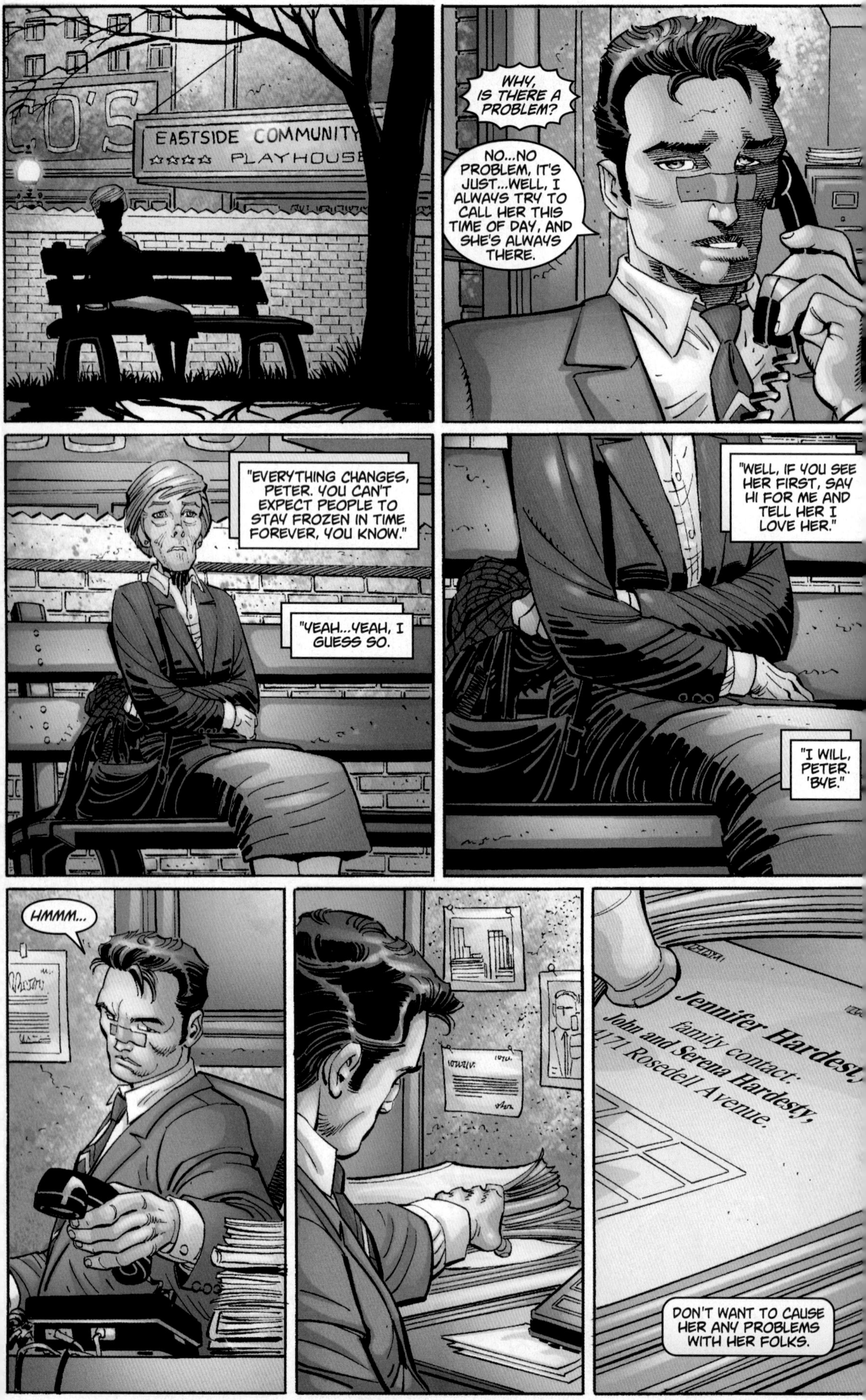
EASTSIDE COMMUNITY
PLAYHOUSE
WHY, IS THERE A PROBLEM?
NO...NO PROBLEM, IT'S JUST...WELL, I ALWAYS TRY TO CALL HER THIS TIME OF DAY, AND SHE'S ALWAYS THERE.
"EVERYTHING CHANGES, PETER. YOU CAN'T EXPECT PEOPLE TO STAY FROZEN IN TIME FOREVER, YOU KNOW."
"YEAH...YEAH, I GUESS SO.
"WELL, IF YOU SEE HER FIRST, SAY HI FOR ME AND TELL HER I LOVE HER."
"I WILL, PETER. 'BYE."
HMMM...
Jennifer Hardesty,
family contact:
John and Serena Hardesty,
4171 Rosedell Avenue.
DON'T WANT TO CAUSE HER ANY PROBLEMS WITH HER FOLKS.

BUT IT PROBABLY WOULDN'T HURT TO WALK HOME A DIFFERENT WAY TODAY.

JUST FOR THE VARIETY.

SPARE SOME CHANGE, MISTER?

CAN I GET A QUARTER FOR FOOD?

CAN WE HAVE SOME MONEY FOR POT? C'MON, AT LEAST WE'RE HONEST ABOUT IT...

HUH...

ADDRESS MATCHES. BUT FROM THE LOOK OF THE PLACE NOBODY'S LIVED HERE FOR AT LEAST A YEAR.

NYC COS CONDEMNED

EXCUSE ME, MA'AM --

I'M NOT A MA'AM, I'M A MISSUS.

I DIDN'T --

MA'AM MEANS MADAM, AND I AIN'T FRENCH AND I AIN'T RUNNING AN ESCORT SERVICE HERE, UNLIKE CERTAIN *OTHER* PEOPLE I COULD NAME ACROSS THE STREET, I DON'T LIKE TO TALK, BUT THERE IT IS --

I JUST WANT TO KNOW --

-- I'M A *MISSUS* WHICH IS *MRS.* WHICH IS *MARRIED* AND I'M *PROUD* OF IT I DON'T CARE *WHAT* MY SISTER SAYS SHE DOESN'T KNOW WHAT I HAVE TO DEAL WITH EVERY DAY, THE NOISE, THE PEOPLE --

HEY!

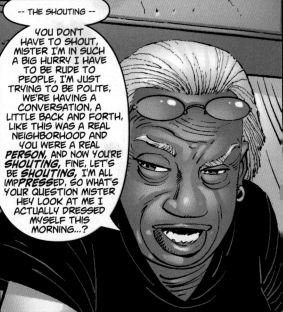

-- THE SHOUTING --

YOU DON'T HAVE TO SHOUT, MISTER I'M IN SUCH A BIG HURRY I HAVE TO BE RUDE TO PEOPLE, I'M JUST TRYING TO BE POLITE, WE'RE HAVING A CONVERSATION, A LITTLE BACK AND FORTH, LIKE THIS WAS A REAL NEIGHBORHOOD AND YOU WERE A REAL *PERSON*, AND NOW YOU'RE *SHOUTING*, FINE, LET'S BE *SHOUTING*, I'M ALL IMPRESSED, SO WHAT'S YOUR QUESTION MISTER HEY LOOK AT ME I ACTUALLY DRESSED MYSELF THIS MORNING...?

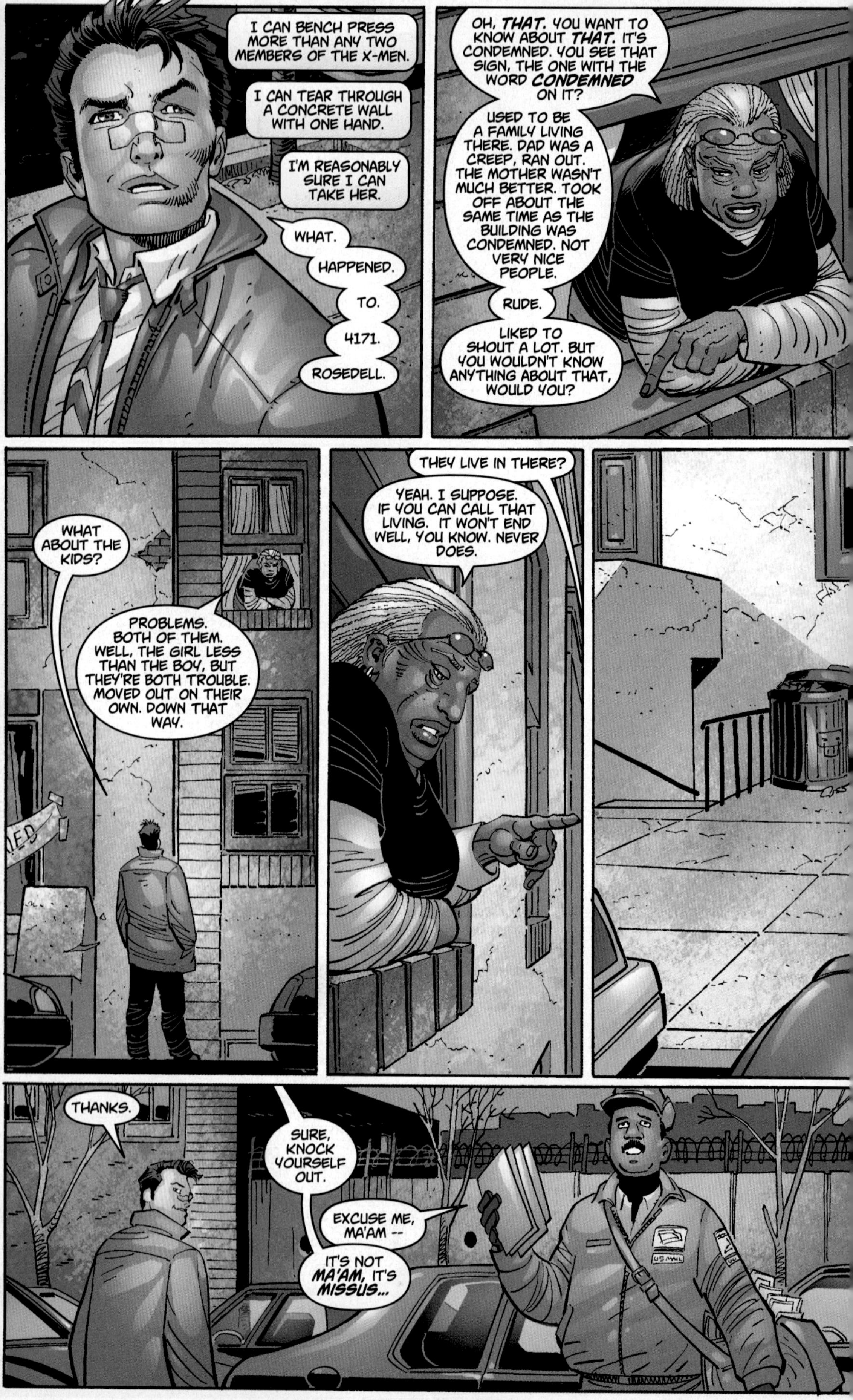

I CAN BENCH PRESS MORE THAN ANY TWO MEMBERS OF THE X-MEN.
I CAN TEAR THROUGH A CONCRETE WALL WITH ONE HAND.
I'M REASONABLY SURE I CAN TAKE HER.
WHAT.
HAPPENED.
TO.
4171.
ROSEDELL.
OH, THAT. YOU WANT TO KNOW ABOUT THAT. IT'S CONDEMNED. YOU SEE THAT SIGN, THE ONE WITH THE WORD CONDEMNED ON IT?
USED TO BE A FAMILY LIVING THERE. DAD WAS A CREEP, RAN OUT. THE MOTHER WASN'T MUCH BETTER. TOOK OFF ABOUT THE SAME TIME AS THE BUILDING WAS CONDEMNED. NOT VERY NICE PEOPLE.
RUDE.
LIKED TO SHOUT A LOT. BUT YOU WOULDN'T KNOW ANYTHING ABOUT THAT, WOULD YOU?
WHAT ABOUT THE KIDS?
PROBLEMS. BOTH OF THEM. WELL, THE GIRL LESS THAN THE BOY, BUT THEY'RE BOTH TROUBLE. MOVED OUT ON THEIR OWN. DOWN THAT WAY.
THEY LIVE IN THERE?
YEAH. I SUPPOSE. IF YOU CAN CALL THAT LIVING. IT WON'T END WELL, YOU KNOW. NEVER DOES.
THANKS.
SURE, KNOCK YOURSELF OUT.
EXCUSE ME, MA'AM --
IT'S NOT MA'AM, IT'S MISSUS...

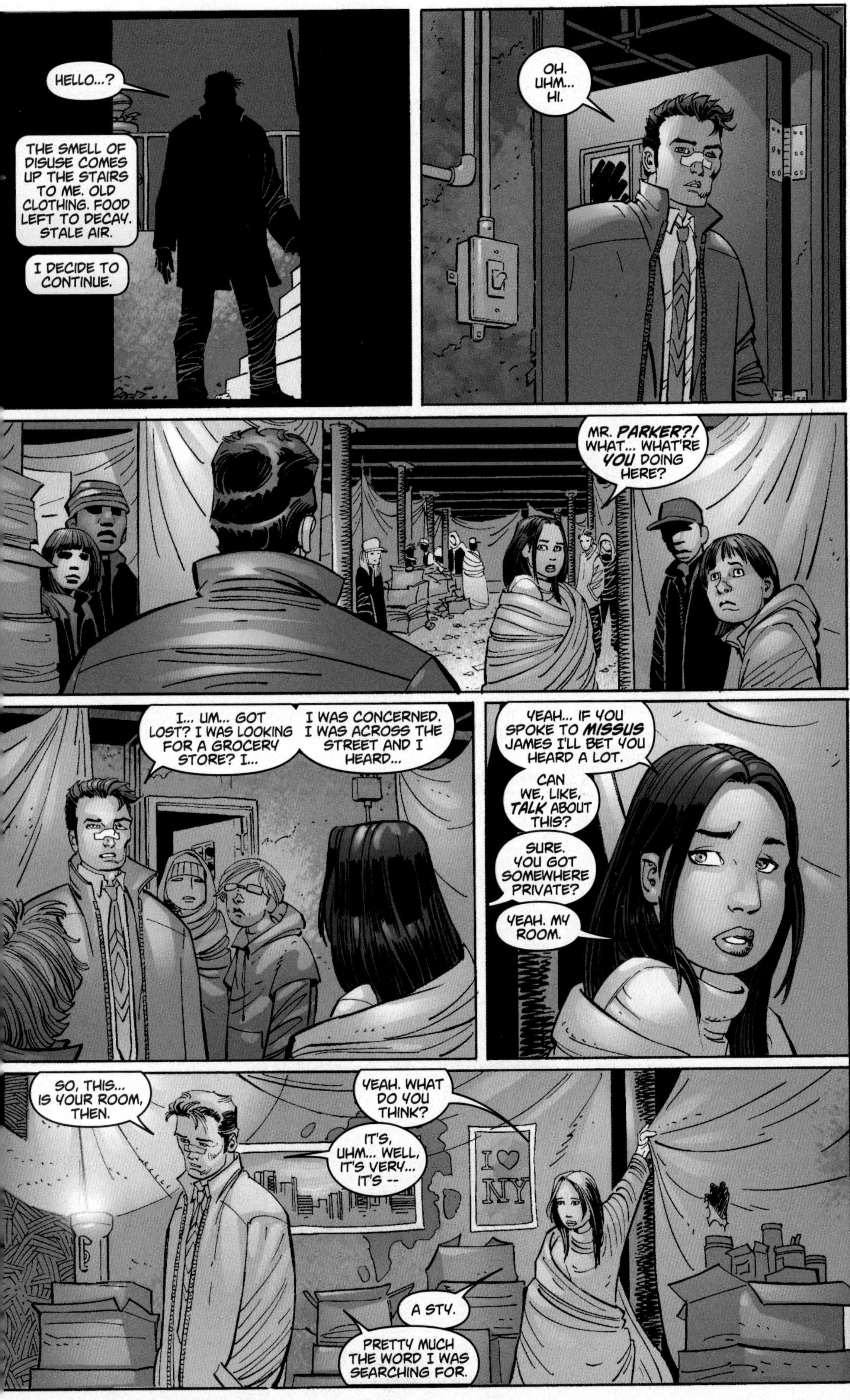
HELLO...?
THE SMELL OF DISUSE COMES UP THE STAIRS TO ME. OLD CLOTHING. FOOD LEFT TO DECAY. STALE AIR.
I DECIDE TO CONTINUE.
OH. UHM... HI.
MR. PARKER?! WHAT... WHAT'RE YOU DOING HERE?
I... UM... GOT LOST? I WAS LOOKING FOR A GROCERY STORE? I...
I WAS CONCERNED. I WAS ACROSS THE STREET AND I HEARD...
YEAH... IF YOU SPOKE TO MISSUS JAMES I'LL BET YOU HEARD A LOT.
CAN WE, LIKE, TALK ABOUT THIS?
SURE. YOU GOT SOMEWHERE PRIVATE?
YEAH. MY ROOM.
SO, THIS... IS YOUR ROOM, THEN.
YEAH. WHAT DO YOU THINK?
IT'S, UHM... WELL, IT'S VERY... IT'S --
A STY.
PRETTY MUCH THE WORD I WAS SEARCHING FOR.
I ♥ NY

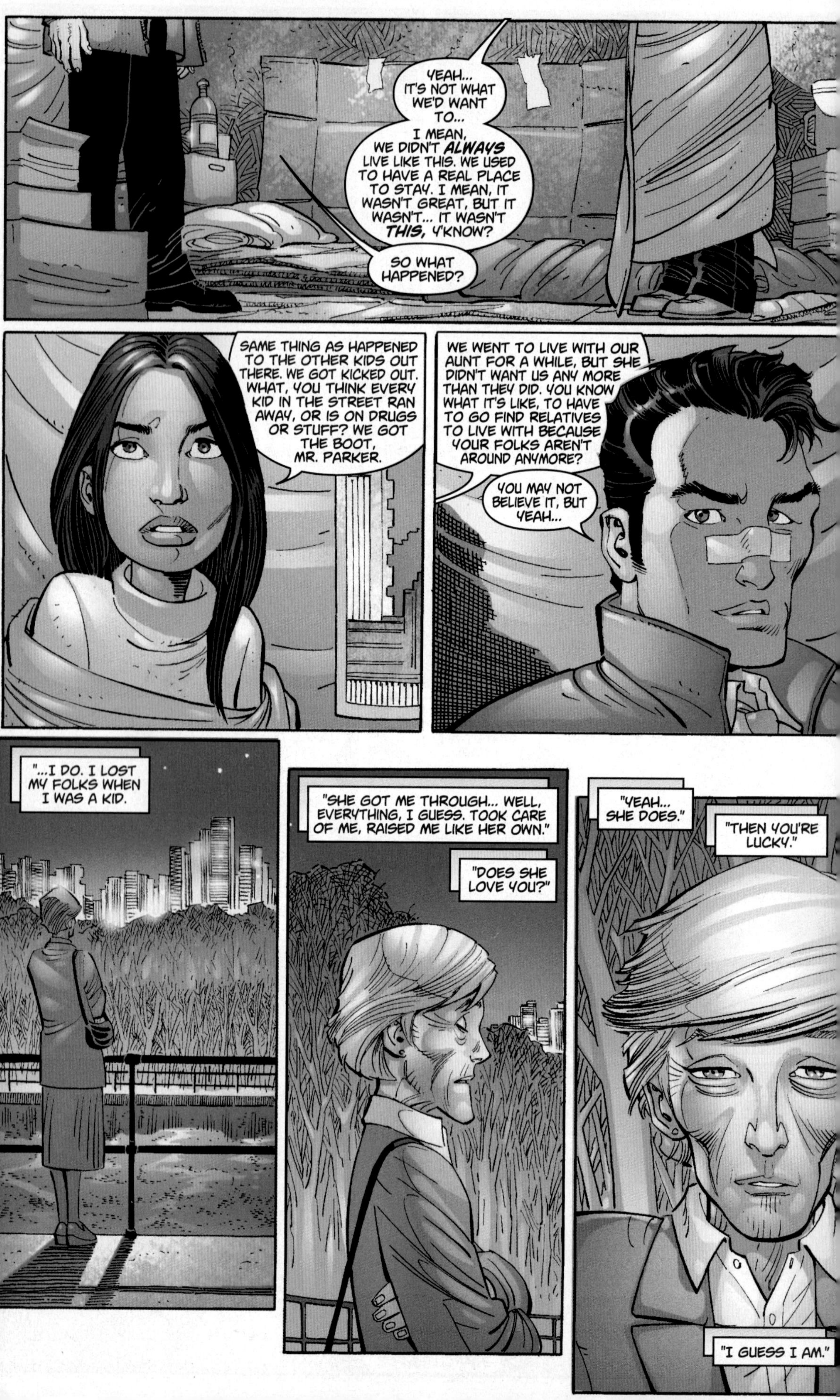
YEAH... IT'S NOT WHAT WE'D WANT TO...
I MEAN, WE DIDN'T ALWAYS LIVE LIKE THIS. WE USED TO HAVE A REAL PLACE TO STAY. I MEAN, IT WASN'T GREAT, BUT IT WASN'T... IT WASN'T THIS, Y'KNOW?
SO WHAT HAPPENED?
SAME THING AS HAPPENED TO THE OTHER KIDS OUT THERE. WE GOT KICKED OUT. WHAT, YOU THINK EVERY KID IN THE STREET RAN AWAY, OR IS ON DRUGS OR STUFF? WE GOT THE BOOT, MR. PARKER.
WE WENT TO LIVE WITH OUR AUNT FOR A WHILE, BUT SHE DIDN'T WANT US ANY MORE THAN THEY DID. YOU KNOW WHAT IT'S LIKE, TO HAVE TO GO FIND RELATIVES TO LIVE WITH BECAUSE YOUR FOLKS AREN'T AROUND ANYMORE?
YOU MAY NOT BELIEVE IT, BUT YEAH...
"...I DO. I LOST MY FOLKS WHEN I WAS A KID.
"SHE GOT ME THROUGH... WELL, EVERYTHING, I GUESS. TOOK CARE OF ME, RAISED ME LIKE HER OWN."
"DOES SHE LOVE YOU?"
"YEAH... SHE DOES."
"THEN YOU'RE LUCKY."
"I GUESS I AM."

WE WEREN'T. FINALLY, STEVE AND I JUST HAD TO GET OUT.

STEVE'S YOUR BROTHER?

YEAH. I KINDA LOOK AFTER HIM. HELP HIM WITH HIS HOMEWORK AND STUFF.

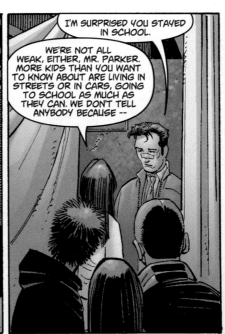

I'M SURPRISED YOU STAYED IN SCHOOL.

WE'RE NOT ALL WEAK, EITHER, MR. PARKER. MORE KIDS THAN YOU WANT TO KNOW ABOUT ARE LIVING IN STREETS OR IN CARS, GOING TO SCHOOL AS MUCH AS THEY CAN. WE DON'T TELL ANYBODY BECAUSE --

WELL, WE JUST CAN'T, THAT'S ALL. THEY'D KICK US OUT, OR WE'D HAVE TO GO TO A FOSTER HOME, AND THE OTHER KIDS...IT'S BETTER THIS WAY.

WE HIT THE STREETS A LOT, ASKING FOR CHANGE AND STUFF. WE GET A FEW BUCKS HERE AND THERE. IT'S NOT SO BAD. WE CAN EVEN EAT AT McDONALD'S ONCE IN A WHILE.

IT'S JUST... IT'S JUST THE WAY THINGS ARE, Y'KNOW?

THERE'S SUCH PAIN IN HER VOICE. BUT ALSO SUCH STRENGTH.

I PASS BY THIS NEIGHBORHOOD A DOZEN TIMES A MONTH. HOW COULD I NOT KNOW THIS WAS HERE? HOW COULD I NOT SEE THIS?

WORST OF ALL... WHEN DID I STOP SEEING THIS?

PLEASE DON'T TELL ON US, MR. PARKER.

I --

PLEASE. THERE'S NOTHING YOU CAN DO UNLESS YOU WANT TO ADOPT ME AND STEVE AND HALF THE KIDS OUT HERE RIGHT NOW. IF YOU TELL ANYBODY, WE'LL END UP IN A FOSTER HOME OR WORSE.

WE'RE SIX MONTHS FROM GRADUATING, SIX MONTHS FROM BEING LEGAL. CAN YOU GIVE US THAT, MR. PARKER? WE'VE COME THIS FAR ON OUR OWN. WE CAN MAKE IT THE REST OF THE WAY. JUST...LET US.

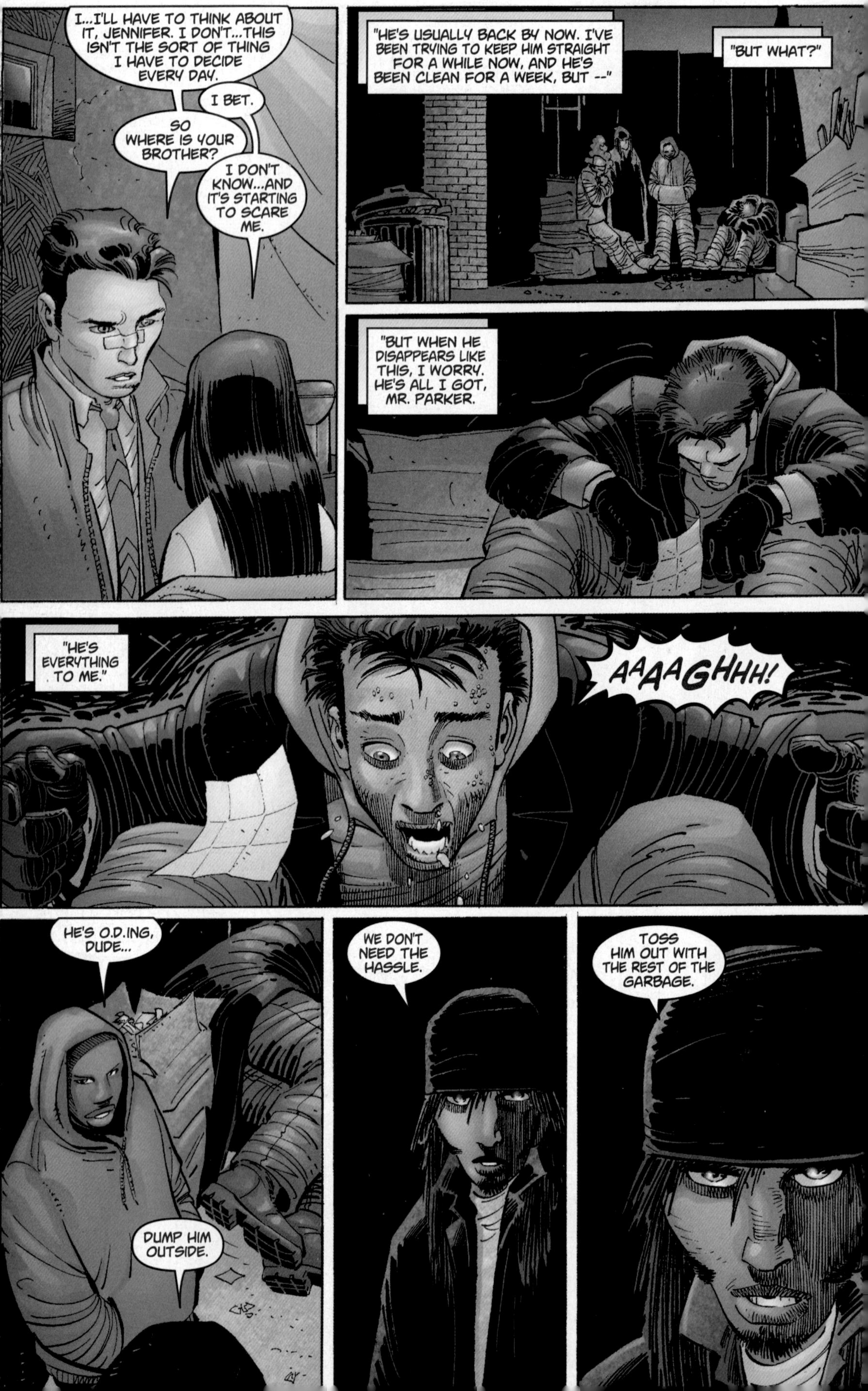
I...I'LL HAVE TO THINK ABOUT IT, JENNIFER. I DON'T...THIS ISN'T THE SORT OF THING I HAVE TO DECIDE EVERY DAY.
I BET.
SO WHERE IS YOUR BROTHER?
I DON'T KNOW...AND IT'S STARTING TO SCARE ME.
"HE'S USUALLY BACK BY NOW. I'VE BEEN TRYING TO KEEP HIM STRAIGHT FOR A WHILE NOW, AND HE'S BEEN CLEAN FOR A WEEK, BUT --"
"BUT WHAT?"
"BUT WHEN HE DISAPPEARS LIKE THIS, I WORRY. HE'S ALL I GOT, MR. PARKER.
"HE'S EVERYTHING TO ME."
AAAAGHHH!
HE'S O.D.ING, DUDE...
DUMP HIM OUTSIDE.
WE DON'T NEED THE HASSLE.
TOSS HIM OUT WITH THE REST OF THE GARBAGE.

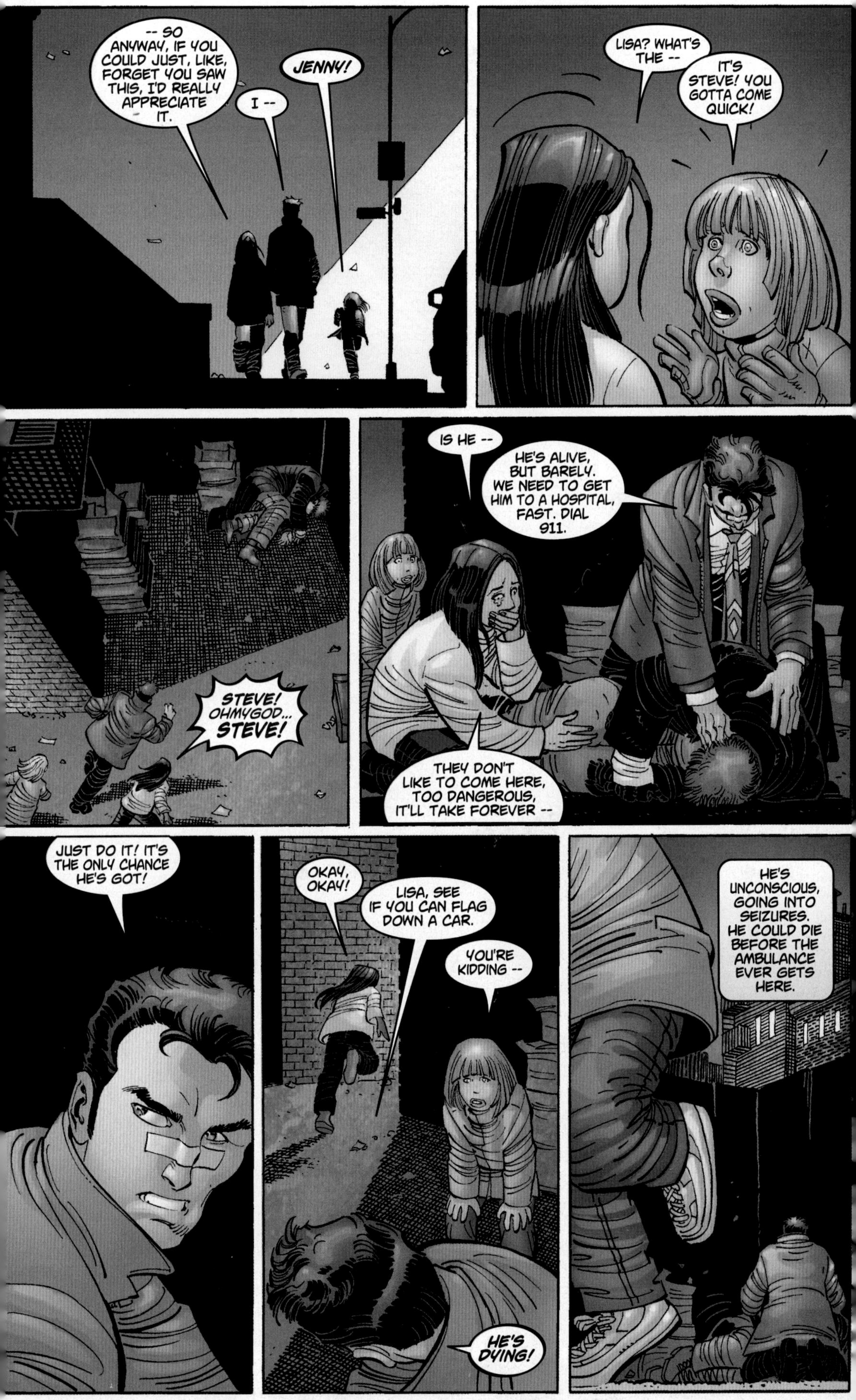

-- SO ANYWAY, IF YOU COULD JUST, LIKE, FORGET YOU SAW THIS, I'D REALLY APPRECIATE IT.
I --
JENNY!
LISA? WHAT'S THE --
IT'S STEVE! YOU GOTTA COME QUICK!
STEVE! OHMYGOD... STEVE!
IS HE --
HE'S ALIVE, BUT BARELY. WE NEED TO GET HIM TO A HOSPITAL, FAST. DIAL 911.
THEY DON'T LIKE TO COME HERE, TOO DANGEROUS, IT'LL TAKE FOREVER --
JUST DO IT! IT'S THE ONLY CHANCE HE'S GOT!
OKAY, OKAY!
LISA, SEE IF YOU CAN FLAG DOWN A CAR.
YOU'RE KIDDING --
HE'S DYING!
HE'S UNCONSCIOUS, GOING INTO SEIZURES. HE COULD DIE BEFORE THE AMBULANCE EVER GETS HERE.

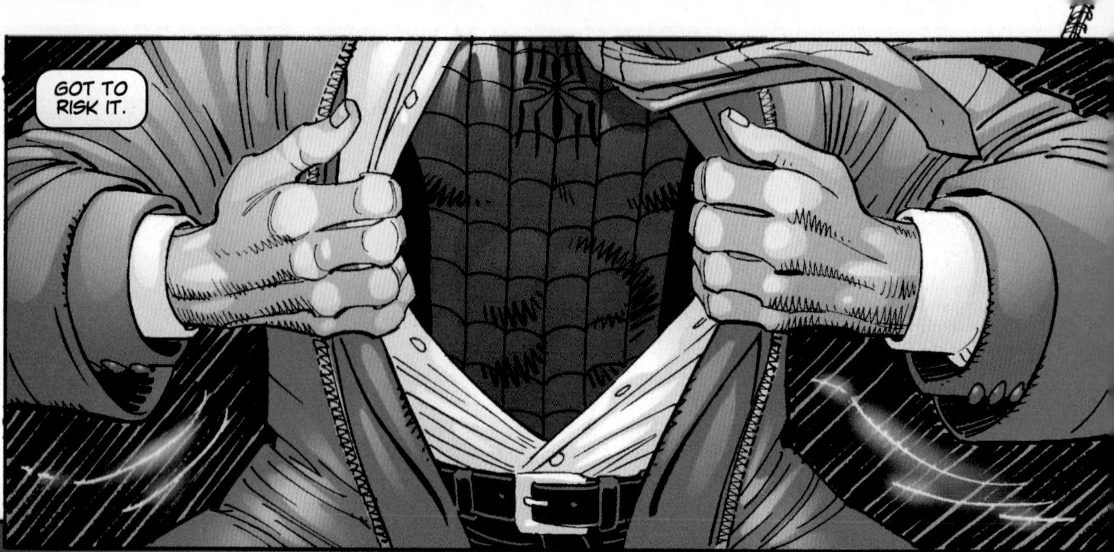
GOT TO RISK IT.

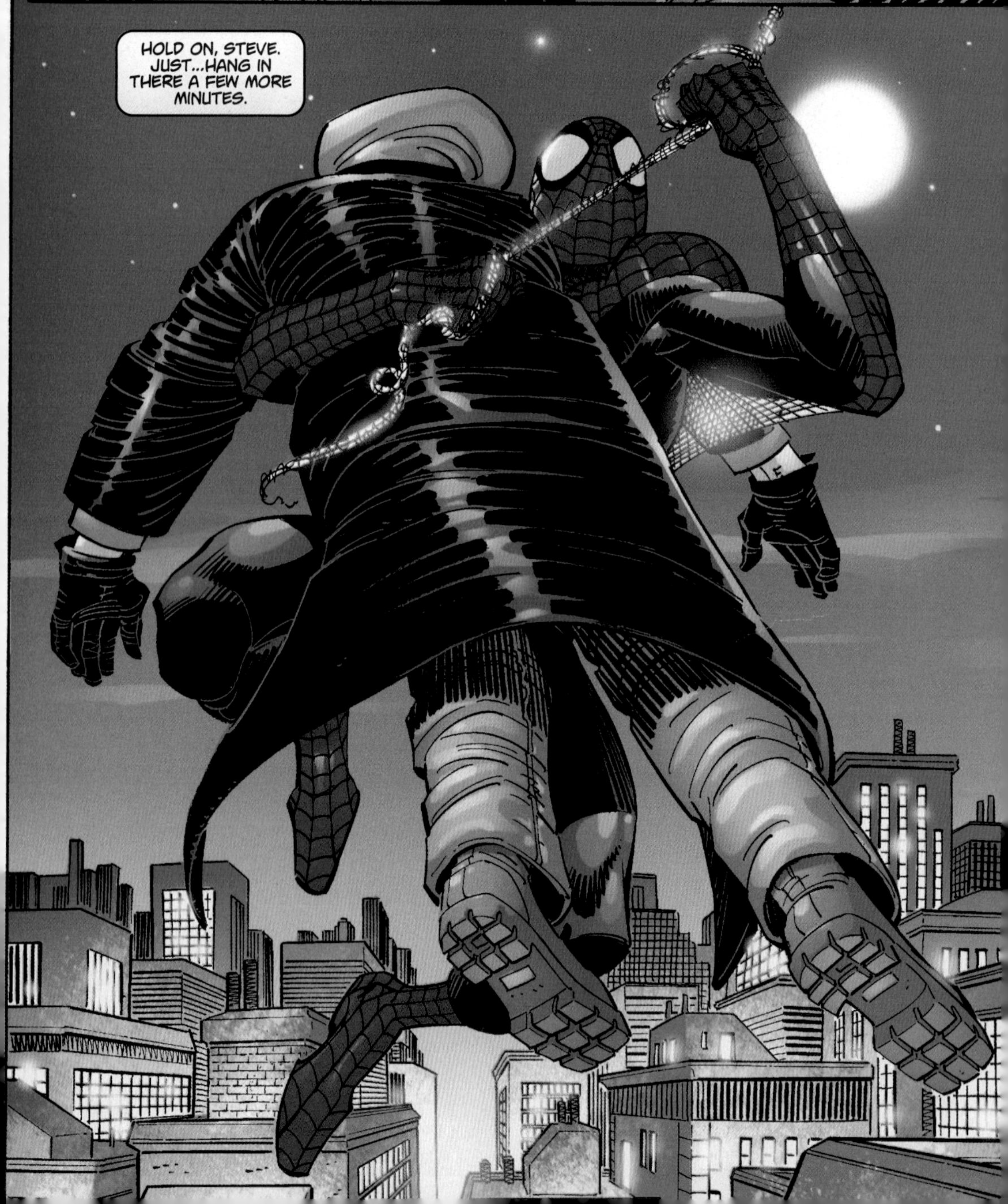
HOLD ON, STEVE. JUST...HANG IN THERE A FEW MORE MINUTES.

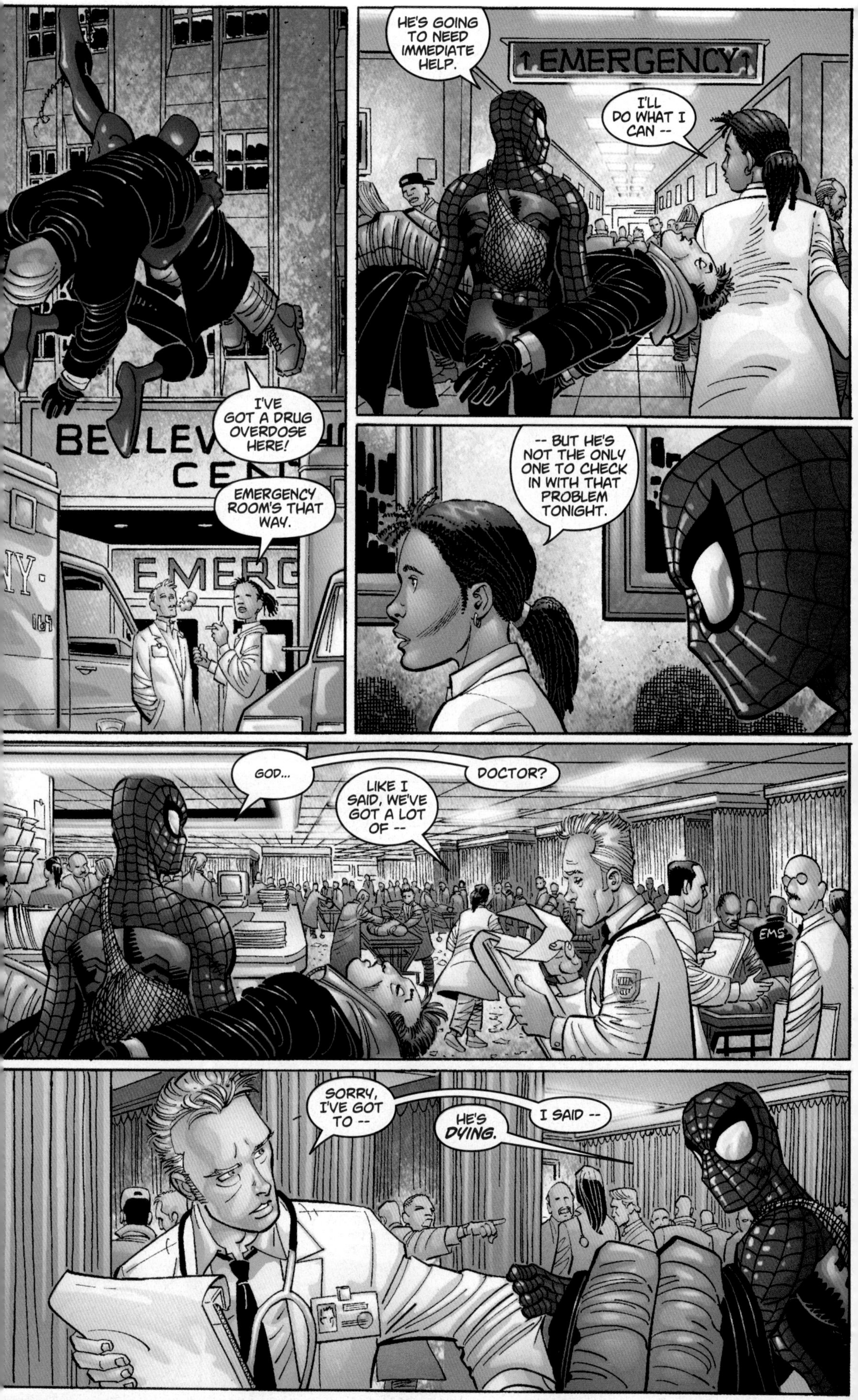
I'VE GOT A DRUG OVERDOSE HERE!
EMERGENCY ROOM'S THAT WAY.
EMERGENCY
HE'S GOING TO NEED IMMEDIATE HELP.
I'LL DO WHAT I CAN --
-- BUT HE'S NOT THE ONLY ONE TO CHECK IN WITH THAT PROBLEM TONIGHT.
GOD...
DOCTOR?
LIKE I SAID, WE'VE GOT A LOT OF --
EMS
SORRY, I'VE GOT TO --
I SAID --
HE'S *DYING.*

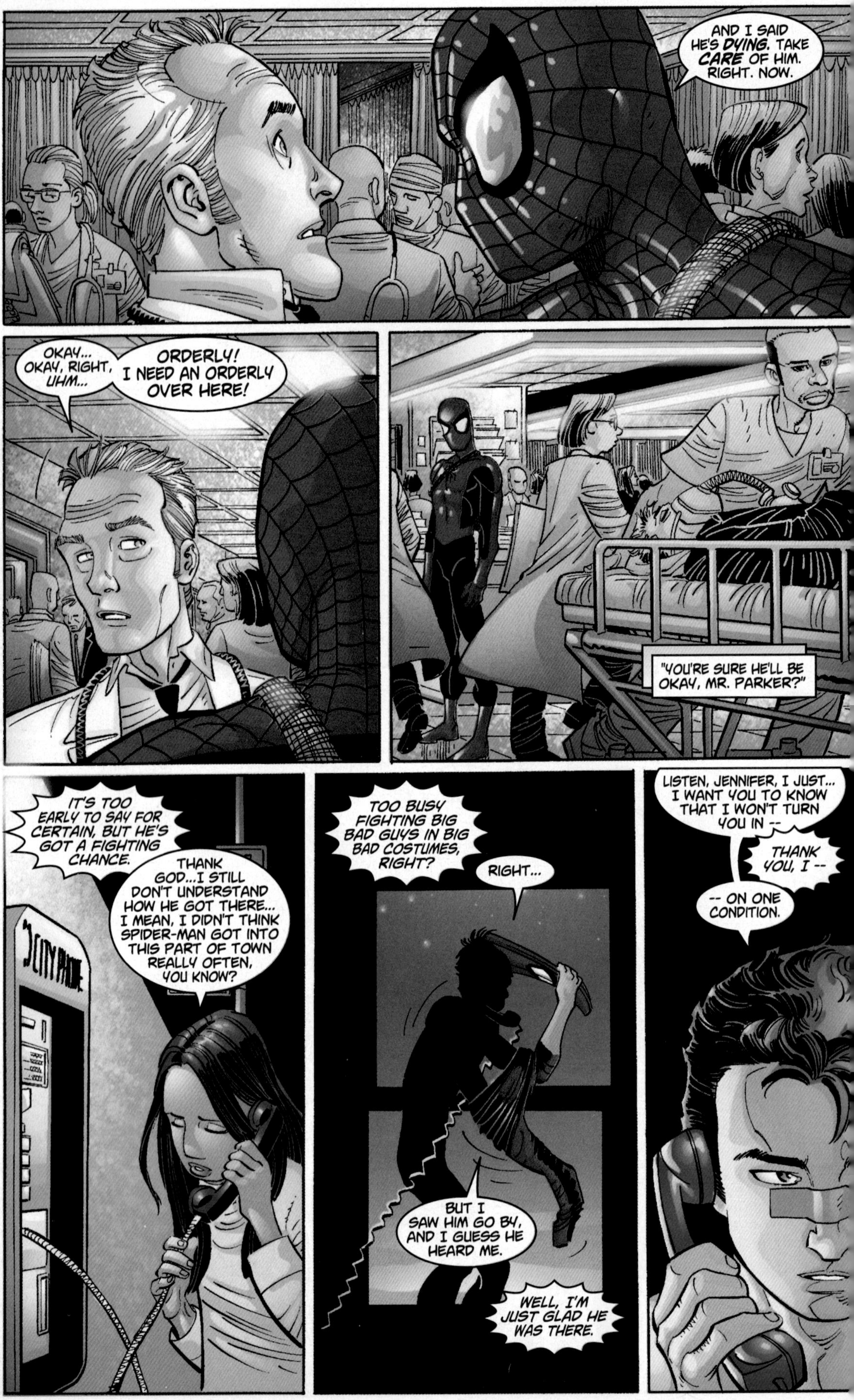

AND I SAID HE'S DYING. TAKE CARE OF HIM. RIGHT. NOW.
OKAY... OKAY, RIGHT, UHM...
ORDERLY! I NEED AN ORDERLY OVER HERE!
"YOU'RE SURE HE'LL BE OKAY, MR. PARKER?"
IT'S TOO EARLY TO SAY FOR CERTAIN, BUT HE'S GOT A FIGHTING CHANCE.
THANK GOD...I STILL DON'T UNDERSTAND HOW HE GOT THERE... I MEAN, I DIDN'T THINK SPIDER-MAN GOT INTO THIS PART OF TOWN REALLY OFTEN, YOU KNOW?
CITY PHONE
TOO BUSY FIGHTING BIG BAD GUYS IN BIG BAD COSTUMES, RIGHT?
RIGHT...
BUT I SAW HIM GO BY, AND I GUESS HE HEARD ME.
WELL, I'M JUST GLAD HE WAS THERE.
LISTEN, JENNIFER, I JUST... I WANT YOU TO KNOW THAT I WON'T TURN YOU IN --
THANK YOU, I --
-- ON ONE CONDITION.

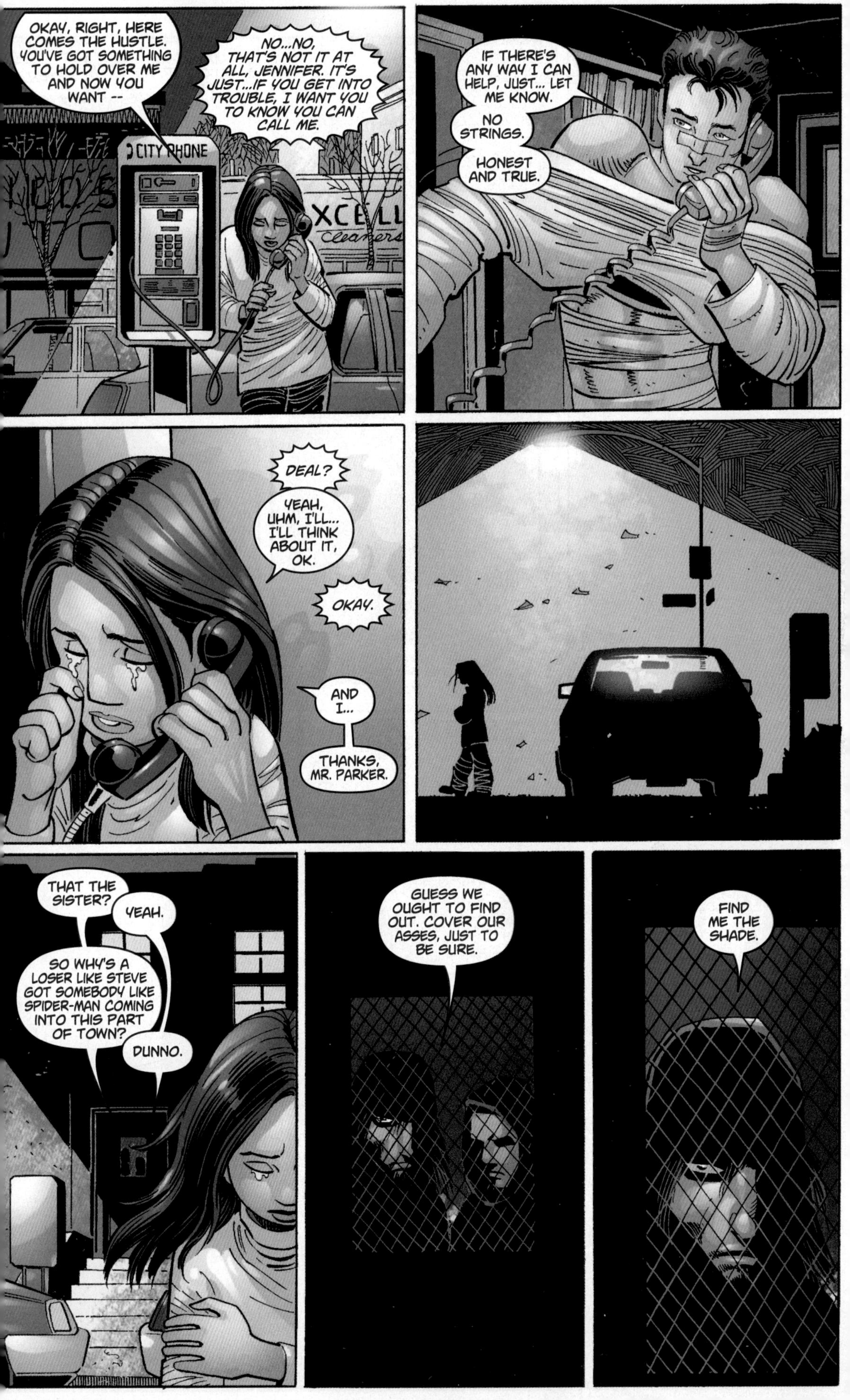
OKAY, RIGHT, HERE COMES THE HUSTLE. YOU'VE GOT SOMETHING TO HOLD OVER ME AND NOW YOU WANT --
NO...NO, THAT'S NOT IT AT ALL, JENNIFER. IT'S JUST...IF YOU GET INTO TROUBLE, I WANT YOU TO KNOW YOU CAN CALL ME.
CITY PHONE
XCELL
Cleaners
IF THERE'S ANY WAY I CAN HELP, JUST... LET ME KNOW.
NO STRINGS.
HONEST AND TRUE.
DEAL?
YEAH, UHM, I'LL... I'LL THINK ABOUT IT, OK.
OKAY.
AND I...
THANKS, MR. PARKER.
THAT THE SISTER?
YEAH.
SO WHY'S A LOSER LIKE STEVE GOT SOMEBODY LIKE SPIDER-MAN COMING INTO THIS PART OF TOWN?
DUNNO.
GUESS WE OUGHT TO FIND OUT. COVER OUR ASSES, JUST TO BE SURE.
FIND ME THE SHADE.

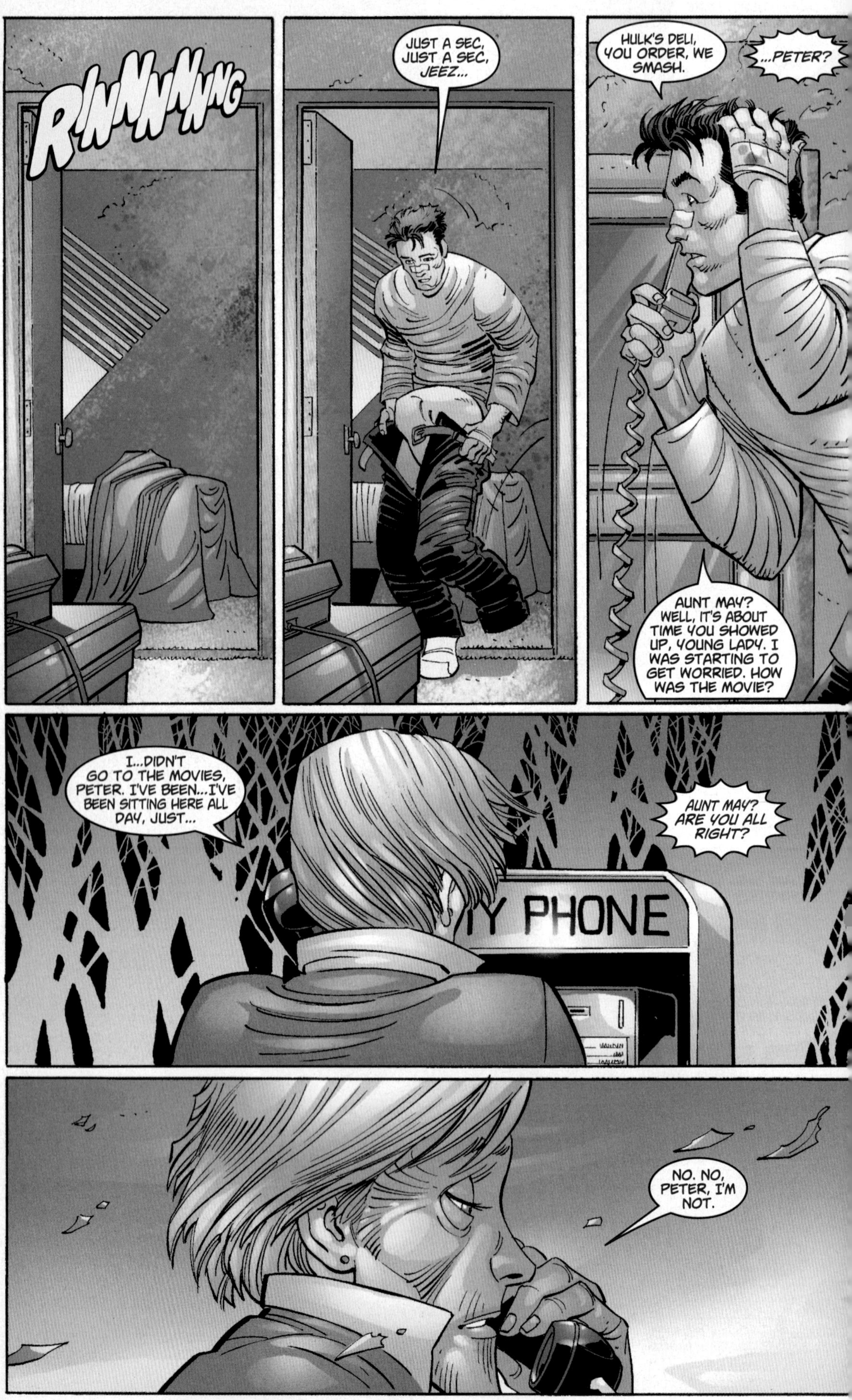
RINNNNNNG
JUST A SEC, JUST A SEC, JEEZ...
HULK'S DELI, YOU ORDER, WE SMASH.
...PETER?
AUNT MAY? WELL, IT'S ABOUT TIME YOU SHOWED UP, YOUNG LADY. I WAS STARTING TO GET WORRIED. HOW WAS THE MOVIE?
I...DIDN'T GO TO THE MOVIES, PETER. I'VE BEEN...I'VE BEEN SITTING HERE ALL DAY, JUST...
AUNT MAY? ARE YOU ALL RIGHT?
Y PHONE
NO. NO, PETER, I'M NOT.

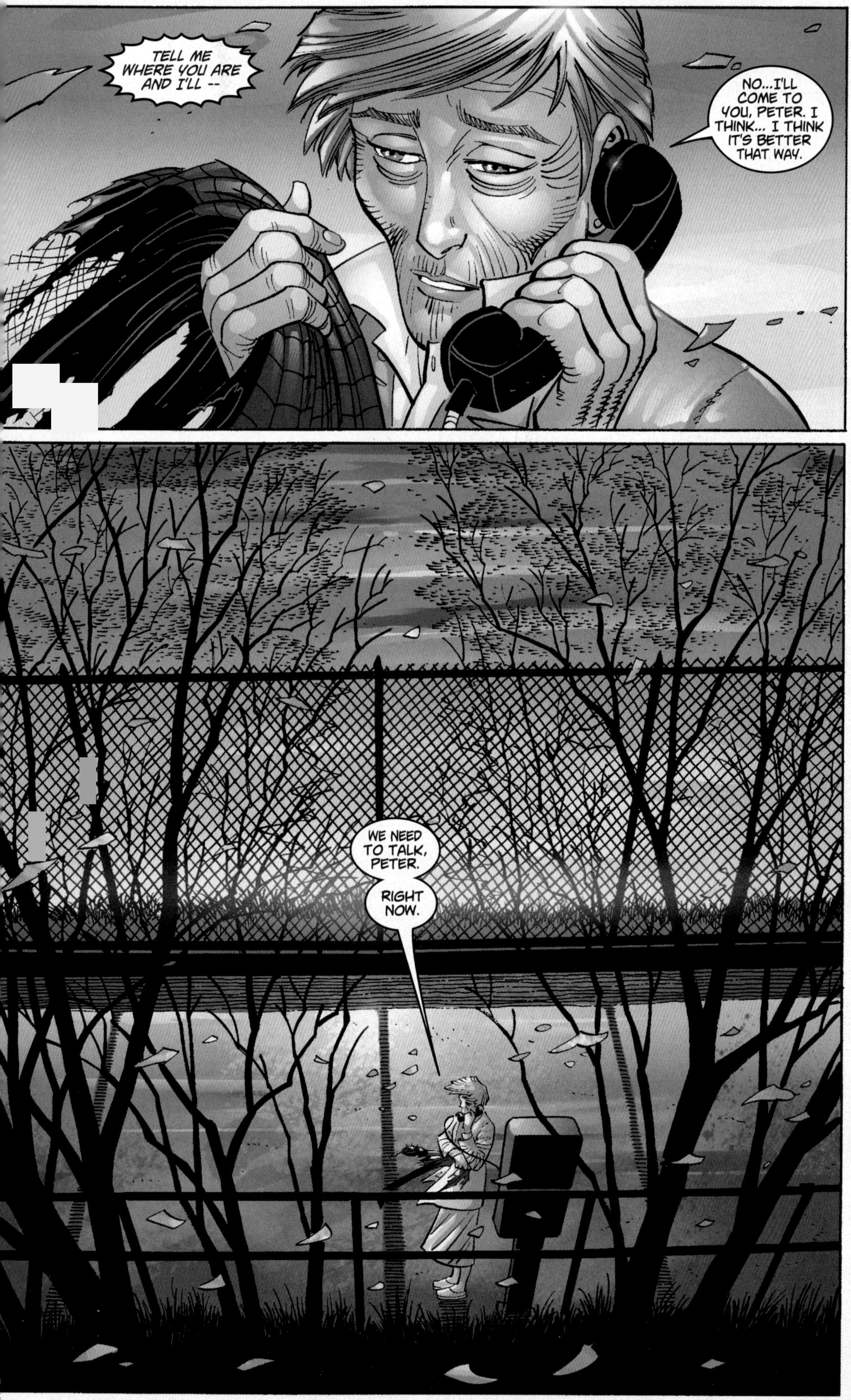
TELL ME WHERE YOU ARE AND I'LL --
NO...I'LL COME TO YOU, PETER. I THINK... I THINK IT'S BETTER THAT WAY.
WE NEED TO TALK, PETER.
RIGHT NOW.

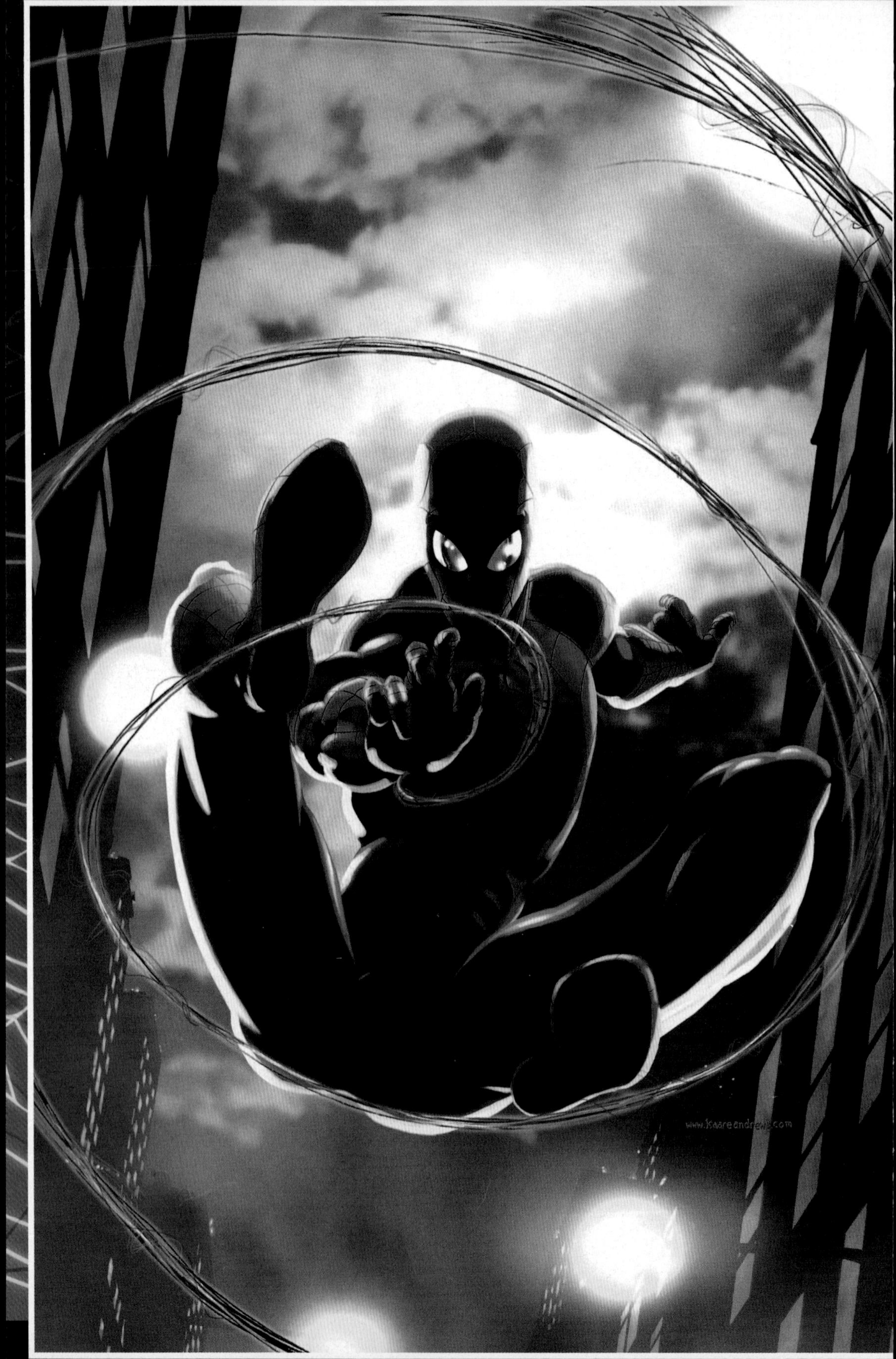
www.kaareandrews.com

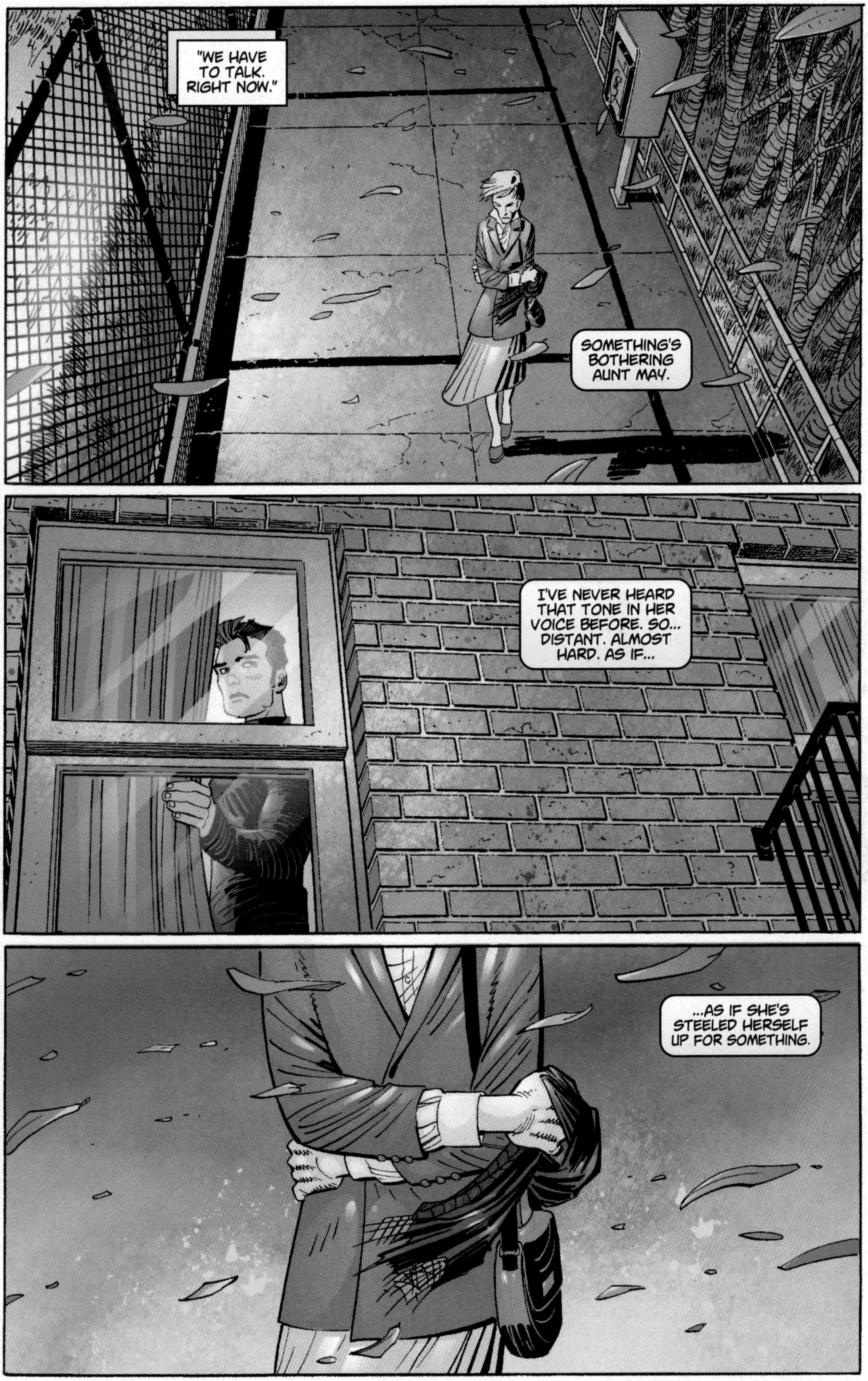
"WE HAVE TO TALK. RIGHT NOW."
SOMETHING'S BOTHERING AUNT MAY.
I'VE NEVER HEARD THAT TONE IN HER VOICE BEFORE. SO... DISTANT. ALMOST HARD. AS IF...
...AS IF SHE'S STEELED HERSELF UP FOR SOMETHING.

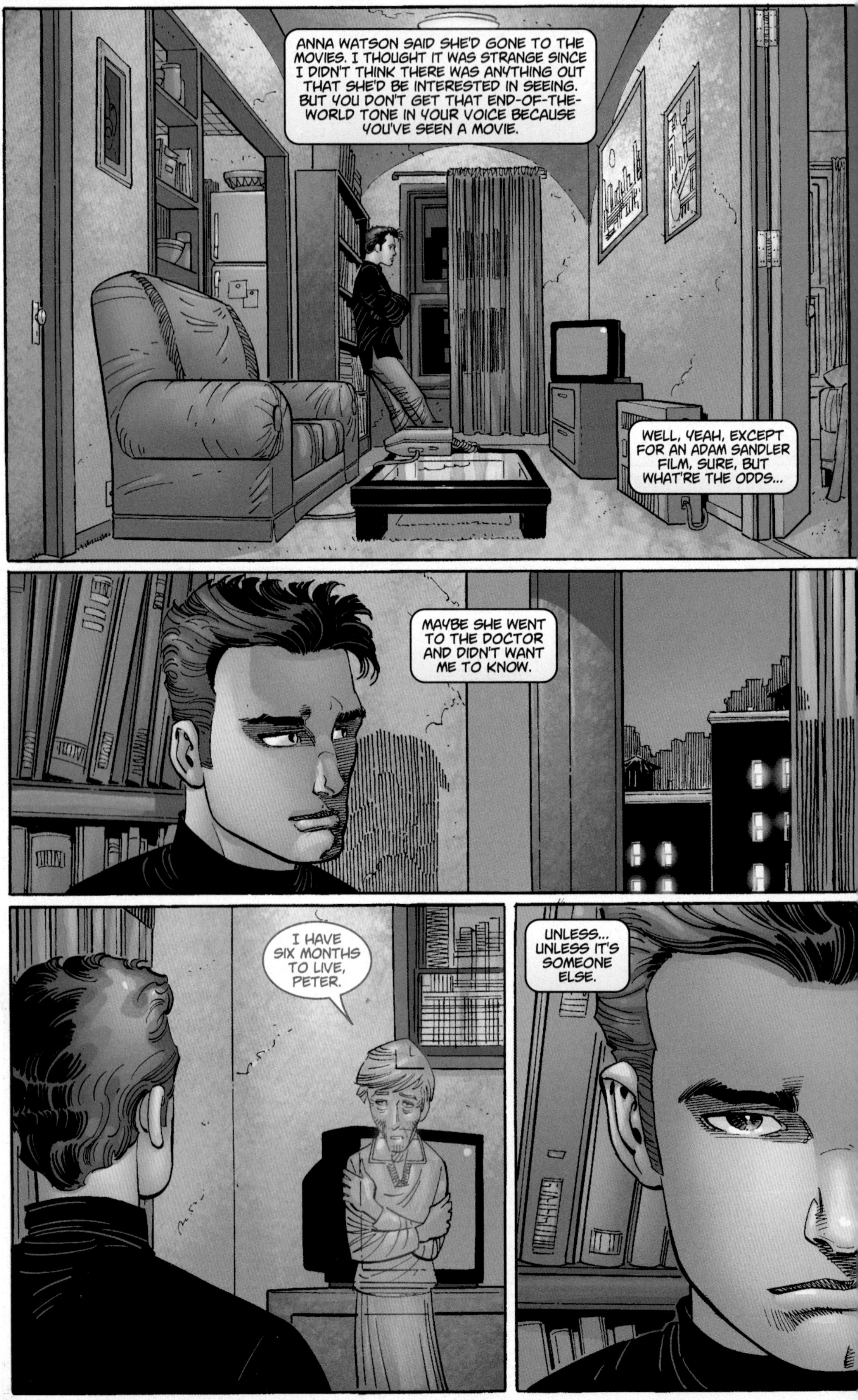
ANNA WATSON SAID SHE'D GONE TO THE MOVIES. I THOUGHT IT WAS STRANGE SINCE I DIDN'T THINK THERE WAS ANYTHING OUT THAT SHE'D BE INTERESTED IN SEEING. BUT YOU DON'T GET THAT END-OF-THE-WORLD TONE IN YOUR VOICE BECAUSE YOU'VE SEEN A MOVIE.
WELL, YEAH, EXCEPT FOR AN ADAM SANDLER FILM, SURE, BUT WHAT'RE THE ODDS...
MAYBE SHE WENT TO THE DOCTOR AND DIDN'T WANT ME TO KNOW.
I HAVE SIX MONTHS TO LIVE, PETER.
UNLESS... UNLESS IT'S SOMEONE ELSE.

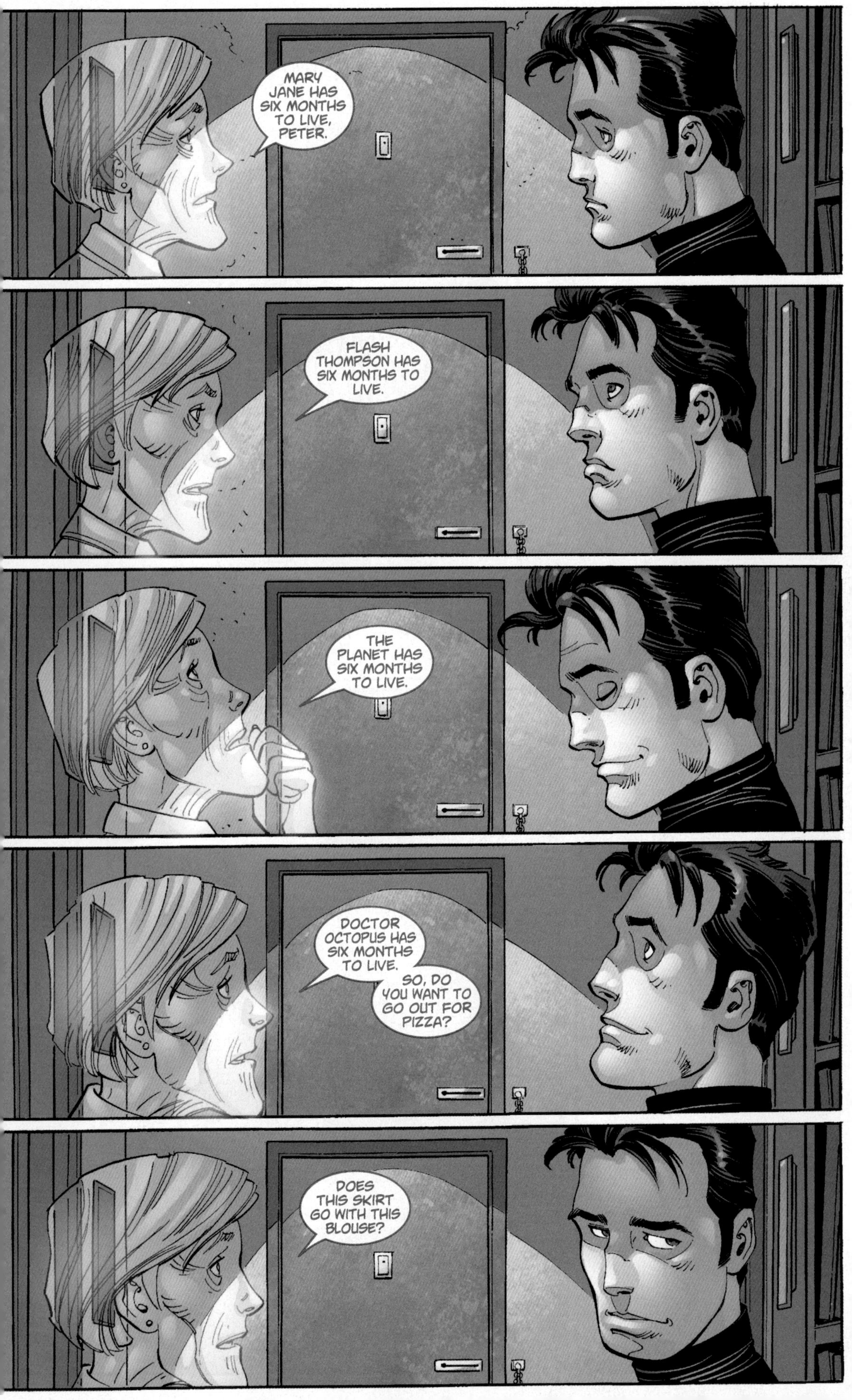
MARY JANE HAS SIX MONTHS TO LIVE, PETER.
FLASH THOMPSON HAS SIX MONTHS TO LIVE.
THE PLANET HAS SIX MONTHS TO LIVE.
DOCTOR OCTOPUS HAS SIX MONTHS TO LIVE.
SO, DO YOU WANT TO GO OUT FOR PIZZA?
DOES THIS SKIRT GO WITH THIS BLOUSE?

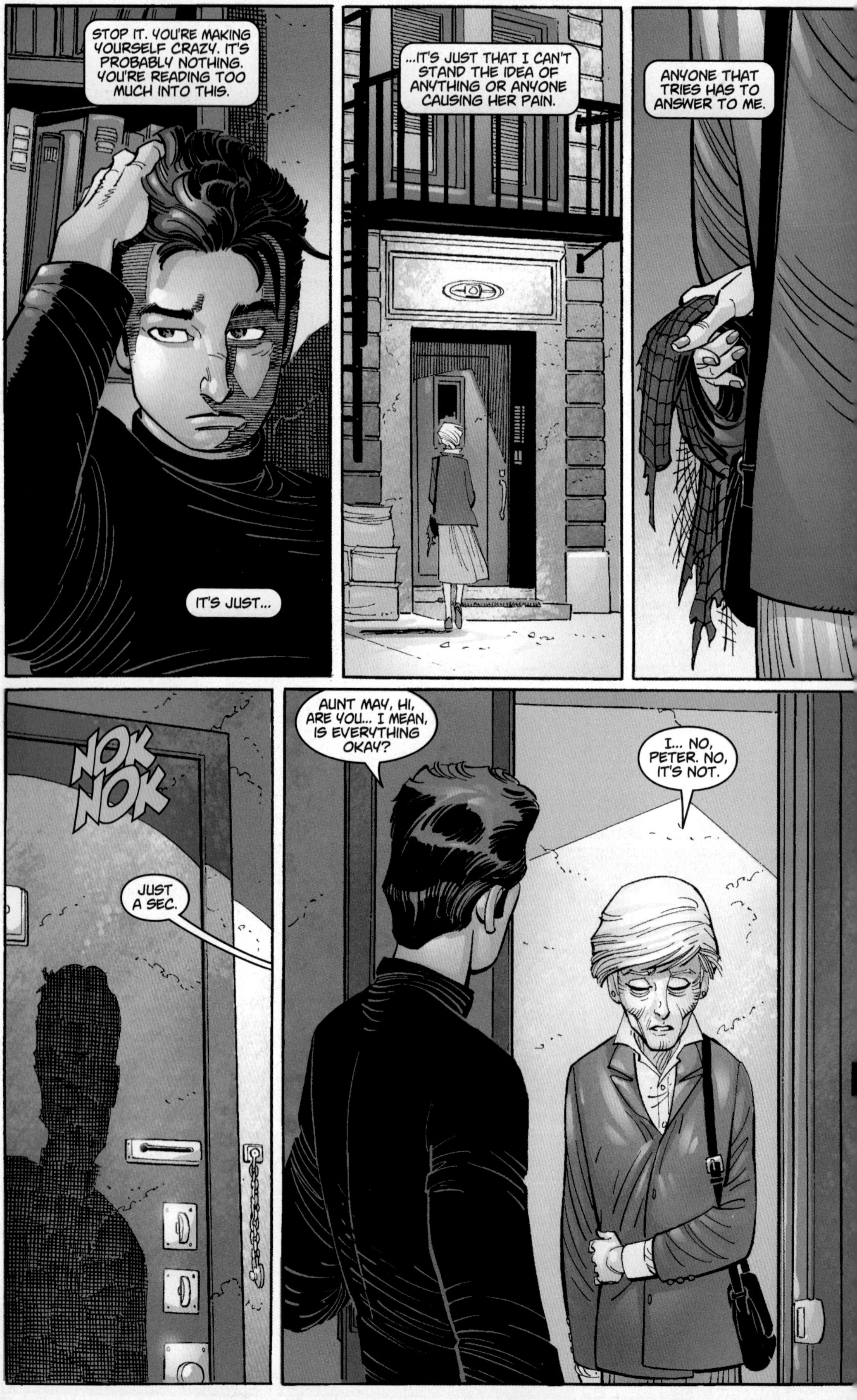

STOP IT. YOU'RE MAKING YOURSELF CRAZY. IT'S PROBABLY NOTHING. YOU'RE READING TOO MUCH INTO THIS.
IT'S JUST...
...IT'S JUST THAT I CAN'T STAND THE IDEA OF ANYTHING OR ANYONE CAUSING HER PAIN.
ANYONE THAT TRIES HAS TO ANSWER TO ME.
NOK NOK
JUST A SEC.
AUNT MAY, HI, ARE YOU... I MEAN, IS EVERYTHING OKAY?
I... NO, PETER. NO, IT'S NOT.

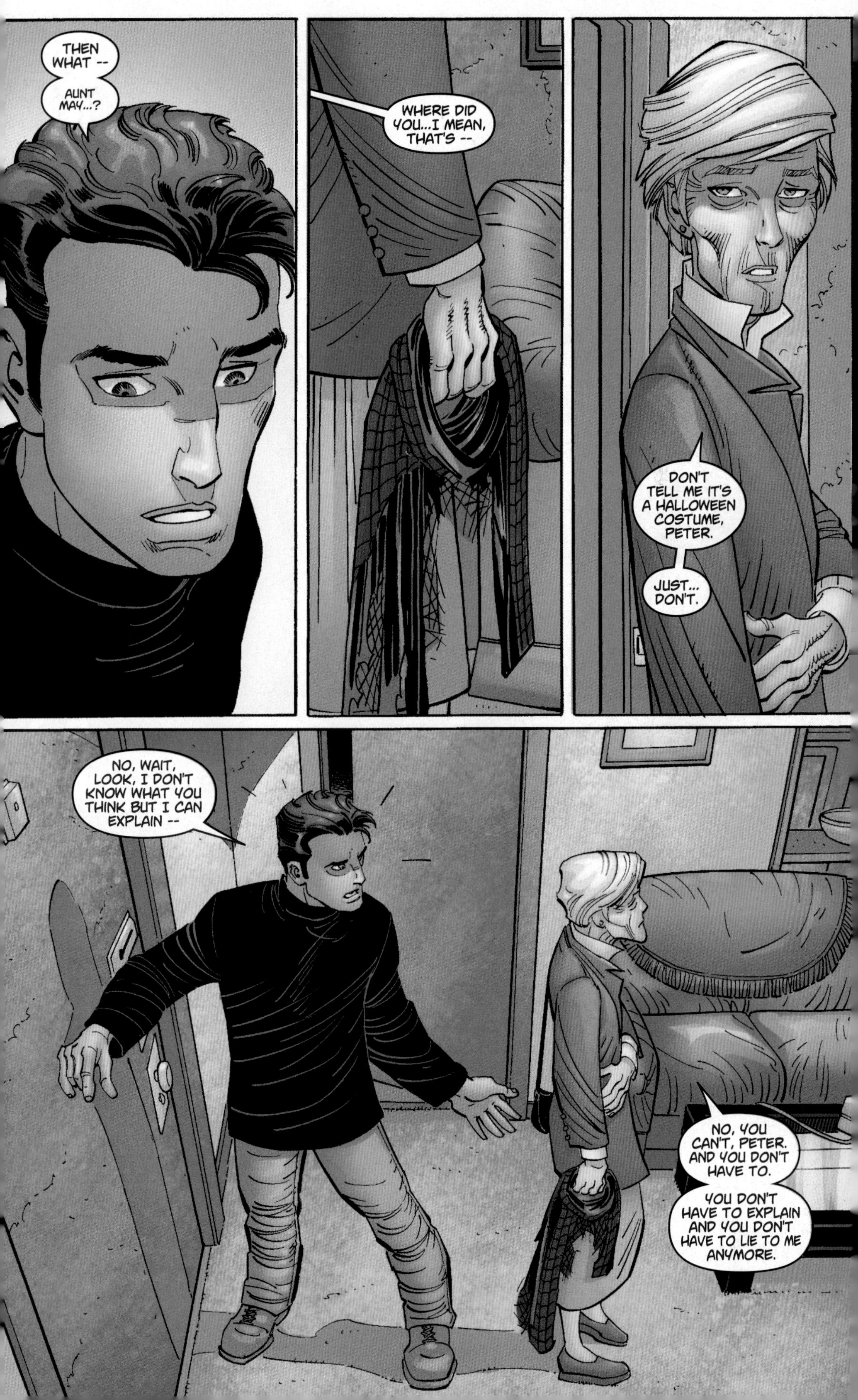
THEN WHAT --
AUNT MAY...?
WHERE DID YOU...I MEAN, THAT'S --
DON'T TELL ME IT'S A HALLOWEEN COSTUME, PETER.
JUST... DON'T.
NO, WAIT, LOOK, I DON'T KNOW WHAT YOU THINK BUT I CAN EXPLAIN --
NO, YOU CAN'T, PETER. AND YOU DON'T HAVE TO.
YOU DON'T HAVE TO EXPLAIN AND YOU DON'T HAVE TO LIE TO ME ANYMORE.

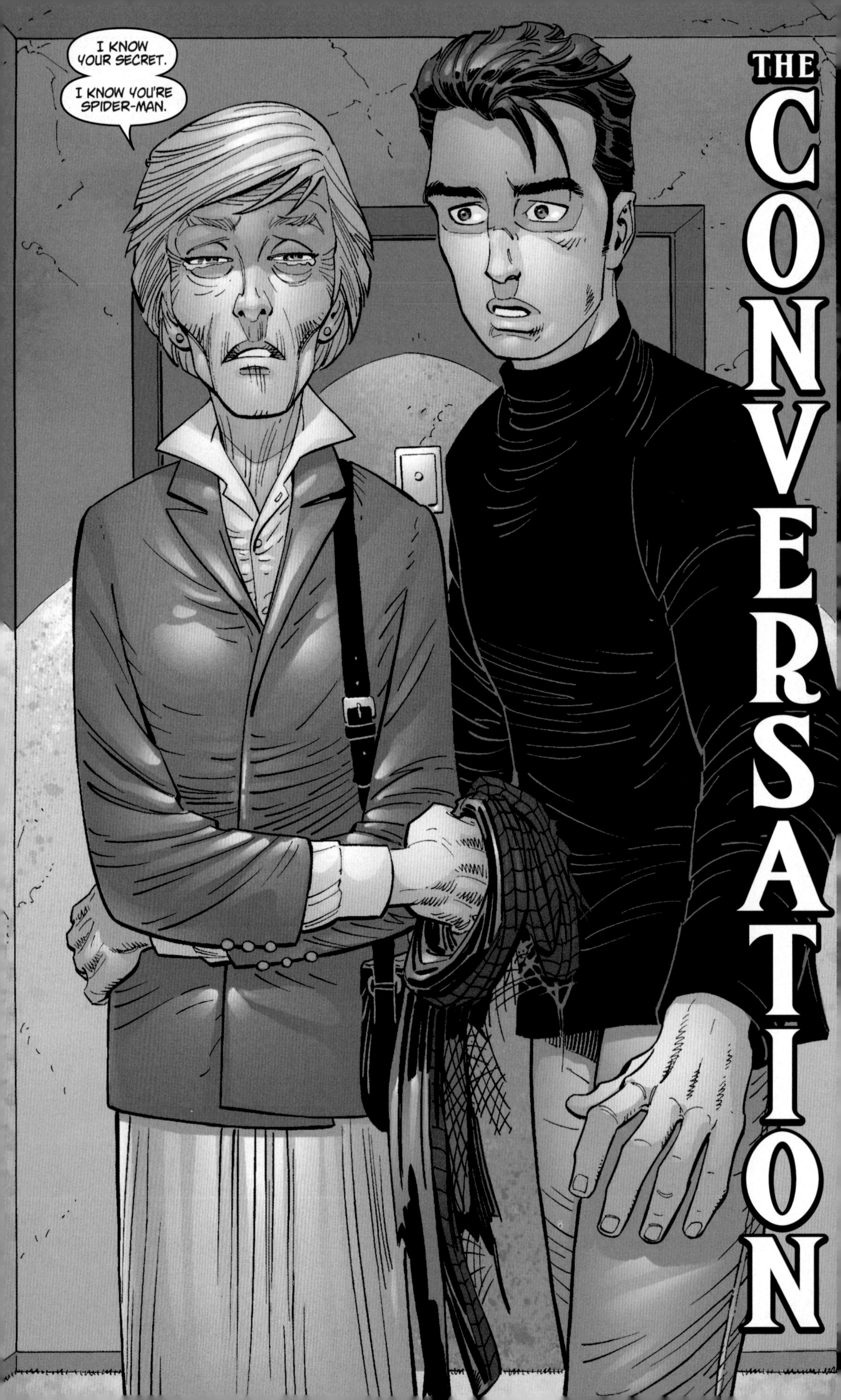
I KNOW YOUR SECRET.
I KNOW YOU'RE SPIDER-MAN.
THE CONVERSATION

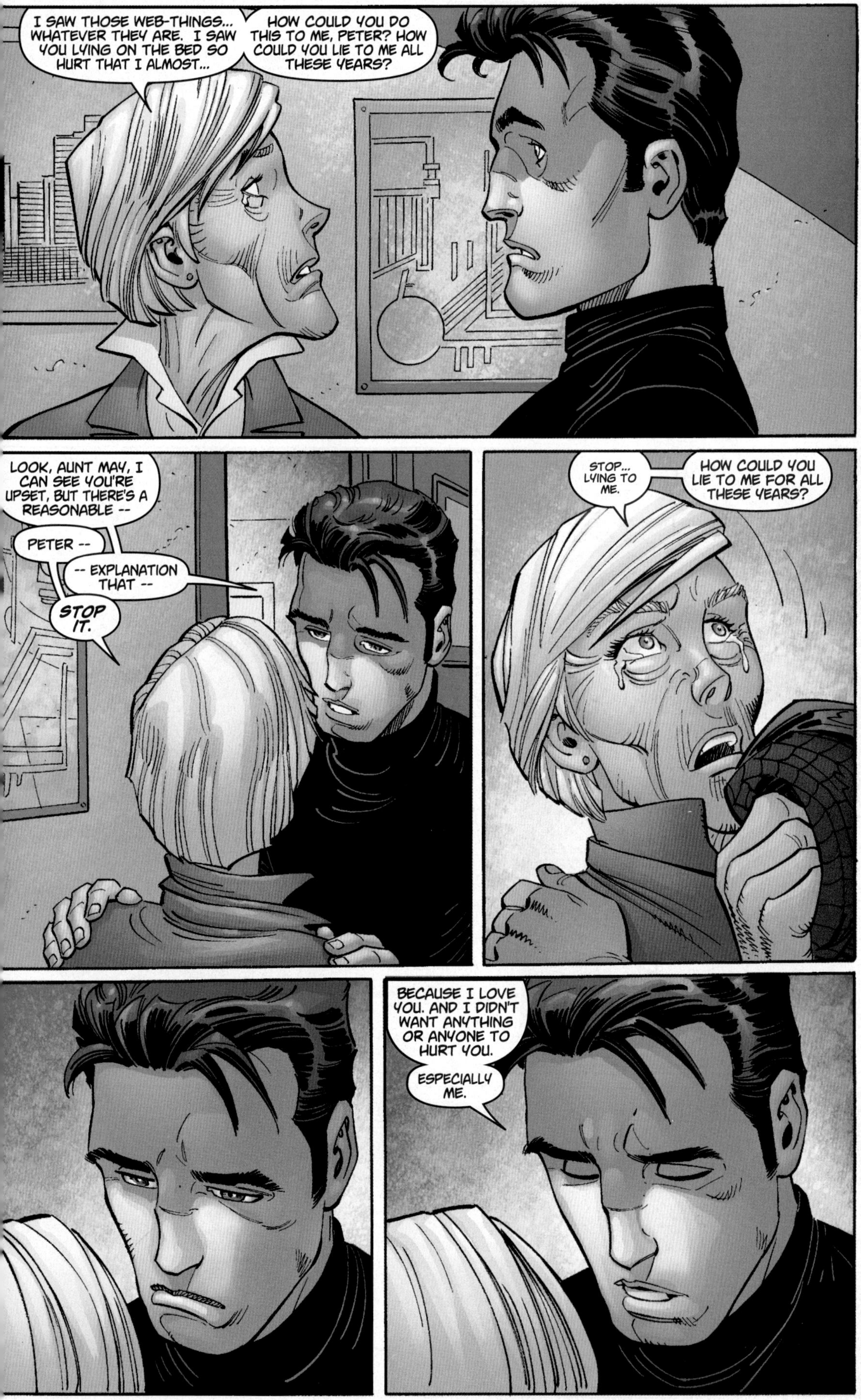
I SAW THOSE WEB-THINGS... WHATEVER THEY ARE. I SAW YOU LYING ON THE BED SO HURT THAT I ALMOST...
HOW COULD YOU DO THIS TO ME, PETER? HOW COULD YOU LIE TO ME ALL THESE YEARS?
LOOK, AUNT MAY, I CAN SEE YOU'RE UPSET, BUT THERE'S A REASONABLE --
PETER --
-- EXPLANATION THAT --
STOP IT.
STOP... LYING TO ME.
HOW COULD YOU LIE TO ME FOR ALL THESE YEARS?
BECAUSE I LOVE YOU. AND I DIDN'T WANT ANYTHING OR ANYONE TO HURT YOU.
ESPECIALLY ME.

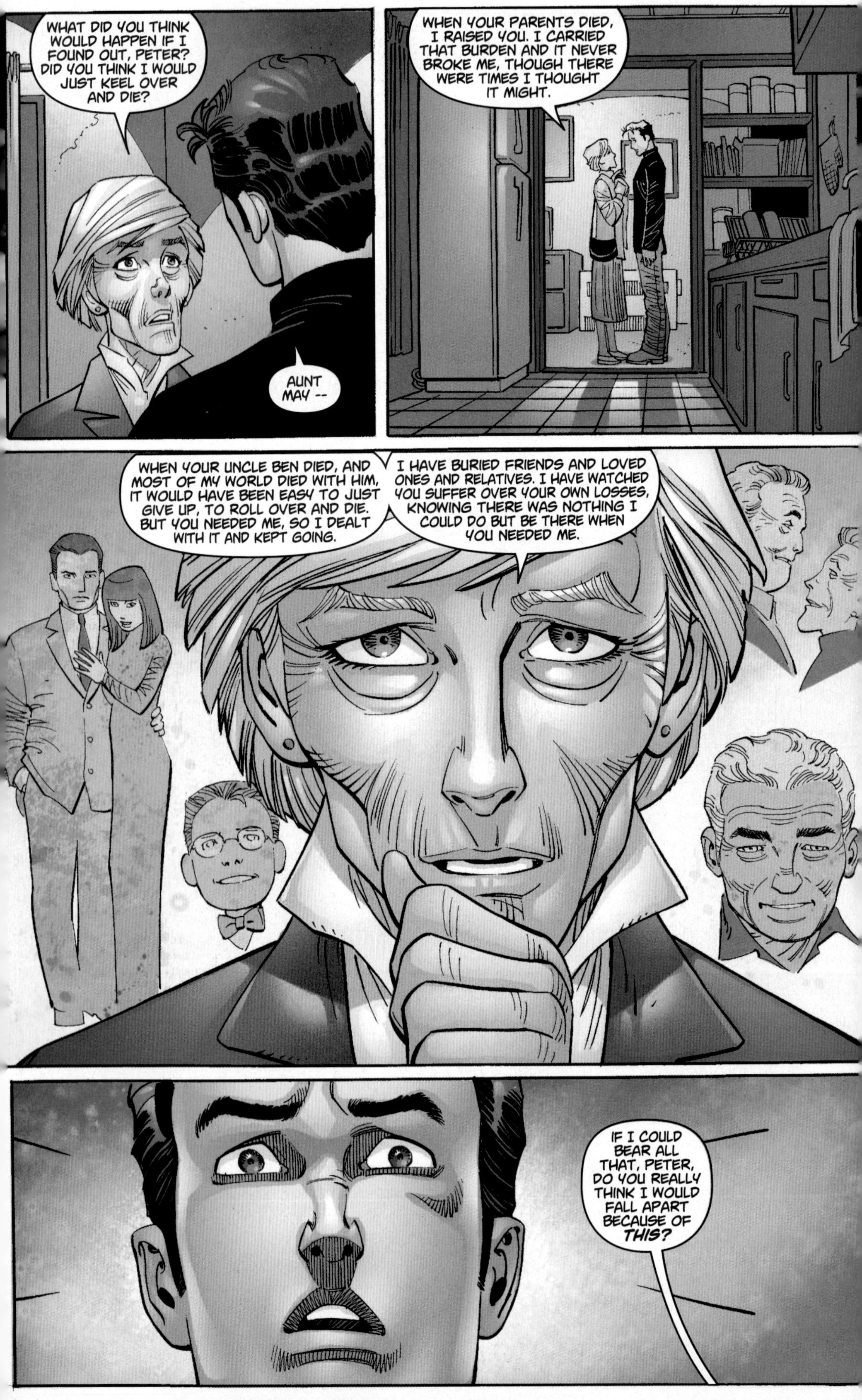
WHAT DID YOU THINK WOULD HAPPEN IF I FOUND OUT, PETER? DID YOU THINK I WOULD JUST KEEL OVER AND DIE?
AUNT MAY --
WHEN YOUR PARENTS DIED, I RAISED YOU. I CARRIED THAT BURDEN AND IT NEVER BROKE ME, THOUGH THERE WERE TIMES I THOUGHT IT MIGHT.
WHEN YOUR UNCLE BEN DIED, AND MOST OF MY WORLD DIED WITH HIM, IT WOULD HAVE BEEN EASY TO JUST GIVE UP, TO ROLL OVER AND DIE. BUT YOU NEEDED ME, SO I DEALT WITH IT AND KEPT GOING.
I HAVE BURIED FRIENDS AND LOVED ONES AND RELATIVES. I HAVE WATCHED YOU SUFFER OVER YOUR OWN LOSSES, KNOWING THERE WAS NOTHING I COULD DO BUT BE THERE WHEN YOU NEEDED ME.
IF I COULD BEAR ALL THAT, PETER, DO YOU REALLY THINK I WOULD FALL APART BECAUSE OF THIS?

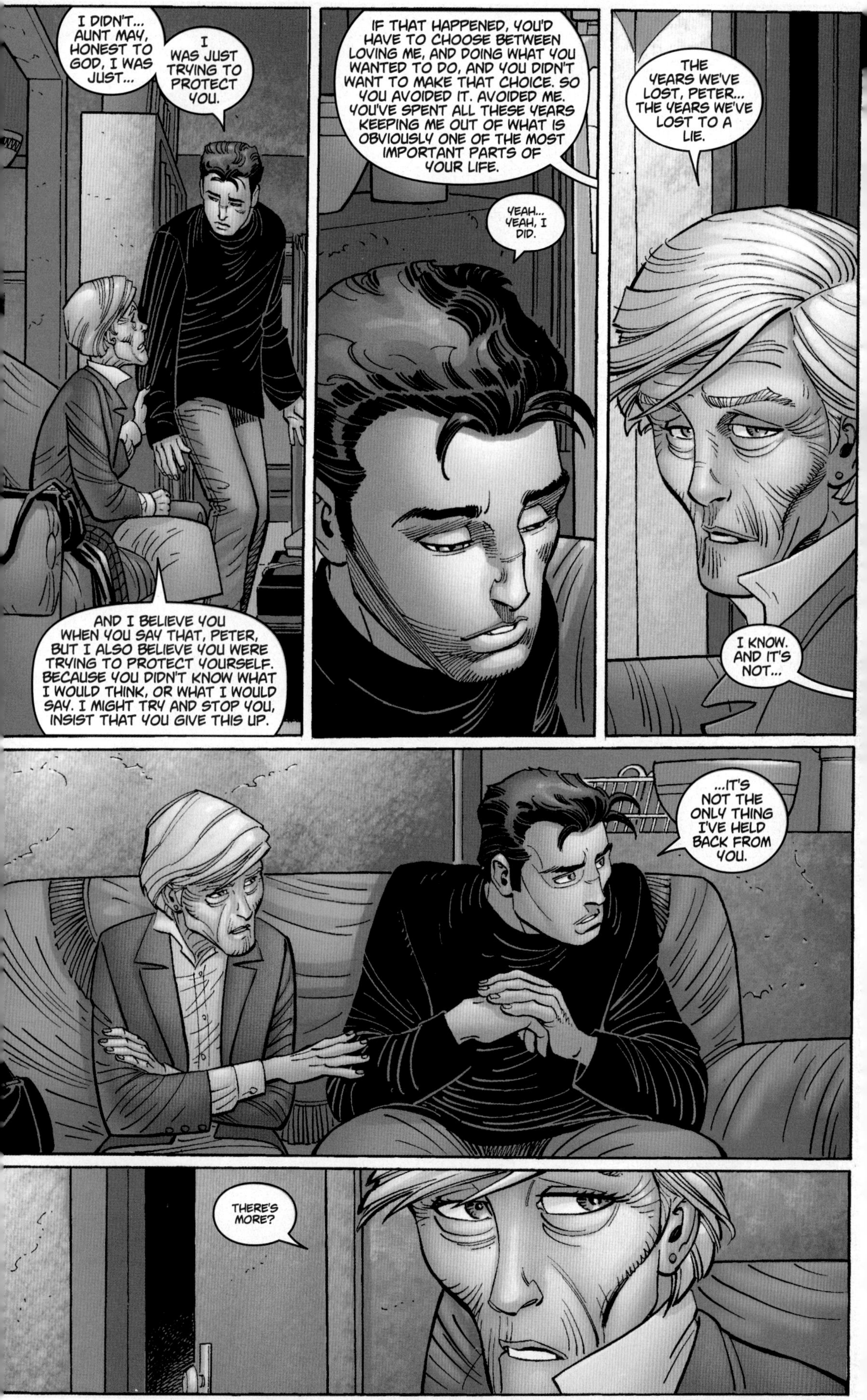

I DIDN'T... AUNT MAY, HONEST TO GOD, I WAS JUST...
I WAS JUST TRYING TO PROTECT YOU.
AND I BELIEVE YOU WHEN YOU SAY THAT, PETER, BUT I ALSO BELIEVE YOU WERE TRYING TO PROTECT YOURSELF. BECAUSE YOU DIDN'T KNOW WHAT I WOULD THINK, OR WHAT I WOULD SAY. I MIGHT TRY AND STOP YOU, INSIST THAT YOU GIVE THIS UP.
IF THAT HAPPENED, YOU'D HAVE TO CHOOSE BETWEEN LOVING ME, AND DOING WHAT YOU WANTED TO DO, AND YOU DIDN'T WANT TO MAKE THAT CHOICE. SO YOU AVOIDED IT. AVOIDED ME. YOU'VE SPENT ALL THESE YEARS KEEPING ME OUT OF WHAT IS OBVIOUSLY ONE OF THE MOST IMPORTANT PARTS OF YOUR LIFE.
YEAH... YEAH, I DID.
THE YEARS WE'VE LOST, PETER... THE YEARS WE'VE LOST TO A LIE.
I KNOW. AND IT'S NOT...
...IT'S NOT THE ONLY THING I'VE HELD BACK FROM YOU.
THERE'S MORE?

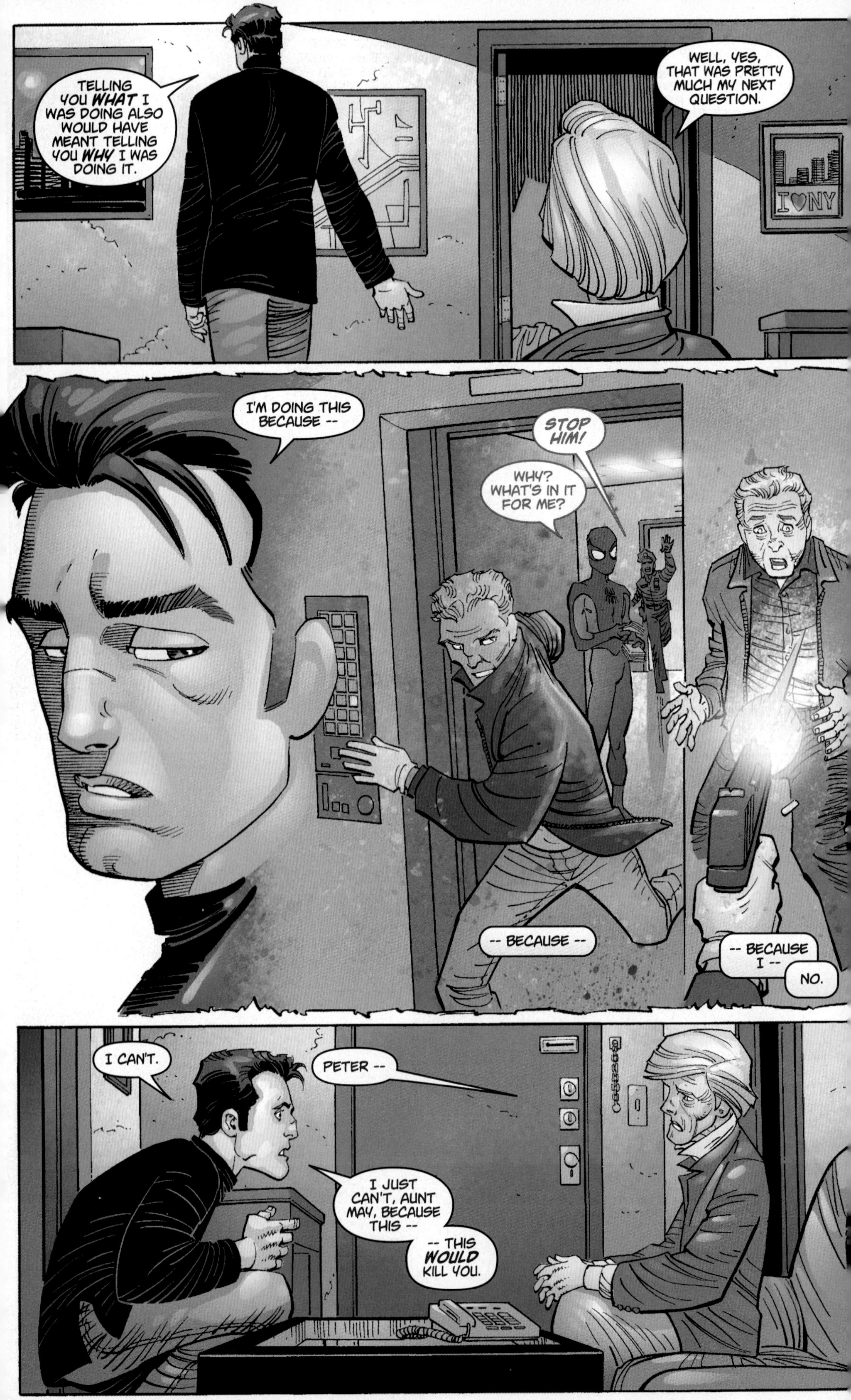
TELLING YOU *WHAT* I WAS DOING ALSO WOULD HAVE MEANT TELLING YOU *WHY* I WAS DOING IT.
WELL, YES, THAT WAS PRETTY MUCH MY NEXT QUESTION.
I♥NY
I'M DOING THIS BECAUSE --
STOP HIM!
WHY? WHAT'S IN IT FOR ME?
-- BECAUSE --
-- BECAUSE I --
NO.
I CAN'T.
PETER --
I JUST CAN'T, AUNT MAY, BECAUSE THIS --
-- THIS *WOULD* KILL YOU.

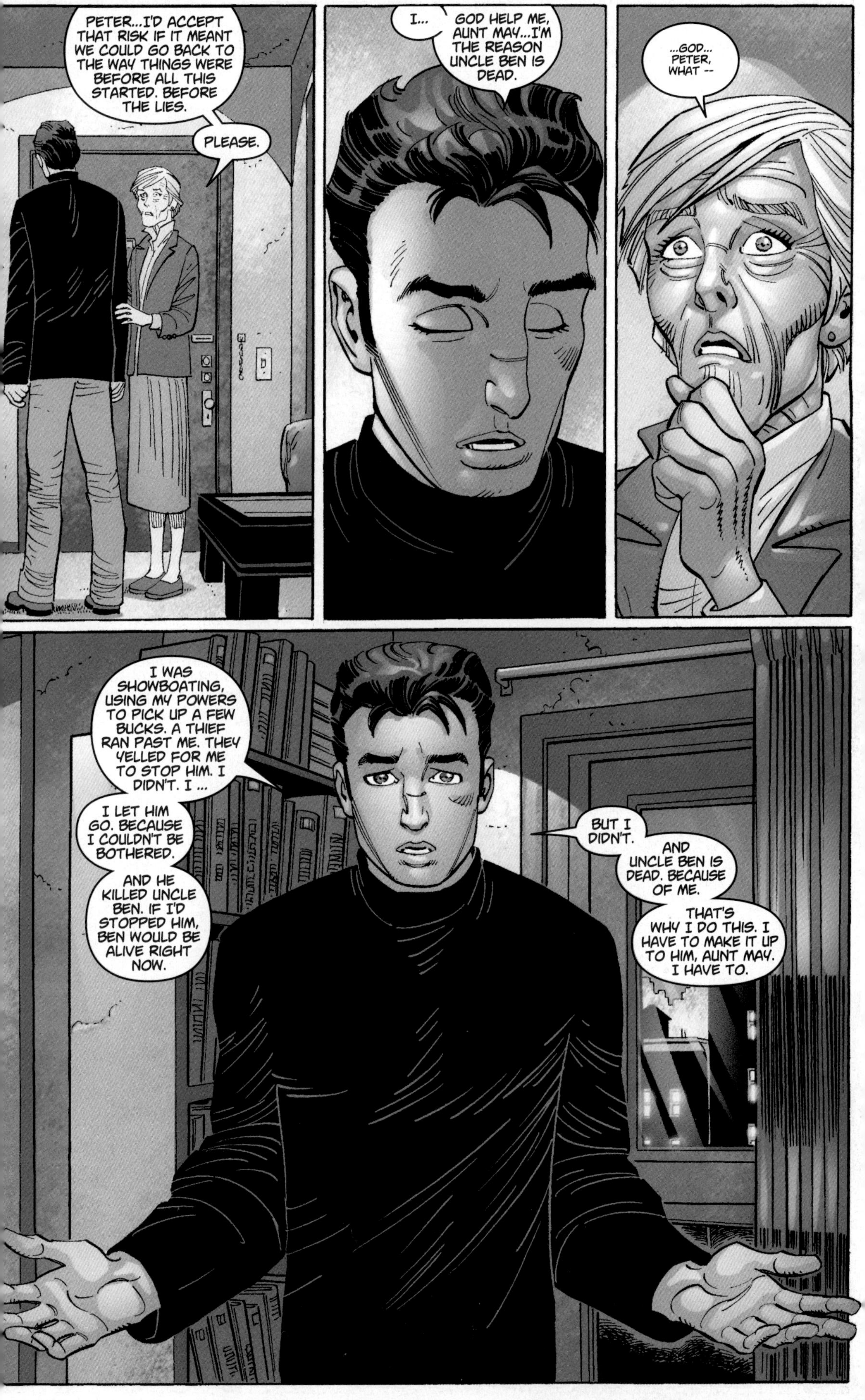
PETER...I'D ACCEPT THAT RISK IF IT MEANT WE COULD GO BACK TO THE WAY THINGS WERE BEFORE ALL THIS STARTED. BEFORE THE LIES.
PLEASE.
I...
GOD HELP ME, AUNT MAY...I'M THE REASON UNCLE BEN IS DEAD.
...GOD... PETER, WHAT --
I WAS SHOWBOATING, USING MY POWERS TO PICK UP A FEW BUCKS. A THIEF RAN PAST ME. THEY YELLED FOR ME TO STOP HIM. I DIDN'T. I ...
I LET HIM GO. BECAUSE I COULDN'T BE BOTHERED.
AND HE KILLED UNCLE BEN. IF I'D STOPPED HIM, BEN WOULD BE ALIVE RIGHT NOW.
BUT I DIDN'T.
AND UNCLE BEN IS DEAD. BECAUSE OF ME.
THAT'S WHY I DO THIS. I HAVE TO MAKE IT UP TO HIM, AUNT MAY. I HAVE TO.

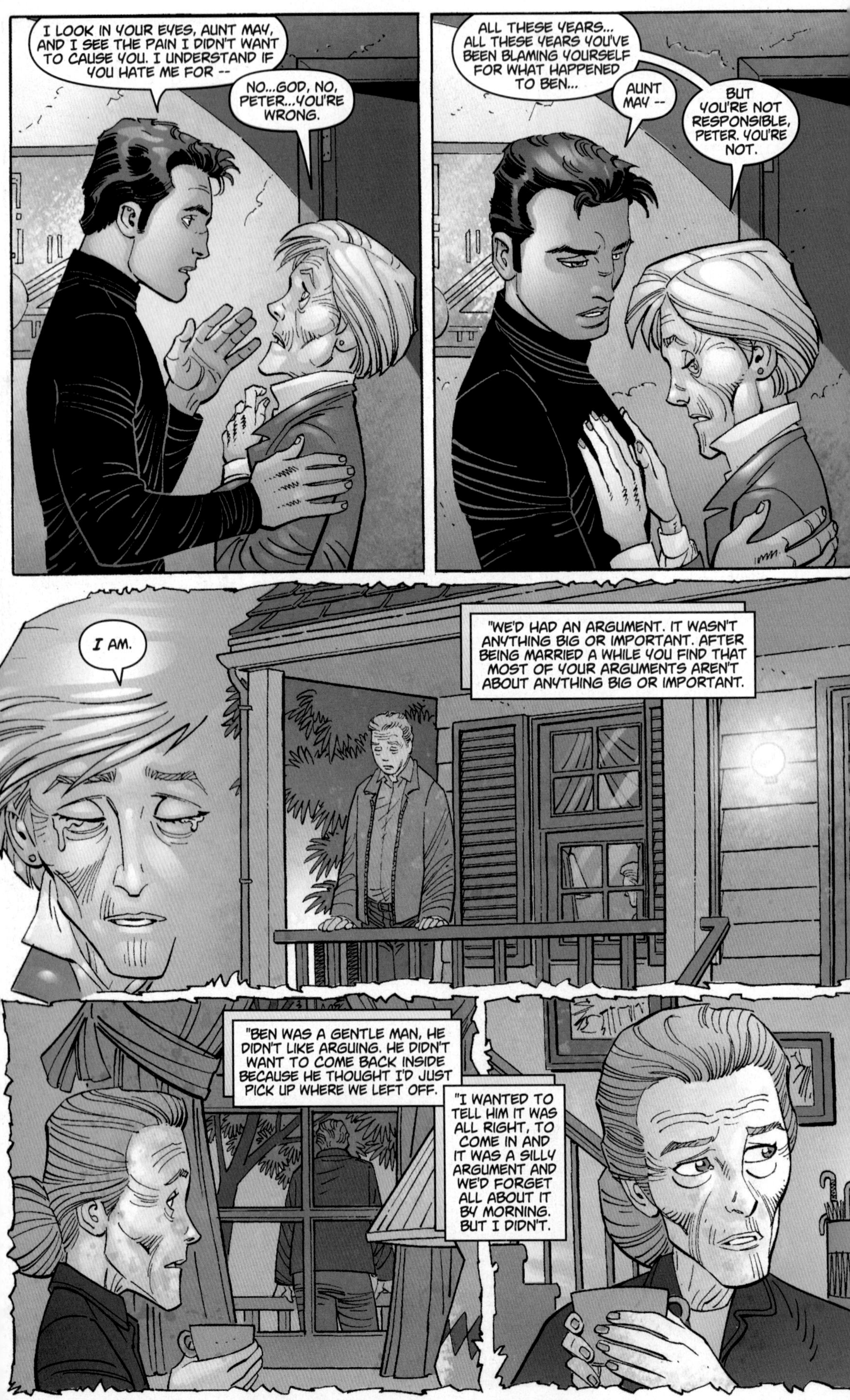
I LOOK IN YOUR EYES, AUNT MAY, AND I SEE THE PAIN I DIDN'T WANT TO CAUSE YOU. I UNDERSTAND IF YOU HATE ME FOR --
NO...GOD, NO, PETER...YOU'RE WRONG.
ALL THESE YEARS... ALL THESE YEARS YOU'VE BEEN BLAMING YOURSELF FOR WHAT HAPPENED TO BEN...
AUNT MAY --
BUT YOU'RE NOT RESPONSIBLE, PETER. YOU'RE NOT.
I AM.
"WE'D HAD AN ARGUMENT. IT WASN'T ANYTHING BIG OR IMPORTANT. AFTER BEING MARRIED A WHILE YOU FIND THAT MOST OF YOUR ARGUMENTS AREN'T ABOUT ANYTHING BIG OR IMPORTANT.
"BEN WAS A GENTLE MAN, HE DIDN'T LIKE ARGUING. HE DIDN'T WANT TO COME BACK INSIDE BECAUSE HE THOUGHT I'D JUST PICK UP WHERE WE LEFT OFF.
"I WANTED TO TELL HIM IT WAS ALL RIGHT, TO COME IN AND IT WAS A SILLY ARGUMENT AND WE'D FORGET ALL ABOUT IT BY MORNING. BUT I DIDN'T.

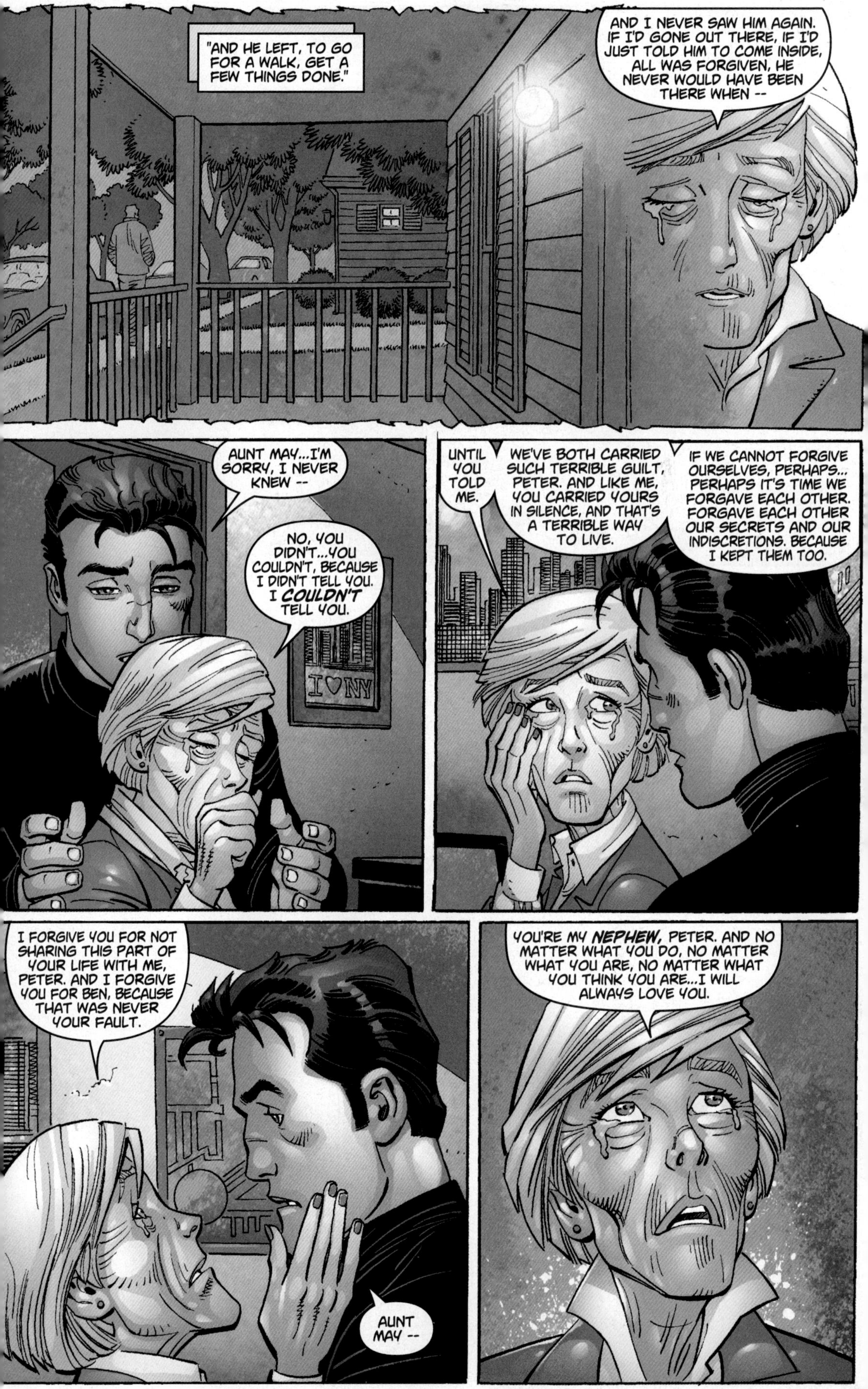

"AND HE LEFT, TO GO FOR A WALK, GET A FEW THINGS DONE."
AND I NEVER SAW HIM AGAIN. IF I'D GONE OUT THERE, IF I'D JUST TOLD HIM TO COME INSIDE, ALL WAS FORGIVEN, HE NEVER WOULD HAVE BEEN THERE WHEN --
AUNT MAY...I'M SORRY, I NEVER KNEW --
NO, YOU DIDN'T...YOU COULDN'T, BECAUSE I DIDN'T TELL YOU. I COULDN'T TELL YOU.
I ♥ NY
UNTIL YOU TOLD ME.
WE'VE BOTH CARRIED SUCH TERRIBLE GUILT, PETER. AND LIKE ME, YOU CARRIED YOURS IN SILENCE, AND THAT'S A TERRIBLE WAY TO LIVE.
IF WE CANNOT FORGIVE OURSELVES, PERHAPS... PERHAPS IT'S TIME WE FORGAVE EACH OTHER. FORGAVE EACH OTHER OUR SECRETS AND OUR INDISCRETIONS. BECAUSE I KEPT THEM TOO.
I FORGIVE YOU FOR NOT SHARING THIS PART OF YOUR LIFE WITH ME, PETER. AND I FORGIVE YOU FOR BEN, BECAUSE THAT WAS NEVER YOUR FAULT.
AUNT MAY --
YOU'RE MY ***NEPHEW***, PETER. AND NO MATTER WHAT YOU DO, NO MATTER WHAT YOU ARE, NO MATTER WHAT YOU THINK YOU ARE...I WILL ALWAYS LOVE YOU.

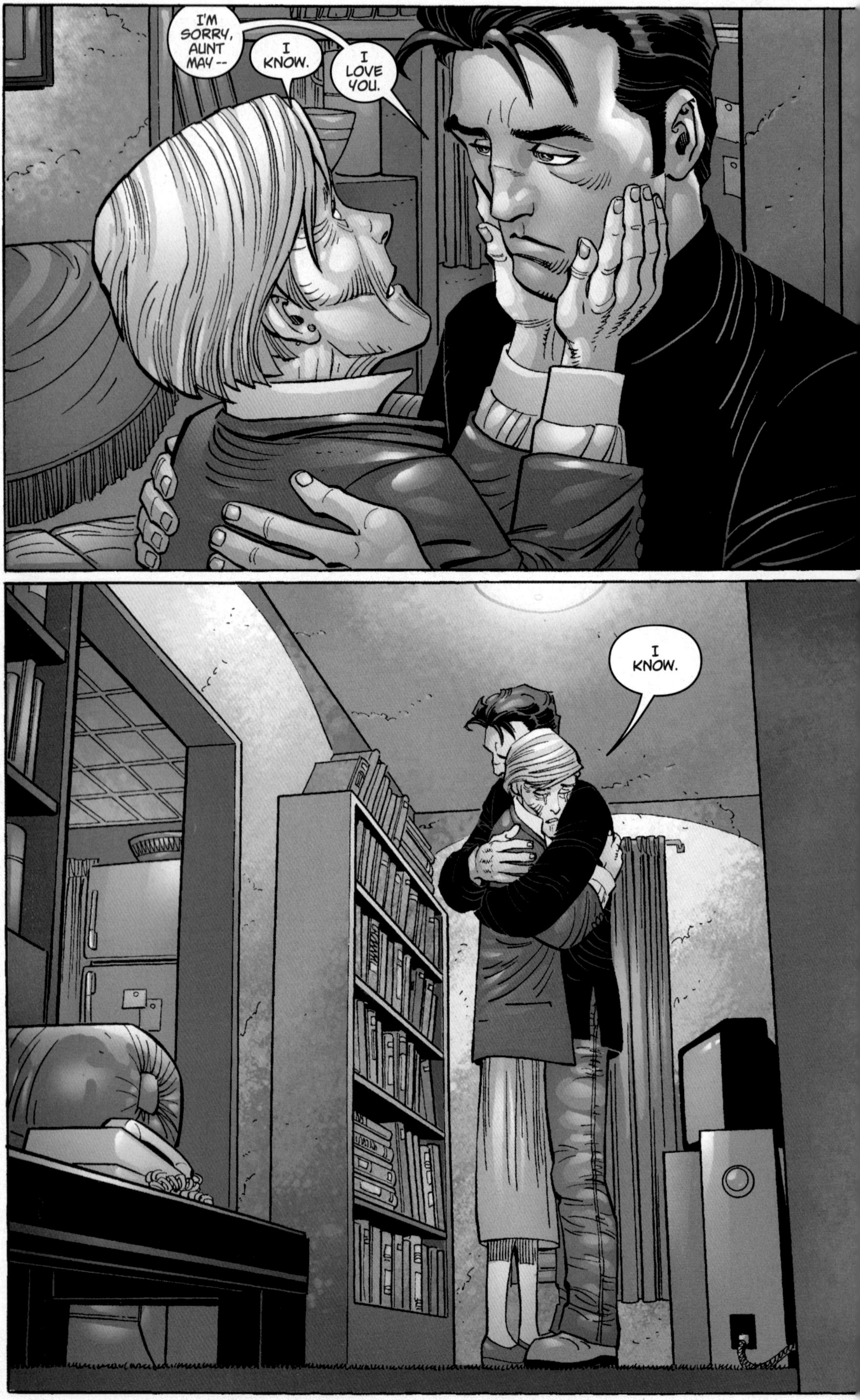
I'M SORRY, AUNT MAY --
I KNOW.
I LOVE YOU.
I KNOW.

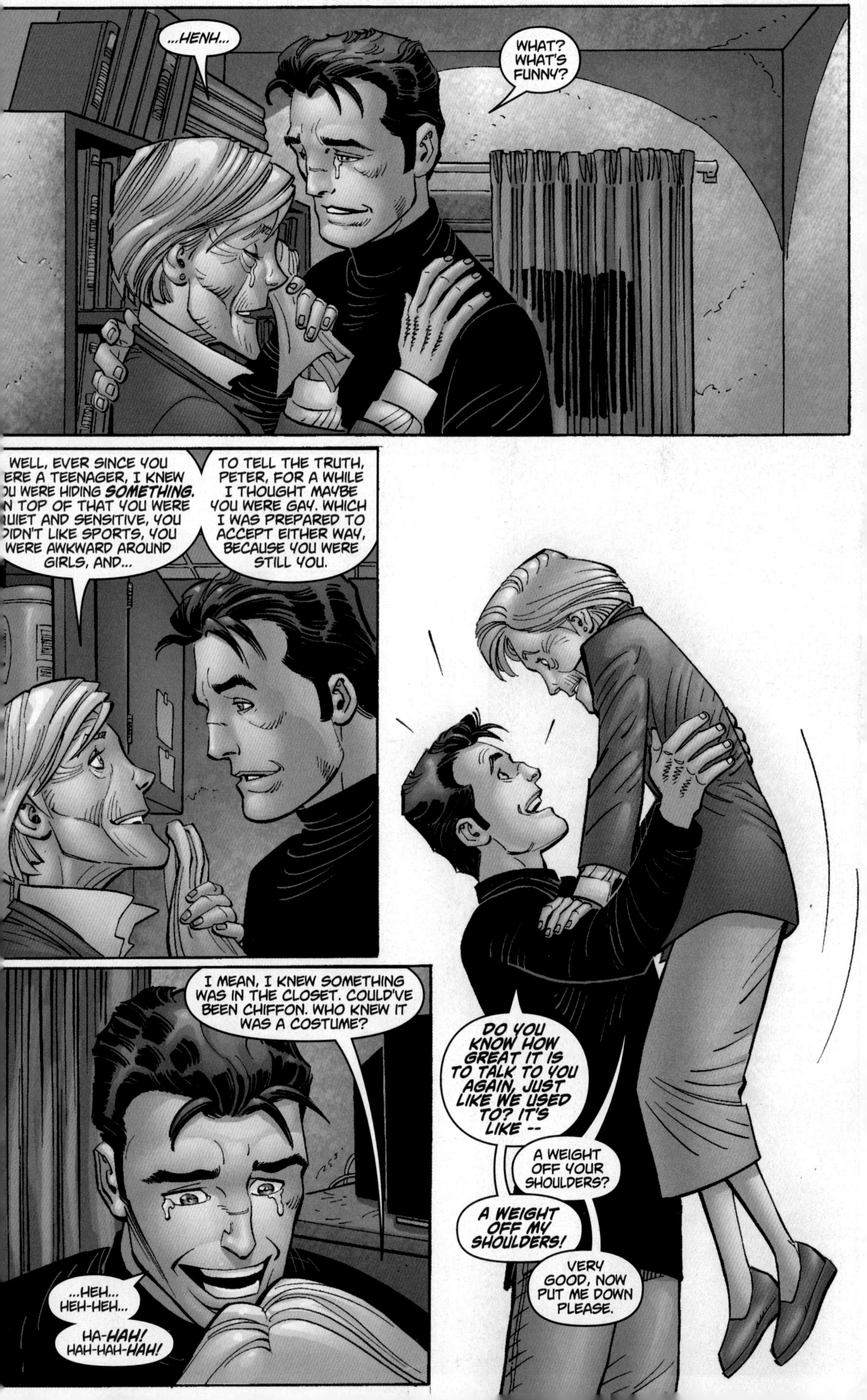

...HENH...
WHAT? WHAT'S FUNNY?
WELL, EVER SINCE YOU ERE A TEENAGER, I KNEW OU WERE HIDING **SOMETHING.** N TOP OF THAT YOU WERE UIET AND SENSITIVE, YOU IDN'T LIKE SPORTS, YOU WERE AWKWARD AROUND GIRLS, AND...
TO TELL THE TRUTH, PETER, FOR A WHILE I THOUGHT MAYBE YOU WERE GAY. WHICH I WAS PREPARED TO ACCEPT EITHER WAY, BECAUSE YOU WERE STILL YOU.
I MEAN, I KNEW SOMETHING WAS IN THE CLOSET. COULD'VE BEEN CHIFFON. WHO KNEW IT WAS A COSTUME?
...HEH... HEH-HEH...
HA-*HAH!* HAH-HAH-*HAH!*
DO YOU KNOW HOW GREAT IT IS TO TALK TO YOU AGAIN, JUST LIKE WE USED TO? IT'S LIKE --
A WEIGHT OFF YOUR SHOULDERS?
A WEIGHT OFF MY SHOULDERS!
VERY GOOD, NOW PUT ME DOWN PLEASE.

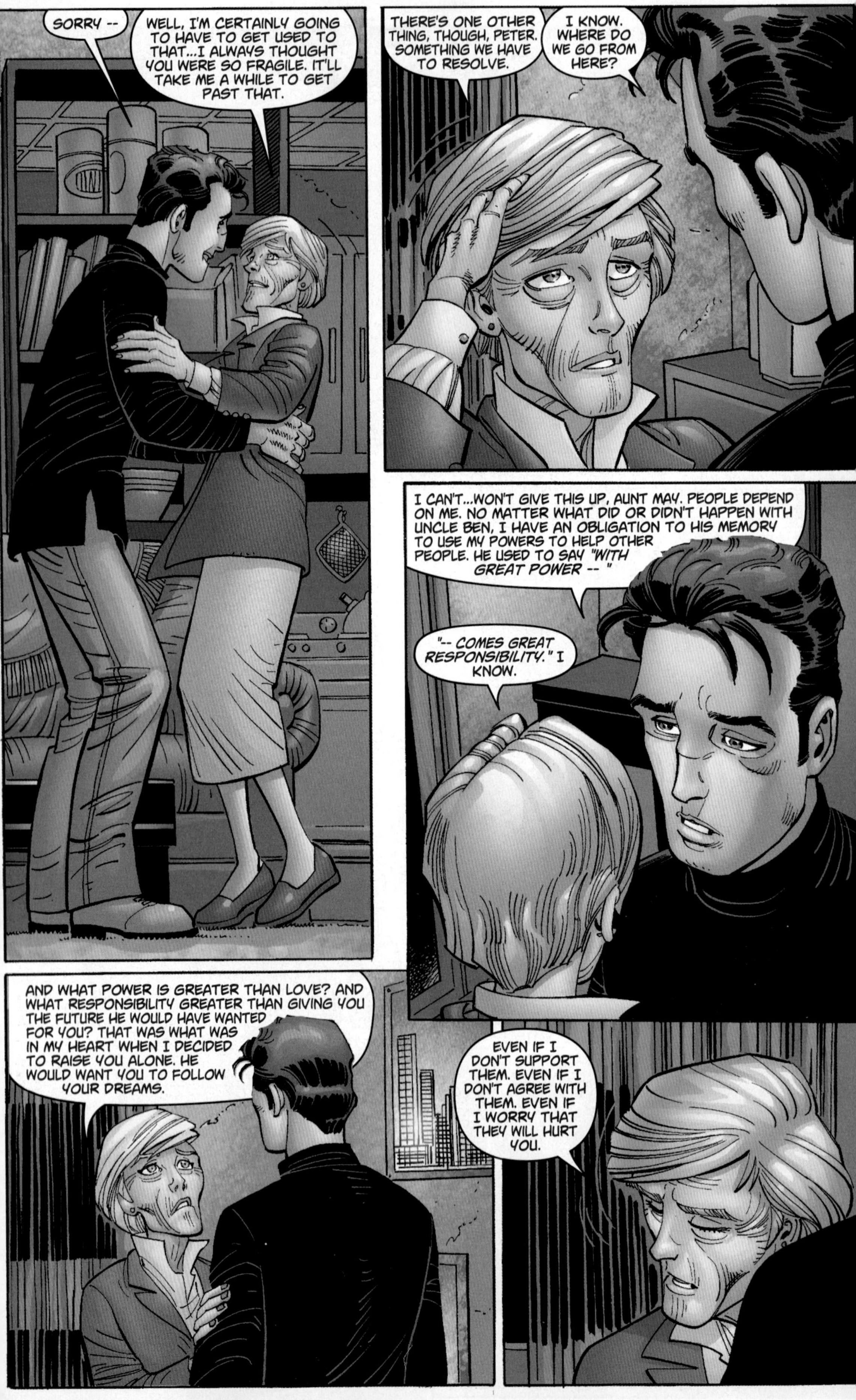
SORRY --
WELL, I'M CERTAINLY GOING TO HAVE TO GET USED TO THAT... I ALWAYS THOUGHT YOU WERE SO FRAGILE. IT'LL TAKE ME A WHILE TO GET PAST THAT.
THERE'S ONE OTHER THING, THOUGH, PETER. SOMETHING WE HAVE TO RESOLVE.
I KNOW. WHERE DO WE GO FROM HERE?
I CAN'T... WON'T GIVE THIS UP, AUNT MAY. PEOPLE DEPEND ON ME. NO MATTER WHAT DID OR DIDN'T HAPPEN WITH UNCLE BEN, I HAVE AN OBLIGATION TO HIS MEMORY TO USE MY POWERS TO HELP OTHER PEOPLE. HE USED TO SAY "WITH GREAT POWER -- "
"-- COMES GREAT RESPONSIBILITY." I KNOW.
AND WHAT POWER IS GREATER THAN LOVE? AND WHAT RESPONSIBILITY GREATER THAN GIVING YOU THE FUTURE HE WOULD HAVE WANTED FOR YOU? THAT WAS WHAT WAS IN MY HEART WHEN I DECIDED TO RAISE YOU ALONE. HE WOULD WANT YOU TO FOLLOW YOUR DREAMS.
EVEN IF I DON'T SUPPORT THEM. EVEN IF I DON'T AGREE WITH THEM. EVEN IF I WORRY THAT THEY WILL HURT YOU.

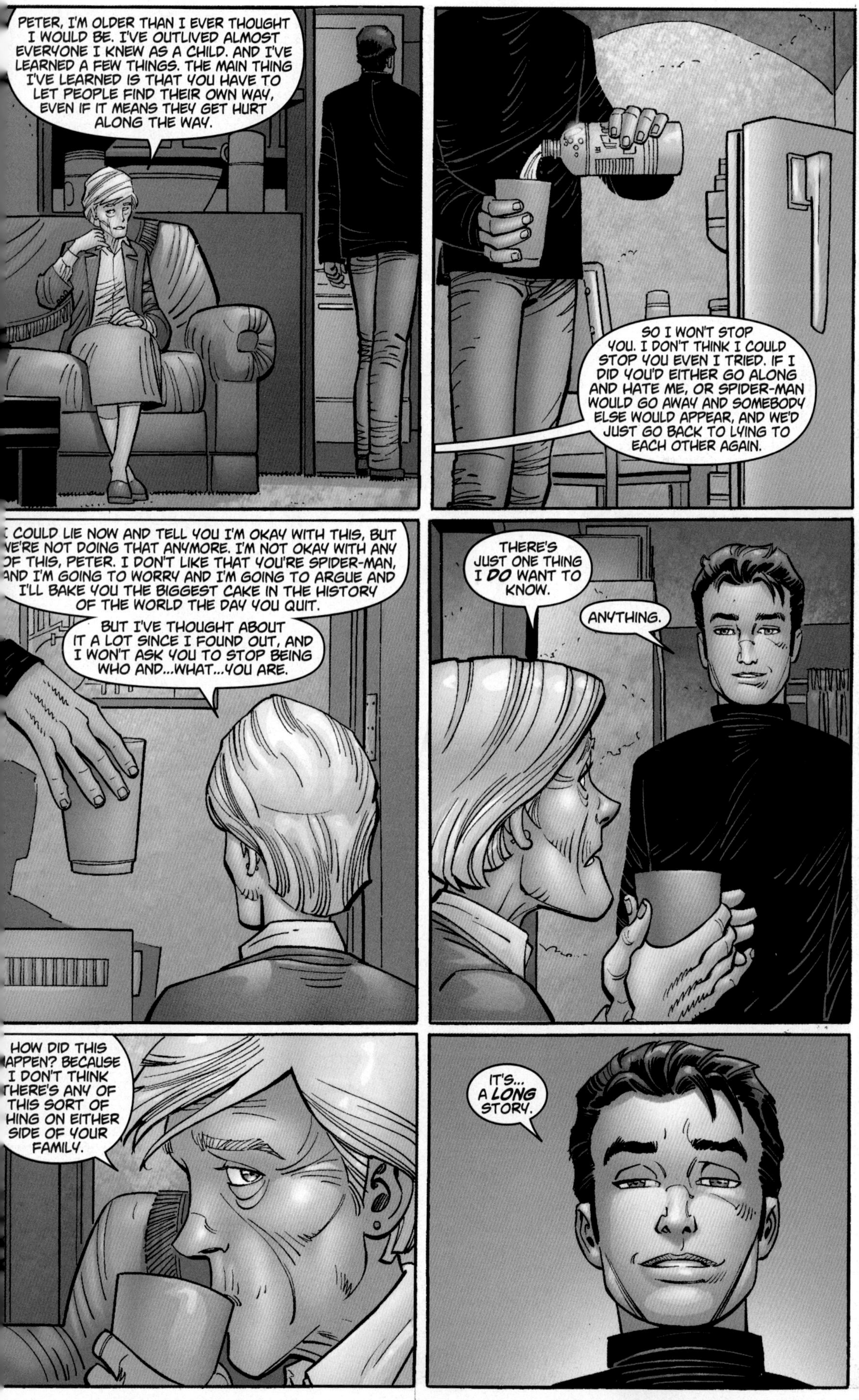

PETER, I'M OLDER THAN I EVER THOUGHT I WOULD BE. I'VE OUTLIVED ALMOST EVERYONE I KNEW AS A CHILD. AND I'VE LEARNED A FEW THINGS. THE MAIN THING I'VE LEARNED IS THAT YOU HAVE TO LET PEOPLE FIND THEIR OWN WAY, EVEN IF IT MEANS THEY GET HURT ALONG THE WAY.
SO I WON'T STOP YOU. I DON'T THINK I COULD STOP YOU EVEN I TRIED. IF I DID YOU'D EITHER GO ALONG AND HATE ME, OR SPIDER-MAN WOULD GO AWAY AND SOMEBODY ELSE WOULD APPEAR, AND WE'D JUST GO BACK TO LYING TO EACH OTHER AGAIN.
COULD LIE NOW AND TELL YOU I'M OKAY WITH THIS, BUT VE'RE NOT DOING THAT ANYMORE. I'M NOT OKAY WITH ANY OF THIS, PETER. I DON'T LIKE THAT YOU'RE SPIDER-MAN, AND I'M GOING TO WORRY AND I'M GOING TO ARGUE AND I'LL BAKE YOU THE BIGGEST CAKE IN THE HISTORY OF THE WORLD THE DAY YOU QUIT.
BUT I'VE THOUGHT ABOUT IT A LOT SINCE I FOUND OUT, AND I WON'T ASK YOU TO STOP BEING WHO AND...WHAT...YOU ARE.
THERE'S JUST ONE THING I **DO** WANT TO KNOW.
ANYTHING.
HOW DID THIS APPEN? BECAUSE I DON'T THINK THERE'S ANY OF THIS SORT OF HING ON EITHER SIDE OF YOUR FAMILY.
IT'S... A **LONG** STORY.

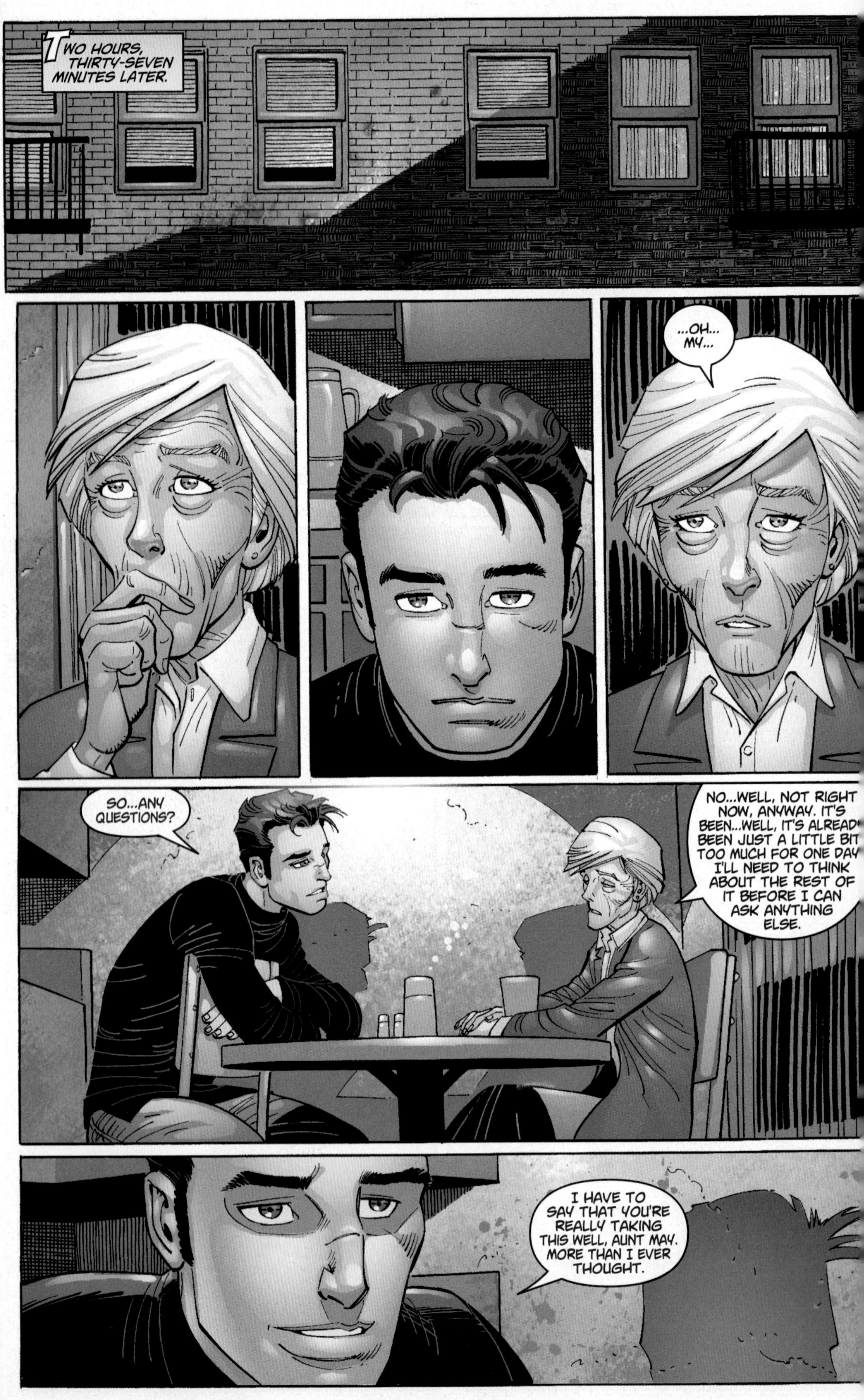
TWO HOURS, THIRTY-SEVEN MINUTES LATER.
...OH... MY...
SO...ANY QUESTIONS?
NO...WELL, NOT RIGHT NOW, ANYWAY. IT'S BEEN...WELL, IT'S ALREAD BEEN JUST A LITTLE BIT TOO MUCH FOR ONE DAY I'LL NEED TO THINK ABOUT THE REST OF IT BEFORE I CAN ASK ANYTHING ELSE.
I HAVE TO SAY THAT YOU'RE REALLY TAKING THIS WELL, AUNT MAY. MORE THAN I EVER THOUGHT.

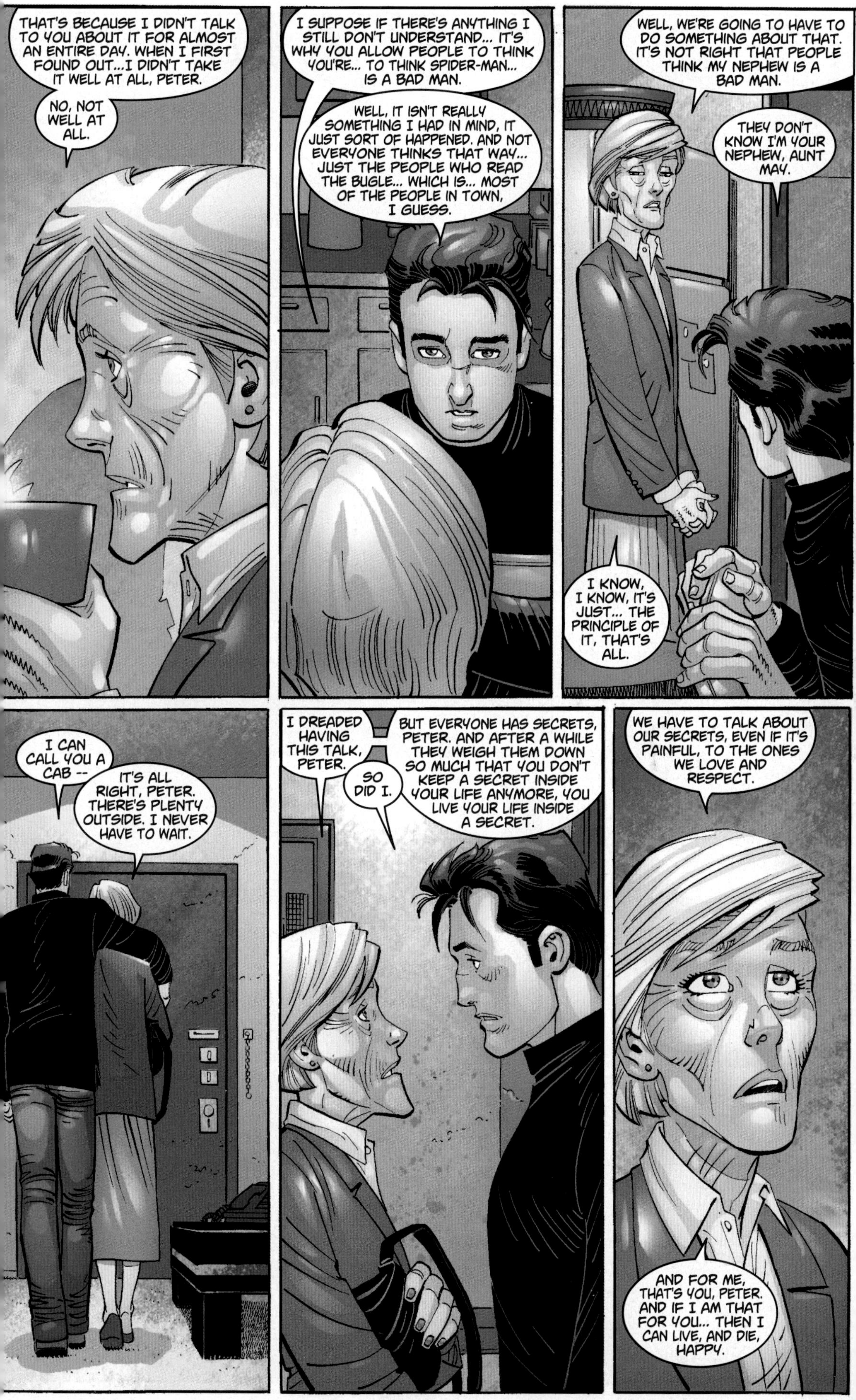
THAT'S BECAUSE I DIDN'T TALK TO YOU ABOUT IT FOR ALMOST AN ENTIRE DAY. WHEN I FIRST FOUND OUT...I DIDN'T TAKE IT WELL AT ALL, PETER.
NO, NOT WELL AT ALL.
I SUPPOSE IF THERE'S ANYTHING I STILL DON'T UNDERSTAND... IT'S WHY YOU ALLOW PEOPLE TO THINK YOU'RE... TO THINK SPIDER-MAN... IS A BAD MAN.
WELL, IT ISN'T REALLY SOMETHING I HAD IN MIND, IT JUST SORT OF HAPPENED. AND NOT EVERYONE THINKS THAT WAY... JUST THE PEOPLE WHO READ THE BUGLE... WHICH IS... MOST OF THE PEOPLE IN TOWN, I GUESS.
WELL, WE'RE GOING TO HAVE TO DO SOMETHING ABOUT THAT. IT'S NOT RIGHT THAT PEOPLE THINK MY NEPHEW IS A BAD MAN.
THEY DON'T KNOW I'M YOUR NEPHEW, AUNT MAY.
I KNOW, I KNOW, IT'S JUST... THE PRINCIPLE OF IT, THAT'S ALL.
I CAN CALL YOU A CAB --
IT'S ALL RIGHT, PETER. THERE'S PLENTY OUTSIDE. I NEVER HAVE TO WAIT.
I DREADED HAVING THIS TALK, PETER.
SO DID I.
BUT EVERYONE HAS SECRETS, PETER. AND AFTER A WHILE THEY WEIGH THEM DOWN SO MUCH THAT YOU DON'T KEEP A SECRET INSIDE YOUR LIFE ANYMORE, YOU LIVE YOUR LIFE INSIDE A SECRET.
WE HAVE TO TALK ABOUT OUR SECRETS, EVEN IF IT'S PAINFUL, TO THE ONES WE LOVE AND RESPECT.
AND FOR ME, THAT'S YOU, PETER. AND IF I AM THAT FOR YOU... THEN I CAN LIVE, AND DIE, HAPPY.

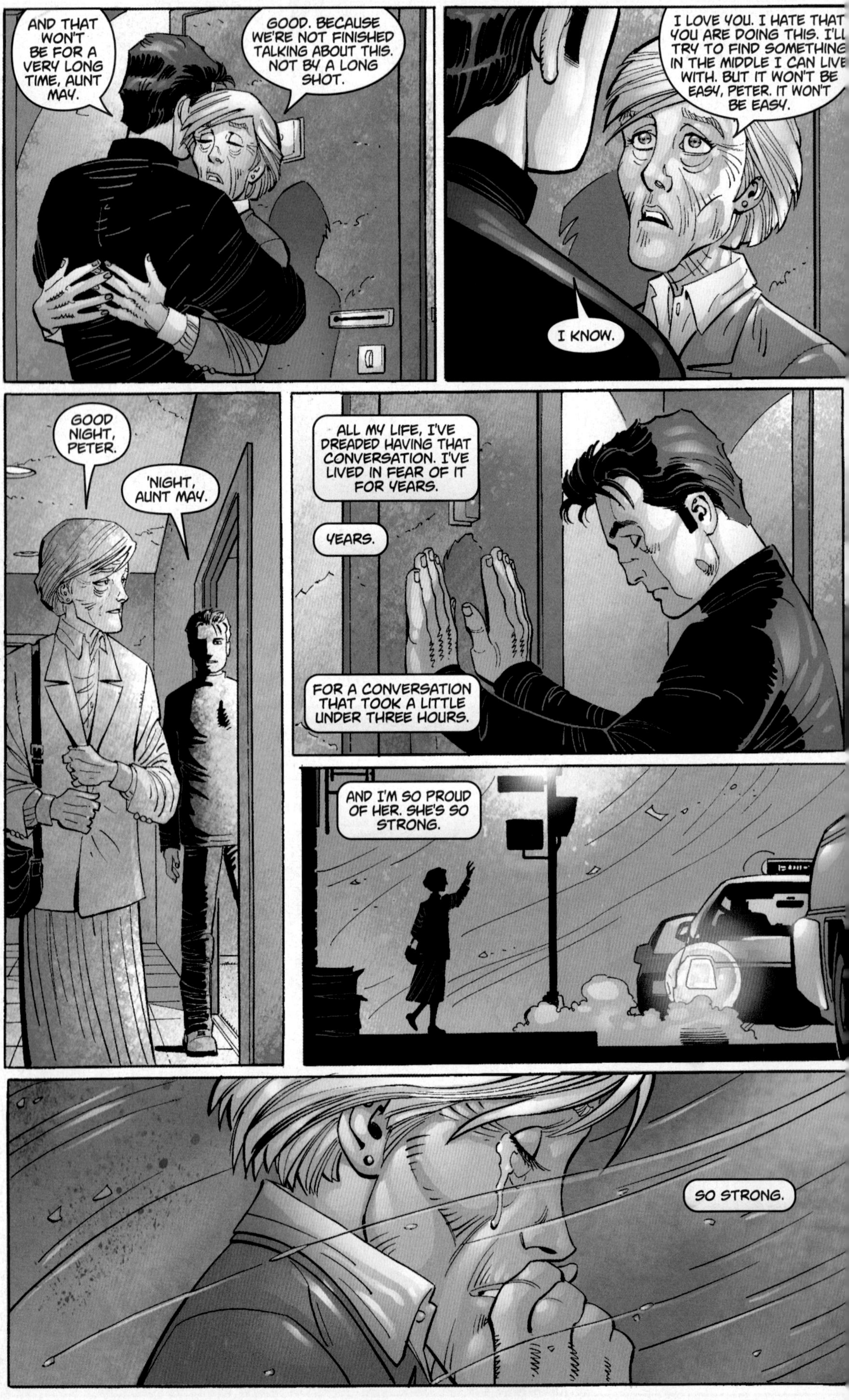
AND THAT WON'T BE FOR A VERY LONG TIME, AUNT MAY.
GOOD. BECAUSE WE'RE NOT FINISHED TALKING ABOUT THIS. NOT BY A LONG SHOT.
I LOVE YOU. I HATE THAT YOU ARE DOING THIS. I'LL TRY TO FIND SOMETHING IN THE MIDDLE I CAN LIVE WITH. BUT IT WON'T BE EASY, PETER. IT WON'T BE EASY.
I KNOW.
GOOD NIGHT, PETER.
'NIGHT, AUNT MAY.
ALL MY LIFE, I'VE DREADED HAVING THAT CONVERSATION. I'VE LIVED IN FEAR OF IT FOR YEARS.
YEARS.
FOR A CONVERSATION THAT TOOK A LITTLE UNDER THREE HOURS.
AND I'M SO PROUD OF HER. SHE'S SO STRONG.
SO STRONG.

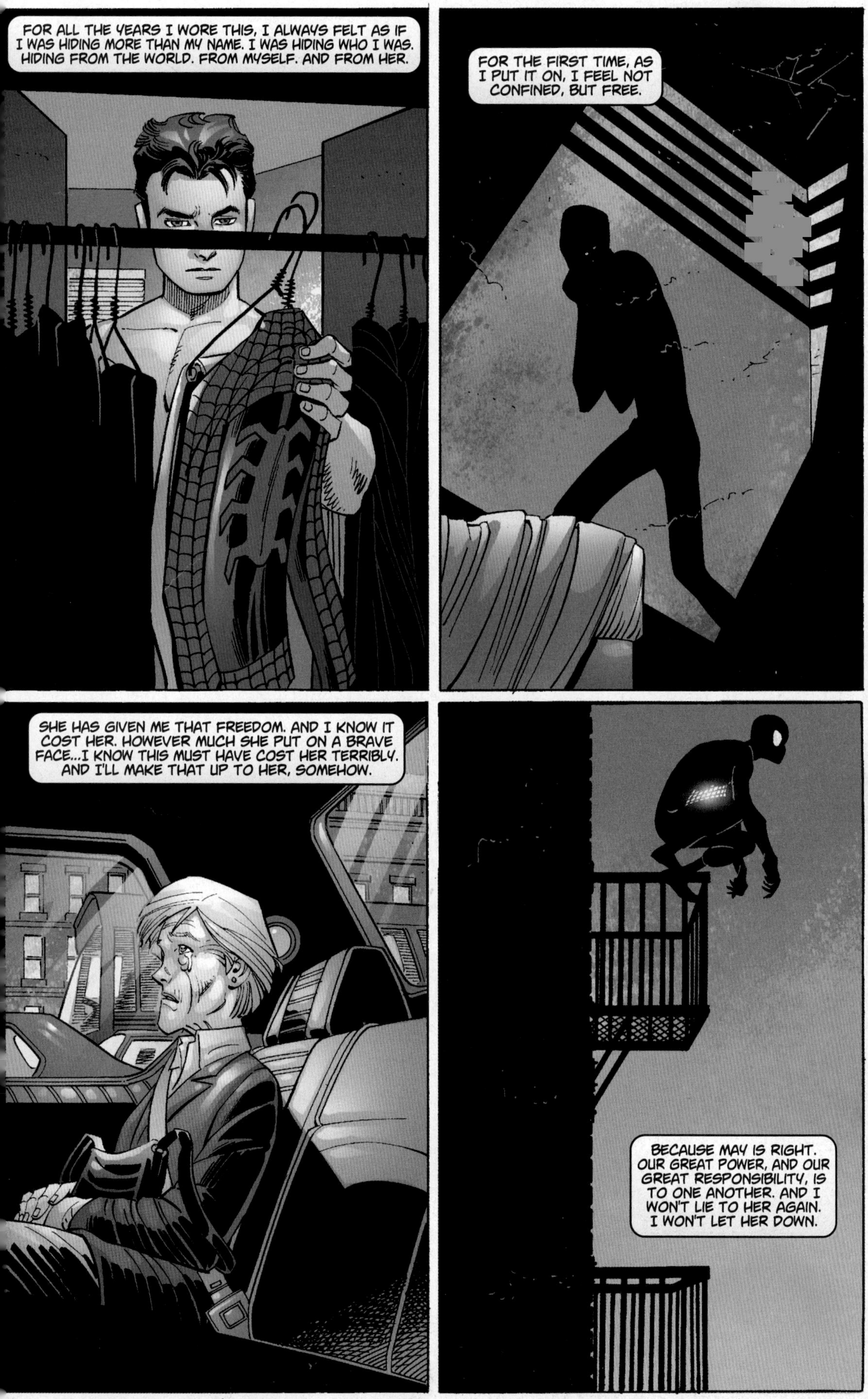
FOR ALL THE YEARS I WORE THIS, I ALWAYS FELT AS IF I WAS HIDING MORE THAN MY NAME. I WAS HIDING WHO I WAS. HIDING FROM THE WORLD. FROM MYSELF. AND FROM HER.
FOR THE FIRST TIME, AS I PUT IT ON, I FEEL NOT CONFINED, BUT FREE.
SHE HAS GIVEN ME THAT FREEDOM. AND I KNOW IT COST HER. HOWEVER MUCH SHE PUT ON A BRAVE FACE...I KNOW THIS MUST HAVE COST HER TERRIBLY. AND I'LL MAKE THAT UP TO HER, SOMEHOW.
BECAUSE MAY IS RIGHT. OUR GREAT POWER, AND OUR GREAT RESPONSIBILITY, IS TO ONE ANOTHER. AND I WON'T LIE TO HER AGAIN. I WON'T LET HER DOWN.

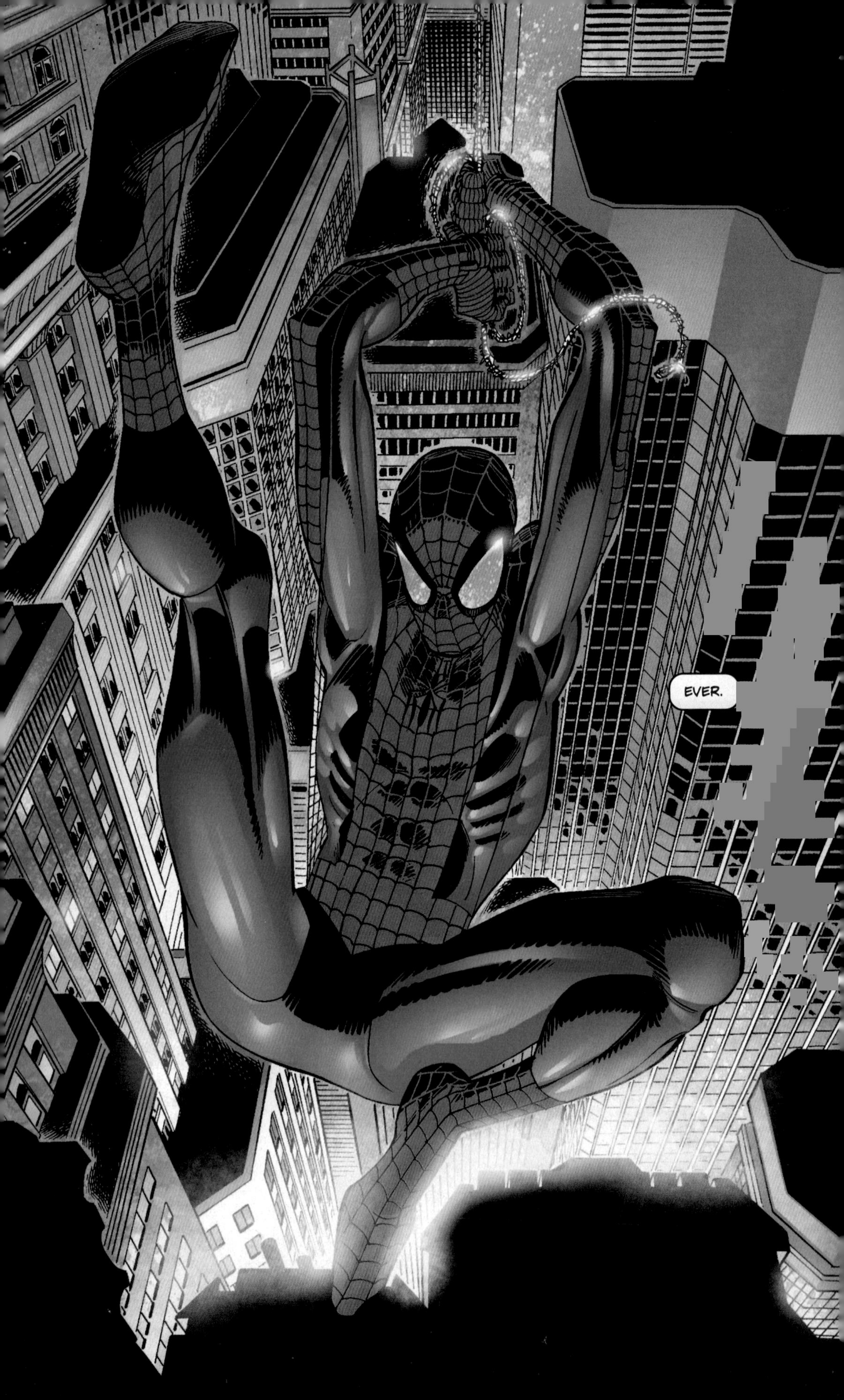
EVER.

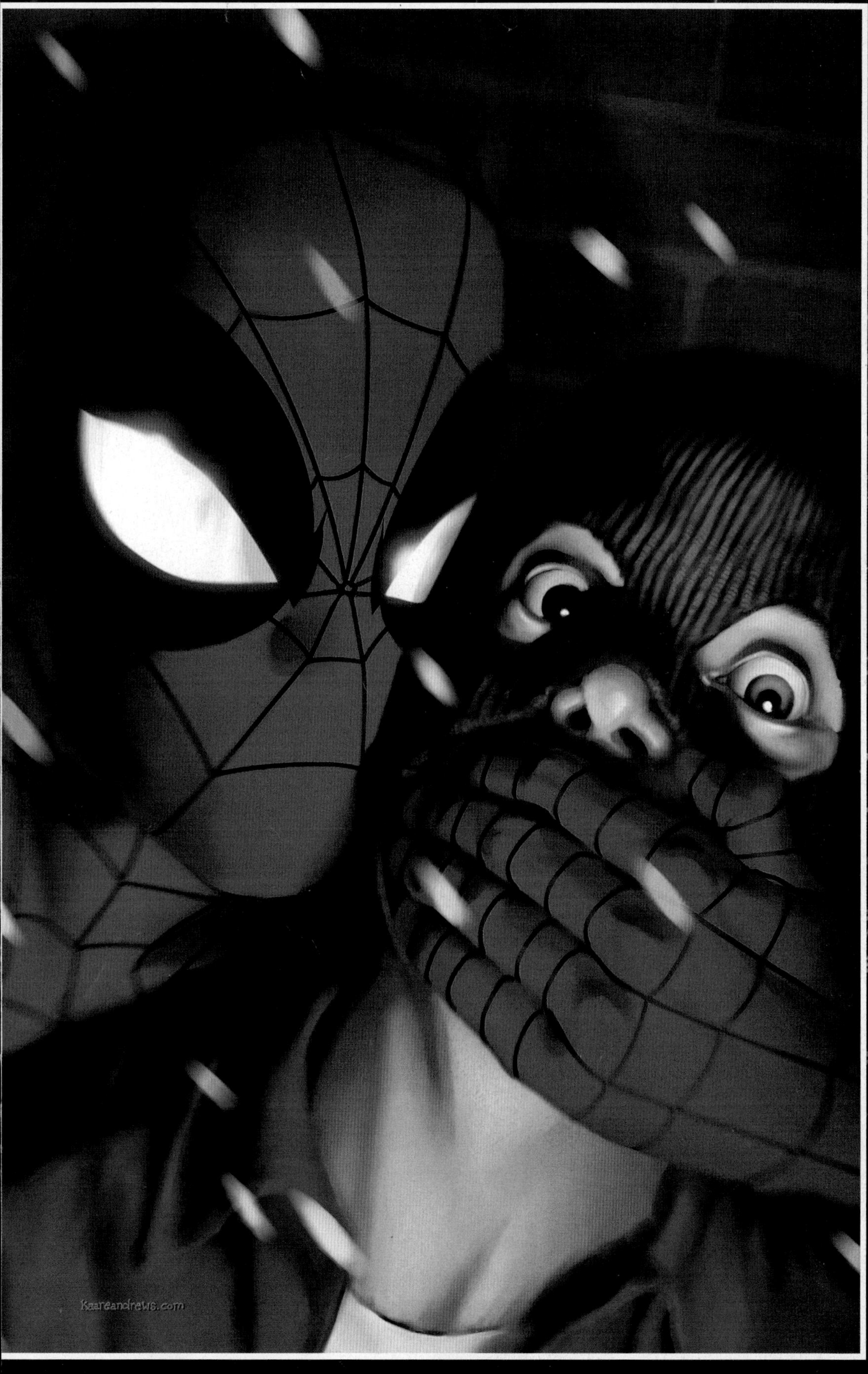
kaareandrews.com

AMAZING SPIDER-MAN #39

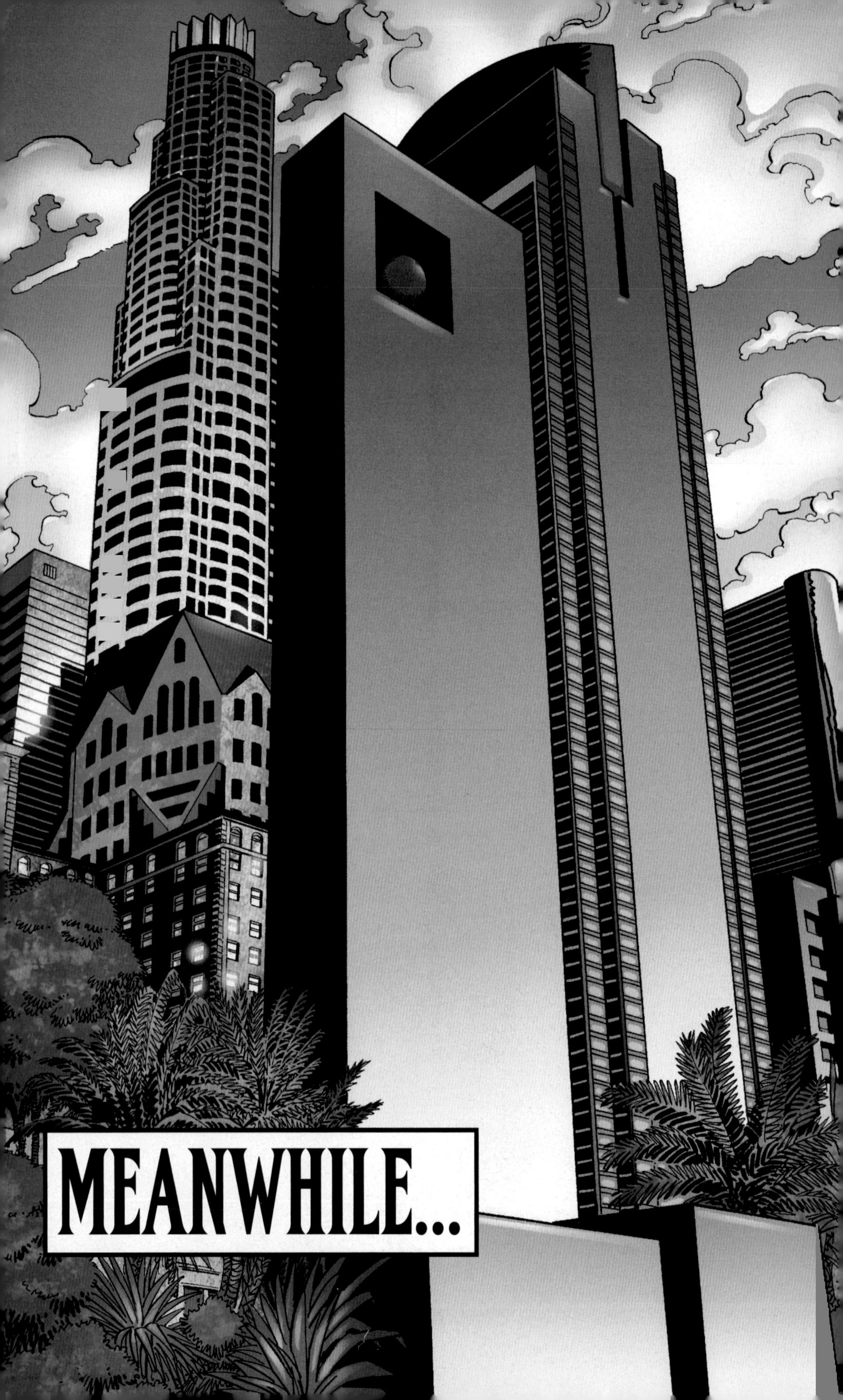
MEANWHILE...

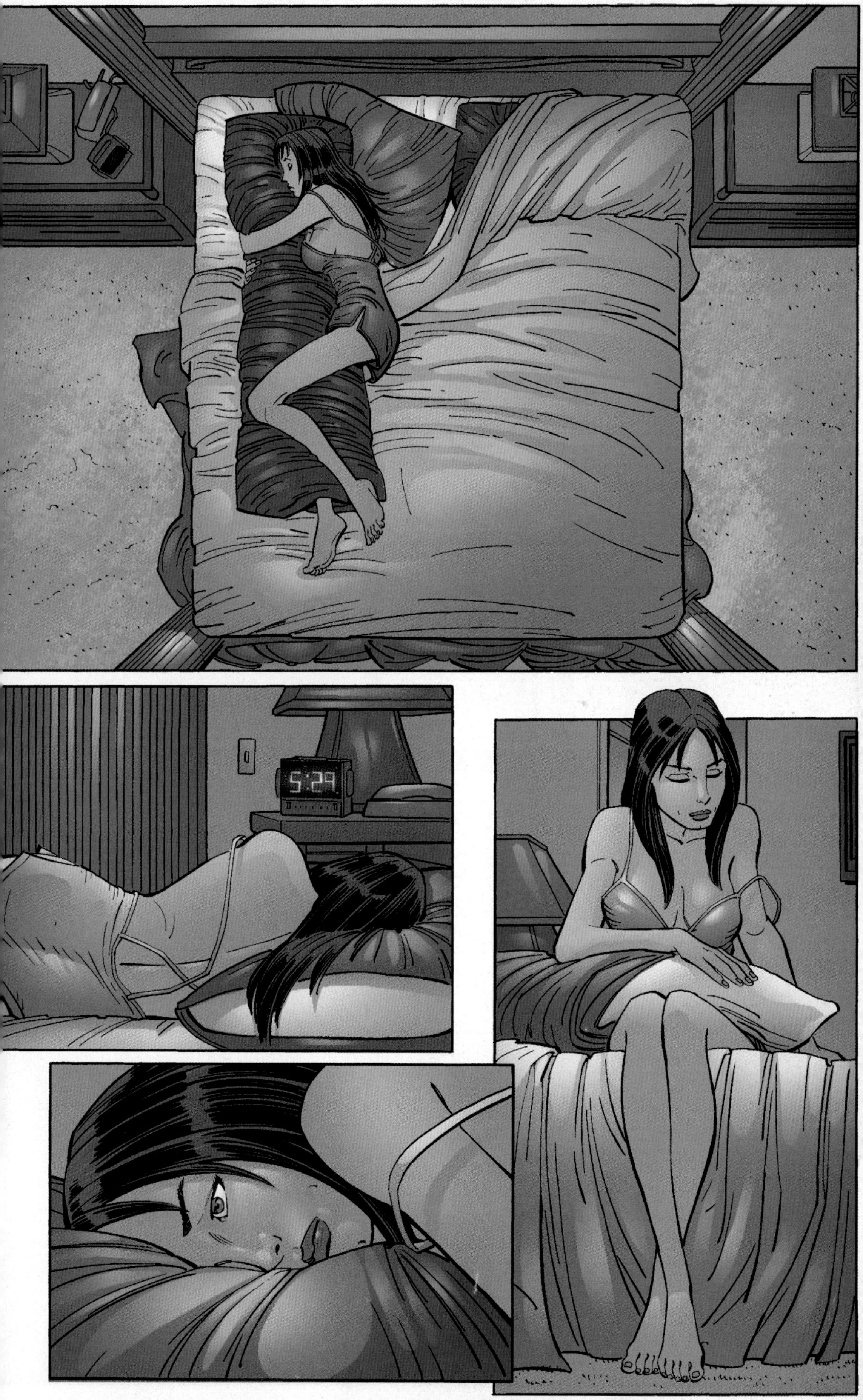
5:29

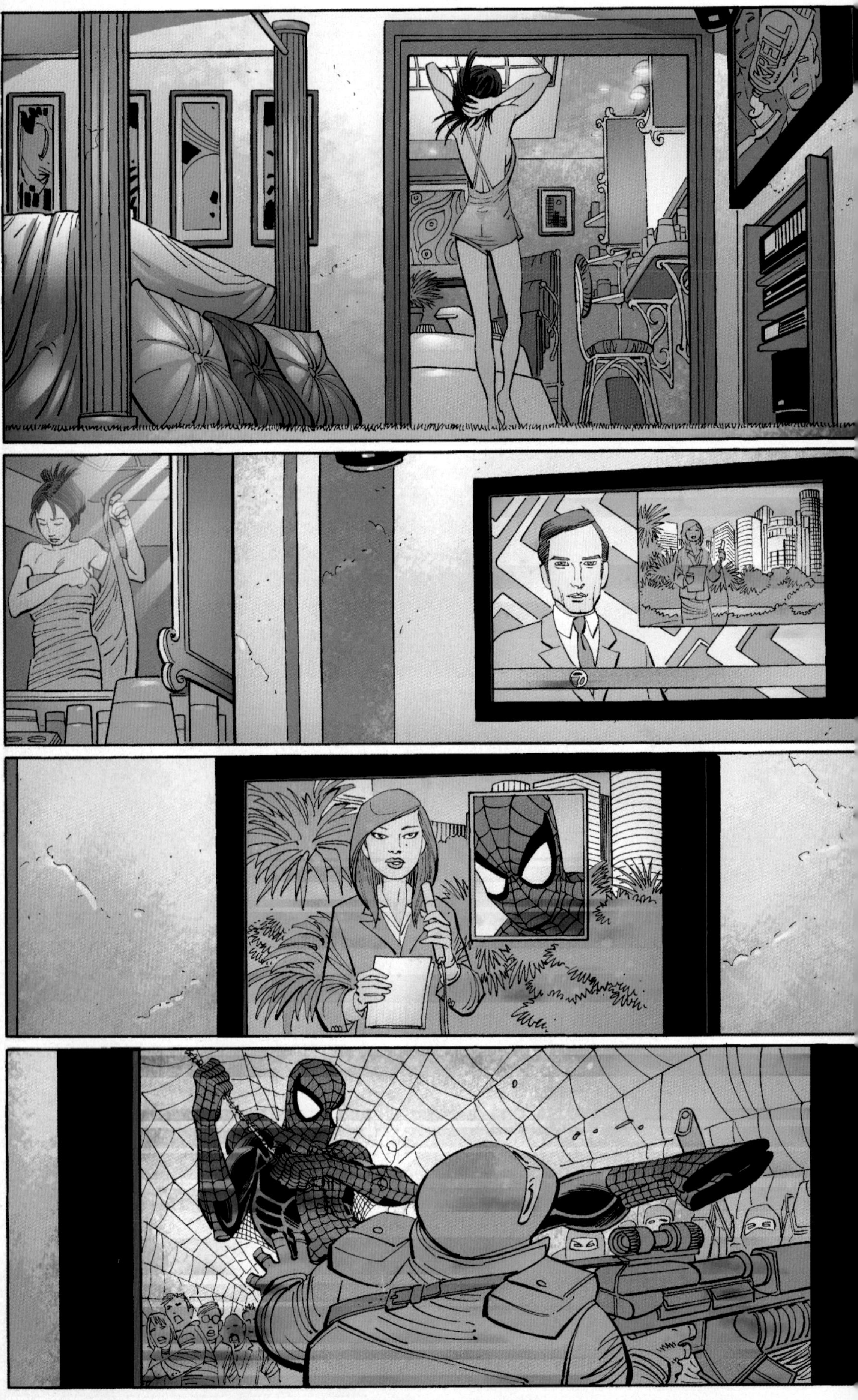
KRELL

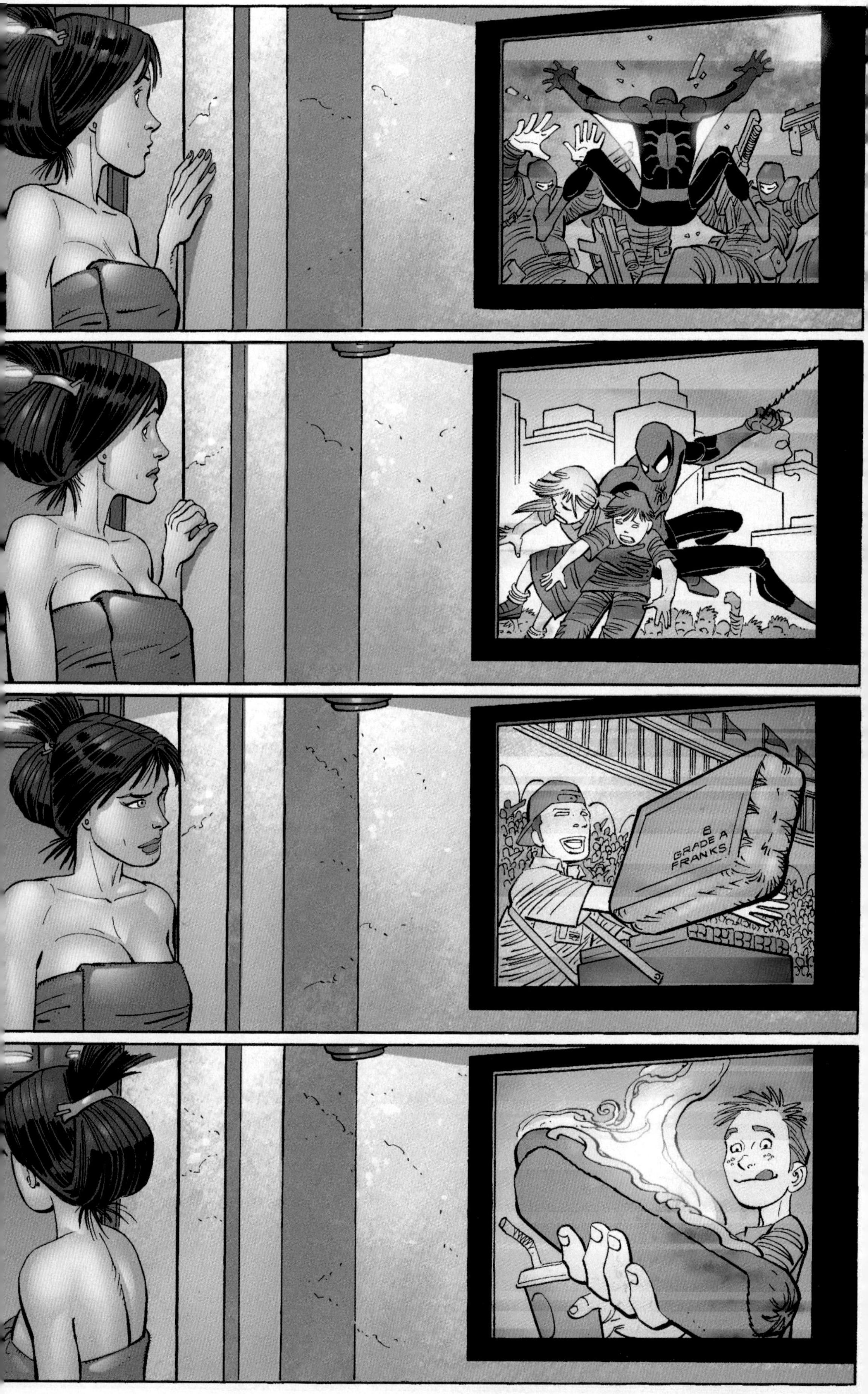
8
GRADE A
FRANKS

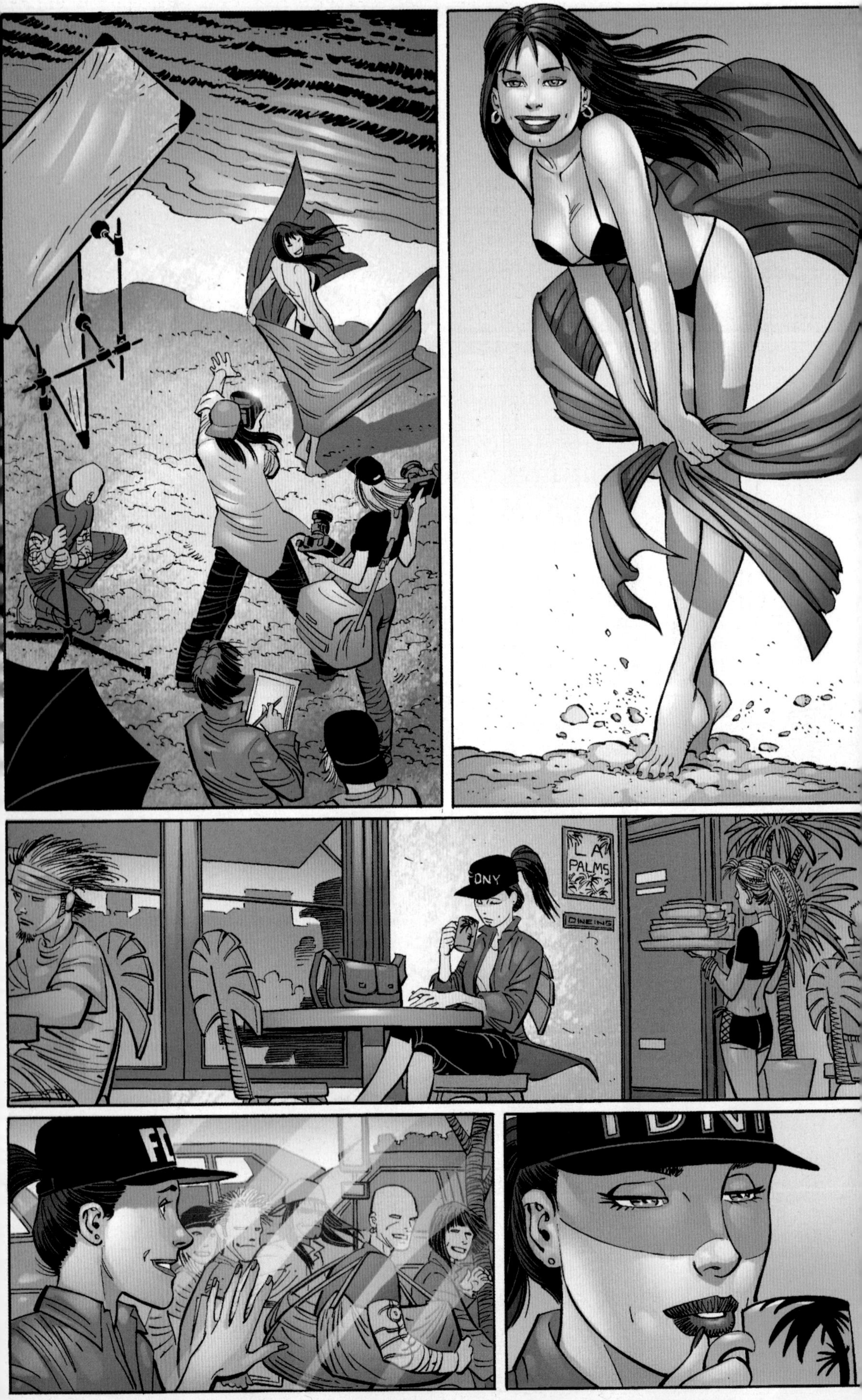
LA PALMS
DINEING

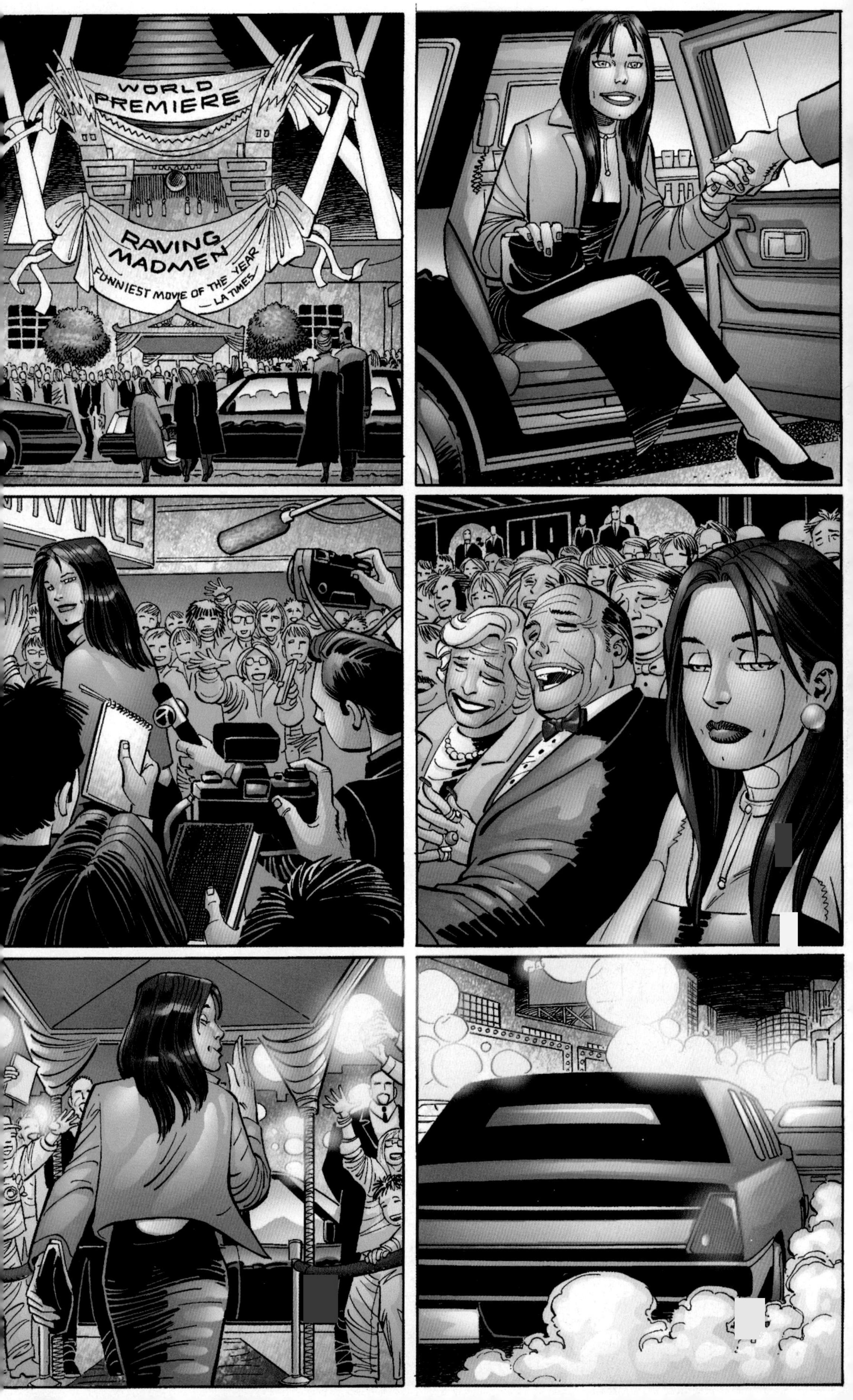
WORLD PREMIERE
RAVING MADMEN
FUNNIEST MOVIE OF THE YEAR
—LA TIMES

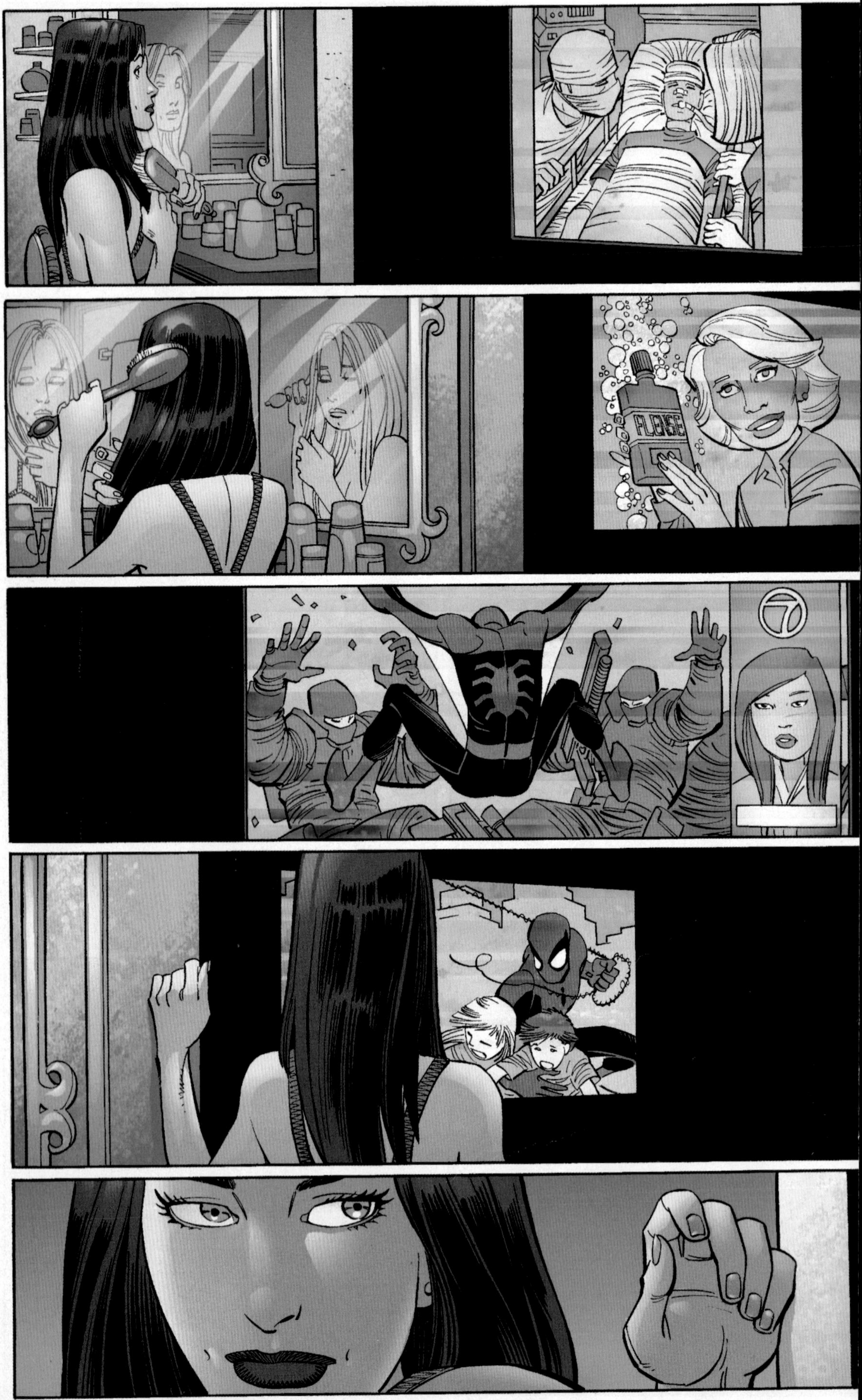
FLENSE

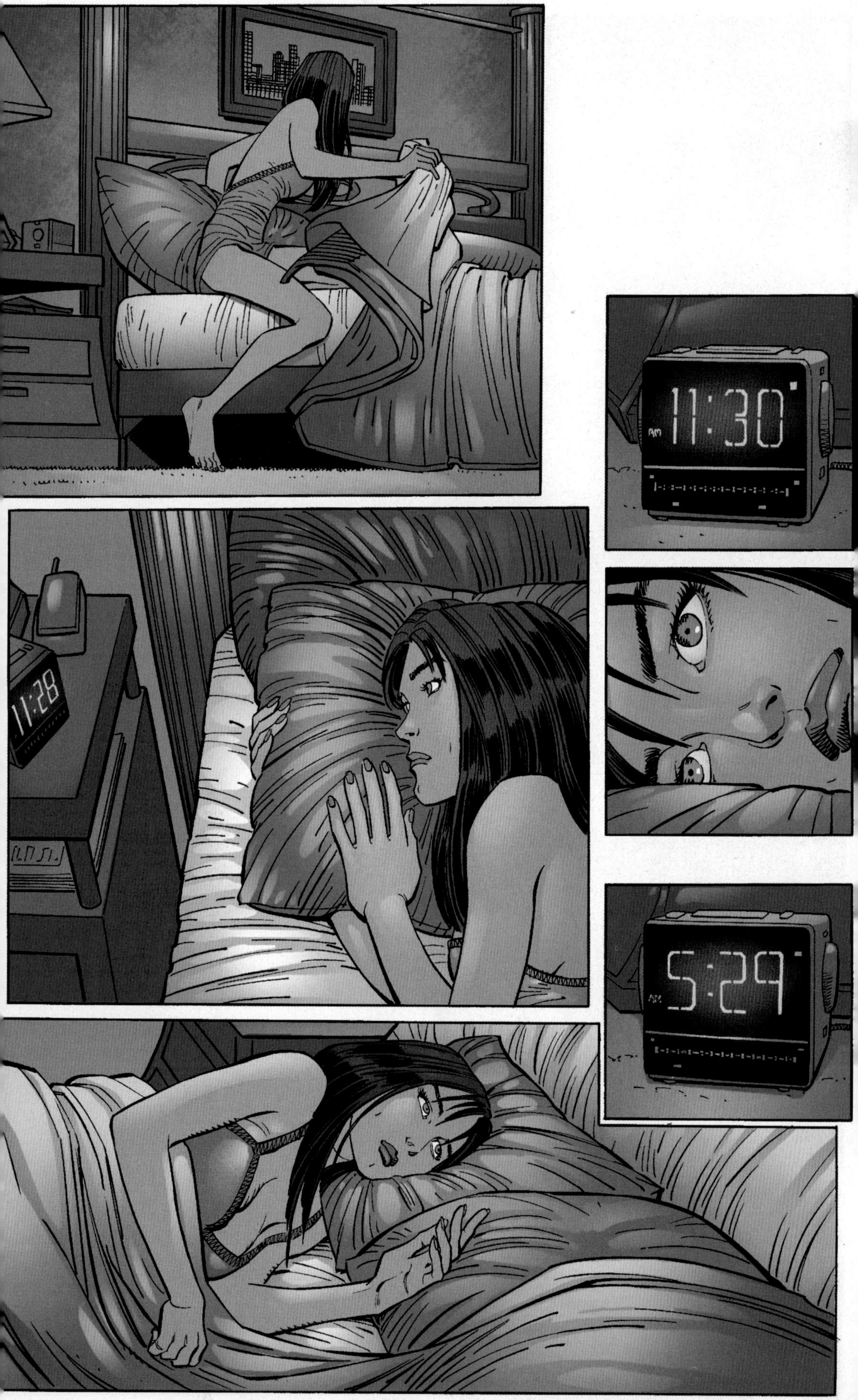
AM 11:30
11:28
AM 5:29

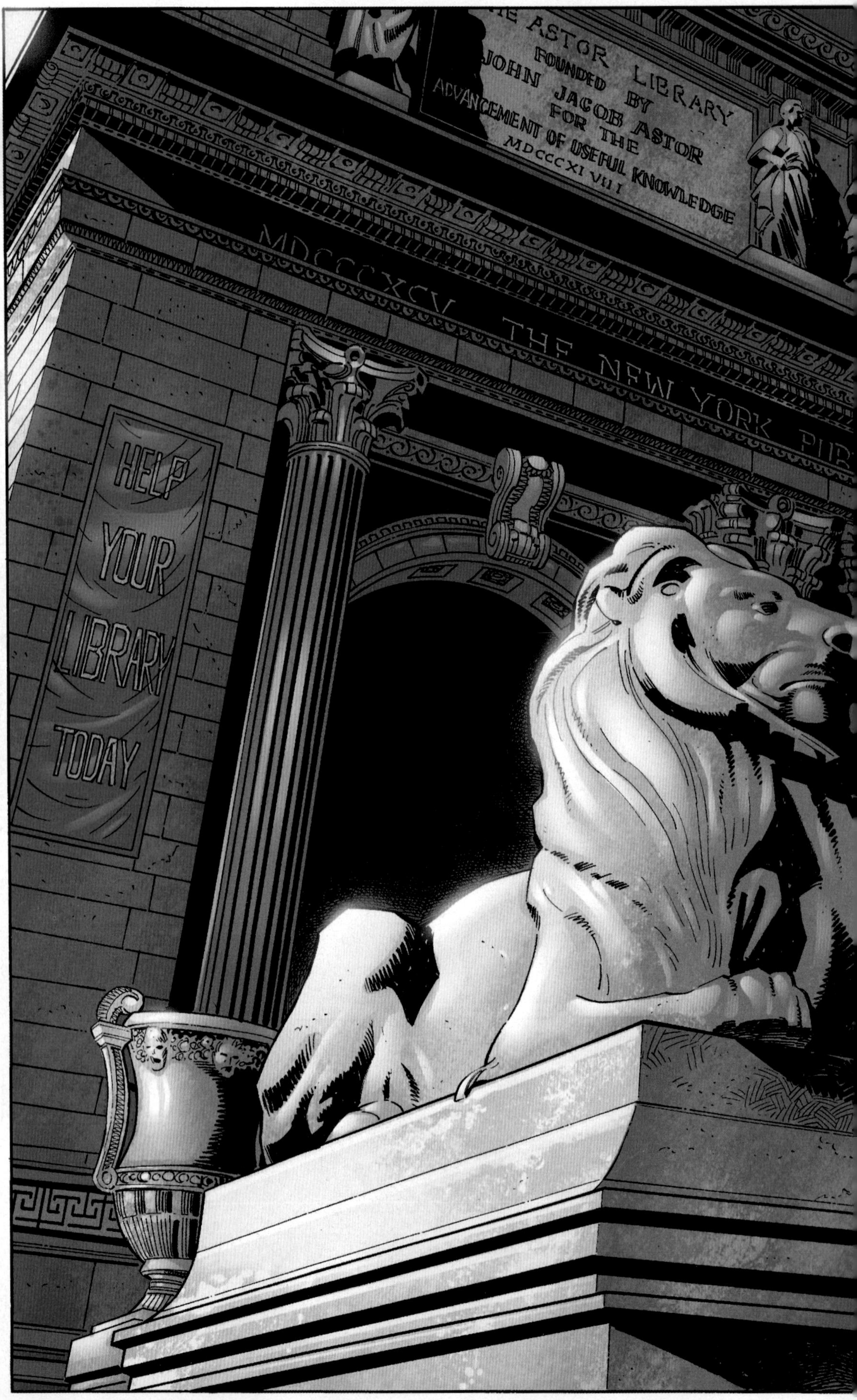
ASTOR LIBRARY
FOUNDED BY
JOHN JACOB ASTOR
FOR THE
ADVANCEMENT OF USEFUL KNOWLEDGE
MDCCCXLVIII
MDCCCXCV THE NEW YORK
HELP YOUR LIBRARY TODAY

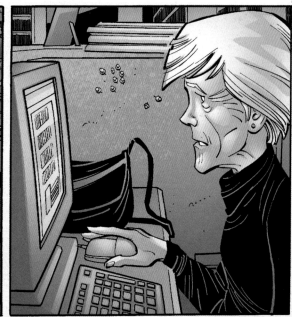

DAILY BUGLE

NEW YORK'S FINEST DAILY NEWSPAPER

SPIDER-MAN:
THREAT OR MENACE?

EDITORIAL BY
J. JONAH JAMESON

New York Herald

SPIDER-MAN
FRIGHTENS RESIDENTS

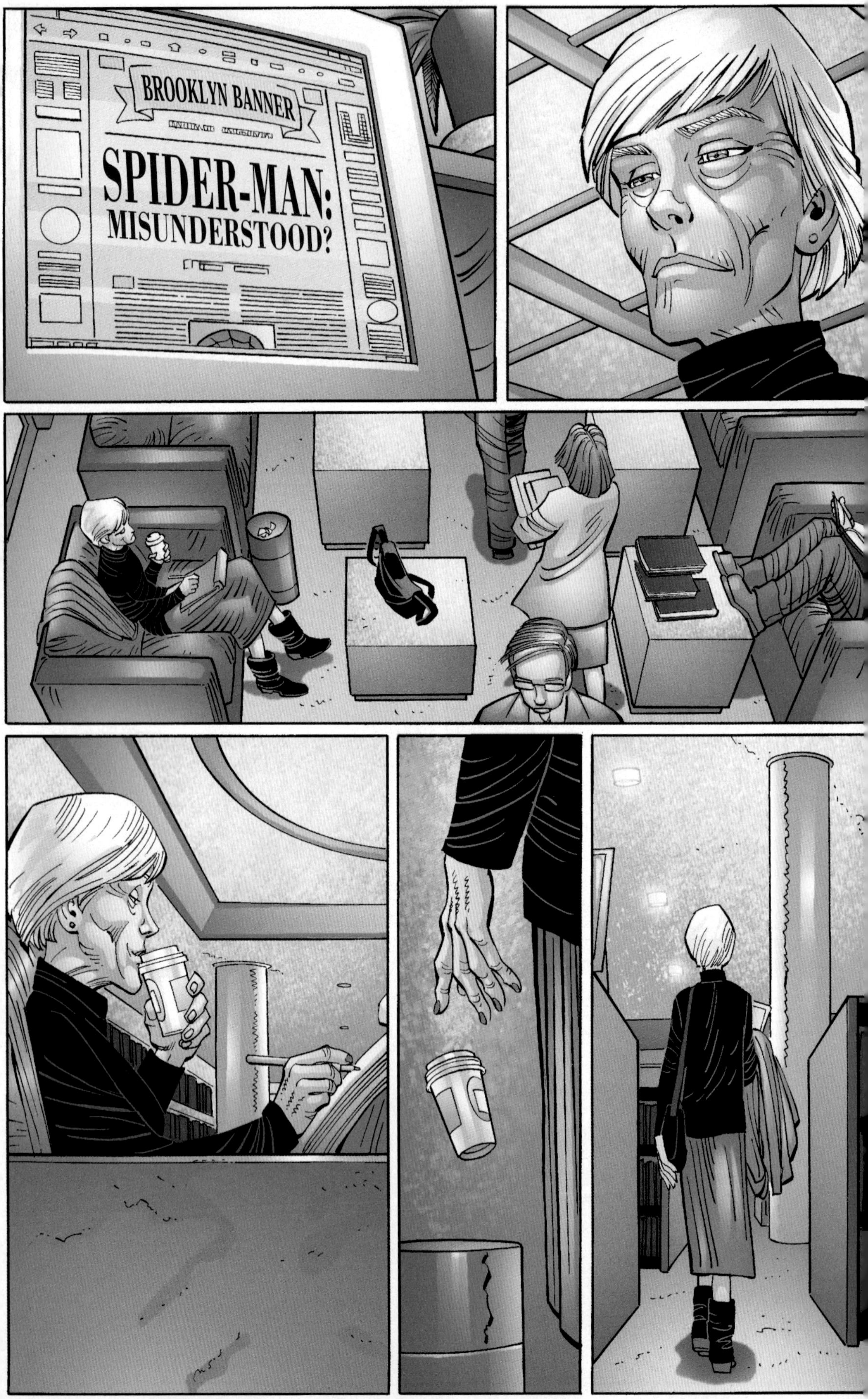

BROOKLYN BANNER
SPIDER-MAN: MISUNDERSTOOD?

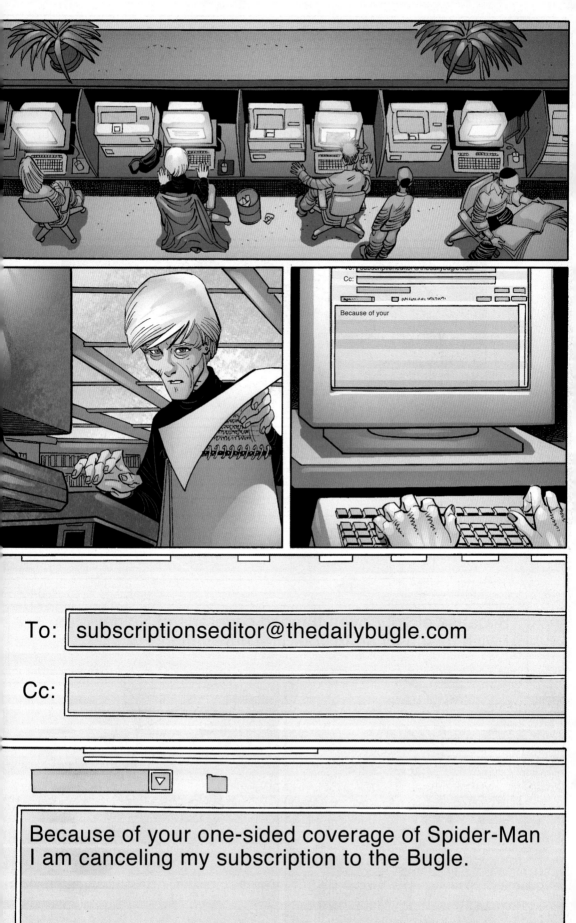

To: subscriptionseditor@thedailybugle.com

Cc:

Because of your one-sided coverage of Spider-Man I am canceling my subscription to the Bugle.

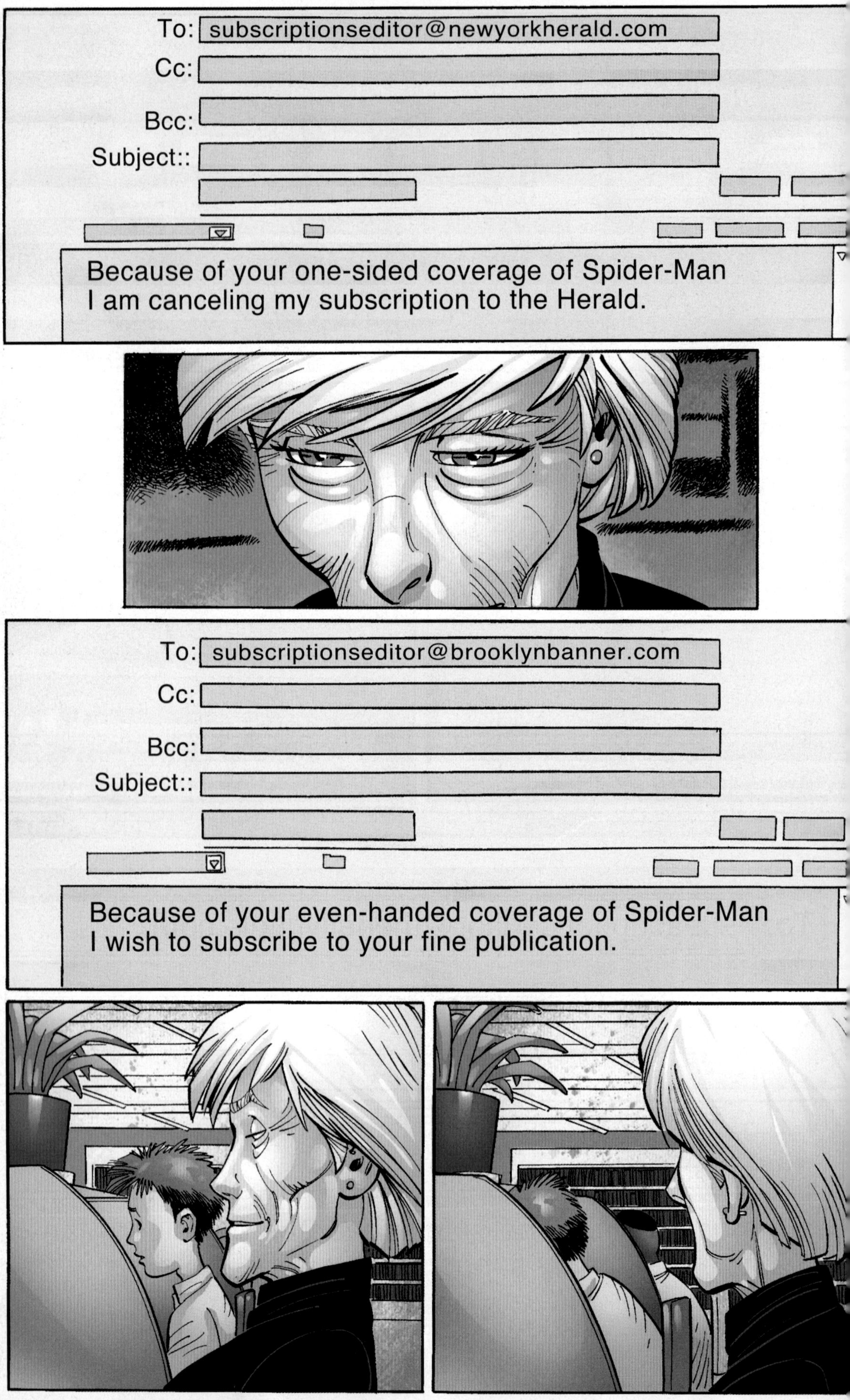
To: subscriptionseditor@newyorkherald.com
Cc:
Bcc:
Subject::
Because of your one-sided coverage of Spider-Man I am canceling my subscription to the Herald.
To: subscriptionseditor@brooklynbanner.com
Cc:
Bcc:
Subject::
Because of your even-handed coverage of Spider-Man I wish to subscribe to your fine publication.

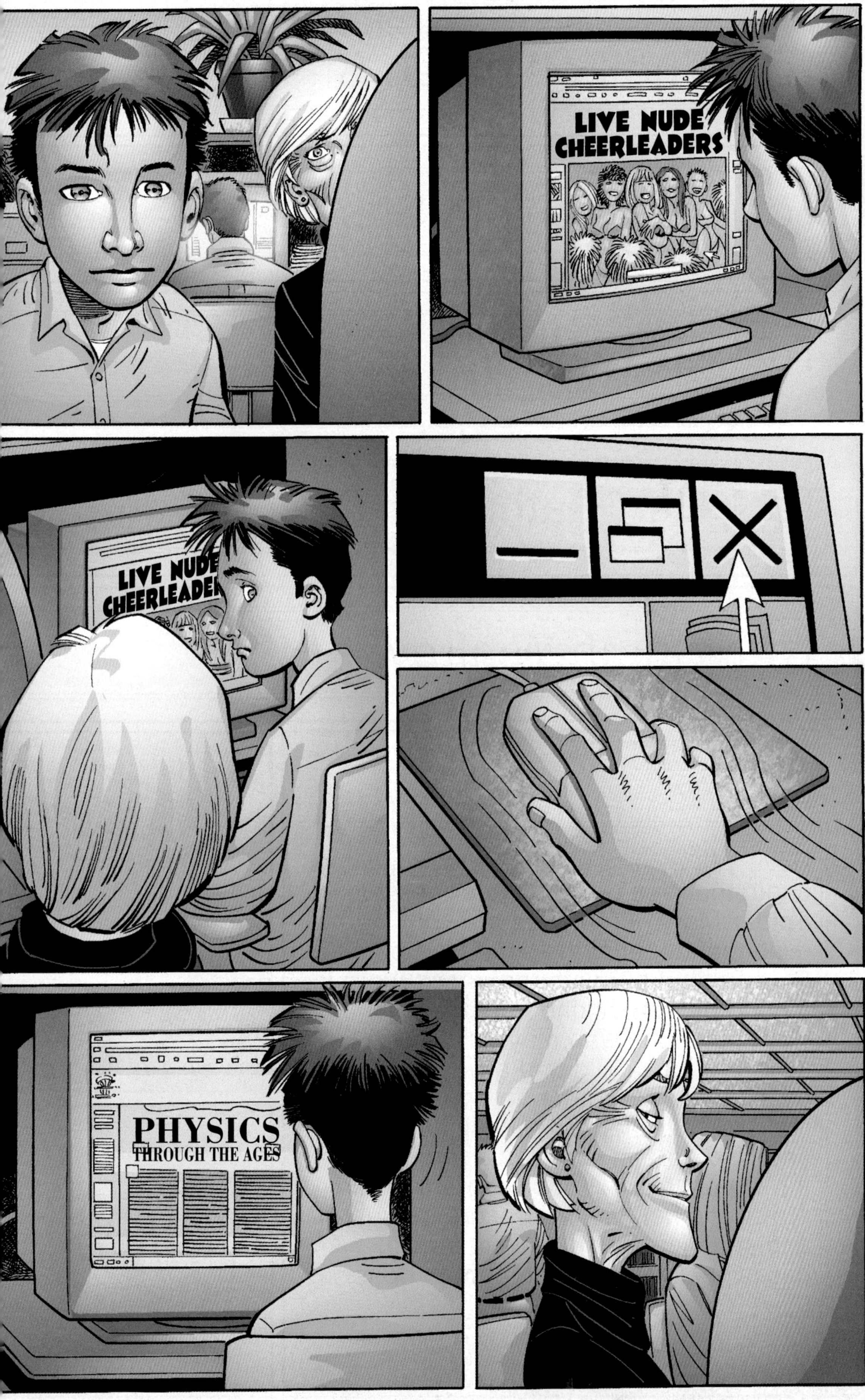
LIVE NUDE
CHEERLEADERS
LIVE NUDE
CHEERLEADER
PHYSICS
THROUGH THE AGES

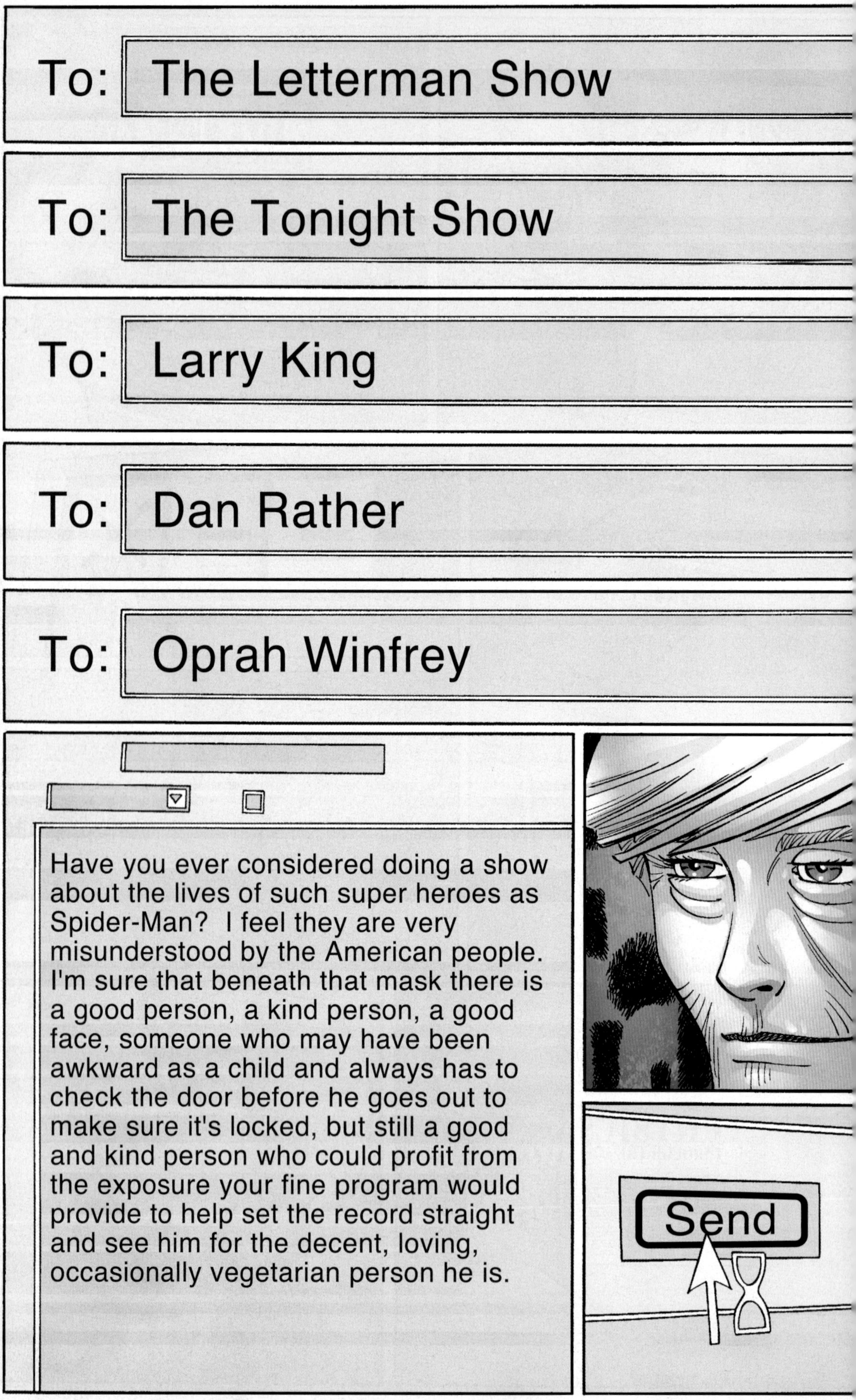

To: The Letterman Show
To: The Tonight Show
To: Larry King
To: Dan Rather
To: Oprah Winfrey
Have you ever considered doing a show about the lives of such super heroes as Spider-Man? I feel they are very misunderstood by the American people. I'm sure that beneath that mask there is a good person, a kind person, a good face, someone who may have been awkward as a child and always has to check the door before he goes out to make sure it's locked, but still a good and kind person who could profit from the exposure your fine program would provide to help set the record straight and see him for the decent, loving, occasionally vegetarian person he is.
Send

To do!
✓ 1. Drop off laundry
✓ 2. Cancel subscriptions to papers that don't like Peter
✓ 3. Try to improve Peter's image!
4. Pick up Zantac and Tucks
5. Keep working to forgive Peter
Keep working to forgive Peter

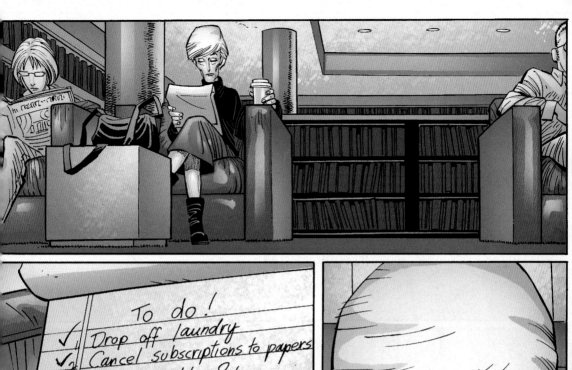

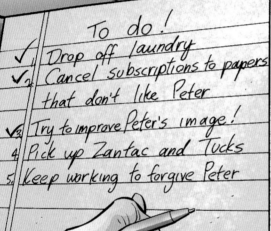

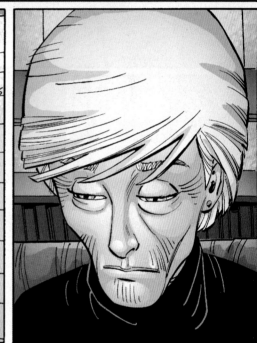

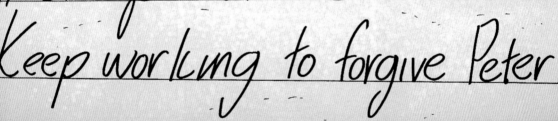

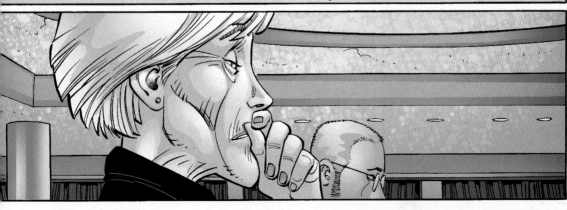

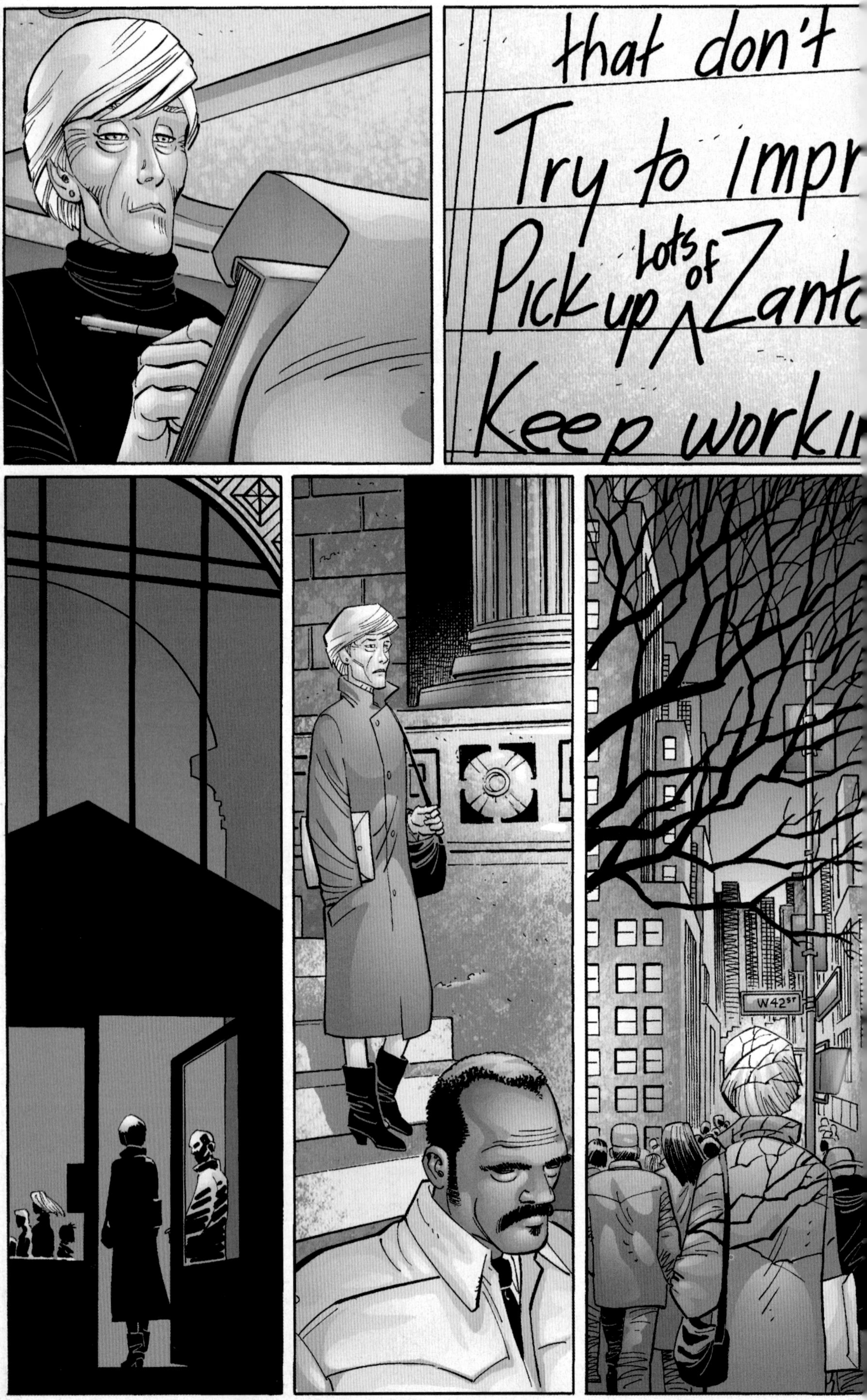
that don't
Try to impr
Pick up lots of Zanta
Keep workin
W 42ST

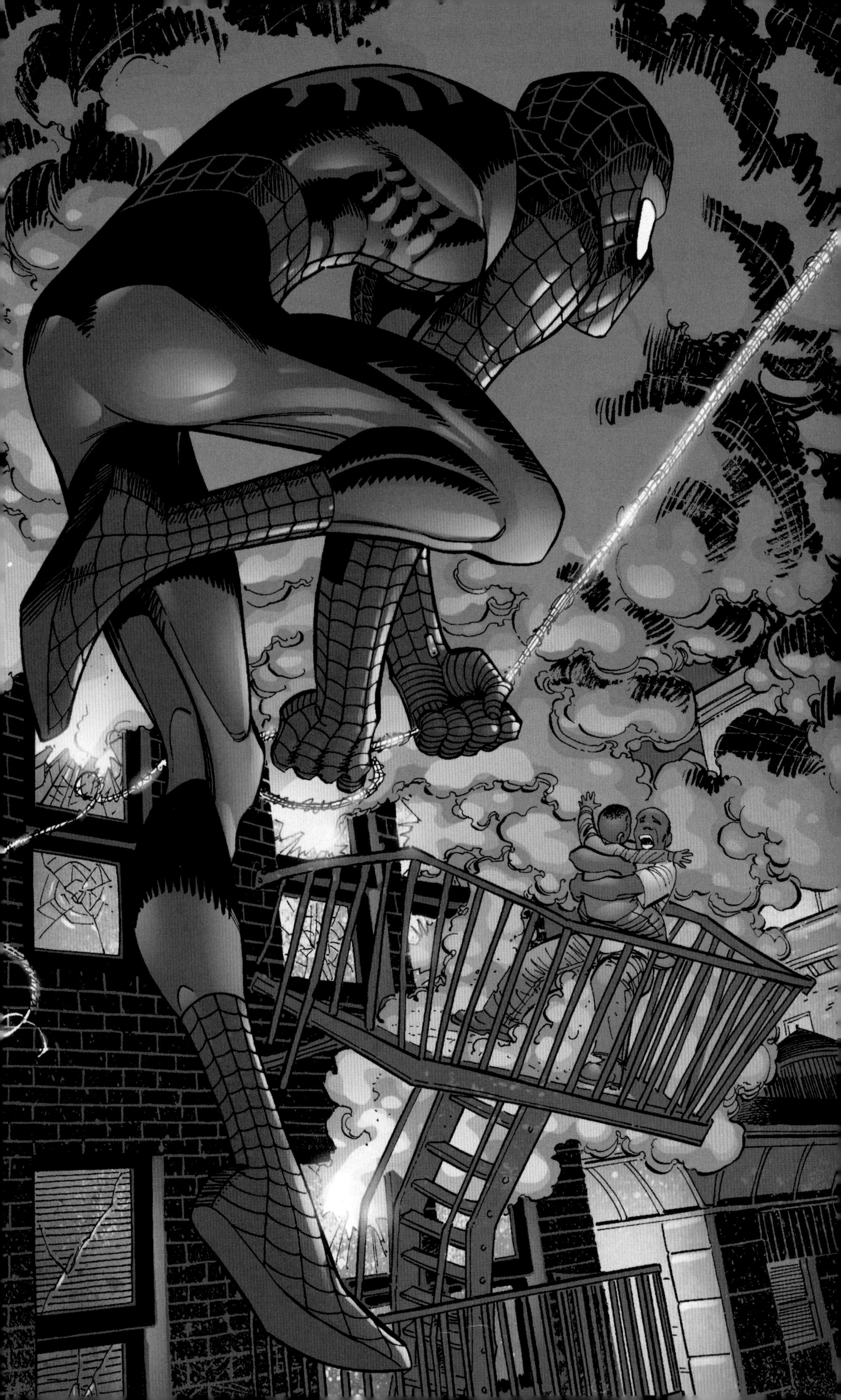

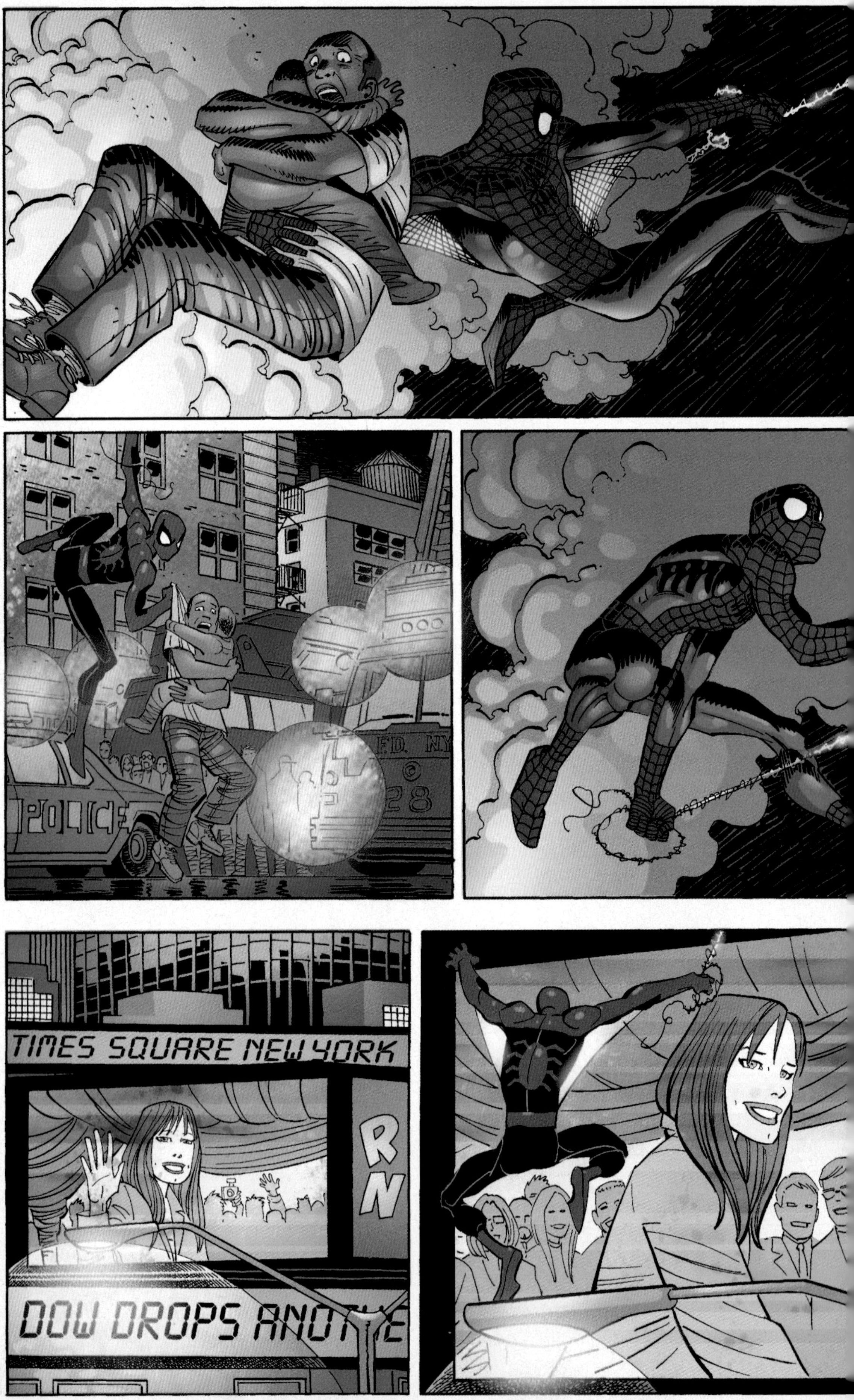
POLICE
F.D. N.Y.
28
TIMES SQUARE NEW YORK
RN
DOW DROPS ANOT

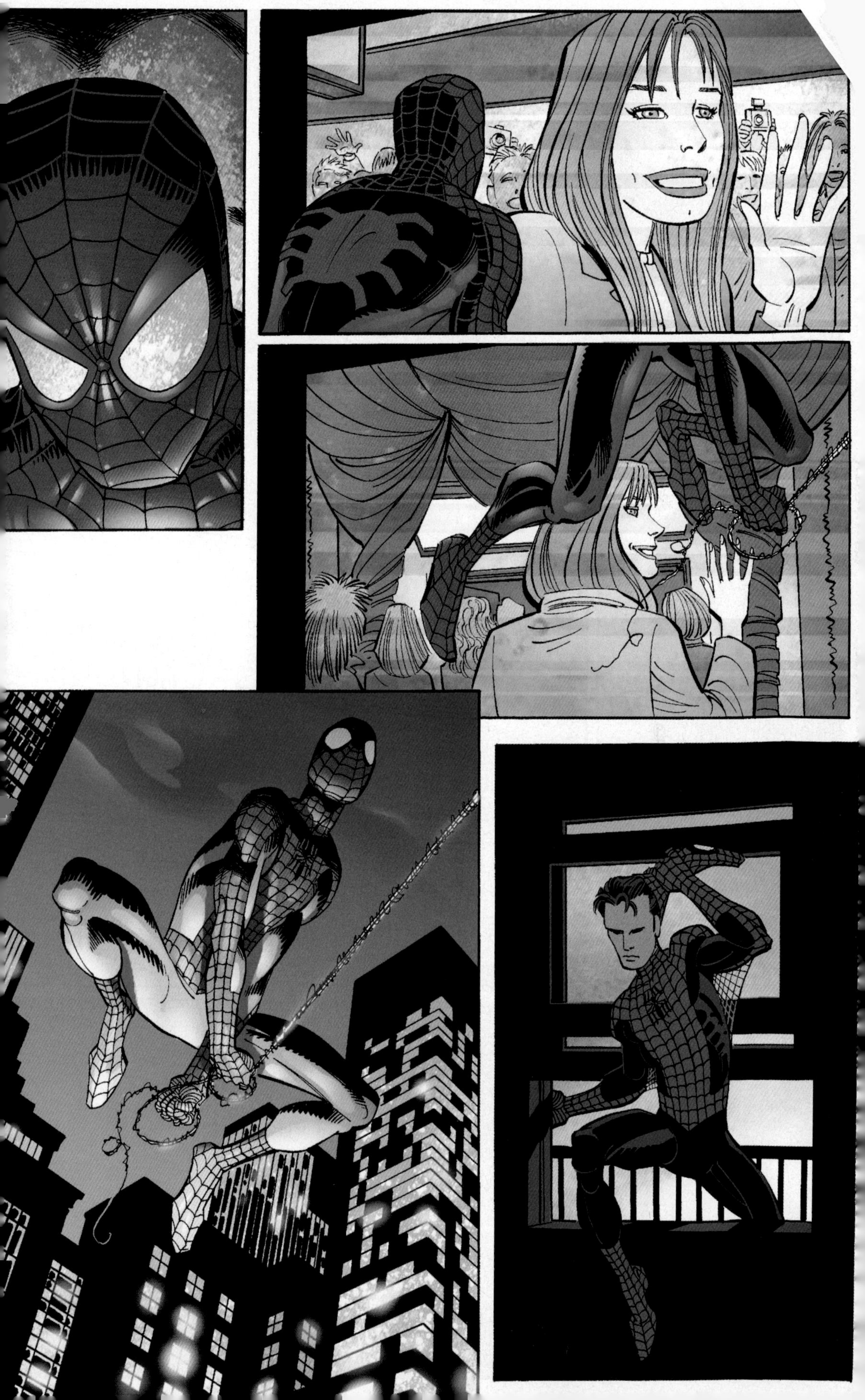

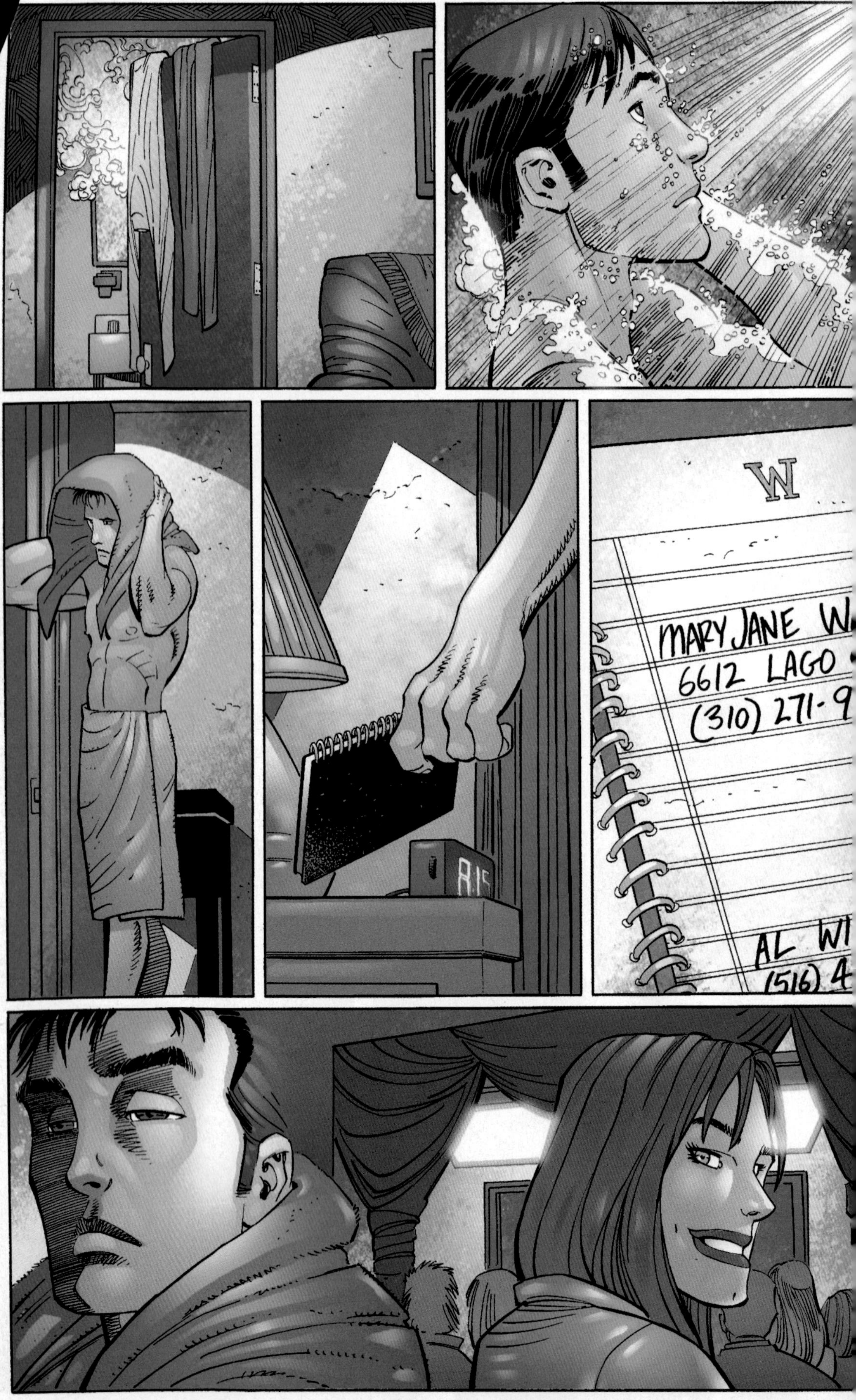

W
MARY JANE W
6612 LAGO
(310) 271-9
AL WI
(516) 4
8:15

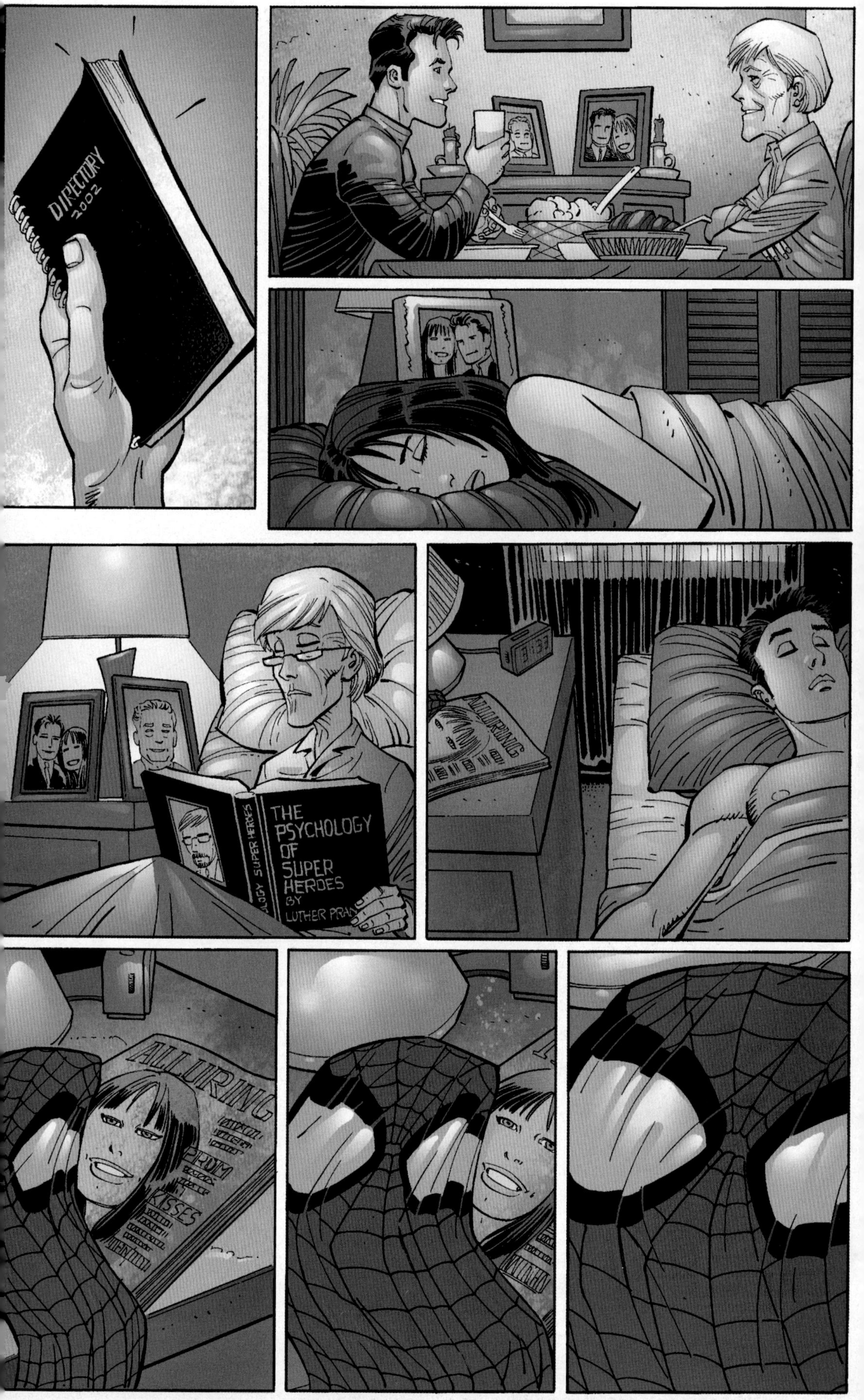

DIRECTORY
2002
THE PSYCHOLOGY OF SUPER HEROES
BY
LUTHER PRAN
ALLURING
ALLURING
PROM
KISSES

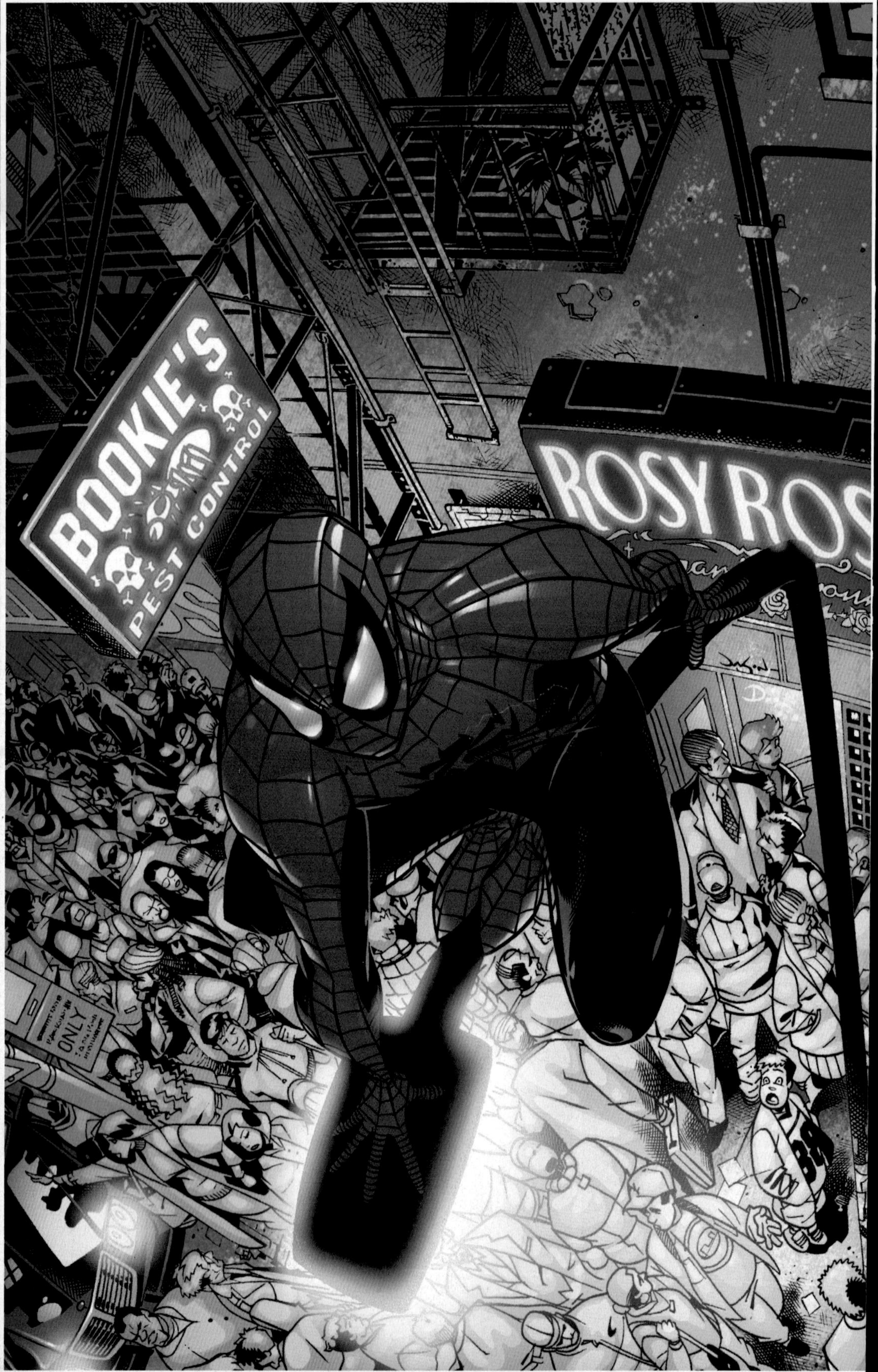
BOOKIE'S
PEST CONTROL
ROSY ROS
ONLY

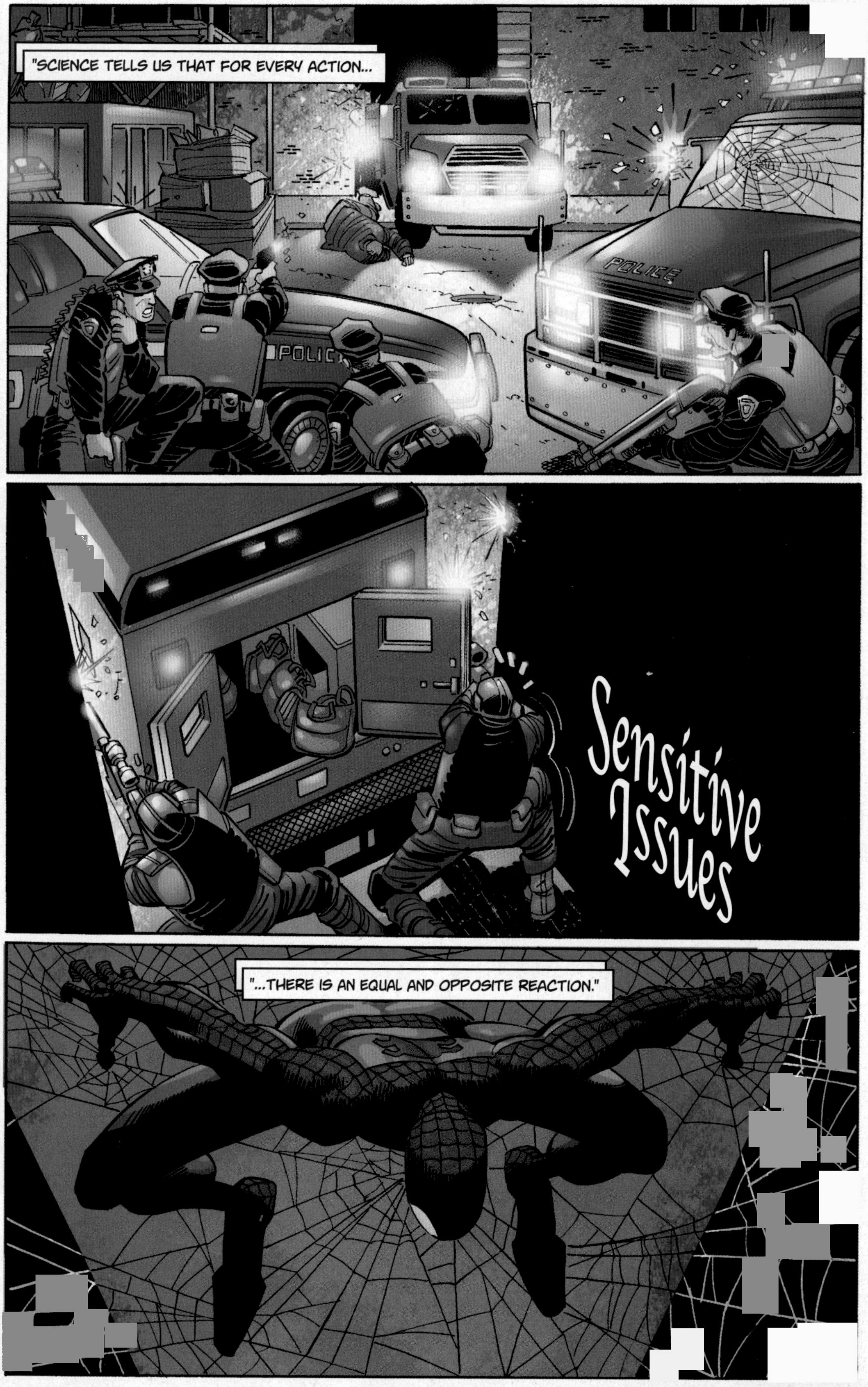

"SCIENCE TELLS US THAT FOR EVERY ACTION...
POLICE
POLIC
Sensitive Issues
"...THERE IS AN EQUAL AND OPPOSITE REACTION."

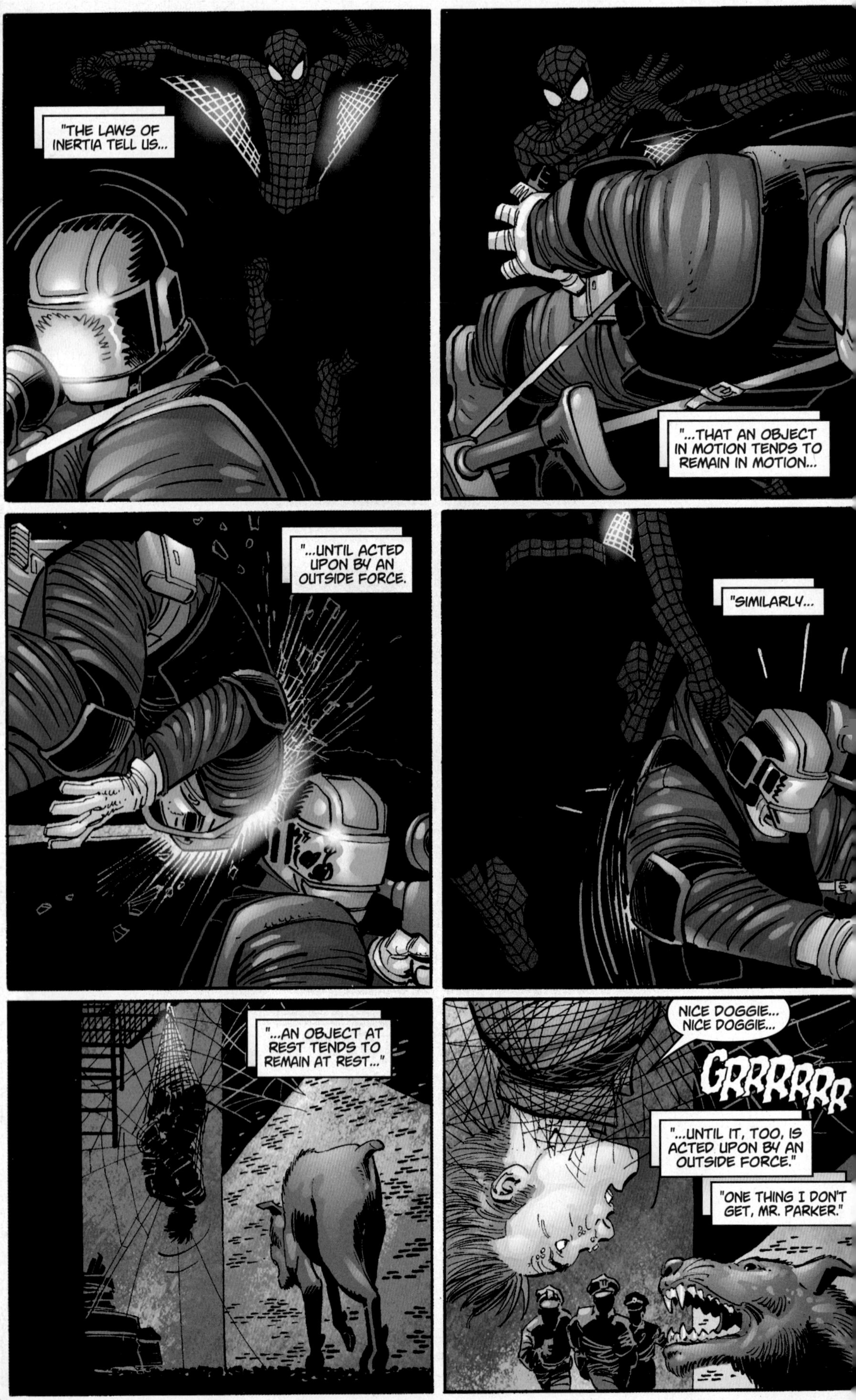
"THE LAWS OF INERTIA TELL US...
"...THAT AN OBJECT IN MOTION TENDS TO REMAIN IN MOTION...
"...UNTIL ACTED UPON BY AN OUTSIDE FORCE.
"SIMILARLY...
"...AN OBJECT AT REST TENDS TO REMAIN AT REST..."
NICE DOGGIE... NICE DOGGIE...
GRRRRRR
"...UNTIL IT, TOO, IS ACTED UPON BY AN OUTSIDE FORCE."
"ONE THING I DON'T GET, MR. PARKER."

I MEAN, THIS IS ALL GREAT, BUT, Y'KNOW, DOES ANYONE EVER ACTUALLY USE ANY OF THIS IN REAL LIFE?

HERE AND THERE...

"FLOOR PLEASE?"

FOURTEEN!

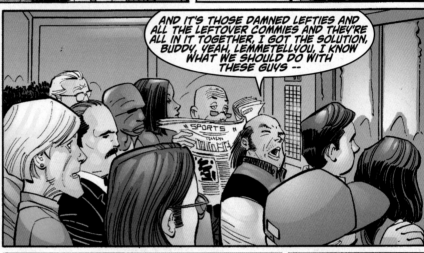

AND IT'S THOSE DAMNED LEFTIES AND ALL THE LEFTOVER COMMIES AND THEY'RE ALL IN IT TOGETHER, I GOT THE SOLUTION, BUDDY, YEAH, LEMMETELLYOU, I KNOW WHAT WE SHOULD DO WITH THESE GUYS --

GONNA FIND ME SOMEBODY TO LISTEN TO ME AND WRITE AN ARTICLE ABOUT THIS AND WE'LL MAKE A MILLION BUCKS IT'S GONNA BE --

DING

I THINK THIS IS YOUR FLOOR.

JUST GOTTA USE HATS! HATS MADE OUTTA TINFOIL, THAT'LL STOP THE RAYS, SEE, AND THE FLUORIDATION OF WATER, MAKIN' EVERYBODY JUST NUTS, BUT I KNOW THE REAL STORY, HEY YOU!

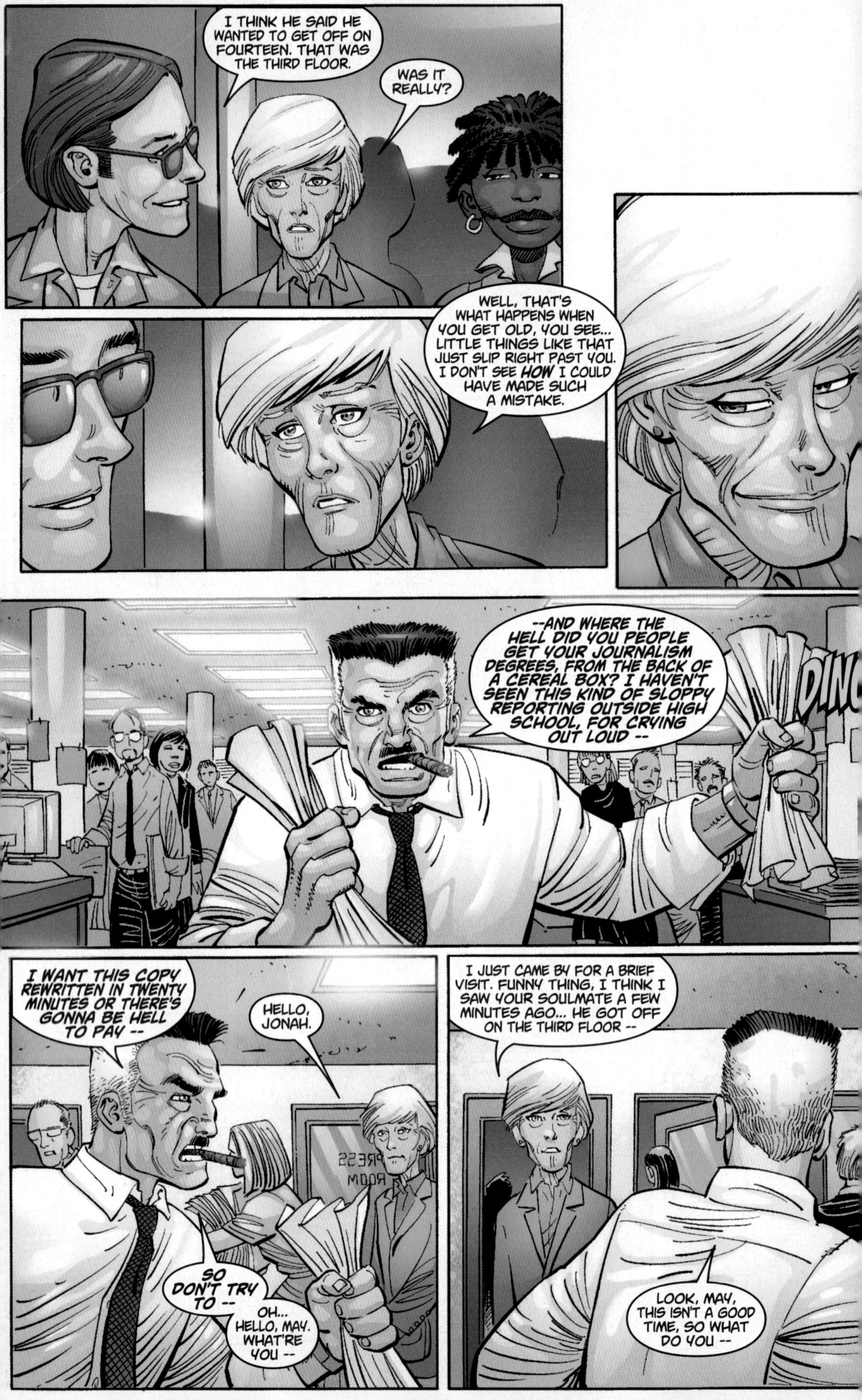

I THINK HE SAID HE WANTED TO GET OFF ON FOURTEEN. THAT WAS THE THIRD FLOOR.
WAS IT REALLY?
WELL, THAT'S WHAT HAPPENS WHEN YOU GET OLD, YOU SEE... LITTLE THINGS LIKE THAT JUST SLIP RIGHT PAST YOU. I DON'T SEE *HOW* I COULD HAVE MADE SUCH A MISTAKE.
--AND WHERE THE HELL DID YOU PEOPLE GET YOUR JOURNALISM DEGREES, FROM THE BACK OF A CEREAL BOX? I HAVEN'T SEEN THIS KIND OF SLOPPY REPORTING OUTSIDE HIGH SCHOOL, FOR CRYING OUT LOUD --
I WANT THIS COPY REWRITTEN IN TWENTY MINUTES OR THERE'S GONNA BE HELL TO PAY --
HELLO, JONAH.
SO DON'T TRY TO --
OH... HELLO, MAY. WHAT'RE YOU --
PRESS ROOM
I JUST CAME BY FOR A BRIEF VISIT. FUNNY THING, I THINK I SAW YOUR SOULMATE A FEW MINUTES AGO... HE GOT OFF ON THE THIRD FLOOR --
LOOK, MAY, THIS ISN'T A GOOD TIME, SO WHAT DO YOU --

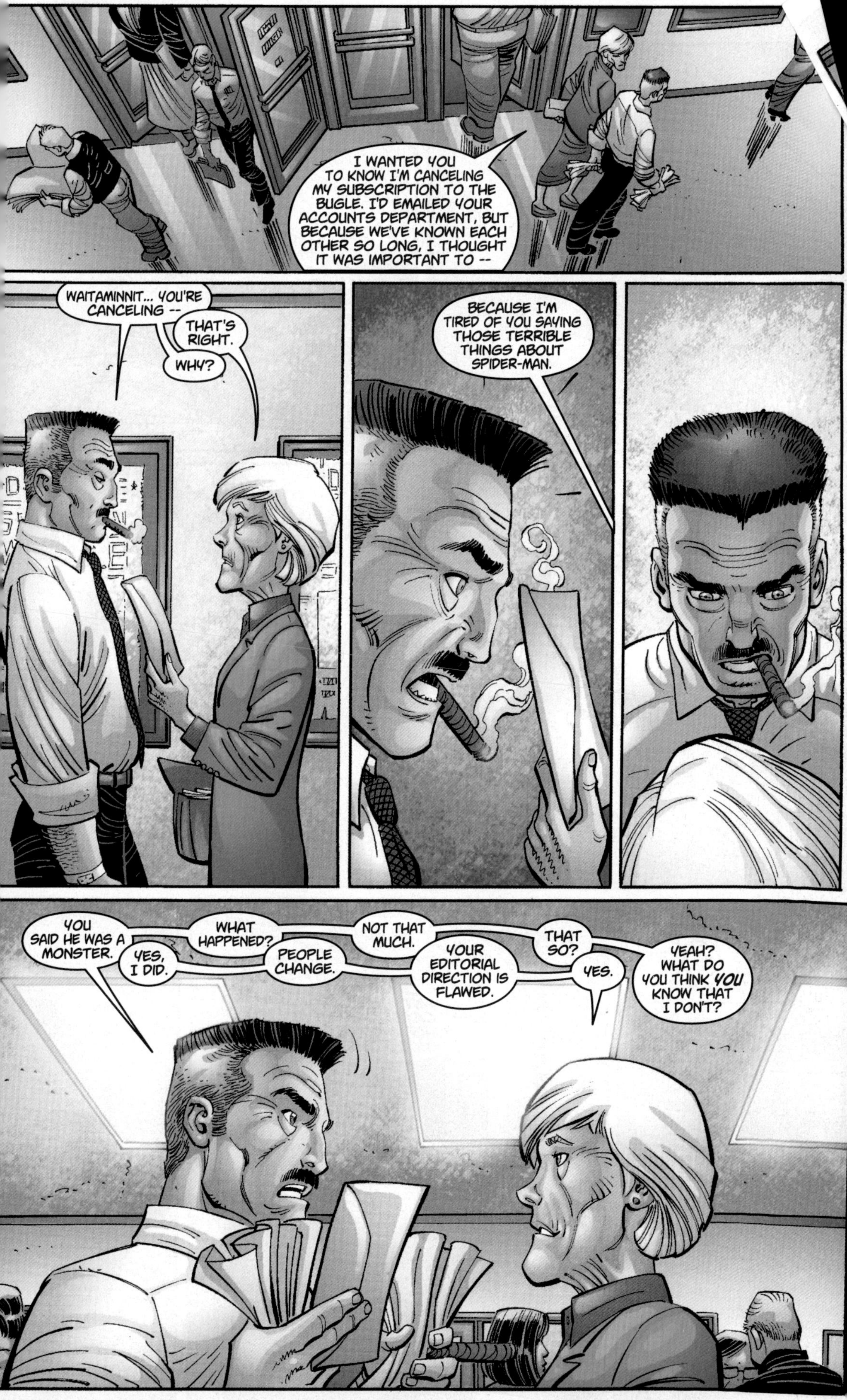
I WANTED YOU TO KNOW I'M CANCELING MY SUBSCRIPTION TO THE BUGLE. I'D EMAILED YOUR ACCOUNTS DEPARTMENT, BUT BECAUSE WE'VE KNOWN EACH OTHER SO LONG, I THOUGHT IT WAS IMPORTANT TO --
WAITAMINNIT... YOU'RE CANCELING --
THAT'S RIGHT.
WHY?
BECAUSE I'M TIRED OF YOU SAYING THOSE TERRIBLE THINGS ABOUT SPIDER-MAN.
YOU SAID HE WAS A MONSTER.
YES, I DID.
WHAT HAPPENED?
PEOPLE CHANGE.
NOT THAT MUCH.
YOUR EDITORIAL DIRECTION IS FLAWED.
THAT SO?
YES.
YEAH? WHAT DO YOU THINK YOU KNOW THAT I DON'T?

VOLUMES, JONAH. VOLUMES.

FINE, WHATEVER, I DON'T HAVE TIME FOR THIS. FIFTY CENTS ON WEEKDAYS, A BUCK ON SUNDAY, I CAN AFFORD THE LOSS.

THANK YOU. GOOD DAY, JONAH.

WOMAN'S LOSING IT. SOME DAYS I THINK THE WHOLE FAMILY'S CRAZY AS A BEDBUG. IT'S --

IT'S THE LEFTIES AND THE LIBERAL MEDIA ELITE AND THE MICROWAVES FROM MARS, THAT'S THE KICKER, THAT'S WHAT WE'VE GOT TO TELL THE WORLD --

--WE GOTTA MAKE UP HELMETS AND WE GOTTA BOMB 'EM AND WE GOTTA STOP TALKING IN FRONT OF THE CATS, THAT'S THE IMPORTANT THING, WE CAN'T TRUST CATS, THEY'RE FROM MARS, EVERYBODY KNOWS THAT --

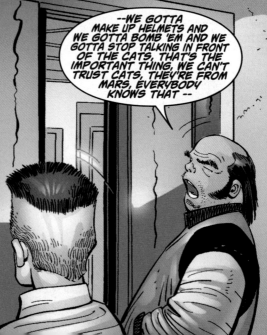

...SIGH...

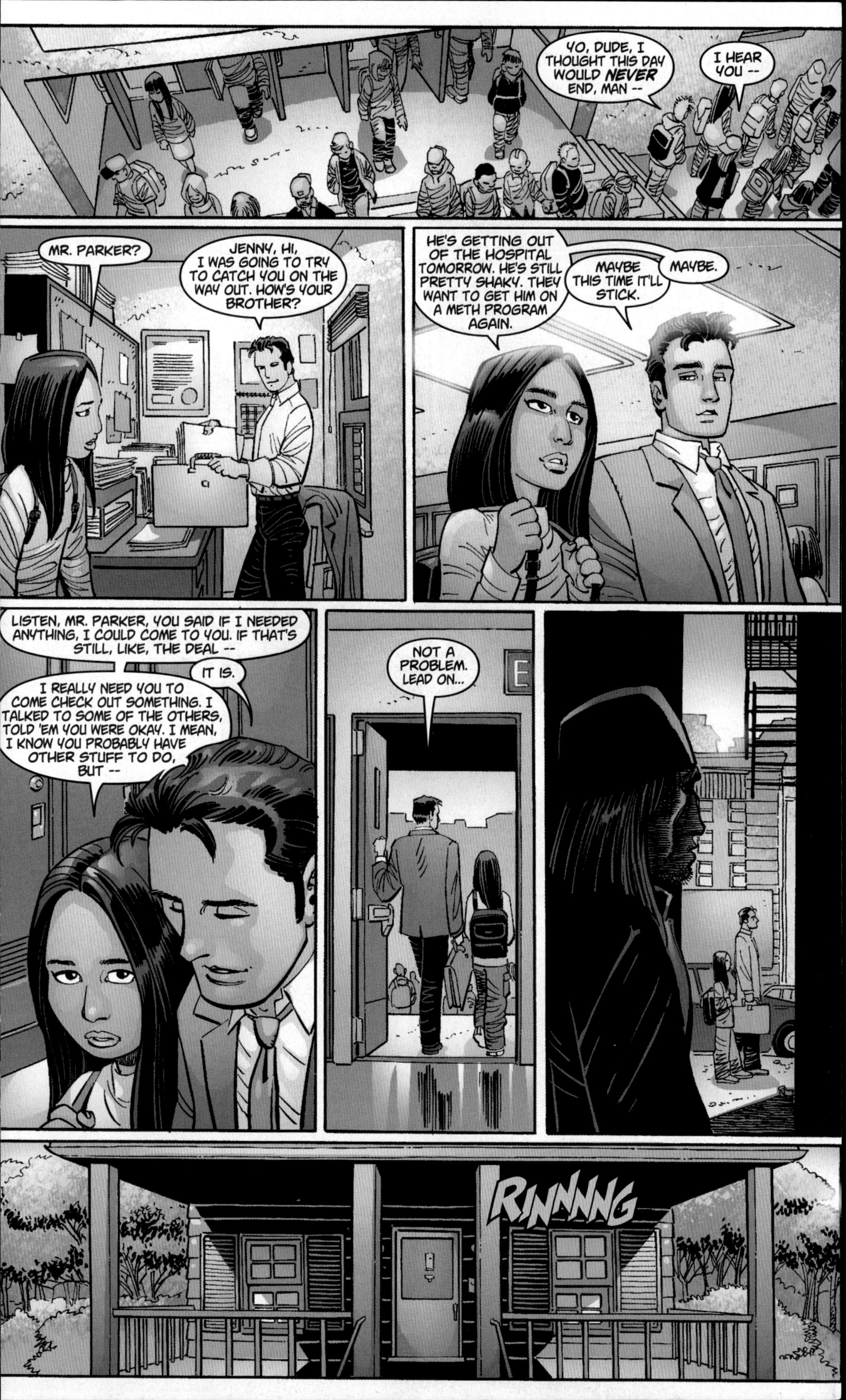

YO, DUDE, I THOUGHT THIS DAY WOULD NEVER END, MAN --
I HEAR YOU --
MR. PARKER?
JENNY, HI, I WAS GOING TO TRY TO CATCH YOU ON THE WAY OUT. HOW'S YOUR BROTHER?
HE'S GETTING OUT OF THE HOSPITAL TOMORROW. HE'S STILL PRETTY SHAKY. THEY WANT TO GET HIM ON A METH PROGRAM AGAIN.
MAYBE THIS TIME IT'LL STICK.
MAYBE.
LISTEN, MR. PARKER, YOU SAID IF I NEEDED ANYTHING, I COULD COME TO YOU. IF THAT'S STILL, LIKE, THE DEAL --
IT IS.
I REALLY NEED YOU TO COME CHECK OUT SOMETHING. I TALKED TO SOME OF THE OTHERS, TOLD 'EM YOU WERE OKAY. I MEAN, I KNOW YOU PROBABLY HAVE OTHER STUFF TO DO, BUT --
NOT A PROBLEM. LEAD ON...
RINNNNG

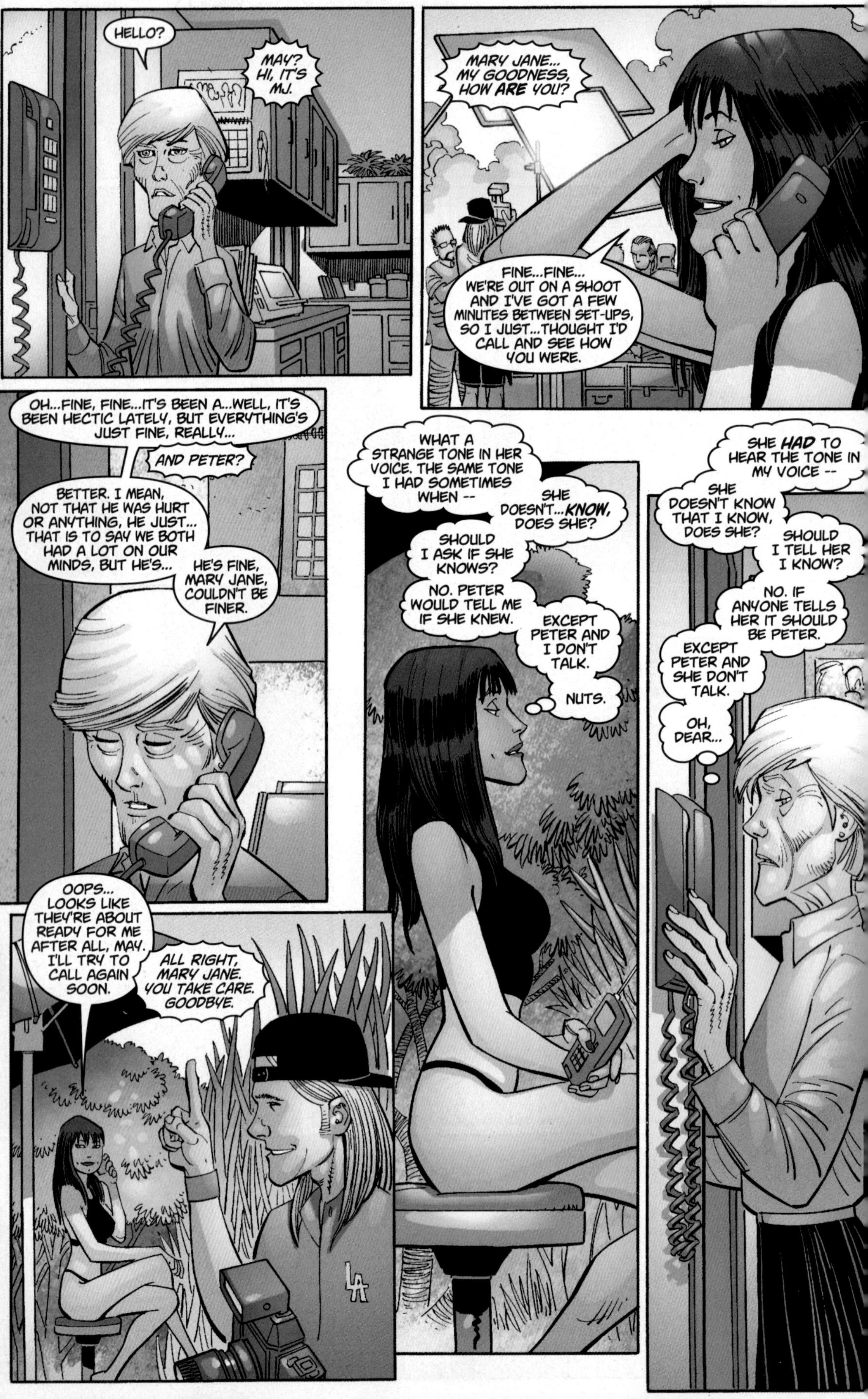
HELLO?
MAY? HI, IT'S MJ.
MARY JANE... MY GOODNESS, HOW ARE YOU?
FINE...FINE... WE'RE OUT ON A SHOOT AND I'VE GOT A FEW MINUTES BETWEEN SET-UPS, SO I JUST...THOUGHT I'D CALL AND SEE HOW YOU WERE.
OH...FINE, FINE...IT'S BEEN A...WELL, IT'S BEEN HECTIC LATELY, BUT EVERYTHING'S JUST FINE, REALLY...
AND PETER?
BETTER. I MEAN, NOT THAT HE WAS HURT OR ANYTHING, HE JUST... THAT IS TO SAY WE BOTH HAD A LOT ON OUR MINDS, BUT HE'S...
HE'S FINE, MARY JANE, COULDN'T BE FINER.
WHAT A STRANGE TONE IN HER VOICE. THE SAME TONE I HAD SOMETIMES WHEN --
SHE DOESN'T...KNOW, DOES SHE?
SHOULD I ASK IF SHE KNOWS?
NO. PETER WOULD TELL ME IF SHE KNEW.
EXCEPT PETER AND I DON'T TALK.
NUTS.
SHE HAD TO HEAR THE TONE IN MY VOICE --
SHE DOESN'T KNOW THAT I KNOW, DOES SHE?
SHOULD I TELL HER I KNOW?
NO. IF ANYONE TELLS HER IT SHOULD BE PETER.
EXCEPT PETER AND SHE DON'T TALK.
OH, DEAR...
OOPS... LOOKS LIKE THEY'RE ABOUT READY FOR ME AFTER ALL, MAY. I'LL TRY TO CALL AGAIN SOON.
ALL RIGHT, MARY JANE. YOU TAKE CARE. GOODBYE.
LA

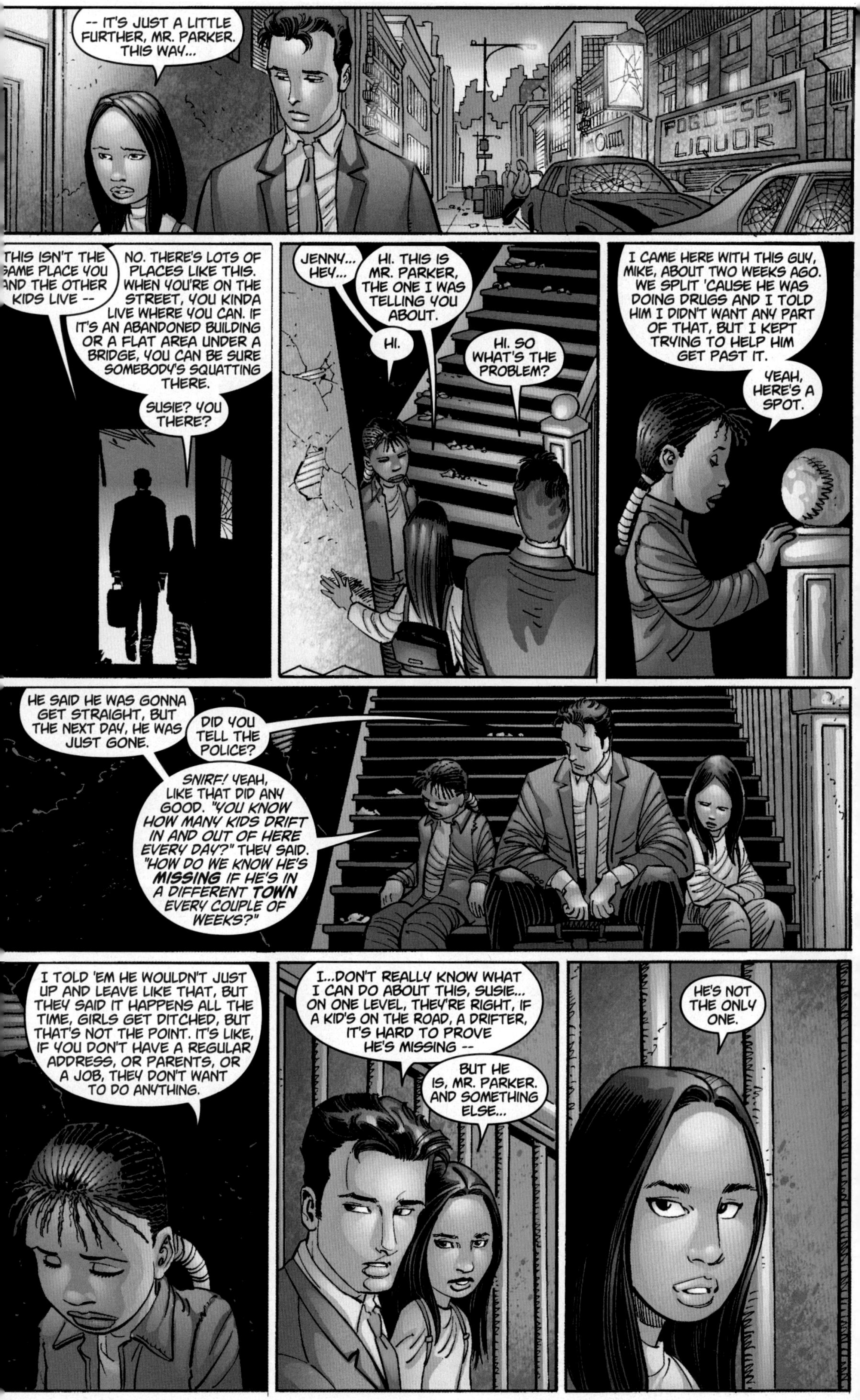
-- IT'S JUST A LITTLE FURTHER, MR. PARKER. THIS WAY...
FOGDESE'S LIQUOR
THIS ISN'T THE SAME PLACE YOU AND THE OTHER KIDS LIVE --
NO. THERE'S LOTS OF PLACES LIKE THIS. WHEN YOU'RE ON THE STREET, YOU KINDA LIVE WHERE YOU CAN. IF IT'S AN ABANDONED BUILDING OR A FLAT AREA UNDER A BRIDGE, YOU CAN BE SURE SOMEBODY'S SQUATTING THERE.
SUSIE? YOU THERE?
JENNY... HEY...
HI. THIS IS MR. PARKER, THE ONE I WAS TELLING YOU ABOUT.
HI.
HI. SO WHAT'S THE PROBLEM?
I CAME HERE WITH THIS GUY, MIKE, ABOUT TWO WEEKS AGO. WE SPLIT 'CAUSE HE WAS DOING DRUGS AND I TOLD HIM I DIDN'T WANT ANY PART OF THAT, BUT I KEPT TRYING TO HELP HIM GET PAST IT.
YEAH, HERE'S A SPOT.
HE SAID HE WAS GONNA GET STRAIGHT, BUT THE NEXT DAY, HE WAS JUST GONE.
DID YOU TELL THE POLICE?
SNIRF! YEAH, LIKE THAT DID ANY GOOD. "YOU KNOW HOW MANY KIDS DRIFT IN AND OUT OF HERE EVERY DAY?" THEY SAID. "HOW DO WE KNOW HE'S **MISSING** IF HE'S IN A DIFFERENT **TOWN** EVERY COUPLE OF WEEKS?"
I TOLD 'EM HE WOULDN'T JUST UP AND LEAVE LIKE THAT, BUT THEY SAID IT HAPPENS ALL THE TIME, GIRLS GET DITCHED, BUT THAT'S NOT THE POINT. IT'S LIKE, IF YOU DON'T HAVE A REGULAR ADDRESS, OR PARENTS, OR A JOB, THEY DON'T WANT TO DO ANYTHING.
I...DON'T REALLY KNOW WHAT I CAN DO ABOUT THIS, SUSIE... ON ONE LEVEL, THEY'RE RIGHT, IF A KID'S ON THE ROAD, A DRIFTER, IT'S HARD TO PROVE HE'S MISSING --
BUT HE IS, MR. PARKER. AND SOMETHING ELSE...
HE'S NOT THE ONLY ONE.

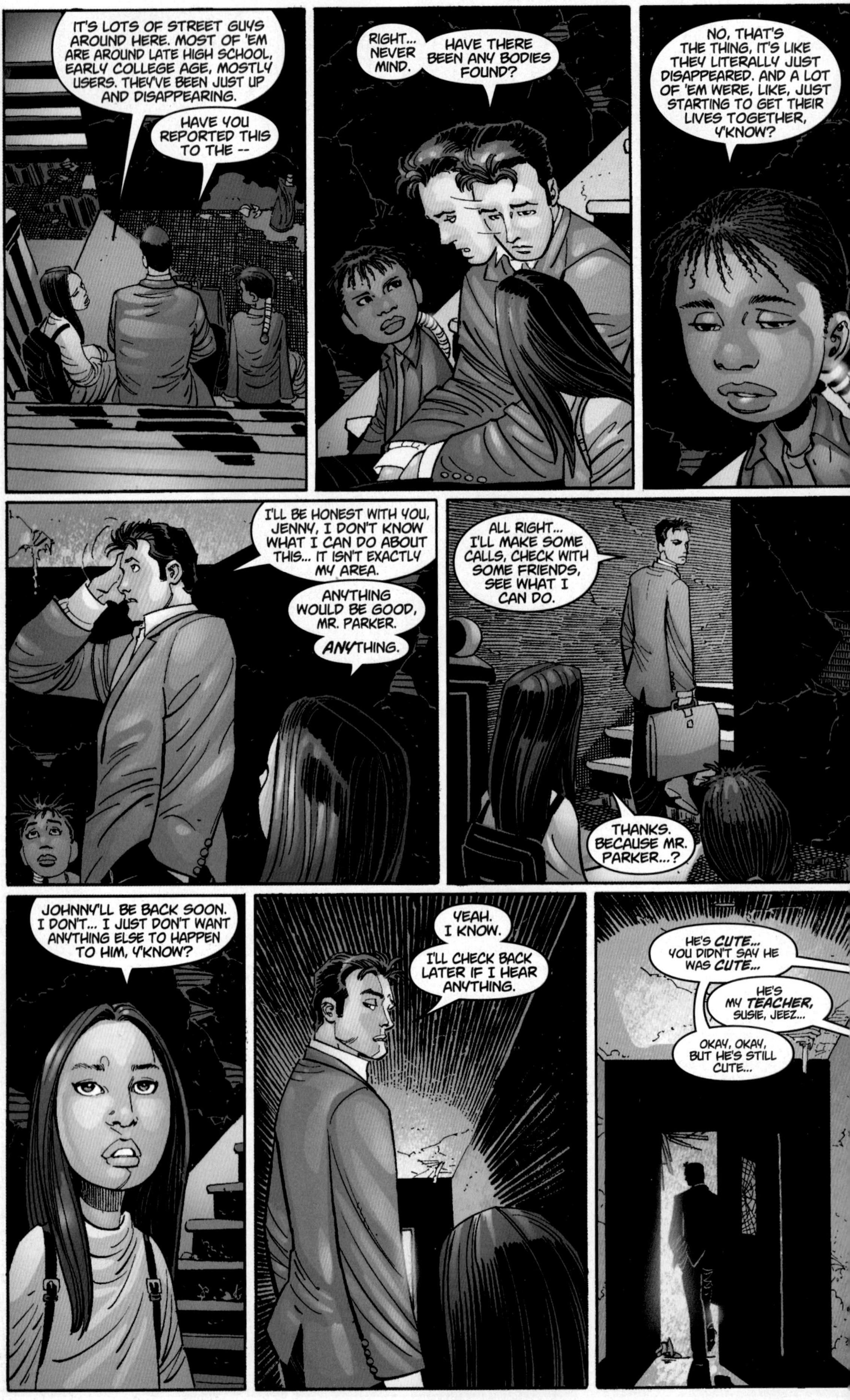
IT'S LOTS OF STREET GUYS AROUND HERE. MOST OF 'EM ARE AROUND LATE HIGH SCHOOL, EARLY COLLEGE AGE, MOSTLY USERS. THEY'VE BEEN JUST UP AND DISAPPEARING.
HAVE YOU REPORTED THIS TO THE --
RIGHT... NEVER MIND.
HAVE THERE BEEN ANY BODIES FOUND?
NO, THAT'S THE THING, IT'S LIKE THEY LITERALLY JUST DISAPPEARED. AND A LOT OF 'EM WERE, LIKE, JUST STARTING TO GET THEIR LIVES TOGETHER, Y'KNOW?
I'LL BE HONEST WITH YOU, JENNY, I DON'T KNOW WHAT I CAN DO ABOUT THIS... IT ISN'T EXACTLY MY AREA.
ANYTHING WOULD BE GOOD, MR. PARKER.
*ANY*THING.
ALL RIGHT... I'LL MAKE SOME CALLS, CHECK WITH SOME FRIENDS, SEE WHAT I CAN DO.
THANKS. BECAUSE MR. PARKER...?
JOHNNY'LL BE BACK SOON. I DON'T... I JUST DON'T WANT ANYTHING ELSE TO HAPPEN TO HIM, Y'KNOW?
YEAH. I KNOW.
I'LL CHECK BACK LATER IF I HEAR ANYTHING.
HE'S *CUTE*... YOU DIDN'T SAY HE WAS *CUTE*...
HE'S MY *TEACHER,* SUSIE, JEEZ...
OKAY, OKAY, BUT HE'S STILL CUTE...

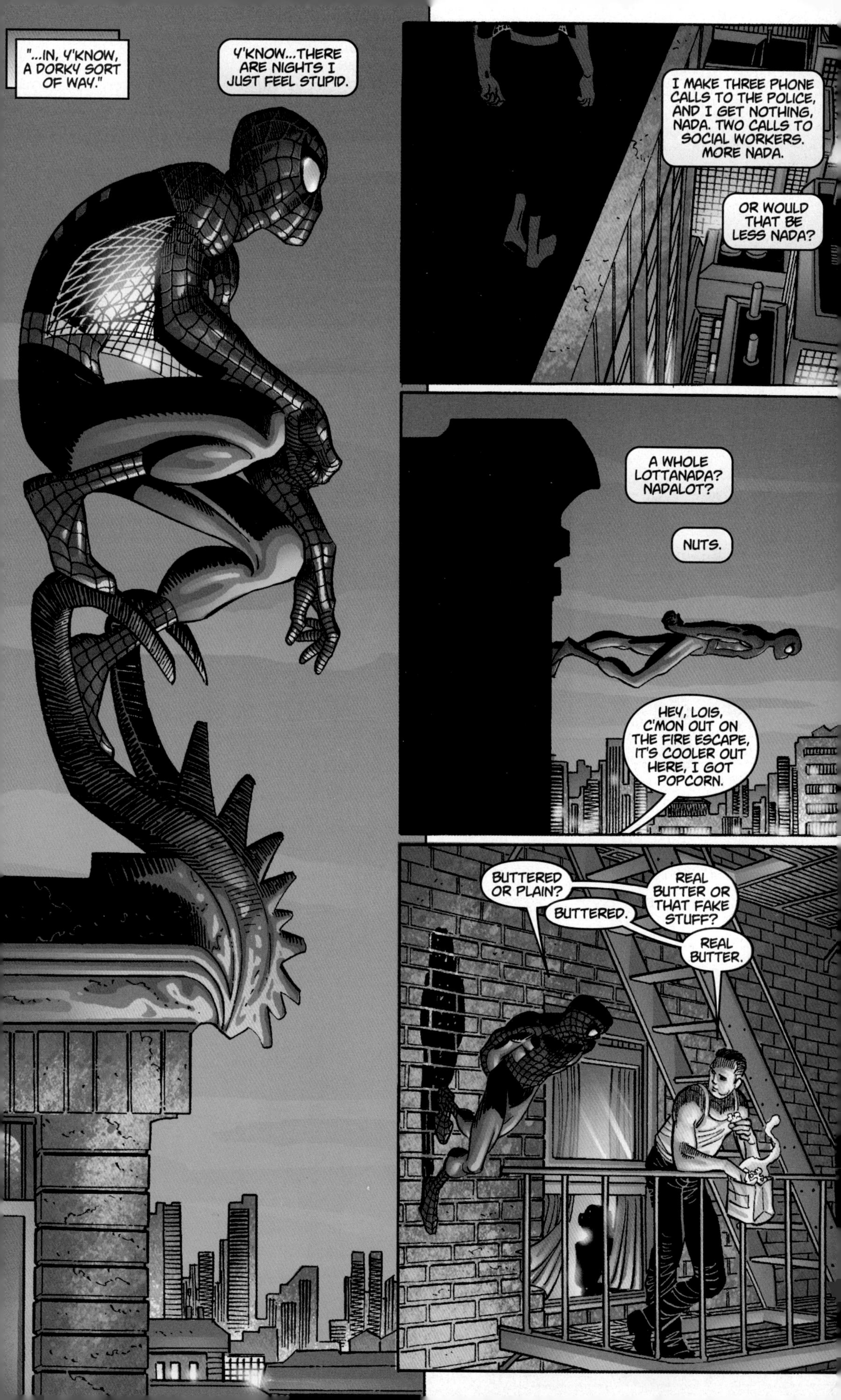
"...IN, Y'KNOW, A DORKY SORT OF WAY."
Y'KNOW...THERE ARE NIGHTS I JUST FEEL STUPID.
I MAKE THREE PHONE CALLS TO THE POLICE, AND I GET NOTHING, NADA. TWO CALLS TO SOCIAL WORKERS. MORE NADA.
OR WOULD THAT BE LESS NADA?
A WHOLE LOTTANADA? NADALOT?
NUTS.
HEY, LOIS, C'MON OUT ON THE FIRE ESCAPE, IT'S COOLER OUT HERE, I GOT POPCORN.
BUTTERED OR PLAIN?
REAL BUTTER OR THAT FAKE STUFF?
BUTTERED.
REAL BUTTER.

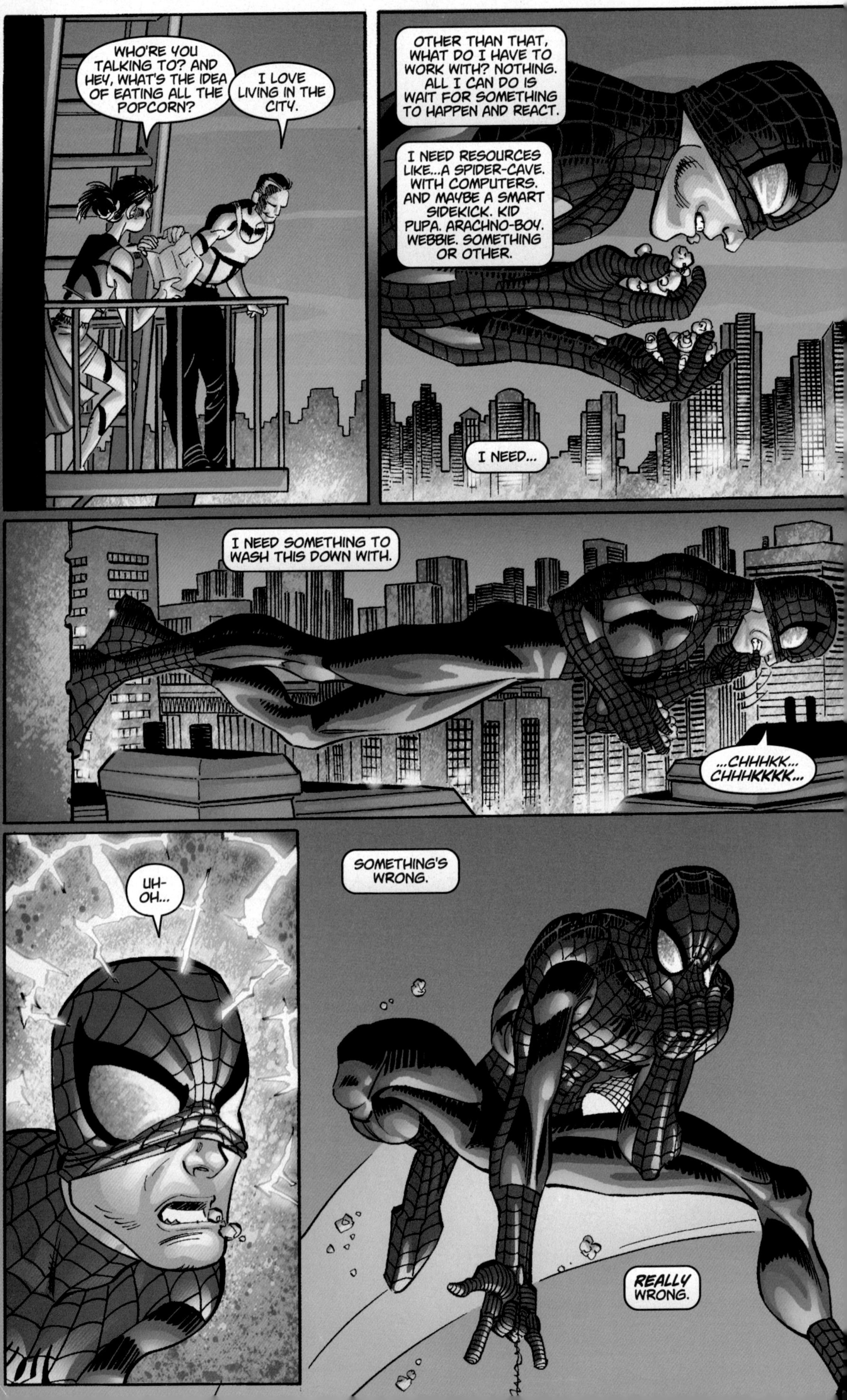
WHO'RE YOU TALKING TO? AND HEY, WHAT'S THE IDEA OF EATING ALL THE POPCORN?
I LOVE LIVING IN THE CITY.
OTHER THAN THAT, WHAT DO I HAVE TO WORK WITH? NOTHING. ALL I CAN DO IS WAIT FOR SOMETHING TO HAPPEN AND REACT.
I NEED RESOURCES LIKE...A SPIDER-CAVE. WITH COMPUTERS. AND MAYBE A SMART SIDEKICK. KID PUPA. ARACHNO-BOY. WEBBIE. SOMETHING OR OTHER.
I NEED...
I NEED SOMETHING TO WASH THIS DOWN WITH.
...CHHHKK... CHHHKKKK...
UH-OH...
SOMETHING'S WRONG.
REALLY WRONG.

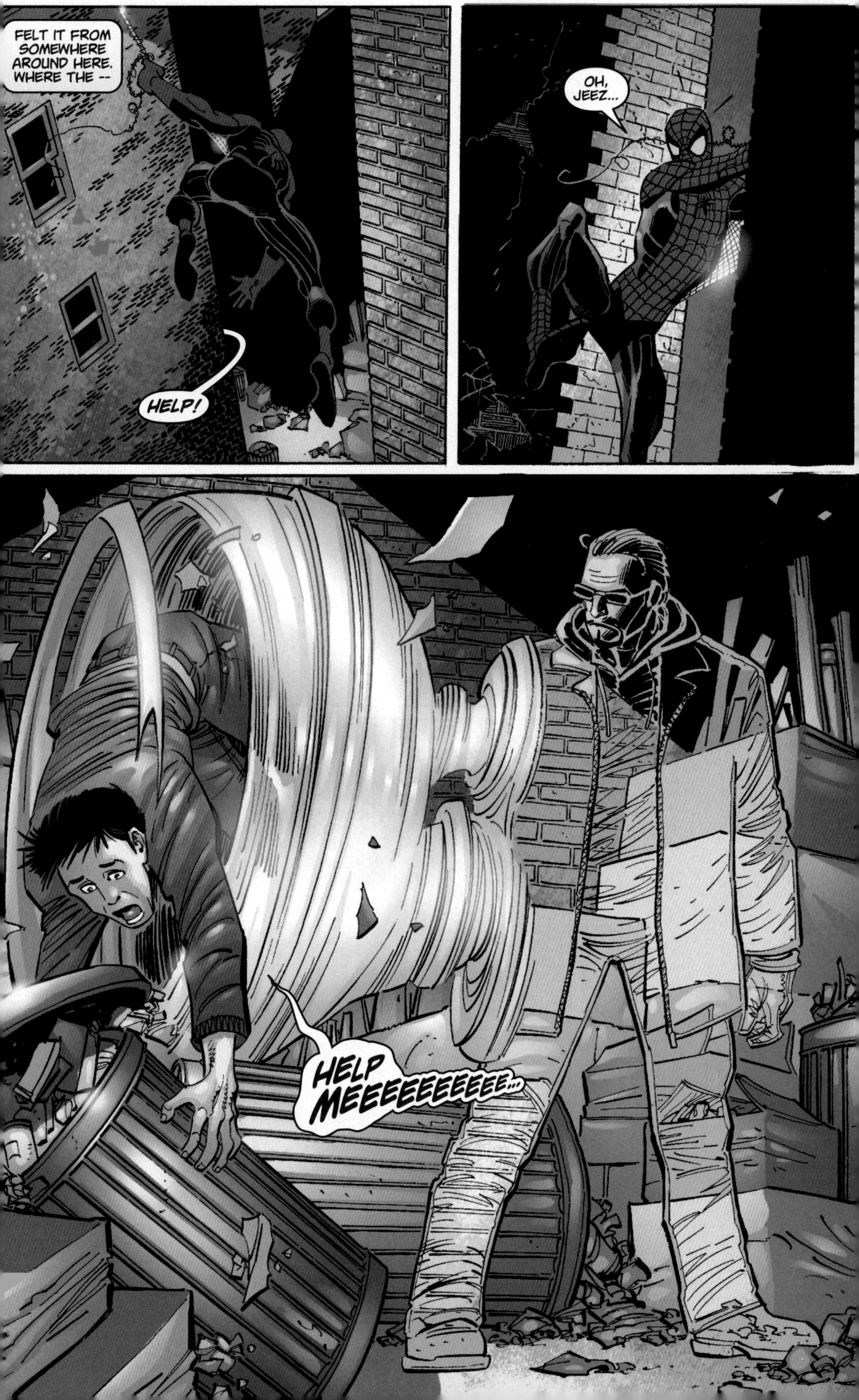
FELT IT FROM SOMEWHERE AROUND HERE. WHERE THE --
HELP!
OH, JEEZ...
HELP MEEEEEEEEEE...

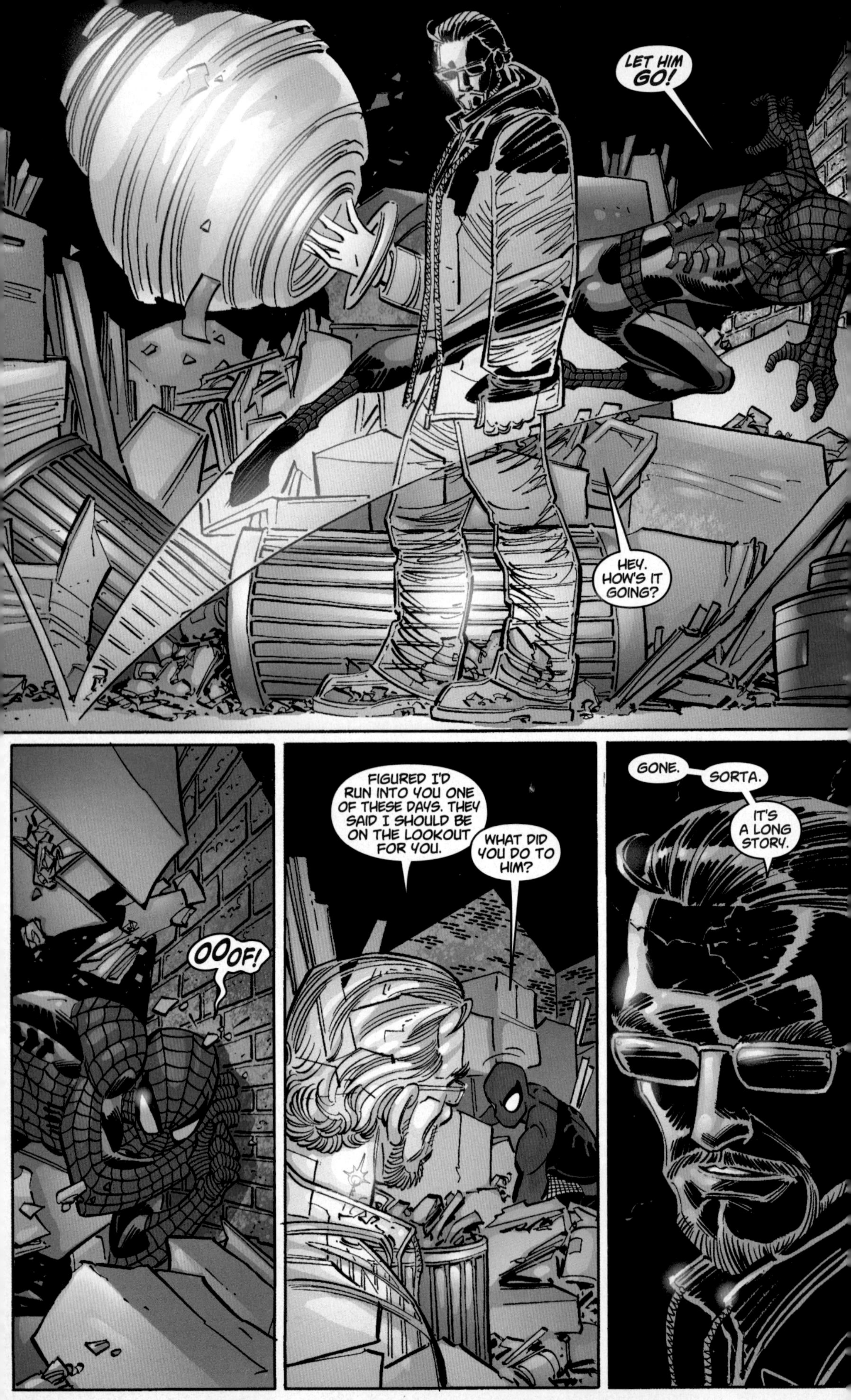
LET HIM GO!
HEY. HOW'S IT GOING?
OOOF!
FIGURED I'D RUN INTO YOU ONE OF THESE DAYS. THEY SAID I SHOULD BE ON THE LOOKOUT FOR YOU.
WHAT DID YOU DO TO HIM?
GONE.
SORTA.
IT'S A LONG STORY.

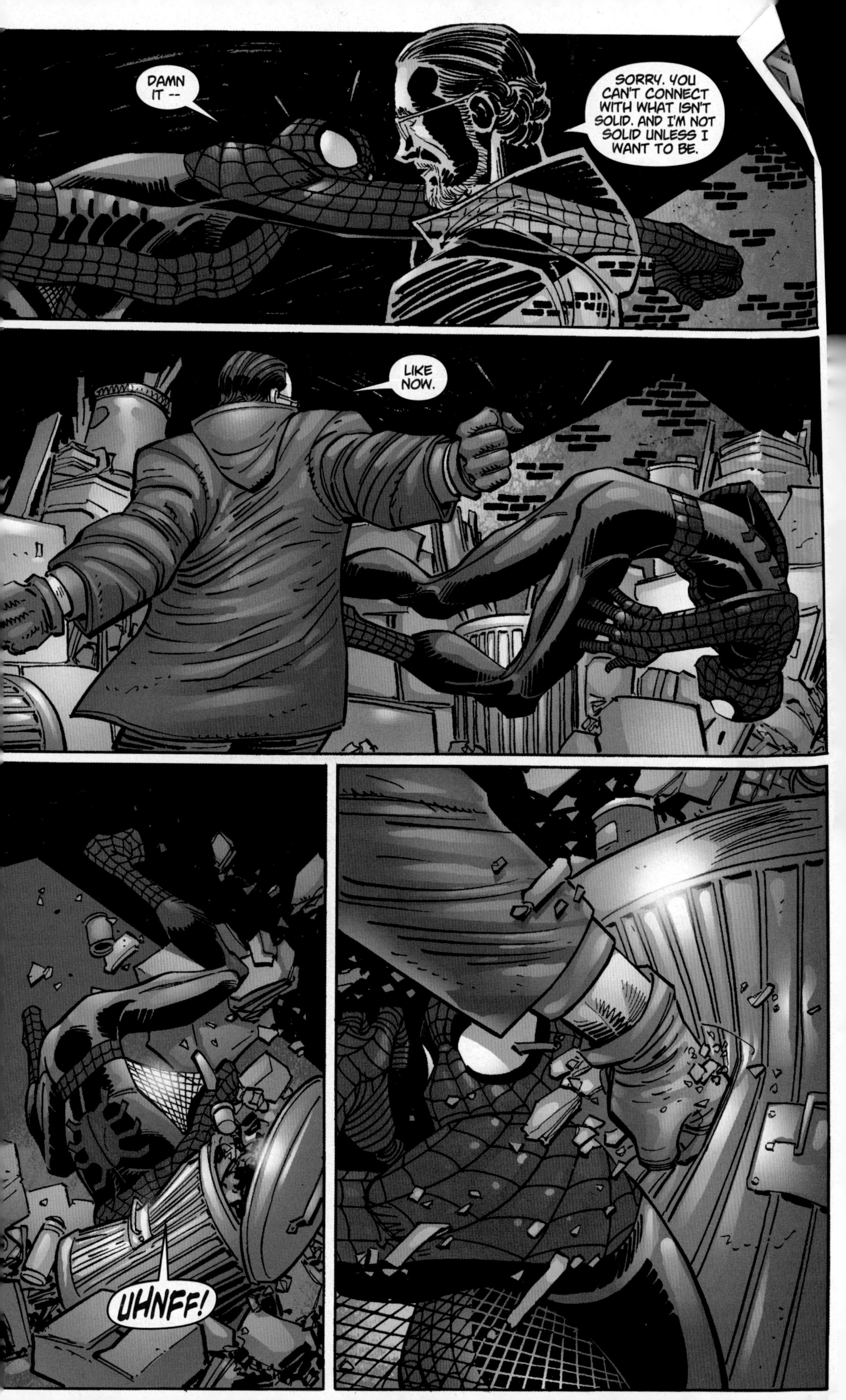
DAMN IT --
SORRY. YOU CAN'T CONNECT WITH WHAT ISN'T SOLID. AND I'M NOT SOLID UNLESS I WANT TO BE.
LIKE NOW.
UHNFF!

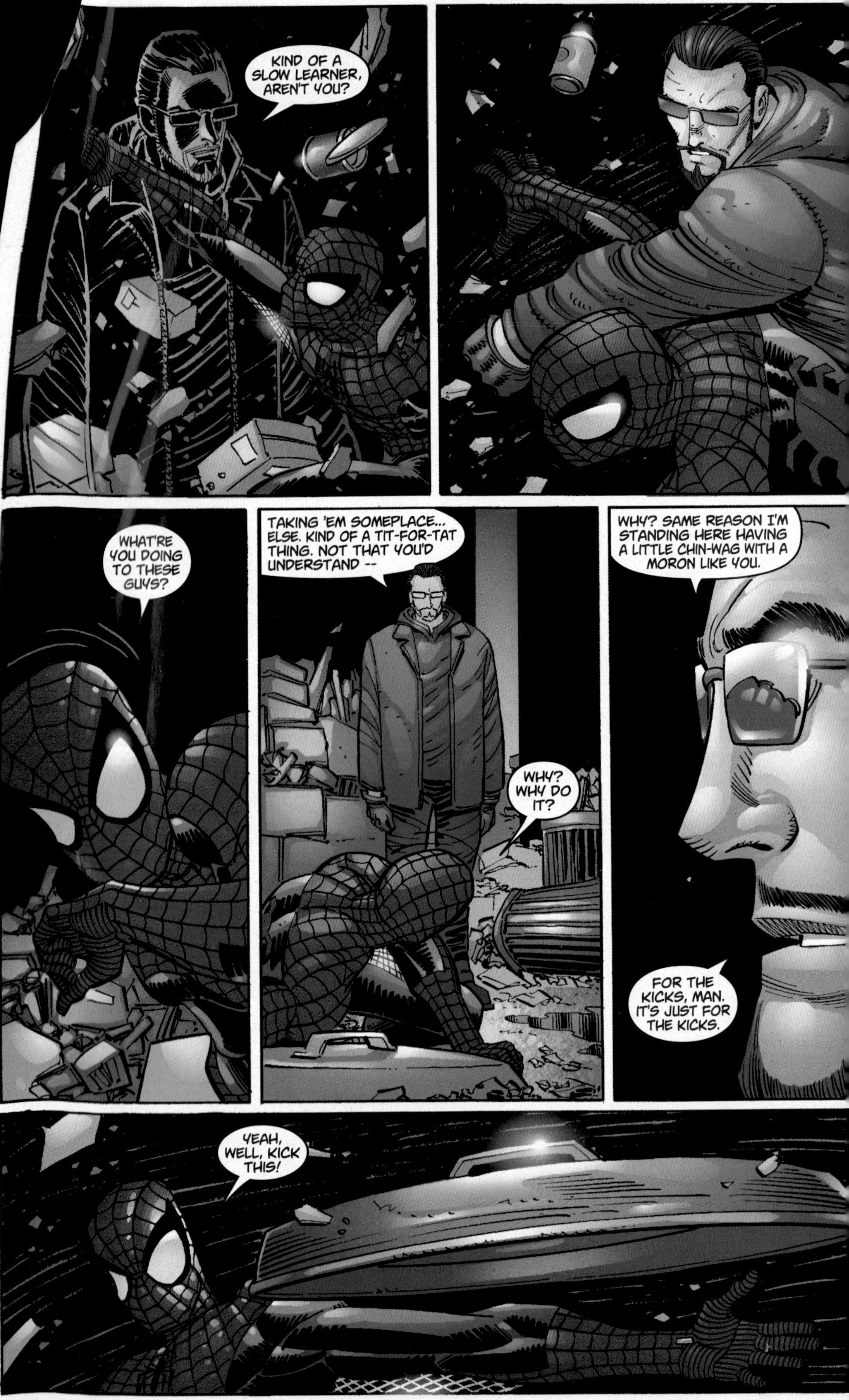
KIND OF A SLOW LEARNER, AREN'T YOU?
WHAT'RE YOU DOING TO THESE GUYS?
TAKING 'EM SOMEPLACE... ELSE. KIND OF A TIT-FOR-TAT THING. NOT THAT YOU'D UNDERSTAND --
WHY? WHY DO IT?
WHY? SAME REASON I'M STANDING HERE HAVING A LITTLE CHIN-WAG WITH A MORON LIKE YOU.
FOR THE KICKS, MAN. IT'S JUST FOR THE KICKS.
YEAH, WELL, KICK THIS!

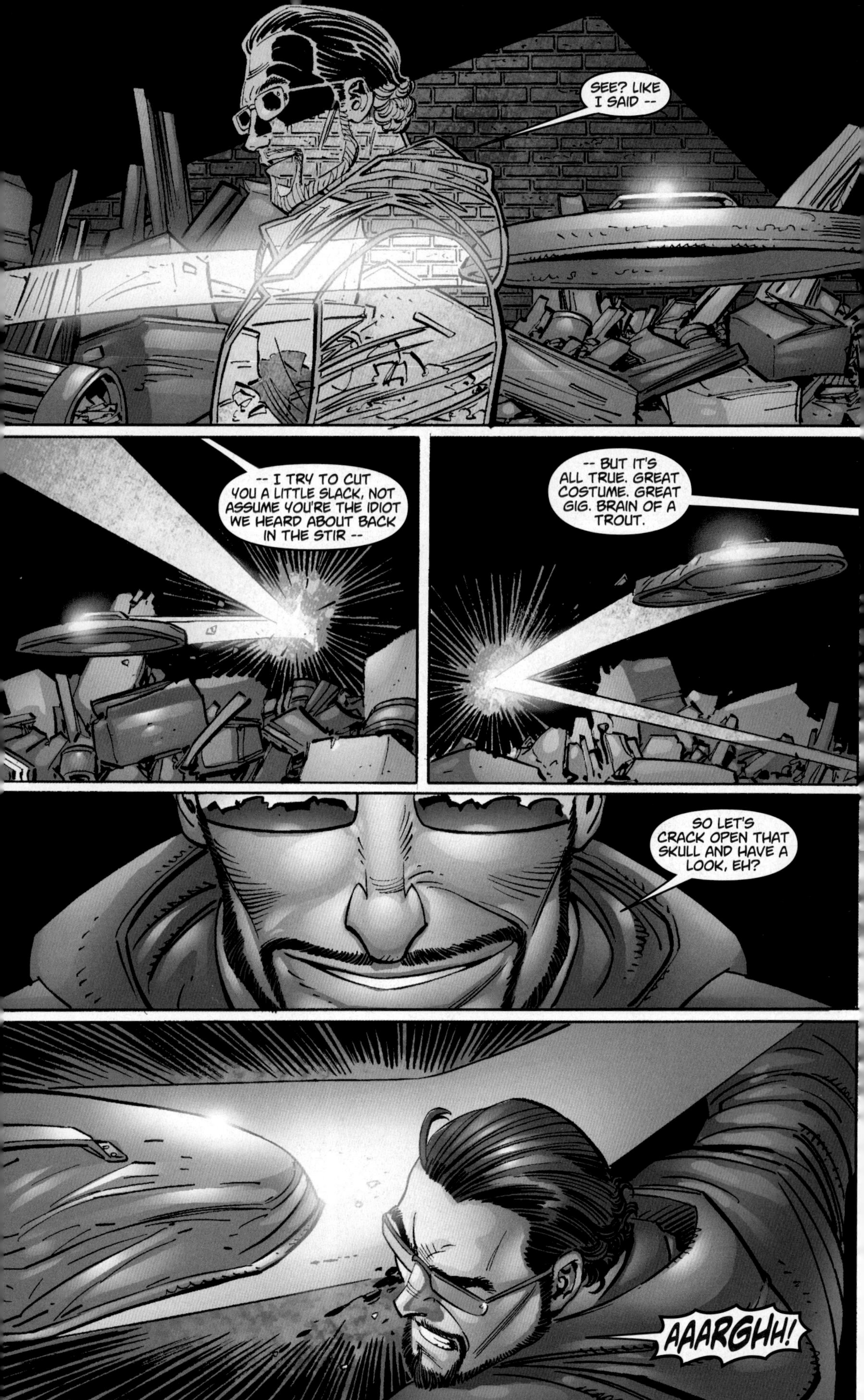
SEE? LIKE I SAID --
-- I TRY TO CUT YOU A LITTLE SLACK, NOT ASSUME YOU'RE THE IDIOT WE HEARD ABOUT BACK IN THE STIR --
-- BUT IT'S ALL TRUE. GREAT COSTUME. GREAT GIG. BRAIN OF A TROUT.
SO LET'S CRACK OPEN THAT SKULL AND HAVE A LOOK, EH?
AAARGHH!

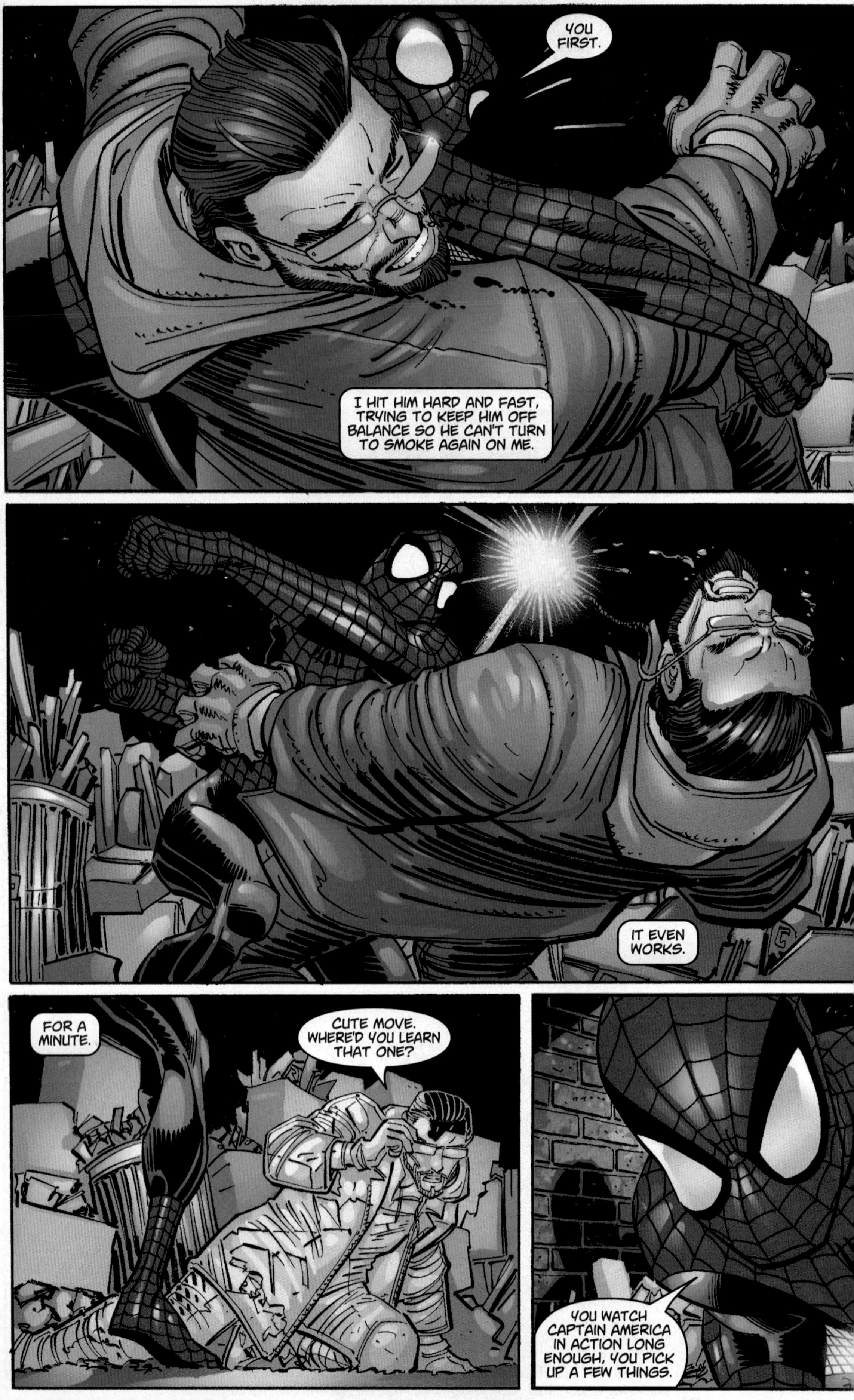
YOU FIRST.
I HIT HIM HARD AND FAST, TRYING TO KEEP HIM OFF BALANCE SO HE CAN'T TURN TO SMOKE AGAIN ON ME.
IT EVEN WORKS.
FOR A MINUTE.
CUTE MOVE. WHERE'D YOU LEARN THAT ONE?
YOU WATCH CAPTAIN AMERICA IN ACTION LONG ENOUGH, YOU PICK UP A FEW THINGS.

YEAH, WELL, I GOTTA GO.

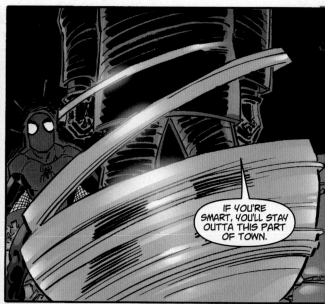

IF YOU'RE SMART, YOU'LL STAY OUTTA THIS PART OF TOWN.

GO FIGHT SOMEBODY IN A CHEAP COSTUME AND STAY OUTTA THE NEIGHBORHOOD. THIS AIN'T YOUR KIND OF PLACE...

HEY!

NUTS.

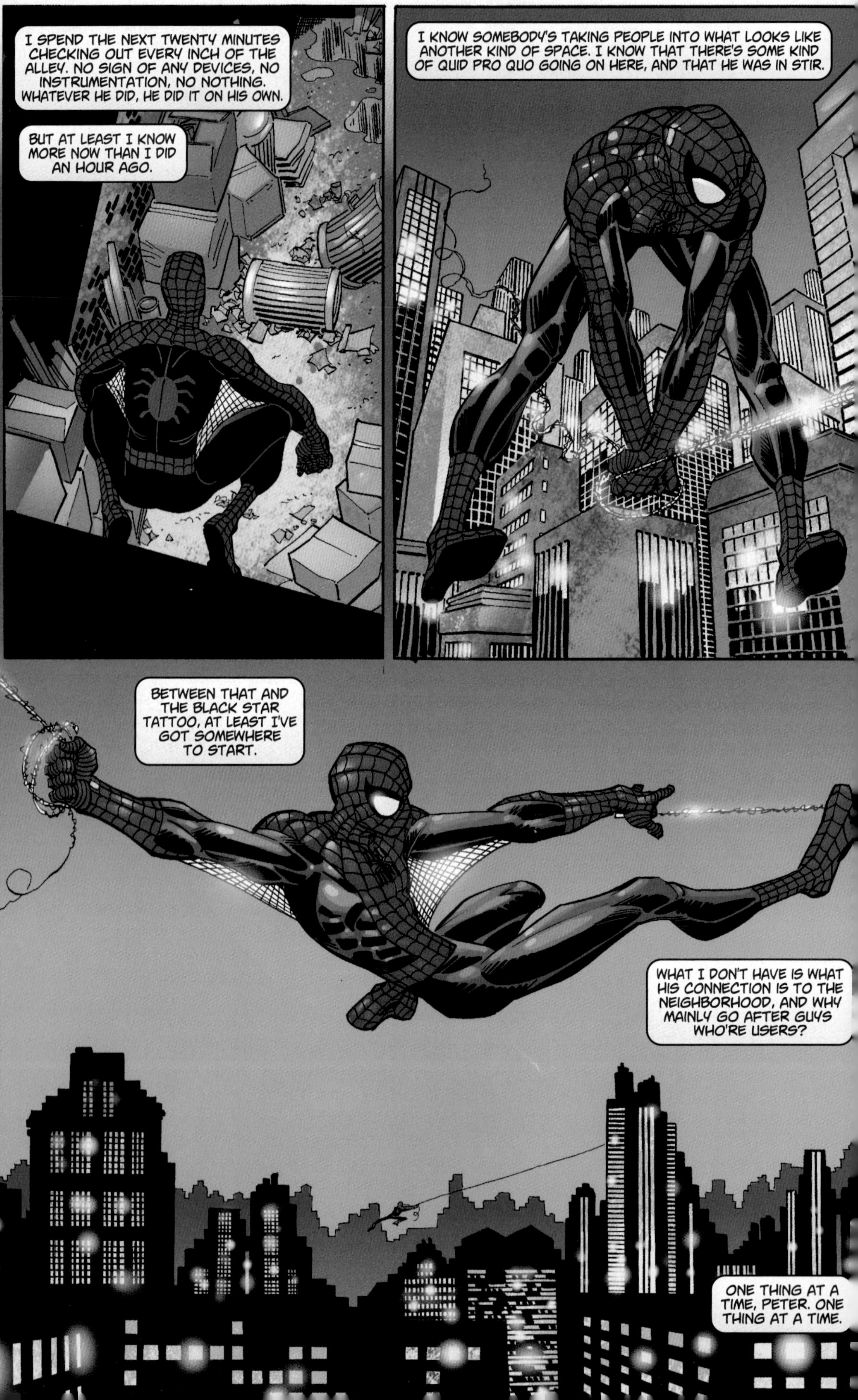
I SPEND THE NEXT TWENTY MINUTES CHECKING OUT EVERY INCH OF THE ALLEY. NO SIGN OF ANY DEVICES, NO INSTRUMENTATION, NO NOTHING. WHATEVER HE DID, HE DID IT ON HIS OWN.
BUT AT LEAST I KNOW MORE NOW THAN I DID AN HOUR AGO.
I KNOW SOMEBODY'S TAKING PEOPLE INTO WHAT LOOKS LIKE ANOTHER KIND OF SPACE. I KNOW THAT THERE'S SOME KIND OF QUID PRO QUO GOING ON HERE, AND THAT HE WAS IN STIR.
BETWEEN THAT AND THE BLACK STAR TATTOO, AT LEAST I'VE GOT SOMEWHERE TO START.
WHAT I DON'T HAVE IS WHAT HIS CONNECTION IS TO THE NEIGHBORHOOD, AND WHY MAINLY GO AFTER GUYS WHO'RE USERS?
ONE THING AT A TIME, PETER. ONE THING AT A TIME.

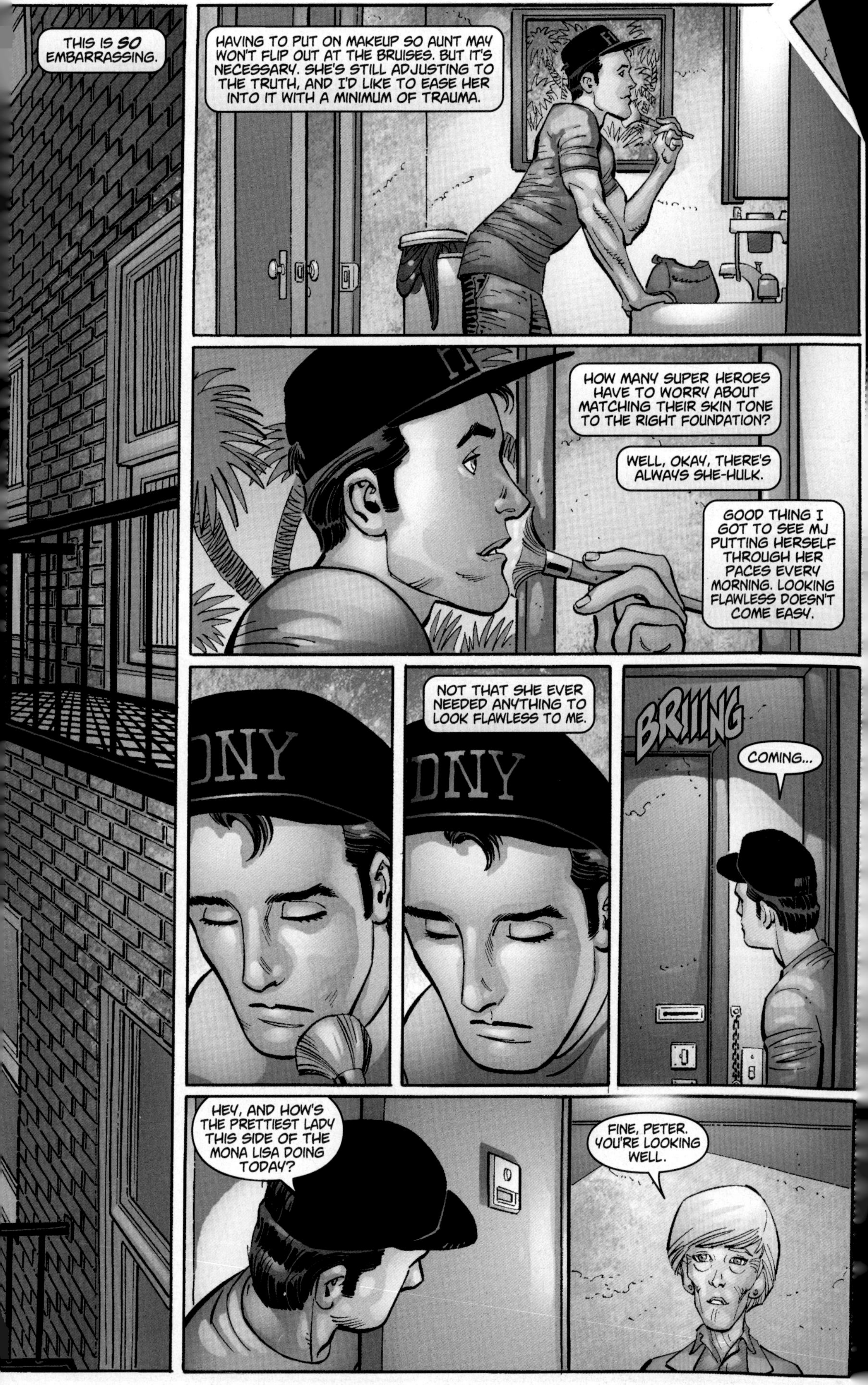
THIS IS SO EMBARRASSING.
HAVING TO PUT ON MAKEUP SO AUNT MAY WON'T FLIP OUT AT THE BRUISES. BUT IT'S NECESSARY. SHE'S STILL ADJUSTING TO THE TRUTH, AND I'D LIKE TO EASE HER INTO IT WITH A MINIMUM OF TRAUMA.
HOW MANY SUPER HEROES HAVE TO WORRY ABOUT MATCHING THEIR SKIN TONE TO THE RIGHT FOUNDATION?
WELL, OKAY, THERE'S ALWAYS SHE-HULK.
GOOD THING I GOT TO SEE MJ PUTTING HERSELF THROUGH HER PACES EVERY MORNING. LOOKING FLAWLESS DOESN'T COME EASY.
DNY
NOT THAT SHE EVER NEEDED ANYTHING TO LOOK FLAWLESS TO ME.
DNY
BRIIING
COMING...
HEY, AND HOW'S THE PRETTIEST LADY THIS SIDE OF THE MONA LISA DOING TODAY?
FINE, PETER. YOU'RE LOOKING WELL.

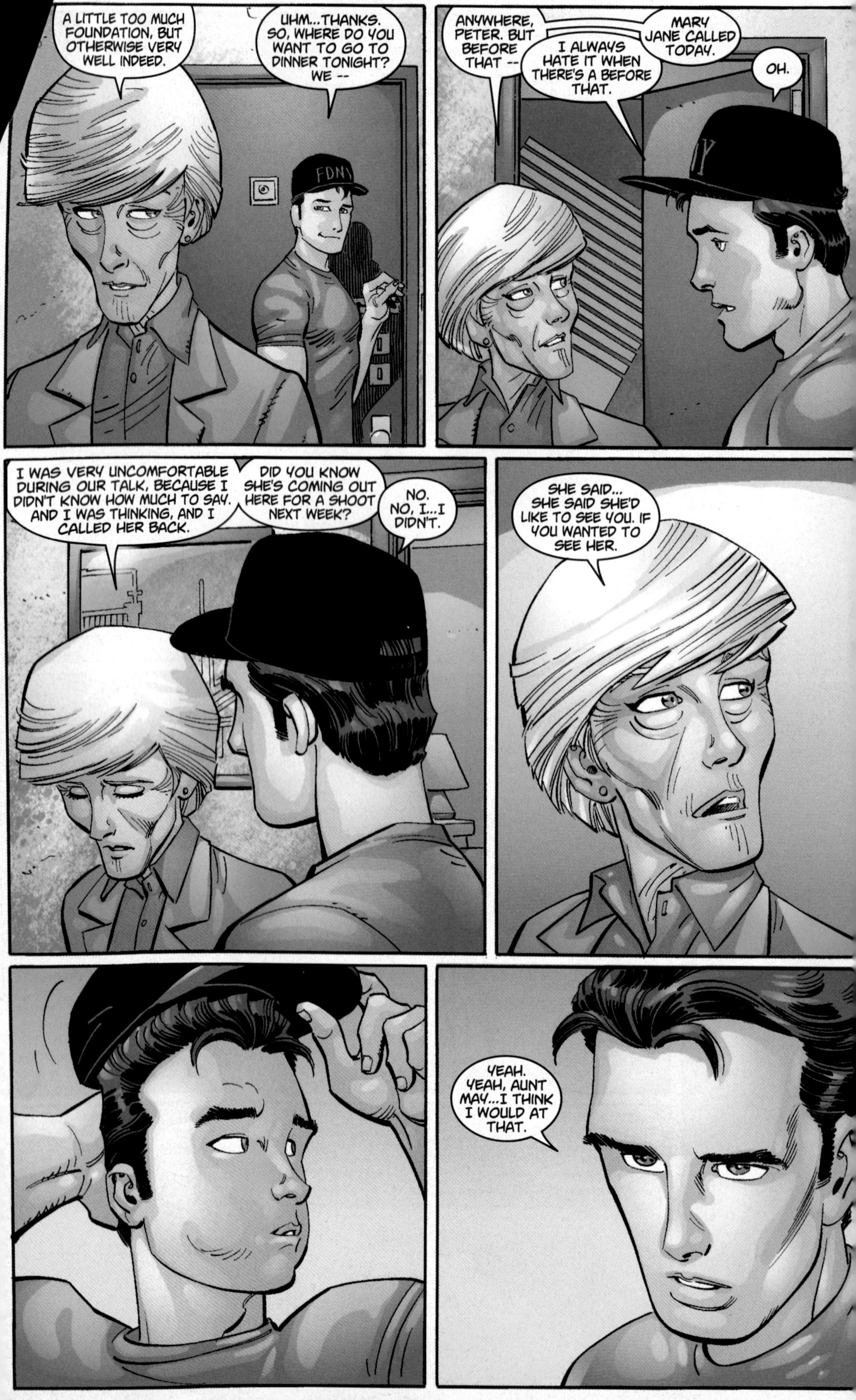
A LITTLE TOO MUCH FOUNDATION, BUT OTHERWISE VERY WELL INDEED.
UHM...THANKS. SO, WHERE DO YOU WANT TO GO TO DINNER TONIGHT? WE --
FDNY
ANYWHERE, PETER. BUT BEFORE THAT --
I ALWAYS HATE IT WHEN THERE'S A BEFORE THAT.
MARY JANE CALLED TODAY.
OH.
I WAS VERY UNCOMFORTABLE DURING OUR TALK, BECAUSE I DIDN'T KNOW HOW MUCH TO SAY. AND I WAS THINKING, AND I CALLED HER BACK.
DID YOU KNOW SHE'S COMING OUT HERE FOR A SHOOT NEXT WEEK?
NO. NO, I...I DIDN'T.
SHE SAID... SHE SAID SHE'D LIKE TO SEE YOU. IF YOU WANTED TO SEE HER.
YEAH. YEAH, AUNT MAY...I THINK I WOULD AT THAT.

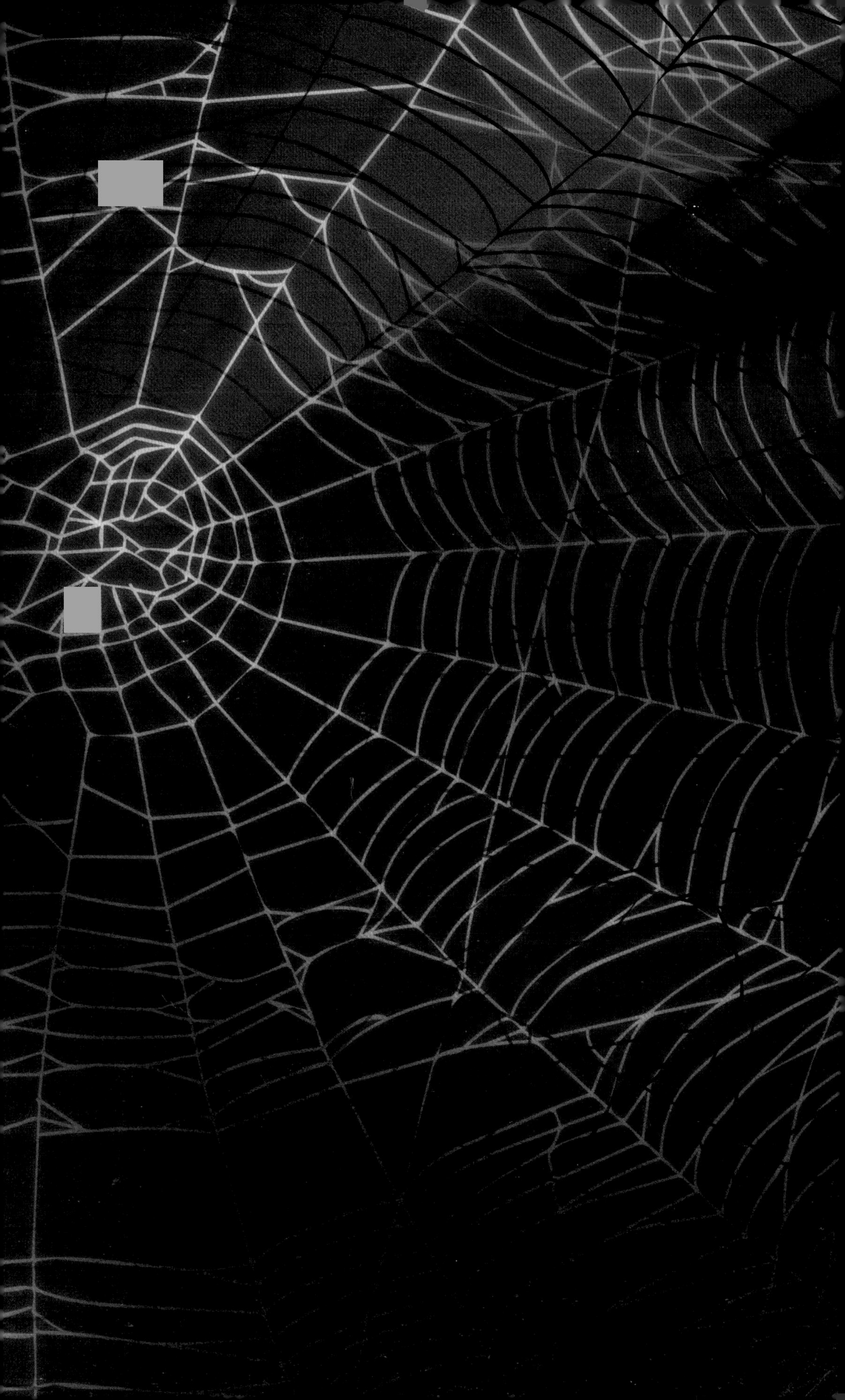

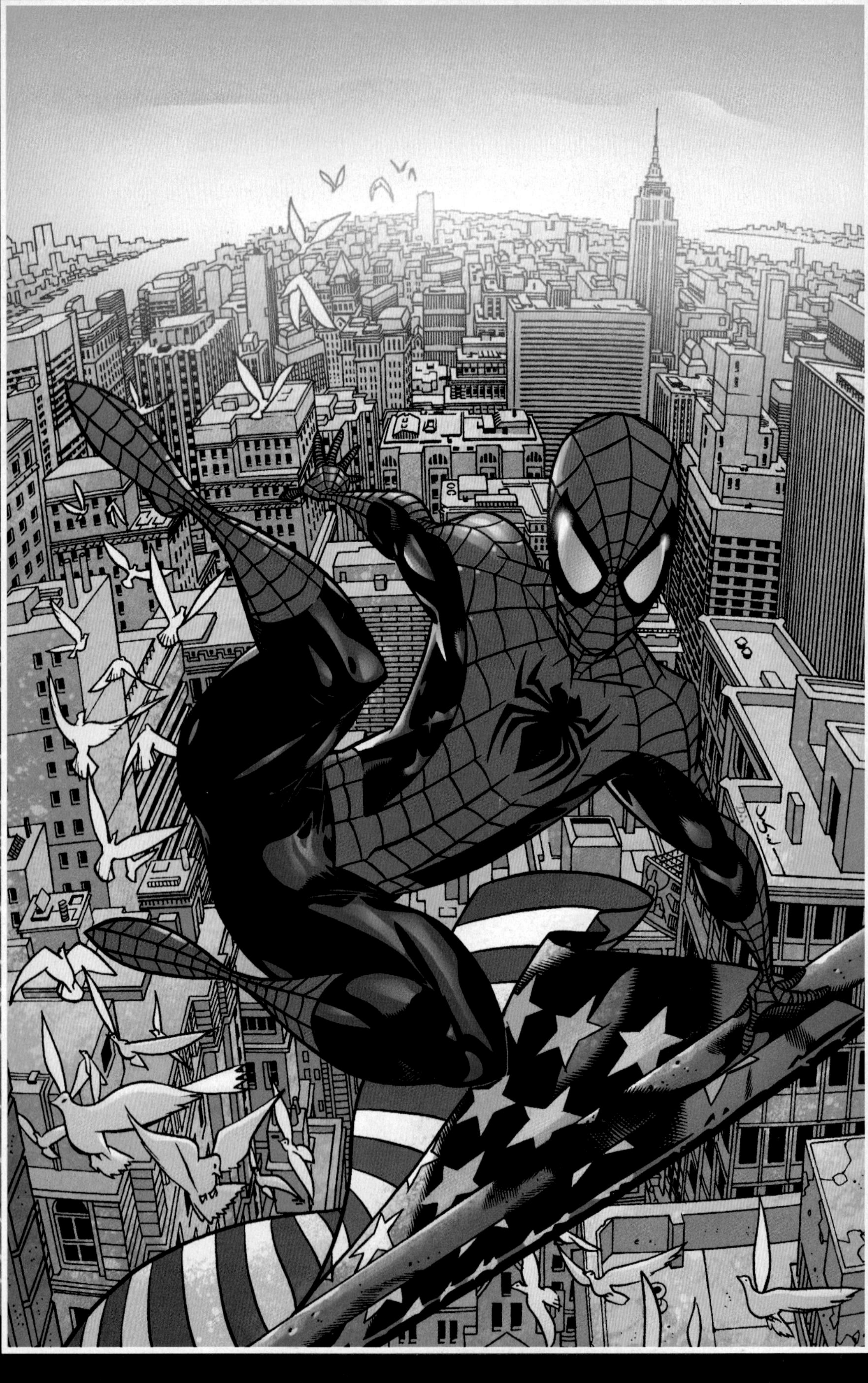

AMAZING SPIDER-MAN #41

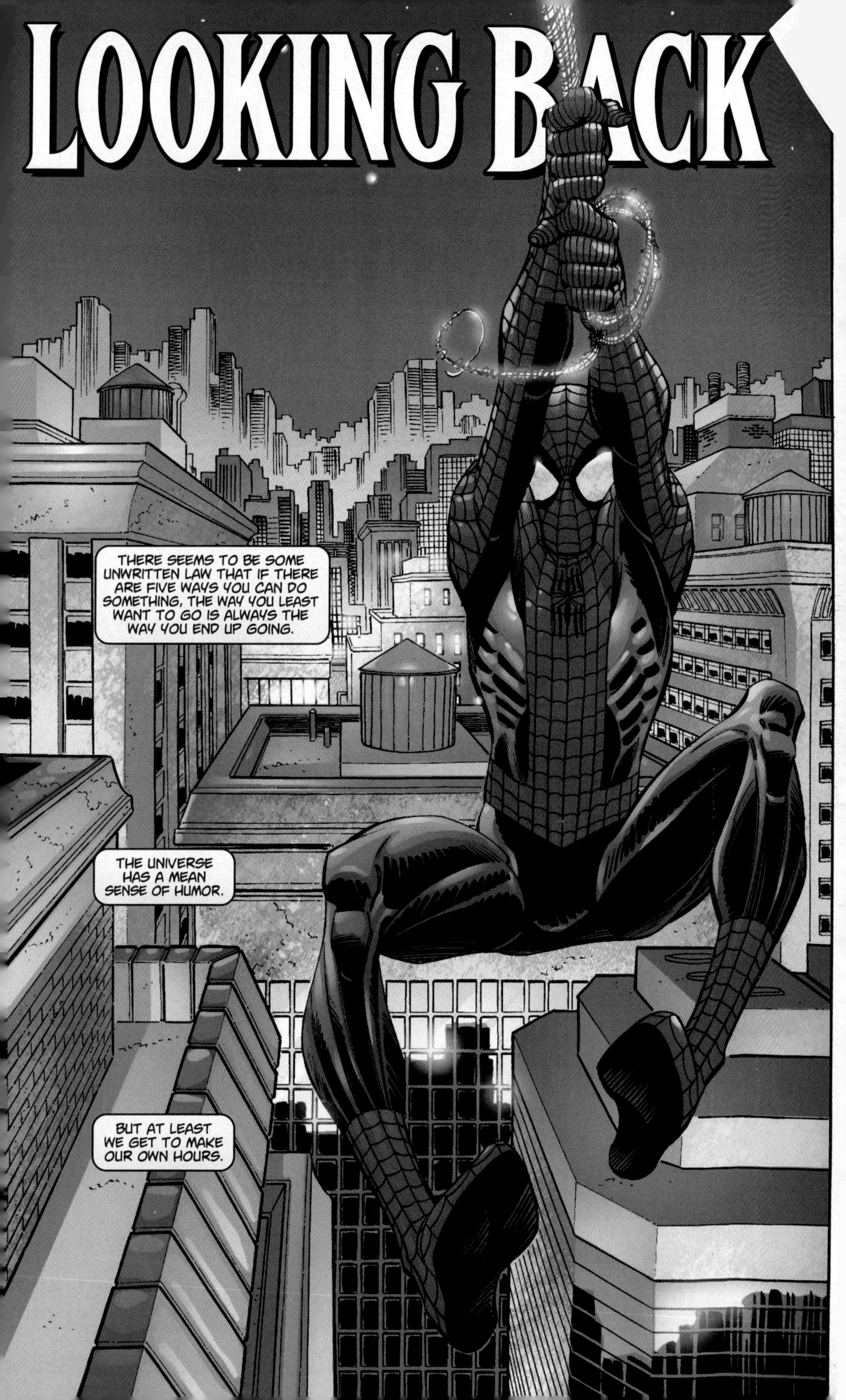
LOOKING BACK
THERE SEEMS TO BE SOME UNWRITTEN LAW THAT IF THERE ARE FIVE WAYS YOU CAN DO SOMETHING, THE WAY YOU LEAST WANT TO GO IS ALWAYS THE WAY YOU END UP GOING.
THE UNIVERSE HAS A MEAN SENSE OF HUMOR.
BUT AT LEAST WE GET TO MAKE OUR OWN HOURS.

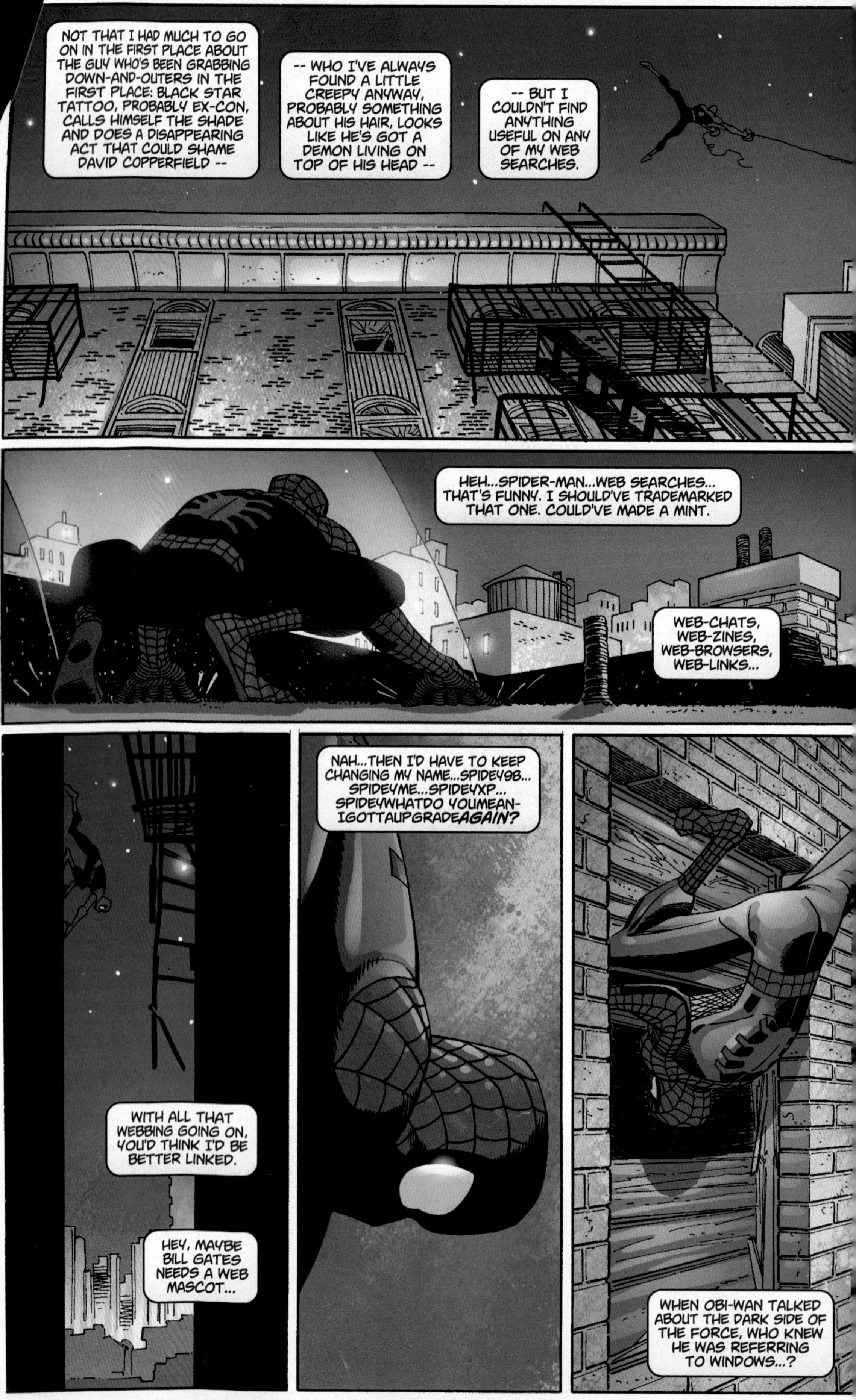
NOT THAT I HAD MUCH TO GO ON IN THE FIRST PLACE ABOUT THE GUY WHO'S BEEN GRABBING DOWN-AND-OUTERS IN THE FIRST PLACE: BLACK STAR TATTOO, PROBABLY EX-CON, CALLS HIMSELF THE SHADE AND DOES A DISAPPEARING ACT THAT COULD SHAME DAVID COPPERFIELD --
-- WHO I'VE ALWAYS FOUND A LITTLE CREEPY ANYWAY, PROBABLY SOMETHING ABOUT HIS HAIR, LOOKS LIKE HE'S GOT A DEMON LIVING ON TOP OF HIS HEAD --
-- BUT I COULDN'T FIND ANYTHING USEFUL ON ANY OF MY WEB SEARCHES.
HEH...SPIDER-MAN...WEB SEARCHES... THAT'S FUNNY. I SHOULD'VE TRADEMARKED THAT ONE. COULD'VE MADE A MINT.
WEB-CHATS, WEB-ZINES, WEB-BROWSERS, WEB-LINKS...
WITH ALL THAT WEBBING GOING ON, YOU'D THINK I'D BE BETTER LINKED.
HEY, MAYBE BILL GATES NEEDS A WEB MASCOT...
NAH...THEN I'D HAVE TO KEEP CHANGING MY NAME...SPIDEY98... SPIDEYME...SPIDEYXP... SPIDEYWHATDO YOUMEAN-IGOTTAUPGRADE*AGAIN?*
WHEN OBI-WAN TALKED ABOUT THE DARK SIDE OF THE FORCE, WHO KNEW HE WAS REFERRING TO WINDOWS...?

AND NOW I GET TO PLAY STUPID LIKE I DON'T KNOW IT'S JENNIFER SINCE SHE'S ONLY MET PETER, NOT ME.

HI, *UHM,* I'M LOOKING FOR JENNIFER.

YEAH, THAT'S ME.

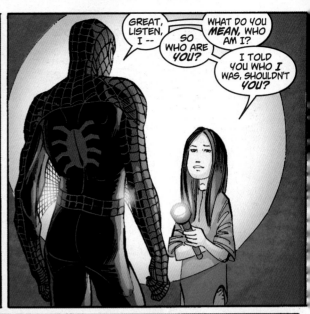

GREAT, LISTEN, I --

SO WHO ARE *YOU?*

WHAT DO YOU *MEAN,* WHO AM I?

I TOLD YOU WHO *I* WAS, SHOULDN'T *YOU?*

YOU LIVE IN NEW YORK?

YOU WATCH THE NEWS?

YEP.

WHEN I'M NEAR A TV... YEP.

YOU EVER DO A WEB SEARCH?

YEAH, BUT WHAT'S THAT GOT TO DO WITH --

SO WHAT DO YOU MEAN YOU DON'T KNOW WHO I AM? I SAVED YOUR BROTHER'S LIFE!

OH, I *KNOW* WHO YOU *ARE...* I JUST WANNA HEAR YOU SAY IT...Y'KNOW, DO THAT WHOLE SUPER HERO *I AM SPIDER-MAN* THING...

C'MON, I LIVE IN AN ABANDONED BASEMENT, I GOTTA GET SOME FUN IN *SOMEWHERE...*

I'M SPIDER-MAN.

HE SAID IT, HE SAID IT, HEE-HEE!

OKAY, WHAT DO YOU WANT TO KNOW?

AND...THANK YOU, REALLY, FOR SAVING JOHNNY. IF I'D LOST HIM --

IT'S OKAY. ALL PART OF THE SERVICE.

I KNOW YOUR BROTHER'S BEEN POPPED BEFORE ON DRUG CHARGES...DOES HE HAVE A REGULAR YOUTH OFFICER ASSIGNED TO HIM?

YES --

DOES THE SAME OFFICER HANDLE OTHER CASES HERE IN THE NEIGHBORHOOD?

I THINK SO...WHY?

I NEED A NAME.

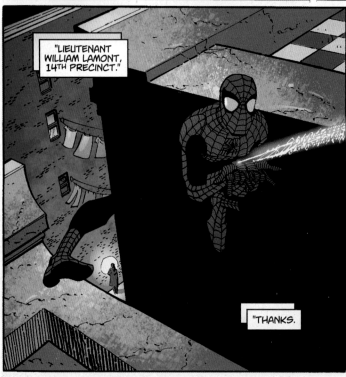

"LIEUTENANT WILLIAM LAMONT, 14TH PRECINCT."

"THANKS.

"I JUST HOPE I CAN GET TO THE BOTTOM OF THIS BEFORE ANYBODY ELSE IS TARGETED."

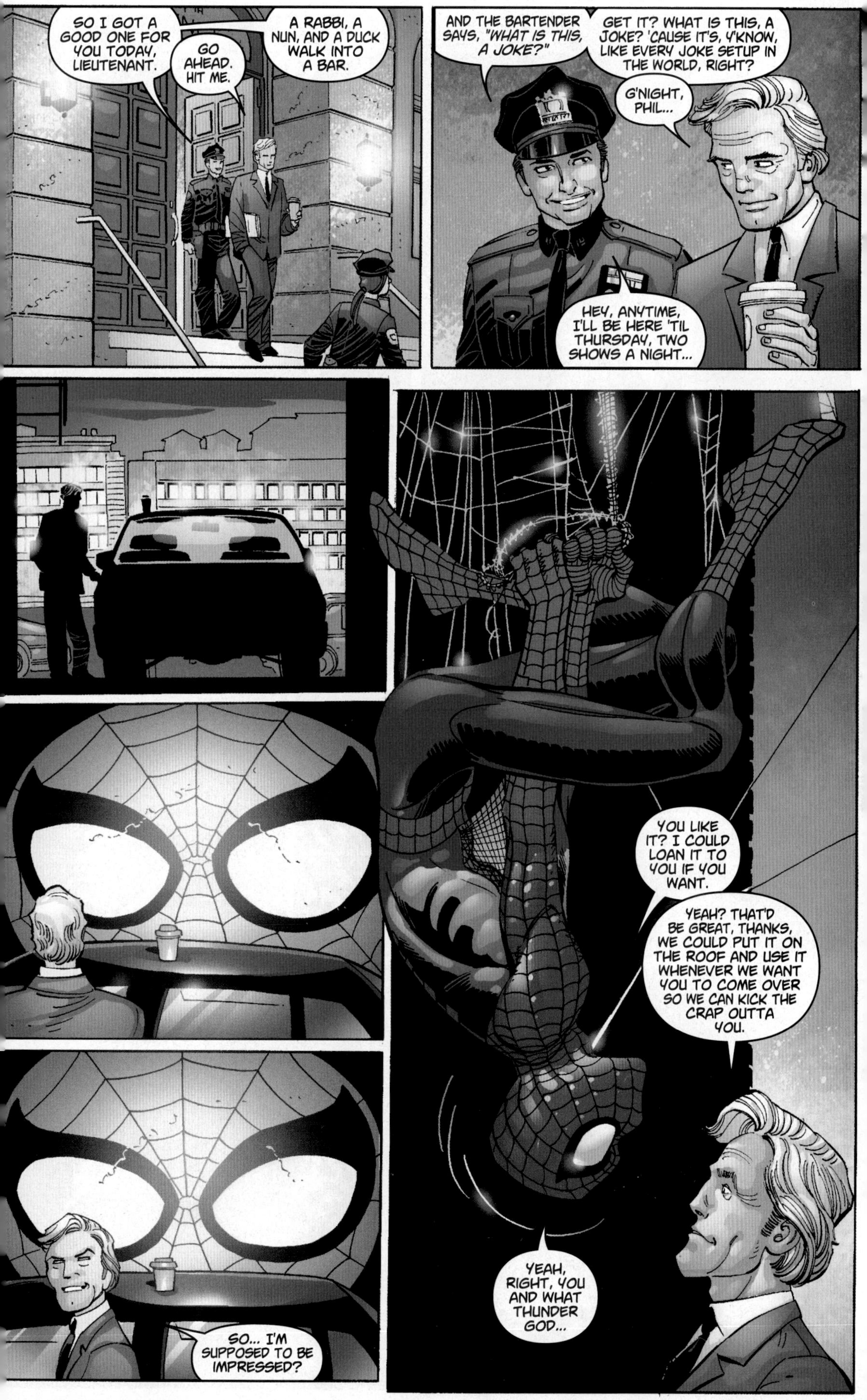
SO I GOT A GOOD ONE FOR YOU TODAY, LIEUTENANT.
GO AHEAD. HIT ME.
A RABBI, A NUN, AND A DUCK WALK INTO A BAR.
AND THE BARTENDER SAYS, "WHAT IS THIS, A JOKE?"
GET IT? WHAT IS THIS, A JOKE? 'CAUSE IT'S, Y'KNOW, LIKE EVERY JOKE SETUP IN THE WORLD, RIGHT?
G'NIGHT, PHIL...
HEY, ANYTIME, I'LL BE HERE 'TIL THURSDAY, TWO SHOWS A NIGHT...
SO... I'M SUPPOSED TO BE IMPRESSED?
YOU LIKE IT? I COULD LOAN IT TO YOU IF YOU WANT.
YEAH? THAT'D BE GREAT, THANKS, WE COULD PUT IT ON THE ROOF AND USE IT WHENEVER WE WANT YOU TO COME OVER SO WE CAN KICK THE CRAP OUTTA YOU.
YEAH, RIGHT, YOU AND WHAT THUNDER GOD...

THERE'S MORE THAN ONE?

SIGH... DOESN'T *ANYONE* READ THE PAPER ANYMORE?

JUST THE BUGLE.

FRASER FRASER

WHAT WAS THAT?

NOTHING, I JUST BURPED. LISTEN, I --

WHATEVER IT IS, I DON'T HAVE TIME FOR THIS. I GOTTA BE AT A --

A BUNCH OF STREET KIDS HAVE GONE MISSING, MOSTLY USERS. NOBODY ELSE SEEMS TO CARE. I'M BETTING YOU DO.

YEAH? WHY?

BECAUSE OF THE WAY THE MOONLIGHT DANCES IN YOUR EYES, YOU BIG STUDLY GUY.

AND THE SISTER OF ONE OF YOUR REGULARS SAID YOU WERE A STAND-UP GUY. YOU GONNA MAKE A LIAR OUT OF HER?

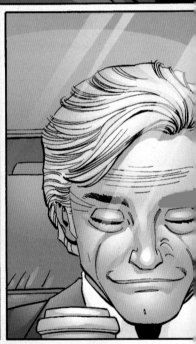

GET IN THE FREAKIN' CAR BEFORE SOMEBODY SEES YOU AND WHIPS OUT A CAN OF RAID.

THANKS. AND I MEANT THAT PART ABOUT THE MOONLIGHT --

SHUDDUP.

SO WHAT DO YOU NEED?

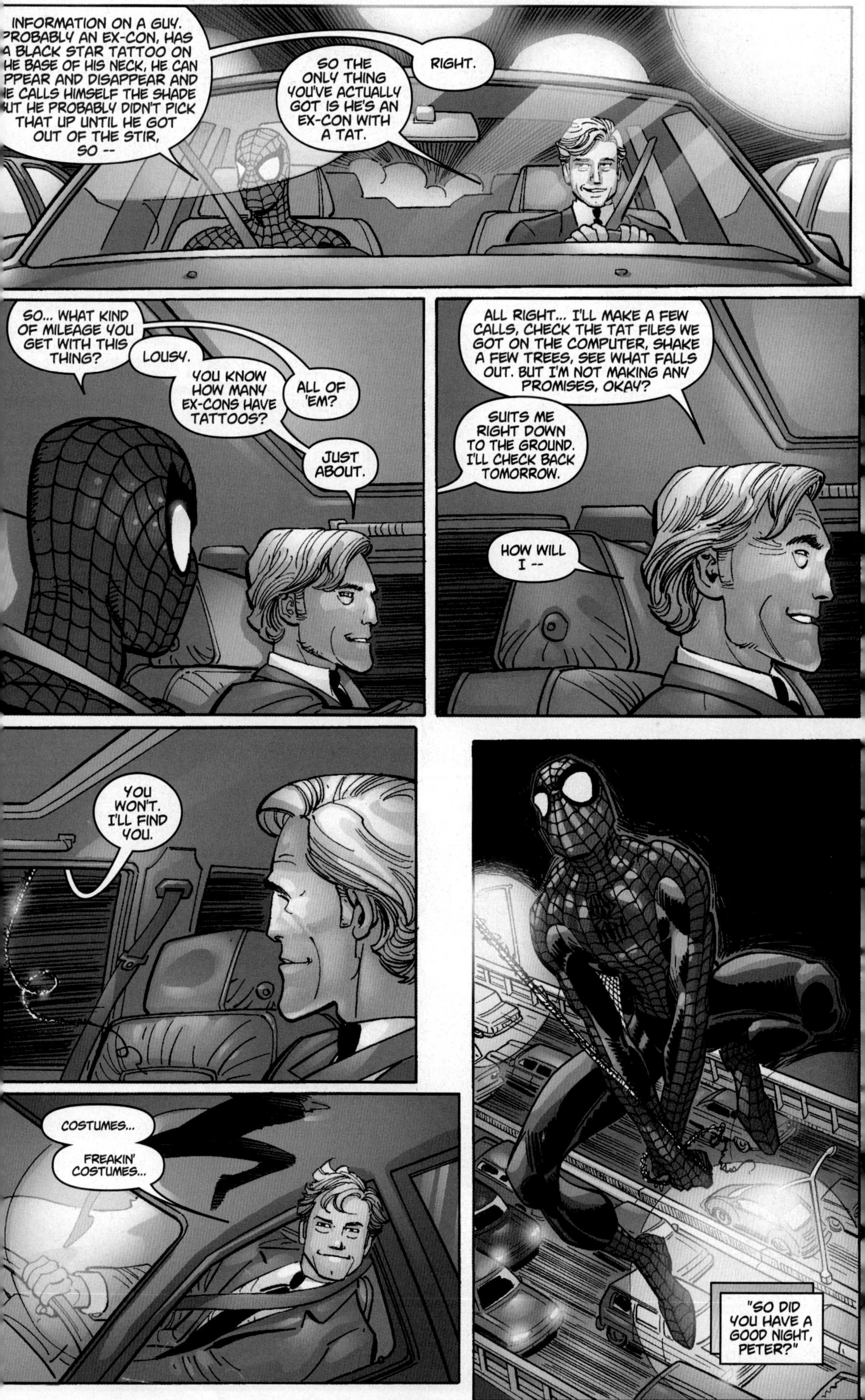
INFORMATION ON A GUY. PROBABLY AN EX-CON, HAS A BLACK STAR TATTOO ON THE BASE OF HIS NECK, HE CAN APPEAR AND DISAPPEAR AND HE CALLS HIMSELF THE SHADE BUT HE PROBABLY DIDN'T PICK THAT UP UNTIL HE GOT OUT OF THE STIR, SO --
RIGHT.
SO THE ONLY THING YOU'VE ACTUALLY GOT IS HE'S AN EX-CON WITH A TAT.
SO... WHAT KIND OF MILEAGE YOU GET WITH THIS THING?
LOUSY.
YOU KNOW HOW MANY EX-CONS HAVE TATTOOS?
ALL OF 'EM?
JUST ABOUT.
ALL RIGHT... I'LL MAKE A FEW CALLS, CHECK THE TAT FILES WE GOT ON THE COMPUTER, SHAKE A FEW TREES, SEE WHAT FALLS OUT. BUT I'M NOT MAKING ANY PROMISES, OKAY?
SUITS ME RIGHT DOWN TO THE GROUND. I'LL CHECK BACK TOMORROW.
HOW WILL I --
YOU WON'T. I'LL FIND YOU.
COSTUMES...
FREAKIN' COSTUMES...
"SO DID YOU HAVE A GOOD NIGHT, PETER?"

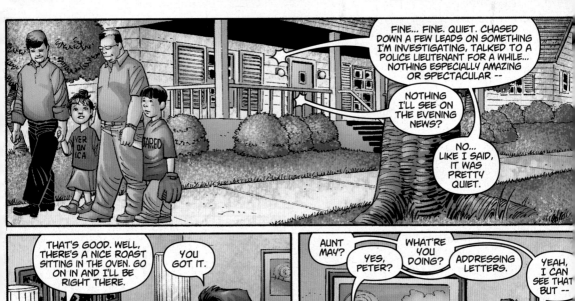

FINE... FINE. QUIET. CHASED DOWN A FEW LEADS ON SOMETHING I'M INVESTIGATING, TALKED TO A POLICE LIEUTENANT FOR A WHILE... NOTHING ESPECIALLY AMAZING OR SPECTACULAR --

NOTHING I'LL SEE ON THE EVENING NEWS?

NO... LIKE I SAID, IT WAS PRETTY QUIET.

THAT'S GOOD. WELL, THERE'S A NICE ROAST SITTING IN THE OVEN. GO ON IN AND I'LL BE RIGHT THERE.

YOU GOT IT.

AUNT MAY?

YES, PETER?

WHAT'RE YOU DOING?

ADDRESSING LETTERS.

YEAH, I CAN SEE THAT BUT --

I'M WRITING TO EVERY NEWSPAPER AND MAGAZINE IN NEW YORK SUGGESTING THAT PEOPLE MIGHT LIKE TO SEE A *POSITIVE* STORY ABOUT SPIDER-MAN ONCE IN A WHILE.

UHM... AUNT MAY --

I SENT THEM E-MAILS TOO, BUT I DON'T THINK ANYBODY REALLY PAYS ATTENTION TO E-MAILS, SO I THOUGHT I'D USE... OH, WHAT DID GORDON CALL IT?

GORDON?

THE NICE COMPUTER BOY WITH THE RED HAIR THAT WORKS AT THE LIBRARY...

SNAIL MAIL. THAT WAS IT. SNAIL MAIL. WHAT AN ODD PHRASE...

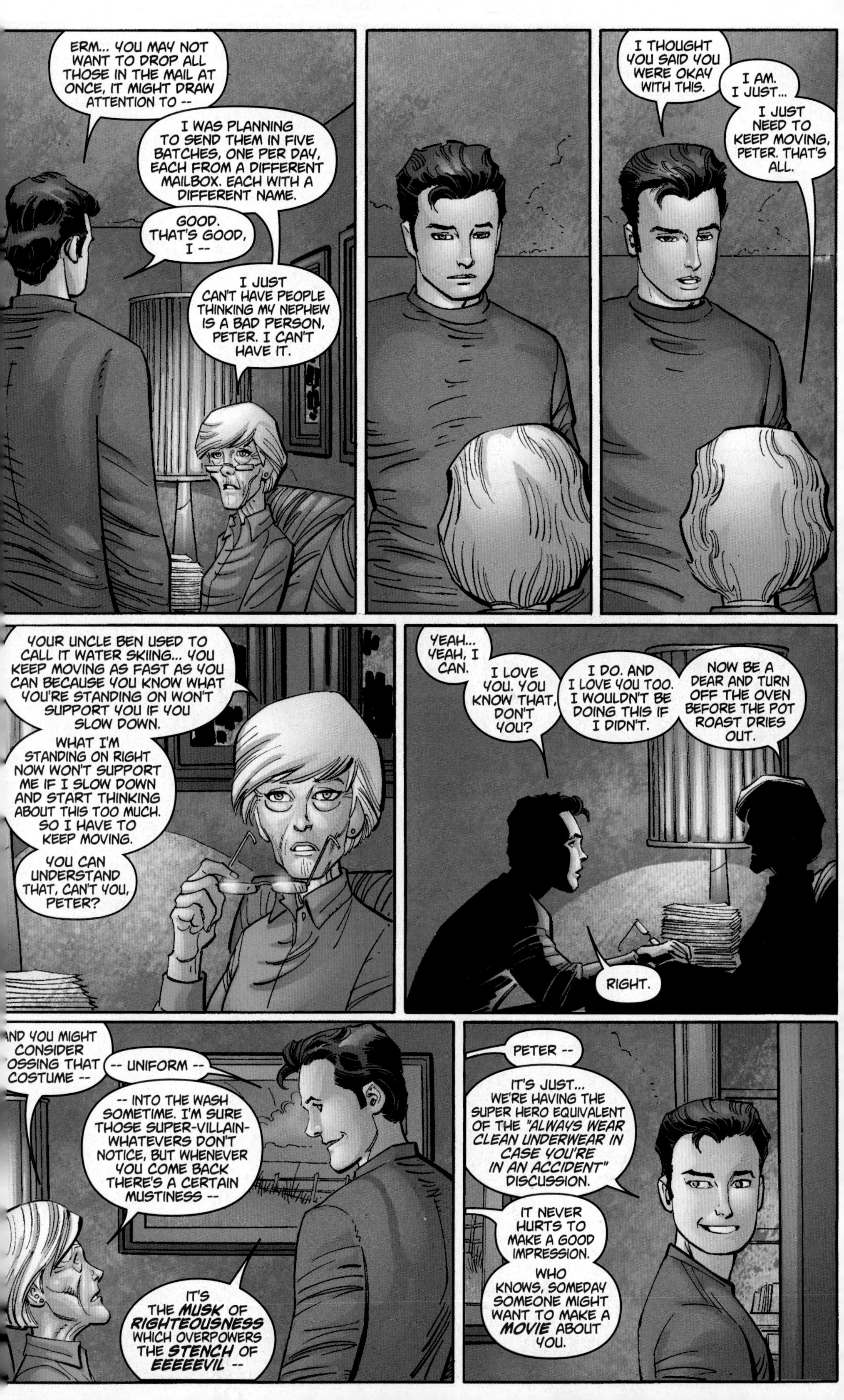
ERM... YOU MAY NOT WANT TO DROP ALL THOSE IN THE MAIL AT ONCE, IT MIGHT DRAW ATTENTION TO --
I WAS PLANNING TO SEND THEM IN FIVE BATCHES, ONE PER DAY, EACH FROM A DIFFERENT MAILBOX. EACH WITH A DIFFERENT NAME.
GOOD. THAT'S GOOD, I --
I JUST CAN'T HAVE PEOPLE THINKING MY NEPHEW IS A BAD PERSON, PETER. I CAN'T HAVE IT.
I THOUGHT YOU SAID YOU WERE OKAY WITH THIS.
I AM. I JUST...
I JUST NEED TO KEEP MOVING, PETER. THAT'S ALL.
YOUR UNCLE BEN USED TO CALL IT WATER SKIING... YOU KEEP MOVING AS FAST AS YOU CAN BECAUSE YOU KNOW WHAT YOU'RE STANDING ON WON'T SUPPORT YOU IF YOU SLOW DOWN.
WHAT I'M STANDING ON RIGHT NOW WON'T SUPPORT ME IF I SLOW DOWN AND START THINKING ABOUT THIS TOO MUCH. SO I HAVE TO KEEP MOVING.
YOU CAN UNDERSTAND THAT, CAN'T YOU, PETER?
YEAH... YEAH, I CAN.
I LOVE YOU. YOU KNOW THAT, DON'T YOU?
I DO. AND I LOVE YOU TOO. I WOULDN'T BE DOING THIS IF I DIDN'T.
NOW BE A DEAR AND TURN OFF THE OVEN BEFORE THE POT ROAST DRIES OUT.
RIGHT.
AND YOU MIGHT CONSIDER TOSSING THAT COSTUME --
-- UNIFORM --
-- INTO THE WASH SOMETIME. I'M SURE THOSE SUPER-VILLAIN-WHATEVERS DON'T NOTICE, BUT WHENEVER YOU COME BACK THERE'S A CERTAIN MUSTINESS --
IT'S THE MUSK OF RIGHTEOUSNESS WHICH OVERPOWERS THE STENCH OF EEEEEVIL --
PETER --
IT'S JUST... WE'RE HAVING THE SUPER HERO EQUIVALENT OF THE "ALWAYS WEAR CLEAN UNDERWEAR IN CASE YOU'RE IN AN ACCIDENT" DISCUSSION.
IT NEVER HURTS TO MAKE A GOOD IMPRESSION.
WHO KNOWS, SOMEDAY SOMEONE MIGHT WANT TO MAKE A MOVIE ABOUT YOU.

YEAH, RIGHT, LIKE THAT'S GONNA HAPPEN.

ALL RIGHT, ALL RIGHT...

IT'S JUST I CAN NEVER REMEMBER IF IT'S WARM-WARM, WARM-COLD OR COLD-COLD, WHAT GETS BLEACH AND WHAT DOESN'T, TOO MUCH AND SUDDENLY I'M THE BEIGE SPIDER...

OH, AND PETER...?

YEAH?

MARY JANE CALLED TO CONFIRM THAT SHE'S FLYING IN ON TUESDAY. SHE'LL ONLY BE HERE FOR ONE NIGHT, SO SHE THOUGHT IT MIGHT BE BEST FOR YOU TO MEET HER AT THE AIRPORT, THAT WAY YOU CAN TALK ON THE WAY INTO TOWN.

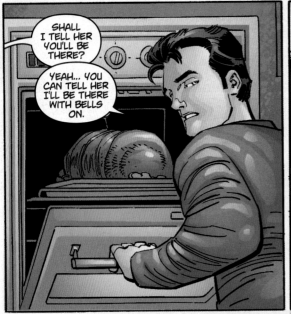

SHALL I TELL HER YOU'LL BE THERE?

YEAH... YOU CAN TELL HER I'LL BE THERE WITH BELLS ON.

I'M SURE THAT WILL GO OVER NICELY WITH THOSE AIRPORT SECURITY SCANNERS.

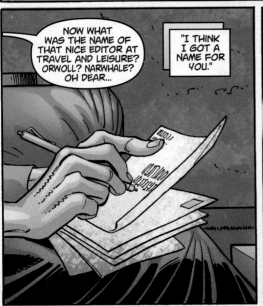

NOW WHAT WAS THE NAME OF THAT NICE EDITOR AT TRAVEL AND LEISURE? ORWOLL? NARWHALE? OH DEAR...

"I THINK I GOT A NAME FOR YOU."

COMPUTER SEARCH TURNED UP A FILE ON A PRISON INMATE AT LATTERBY WHO HAD A BLACK STAR TATTOO ON HIS NECK, SAME AS THE ONE YOU DESCRIBE.

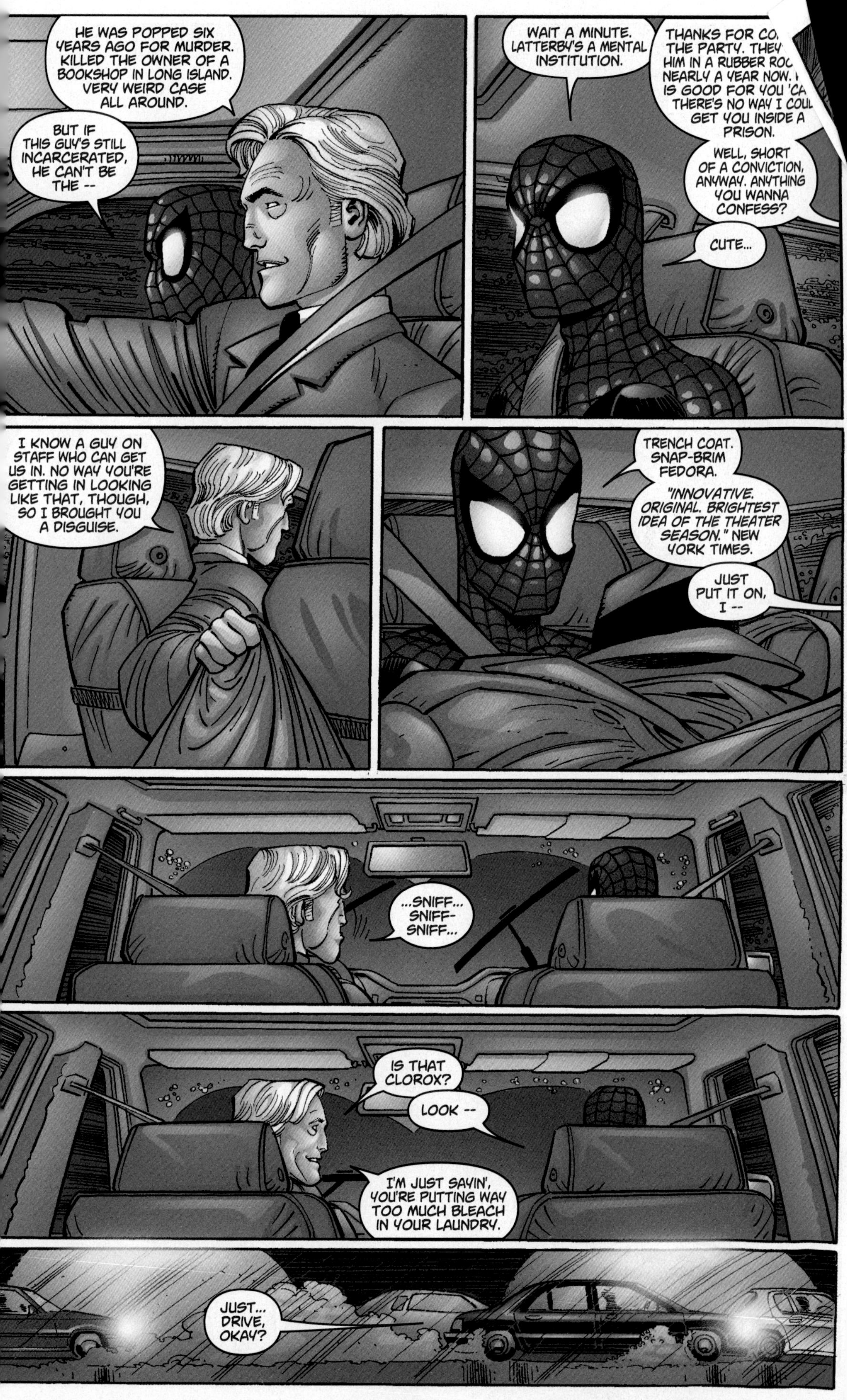
HE WAS POPPED SIX YEARS AGO FOR MURDER. KILLED THE OWNER OF A BOOKSHOP IN LONG ISLAND. VERY WEIRD CASE ALL AROUND.
BUT IF THIS GUY'S STILL INCARCERATED, HE CAN'T BE THE --
WAIT A MINUTE. LATTERBY'S A MENTAL INSTITUTION.
THANKS FOR CO THE PARTY. THEY HIM IN A RUBBER ROO NEARLY A YEAR NOW. IS GOOD FOR YOU 'CA THERE'S NO WAY I COUL GET YOU INSIDE A PRISON.
WELL, SHORT OF A CONVICTION, ANYWAY. ANYTHING YOU WANNA CONFESS?
CUTE...
I KNOW A GUY ON STAFF WHO CAN GET US IN. NO WAY YOU'RE GETTING IN LOOKING LIKE THAT, THOUGH, SO I BROUGHT YOU A DISGUISE.
TRENCH COAT. SNAP-BRIM FEDORA.
"INNOVATIVE. ORIGINAL. BRIGHTEST IDEA OF THE THEATER SEASON." NEW YORK TIMES.
JUST PUT IT ON, I --
...SNIFF... SNIFF-SNIFF...
IS THAT CLOROX?
LOOK --
I'M JUST SAYIN', YOU'RE PUTTING WAY TOO MUCH BLEACH IN YOUR LAUNDRY.
JUST... DRIVE, OKAY?

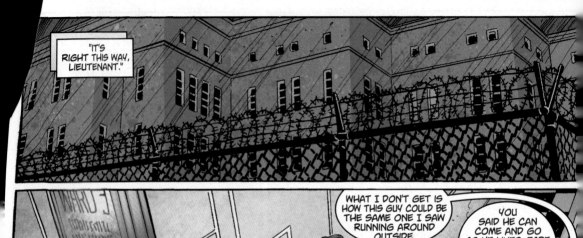

"IT'S RIGHT THIS WAY, LIEUTENANT."

WHAT I DON'T GET IS HOW THIS GUY COULD BE THE SAME ONE I SAW RUNNING AROUND OUTSIDE.

YOU SAID HE CAN COME AND GO AS HE LIKES, FADE IN AND FADE OUT, JUST LIKE ONE OF THOSE SCREEN-PLAYS --

THAT'S TRUE, SO I FOLLOW THE GETTING OUT OF HERE PART --

-- IT'S THE "WHY WOULD ANYBODY COME BACK" PART THAT'S GOT ME PUZZLED.

...SNIFF! HEY! HEY YOU! YOU SMELL ALL PRETTY. SMELL NICE. WANNA COME BE MY GIRLY GIRL, LITTLE PRETTY?

HAH!

...SOMEDAY THEY'LL MAKE A MOVIE...SOMEDAY THEY'LL MAKE A MOVIE...SOMEDAY THEY'LL MAKE A MOVIE...

HERE HE IS.

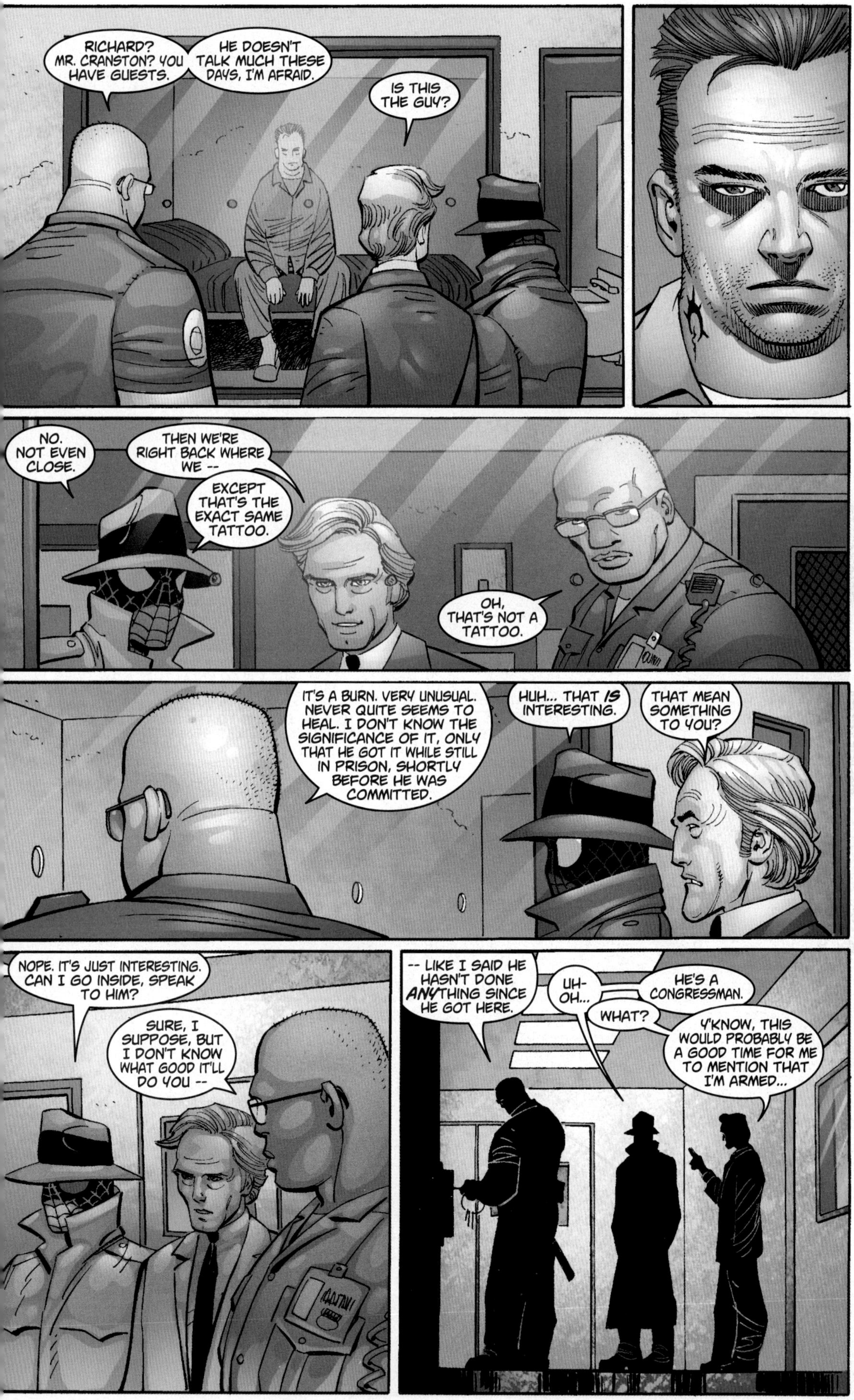

RICHARD? MR. CRANSTON? YOU HAVE GUESTS.
HE DOESN'T TALK MUCH THESE DAYS, I'M AFRAID.
IS THIS THE GUY?
NO. NOT EVEN CLOSE.
THEN WE'RE RIGHT BACK WHERE WE --
EXCEPT THAT'S THE EXACT SAME TATTOO.
OH, THAT'S NOT A TATTOO.
IT'S A BURN. VERY UNUSUAL. NEVER QUITE SEEMS TO HEAL. I DON'T KNOW THE SIGNIFICANCE OF IT, ONLY THAT HE GOT IT WHILE STILL IN PRISON, SHORTLY BEFORE HE WAS COMMITTED.
HUH... THAT *IS* INTERESTING.
THAT MEAN SOMETHING TO YOU?
NOPE. IT'S JUST INTERESTING. CAN I GO INSIDE, SPEAK TO HIM?
SURE, I SUPPOSE, BUT I DON'T KNOW WHAT GOOD IT'LL DO YOU --
-- LIKE I SAID HE HASN'T DONE *ANY*THING SINCE HE GOT HERE.
UH-OH...
HE'S A CONGRESSMAN.
WHAT?
Y'KNOW, THIS WOULD PROBABLY BE A GOOD TIME FOR ME TO MENTION THAT I'M ARMED...

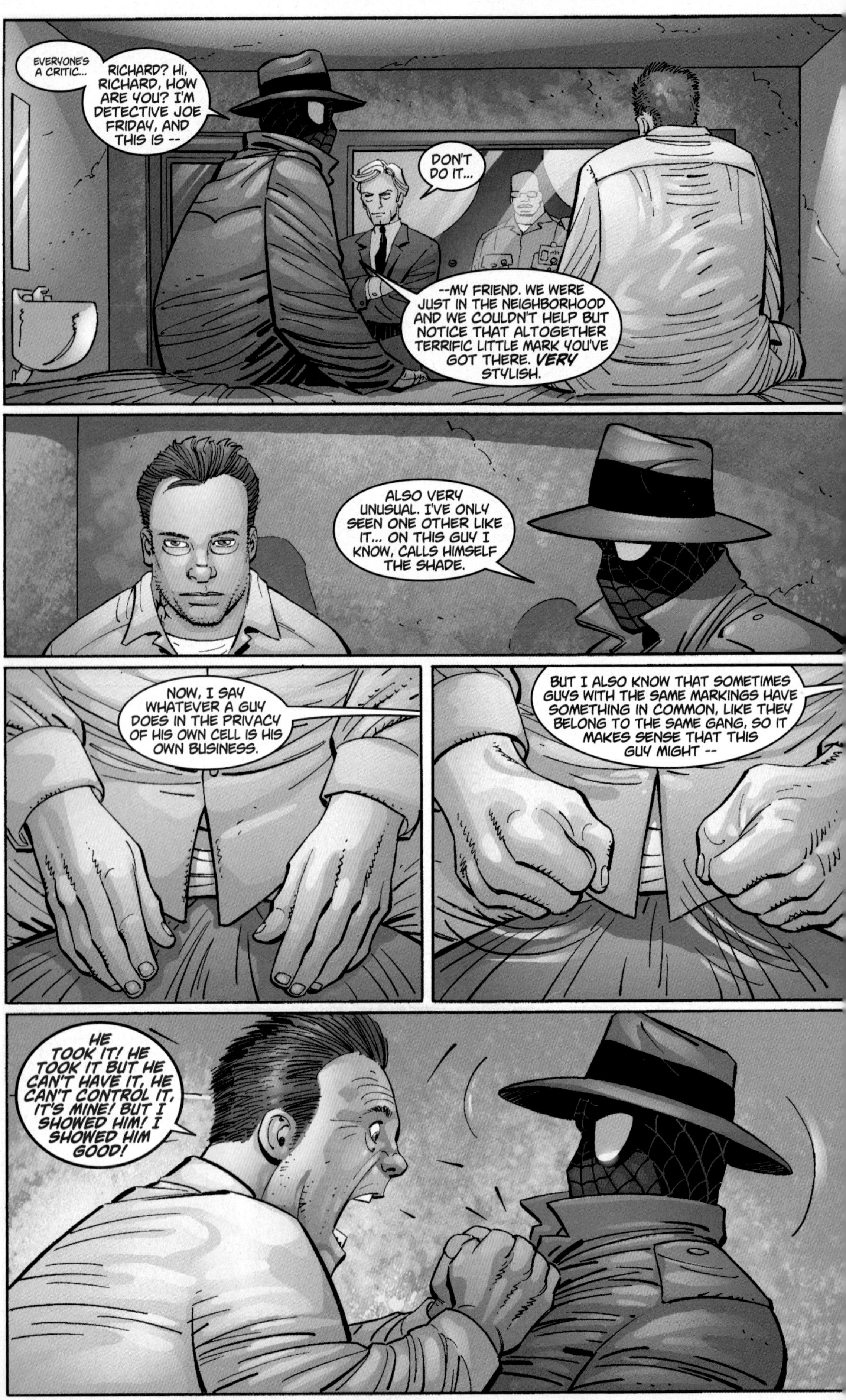
EVERYONE'S A CRITIC...
RICHARD? HI, RICHARD, HOW ARE YOU? I'M DETECTIVE JOE FRIDAY, AND THIS IS --
DON'T DO IT...
--MY FRIEND. WE WERE JUST IN THE NEIGHBORHOOD AND WE COULDN'T HELP BUT NOTICE THAT ALTOGETHER TERRIFIC LITTLE MARK YOU'VE GOT THERE. VERY STYLISH.
ALSO VERY UNUSUAL. I'VE ONLY SEEN ONE OTHER LIKE IT... ON THIS GUY I KNOW, CALLS HIMSELF THE SHADE.
NOW, I SAY WHATEVER A GUY DOES IN THE PRIVACY OF HIS OWN CELL IS HIS OWN BUSINESS.
BUT I ALSO KNOW THAT SOMETIMES GUYS WITH THE SAME MARKINGS HAVE SOMETHING IN COMMON, LIKE THEY BELONG TO THE SAME GANG, SO IT MAKES SENSE THAT THIS GUY MIGHT --
HE TOOK IT! HE TOOK IT BUT HE CAN'T HAVE IT, HE CAN'T CONTROL IT, IT'S MINE! BUT I SHOWED HIM! I SHOWED HIM GOOD!

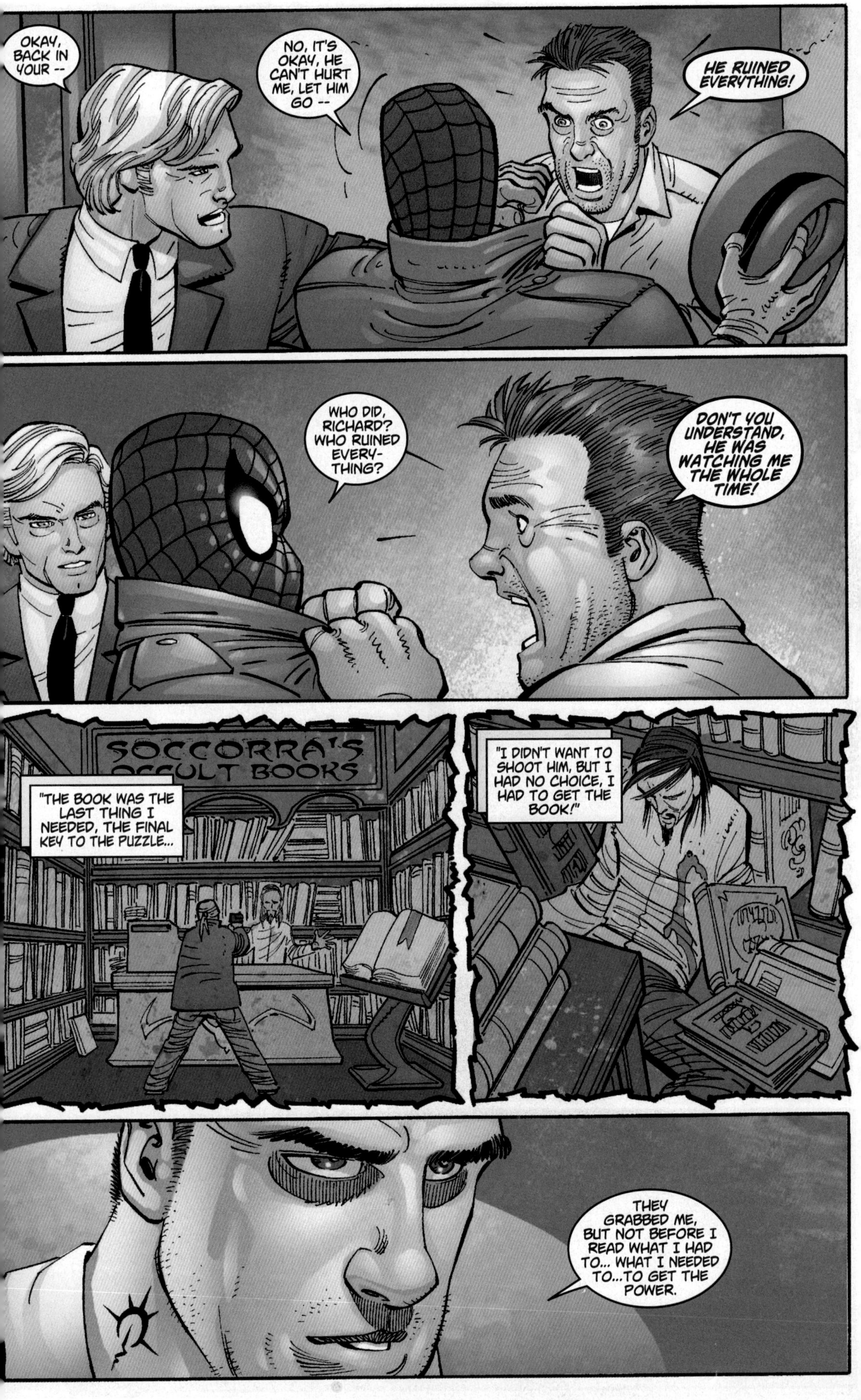
OKAY, BACK IN YOUR --
NO, IT'S OKAY, HE CAN'T HURT ME, LET HIM GO --
HE RUINED EVERYTHING!
WHO DID, RICHARD? WHO RUINED EVERY-THING?
DON'T YOU UNDERSTAND, HE WAS WATCHING ME THE WHOLE TIME!
SOCCORRA'S OCCULT BOOKS
"THE BOOK WAS THE LAST THING I NEEDED, THE FINAL KEY TO THE PUZZLE...
"I DIDN'T WANT TO SHOOT HIM, BUT I HAD NO CHOICE, I HAD TO GET THE BOOK!"
THEY GRABBED ME, BUT NOT BEFORE I READ WHAT I HAD TO... WHAT I NEEDED TO...TO GET THE POWER.

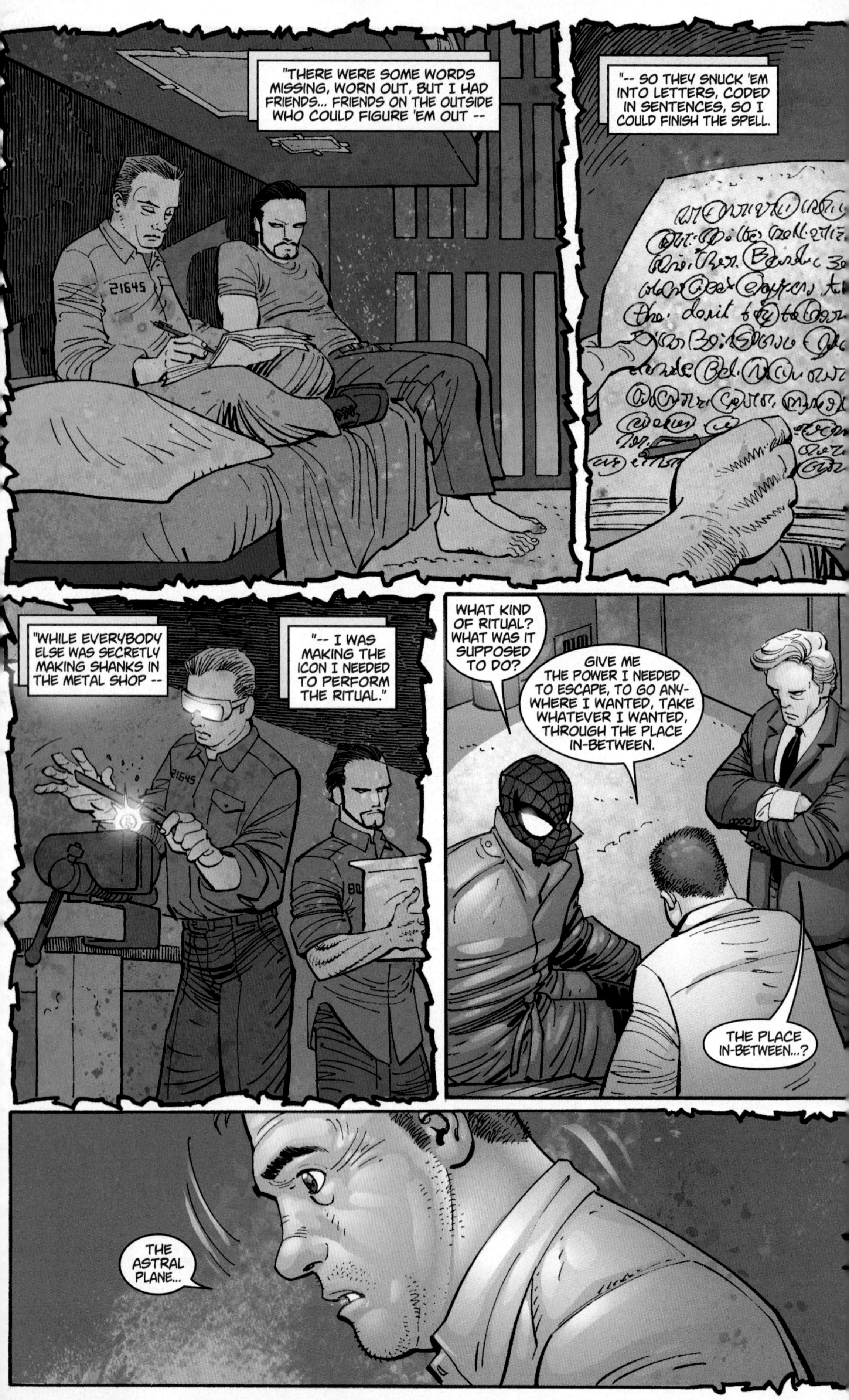
"THERE WERE SOME WORDS MISSING, WORN OUT, BUT I HAD FRIENDS... FRIENDS ON THE OUTSIDE WHO COULD FIGURE 'EM OUT --
"-- SO THEY SNUCK 'EM INTO LETTERS, CODED IN SENTENCES, SO I COULD FINISH THE SPELL.
"WHILE EVERYBODY ELSE WAS SECRETLY MAKING SHANKS IN THE METAL SHOP --
"-- I WAS MAKING THE ICON I NEEDED TO PERFORM THE RITUAL."
WHAT KIND OF RITUAL? WHAT WAS IT SUPPOSED TO DO?
GIVE ME THE POWER I NEEDED TO ESCAPE, TO GO ANYWHERE I WANTED, TAKE WHATEVER I WANTED, THROUGH THE PLACE IN-BETWEEN.
THE PLACE IN-BETWEEN...?
THE ASTRAL PLANE...

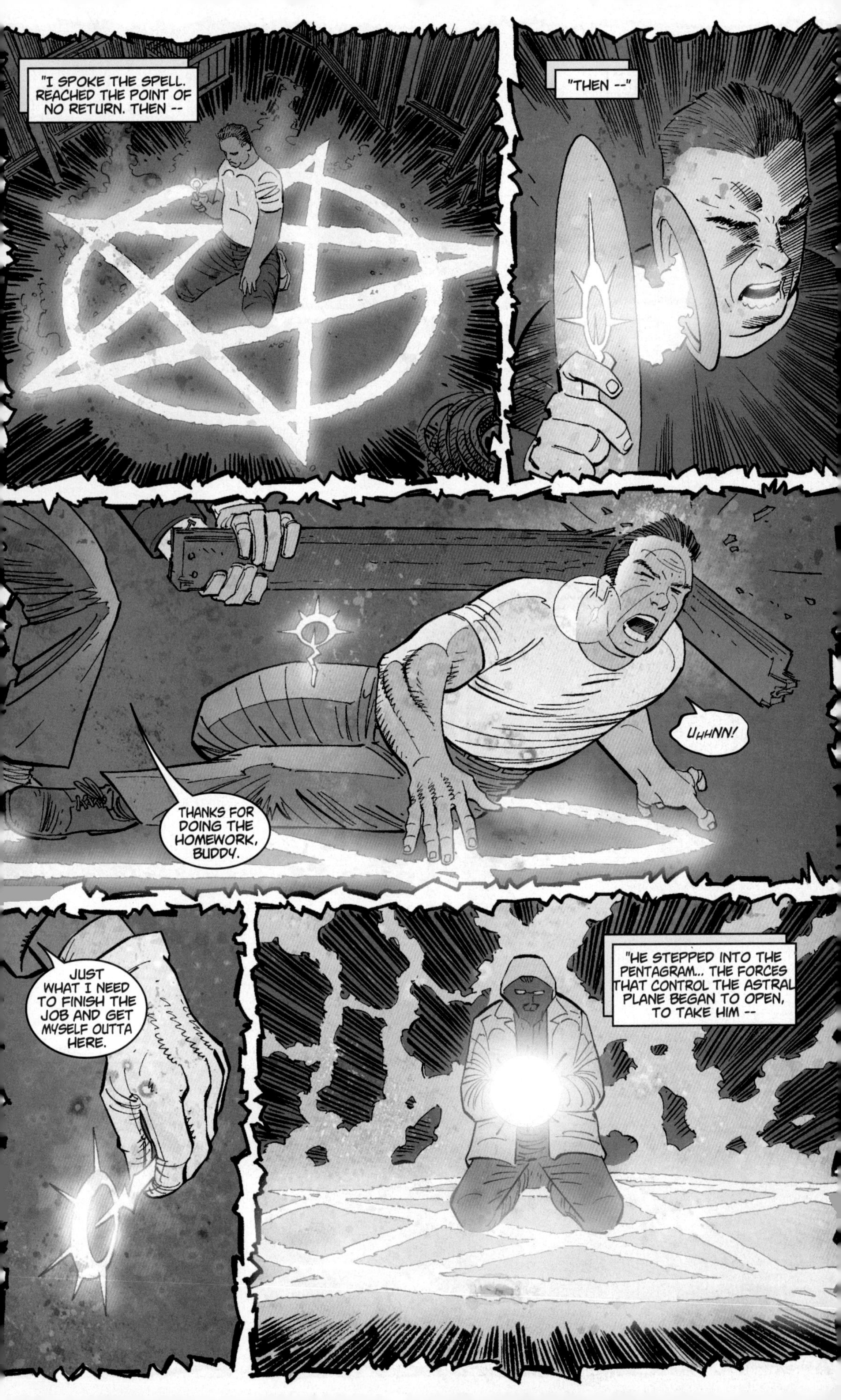
"I SPOKE THE SPELL. REACHED THE POINT OF NO RETURN. THEN --
"THEN --"
UHHNN!
THANKS FOR DOING THE HOMEWORK, BUDDY.
JUST WHAT I NEED TO FINISH THE JOB AND GET MYSELF OUTTA HERE.
"HE STEPPED INTO THE PENTAGRAM... THE FORCES THAT CONTROL THE ASTRAL PLANE BEGAN TO OPEN, TO TAKE HIM --

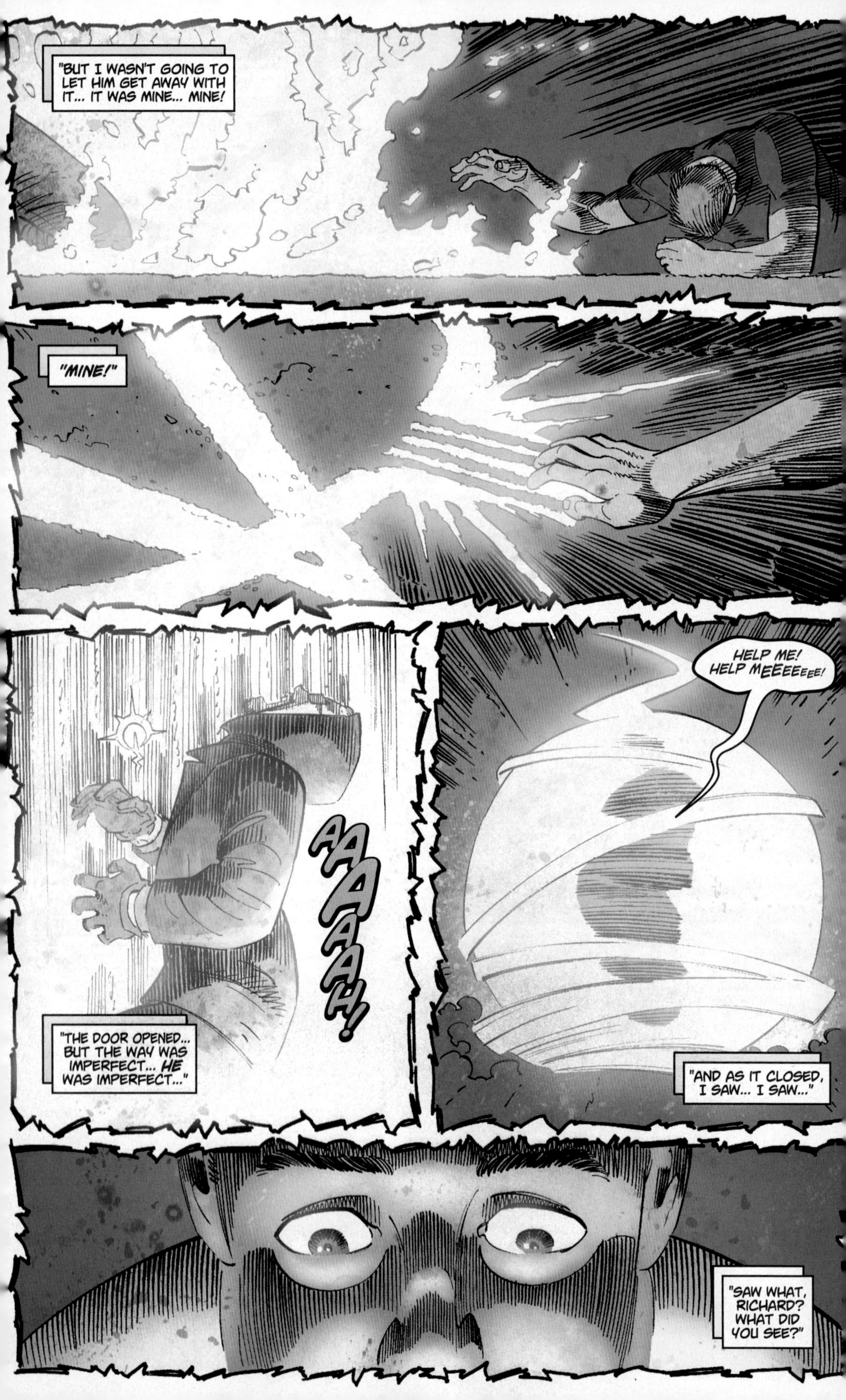
"BUT I WASN'T GOING TO LET HIM GET AWAY WITH IT... IT WAS MINE... MINE!
"MINE!"
"THE DOOR OPENED... BUT THE WAY WAS IMPERFECT... HE WAS IMPERFECT..."
AAAAAAH!
HELP ME! HELP MEEEEEEE!
"AND AS IT CLOSED, I SAW... I SAW..."
"SAW WHAT, RICHARD? WHAT DID YOU SEE?"

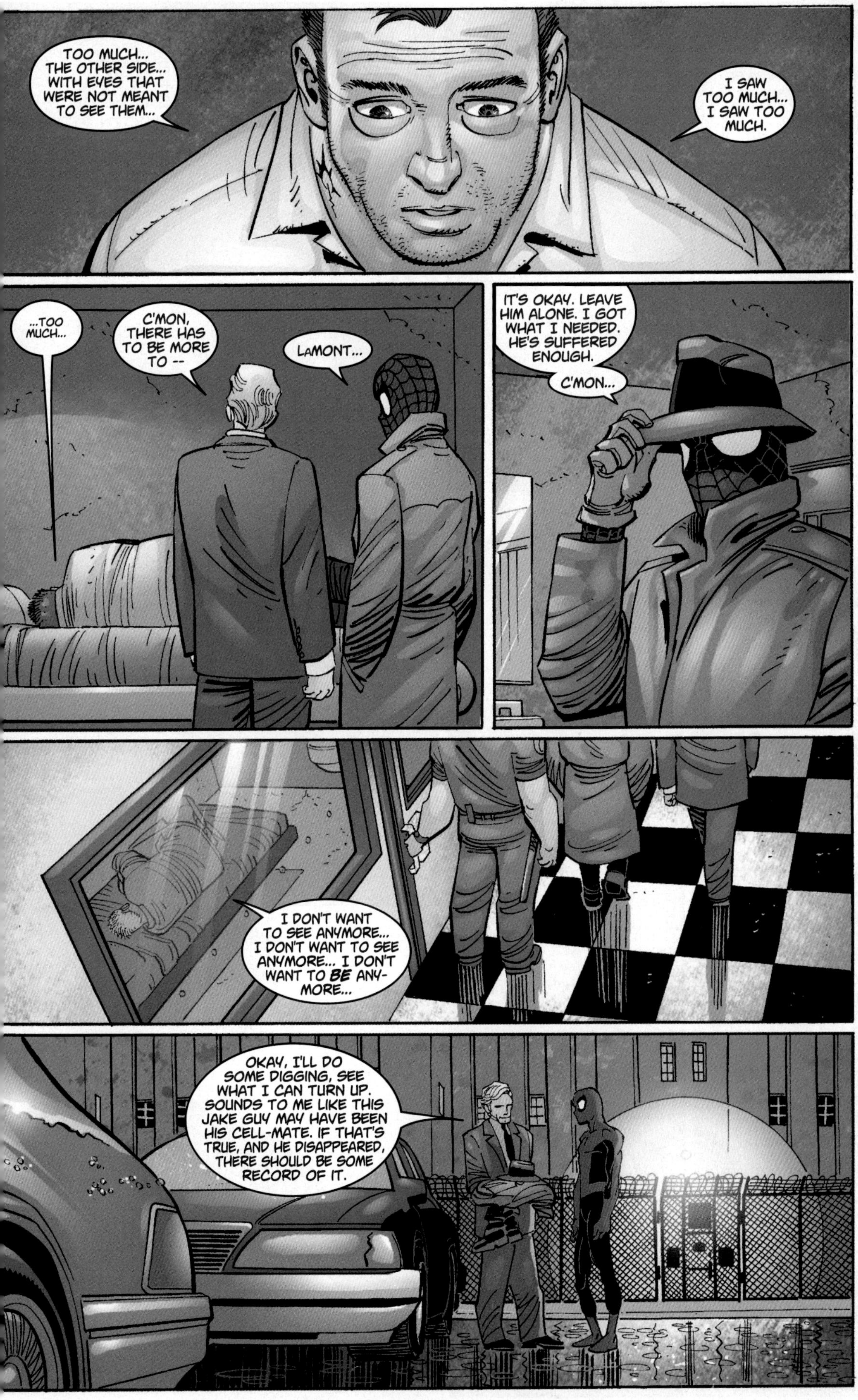
TOO MUCH... THE OTHER SIDE... WITH EYES THAT WERE NOT MEANT TO SEE THEM...
I SAW TOO MUCH... I SAW TOO MUCH.
...TOO MUCH...
C'MON, THERE HAS TO BE MORE TO --
LAMONT...
IT'S OKAY. LEAVE HIM ALONE. I GOT WHAT I NEEDED. HE'S SUFFERED ENOUGH.
C'MON...
I DON'T WANT TO SEE ANYMORE... I DON'T WANT TO SEE ANYMORE... I DON'T WANT TO BE ANY-MORE...
OKAY, I'LL DO SOME DIGGING, SEE WHAT I CAN TURN UP. SOUNDS TO ME LIKE THIS JAKE GUY MAY HAVE BEEN HIS CELL-MATE. IF THAT'S TRUE, AND HE DISAPPEARED, THERE SHOULD BE SOME RECORD OF IT.

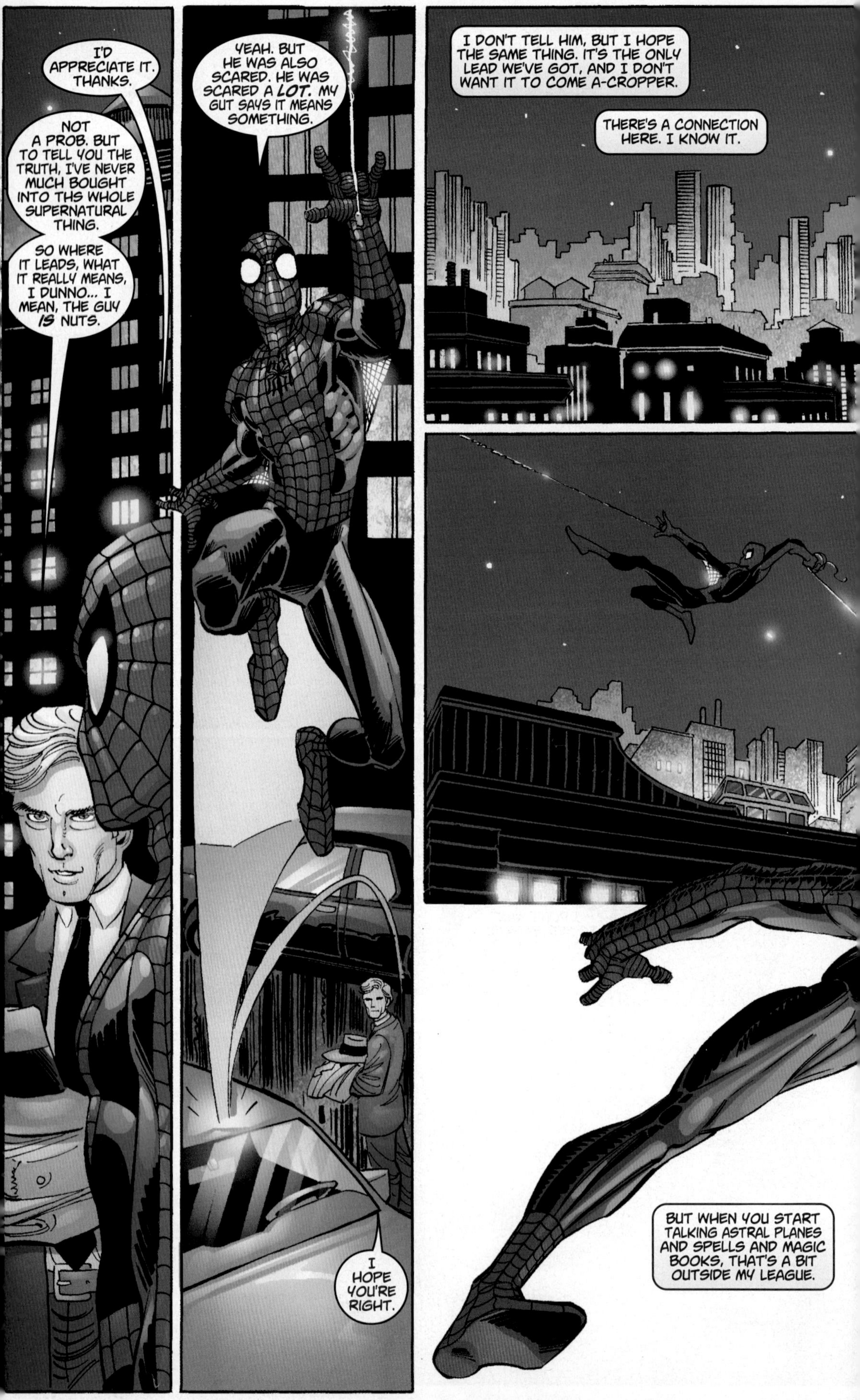
I'D APPRECIATE IT. THANKS.
NOT A PROB. BUT TO TELL YOU THE TRUTH, I'VE NEVER MUCH BOUGHT INTO THS WHOLE SUPERNATURAL THING.
SO WHERE IT LEADS, WHAT IT REALLY MEANS, I DUNNO... I MEAN, THE GUY IS NUTS.
YEAH. BUT HE WAS ALSO SCARED. HE WAS SCARED A LOT. MY GUT SAYS IT MEANS SOMETHING.
I HOPE YOU'RE RIGHT.
I DON'T TELL HIM, BUT I HOPE THE SAME THING. IT'S THE ONLY LEAD WE'VE GOT, AND I DON'T WANT IT TO COME A-CROPPER.
THERE'S A CONNECTION HERE. I KNOW IT.
BUT WHEN YOU START TALKING ASTRAL PLANES AND SPELLS AND MAGIC BOOKS, THAT'S A BIT OUTSIDE MY LEAGUE.

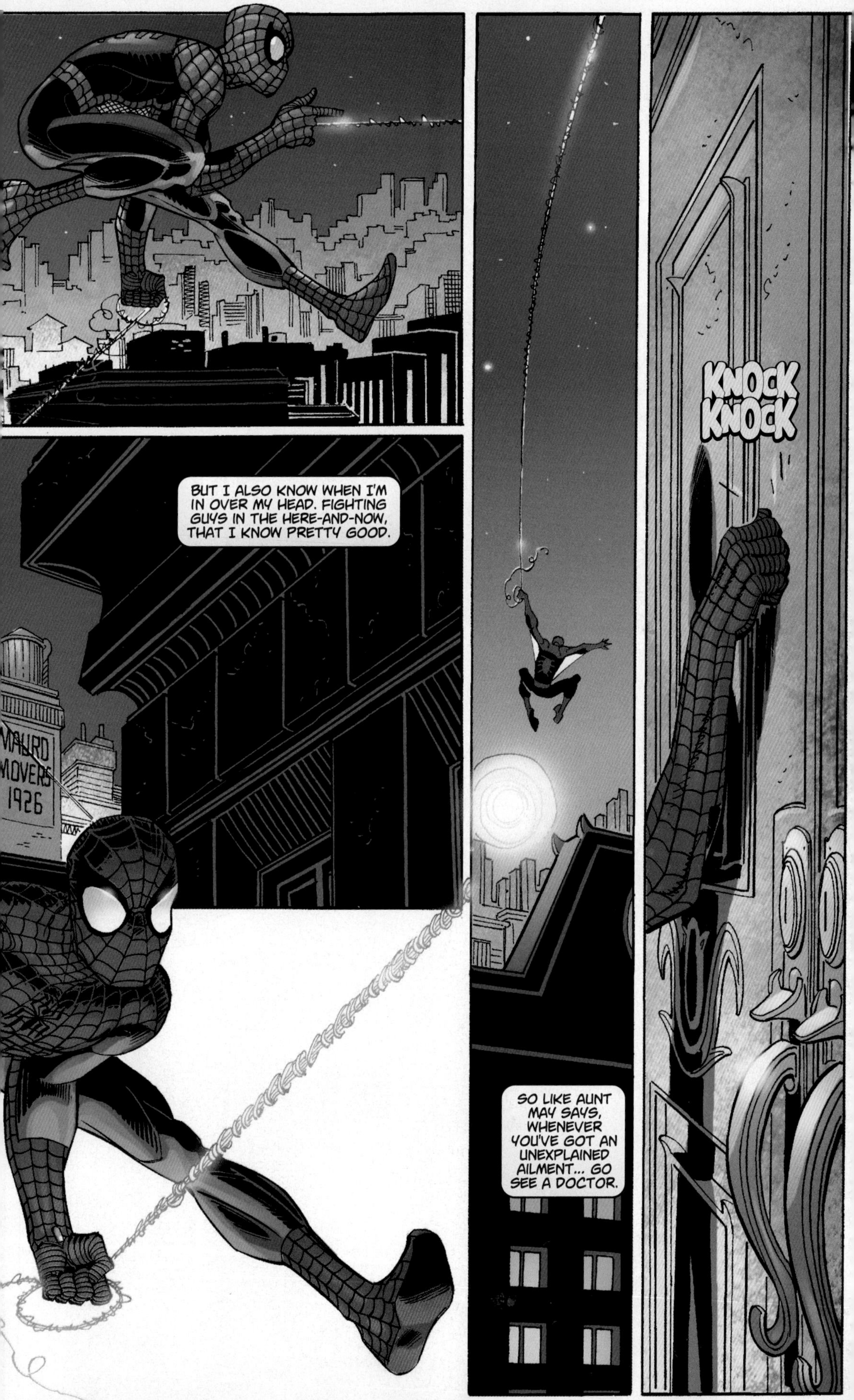

BUT I ALSO KNOW WHEN I'M IN OVER MY HEAD. FIGHTING GUYS IN THE HERE-AND-NOW, THAT I KNOW PRETTY GOOD.
MAURO MOVERS 1926
SO LIKE AUNT MAY SAYS, WHENEVER YOU'VE GOT AN UNEXPLAINED AILMENT... GO SEE A DOCTOR.
KNOCK KNOCK

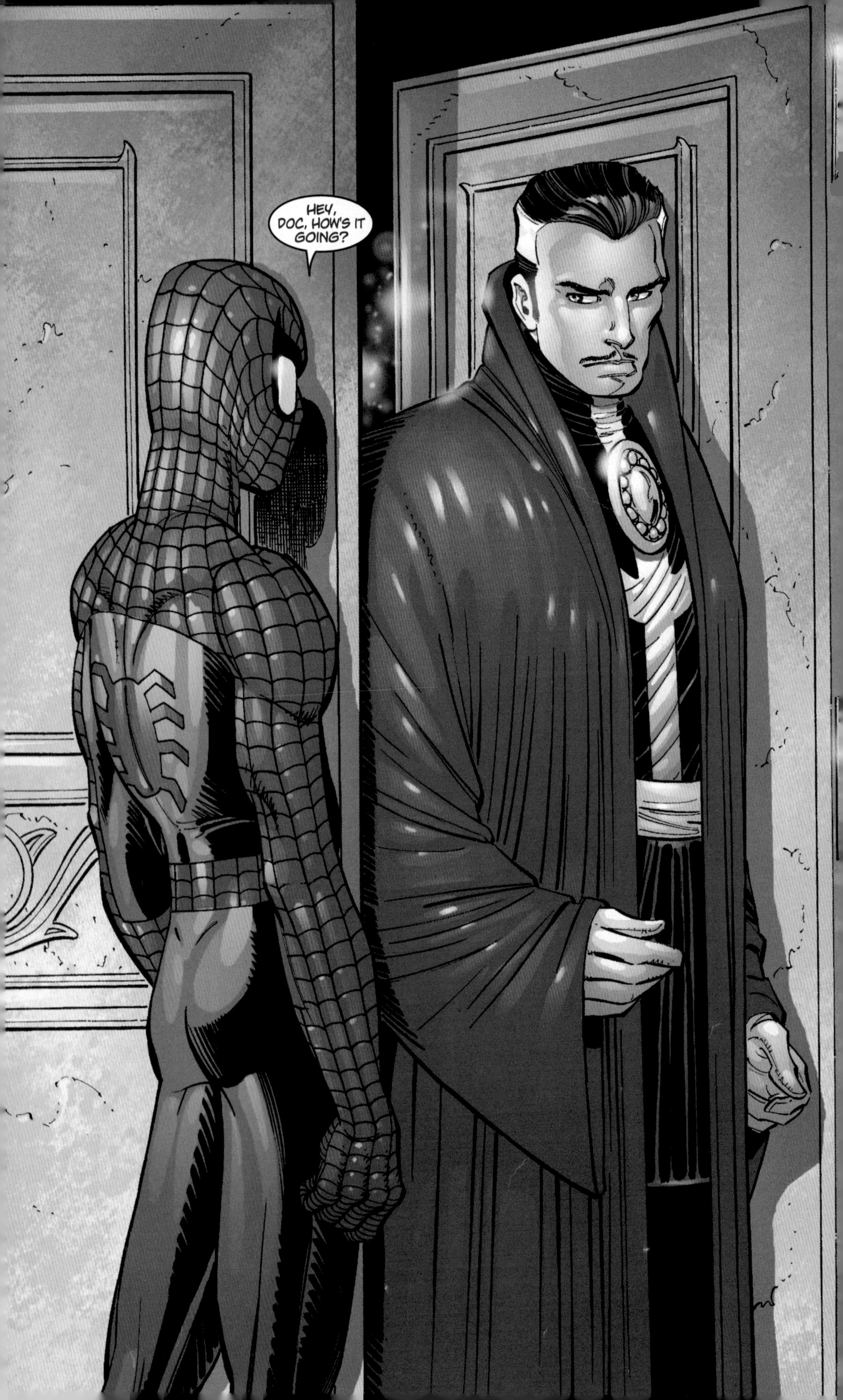
HEY, DOC, HOW'S IT GOING?

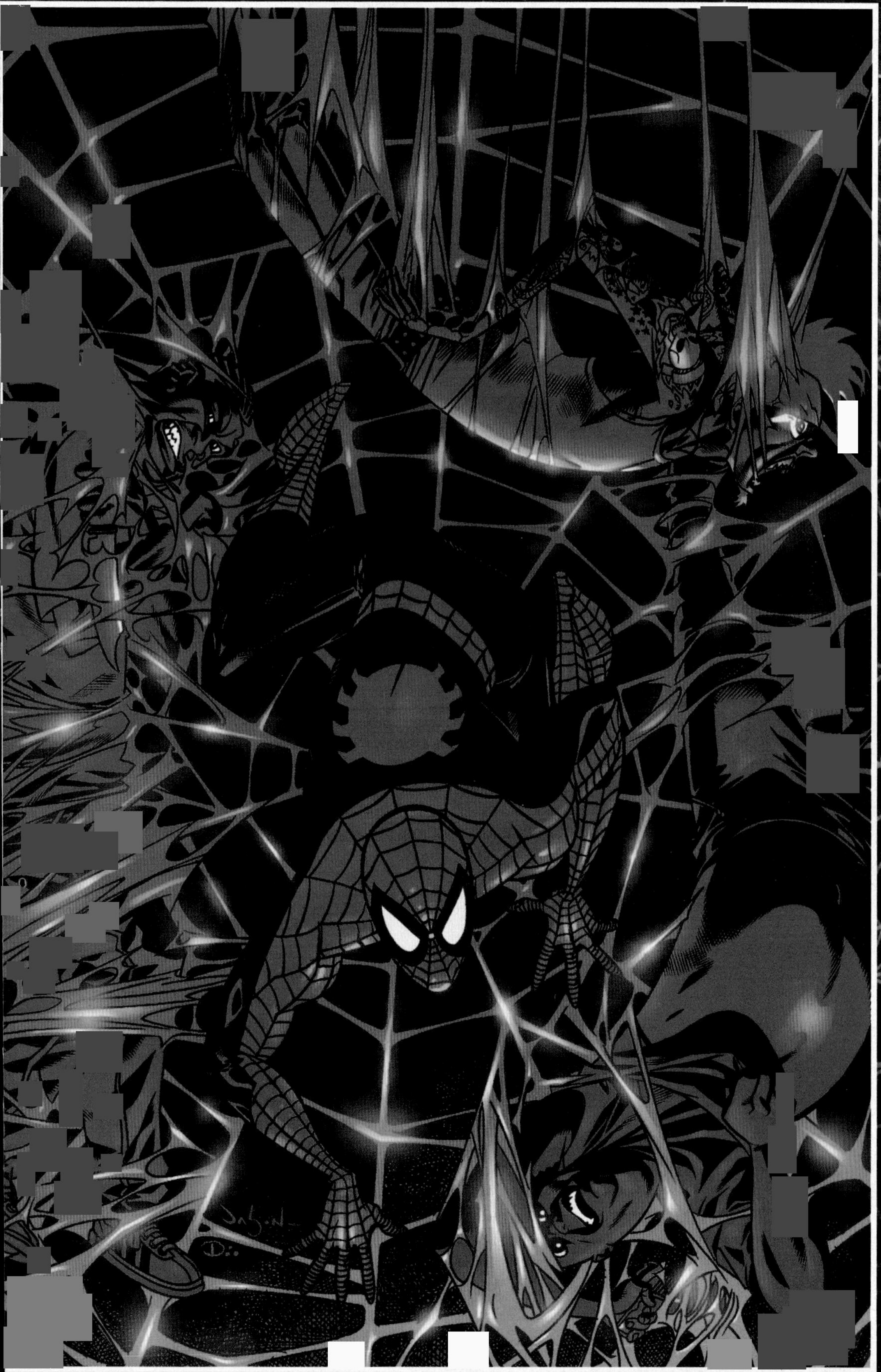

AMAZING SPIDER-MAN #42

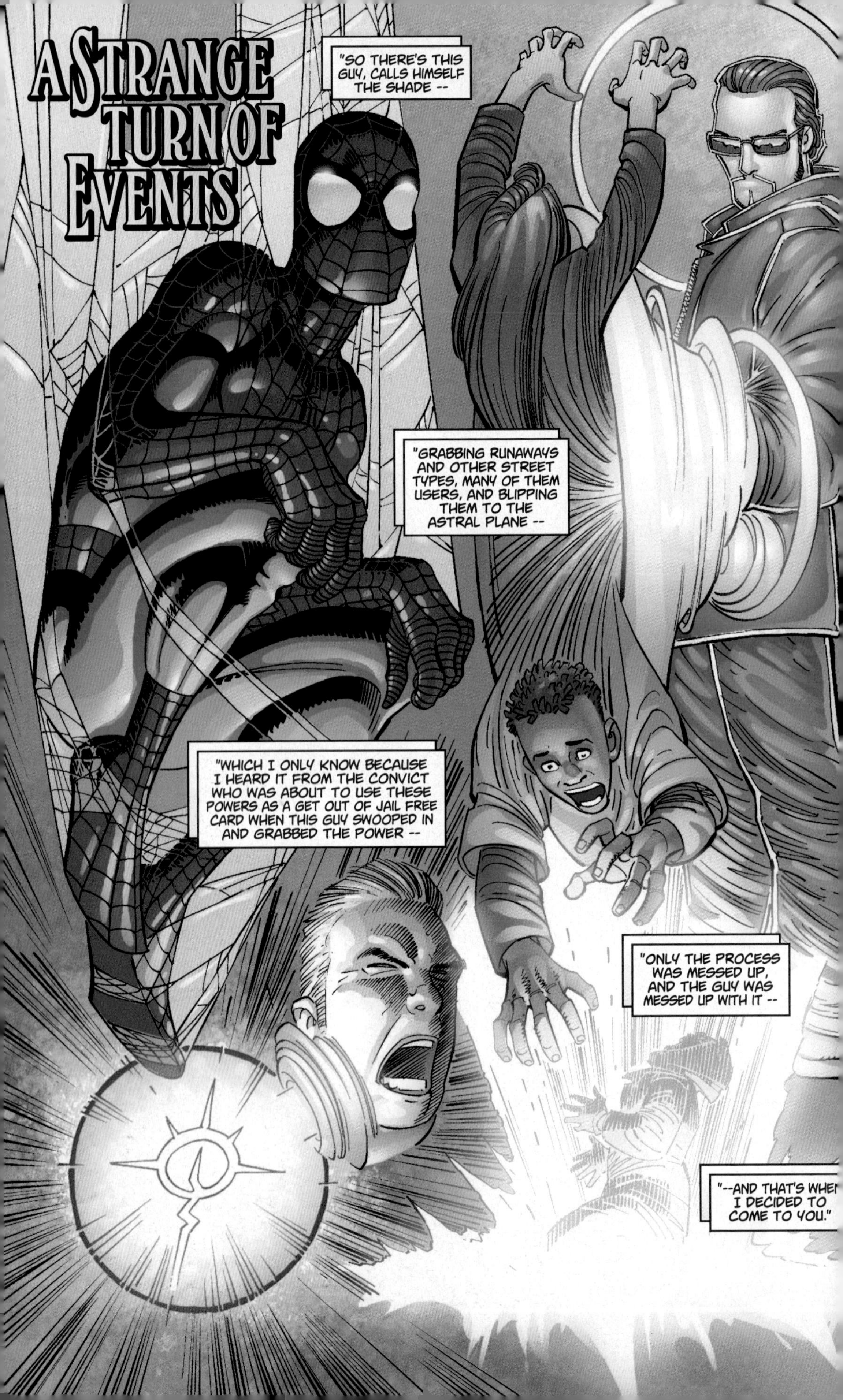
A STRANGE TURN OF EVENTS
"SO THERE'S THIS GUY, CALLS HIMSELF THE SHADE --
"GRABBING RUNAWAYS AND OTHER STREET TYPES, MANY OF THEM USERS, AND BLIPPING THEM TO THE ASTRAL PLANE --
"WHICH I ONLY KNOW BECAUSE I HEARD IT FROM THE CONVICT WHO WAS ABOUT TO USE THESE POWERS AS A GET OUT OF JAIL FREE CARD WHEN THIS GUY SWOOPED IN AND GRABBED THE POWER --
"ONLY THE PROCESS WAS MESSED UP, AND THE GUY WAS MESSED UP WITH IT --
"--AND THAT'S WHEN I DECIDED TO COME TO YOU."

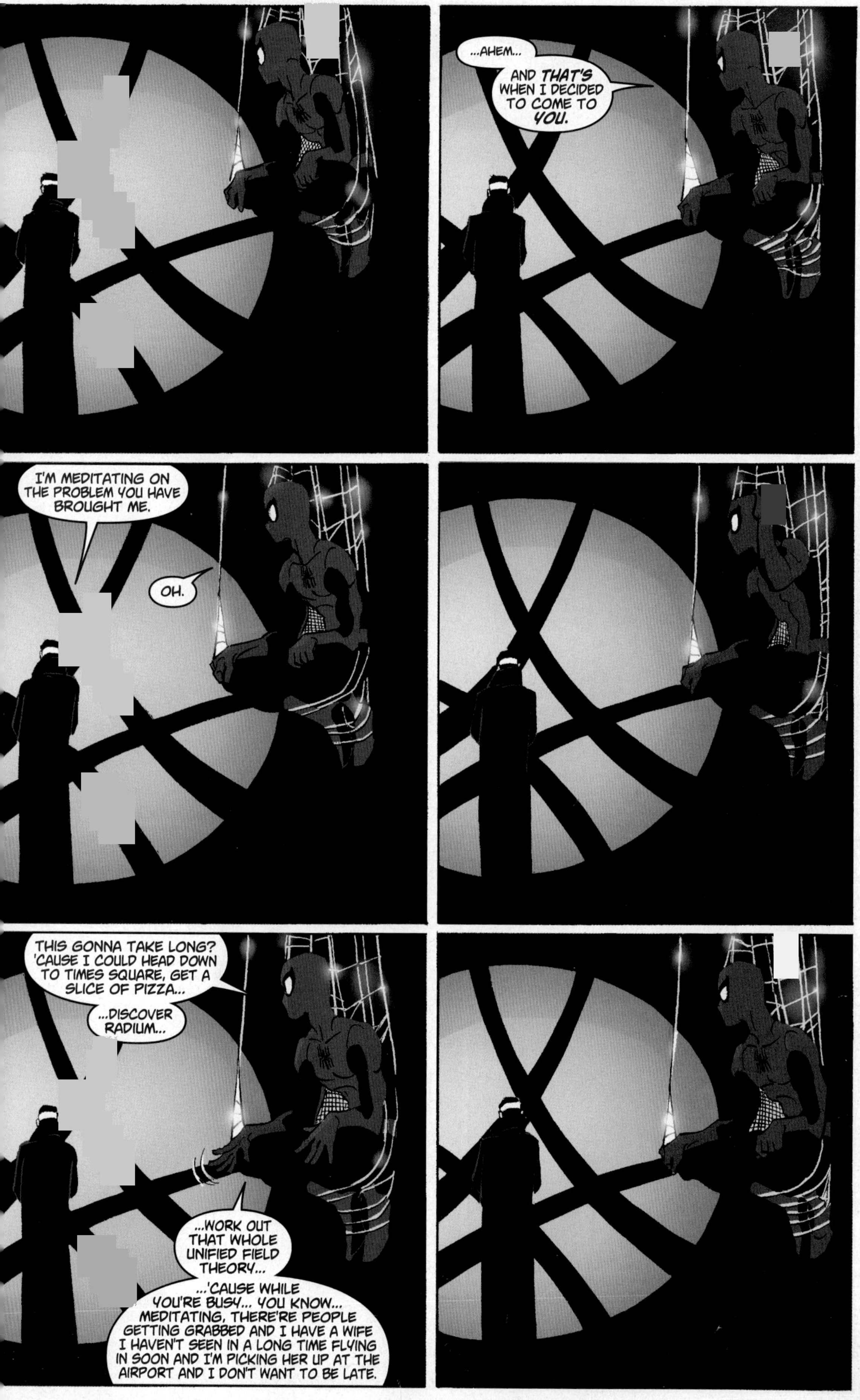
...AHEM...
AND THAT'S WHEN I DECIDED TO COME TO YOU.
I'M MEDITATING ON THE PROBLEM YOU HAVE BROUGHT ME.
OH.
THIS GONNA TAKE LONG? 'CAUSE I COULD HEAD DOWN TO TIMES SQUARE, GET A SLICE OF PIZZA...
...DISCOVER RADIUM...
...WORK OUT THAT WHOLE UNIFIED FIELD THEORY...
...'CAUSE WHILE YOU'RE BUSY... YOU KNOW... MEDITATING, THERE'RE PEOPLE GETTING GRABBED AND I HAVE A WIFE I HAVEN'T SEEN IN A LONG TIME FLYING IN SOON AND I'M PICKING HER UP AT THE AIRPORT AND I DON'T WANT TO BE LATE.

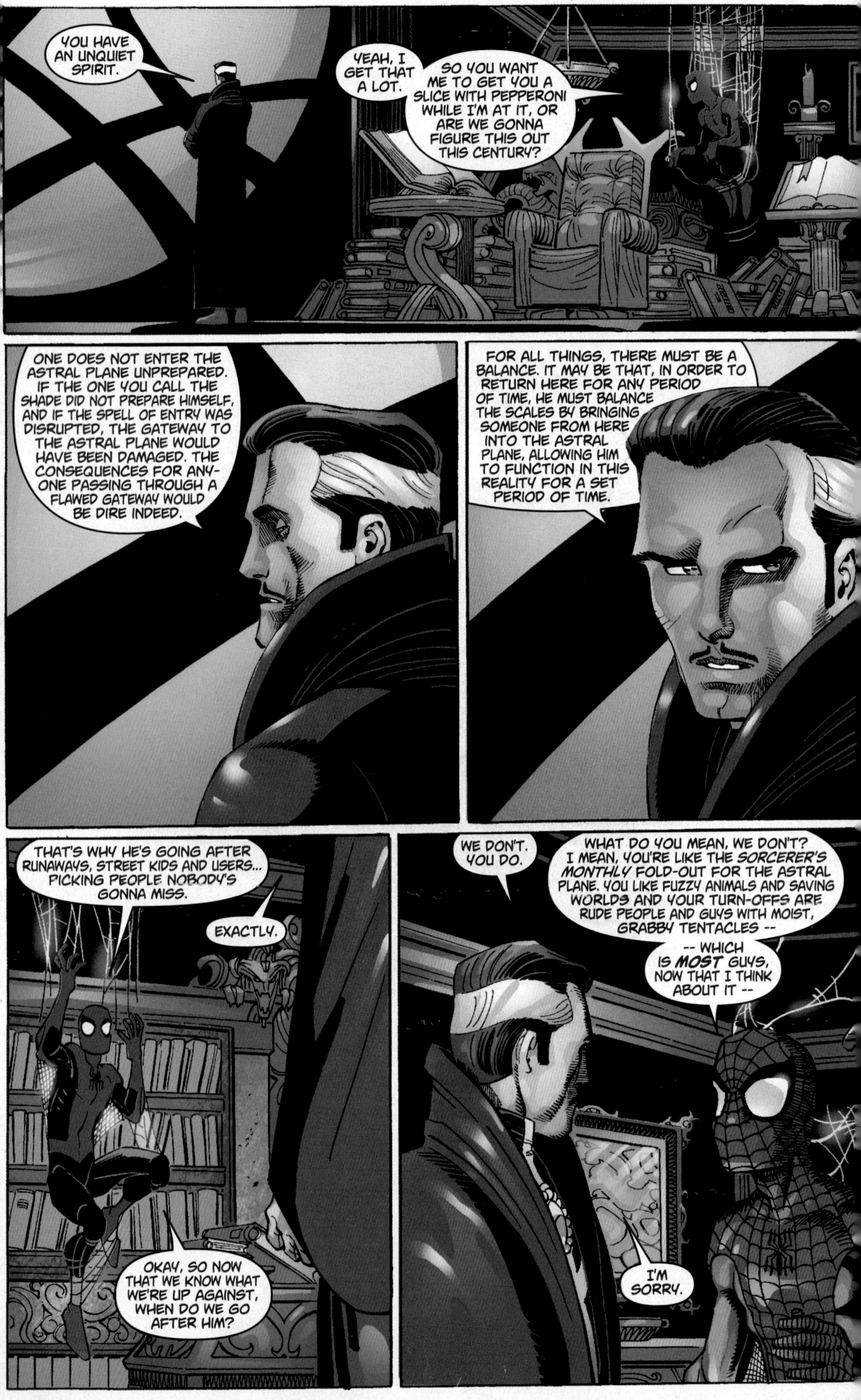
YOU HAVE AN UNQUIET SPIRIT.
YEAH, I GET THAT A LOT.
SO YOU WANT ME TO GET YOU A SLICE WITH PEPPERONI WHILE I'M AT IT, OR ARE WE GONNA FIGURE THIS OUT THIS CENTURY?
ONE DOES NOT ENTER THE ASTRAL PLANE UNPREPARED. IF THE ONE YOU CALL THE SHADE DID NOT PREPARE HIMSELF, AND IF THE SPELL OF ENTRY WAS DISRUPTED, THE GATEWAY TO THE ASTRAL PLANE WOULD HAVE BEEN DAMAGED. THE CONSEQUENCES FOR ANY-ONE PASSING THROUGH A FLAWED GATEWAY WOULD BE DIRE INDEED.
FOR ALL THINGS, THERE MUST BE A BALANCE. IT MAY BE THAT, IN ORDER TO RETURN HERE FOR ANY PERIOD OF TIME, HE MUST BALANCE THE SCALES BY BRINGING SOMEONE FROM HERE INTO THE ASTRAL PLANE, ALLOWING HIM TO FUNCTION IN THIS REALITY FOR A SET PERIOD OF TIME.
THAT'S WHY HE'S GOING AFTER RUNAWAYS, STREET KIDS AND USERS... PICKING PEOPLE NOBODY'S GONNA MISS.
EXACTLY.
OKAY, SO NOW THAT WE KNOW WHAT WE'RE UP AGAINST, WHEN DO WE GO AFTER HIM?
WE DON'T. YOU DO.
WHAT DO YOU MEAN, WE DON'T? I MEAN, YOU'RE LIKE THE SORCERER'S MONTHLY FOLD-OUT FOR THE ASTRAL PLANE. YOU LIKE FUZZY ANIMALS AND SAVING WORLDS AND YOUR TURN-OFFS ARE RUDE PEOPLE AND GUYS WITH MOIST, GRABBY TENTACLES --
-- WHICH IS MOST GUYS, NOW THAT I THINK ABOUT IT --
I'M SORRY.

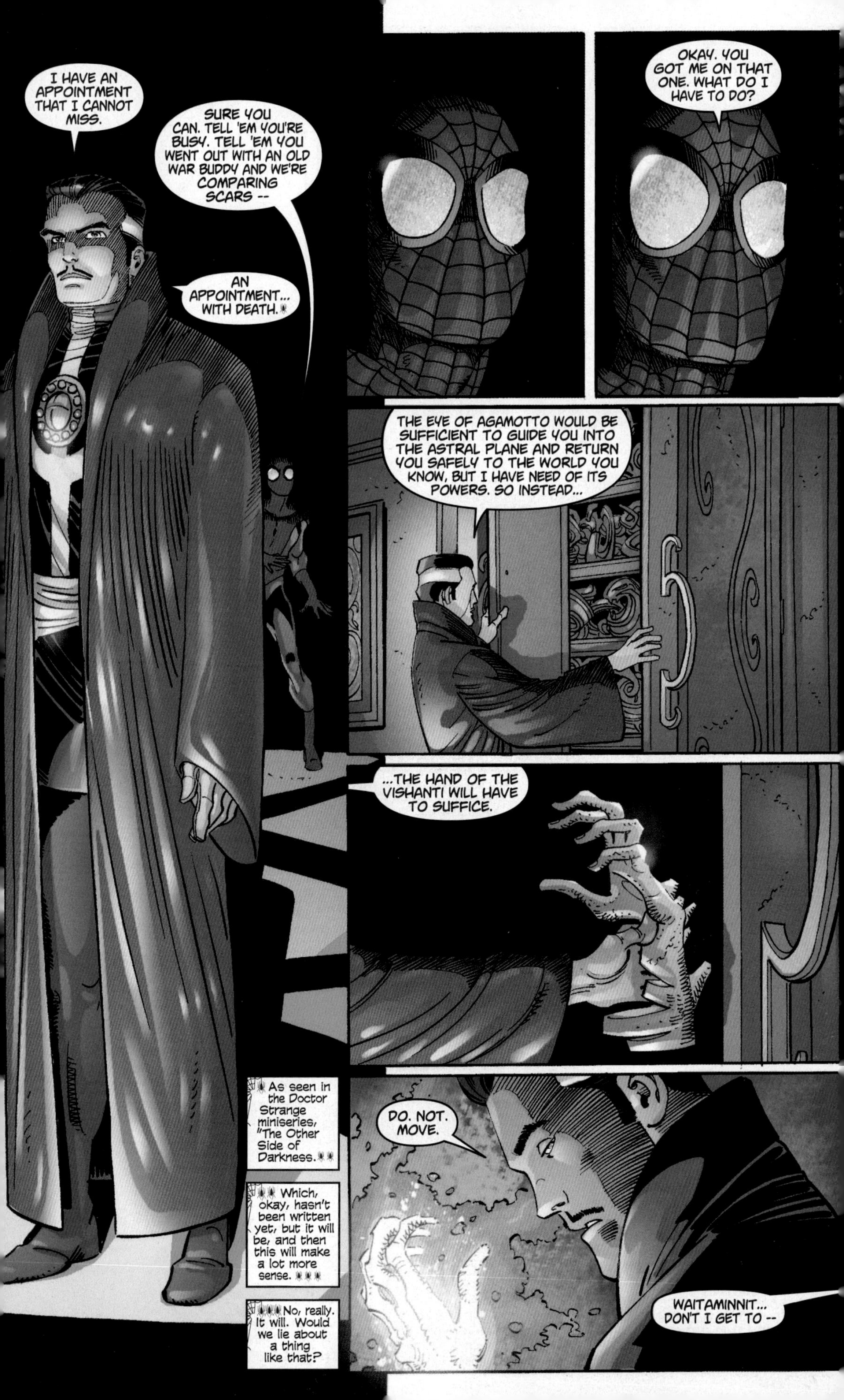
I HAVE AN APPOINTMENT THAT I CANNOT MISS.
SURE YOU CAN. TELL 'EM YOU'RE BUSY. TELL 'EM YOU WENT OUT WITH AN OLD WAR BUDDY AND WE'RE COMPARING SCARS --
AN APPOINTMENT... WITH DEATH.*
OKAY. YOU GOT ME ON THAT ONE. WHAT DO I HAVE TO DO?
THE EYE OF AGAMOTTO WOULD BE SUFFICIENT TO GUIDE YOU INTO THE ASTRAL PLANE AND RETURN YOU SAFELY TO THE WORLD YOU KNOW, BUT I HAVE NEED OF ITS POWERS. SO INSTEAD...
...THE HAND OF THE VISHANTI WILL HAVE TO SUFFICE.
*As seen in the Doctor Strange miniseries, "The Other Side of Darkness.**
Which, okay, hasn't been written yet, but it will be, and then this will make a lot more sense. *
***No, really. It will. Would we lie about a thing like that?
DO. NOT. MOVE.
WAITAMINNIT... DON'T I GET TO --

AAAAAGGGG!

OWW...

OH, MAAAANNNN... WHERE THE HELL DID THAT TRUCK COME FROM?

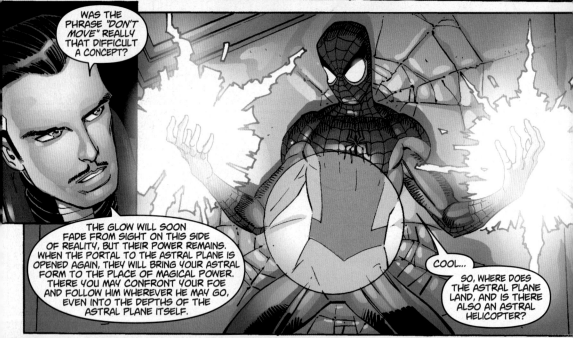

WAS THE PHRASE "DON'T MOVE" REALLY THAT DIFFICULT A CONCEPT?

THE GLOW WILL SOON FADE FROM SIGHT ON THIS SIDE OF REALITY, BUT THEIR POWER REMAINS. WHEN THE PORTAL TO THE ASTRAL PLANE IS OPENED AGAIN, THEY WILL BRING YOUR ASTRAL FORM TO THE PLACE OF MAGICAL POWER. THERE YOU MAY CONFRONT YOUR FOE AND FOLLOW HIM WHEREVER HE MAY GO, EVEN INTO THE DEPTHS OF THE ASTRAL PLANE ITSELF.

COOL... SO, WHERE DOES THE ASTRAL PLANE LAND, AND IS THERE ALSO AN ASTRAL HELICOPTER?

CERTAIN THINGS SHOULD NOT BE JOKED ABOUT. YOU MUST APPROACH THIS SITUATION WITH CAUTION, REVERENCE, AND GREAT SERIOUSNESS.

HMMM... AND ONE OTHER THING...

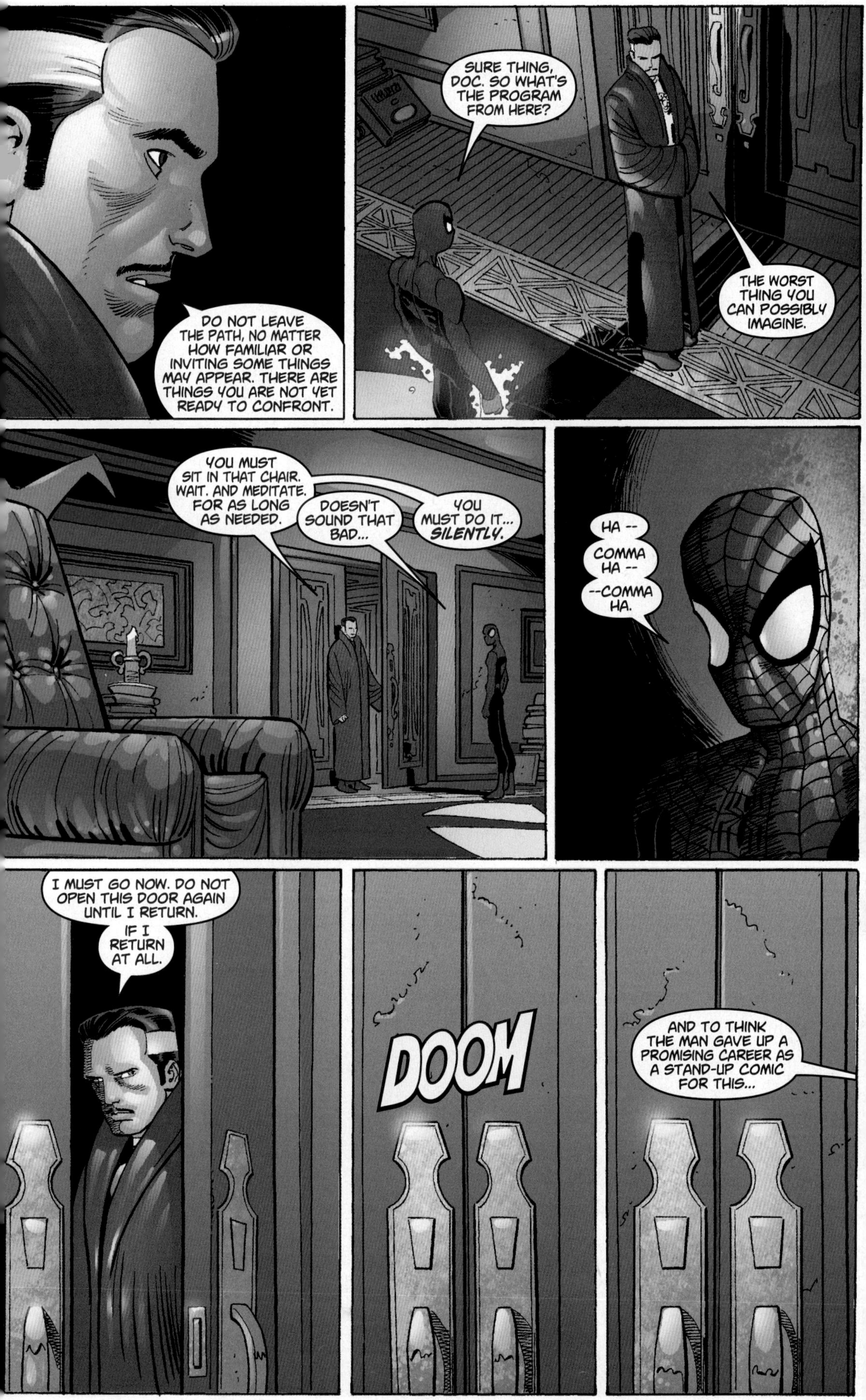
DO NOT LEAVE THE PATH, NO MATTER HOW FAMILIAR OR INVITING SOME THINGS MAY APPEAR. THERE ARE THINGS YOU ARE NOT YET READY TO CONFRONT.
SURE THING, DOC. SO WHAT'S THE PROGRAM FROM HERE?
THE WORST THING YOU CAN POSSIBLY IMAGINE.
YOU MUST SIT IN THAT CHAIR. WAIT. AND MEDITATE. FOR AS LONG AS NEEDED.
DOESN'T SOUND THAT BAD...
YOU MUST DO IT... SILENTLY.
HA --
COMMA HA --
--COMMA HA.
I MUST GO NOW. DO NOT OPEN THIS DOOR AGAIN UNTIL I RETURN.
IF I RETURN AT ALL.
DOOM
AND TO THINK THE MAN GAVE UP A PROMISING CAREER AS A STAND-UP COMIC FOR THIS...

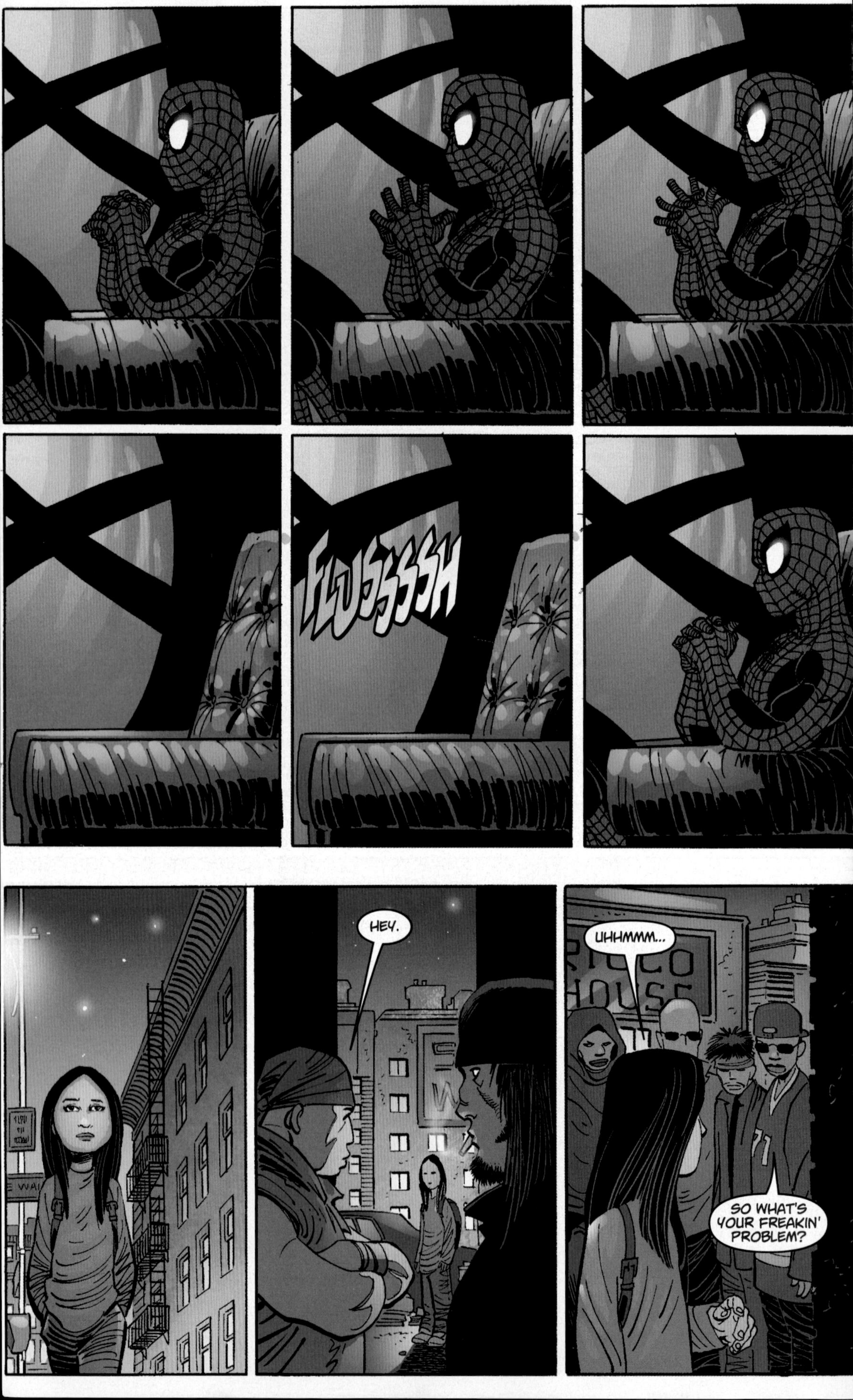
FLUSSSSH
HEY.
UHHMMM...
SO WHAT'S YOUR FREAKIN' PROBLEM?

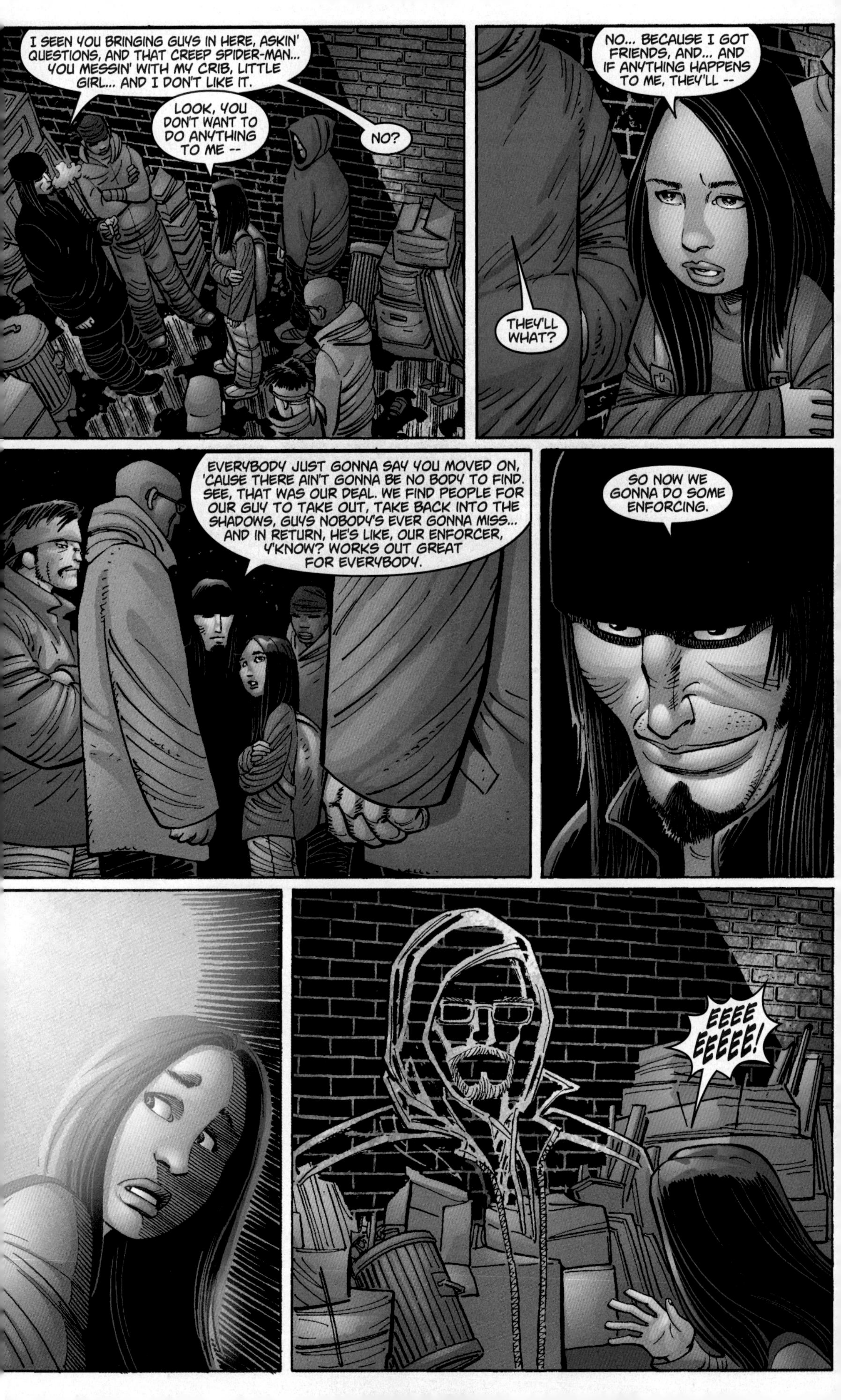
I SEEN YOU BRINGING GUYS IN HERE, ASKIN' QUESTIONS, AND THAT CREEP SPIDER-MAN... YOU MESSIN' WITH MY CRIB, LITTLE GIRL... AND I DON'T LIKE IT.
LOOK, YOU DON'T WANT TO DO ANYTHING TO ME --
NO?
NO... BECAUSE I GOT FRIENDS, AND... AND IF ANYTHING HAPPENS TO ME, THEY'LL --
THEY'LL WHAT?
EVERYBODY JUST GONNA SAY YOU MOVED ON, 'CAUSE THERE AIN'T GONNA BE NO BODY TO FIND. SEE, THAT WAS OUR DEAL. WE FIND PEOPLE FOR OUR GUY TO TAKE OUT, TAKE BACK INTO THE SHADOWS, GUYS NOBODY'S EVER GONNA MISS... AND IN RETURN, HE'S LIKE, OUR ENFORCER, Y'KNOW? WORKS OUT GREAT FOR EVERYBODY.
SO NOW WE GONNA DO SOME ENFORCING.
EEEE EEEEE!

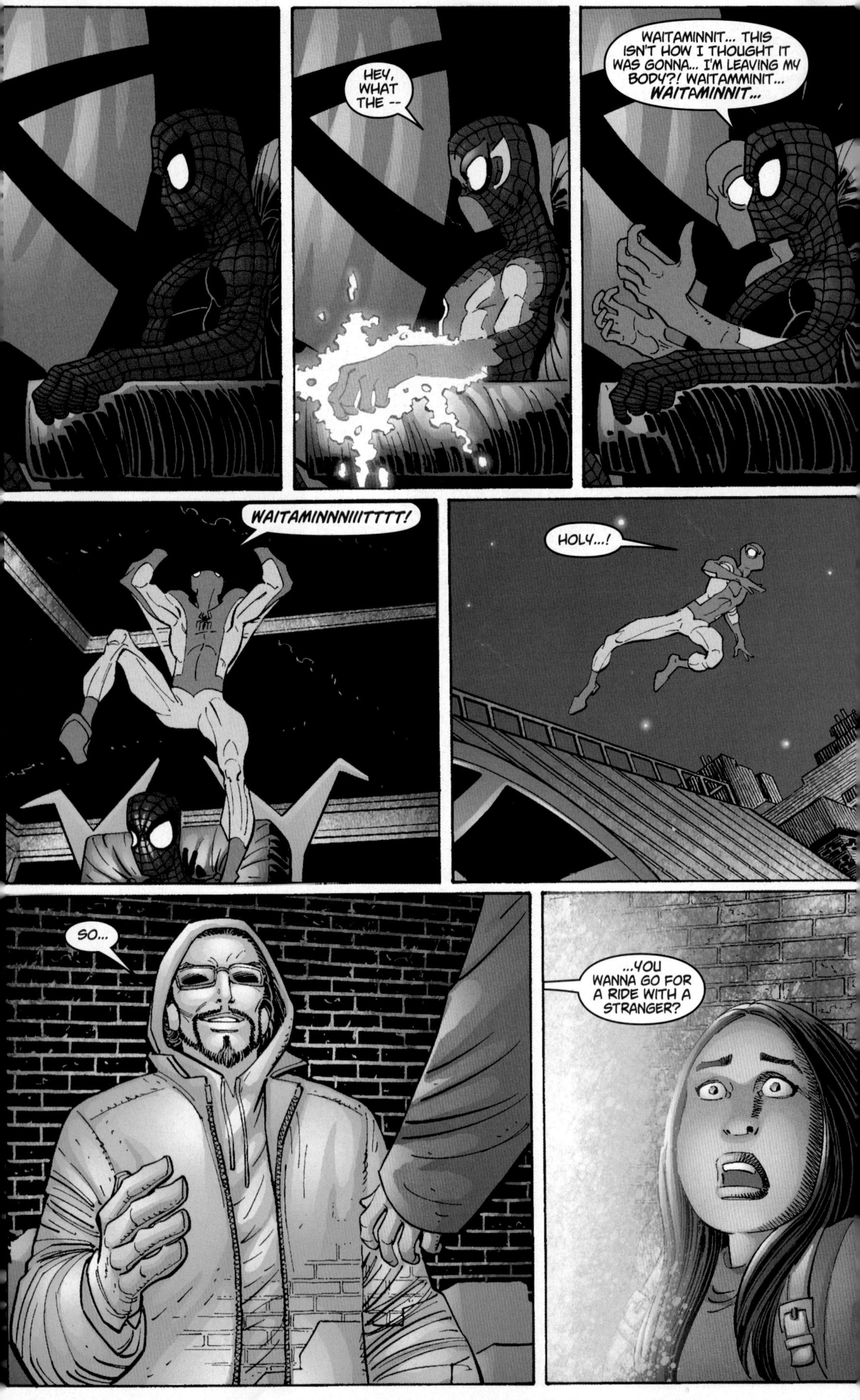
HEY, WHAT THE --
WAITAMINNIT... THIS ISN'T HOW I THOUGHT IT WAS GONNA... I'M LEAVING MY BODY?! WAITAMMINIT... WAITAMINNIT...
WAITAMINNNIIITTTT!
HOLY...!
SO...
...YOU WANNA GO FOR A RIDE WITH A STRANGER?

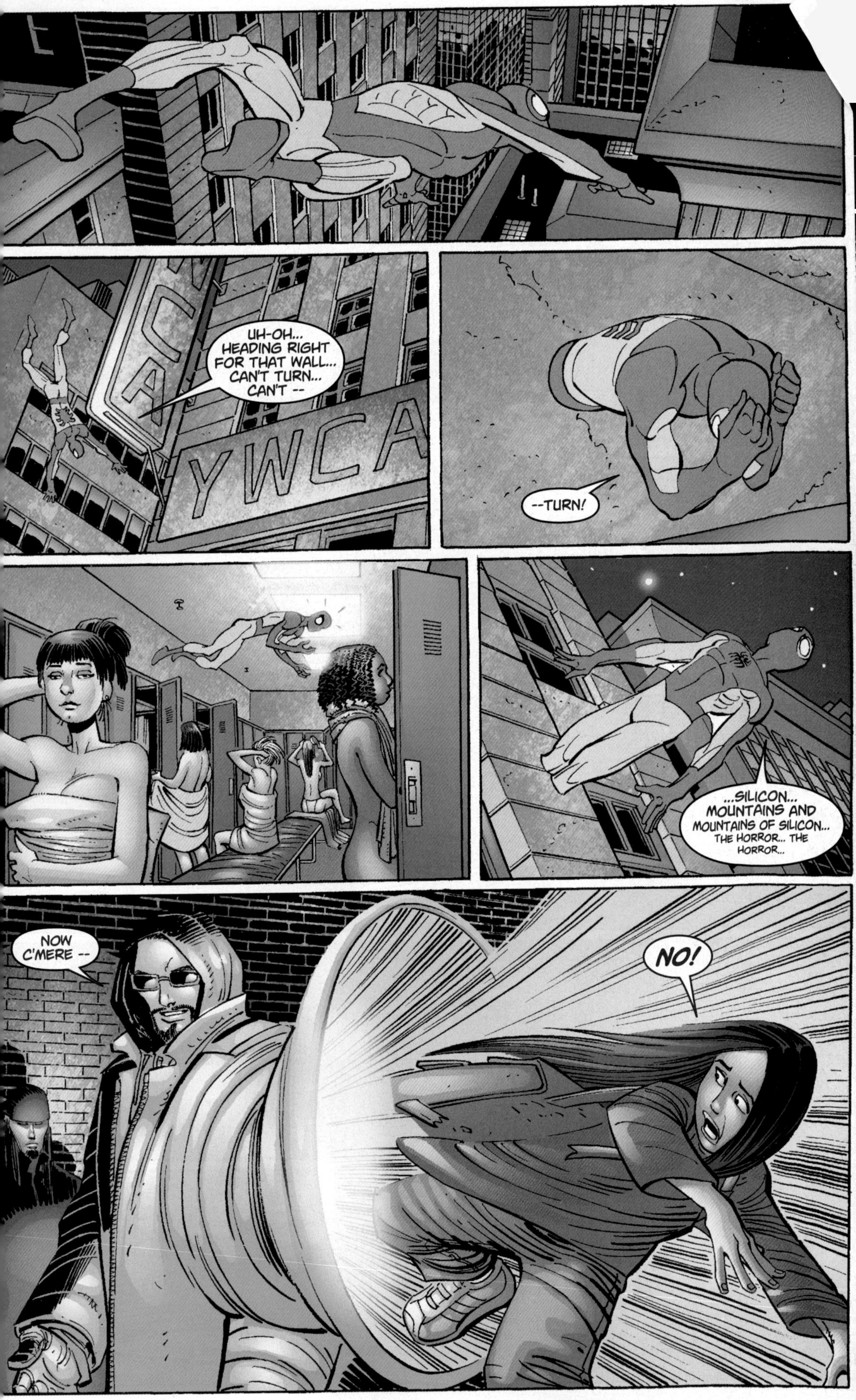
UH-OH... HEADING RIGHT FOR THAT WALL... CAN'T TURN... CAN'T --
YWCA
--TURN!
...SILICON... MOUNTAINS AND MOUNTAINS OF SILICON... THE HORROR... THE HORROR...
NOW C'MERE --
NO!

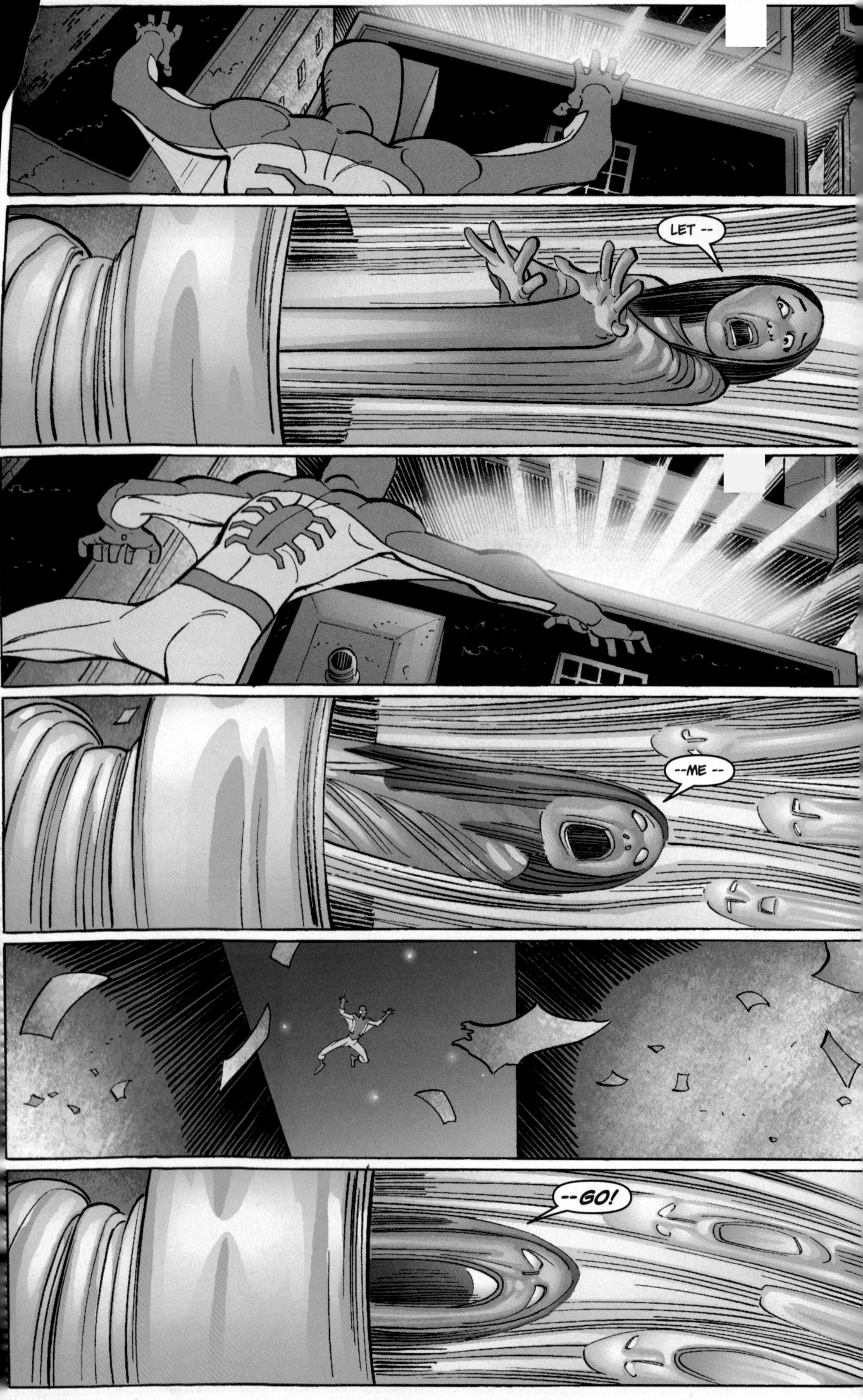
LET --
--ME --
--GO!

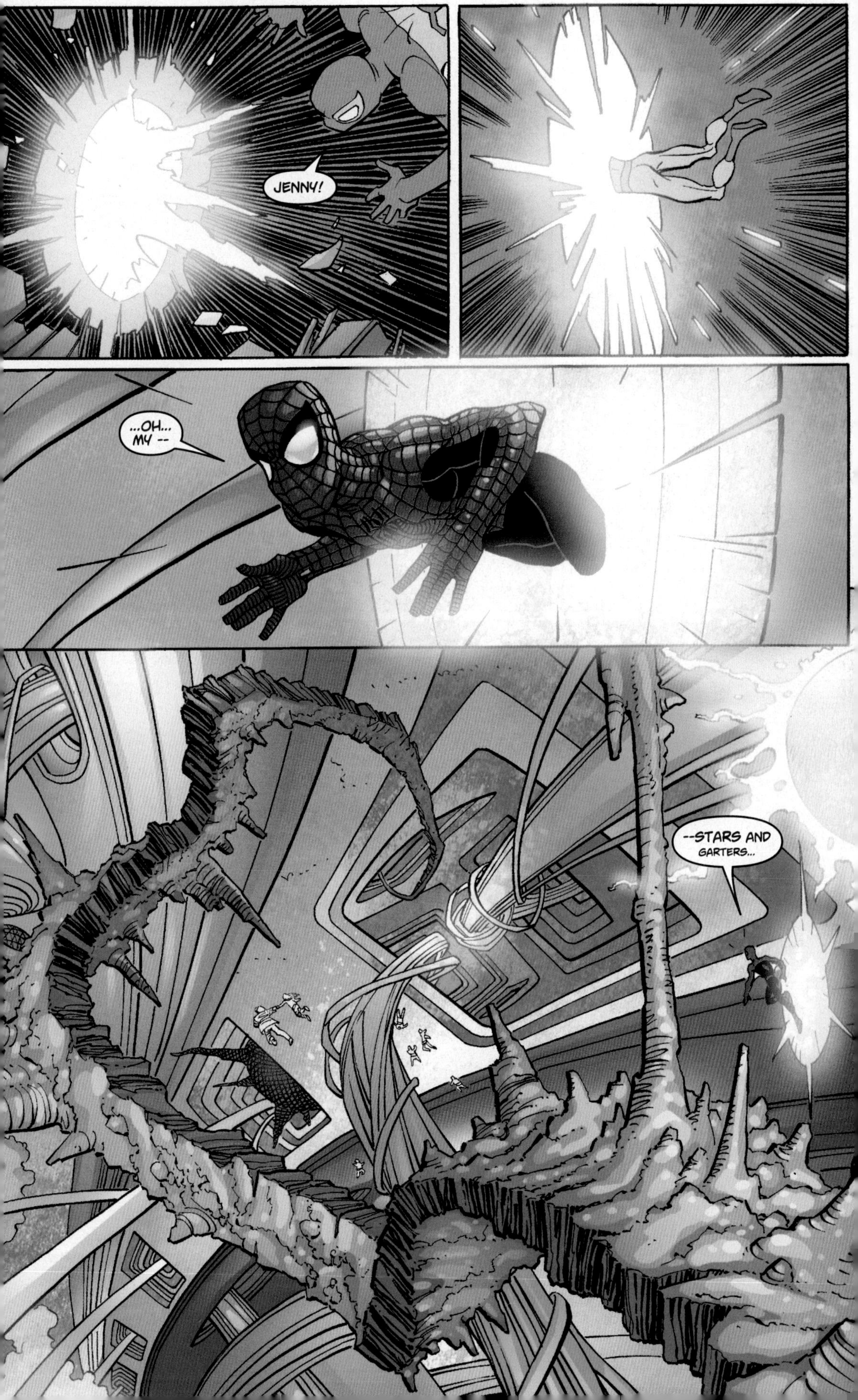
JENNY!
...OH... MY --
--STARS AND GARTERS...

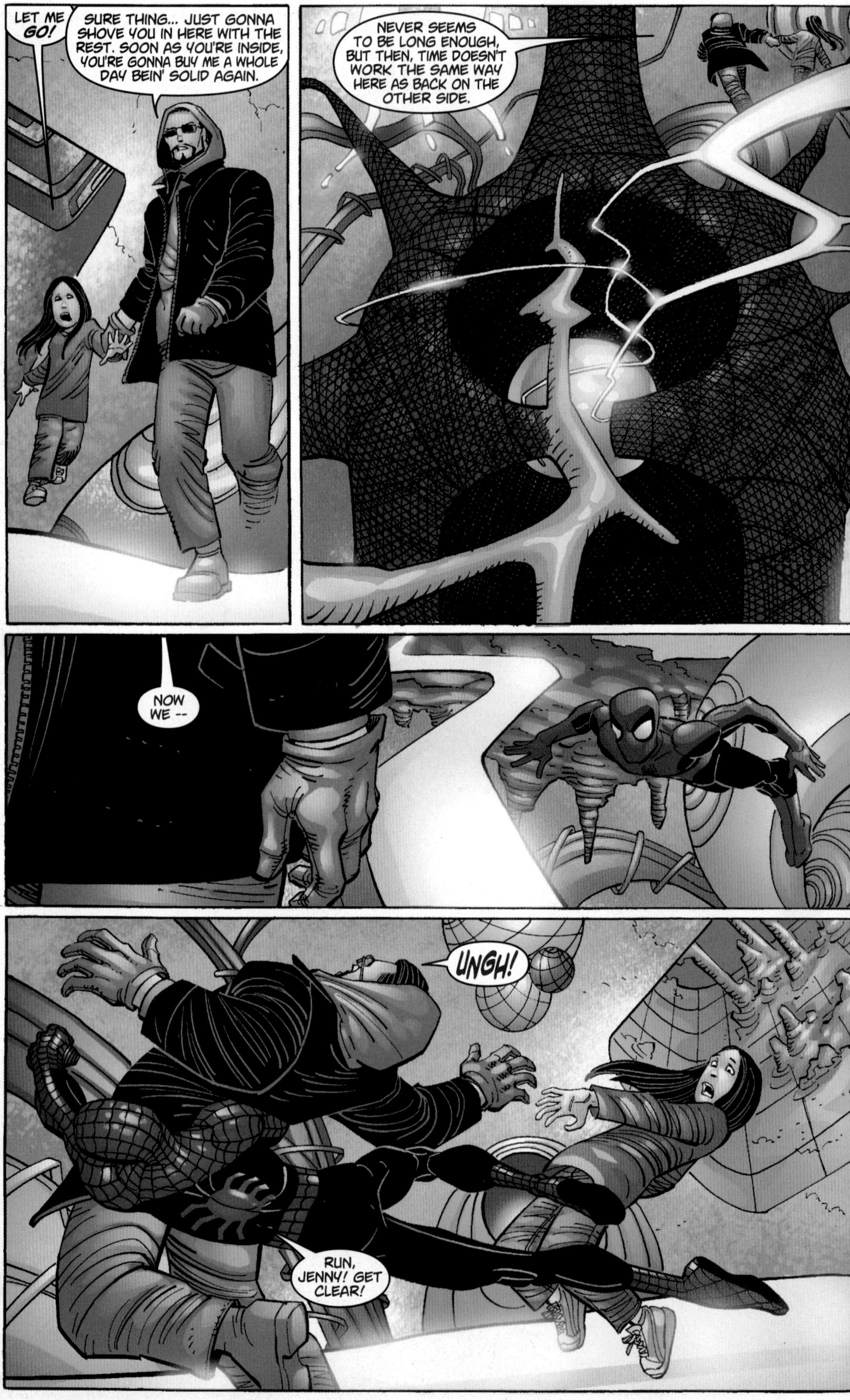
LET ME GO!
SURE THING... JUST GONNA SHOVE YOU IN HERE WITH THE REST. SOON AS YOU'RE INSIDE, YOU'RE GONNA BUY ME A WHOLE DAY BEIN' SOLID AGAIN.
NEVER SEEMS TO BE LONG ENOUGH, BUT THEN, TIME DOESN'T WORK THE SAME WAY HERE AS BACK ON THE OTHER SIDE.
NOW WE --
UNGH!
RUN, JENNY! GET CLEAR!

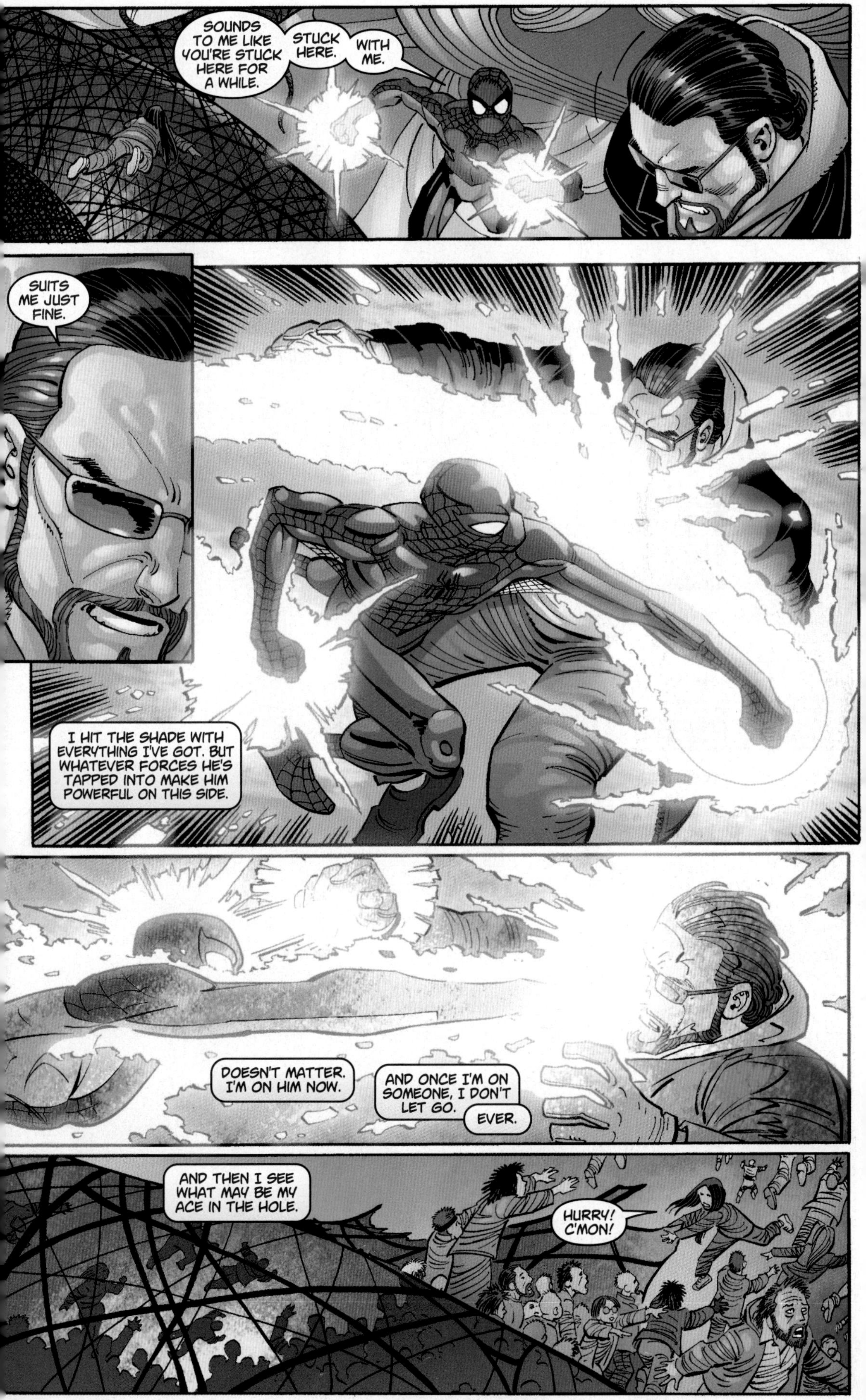
SOUNDS TO ME LIKE YOU'RE STUCK HERE FOR A WHILE.
STUCK HERE.
WITH ME.
SUITS ME JUST FINE.
I HIT THE SHADE WITH EVERYTHING I'VE GOT. BUT WHATEVER FORCES HE'S TAPPED INTO MAKE HIM POWERFUL ON THIS SIDE.
DOESN'T MATTER. I'M ON HIM NOW.
AND ONCE I'M ON SOMEONE, I DON'T LET GO.
EVER.
AND THEN I SEE WHAT MAY BE MY ACE IN THE HOLE.
HURRY! C'MON!

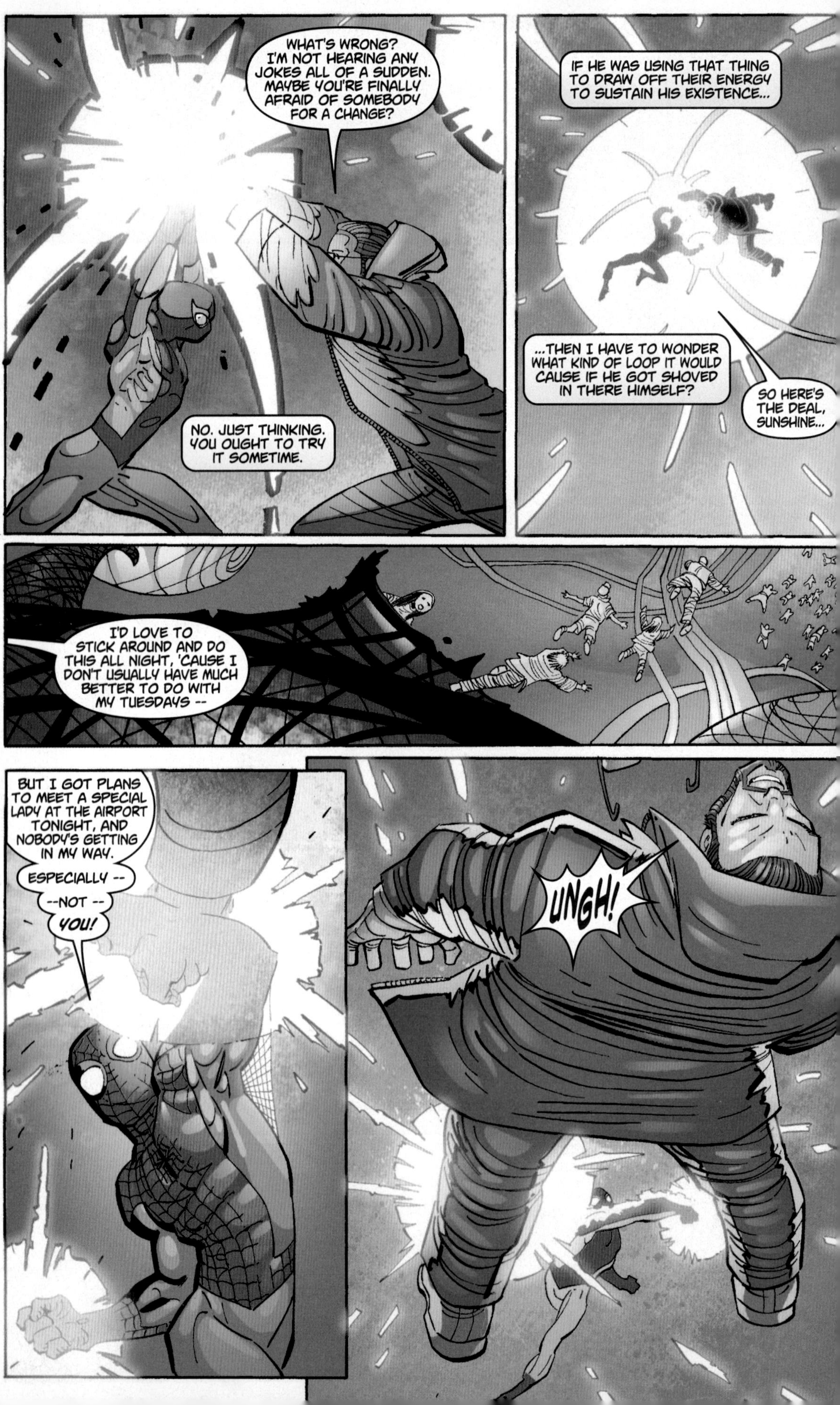
WHAT'S WRONG? I'M NOT HEARING ANY JOKES ALL OF A SUDDEN. MAYBE YOU'RE FINALLY AFRAID OF SOMEBODY FOR A CHANGE?
NO. JUST THINKING. YOU OUGHT TO TRY IT SOMETIME.
IF HE WAS USING THAT THING TO DRAW OFF THEIR ENERGY TO SUSTAIN HIS EXISTENCE...
...THEN I HAVE TO WONDER WHAT KIND OF LOOP IT WOULD CAUSE IF HE GOT SHOVED IN THERE HIMSELF?
SO HERE'S THE DEAL, SUNSHINE...
I'D LOVE TO STICK AROUND AND DO THIS ALL NIGHT, 'CAUSE I DON'T USUALLY HAVE MUCH BETTER TO DO WITH MY TUESDAYS --
BUT I GOT PLANS TO MEET A SPECIAL LADY AT THE AIRPORT TONIGHT, AND NOBODY'S GETTING IN MY WAY.
ESPECIALLY --
--NOT --
YOU!
UNGH!

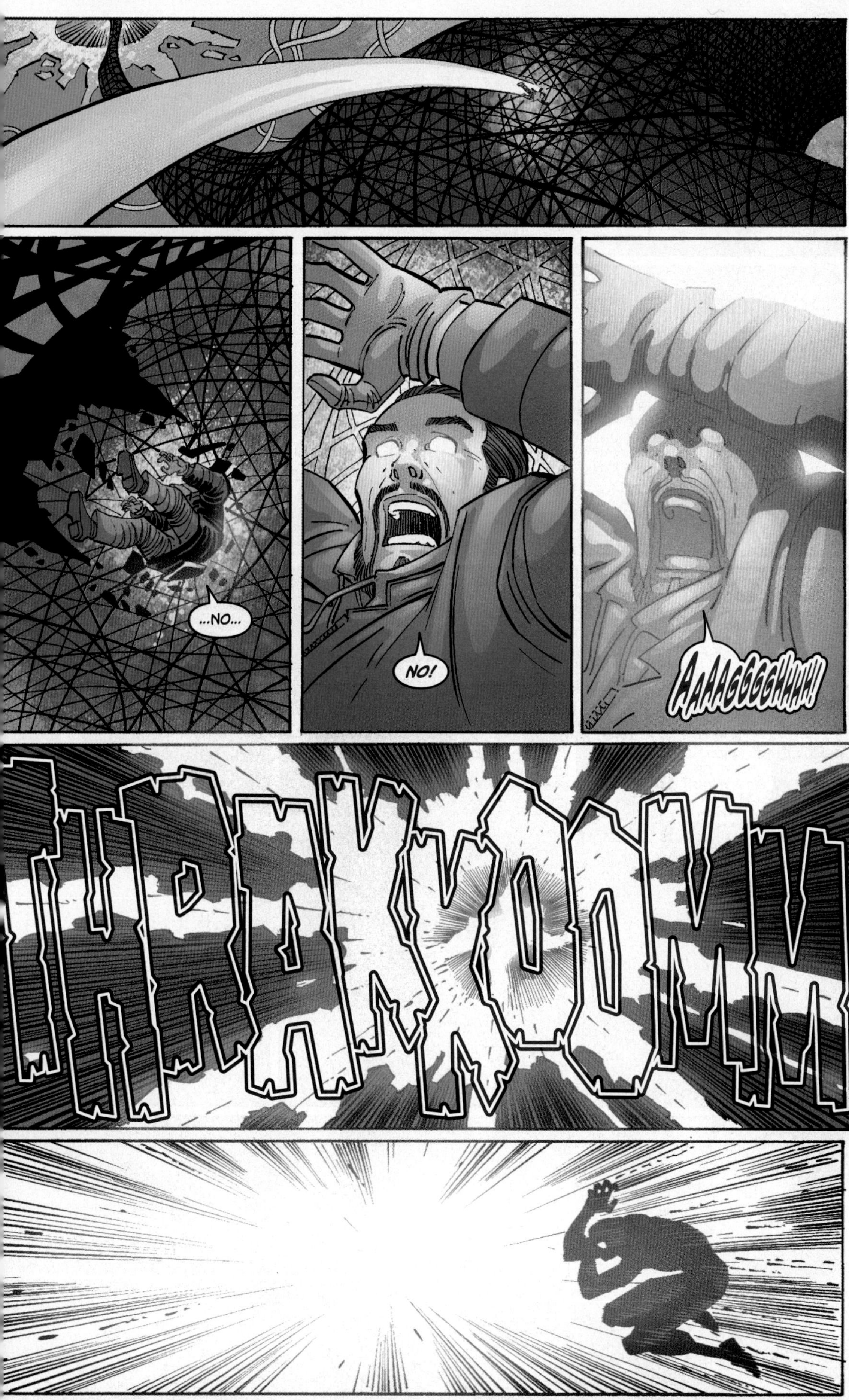
...NO...
NO!
AAAAGGGGHHHH!
THRAKXOOMM

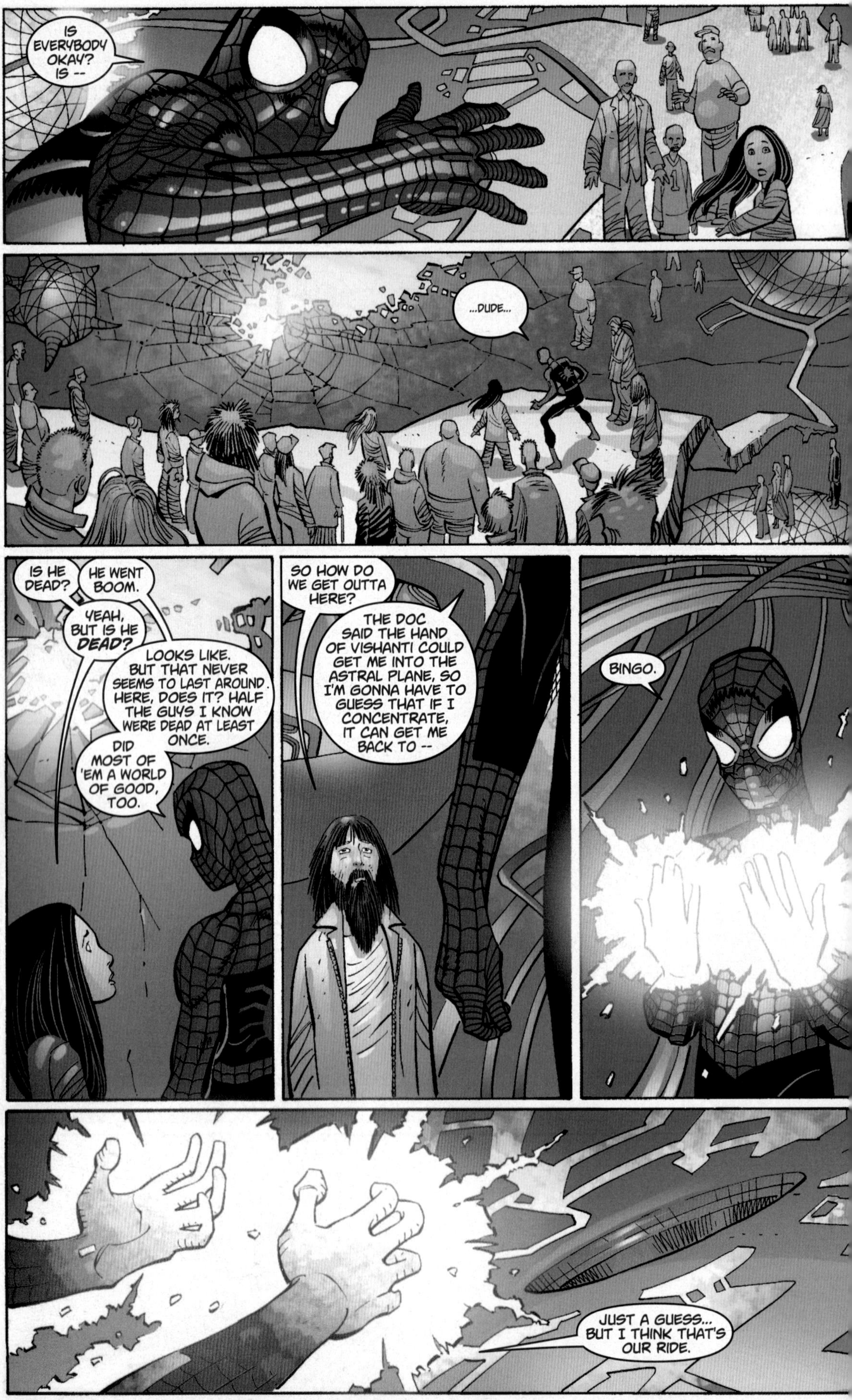
IS EVERYBODY OKAY? IS --
...DUDE...
IS HE DEAD?
HE WENT BOOM.
YEAH, BUT IS HE *DEAD?*
LOOKS LIKE. BUT THAT NEVER SEEMS TO LAST AROUND HERE, DOES IT? HALF THE GUYS I KNOW WERE DEAD AT LEAST ONCE.
DID MOST OF 'EM A WORLD OF GOOD, TOO.
SO HOW DO WE GET OUTTA HERE?
THE DOC SAID THE HAND OF VISHANTI COULD GET ME INTO THE ASTRAL PLANE, SO I'M GONNA HAVE TO GUESS THAT IF I CONCENTRATE, IT CAN GET ME BACK TO --
BINGO.
JUST A GUESS... BUT I THINK THAT'S OUR RIDE.

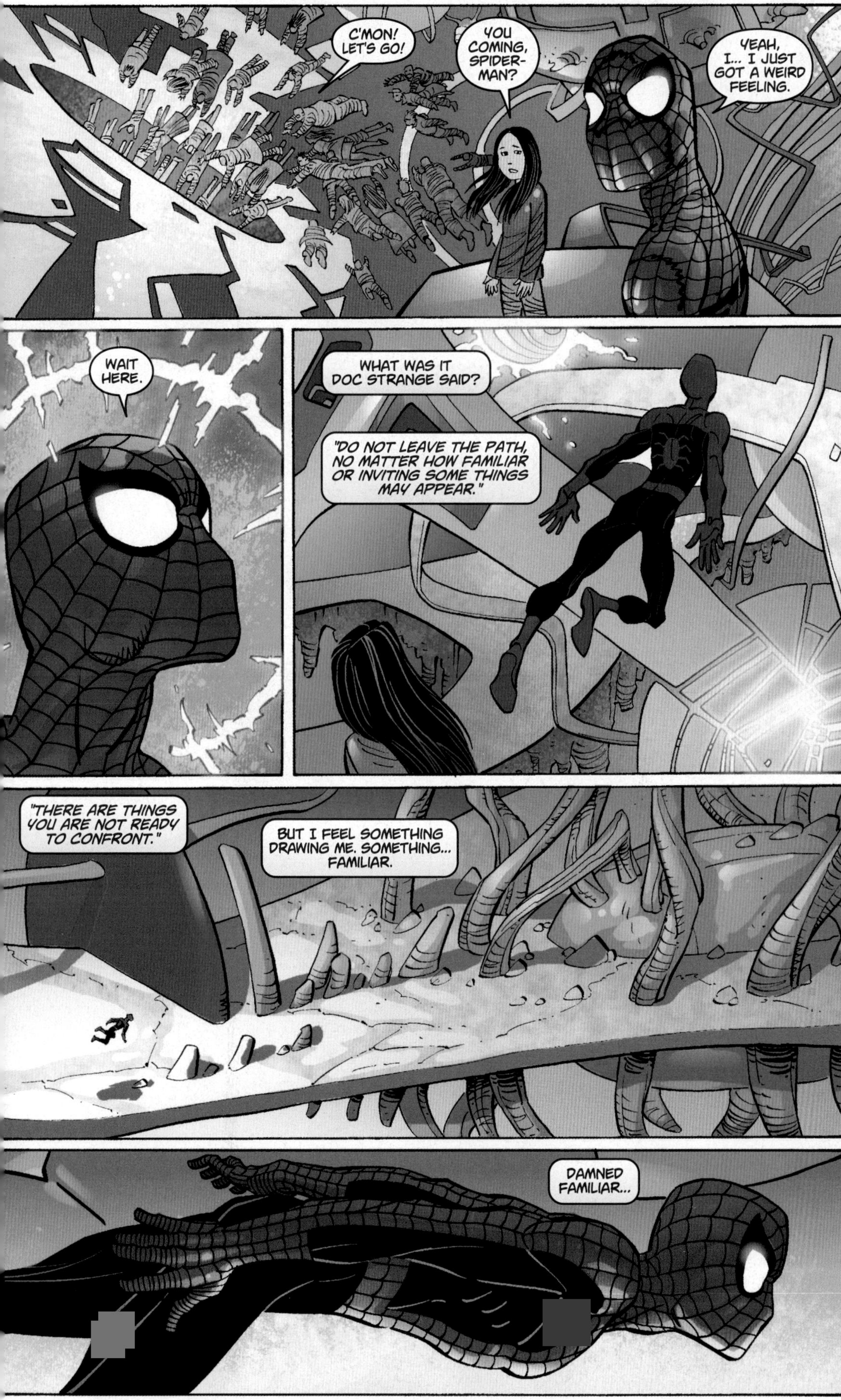
C'MON! LET'S GO!
YOU COMING, SPIDER-MAN?
YEAH, I... I JUST GOT A WEIRD FEELING.
WAIT HERE.
WHAT WAS IT DOC STRANGE SAID?
"DO NOT LEAVE THE PATH, NO MATTER HOW FAMILIAR OR INVITING SOME THINGS MAY APPEAR."
"THERE ARE THINGS YOU ARE NOT READY TO CONFRONT."
BUT I FEEL SOMETHING DRAWING ME. SOMETHING... FAMILIAR.
DAMNED FAMILIAR...

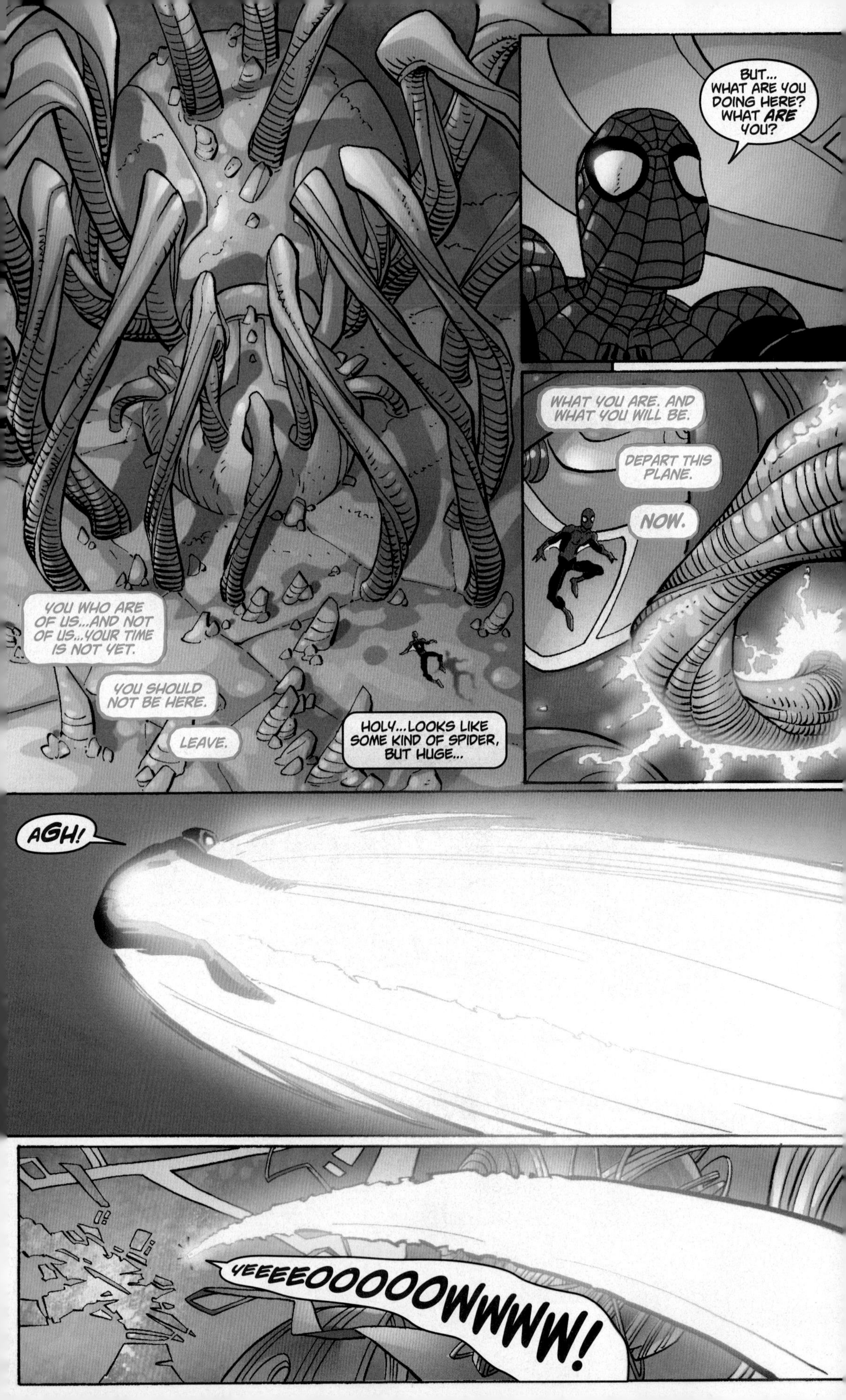
YOU WHO ARE OF US...AND NOT OF US...YOUR TIME IS NOT YET.
YOU SHOULD NOT BE HERE.
LEAVE.
HOLY...LOOKS LIKE SOME KIND OF SPIDER, BUT HUGE...
BUT... WHAT ARE YOU DOING HERE? WHAT ARE YOU?
WHAT YOU ARE. AND WHAT YOU WILL BE.
DEPART THIS PLANE.
NOW.
AGH!
YEEEEOOOOOWWWW!

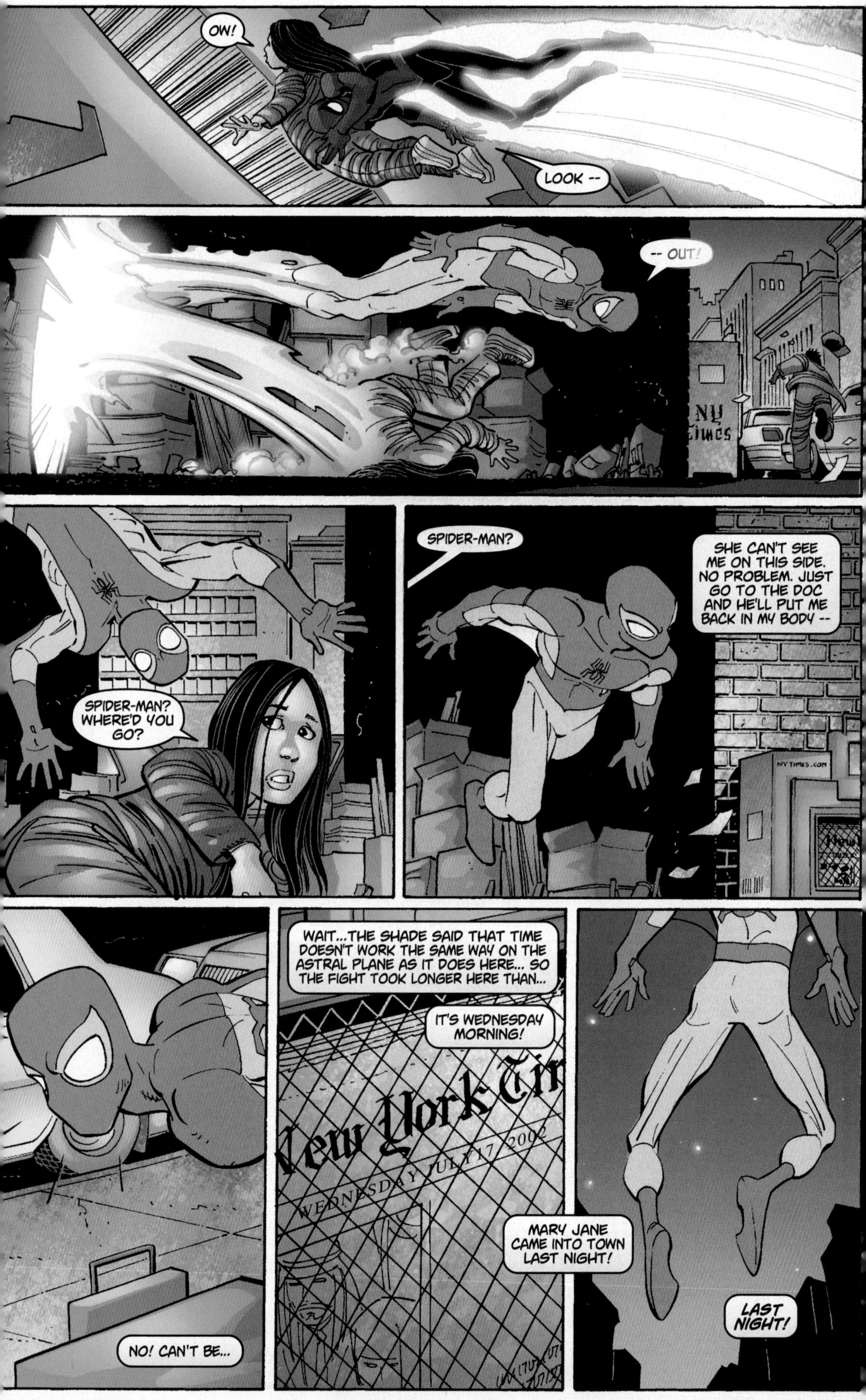
OW!
LOOK --
-- OUT!
SPIDER-MAN? WHERE'D YOU GO?
SPIDER-MAN?
SHE CAN'T SEE ME ON THIS SIDE. NO PROBLEM. JUST GO TO THE DOC AND HE'LL PUT ME BACK IN MY BODY --
NO! CAN'T BE...
WAIT...THE SHADE SAID THAT TIME DOESN'T WORK THE SAME WAY ON THE ASTRAL PLANE AS IT DOES HERE... SO THE FIGHT TOOK LONGER HERE THAN...
IT'S WEDNESDAY MORNING!
WEDNESDAY JULY 17, 2002
MARY JANE CAME INTO TOWN LAST NIGHT!
LAST NIGHT!

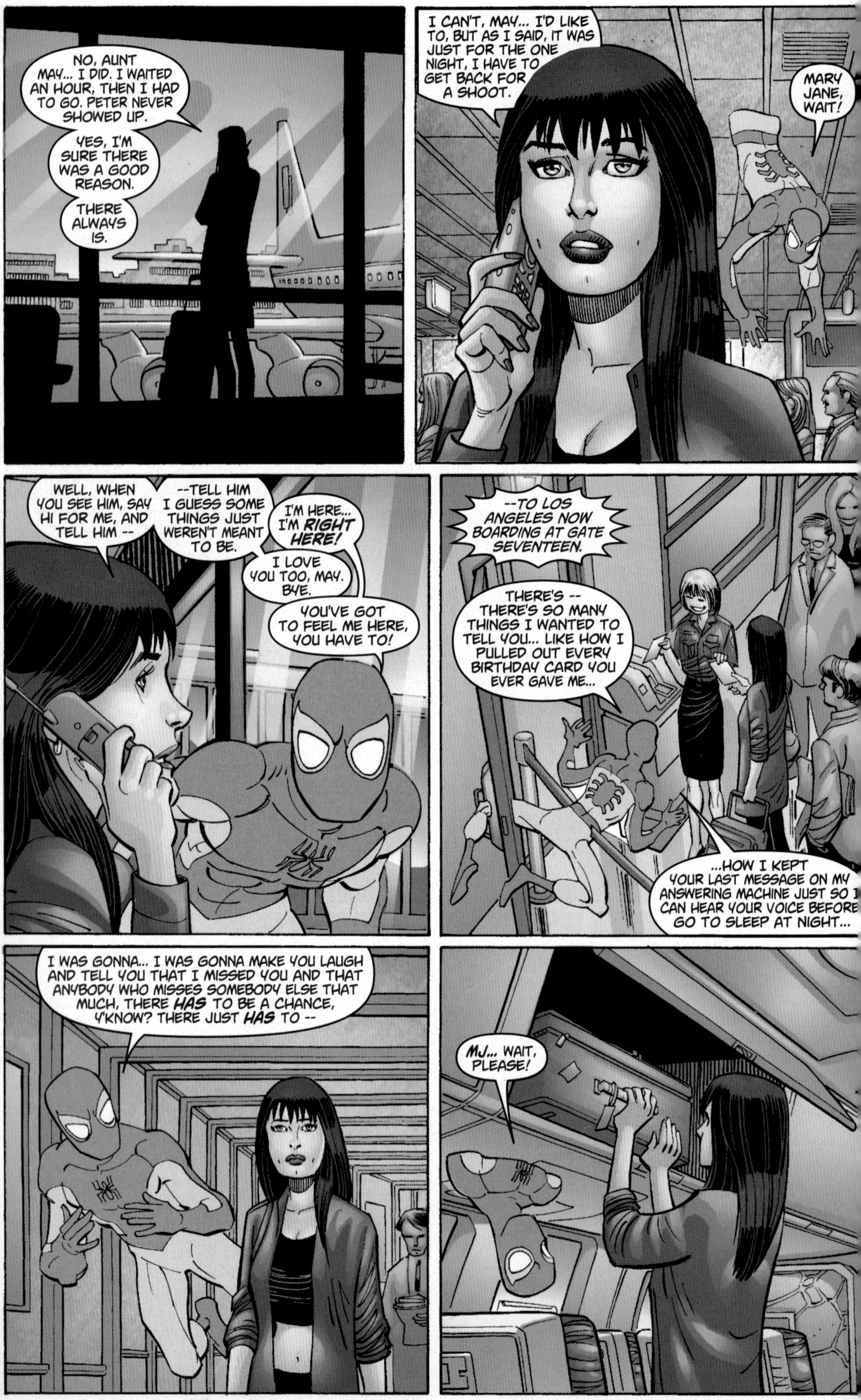
NO, AUNT MAY... I DID. I WAITED AN HOUR, THEN I HAD TO GO. PETER NEVER SHOWED UP.
YES, I'M SURE THERE WAS A GOOD REASON.
THERE ALWAYS IS.
I CAN'T, MAY... I'D LIKE TO, BUT AS I SAID, IT WAS JUST FOR THE ONE NIGHT, I HAVE TO GET BACK FOR A SHOOT.
MARY JANE, WAIT!
WELL, WHEN YOU SEE HIM, SAY HI FOR ME, AND TELL HIM --
--TELL HIM I GUESS SOME THINGS JUST WEREN'T MEANT TO BE.
I'M HERE... I'M RIGHT HERE!
I LOVE YOU TOO, MAY. BYE.
YOU'VE GOT TO FEEL ME HERE, YOU HAVE TO!
--TO LOS ANGELES NOW BOARDING AT GATE SEVENTEEN.
THERE'S -- THERE'S SO MANY THINGS I WANTED TO TELL YOU... LIKE HOW I PULLED OUT EVERY BIRTHDAY CARD YOU EVER GAVE ME...
...HOW I KEPT YOUR LAST MESSAGE ON MY ANSWERING MACHINE JUST SO I CAN HEAR YOUR VOICE BEFORE I GO TO SLEEP AT NIGHT...
I WAS GONNA... I WAS GONNA MAKE YOU LAUGH AND TELL YOU THAT I MISSED YOU AND THAT ANYBODY WHO MISSES SOMEBODY ELSE THAT MUCH, THERE HAS TO BE A CHANCE, Y'KNOW? THERE JUST HAS TO --
MJ... WAIT, PLEASE!

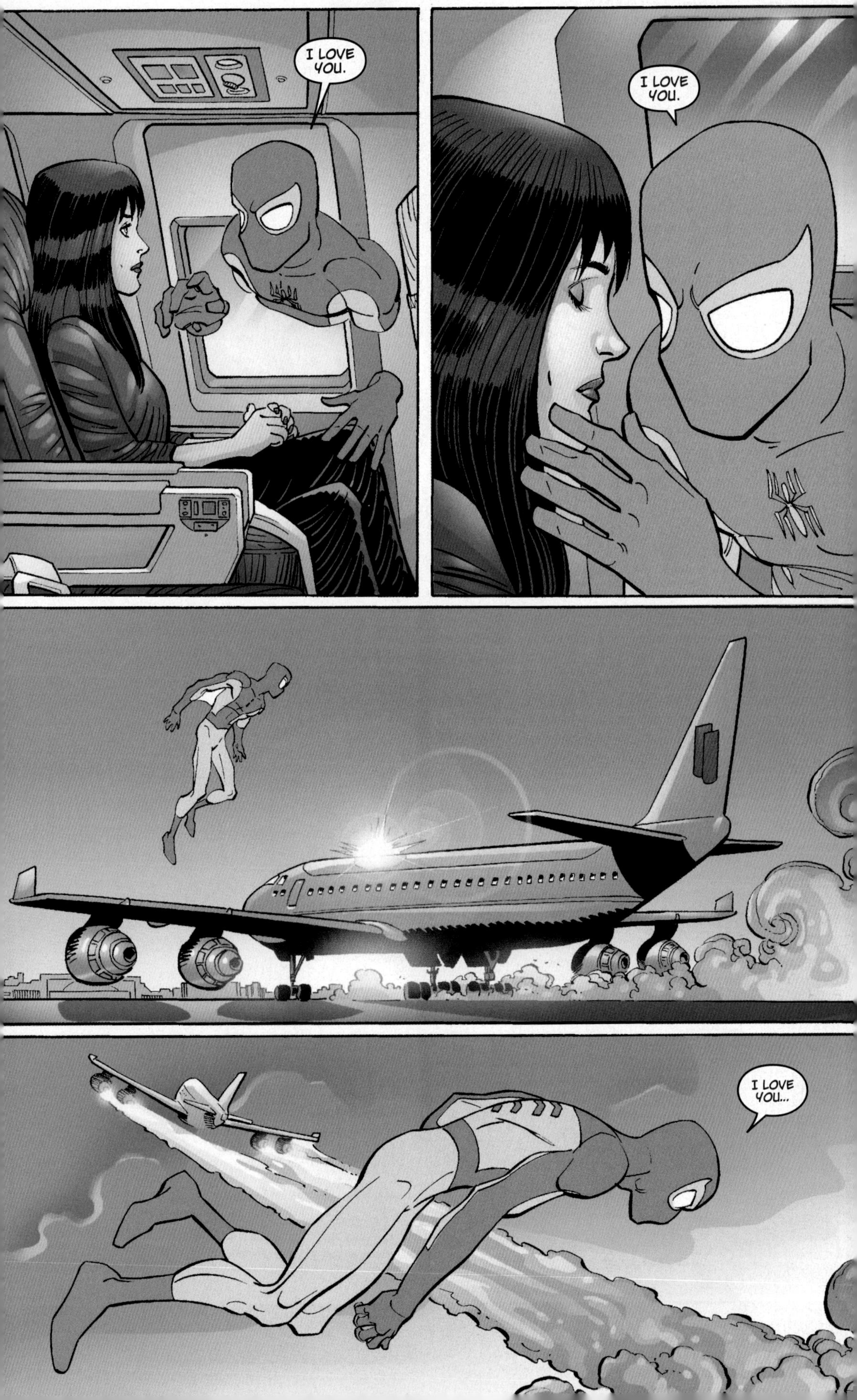
I LOVE YOU.
I LOVE YOU.
I LOVE YOU...

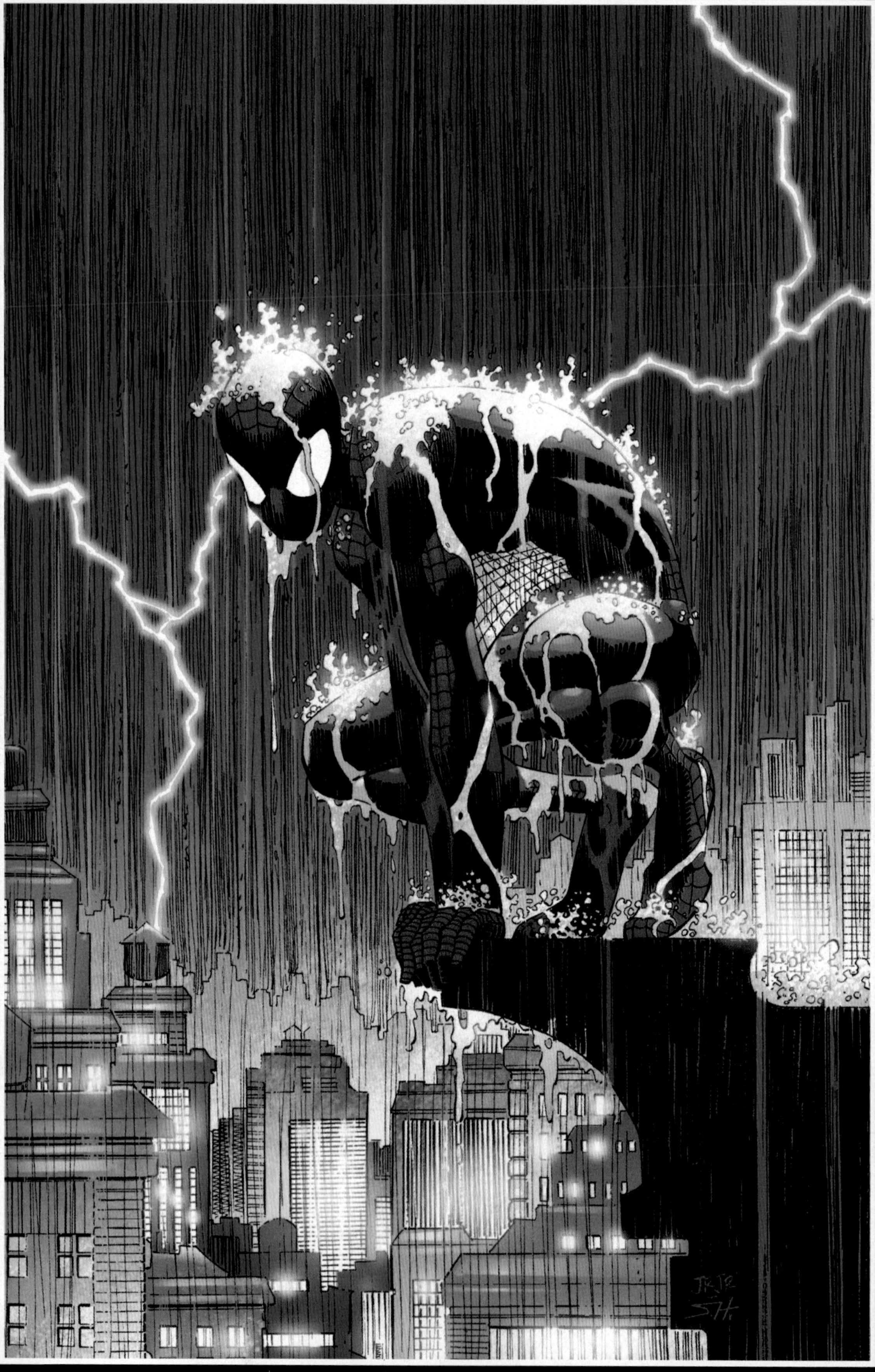

AMAZING SPIDER-MAN #43

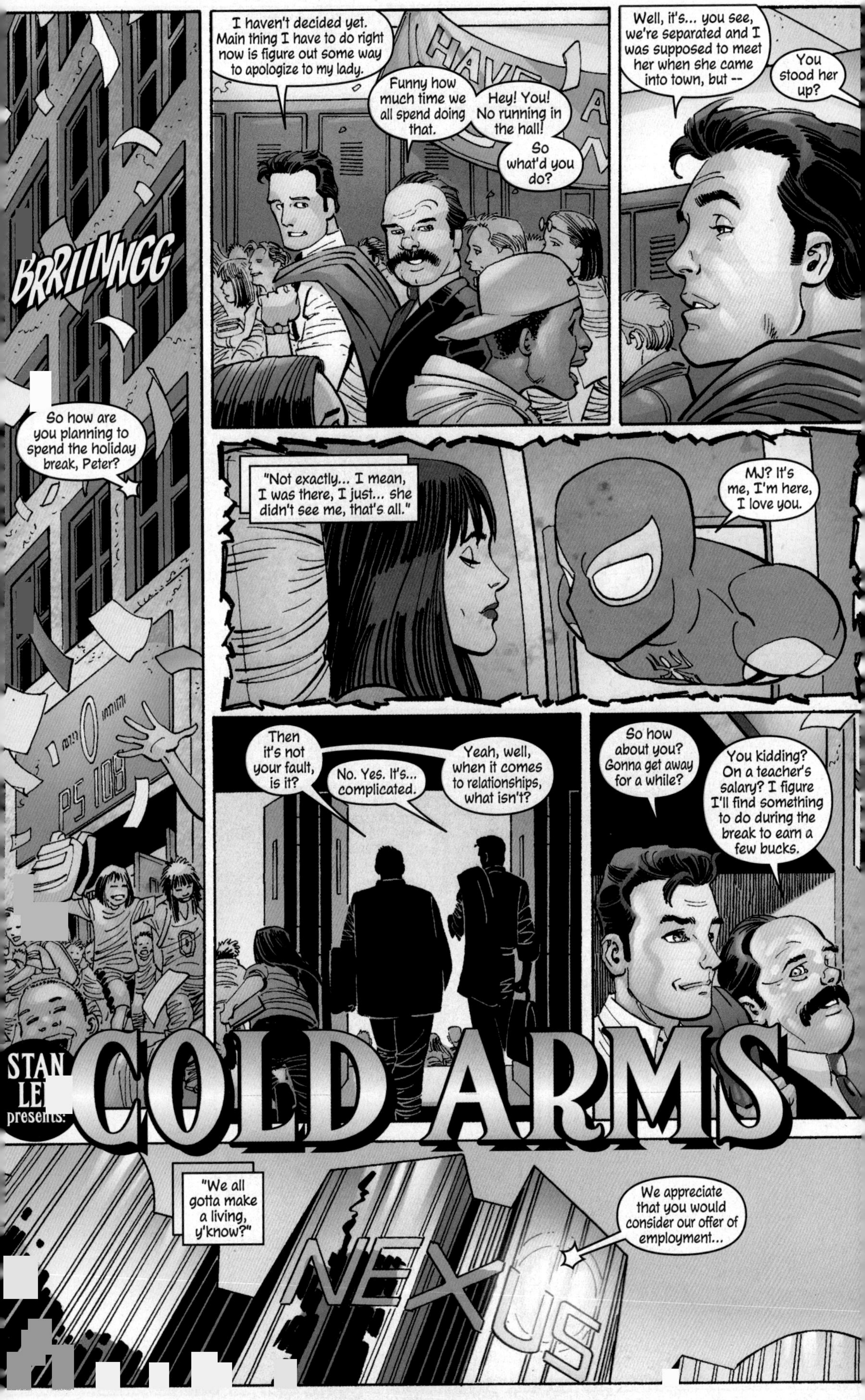
BRRIINNGG
So how are you planning to spend the holiday break, Peter?
I haven't decided yet. Main thing I have to do right now is figure out some way to apologize to my lady.
Funny how much time we all spend doing that.
Hey! You! No running in the hall!
So what'd you do?
Well, it's... you see, we're separated and I was supposed to meet her when she came into town, but --
You stood her up?
"Not exactly... I mean, I was there, I just... she didn't see me, that's all."
MJ? It's me, I'm here, I love you.
Then it's not your fault, is it?
No. Yes. It's... complicated.
Yeah, well, when it comes to relationships, what isn't?
So how about you? Gonna get away for a while?
You kidding? On a teacher's salary? I figure I'll find something to do during the break to earn a few bucks.
PS 108
STAN LEE presents:
COLD ARMS
"We all gotta make a living, y'know?"
We appreciate that you would consider our offer of employment...
NEXUS

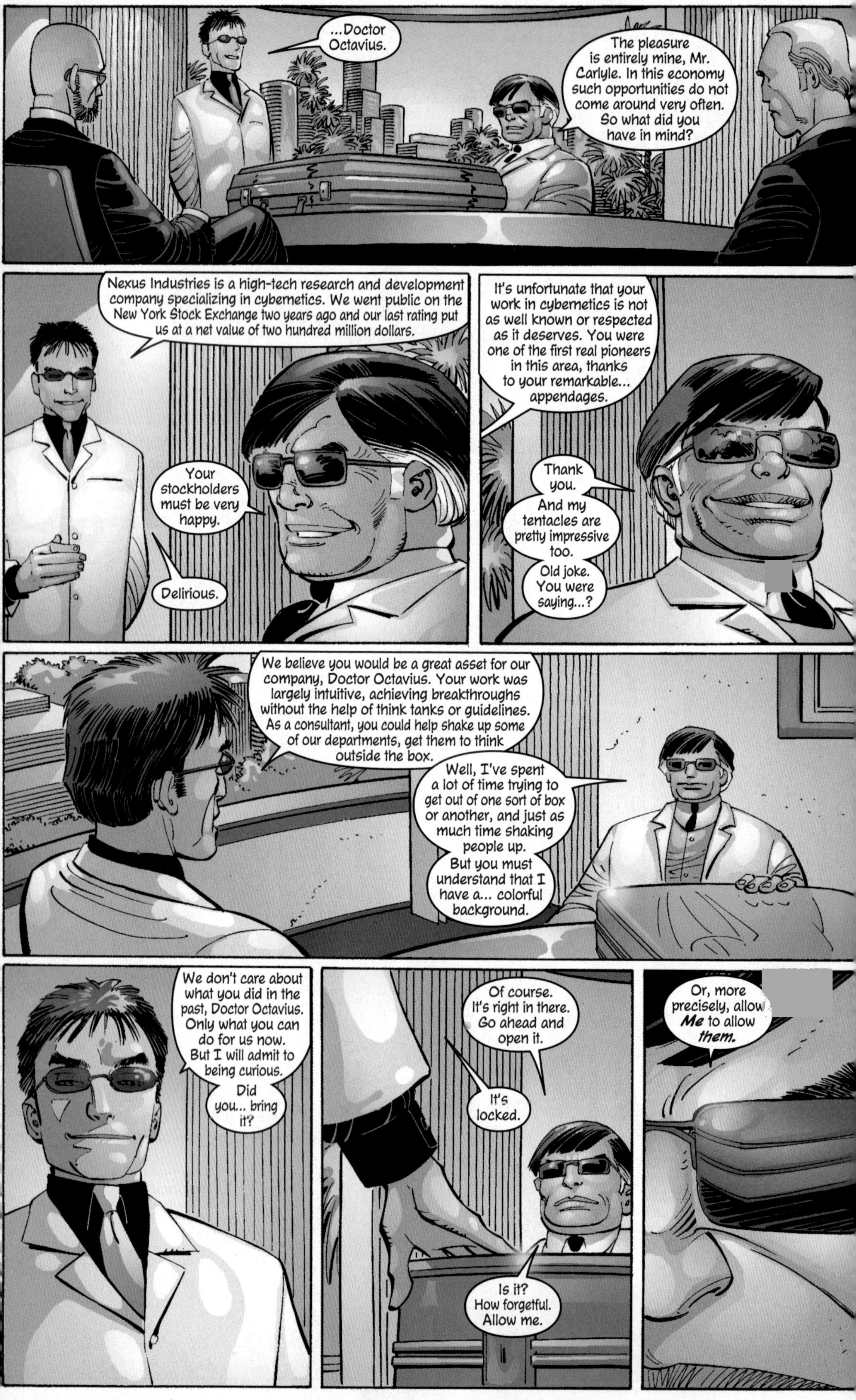

...Doctor Octavius.
The pleasure is entirely mine, Mr. Carlyle. In this economy such opportunities do not come around very often. So what did you have in mind?
Nexus Industries is a high-tech research and development company specializing in cybernetics. We went public on the New York Stock Exchange two years ago and our last rating put us at a net value of two hundred million dollars.
Your stockholders must be very happy.
Delirious.
It's unfortunate that your work in cybernetics is not as well known or respected as it deserves. You were one of the first real pioneers in this area, thanks to your remarkable... appendages.
Thank you.
And my tentacles are pretty impressive too.
Old joke. You were saying...?
We believe you would be a great asset for our company, Doctor Octavius. Your work was largely intuitive, achieving breakthroughs without the help of think tanks or guidelines. As a consultant, you could help shake up some of our departments, get them to think outside the box.
Well, I've spent a lot of time trying to get out of one sort of box or another, and just as much time shaking people up.
But you must understand that I have a... colorful background.
We don't care about what you did in the past, Doctor Octavius. Only what you can do for us now.
But I will admit to being curious.
Did you... bring it?
Of course. It's right in there. Go ahead and open it.
It's locked.
Is it? How forgetful. Allow me.
Or, more precisely, allow *Me* to allow *them.*

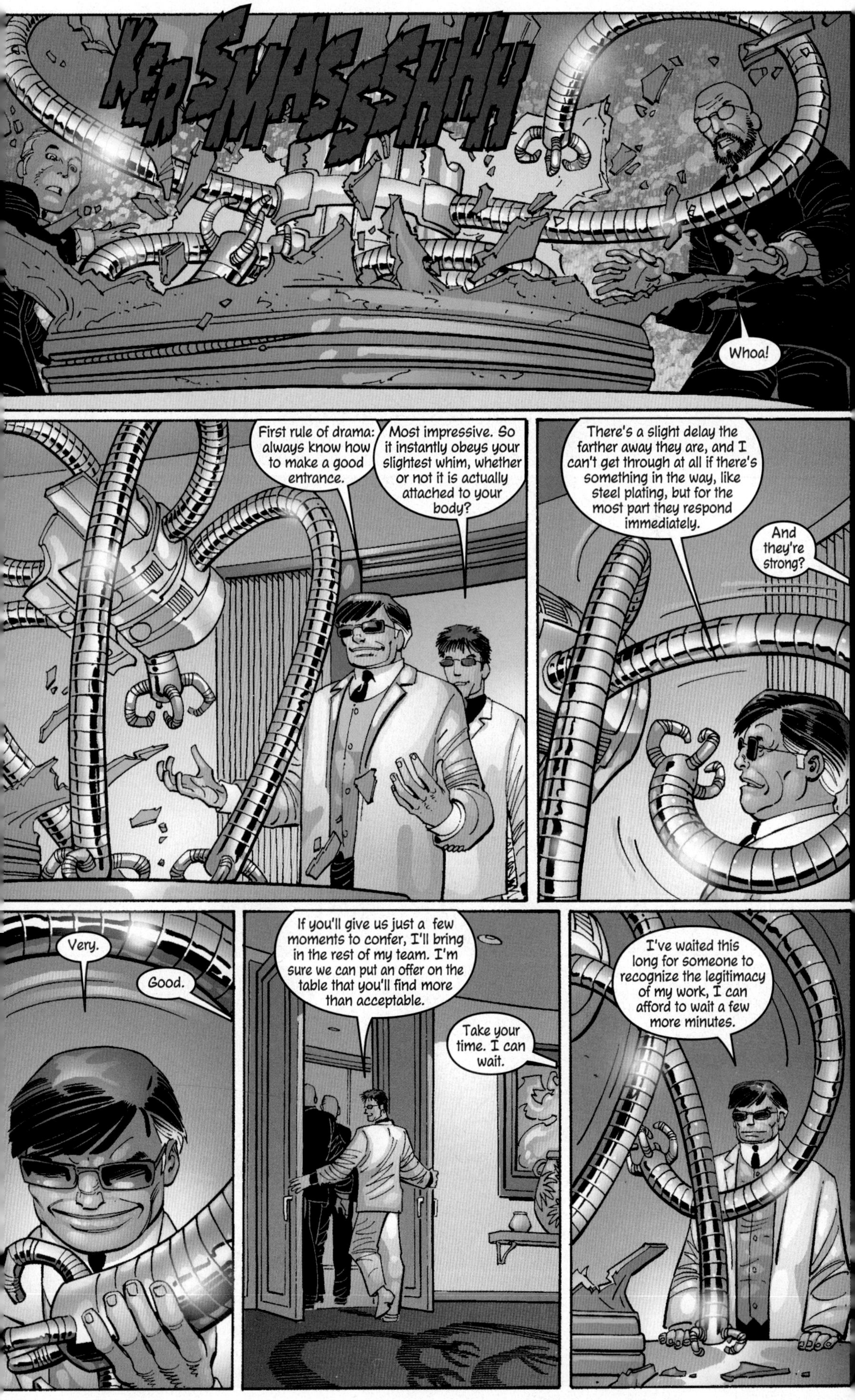
KERSMASSSHHH
Whoa!
First rule of drama: always know how to make a good entrance.
Most impressive. So it instantly obeys your slightest whim, whether or not it is actually attached to your body?
There's a slight delay the farther away they are, and I can't get through at all if there's something in the way, like steel plating, but for the most part they respond immediately.
And they're strong?
Very.
Good.
If you'll give us just a few moments to confer, I'll bring in the rest of my team. I'm sure we can put an offer on the table that you'll find more than acceptable.
Take your time. I can wait.
I've waited this long for someone to recognize the legitimacy of my work, I can afford to wait a few more minutes.

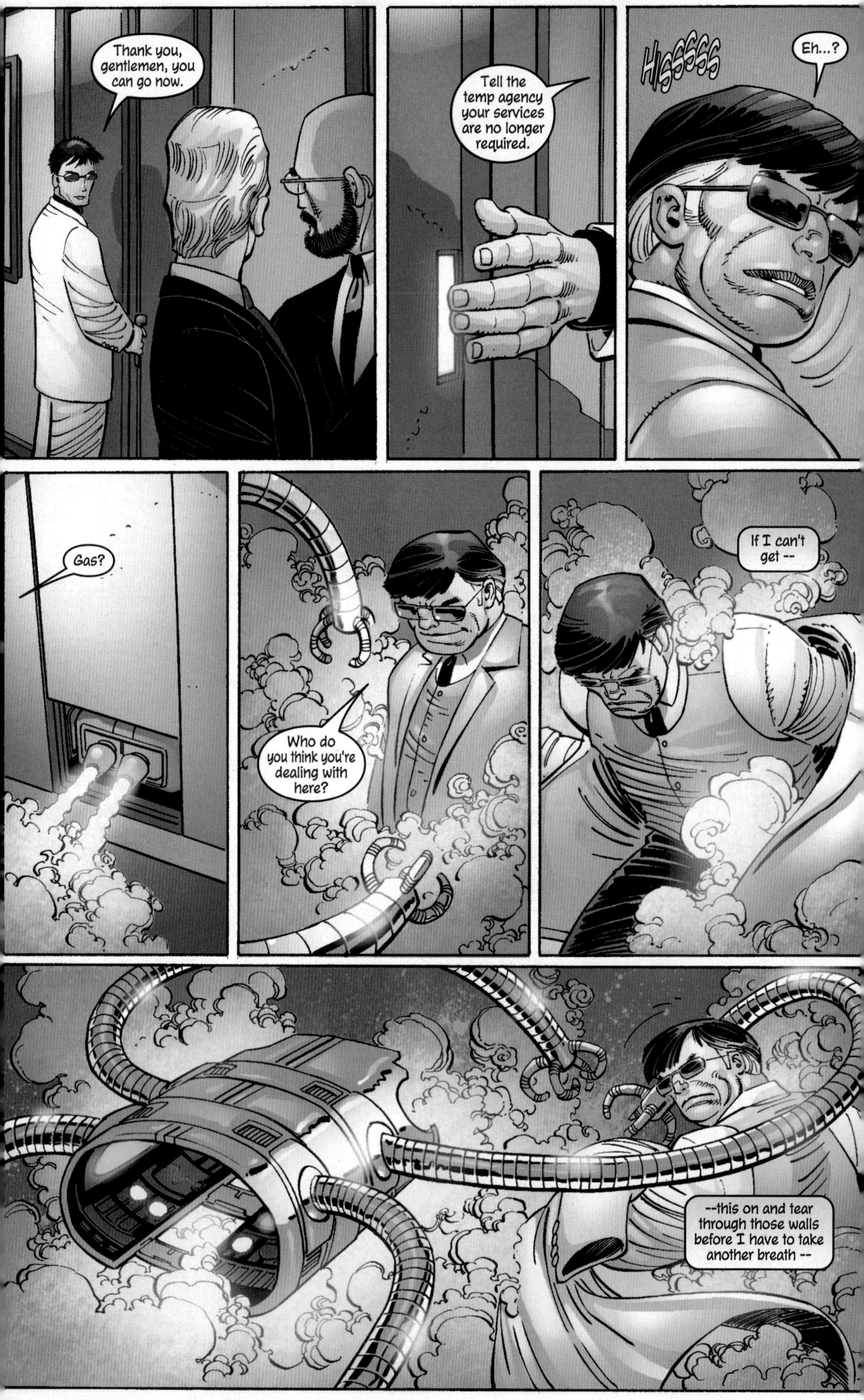
Thank you, gentlemen, you can go now.
Tell the temp agency your services are no longer required.
HISSSSS
Eh...?
Gas?
Who do you think you're dealing with here?
If I can't get --
--this on and tear through those walls before I have to take another breath --

SHUNNNK

--I don't deserve the name --

--of Doctor Octavius.

Wood against tempered steel. This isn't even a contest.

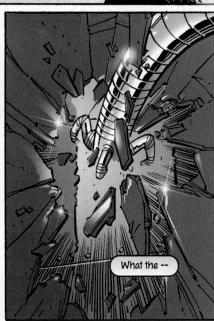

What the --

No --

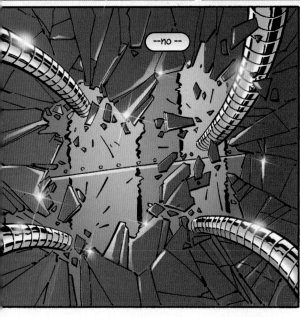

--no --

...no...

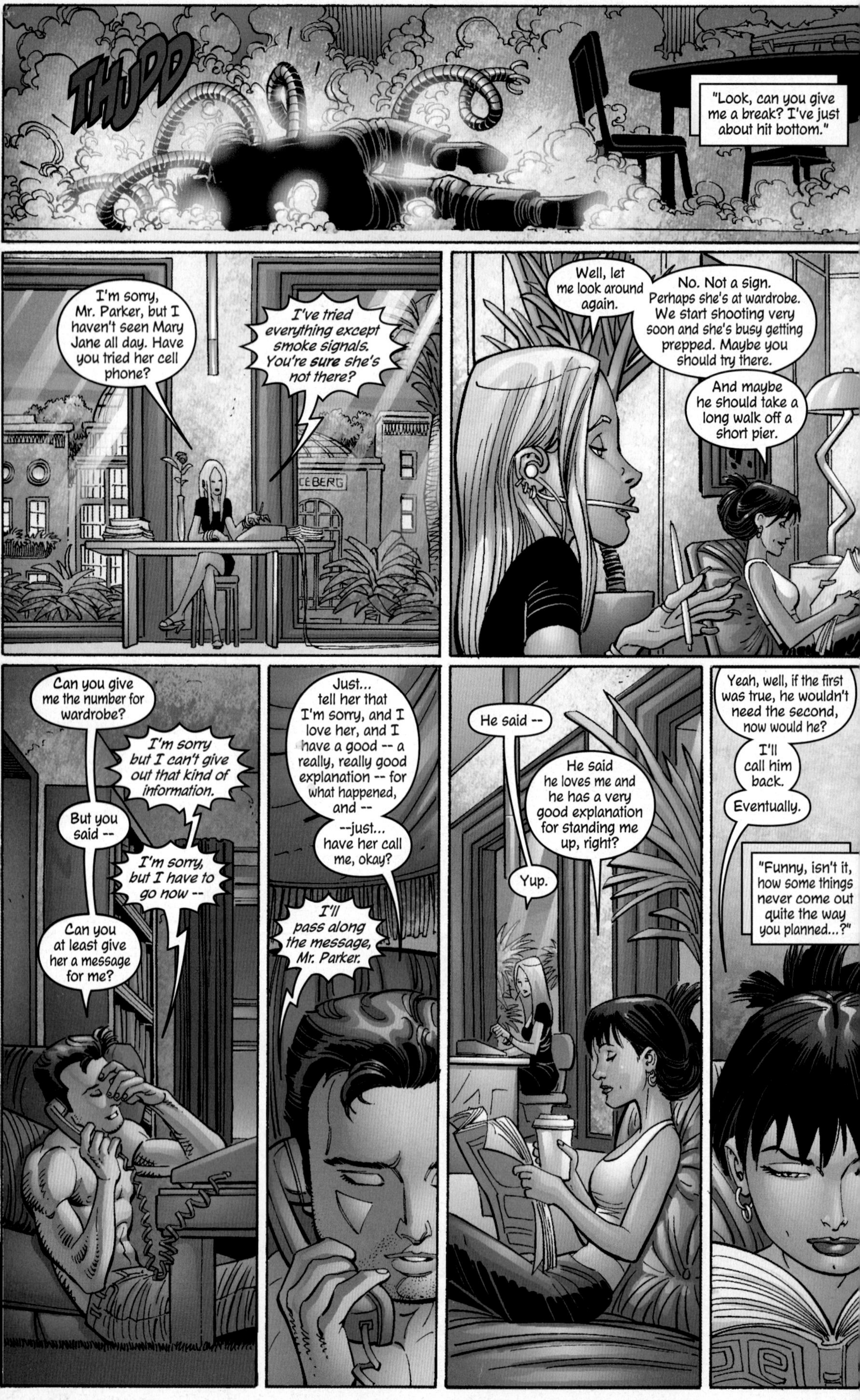

THUDD
"Look, can you give me a break? I've just about hit bottom."
I'm sorry, Mr. Parker, but I haven't seen Mary Jane all day. Have you tried her cell phone?
I've tried everything except smoke signals. You're sure she's not there?
CEBERG
Well, let me look around again.
No. Not a sign. Perhaps she's at wardrobe. We start shooting very soon and she's busy getting prepped. Maybe you should try there.
And maybe he should take a long walk off a short pier.
Can you give me the number for wardrobe?
I'm sorry but I can't give out that kind of information.
But you said --
I'm sorry, but I have to go now --
Can you at least give her a message for me?
Just... tell her that I'm sorry, and I love her, and I have a good -- a really, really good explanation -- for what happened, and --
--just... have her call me, okay?
I'll pass along the message, Mr. Parker.
He said --
He said he loves me and he has a very good explanation for standing me up, right?
Yup.
Yeah, well, if the first was true, he wouldn't need the second, now would he?
I'll call him back.
Eventually.
"Funny, isn't it, how some things never come out quite the way you planned...?"

You came here five days ago hoping to be hired as a consultant. And a consultant you've been... just not in quite the way you had in mind.

Five... *Days?*

Actually, I thought it would take a lot longer to get the job done. But you hire the right people, you get the job done fast.

I'm just glad I won't be here when they try to cash the checks.

I don't... understand...

Of course not. Your mind is still cloudy from the drugs. And the news hasn't hit the networks yet. But since it'll come out any time now... no reason not to give you a preview.

"I came aboard Nexus because they needed someone to be the mouth, to help promote and advance the public image of the company, raise the value of the stocks.

"It's just good they needed someone in a hurry and didn't go as deep in their background checks as they should have gone.

"Thing is, nobody wants to give you money if they think you actually need it. Guys with flash only give money to guys with even more flash, because they know they'll get it back, with interest.

"So I made sure we had all the flash-and-dazzle anybody could ask for.

"Sometimes the money coming in even equaled the money going out. And sometimes it didn't. But those are the breaks, right? You gotta spend money to make money, right? Of course right.

"What did come in, went back out in acquisitions of other businesses. I even set up some dummy subsidiaries and financed them from inside the company, counting their assets as revenue to make the company look bigger and stronger on the stock market.

"And it worked.

"At least on paper.

"For a while.

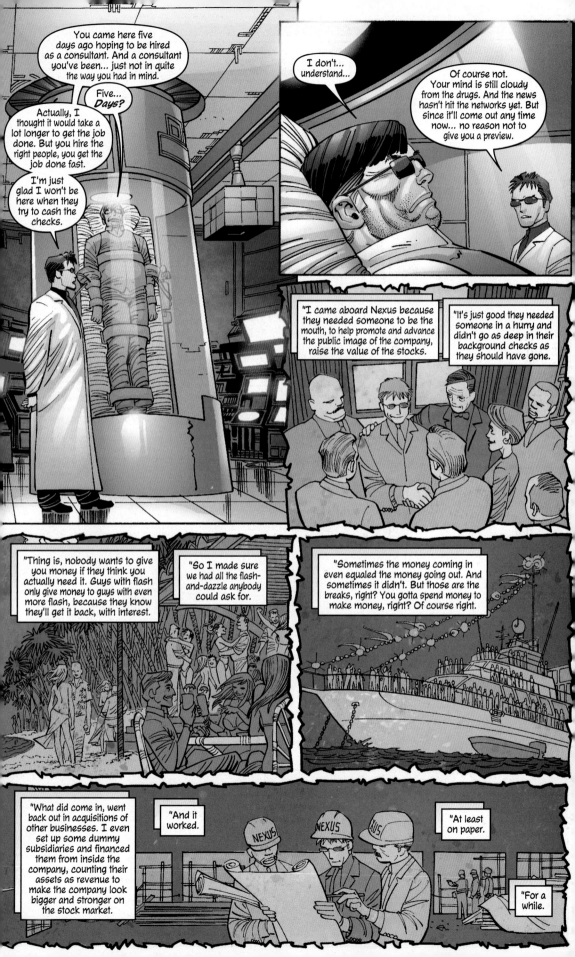

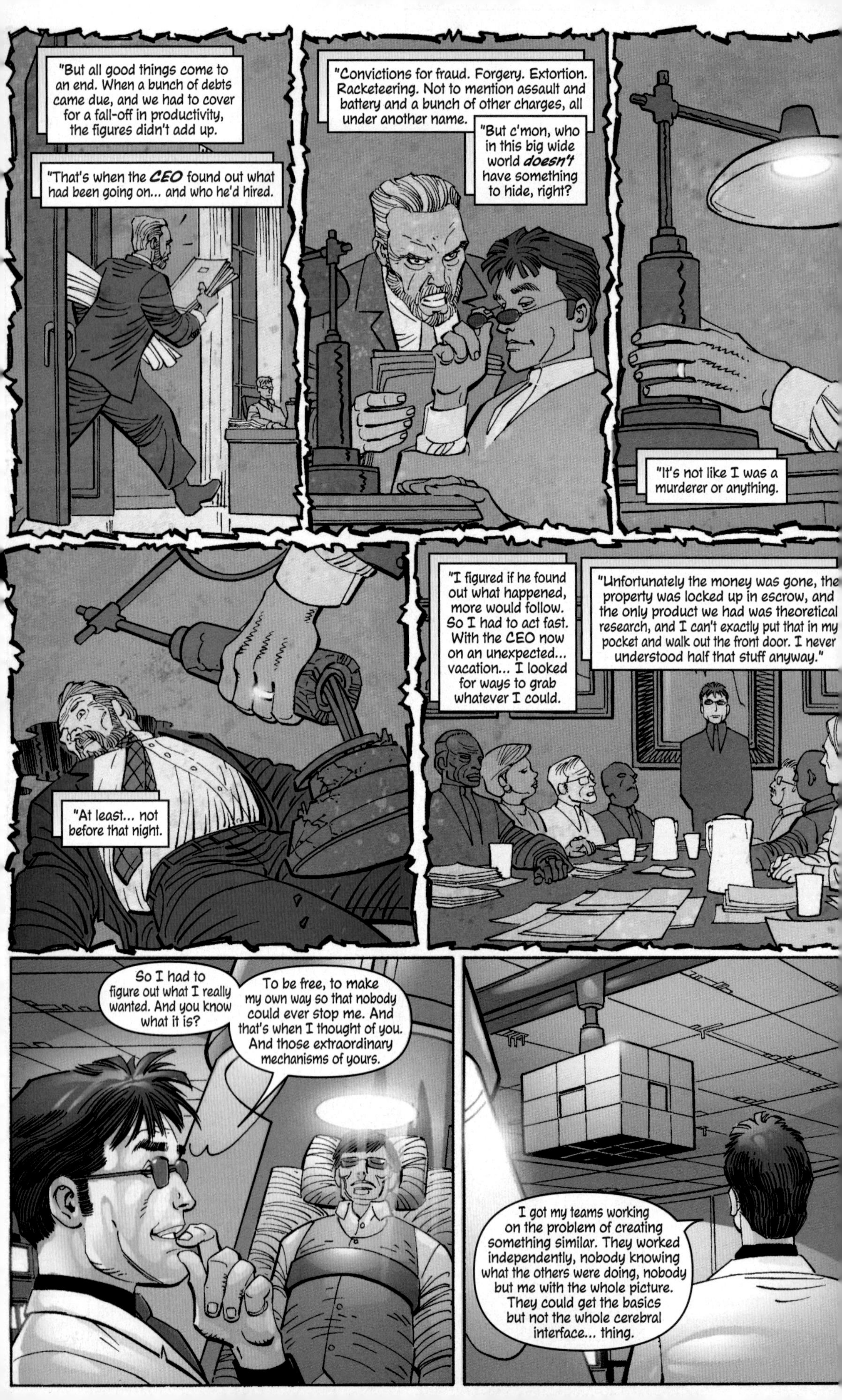
"But all good things come to an end. When a bunch of debts came due, and we had to cover for a fall-off in productivity, the figures didn't add up.
"That's when the CEO found out what had been going on... and who he'd hired.
"Convictions for fraud. Forgery. Extortion. Racketeering. Not to mention assault and battery and a bunch of other charges, all under another name.
"But c'mon, who in this big wide world doesn't have something to hide, right?
"It's not like I was a murderer or anything.
"At least... not before that night.
"I figured if he found out what happened, more would follow. So I had to act fast. With the CEO now on an unexpected... vacation... I looked for ways to grab whatever I could.
"Unfortunately the money was gone, the property was locked up in escrow, and the only product we had was theoretical research, and I can't exactly put that in my pocket and walk out the front door. I never understood half that stuff anyway."
So I had to figure out what I really wanted. And you know what it is?
To be free, to make my own way so that nobody could ever stop me. And that's when I thought of you. And those extraordinary mechanisms of yours.
I got my teams working on the problem of creating something similar. They worked independently, nobody knowing what the others were doing, nobody but me with the whole picture. They could get the basics but not the whole cerebral interface... thing.

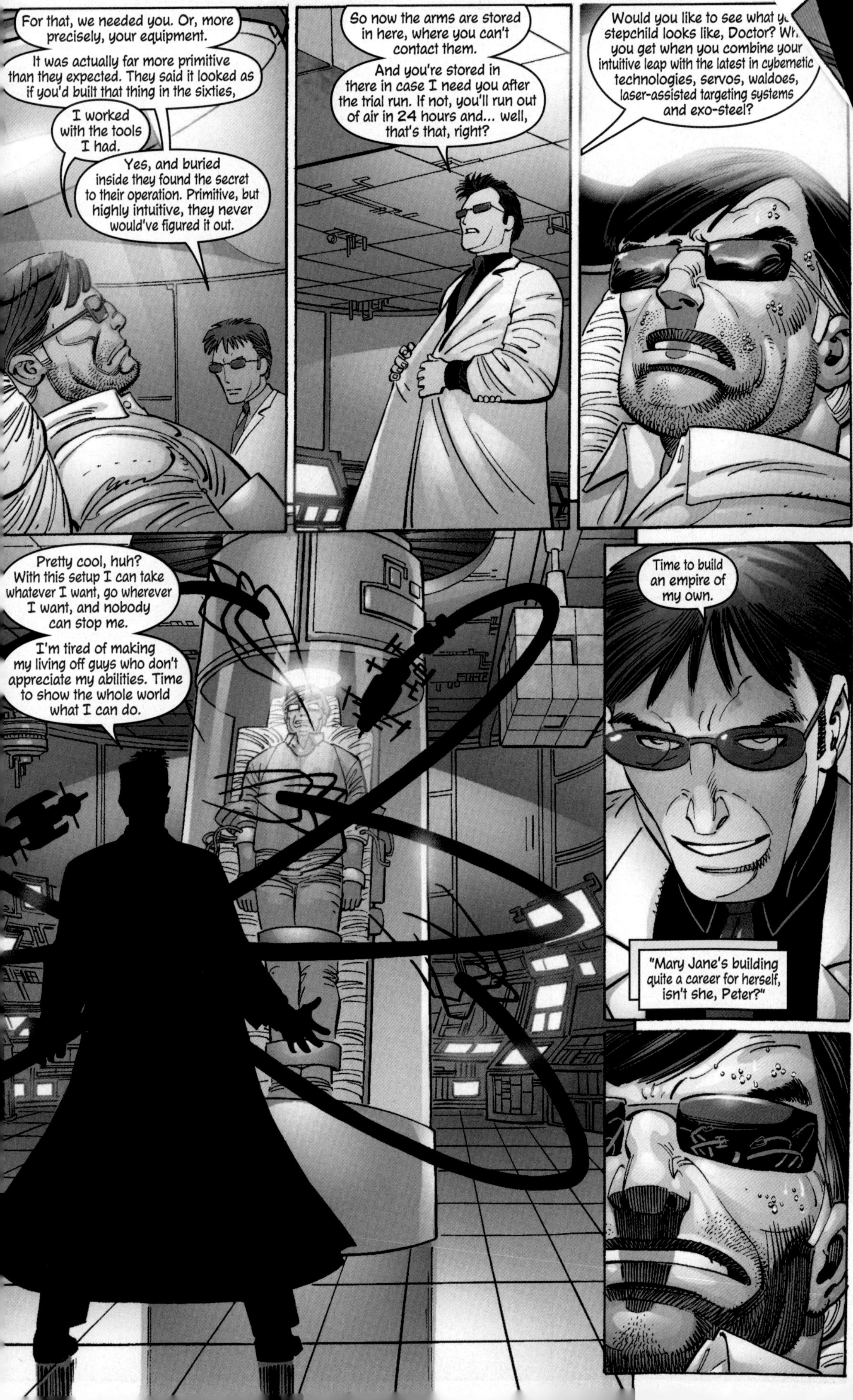
For that, we needed you. Or, more precisely, your equipment.
It was actually far more primitive than they expected. They said it looked as if you'd built that thing in the sixties,
I worked with the tools I had.
Yes, and buried inside they found the secret to their operation. Primitive, but highly intuitive, they never would've figured it out.
So now the arms are stored in here, where you can't contact them.
And you're stored in there in case I need you after the trial run. If not, you'll run out of air in 24 hours and... well, that's that, right?
Would you like to see what yo stepchild looks like, Doctor? Wh you get when you combine your intuitive leap with the latest in cybernetic technologies, servos, waldoes, laser-assisted targeting systems and exo-steel?
Pretty cool, huh? With this setup I can take whatever I want, go wherever I want, and nobody can stop me.
I'm tired of making my living off guys who don't appreciate my abilities. Time to show the whole world what I can do.
Time to build an empire of my own.
"Mary Jane's building quite a career for herself, isn't she, Peter?"

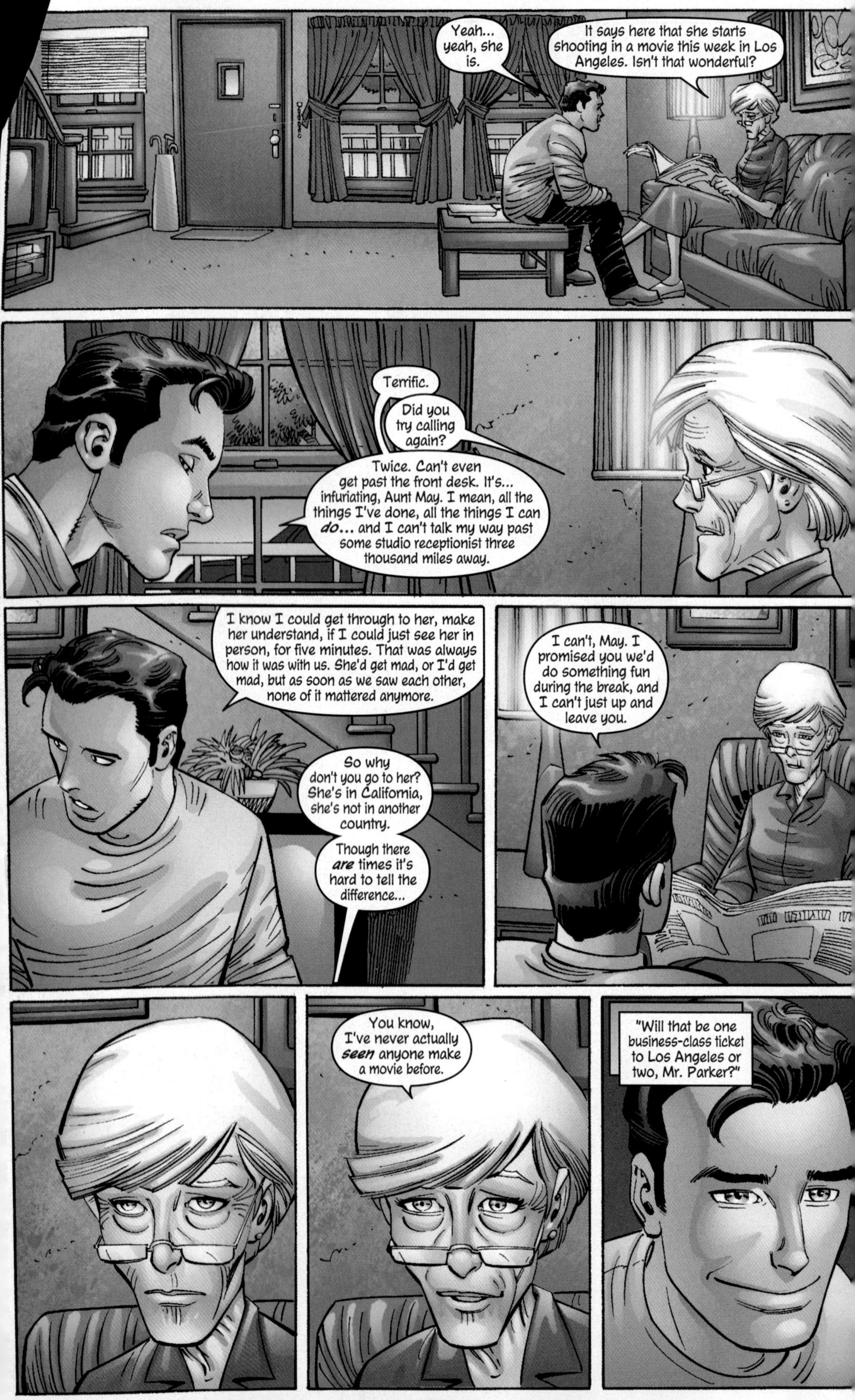
Yeah... yeah, she is.
It says here that she starts shooting in a movie this week in Los Angeles. Isn't that wonderful?
Terrific.
Did you try calling again?
Twice. Can't even get past the front desk. It's... infuriating, Aunt May. I mean, all the things I've done, all the things I can *do...* and I can't talk my way past some studio receptionist three thousand miles away.
I know I could get through to her, make her understand, if I could just see her in person, for five minutes. That was always how it was with us. She'd get mad, or I'd get mad, but as soon as we saw each other, none of it mattered anymore.
So why don't you go to her? She's in California, she's not in another country.
Though there *are* times it's hard to tell the difference...
I can't, May. I promised you we'd do something fun during the break, and I can't just up and leave you.
You know, I've never actually *seen* anyone make a movie before.
"Will that be one business-class ticket to Los Angeles or two, Mr. Parker?"

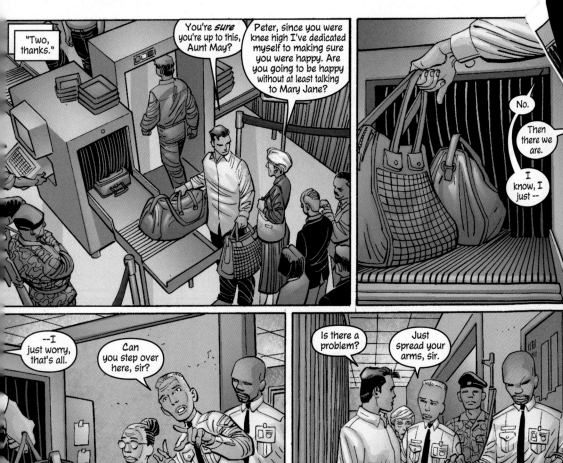

"Two, thanks."

You're **sure** you're up to this, Aunt May?

Peter, since you were knee high I've dedicated myself to making sure you were happy. Are you going to be happy without at least talking to Mary Jane?

No.

Then there we are.

I know, I just --

--I just worry, that's all.

Can you step over here, sir?

Is there a problem?

Just spread your arms, sir.

I can open that for you --

Please don't move, sir.

Long-johns. I get chills.

Ever since he was a little boy.

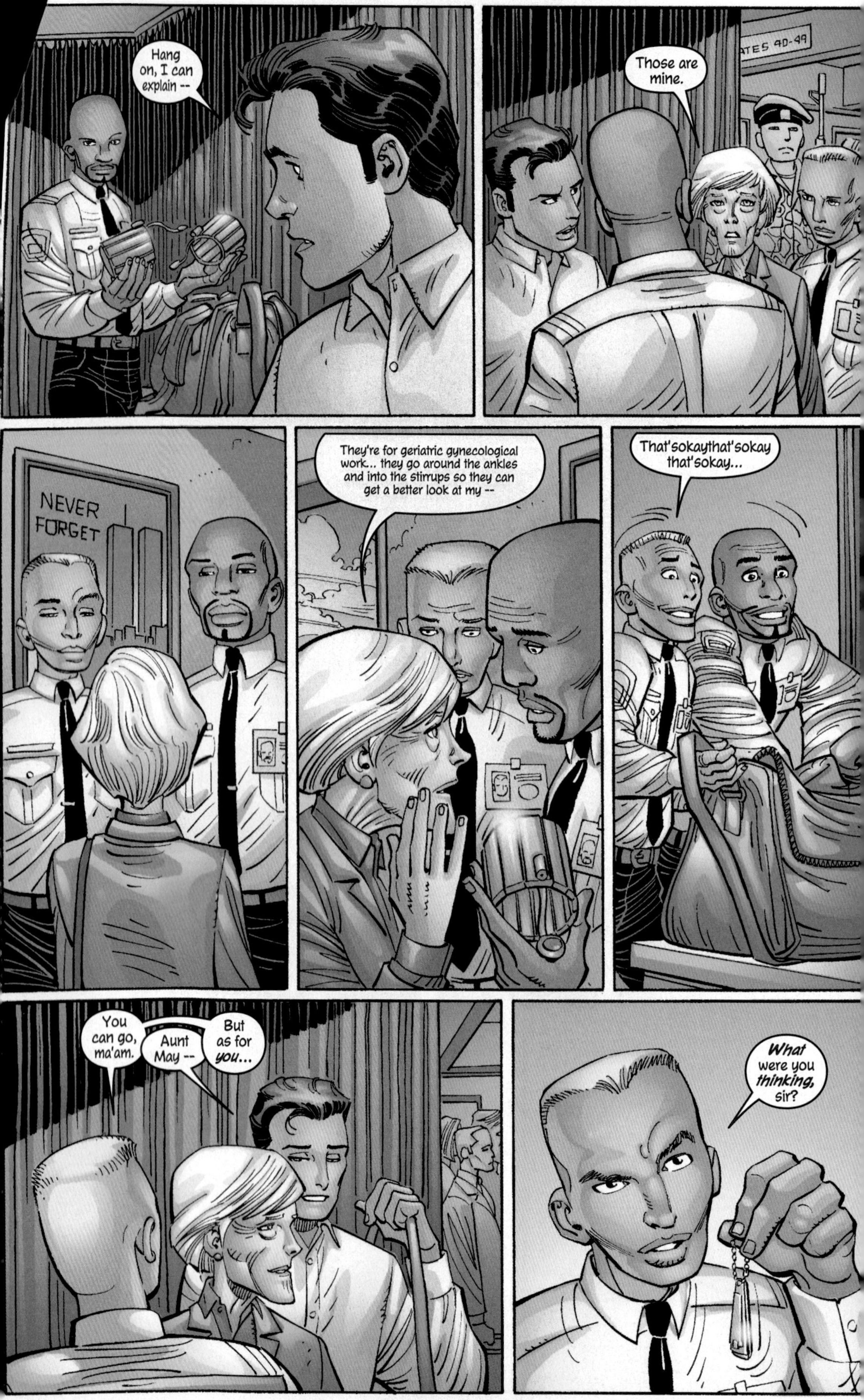

Hang on, I can explain --
Those are mine.
ATES 40-49
NEVER FORGET
They're for geriatric gynecological work... they go around the ankles and into the stirrups so they can get a better look at my --
That'sokaythat'sokay that'sokay...
You can go, ma'am.
Aunt May --
But as for *you...*
What were you ***thinking,*** sir?

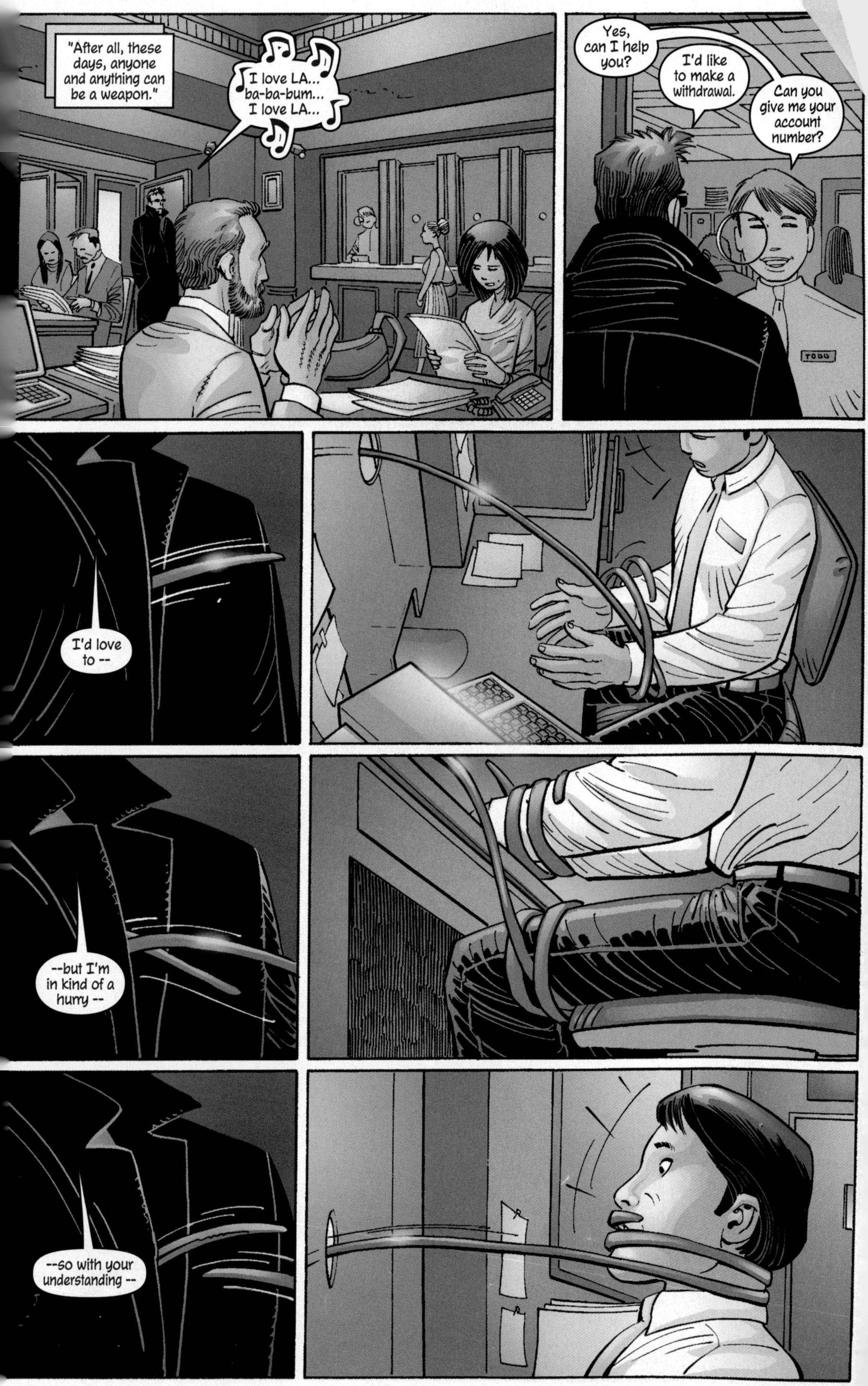
"After all, these days, anyone and anything can be a weapon."
I love LA... ba-ba-bum... I love LA...
Yes, can I help you?
I'd like to make a withdrawal.
Can you give me your account number?
TODD
I'd love to --
--but I'm in kind of a hurry --
--so with your understanding --

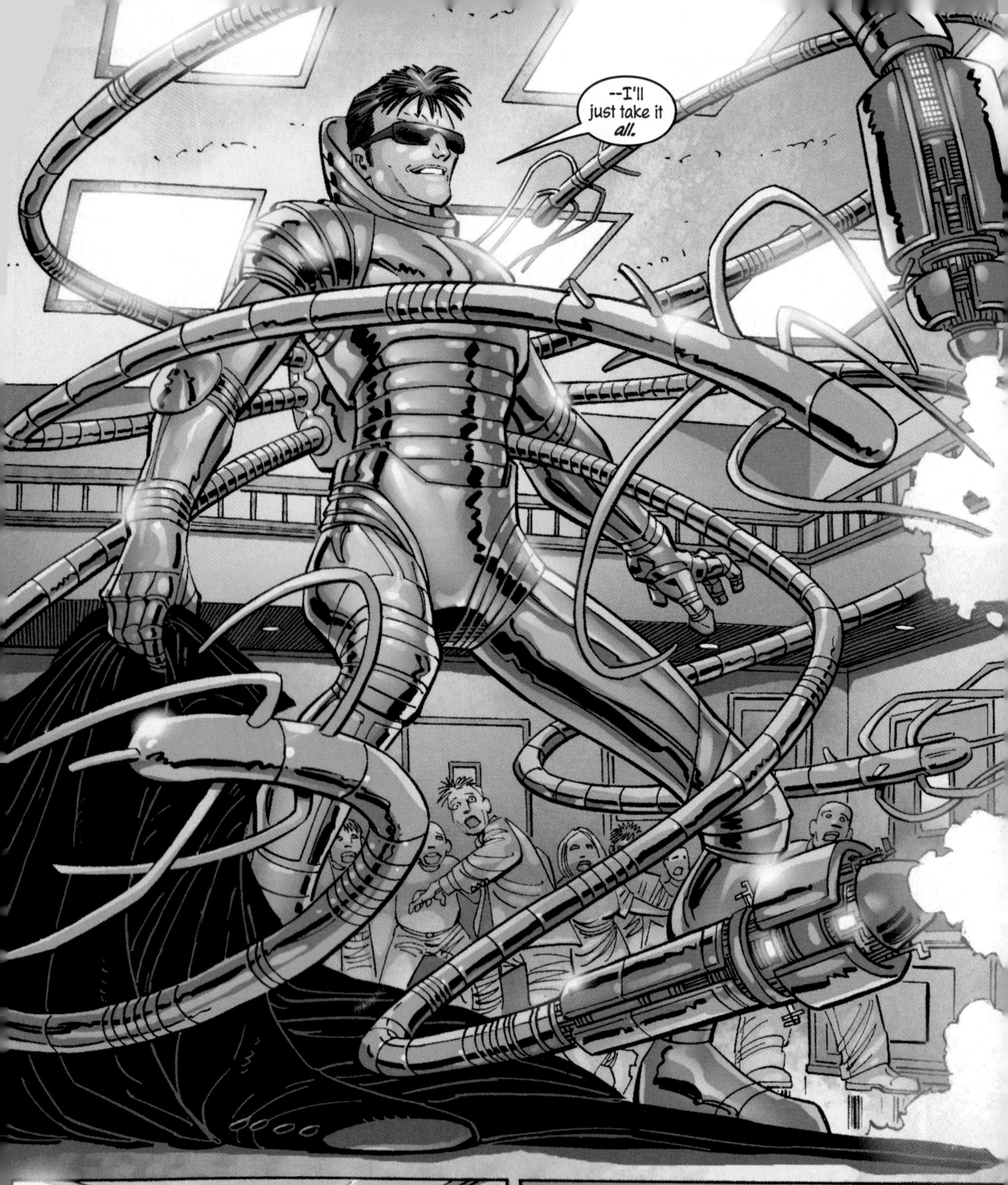
--I'll just take it *all.*

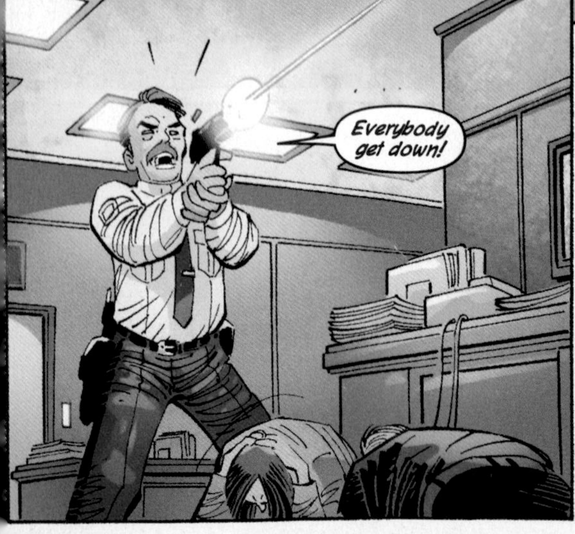
Everybody get down!

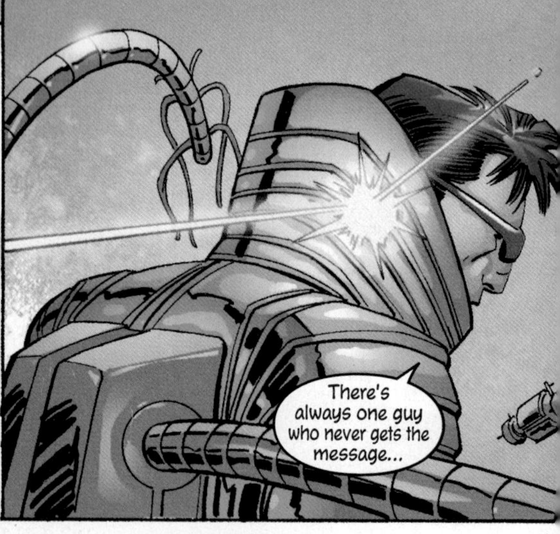
There's always one guy who never gets the message...

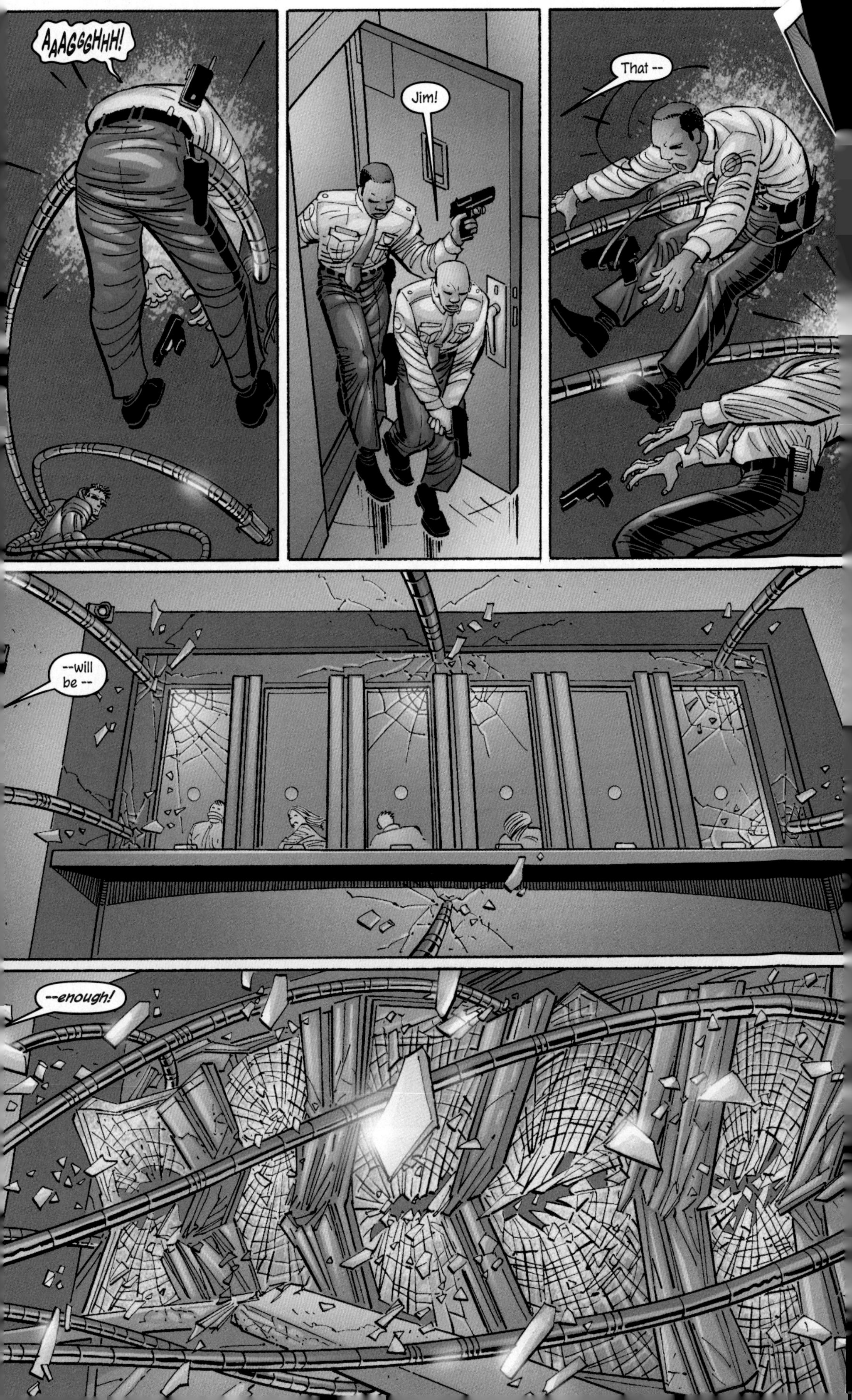

AAAGGGHHH!
Jim!
That --
--will be --
--enough!

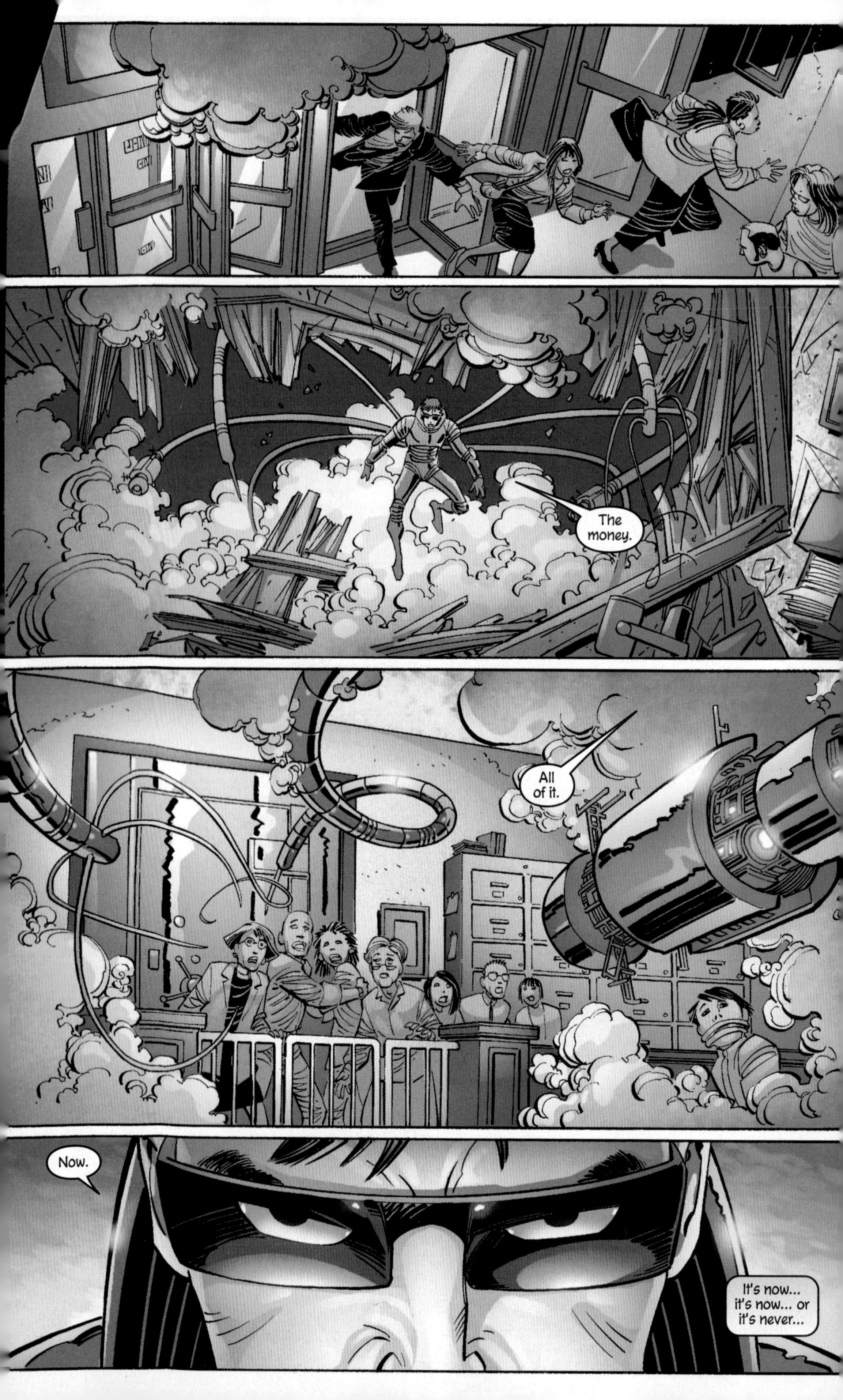
The money.
All of it.
Now.
It's now... it's now... or it's never...

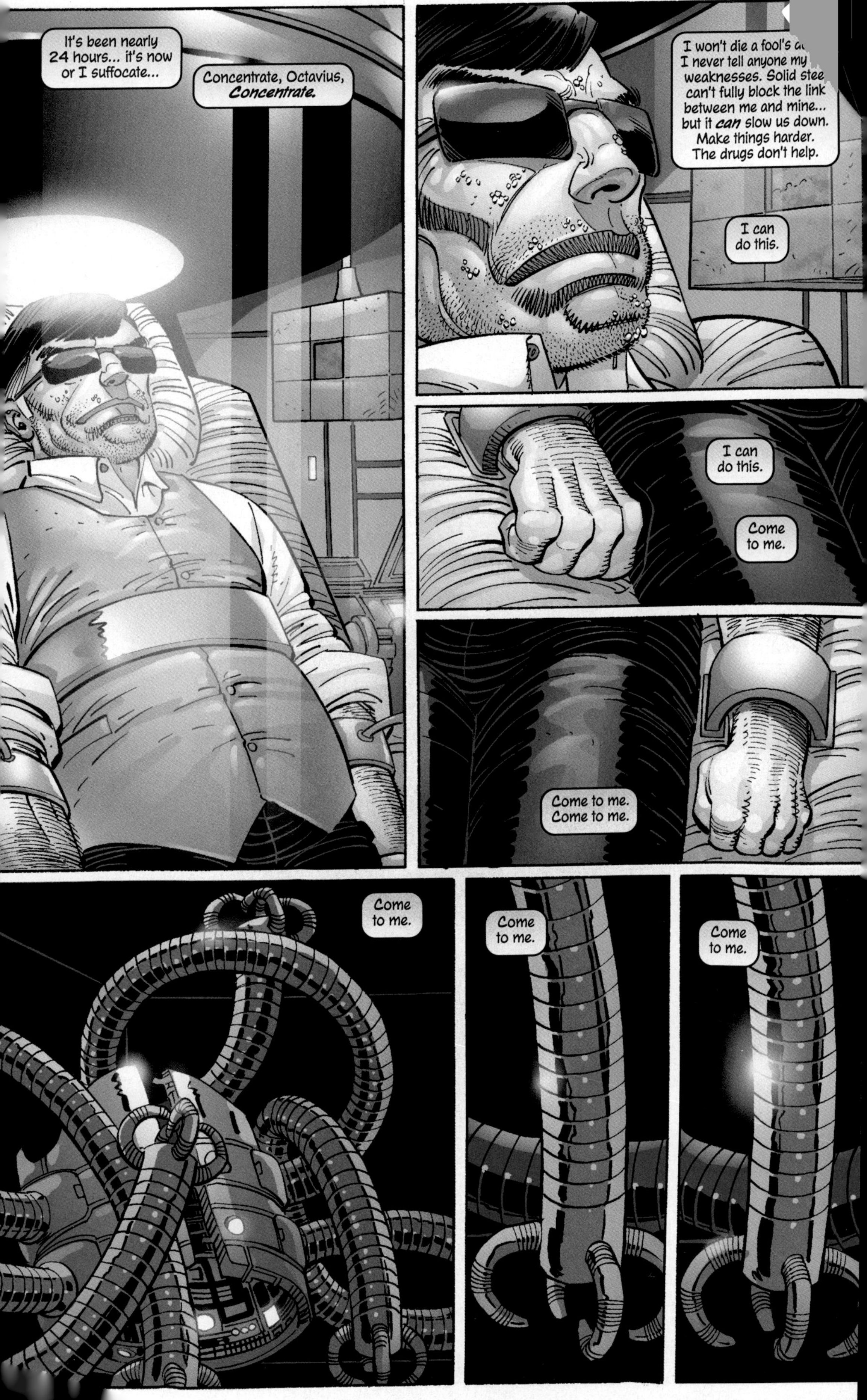

It's been nearly 24 hours... it's now or I suffocate...
Concentrate, Octavius, *Concentrate.*
I won't die a fool's
I never tell anyone my
weaknesses. Solid stee
can't fully block the link between me and mine... but it *can* slow us down. Make things harder. The drugs don't help.
I can do this.
I can do this.
Come to me.
Come to me. Come to me.
Come to me.
Come to me.
Come to me.

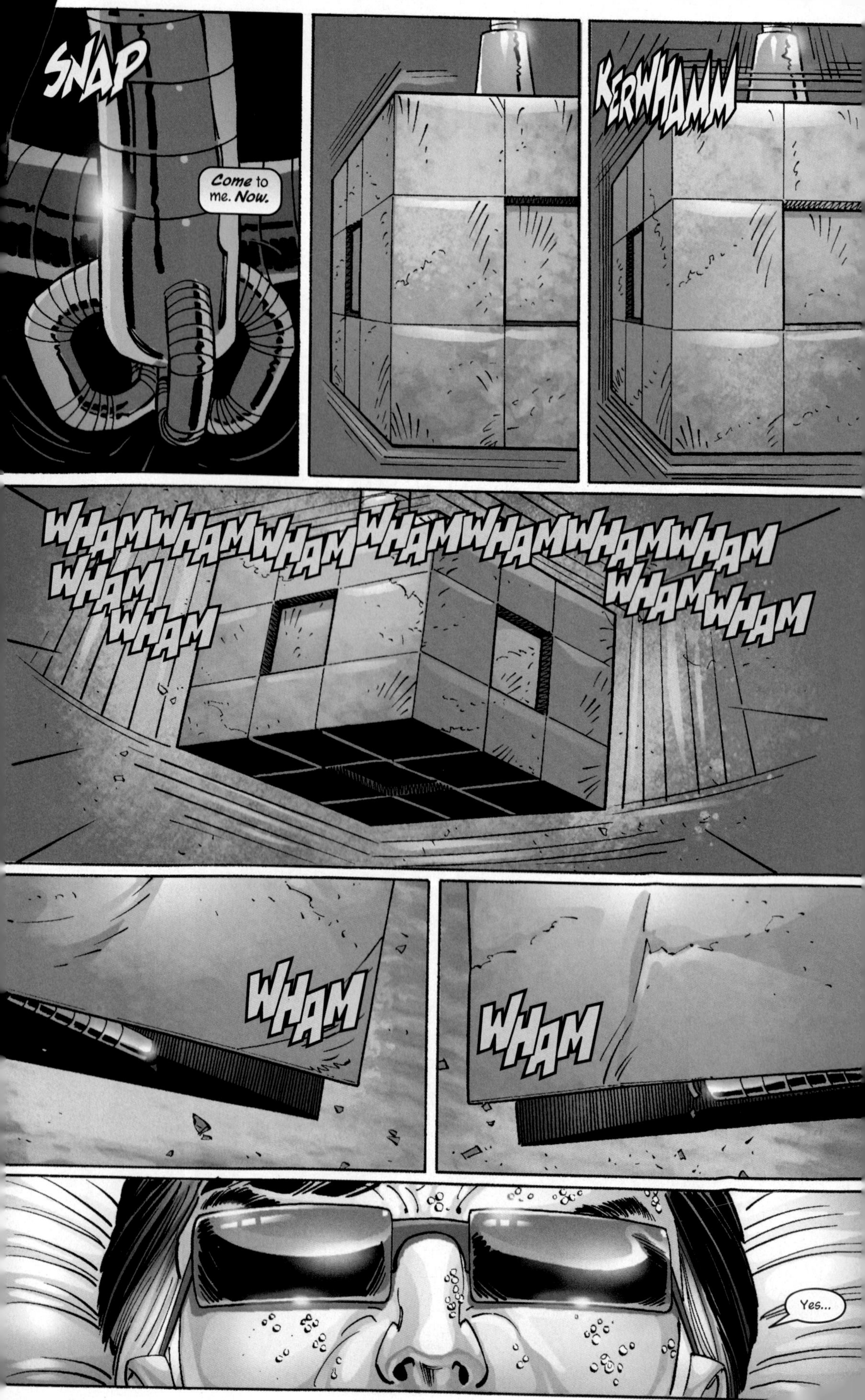
SNAP
Come to me. Now.
KERWHAMM
WHAMWHAMWHAMWHAMWHAMWHAMWHAM
WHAM
WHAM
WHAMWHAM
WHAM
WHAM
Yes...

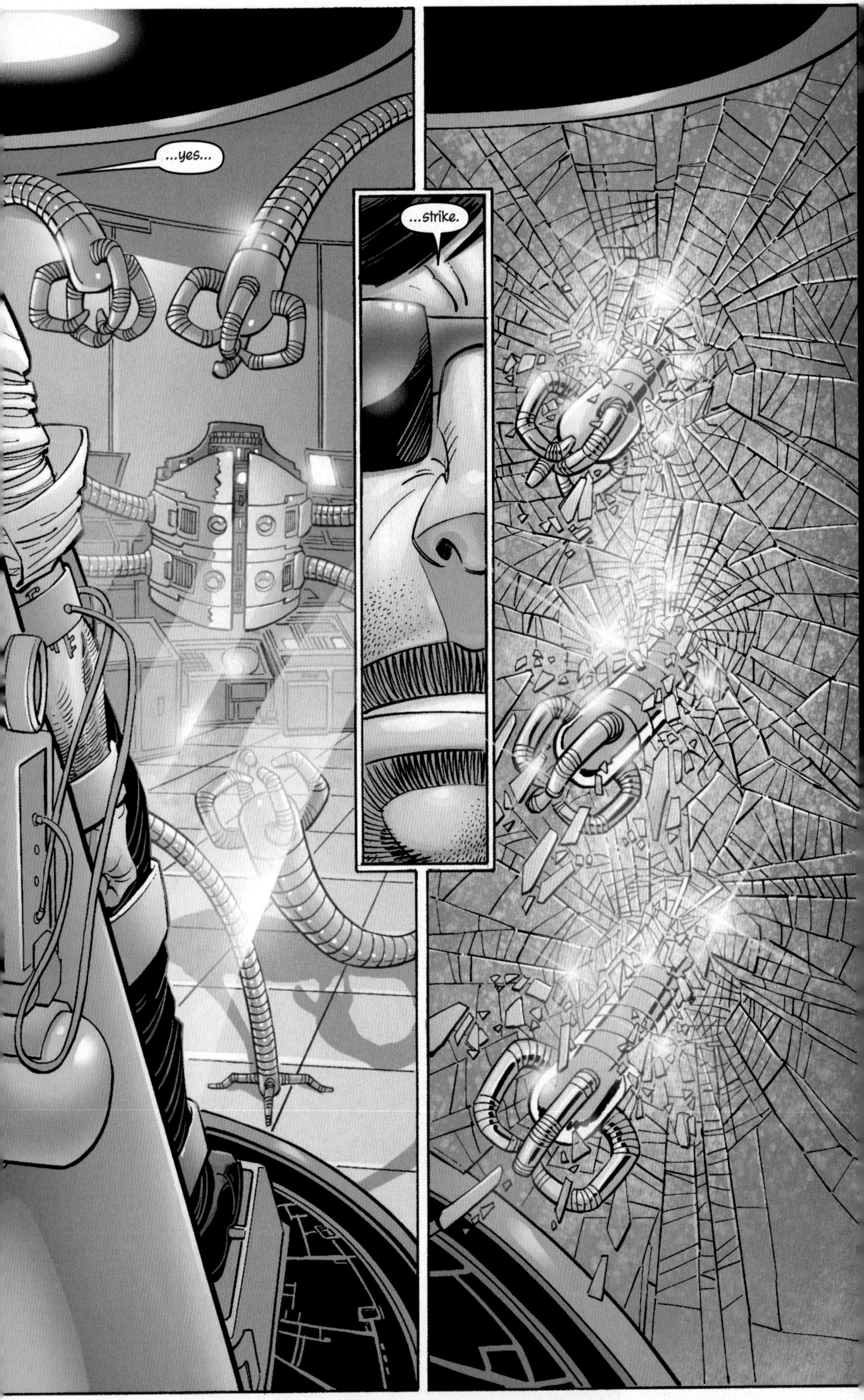
...yes...
...strike.

Too drugged to stand...

Take me away from here. Quickly.

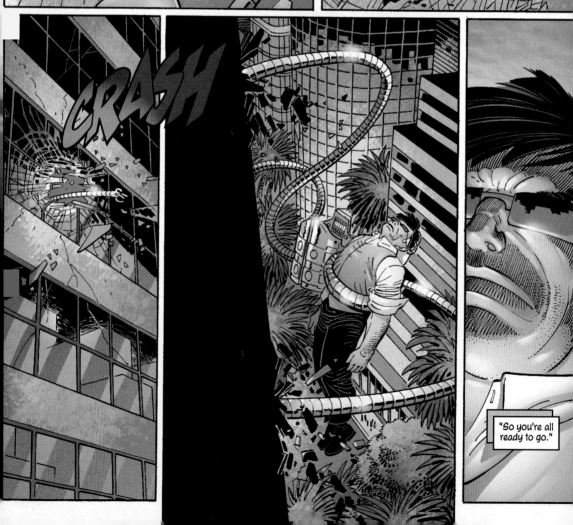

CRASH

"So you're all ready to go."

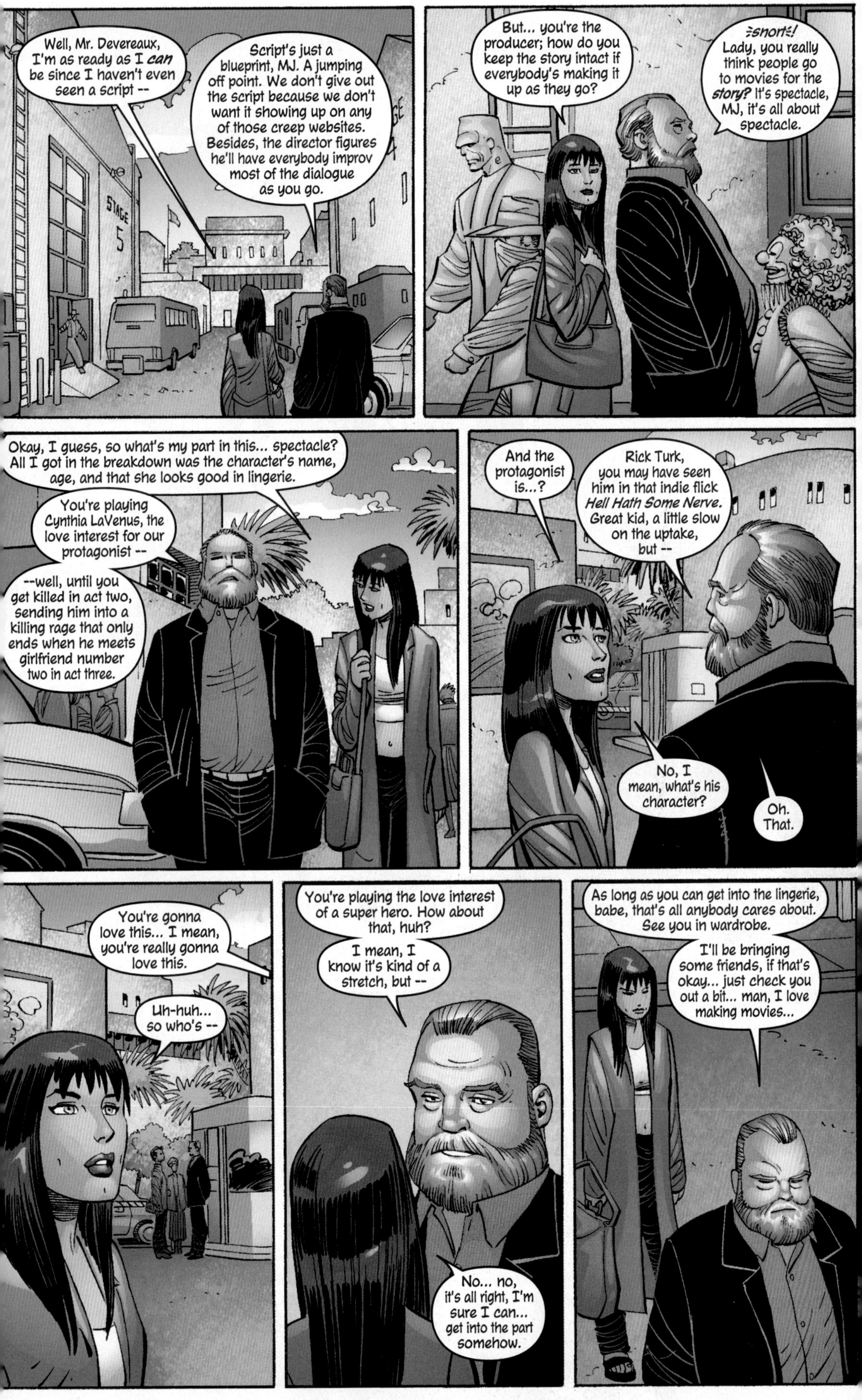

Well, Mr. Devereaux, I'm as ready as I *can* be since I haven't even seen a script --
Script's just a blueprint, MJ. A jumping off point. We don't give out the script because we don't want it showing up on any of those creep websites. Besides, the director figures he'll have everybody improv most of the dialogue as you go.
STAGE 5
But... you're the producer; how do you keep the story intact if everybody's making it up as they go?
snort!
Lady, you really think people go to movies for the ***story?*** It's spectacle, MJ, it's all about spectacle.
Okay, I guess, so what's my part in this... spectacle? All I got in the breakdown was the character's name, age, and that she looks good in lingerie.
You're playing Cynthia LaVenus, the love interest for our protagonist --
--well, until you get killed in act two, sending him into a killing rage that only ends when he meets girlfriend number two in act three.
And the protagonist is...?
Rick Turk, you may have seen him in that indie flick *Hell Hath Some Nerve.* Great kid, a little slow on the uptake, but --
No, I mean, what's his character?
Oh. That.
You're gonna love this... I mean, you're really gonna love this.
Uh-huh... so who's --
You're playing the love interest of a super hero. How about that, huh?
I mean, I know it's kind of a stretch, but --
No... no, it's all right, I'm sure I can... get into the part somehow.
As long as you can get into the lingerie, babe, that's all anybody cares about. See you in wardrobe.
I'll be bringing some friends, if that's okay... just check you out a bit... man, I love making movies...

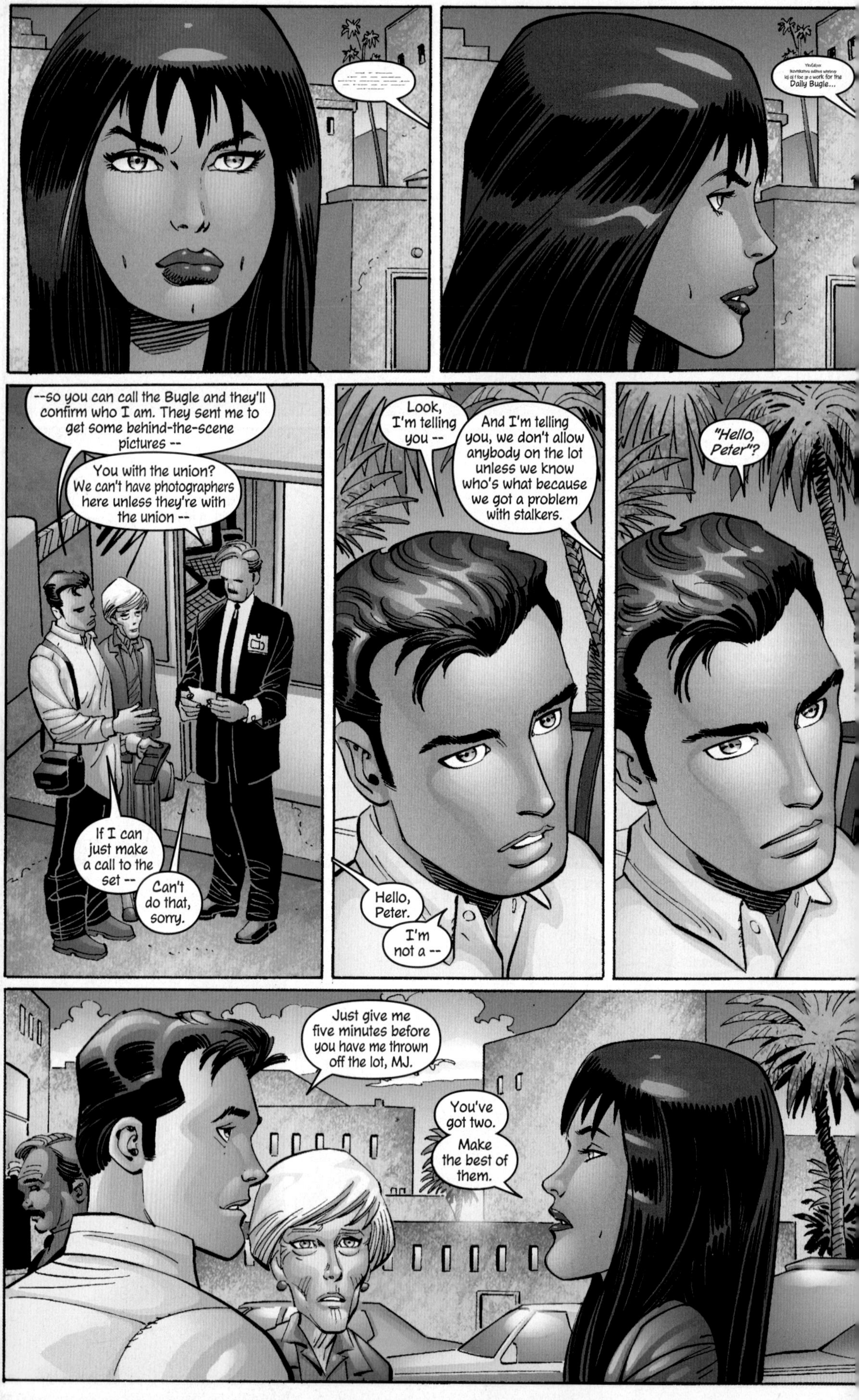

work for the Daily Bugle...
--so you can call the Bugle and they'll confirm who I am. They sent me to get some behind-the-scene pictures --
You with the union? We can't have photographers here unless they're with the union --
If I can just make a call to the set --
Can't do that, sorry.
Look, I'm telling you --
And I'm telling you, we don't allow anybody on the lot unless we know who's what because we got a problem with stalkers.
Hello, Peter.
I'm not a --
"Hello, Peter"?
Just give me five minutes before you have me thrown off the lot, MJ.
You've got two.
Make the best of them.

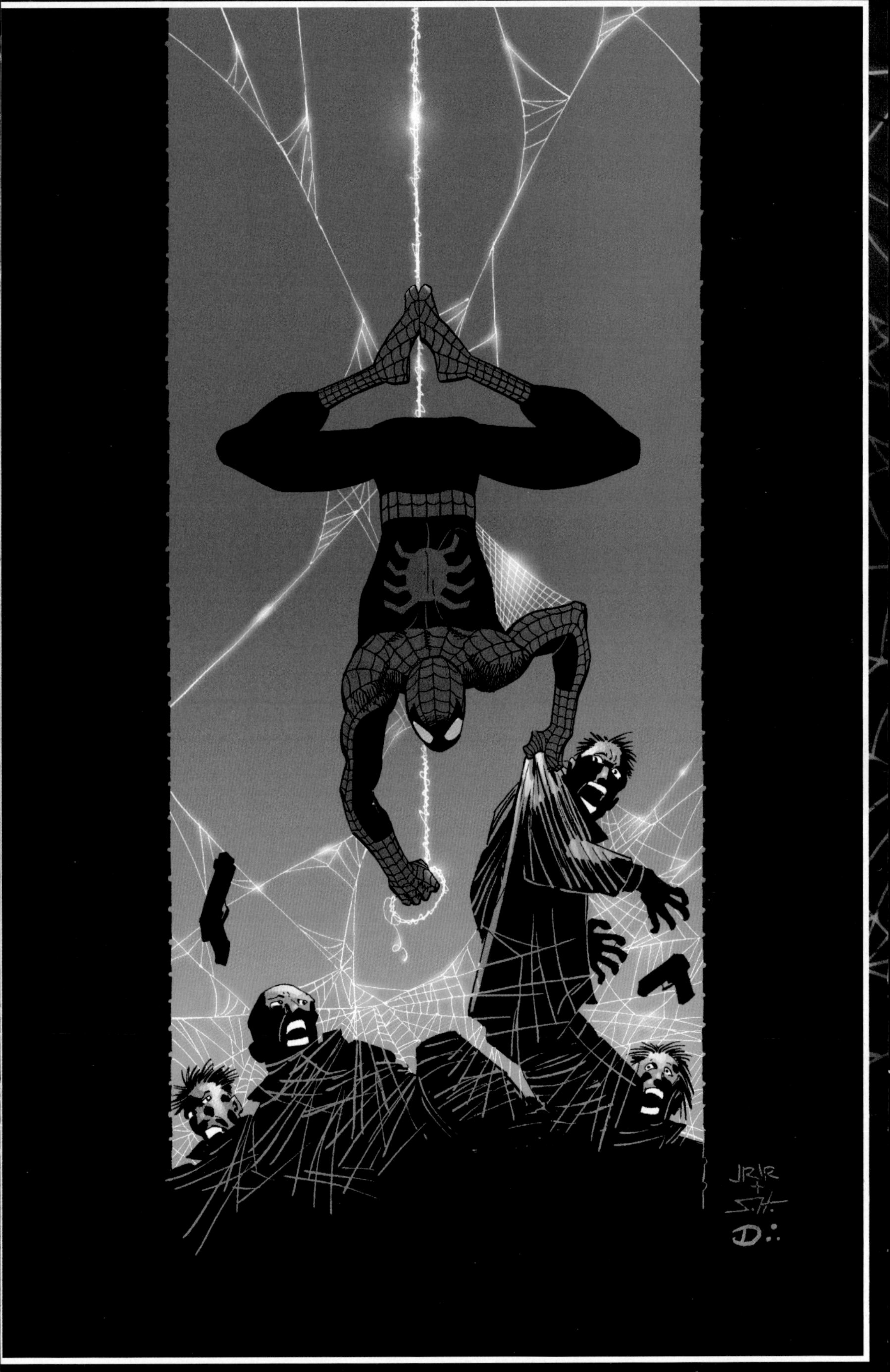

AMAZING SPIDER-MAN #44

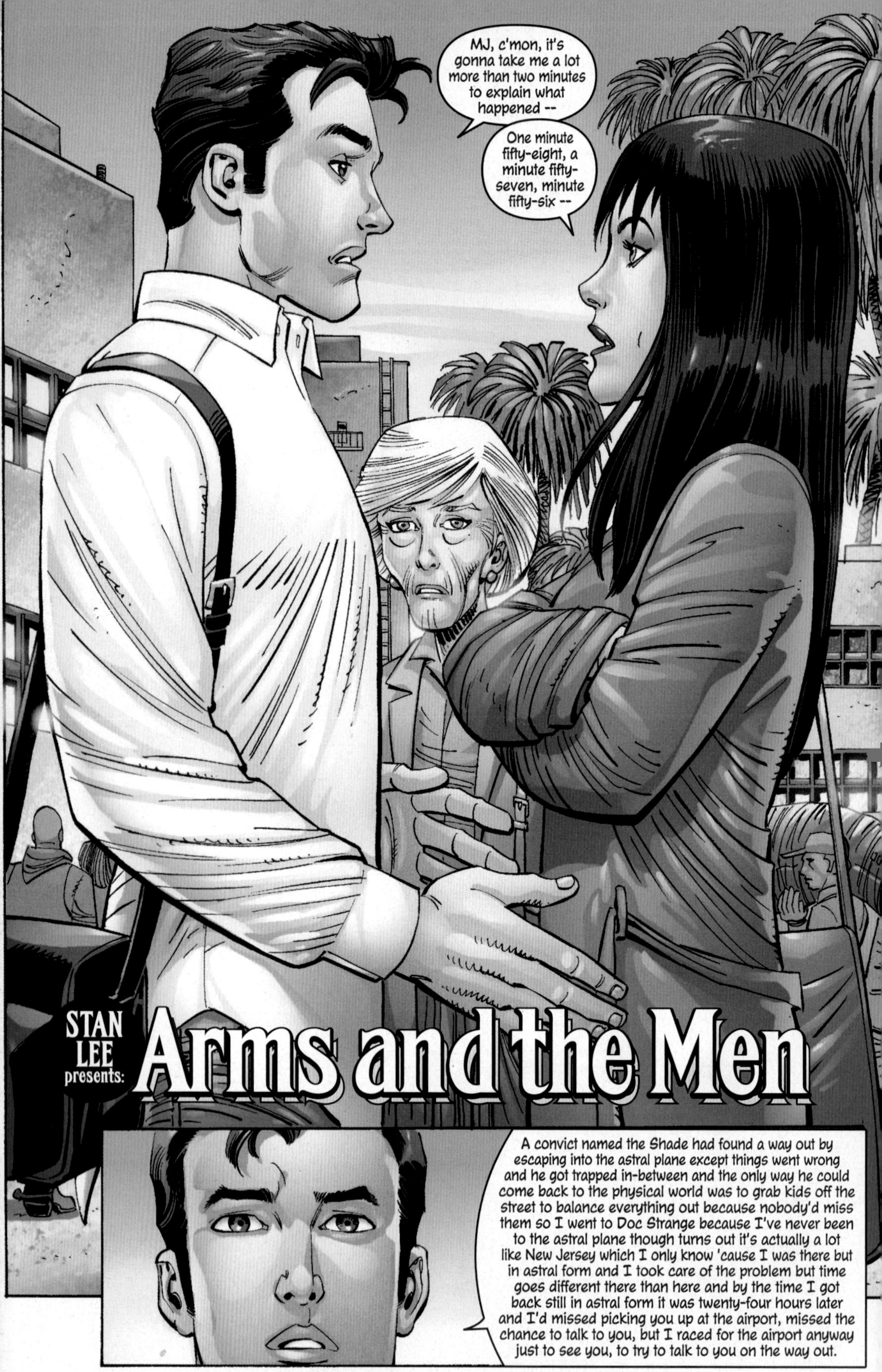
MJ, c'mon, it's gonna take me a lot more than two minutes to explain what happened --
One minute fifty-eight, a minute fifty-seven, minute fifty-six --
STAN LEE presents:
Arms and the Men
A convict named the Shade had found a way out by escaping into the astral plane except things went wrong and he got trapped in-between and the only way he could come back to the physical world was to grab kids off the street to balance everything out because nobody'd miss them so I went to Doc Strange because I've never been to the astral plane though turns out it's actually a lot like New Jersey which I only know 'cause I was there but in astral form and I took care of the problem but time goes different there than here and by the time I got back still in astral form it was twenty-four hours later and I'd missed picking you up at the airport, missed the chance to talk to you, but I raced for the airport anyway just to see you, to try to talk to you on the way out.

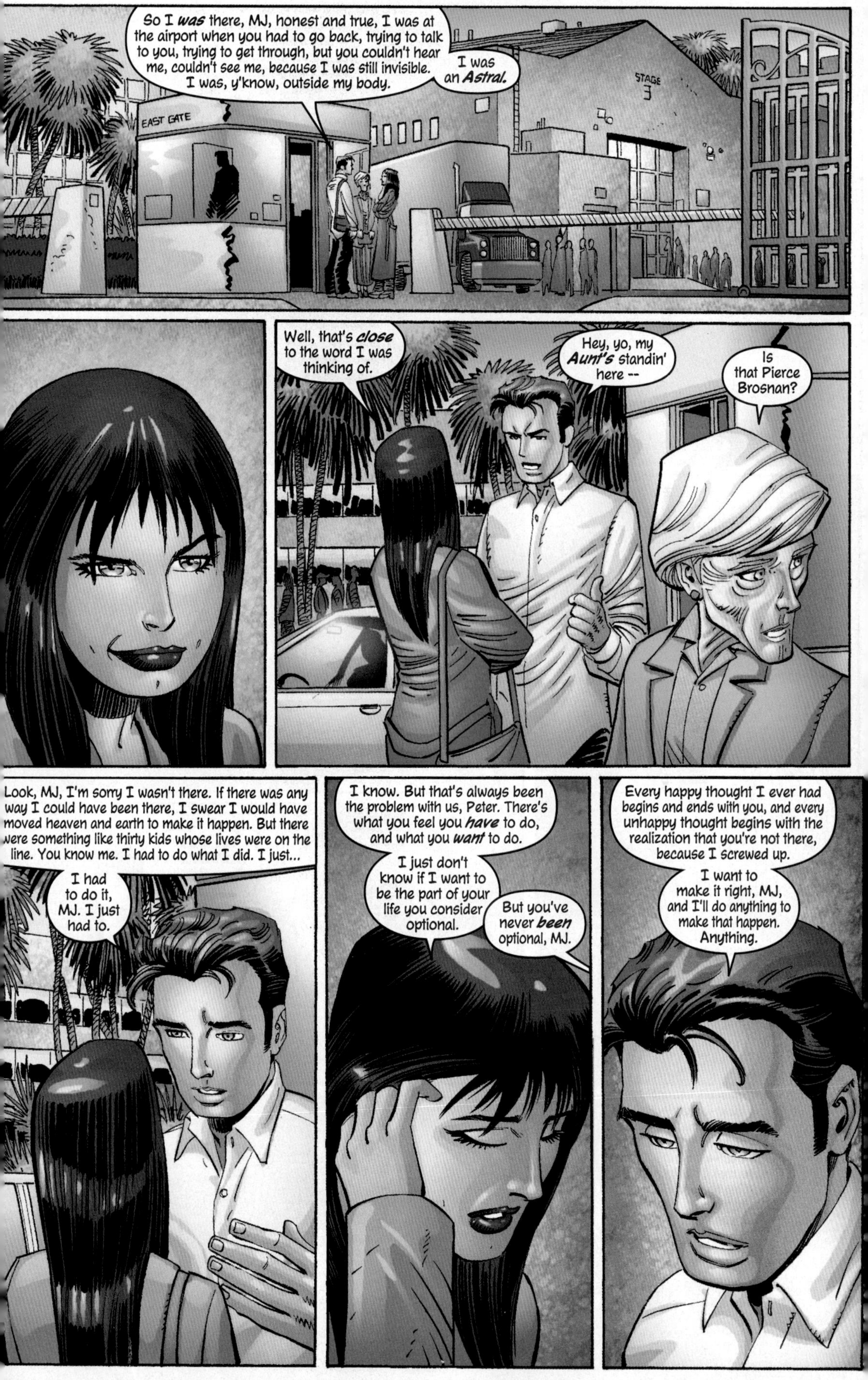

So I *was* there, MJ, honest and true, I was at the airport when you had to go back, trying to talk to you, trying to get through, but you couldn't hear me, couldn't see me, because I was still invisible. I was, y'know, outside my body.
I was an *Astral.*
EAST GATE
STAGE 3
Well, that's *close* to the word I was thinking of.
Hey, yo, my *Aunt's* standin' here --
Is that Pierce Brosnan?
Look, MJ, I'm sorry I wasn't there. If there was any way I could have been there, I swear I would have moved heaven and earth to make it happen. But there were something like thirty kids whose lives were on the line. You know me. I had to do what I did. I just...
I had to do it, MJ. I just had to.
I know. But that's always been the problem with us, Peter. There's what you feel you *have* to do, and what you *want* to do.
I just don't know if I want to be the part of your life you consider optional.
But you've never *been* optional, MJ.
Every happy thought I ever had begins and ends with you, and every unhappy thought begins with the realization that you're not there, because I screwed up.
I want to make it right, MJ, and I'll do anything to make that happen. Anything.

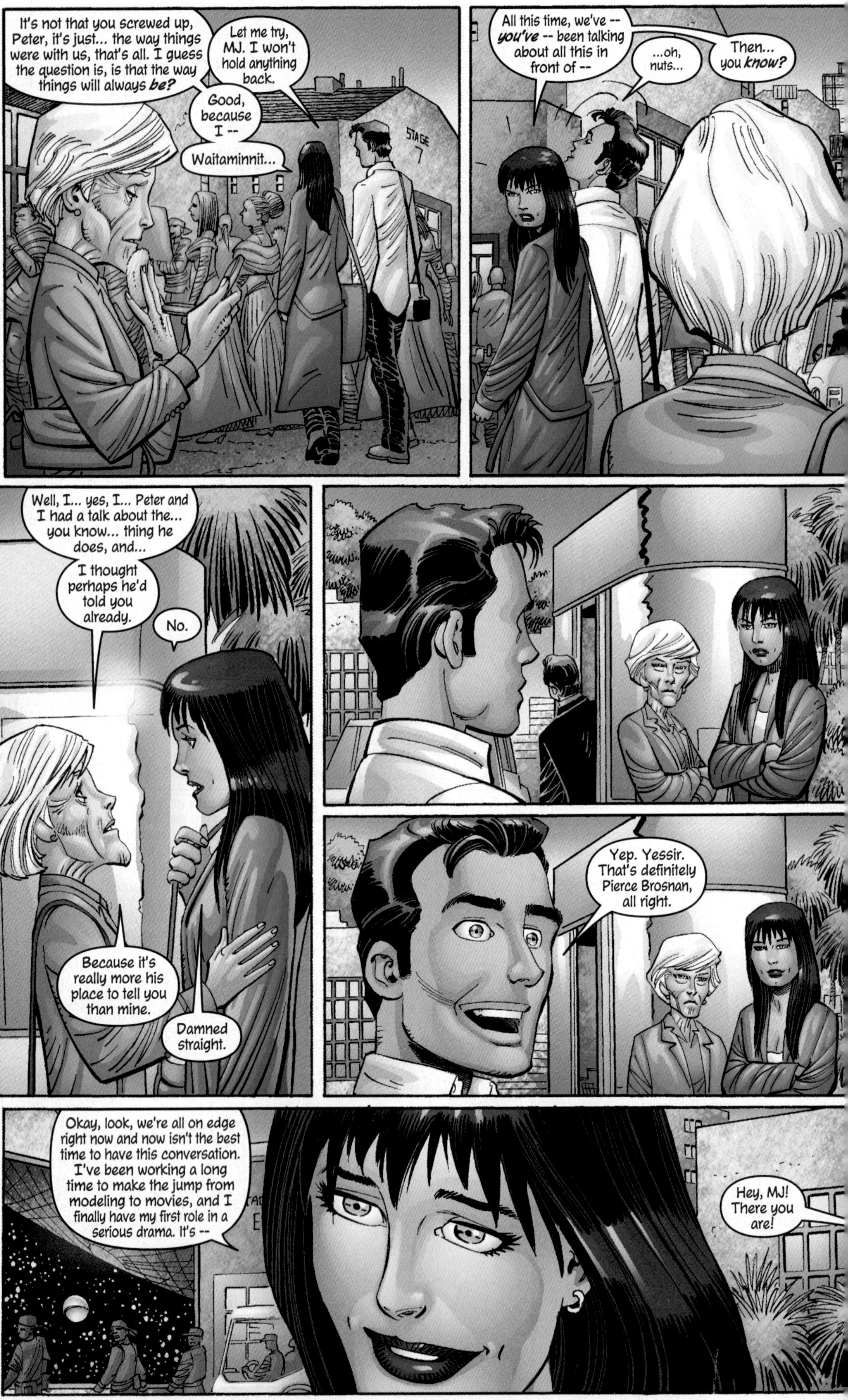
It's not that you screwed up, Peter, it's just... the way things were with us, that's all. I guess the question is, is that the way things will always *be?*
Let me try, MJ. I won't hold anything back.
Good, because I --
Waitaminnit...
STAGE 7
All this time, we've -- *you've* -- been talking about all this in front of --
...oh, nuts...
Then... you *know?*
Well, I... yes, I... Peter and I had a talk about the... you know... thing he does, and...
I thought perhaps he'd told you already.
No.
Because it's really more his place to tell you than mine.
Damned straight.
Yep. Yessir. That's definitely Pierce Brosnan, all right.
Okay, look, we're all on edge right now and now isn't the best time to have this conversation. I've been working a long time to make the jump from modeling to movies, and I finally have my first role in a serious drama. It's --
Hey, MJ! There you are!

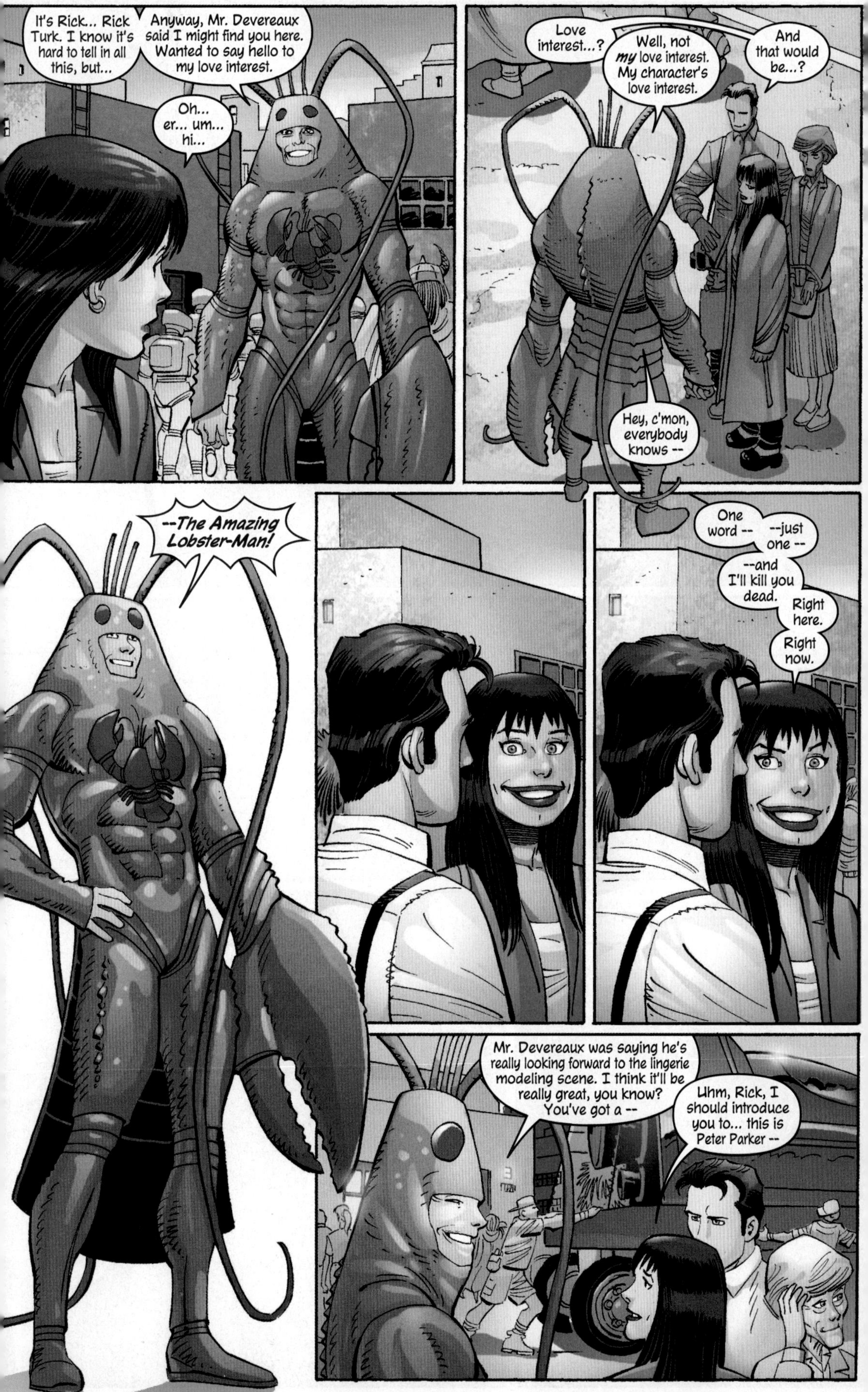
It's Rick... Rick Turk. I know it's hard to tell in all this, but...
Anyway, Mr. Devereaux said I might find you here. Wanted to say hello to my love interest.
Oh... er... um... hi...
Love interest...?
Well, not *my* love interest. My character's love interest.
And that would be...?
Hey, c'mon, everybody knows --
--The Amazing Lobster-Man!
One word --
--just one --
--and I'll kill you dead.
Right here.
Right now.
Mr. Devereaux was saying he's really looking forward to the lingerie modeling scene. I think it'll be really great, you know? You've got a --
Uhm, Rick, I should introduce you to... this is Peter Parker --

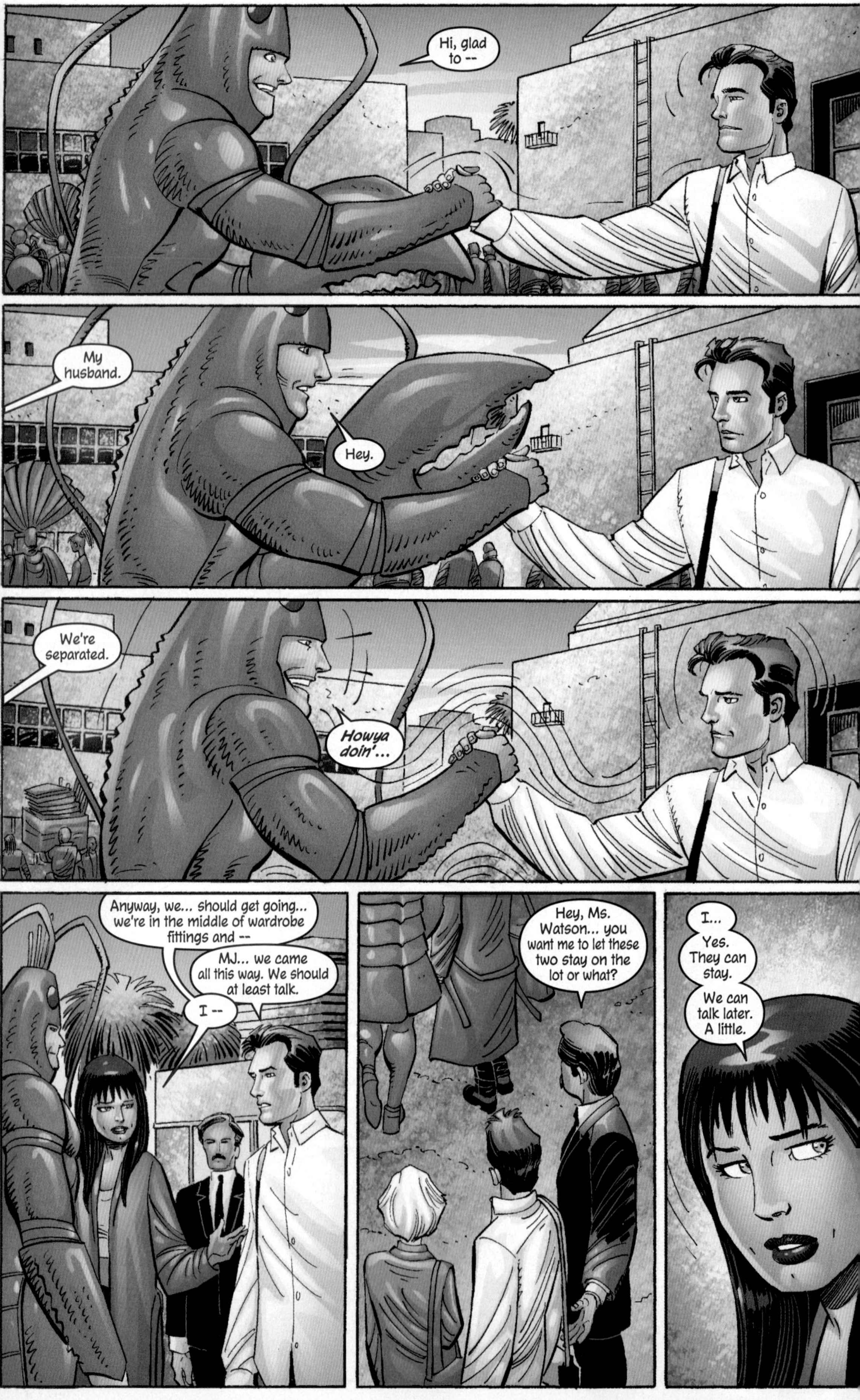

Hi, glad to --
My husband.
Hey.
We're separated.
Howya doin'...
Anyway, we... should get going... we're in the middle of wardrobe fittings and --
MJ... we came all this way. We should at least talk.
I --
Hey, Ms. Watson... you want me to let these two stay on the lot or what?
I...
Yes. They can stay.
We can talk later. A little.

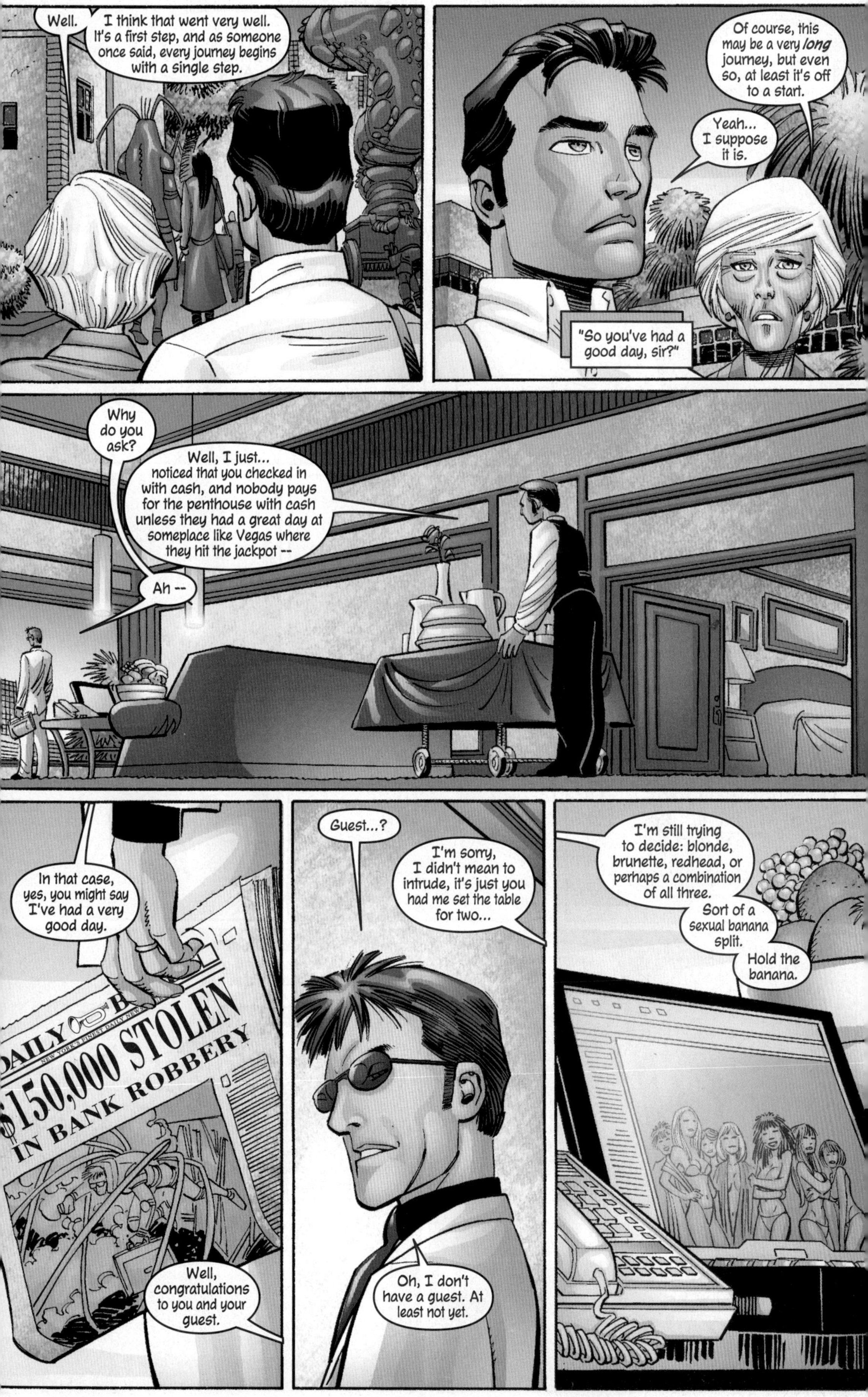

Well.
I think that went very well. It's a first step, and as someone once said, every journey begins with a single step.
Of course, this may be a very *long* journey, but even so, at least it's off to a start.
Yeah... I suppose it is.
"So you've had a good day, sir?"
Why do you ask?
Well, I just... noticed that you checked in with cash, and nobody pays for the penthouse with cash unless they had a great day at someplace like Vegas where they hit the jackpot --
Ah --
In that case, yes, you might say I've had a very good day.
DAILY B
$150,000 STOLEN IN BANK ROBBERY
Well, congratulations to you and your guest.
Guest...?
I'm sorry, I didn't mean to intrude, it's just you had me set the table for two...
Oh, I don't have a guest. At least not yet.
I'm still trying to decide: blonde, brunette, redhead, or perhaps a combination of all three.
Sort of a sexual banana split.
Hold the banana.

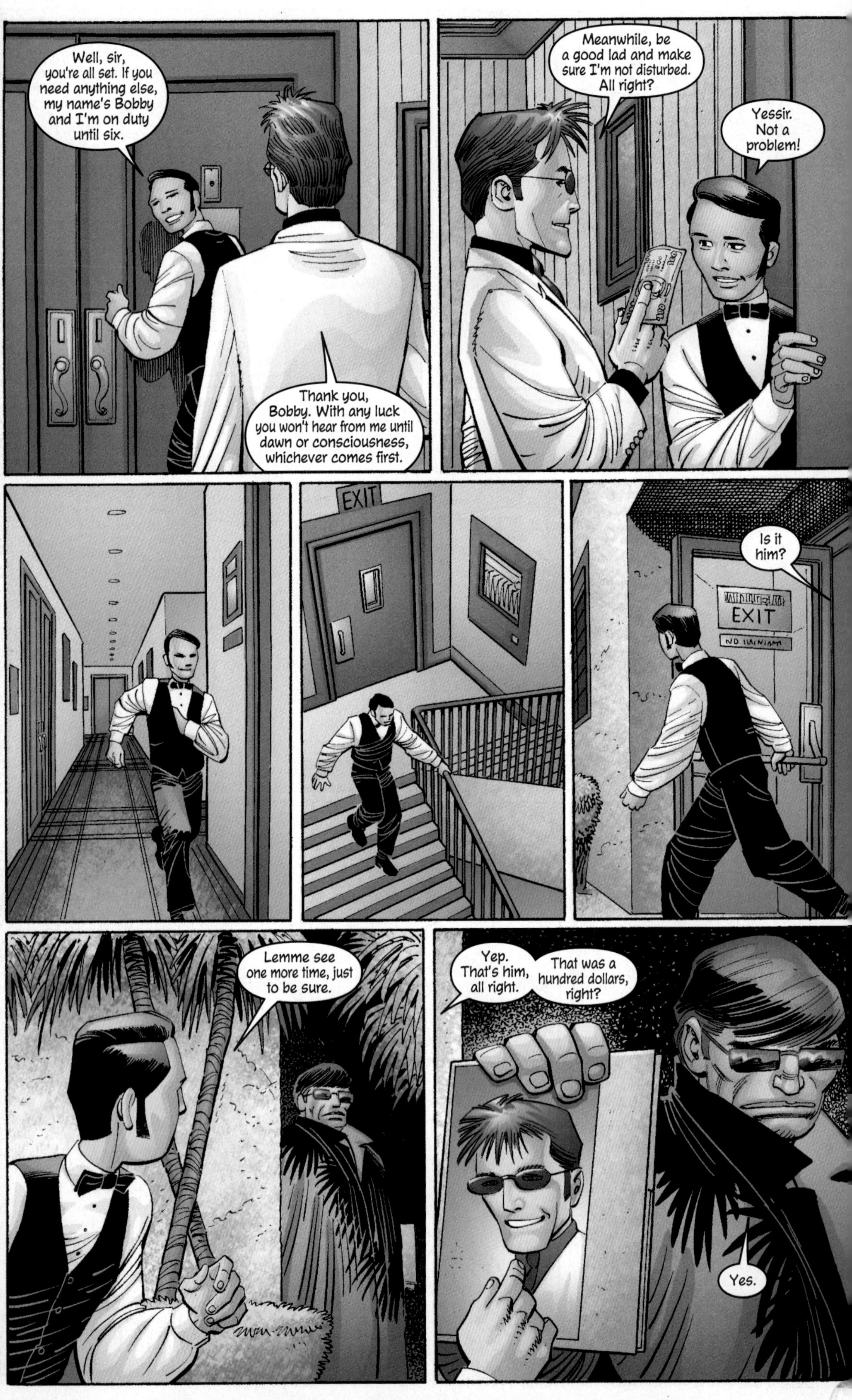

Well, sir, you're all set. If you need anything else, my name's Bobby and I'm on duty until six.
Thank you, Bobby. With any luck you won't hear from me until dawn or consciousness, whichever comes first.
Meanwhile, be a good lad and make sure I'm not disturbed. All right?
Yessir. Not a problem!
EXIT
EXIT
Is it him?
Lemme see one more time, just to be sure.
Yep. That's him, all right.
That was a hundred dollars, right?
Yes.

Thank you for your service.

Hey, anytime, mister. Just as long as there's no trouble, right?

No... no trouble at all.

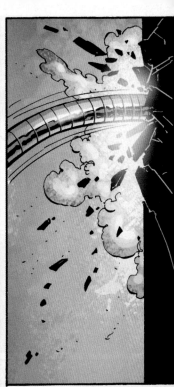

Now you just sit there and enjoy the view, honey, we'll go down to dinner in just a minute.

All right... but it's *boring*.

Mommmm!

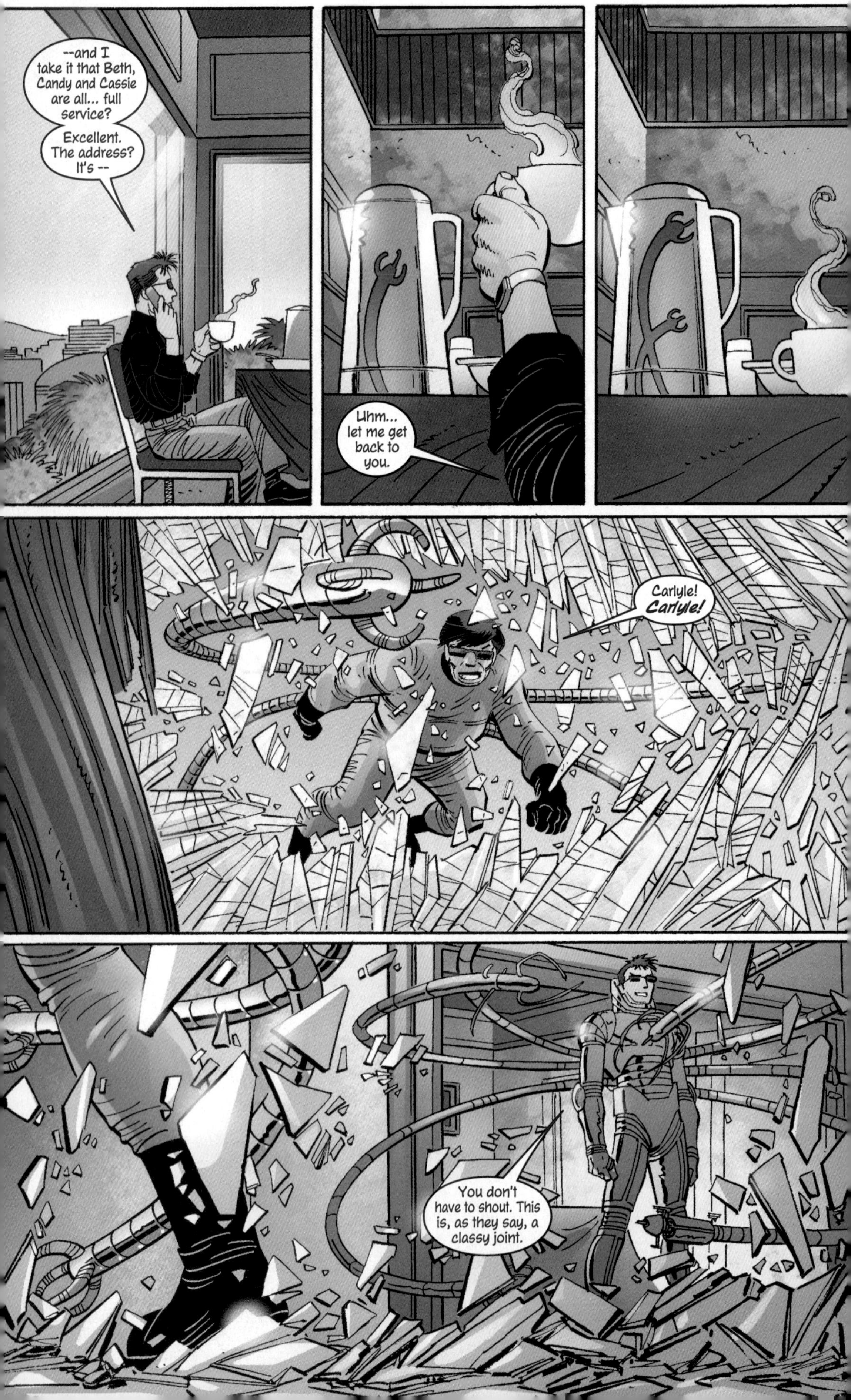
--and I take it that Beth, Candy and Cassie are all... full service?
Excellent. The address? It's --
Uhm... let me get back to you.
Carlyle! Carlyle!
You don't have to shout. This is, as they say, a classy joint.

Take. That. Off.

Sigh... you're the *last* person in the world I wanted to hear utter those words while I was in the bedroom.

But you'll do.

I was reading a book on this hotel and they say this floor is supposed to be haunted --

--snort! --

Gimme a break. That's just to bring in the tourists and the ghost-nuts. Nothing that weird goes on in real life --

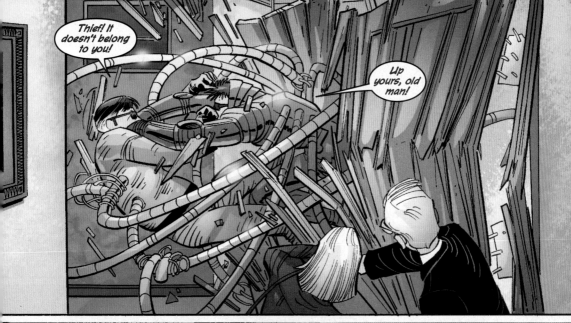

Thief! It doesn't belong to you!

Up yours, old man!

Aaaaghhh!

Maybe we should try another hotel...

Yeah, maybe...

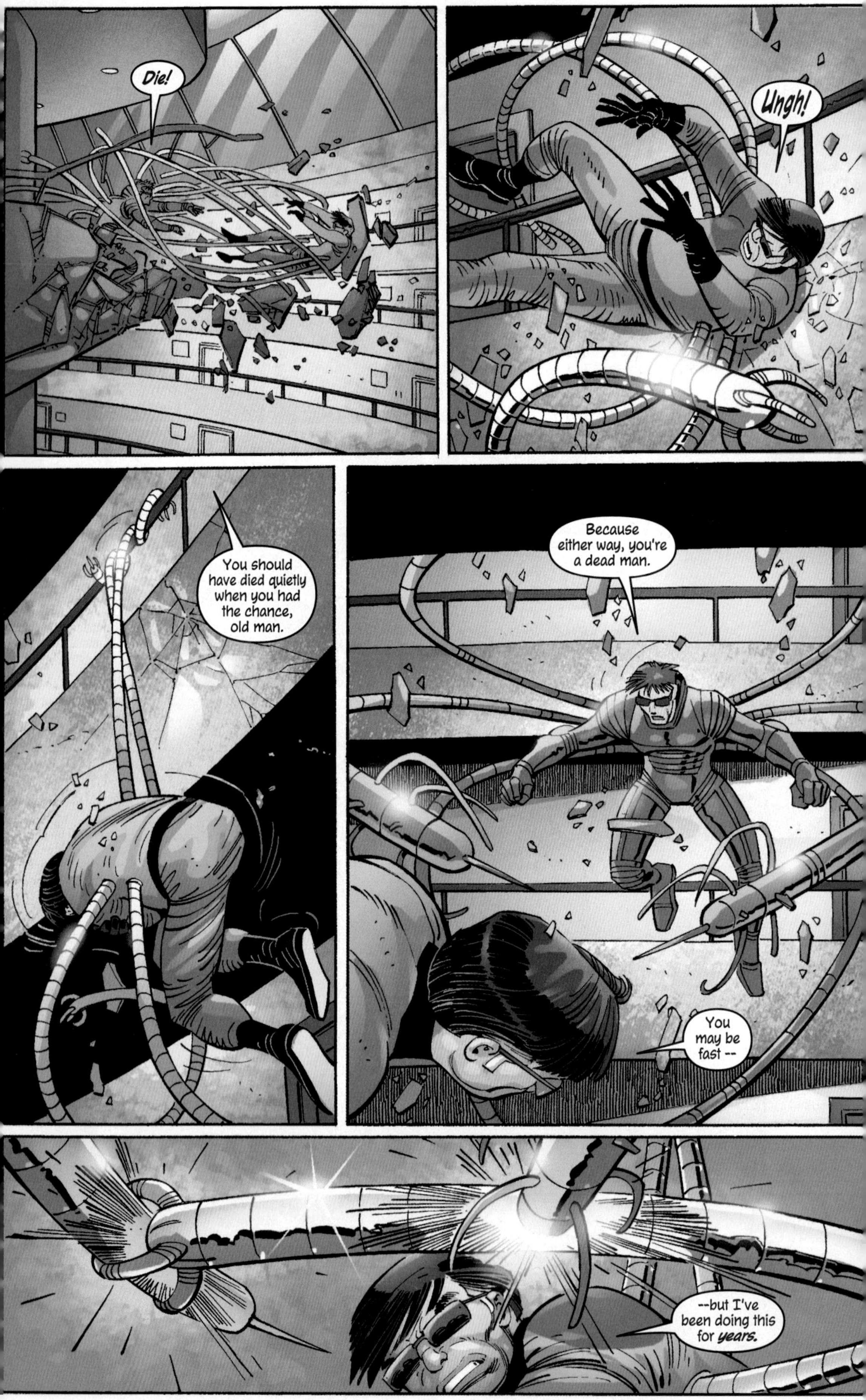

Die!
Ungh!
You should have died quietly when you had the chance, old man.
Because either way, you're a dead man.
You may be fast --
--but I've been doing this for *years.*

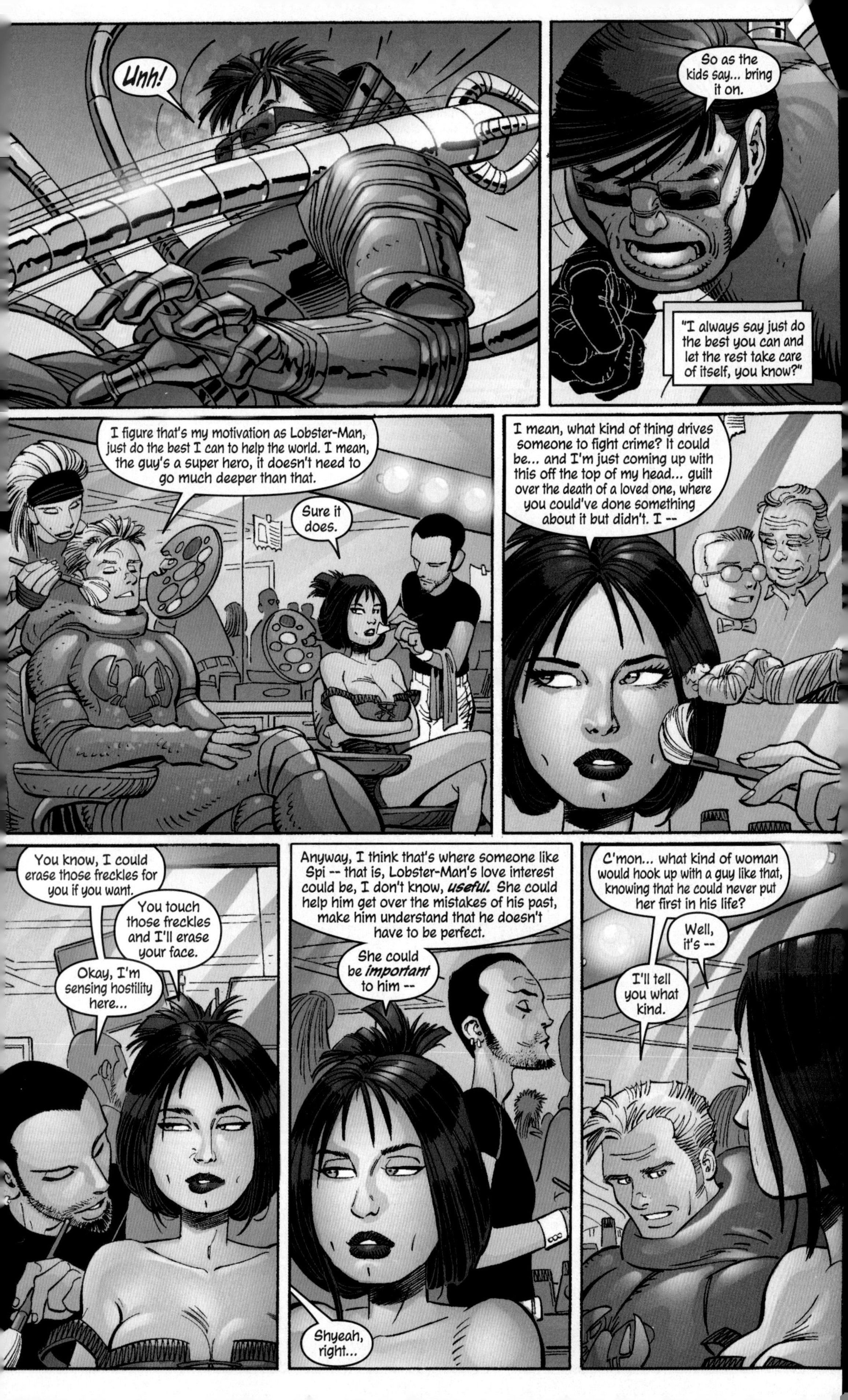

Unh!
So as the kids say... bring it on.
"I always say just do the best you can and let the rest take care of itself, you know?"
I figure that's my motivation as Lobster-Man, just do the best I can to help the world. I mean, the guy's a super hero, it doesn't need to go much deeper than that.
Sure it does.
I mean, what kind of thing drives someone to fight crime? It could be... and I'm just coming up with this off the top of my head... guilt over the death of a loved one, where you could've done something about it but didn't. I --
You know, I could erase those freckles for you if you want.
You touch those freckles and I'll erase your face.
Okay, I'm sensing hostility here...
Anyway, I think that's where someone like Spi -- that is, Lobster-Man's love interest could be, I don't know, *useful.* She could help him get over the mistakes of his past, make him understand that he doesn't have to be perfect.
She could be *important* to him --
Shyeah, right...
C'mon... what kind of woman would hook up with a guy like that, knowing that he could never put her first in his life?
Well, it's --
I'll tell you what kind.

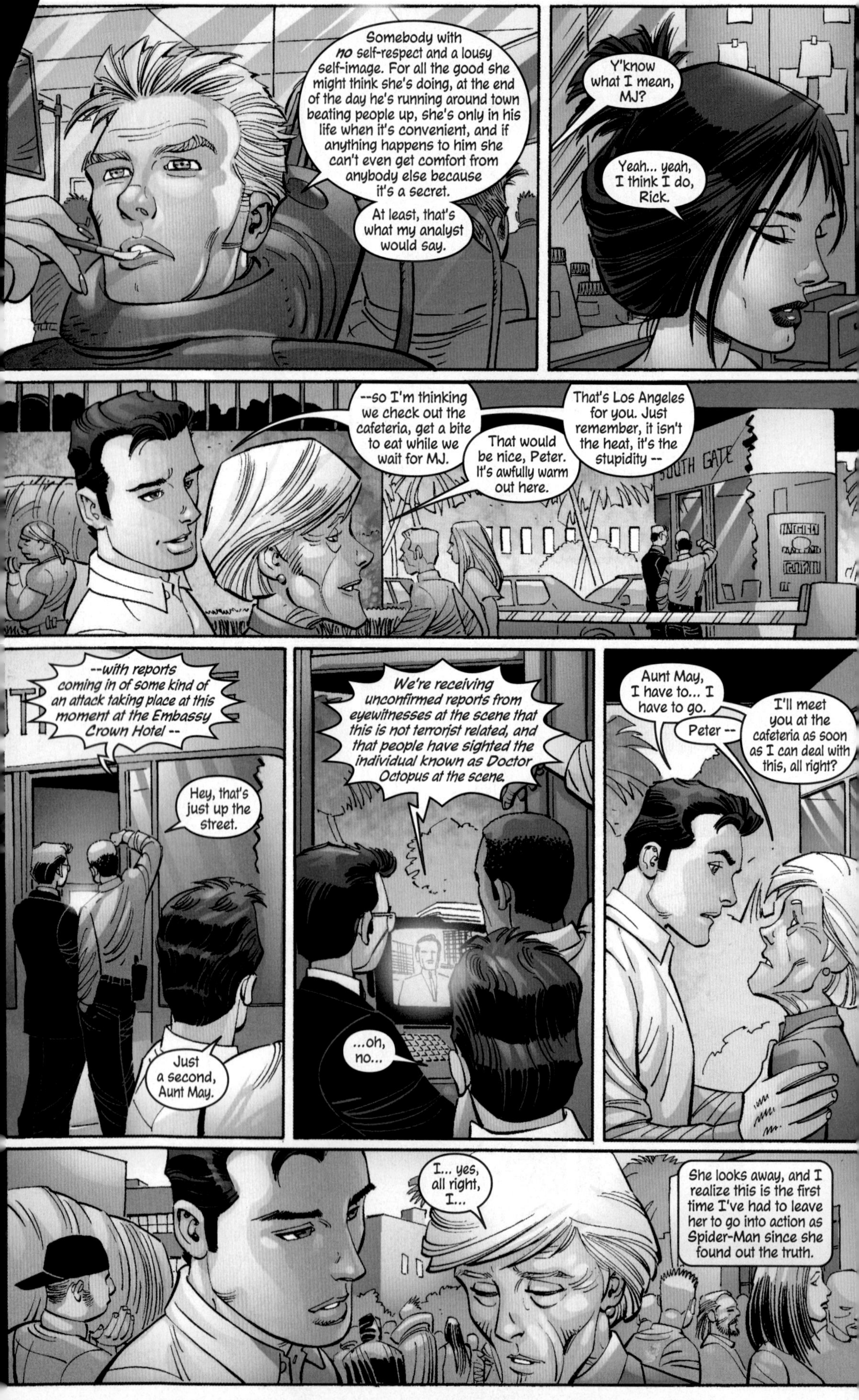
Somebody with *no* self-respect and a lousy self-image. For all the good she might think she's doing, at the end of the day he's running around town beating people up, she's only in his life when it's convenient, and if anything happens to him she can't even get comfort from anybody else because it's a secret.
At least, that's what my analyst would say.
Y'know what I mean, MJ?
Yeah... yeah, I think I do, Rick.
--so I'm thinking we check out the cafeteria, get a bite to eat while we wait for MJ.
That would be nice, Peter. It's awfully warm out here.
That's Los Angeles for you. Just remember, it isn't the heat, it's the stupidity --
SOUTH GATE
--with reports coming in of some kind of an attack taking place at this moment at the Embassy Crown Hotel --
Hey, that's just up the street.
Just a second, Aunt May.
We're receiving unconfirmed reports from eyewitnesses at the scene that this is not terrorist related, and that people have sighted the individual known as Doctor Octopus at the scene.
...oh, no...
Aunt May, I have to... I have to go.
Peter --
I'll meet you at the cafeteria as soon as I can deal with this, all right?
I... yes, all right, I...
She looks away, and I realize this is the first time I've had to leave her to go into action as Spider-Man since she found out the truth.

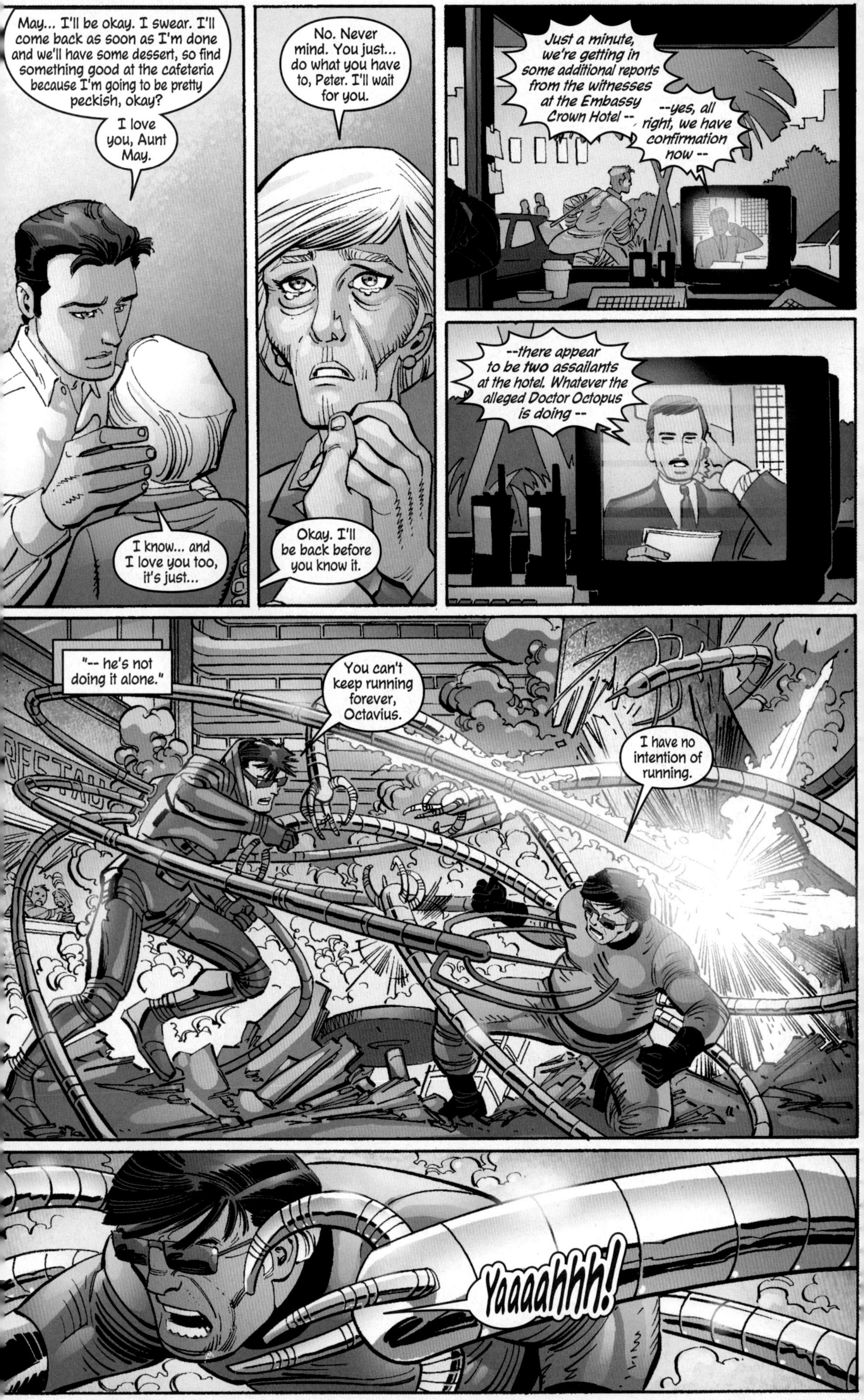
May... I'll be okay. I swear. I'll come back as soon as I'm done and we'll have some dessert, so find something good at the cafeteria because I'm going to be pretty peckish, okay?
I love you, Aunt May.
I know... and I love you too, it's just...
No. Never mind. You just... do what you have to, Peter. I'll wait for you.
Okay. I'll be back before you know it.
Just a minute, we're getting in some additional reports from the witnesses at the Embassy Crown Hotel --
--yes, all right, we have confirmation now --
--there appear to be two assailants at the hotel. Whatever the alleged Doctor Octopus is doing --
"-- he's not doing it alone."
You can't keep running forever, Octavius.
I have no intention of running.
Yaaaahhh!

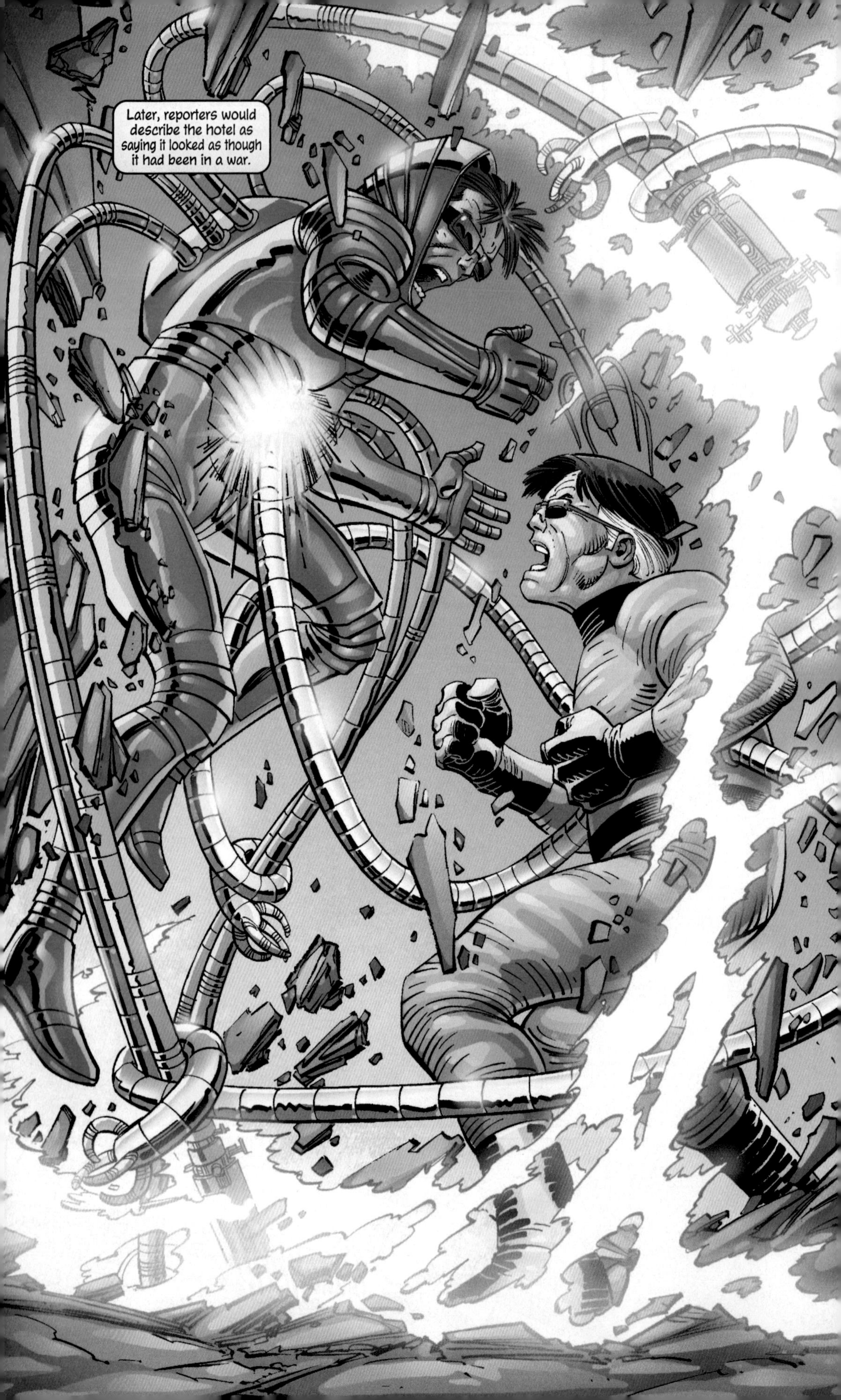
Later, reporters would describe the hotel as saying it looked as though it had been in a war.

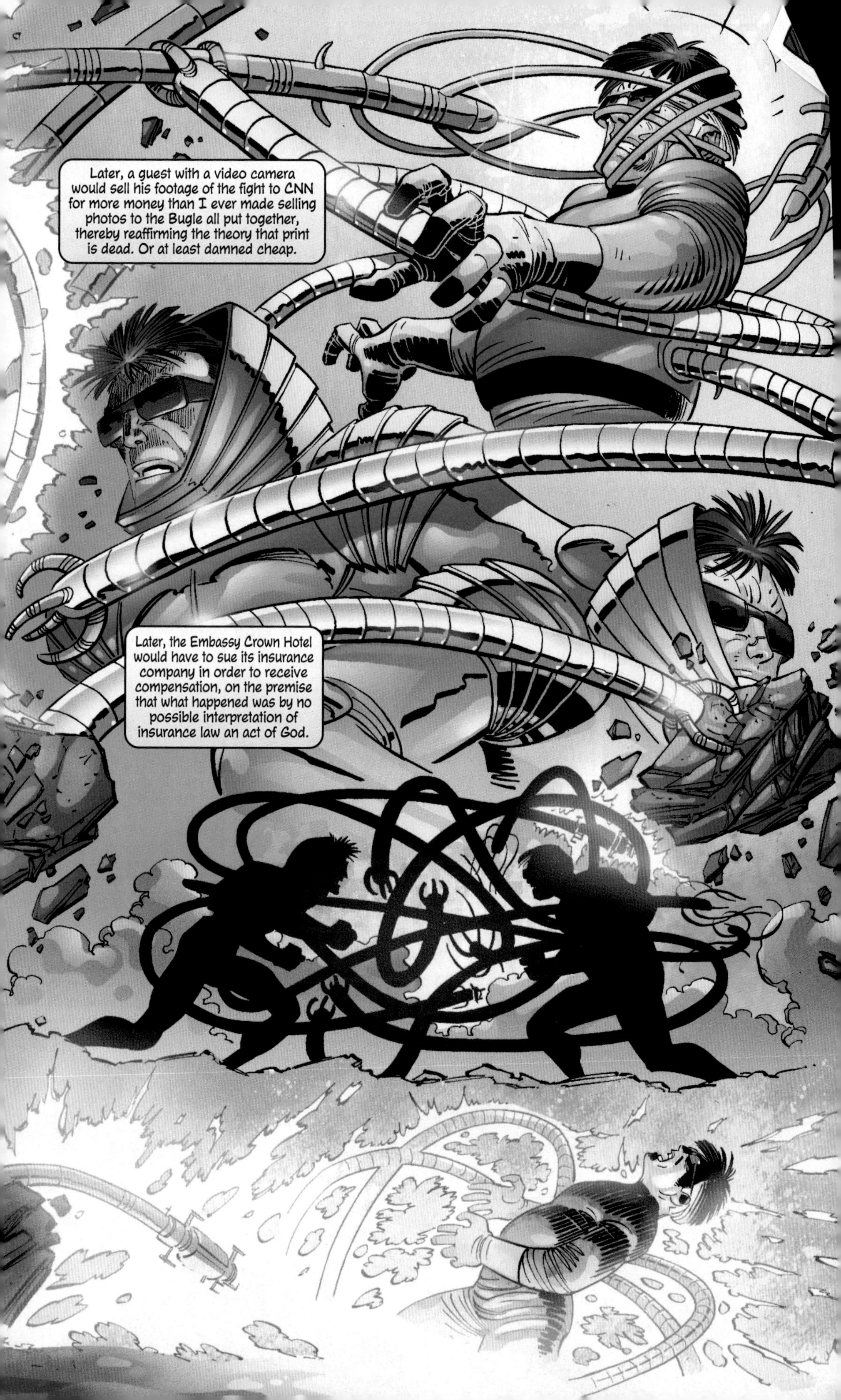
Later, a guest with a video camera would sell his footage of the fight to CNN for more money than I ever made selling photos to the Bugle all put together, thereby reaffirming the theory that print is dead. Or at least damned cheap.
Later, the Embassy Crown Hotel would have to sue its insurance company in order to receive compensation, on the premise that what happened was by no possible interpretation of insurance law an act of God.

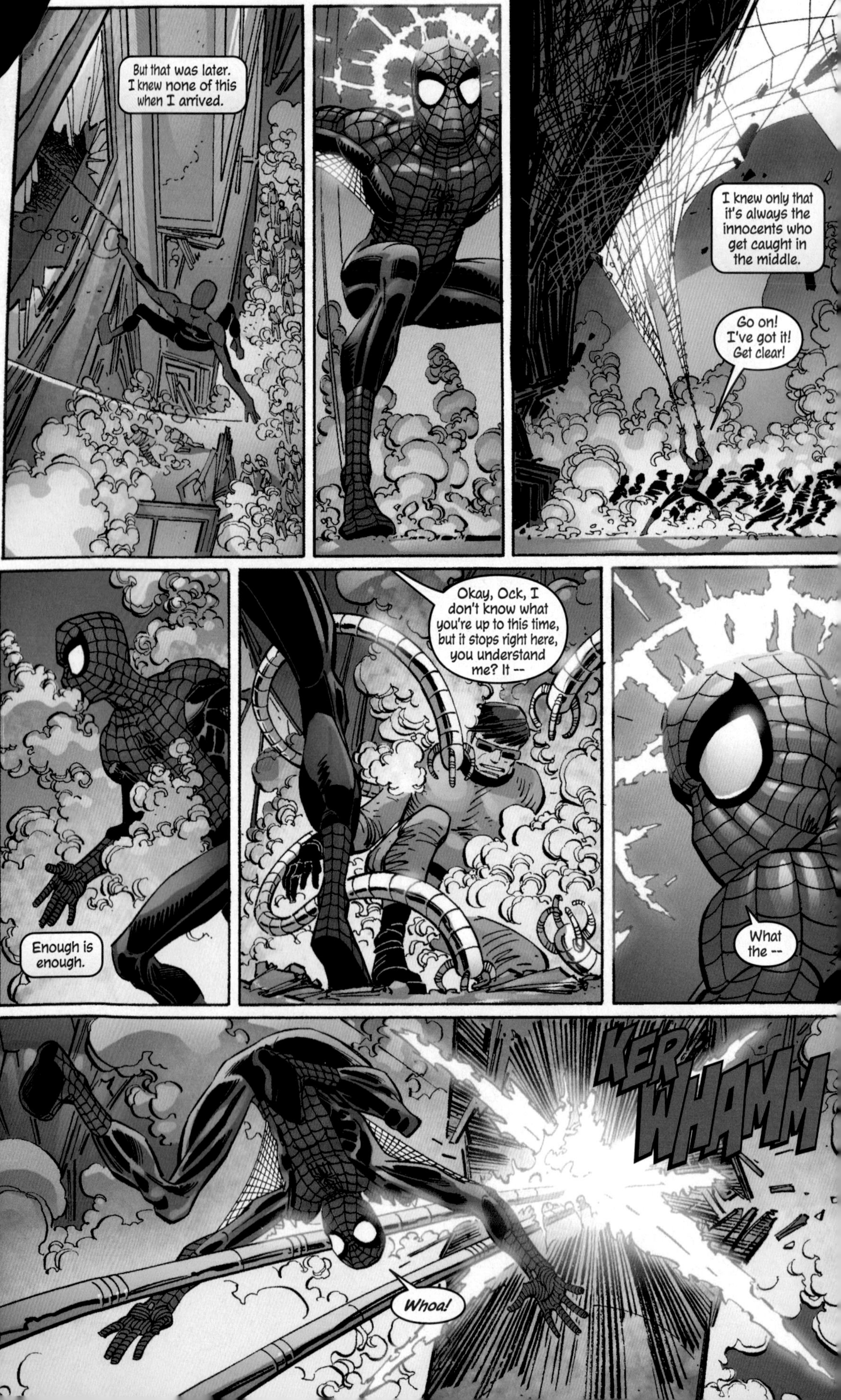
But that was later. I knew none of this when I arrived.
I knew only that it's always the innocents who get caught in the middle.
Go on! I've got it! Get clear!
Enough is enough.
Okay, Ock, I don't know what you're up to this time, but it stops right here, you understand me? It --
What the --
KER WHAMM
Whoa!

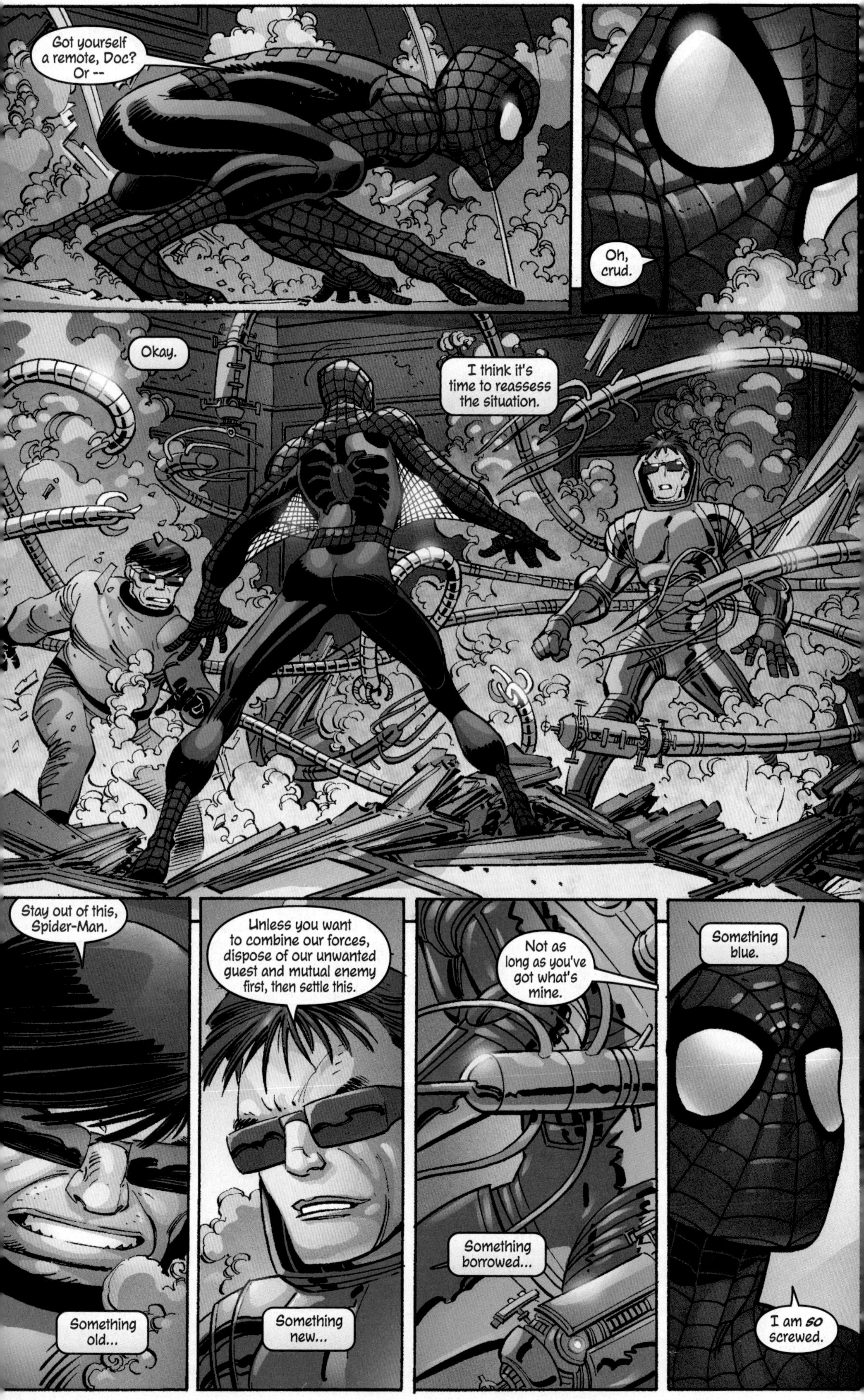
Got yourself a remote, Doc? Or --
Oh, crud.
Okay.
I think it's time to reassess the situation.
Stay out of this, Spider-Man.
Something old...
Unless you want to combine our forces, dispose of our unwanted guest and mutual enemy first, then settle this.
Something new...
Not as long as you've got what's mine.
Something borrowed...
Something blue.
I am *so* screwed.

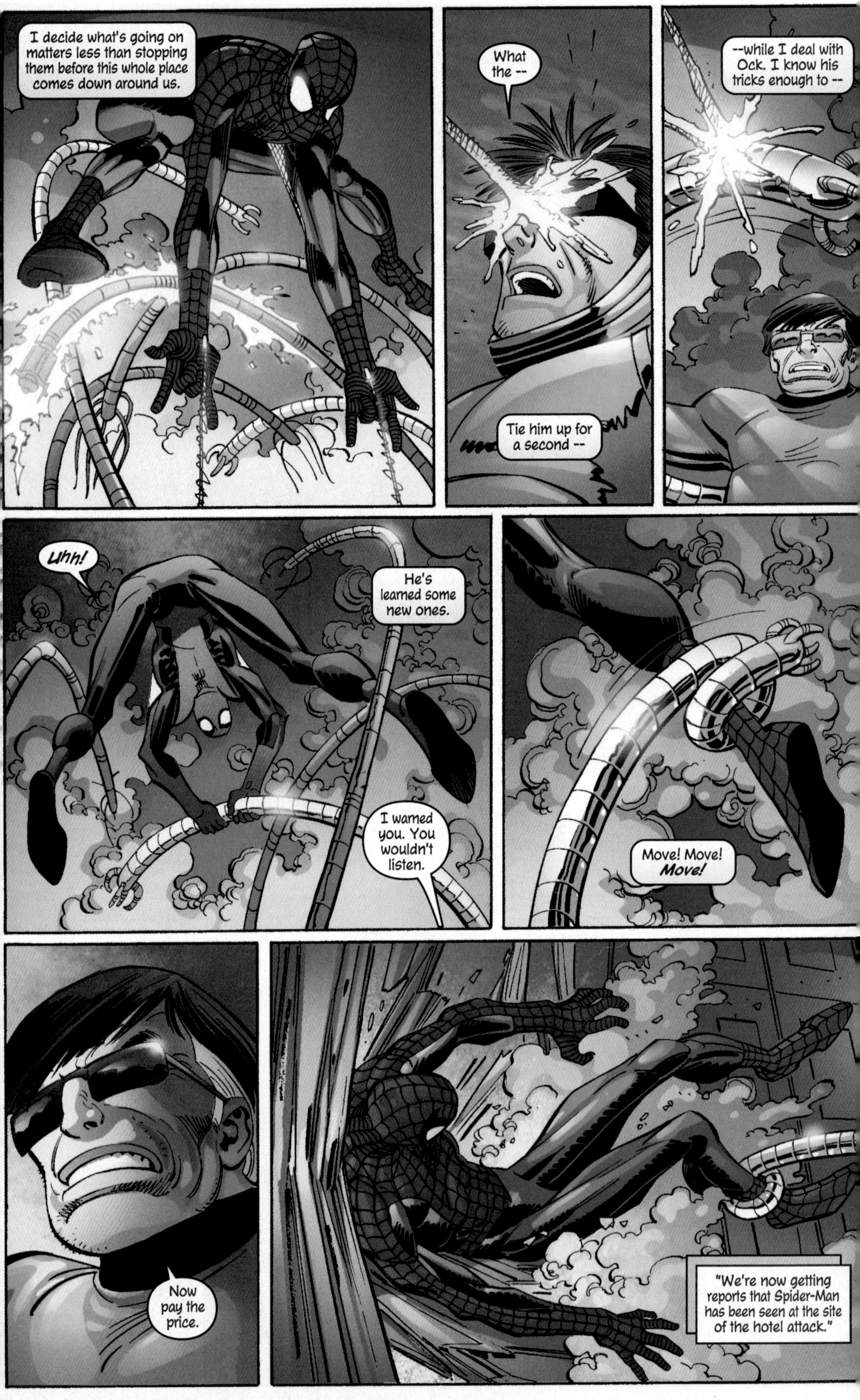

I decide what's going on matters less than stopping them before this whole place comes down around us.
What the --
Tie him up for a second --
--while I deal with Ock. I know his tricks enough to --
Uhn!
He's learned some new ones.
I warned you. You wouldn't listen.
Move! Move! Move!
Now pay the price.
"We're now getting reports that Spider-Man has been seen at the site of the hotel attack."

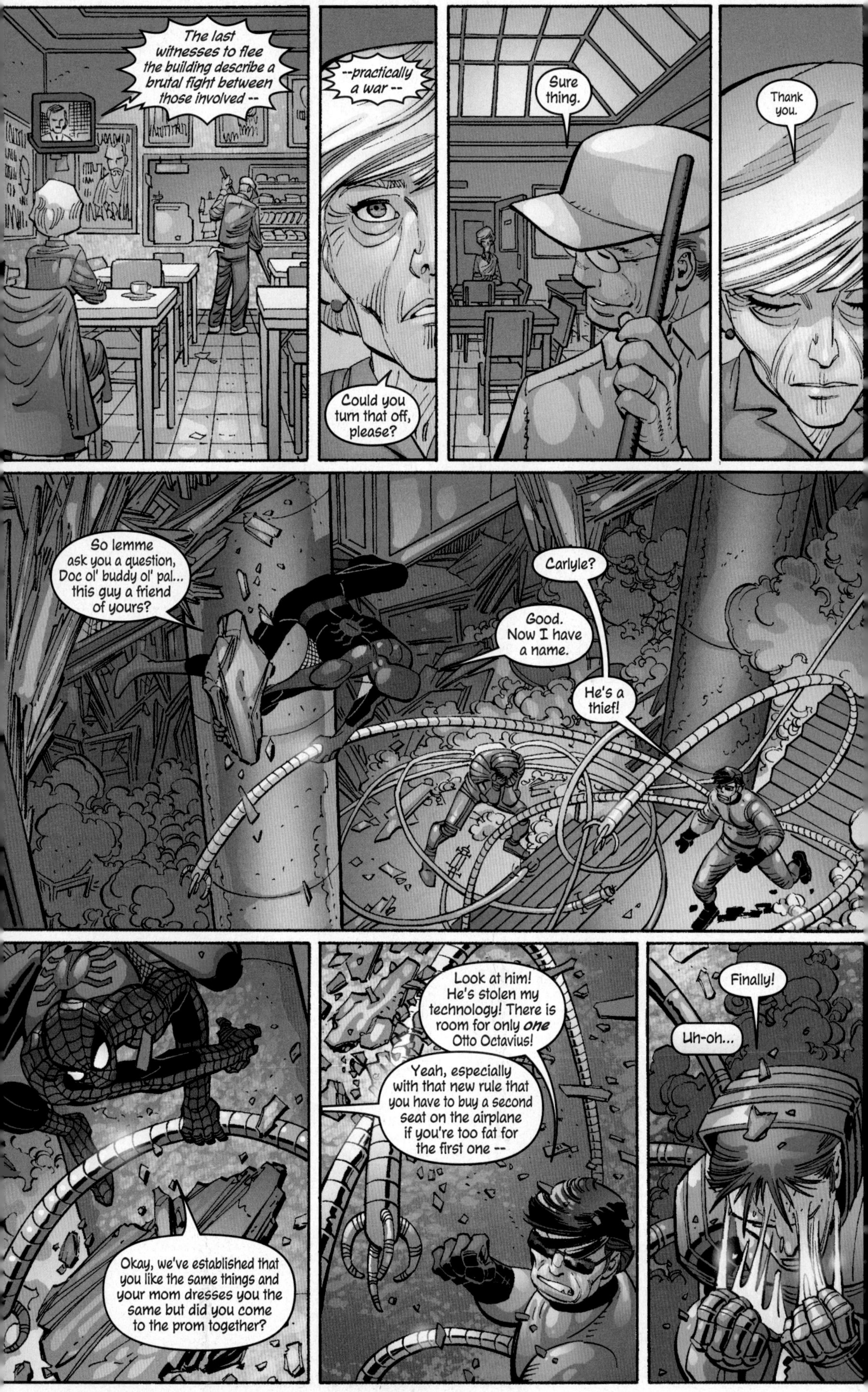
The last witnesses to flee the building describe a brutal fight between those involved --
--practically a war --
Could you turn that off, please?
Sure thing.
Thank you.
So lemme ask you a question, Doc ol' buddy ol' pal... this guy a friend of yours?
Carlyle?
Good. Now I have a name.
He's a thief!
Okay, we've established that you like the same things and your mom dresses you the same but did you come to the prom together?
Look at him! He's stolen my technology! There is room for only *one* Otto Octavius!
Yeah, especially with that new rule that you have to buy a second seat on the airplane if you're too fat for the first one --
Finally!
Uh-oh...

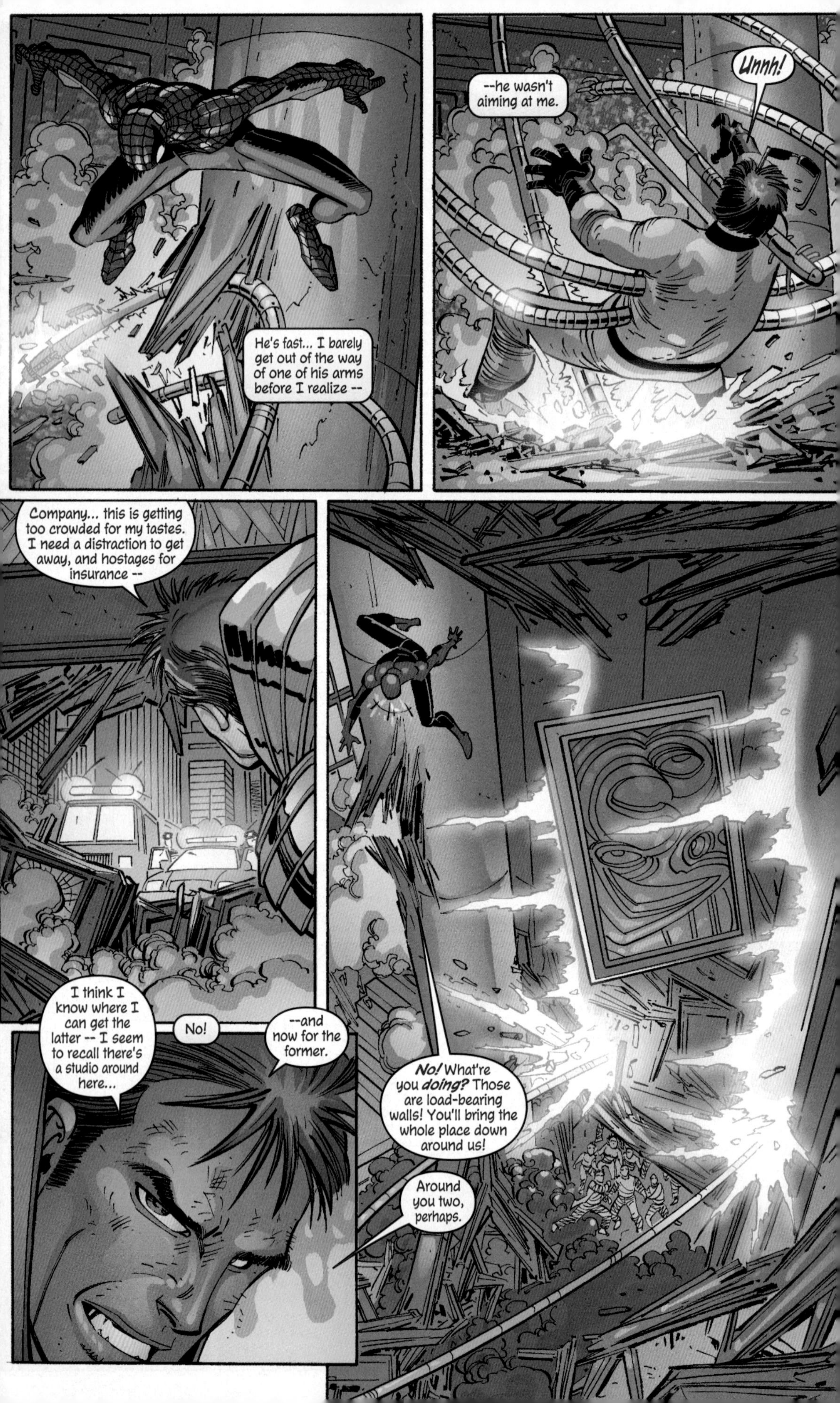
He's fast... I barely get out of the way of one of his arms before I realize --
--he wasn't aiming at me.
Unnh!
Company... this is getting too crowded for my tastes. I need a distraction to get away, and hostages for insurance --
I think I know where I can get the latter -- I seem to recall there's a studio around here...
No!
--and now for the former.
No! What're you doing? Those are load-bearing walls! You'll bring the whole place down around us!
Around you two, perhaps.

But not me!

Doc! You gotta help me keep it together until the civilians can get out!

Please!

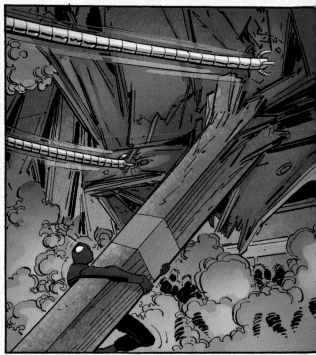

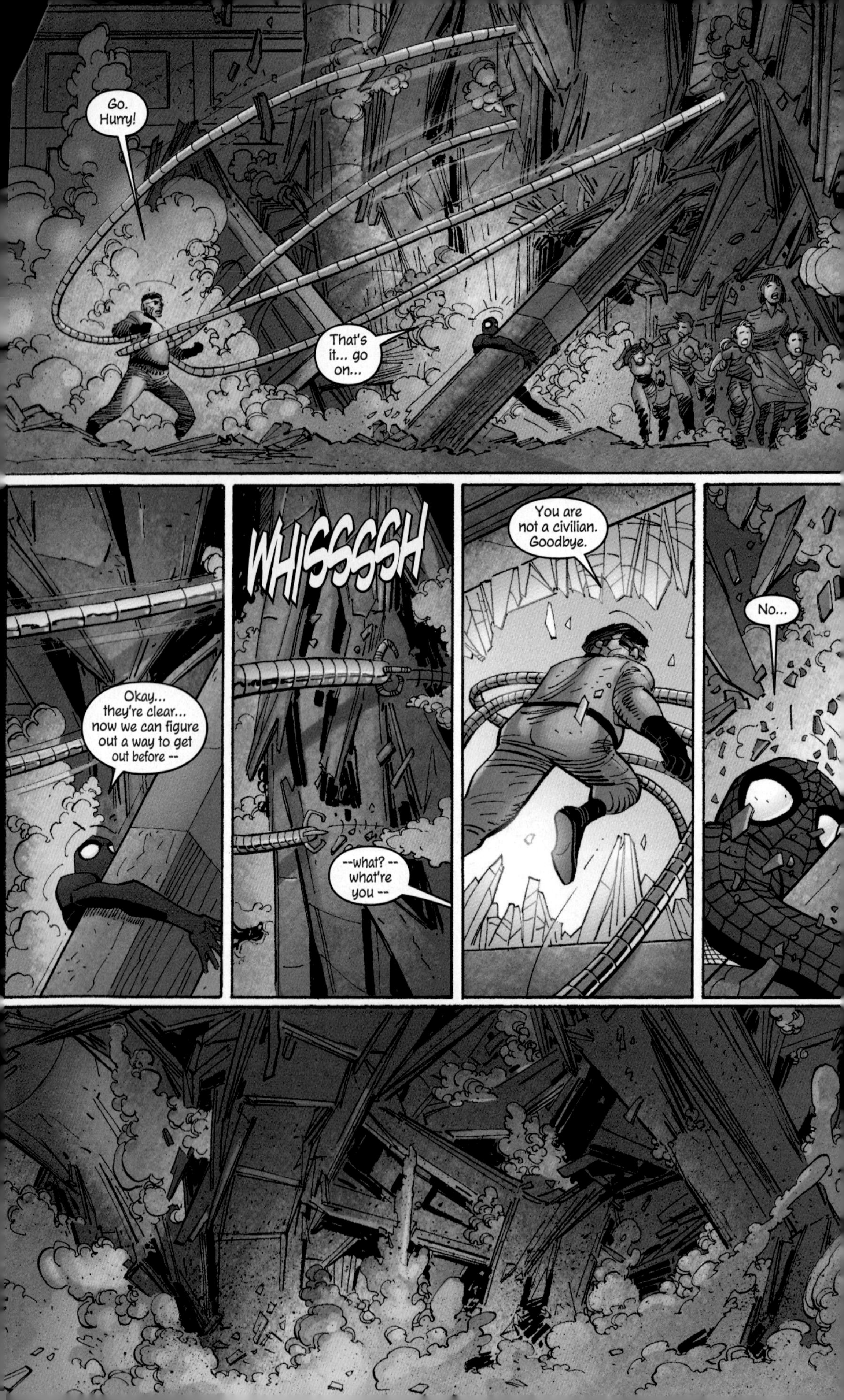
Go. Hurry!
That's it... go on...
Okay... they're clear... now we can figure out a way to get out before --
WHISSSSH
--what? -- what're you --
You are not a civilian. Goodbye.
No...

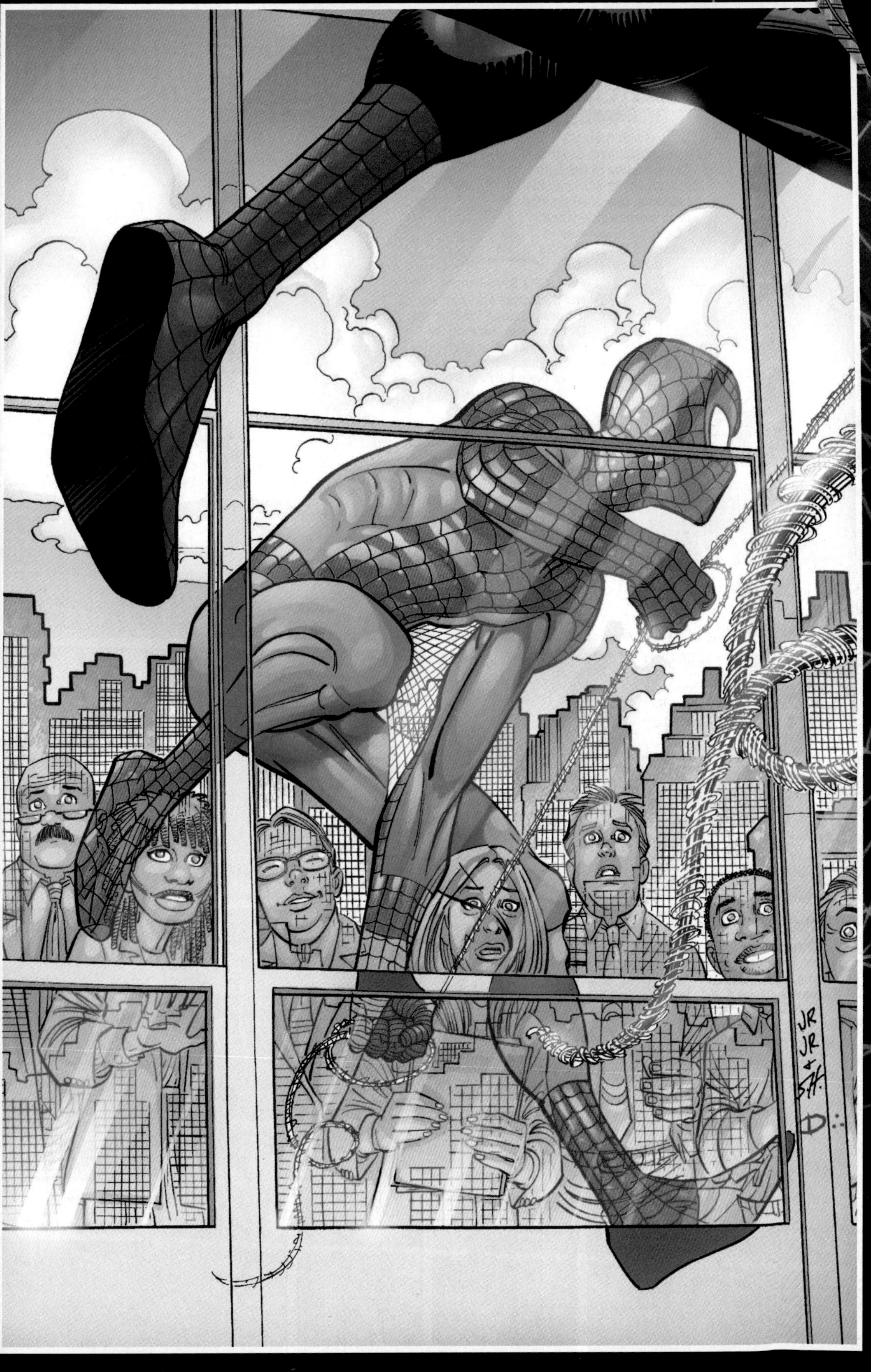

AMAZING SPIDER-MAN #45

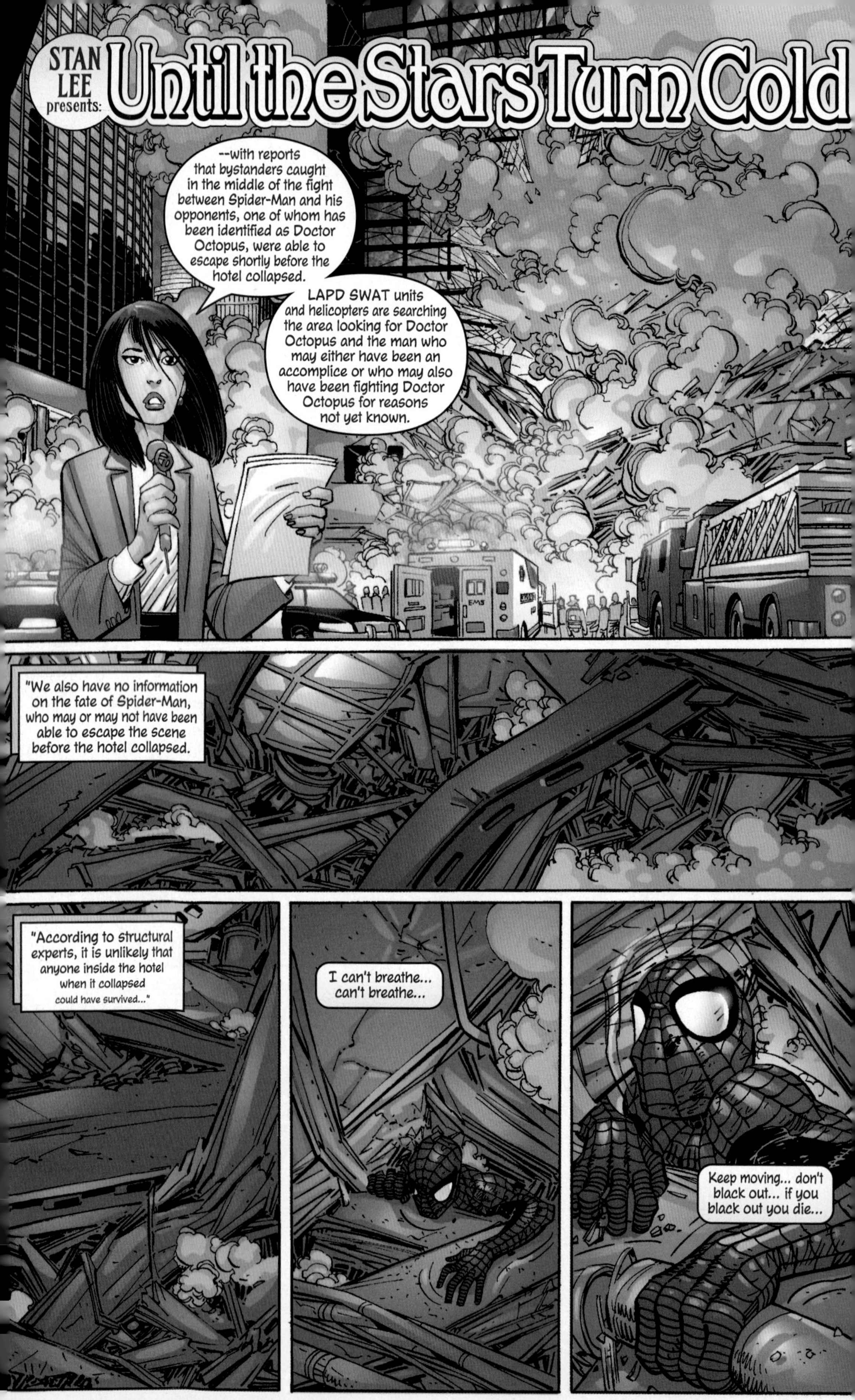
STAN LEE presents:
Until the Stars Turn Cold
--with reports that bystanders caught in the middle of the fight between Spider-Man and his opponents, one of whom has been identified as Doctor Octopus, were able to escape shortly before the hotel collapsed.
LAPD SWAT units and helicopters are searching the area looking for Doctor Octopus and the man who may either have been an accomplice or who may also have been fighting Doctor Octopus for reasons not yet known.
"We also have no information on the fate of Spider-Man, who may or may not have been able to escape the scene before the hotel collapsed.
"According to structural experts, it is unlikely that anyone inside the hotel when it collapsed could have survived..."
I can't breathe... can't breathe...
Keep moving... don't black out... if you black out you die...

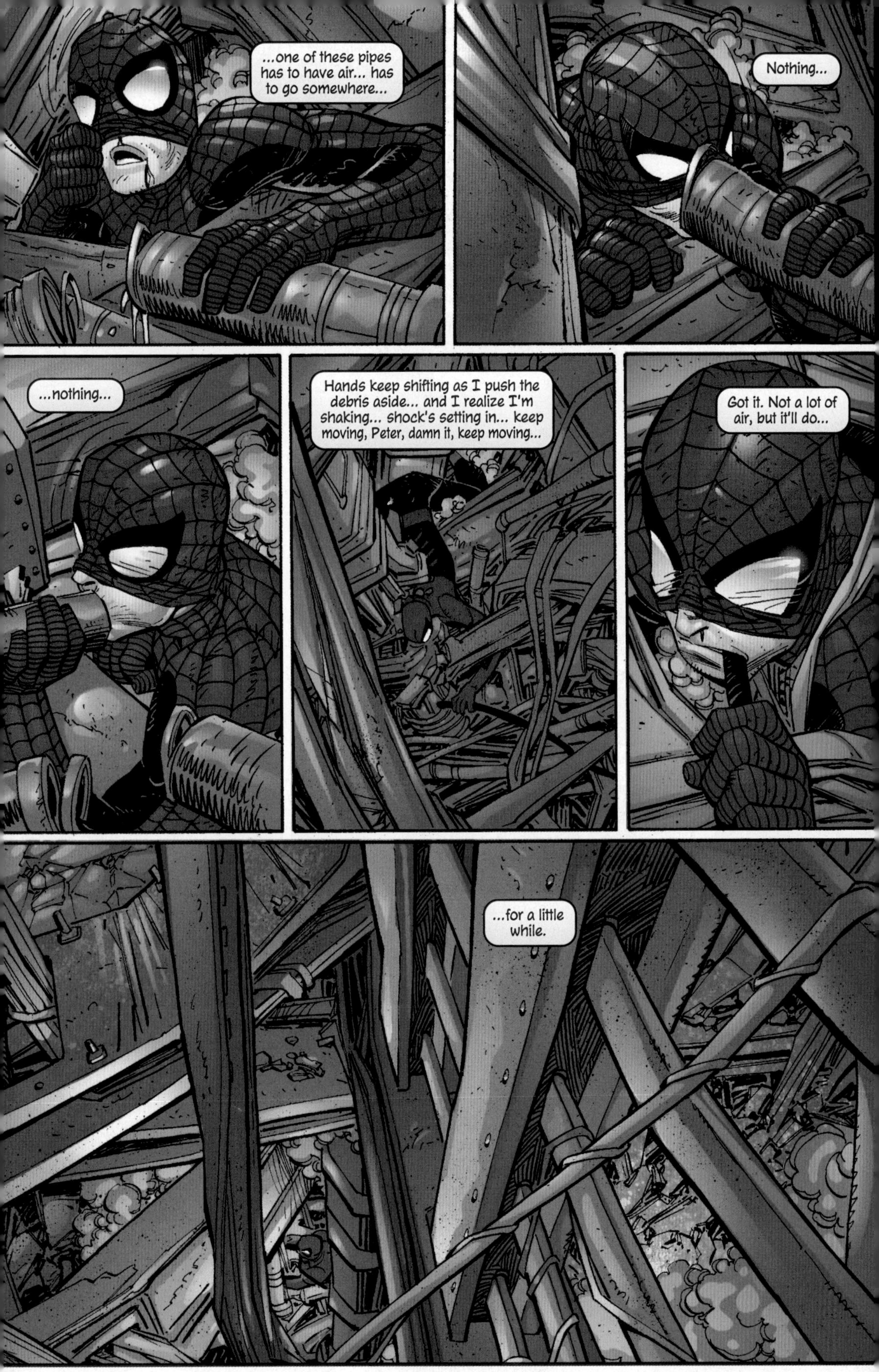
...one of these pipes has to have air... has to go somewhere...
Nothing...
...nothing...
Hands keep shifting as I push the debris aside... and I realize I'm shaking... shock's setting in... keep moving, Peter, damn it, keep moving...
Got it. Not a lot of air, but it'll do...
...for a little while.

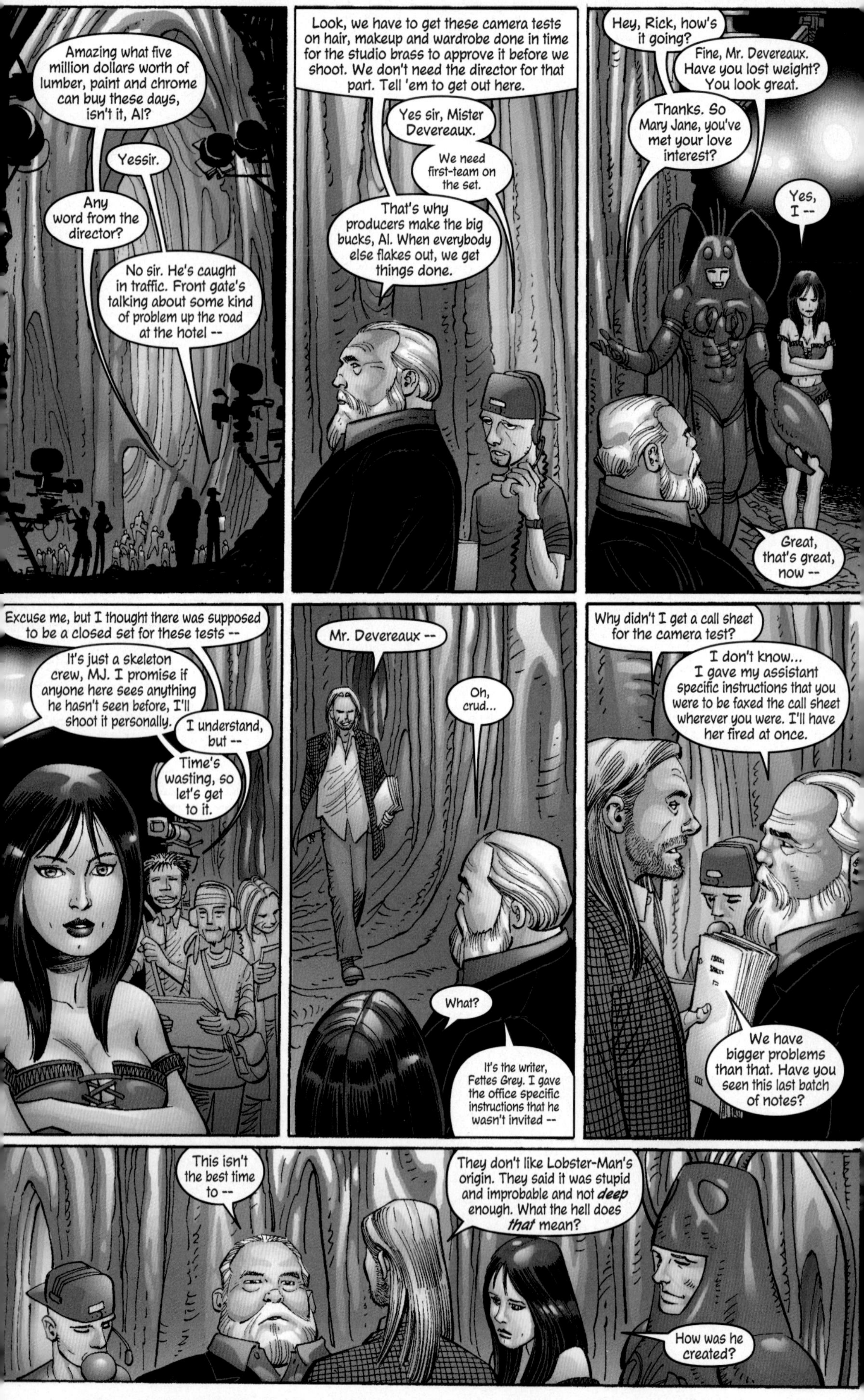

Amazing what five million dollars worth of lumber, paint and chrome can buy these days, isn't it, Al?
Yessir.
Any word from the director?
No sir. He's caught in traffic. Front gate's talking about some kind of problem up the road at the hotel --
Look, we have to get these camera tests on hair, makeup and wardrobe done in time for the studio brass to approve it before we shoot. We don't need the director for that part. Tell 'em to get out here.
Yes sir, Mister Devereaux.
We need first-team on the set.
That's why producers make the big bucks, Al. When everybody else flakes out, we get things done.
Hey, Rick, how's it going?
Fine, Mr. Devereaux. Have you lost weight? You look great.
Thanks. So Mary Jane, you've met your love interest?
Yes, I --
Great, that's great, now --
Excuse me, but I thought there was supposed to be a closed set for these tests --
It's just a skeleton crew, MJ. I promise if anyone here sees anything he hasn't seen before, I'll shoot it personally.
I understand, but --
Time's wasting, so let's get to it.
Mr. Devereaux --
Oh, crud...
What?
It's the writer, Fettes Grey. I gave the office specific instructions that he wasn't invited --
Why didn't I get a call sheet for the camera test?
I don't know... I gave my assistant specific instructions that you were to be faxed the call sheet wherever you were. I'll have her fired at once.
We have bigger problems than that. Have you seen this last batch of notes?
This isn't the best time to --
They don't like Lobster-Man's origin. They said it was stupid and improbable and not *deep* enough. What the hell does *that* mean?
How was he created?

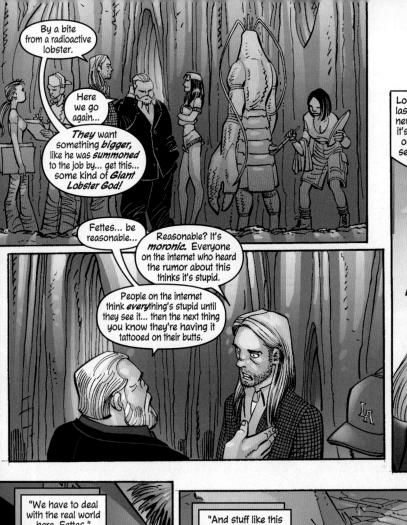

By a bite from a radioactive lobster.

Here we go again...

They want something *bigger,* like he was *summoned* to the job by... get this... some kind of *Giant Lobster God!*

Fettes... be reasonable...

Reasonable? It's *moronic.* Everyone on the internet who heard the rumor about this thinks it's stupid.

People on the internet think *every*thing's stupid until they see it... then the next thing you know they're having it tattooed on their butts.

Look, Fettes... radiation is passe. It is *so* last-century. We have to move on, create new myths for a new audience. Besides, if it's a Lobster God rather than a one-time-only accident we can have all *kinds* of sequels... Lobster-Boy and Lobster-Girl and the Evil Lobster-Man, you name it.

"We have to deal with the real world here, Fettes."

--estimating that it will be days before rescuers can reach the bottom of the collapsed hotel --

"And stuff like this just doesn't happen in the real world."

Sorry, pal, but you've got something I need.

Building after building filled with rich, high-profile hostages...

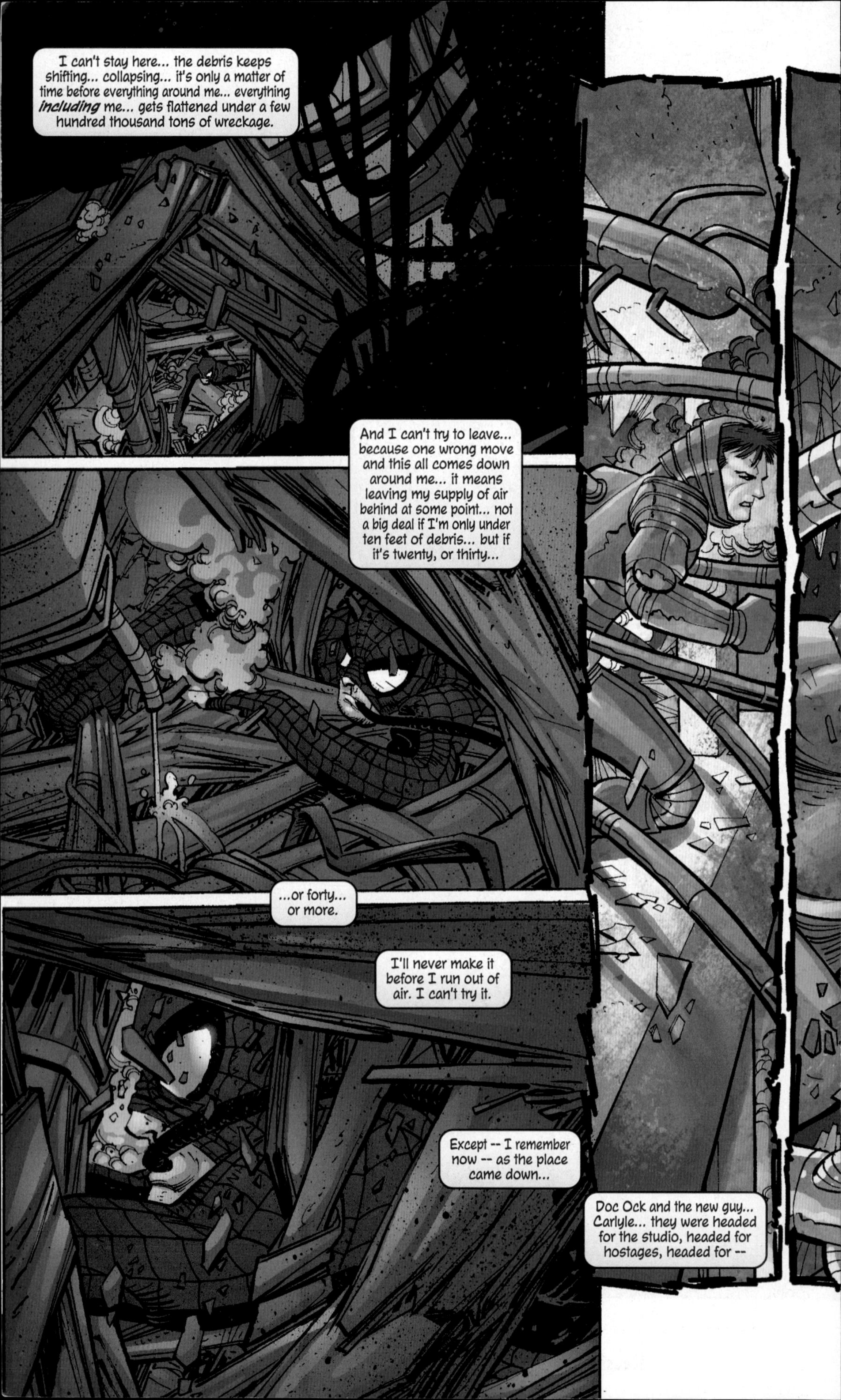
I can't stay here... the debris keeps shifting... collapsing... it's only a matter of time before everything around me... everything *including* me... gets flattened under a few hundred thousand tons of wreckage.
And I can't try to leave... because one wrong move and this all comes down around me... it means leaving my supply of air behind at some point... not a big deal if I'm only under ten feet of debris... but if it's twenty, or thirty...
...or forty... or more.
I'll never make it before I run out of air. I can't try it.
Except -- I remember now -- as the place came down...
Doc Ock and the new guy... Carlyle... they were headed for the studio, headed for hostages, headed for --

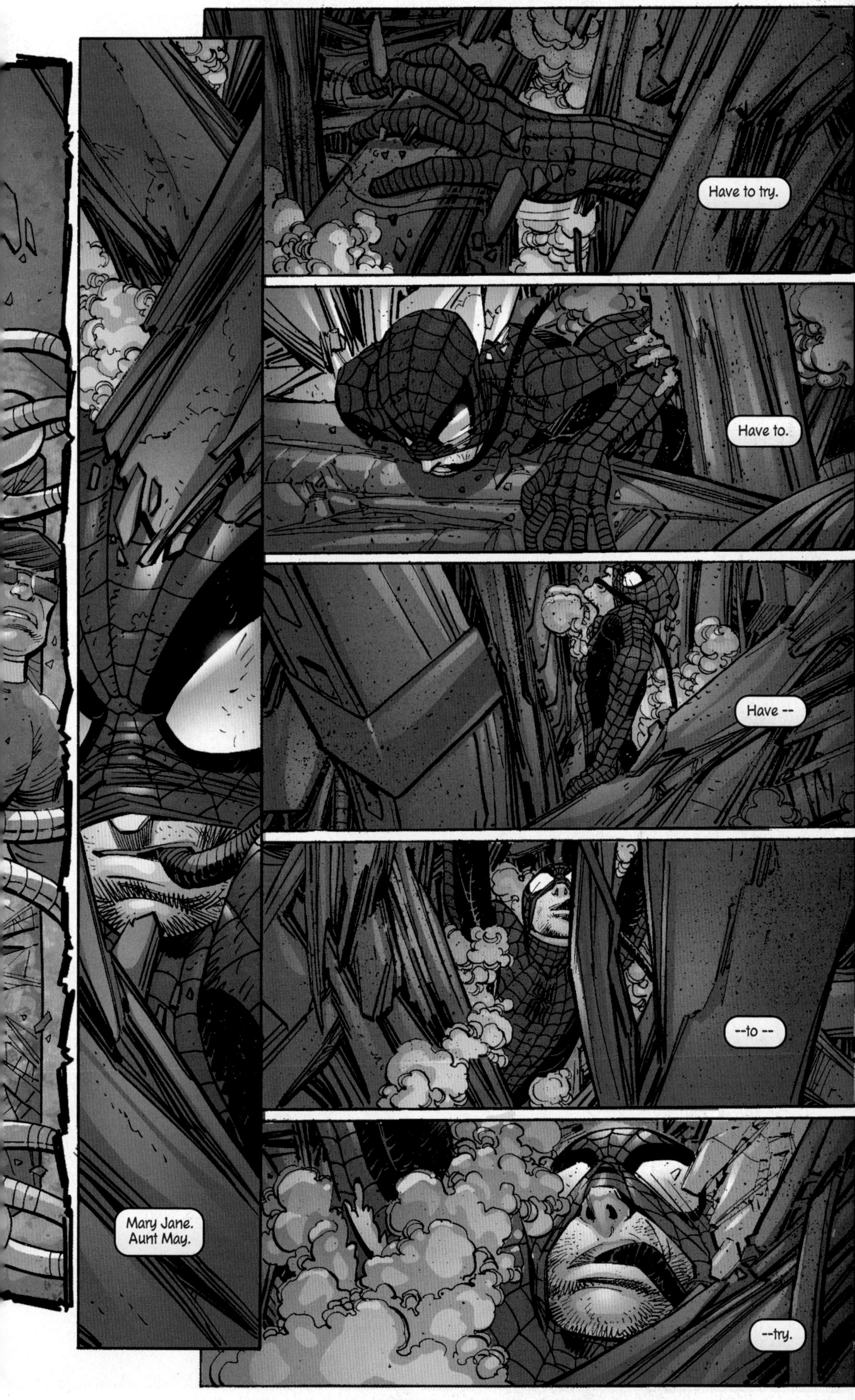
Mary Jane.
Aunt May.
Have to try.
Have to.
Have --
--to --
--try.

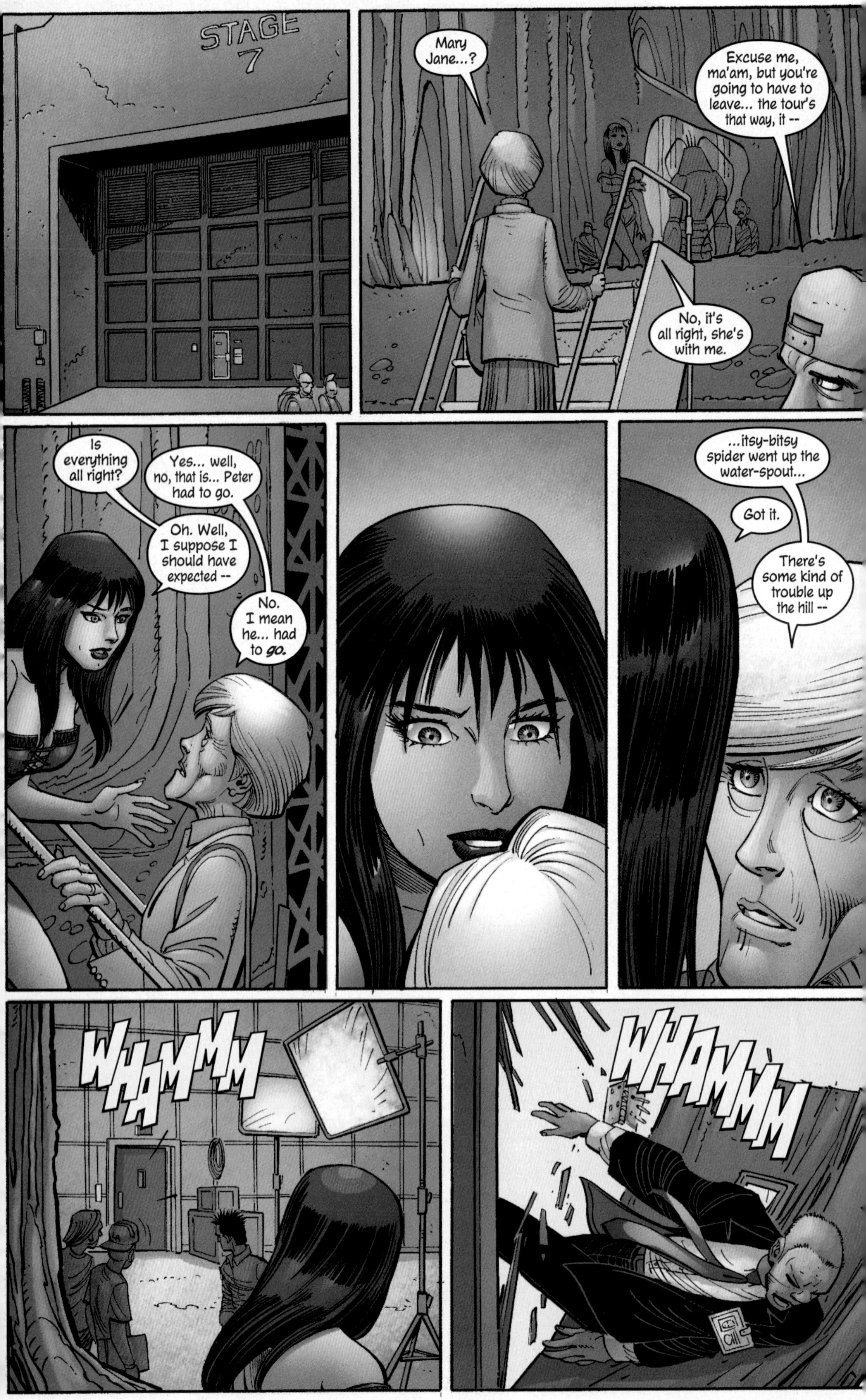
STAGE 7
Mary Jane...?
Excuse me, ma'am, but you're going to have to leave... the tour's that way, it --
No, it's all right, she's with me.
Is everything all right?
Yes... well, no, that is... Peter had to go.
Oh. Well, I suppose I should have expected --
No. I mean he... had to *go.*
...itsy-bitsy spider went up the water-spout...
Got it.
There's some kind of trouble up the hill --
WHAMMMM
WHAMMMM

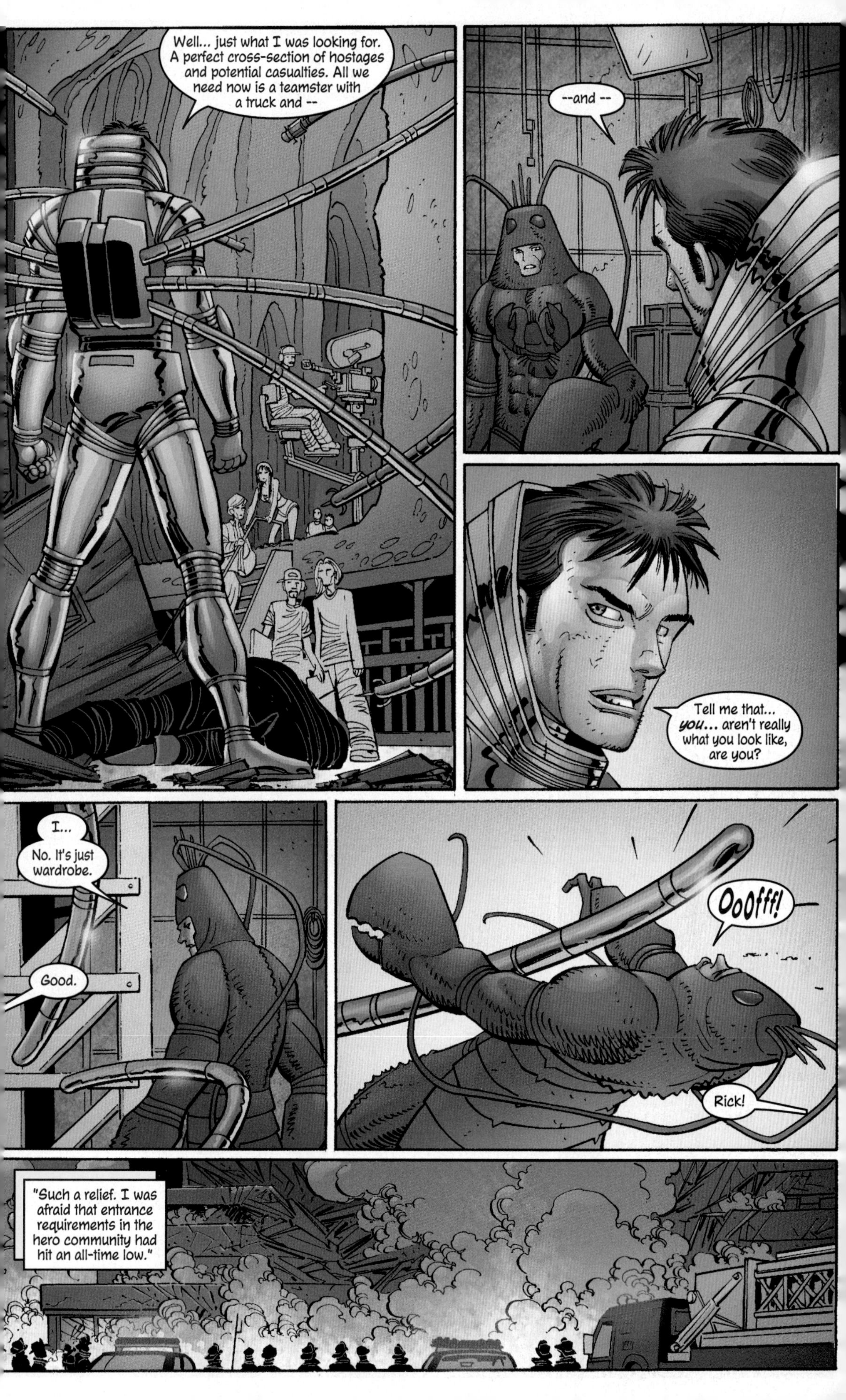
Well... just what I was looking for. A perfect cross-section of hostages and potential casualties. All we need now is a teamster with a truck and --
--and --
Tell me that... *you*... aren't really what you look like, are you?
I...
No. It's just wardrobe.
Good.
OoOfff!
Rick!
"Such a relief. I was afraid that entrance requirements in the hero community had hit an all-time low."

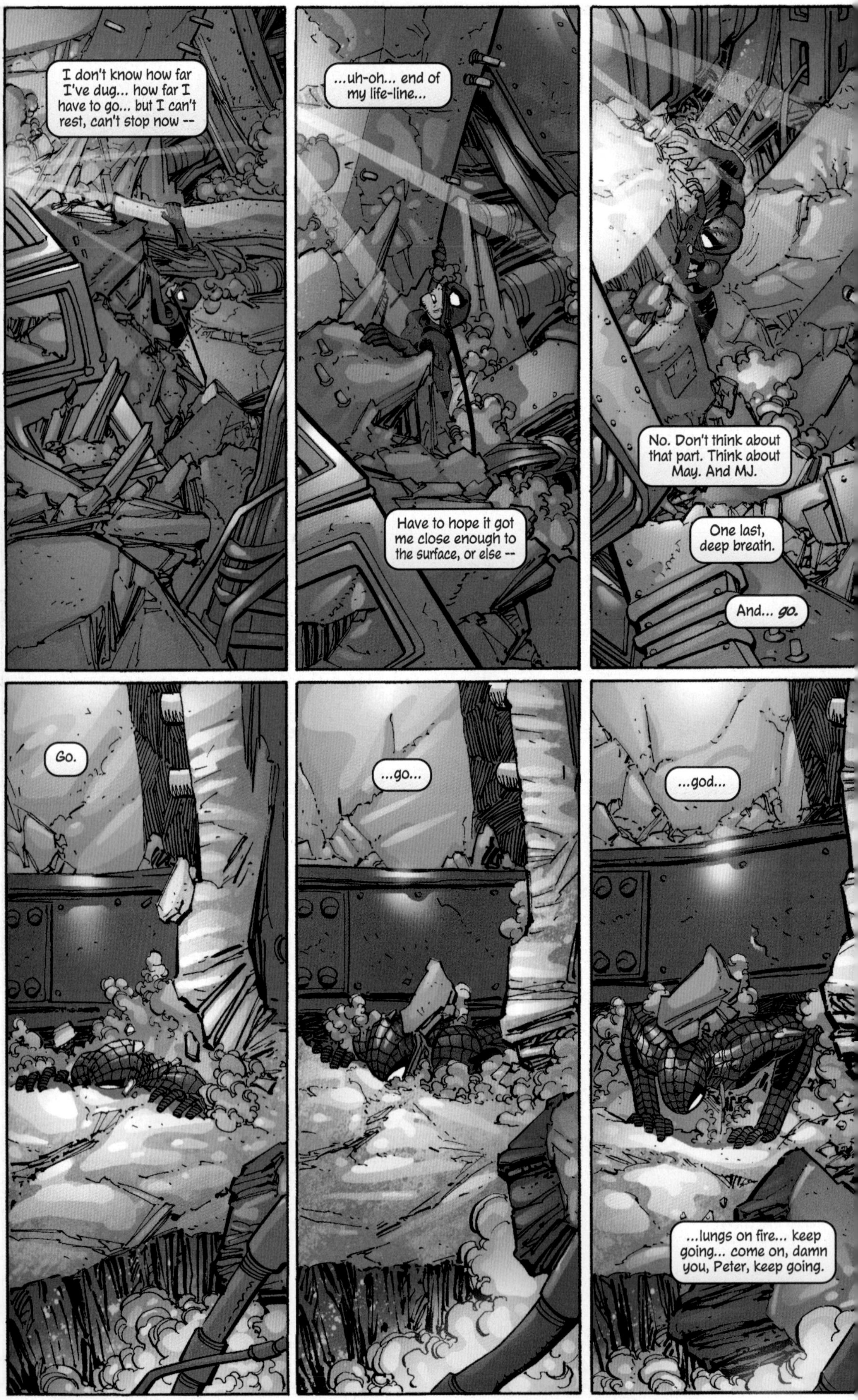
I don't know how far I've dug... how far I have to go... but I can't rest, can't stop now --
...uh-oh... end of my life-line...
Have to hope it got me close enough to the surface, or else --
No. Don't think about that part. Think about May. And MJ.
One last, deep breath.
And... *go.*
Go.
...go...
...god...
...lungs on fire... keep going... come on, damn you, Peter, keep going.

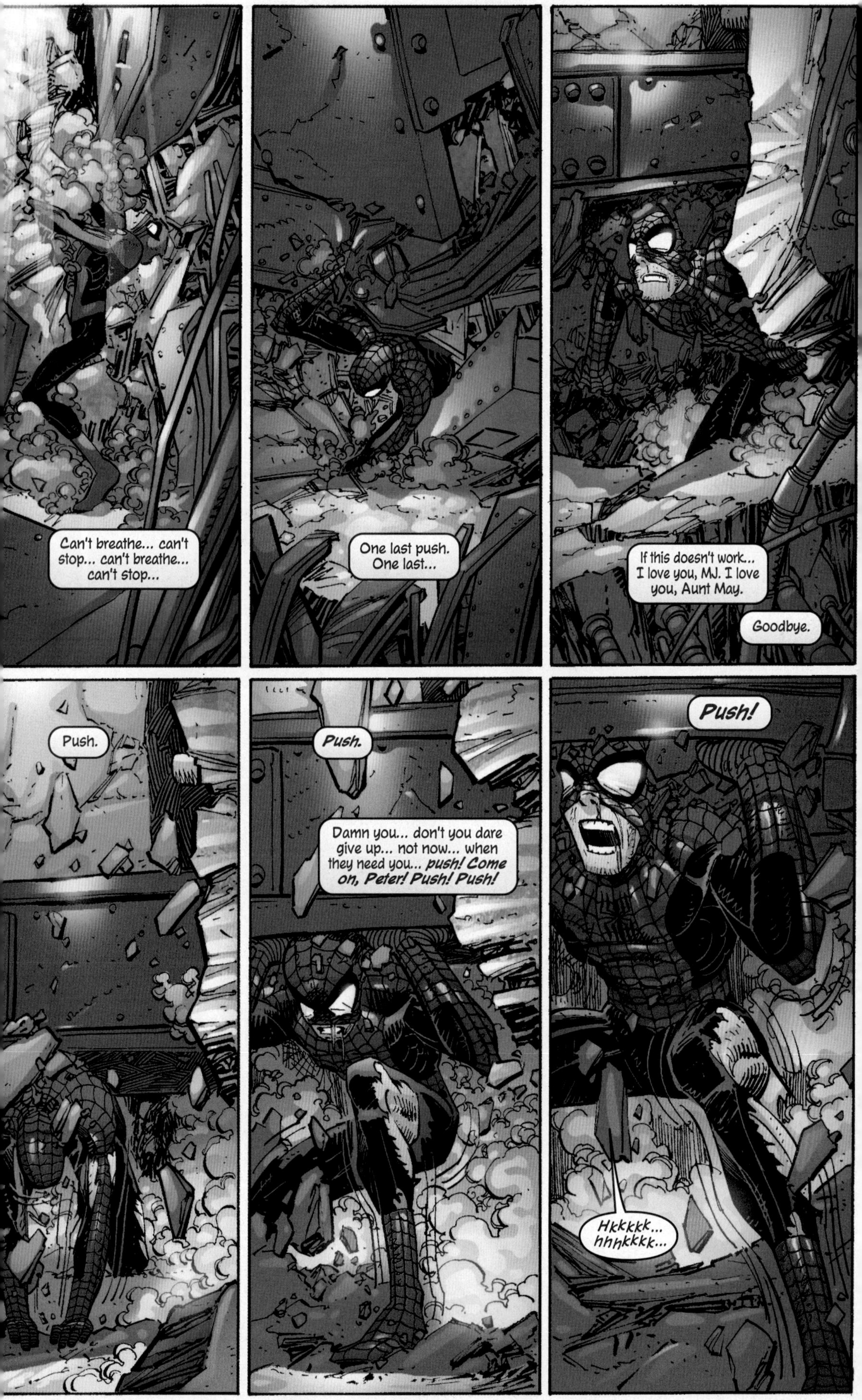

Can't breathe... can't stop... can't breathe... can't stop...
One last push. One last...
If this doesn't work... I love you, MJ. I love you, Aunt May.
Goodbye.
Push.
Push.
Damn you... don't you dare give up... not now... when they need you... push! Come on, Peter! Push! Push!
Push!
Hkkkkk... hhhkkkk...

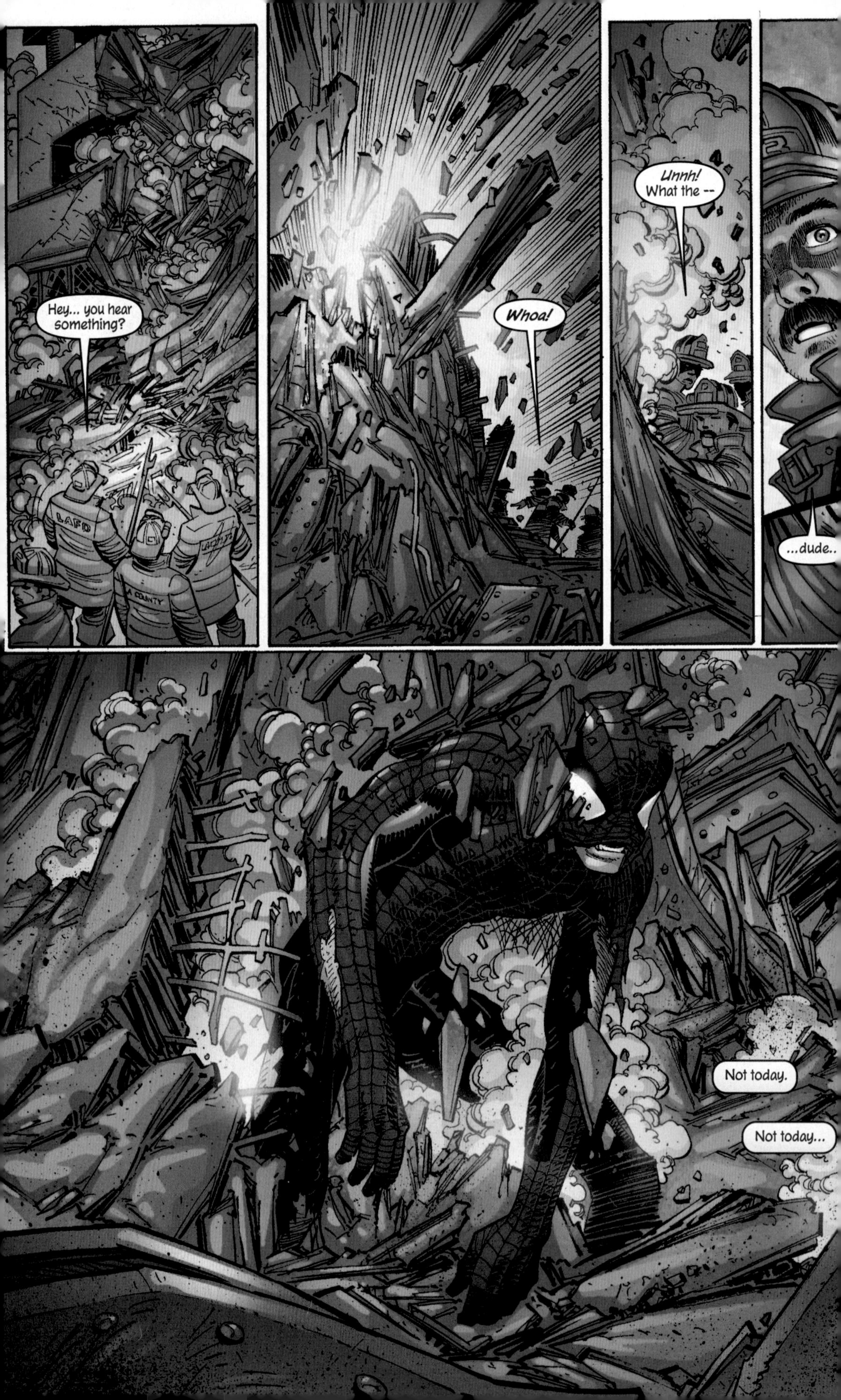

Hey... you hear something?
Whoa!
Unnh! What the --
...dude..
Not today.
Not today...

Look, whoever you are, if you're smart you'll take a hike and get away while you still can.

While I still *can?* Are *you* threatening *me*... in *that?*

If you harm us, there's no way on earth you're getting out of here in one piece. The LAPD has a policy: they don't negotiate over hostages. No one will.

Well, now, let's not be hasty.

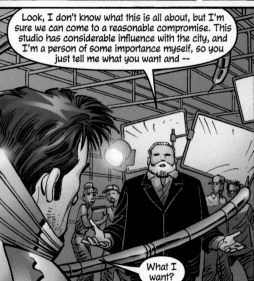

Look, I don't know what this is all about, but I'm sure we can come to a reasonable compromise. This studio has considerable influence with the city, and I'm a person of some importance myself, so you just tell me what you want and --

What I want?

I want a fast car out of here, no pursuit, and no interference from *anyone*. But I know they won't take me seriously, no one ever does.

Until someone dies. So I have to make them understand just how serious I am.

But to show I'm not completely heartless, I should pick someone... expendable. Someone who's already had a good, long life.

So, ma'am, let me ask you a question.

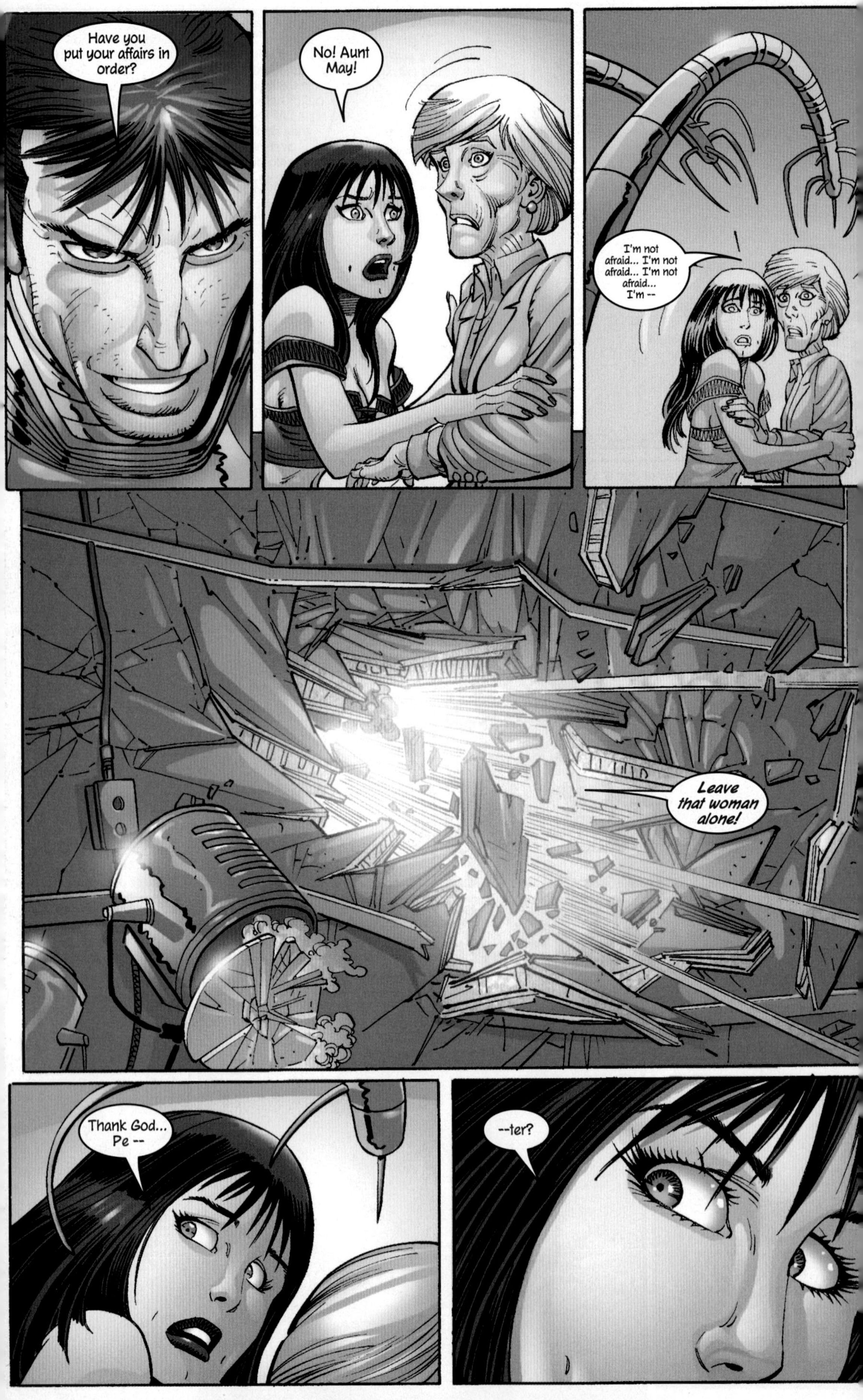
Have you put your affairs in order?
No! Aunt May!
I'm not afraid... I'm not afraid... I'm not afraid... I'm --
Leave that woman alone!
Thank God... Pe --
--ter?

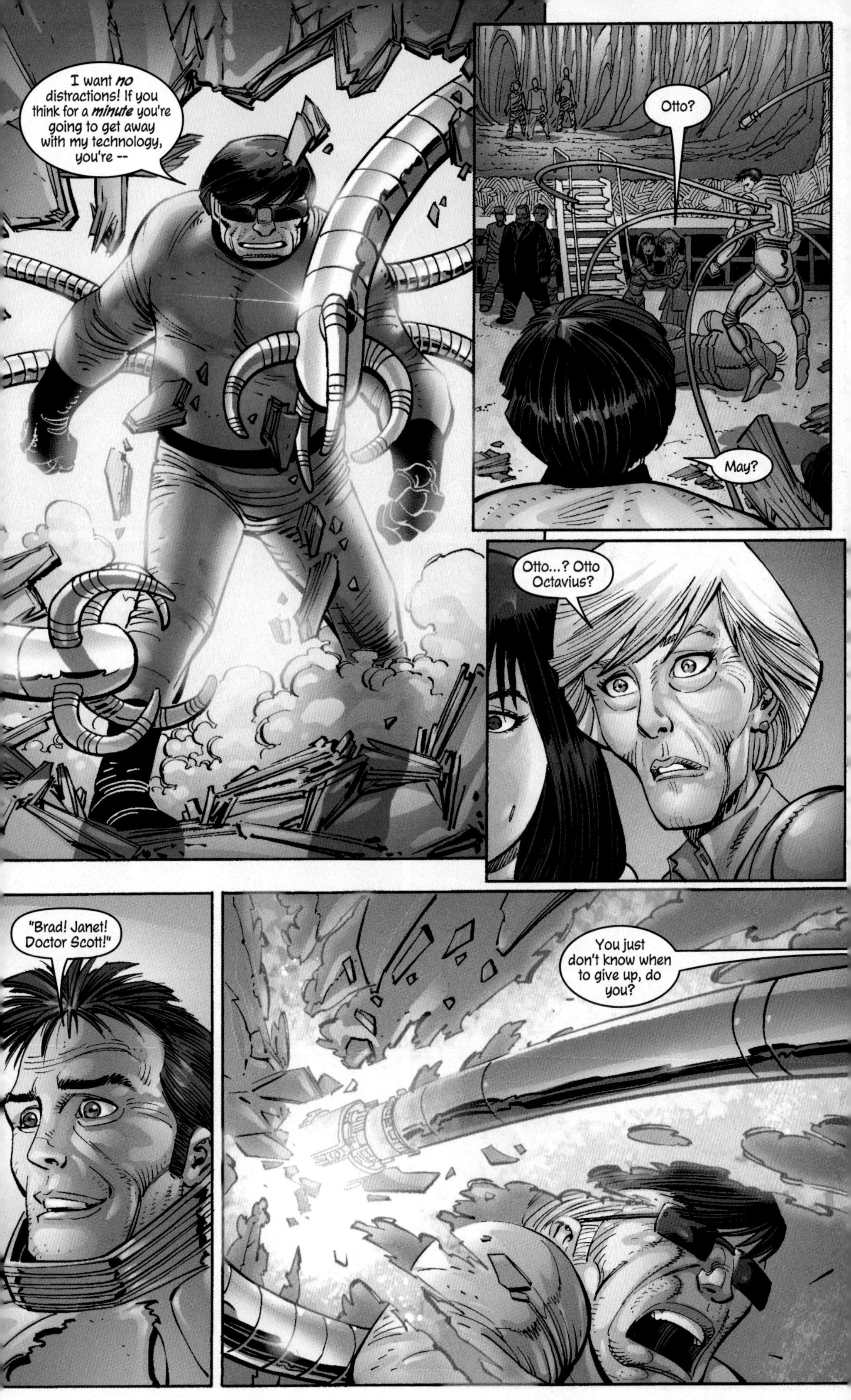
I want *no* distractions! If you think for a *minute* you're going to get away with my technology, you're --
Otto?
May?
Otto...? Otto Octavius?
"Brad! Janet! Doctor Scott!"
You just don't know when to give up, do you?

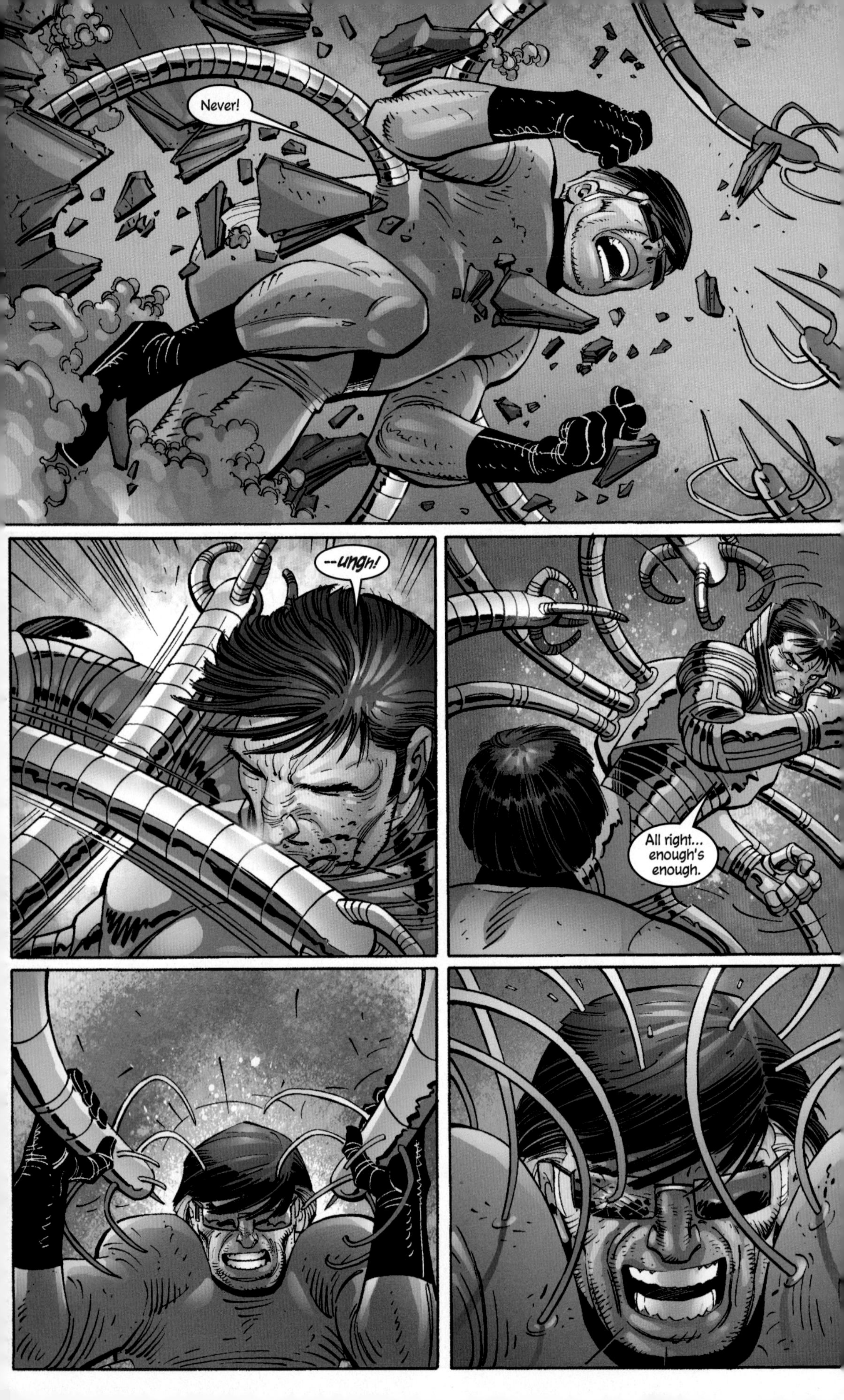
Never!
--ungh!
All right... enough's enough.

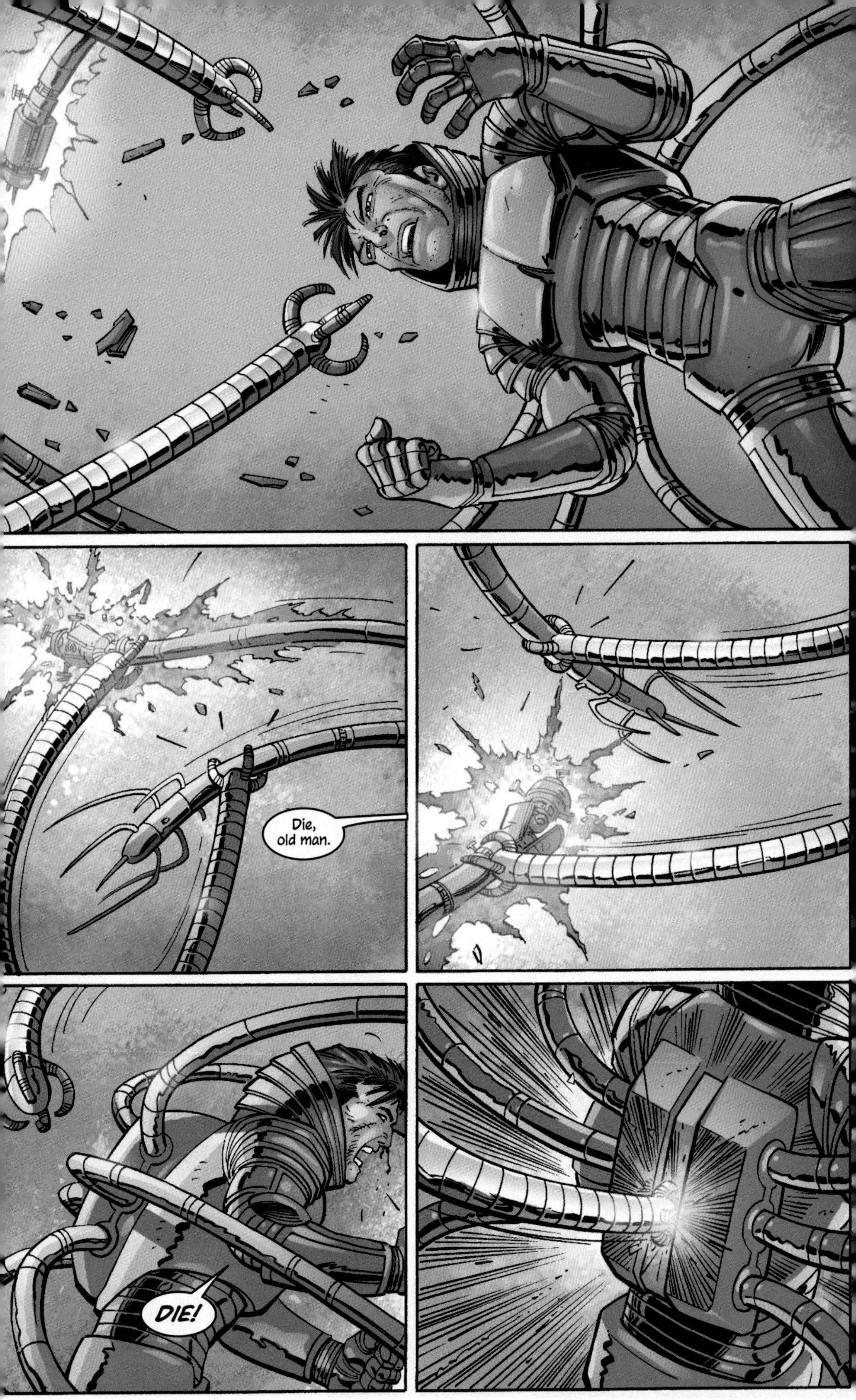
Die,
old man.
DIE!

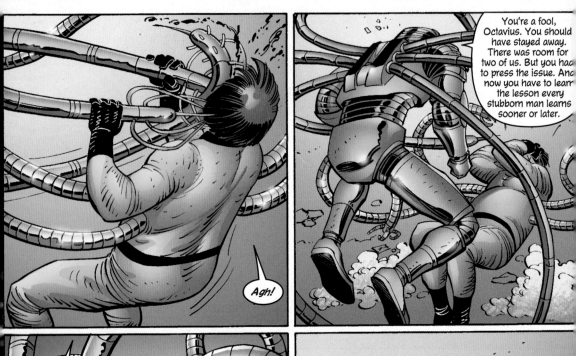

Agh!

You're a fool, Octavius. You should have stayed away. There was room for two of us. But you had to press the issue. And now you have to learn the lesson every stubborn man learns sooner or later.

Whoever has the most advanced technology always wins in the end.

What the --

Thanks for pointing out the obvious.

But it only works if there's nobody else in town more advanced than you are.

Which would include pretty much anybody else shopping at the Sharper Image these days.

Is that--

Yes...But I... think you should stay under here for a while. It's...it's safer.

I catch MJ keeping Aunt May away, where she can't see what shape I'm in, and where she's safe.

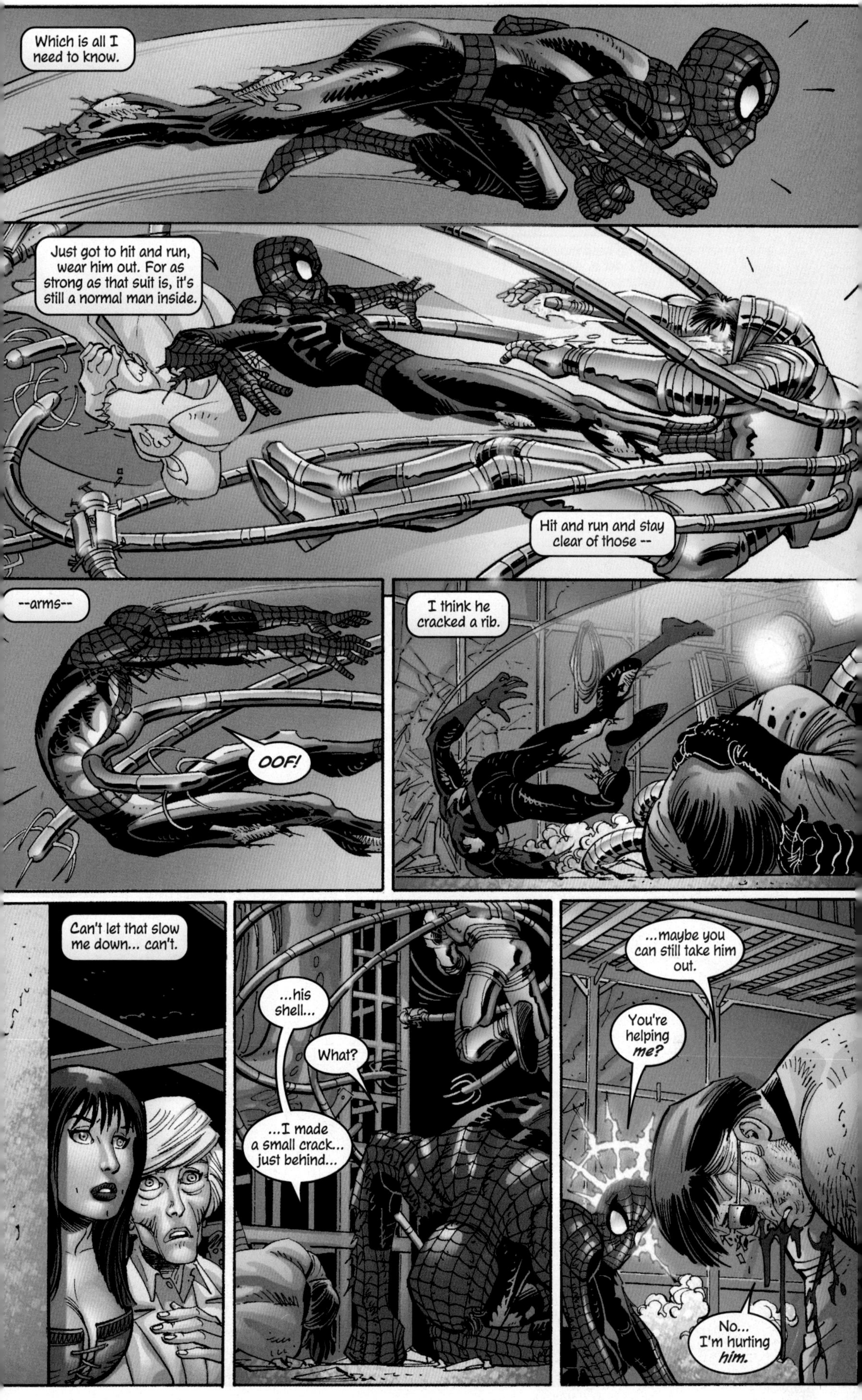
Which is all I need to know.
Just got to hit and run, wear him out. For as strong as that suit is, it's still a normal man inside.
Hit and run and stay clear of those --
--arms--
OOF!
I think he cracked a rib.
Can't let that slow me down... can't.
...his shell...
What?
...I made a small crack... just behind...
...maybe you can still take him out.
You're helping *me?*
No... I'm hurting *him.*

Got to keep moving... if I get close I risk getting snared...those arms can rip me in two if they get a good grip.
Just got to hold on and try to find it.
And pray.
What're you --
I'm trying to decide what to call you. If he's Doctor Octopus, does that make you--
uhhn
Carlyle Calamari?
C'mon, where is it...where *is* it?
...where...
GOT IT!
Room's spinning...no time... no time to try and wrestle it free...just one chance--
PSSSSSHHHH
Just have to try...to gum up the works. Empty the whole thing. Let the webbing expand inside the suit.

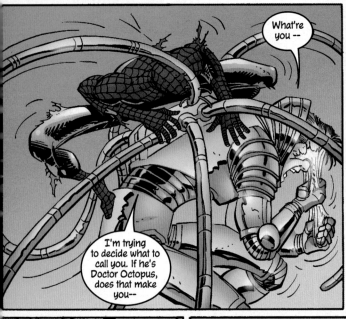

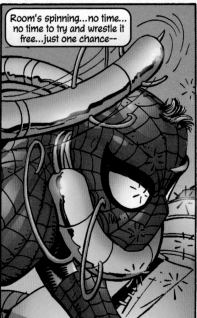

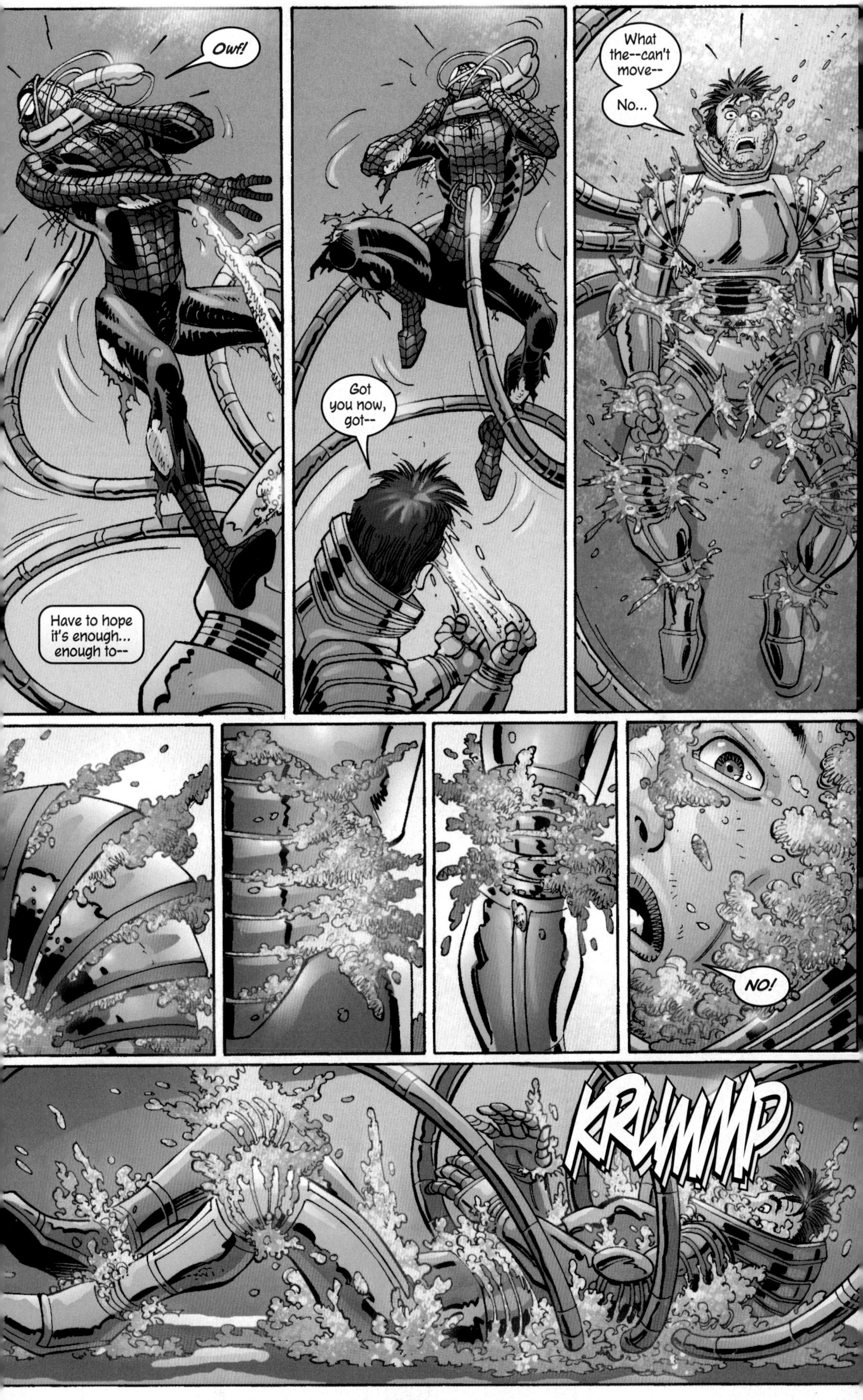
Owf!
Have to hope it's enough... enough to--
Got you now, got--
What the--can't move--
No...
NO!
KRUMMP

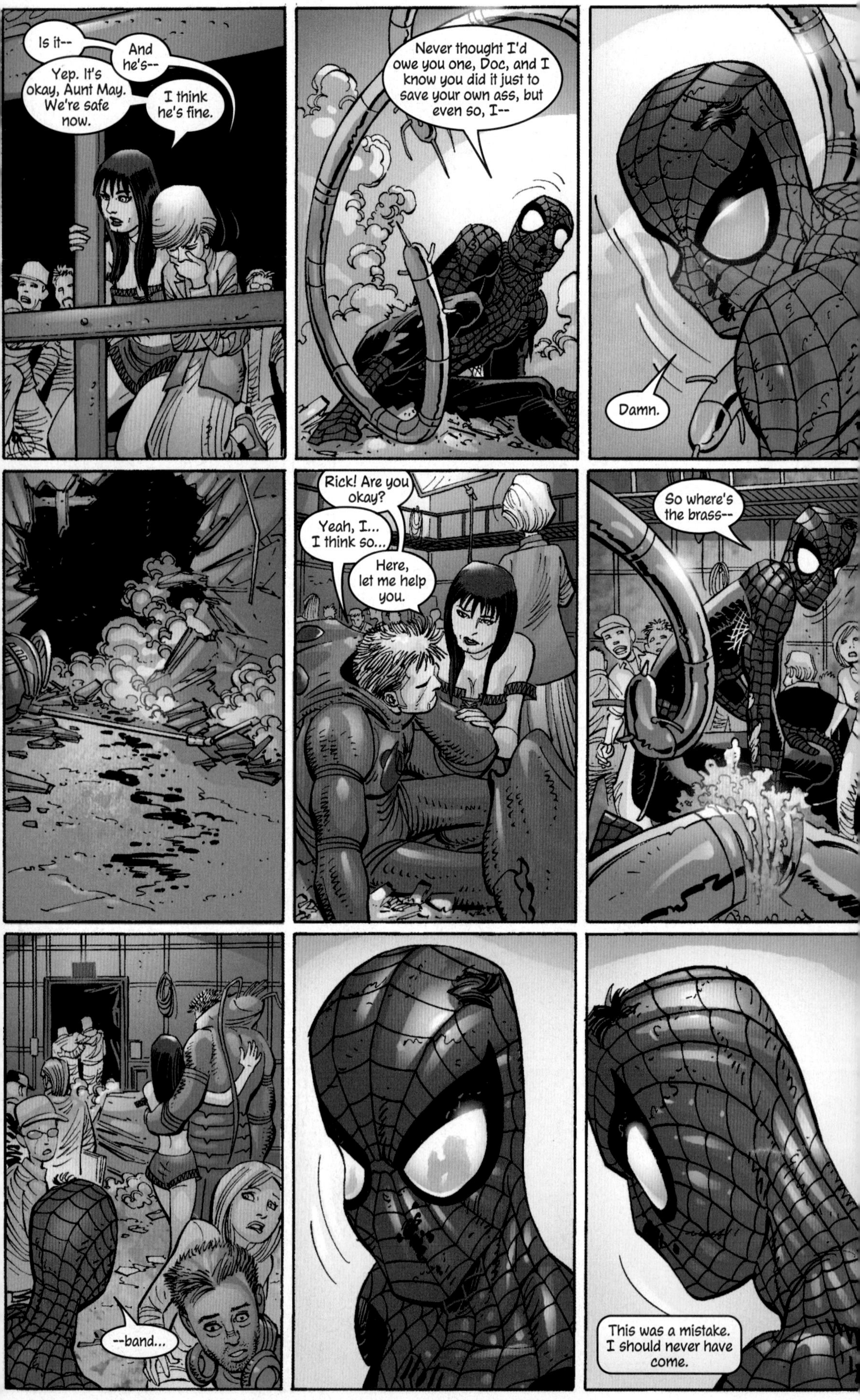

Is it--
And he's--
Yep. It's okay, Aunt May. We're safe now.
I think he's fine.
Never thought I'd owe you one, Doc, and I know you did it just to save your own ass, but even so, I--
Damn.
Rick! Are you okay?
Yeah, I... I think so...
Here, let me help you.
So where's the brass--
--band...
This was a mistake. I should never have come.

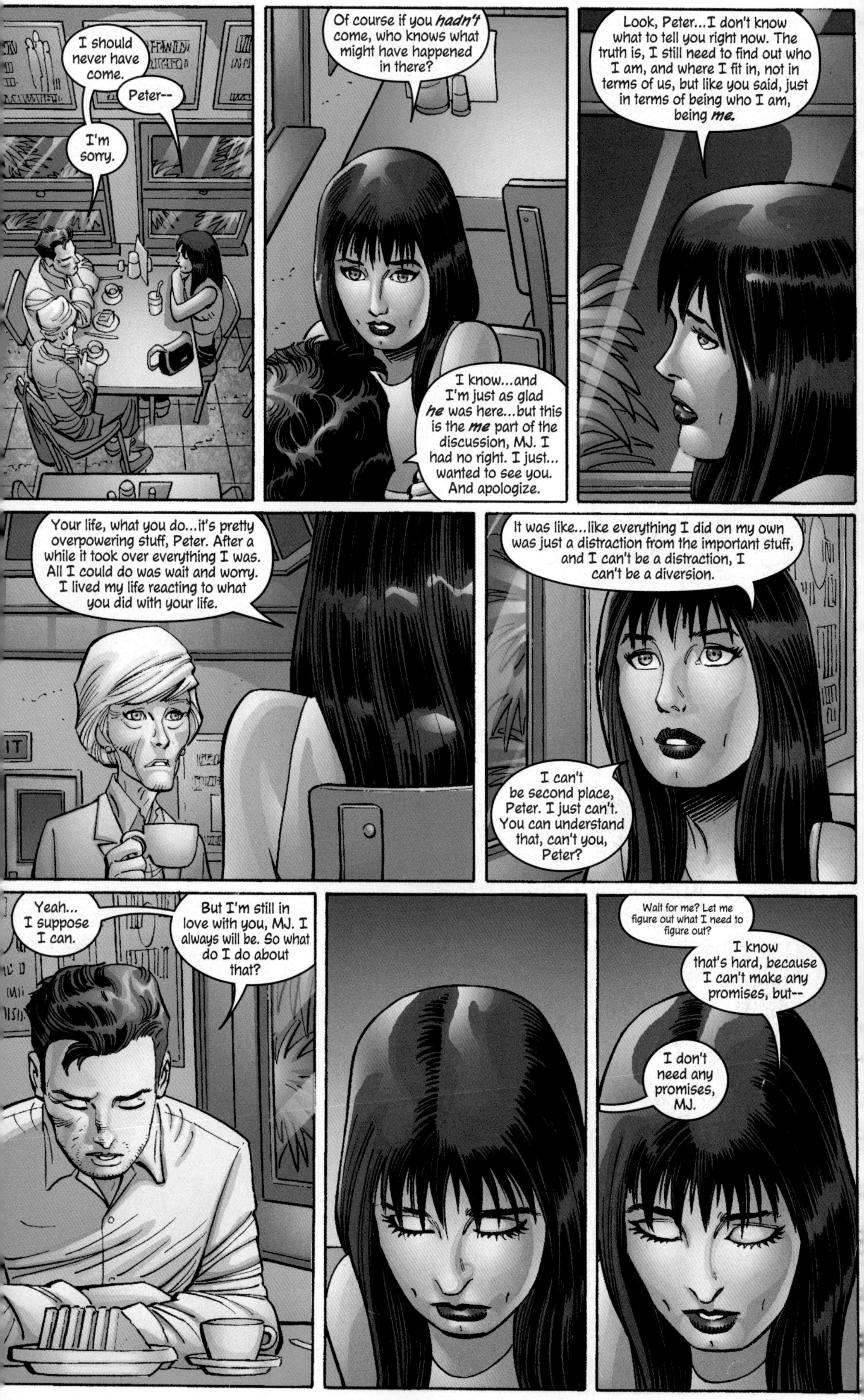
I should never have come.
Peter--
I'm sorry.
Of course if you *hadn't* come, who knows what might have happened in there?
I know...and I'm just as glad *he* was here...but this is the *me* part of the discussion, MJ. I had no right. I just... wanted to see you. And apologize.
Look, Peter...I don't know what to tell you right now. The truth is, I still need to find out who I am, and where I fit in, not in terms of us, but like you said, just in terms of being who I am, being *me.*
Your life, what you do...it's pretty overpowering stuff, Peter. After a while it took over everything I was. All I could do was wait and worry. I lived my life reacting to what you did with your life.
It was like...like everything I did on my own was just a distraction from the important stuff, and I can't be a distraction, I can't be a diversion.
I can't be second place, Peter. I just can't. You can understand that, can't you, Peter?
Yeah... I suppose I can.
But I'm still in love with you, MJ. I always will be. So what do I do about that?
Wait for me? Let me figure out what I need to figure out?
I know that's hard, because I can't make any promises, but--
I don't need any promises, MJ.

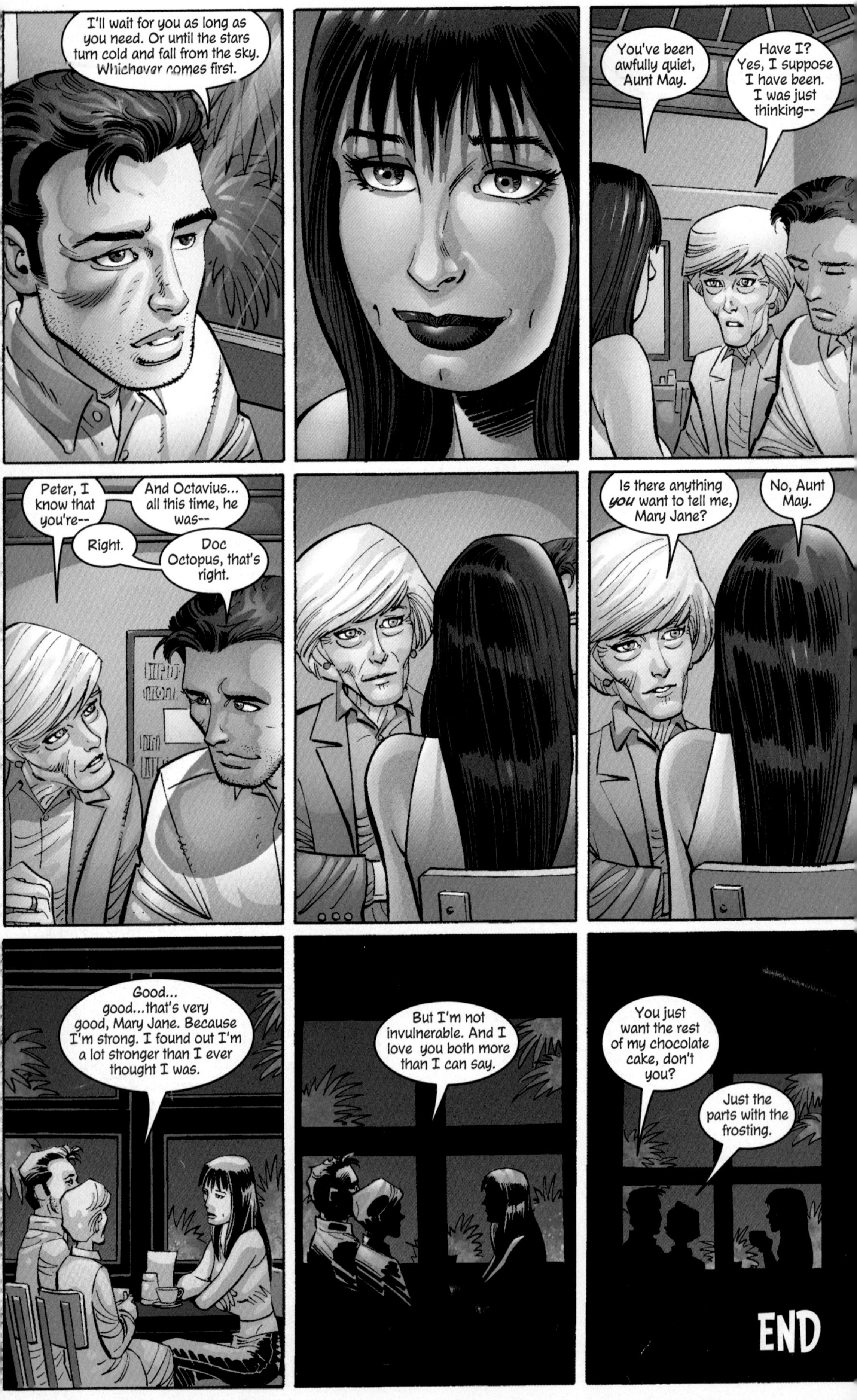
I'll wait for you as long as you need. Or until the stars turn cold and fall from the sky. Whichever comes first.
You've been awfully quiet, Aunt May.
Have I? Yes, I suppose I have been. I was just thinking--
Peter, I know that you're--
Right.
And Octavius... all this time, he was--
Doc Octopus, that's right.
Is there anything *you* want to tell me, Mary Jane?
No, Aunt May.
Good... good...that's very good, Mary Jane. Because I'm strong. I found out I'm a lot stronger than I ever thought I was.
But I'm not invulnerable. And I love you both more than I can say.
You just want the rest of my chocolate cake, don't you?
Just the parts with the frosting.
END

the AMAZING SPIDER-MAN

ISSUE #39
WRITER: J. MICHAEL STRACZYNSKI
PENCILS: JOHN ROMITA JR.
INKS: SCOTT HANNA
COLORS: DAN KEMP

PAGE ONE

FULL PAGE
A penthouse building in Los Angeles. Dawn.

1 T&C   "MEANWHILE...."

J. MICAEL STRACZYNSKI - WRITER
JOHN ROMITA, JR. - PENCILS
SCOTT HANNA - INKS
BRIAN HABERLIN - COLORS
COMICRAFT - LETTERS
AXEL ALONSO - EDITOR
JOE QUESADA - CHIEF
BILL JEMAS - PRES

PAGE TWO

PANEL ONE
Mary Jane in something knee-bucklingly revealing. She's lying on one side of the bed. What you do when you've been used to sleeping with someone for a long time and they're not there anymore. The other side of the bedding is barely even pulled back. She's facing —

PANEL TWO
The alarm clock. 5:29 A.M.

PANEL THREE
Close on Mary Jane's face. Sad.

PANEL FOUR
She's getting up, slipping off the shoulder strap as she rises.

PAGE THREE

PANEL ONE
The bedroom leading to the bathroom. The TV is on, silent, at one end of the bedroom. There's a commercial for Krell Toothpaste. We get a sense of MJ inside the bathroom, going about her business.

PANEL TWO
Same exact angle, a little later. There's a newscaster on the TV now, sitting somewhere inside a studio.

PANEL THREE
Same again, but now a reporter in the field, outside, with a hand mike, is on camera. MJ still hasn't come out.

PANEL FOUR
There's now footage of Spider-Man swinging by, in action, saving people from a terrorist-looking guy firing a huge gun.

PAGE FOUR

PANEL ONE
MJ has emerged, barely wearing a towel, and is now standing in front of the TV, watching the report on Spider-Man.

PANEL TWO
Ditto. He's carrying people out of harm's way. She hasn't moved.

PANEL THREE
We've gone to commercial. Fandangoing frankfurters onscreen. She's heading back to the bathroom.

PANEL FOUR
She's back inside the bathroom, the commercial continuing out here.

PAGE FIVE

PANEL ONE
MJ on a beach in LA, modeling a micro-small bathing suit, smiling a million-dollar smile for the photographer and his support crew.

PANEL TWO
Flashbulbs go off; she's turning it all loose.

PANEL THREE
Later. She's sitting by herself in an outdoor coffee shop. Eyes down. Lost in thought.

PANEL FOUR
Some of the crew goes by, waving. She's all smiles again, waving back.

PANEL FIVE
Same as panel three. When they're gone, the pretense falls away.

PAGE SIX

PANEL ONE
A big Hollywood premiere at the Chinese Theater. Limos. Spotlights. Fans piled behind red velvet ropes. A red carpet leading to the theater. The movie's title is RAVING MADMEN, and a banner says THE FUNNIEST MOVIE OF THE YEAR - Los Angeles Times.

PANEL TWO
A limo has pulled up and MJ is getting out. More flashbulbs, more of the million-dollar smile.

PANEL THREE
She moves down the red carpet, smiling and waving, more flashbulbs.

PANEL FOUR
A raking angle past MJ in one of the theater seats, so we see those behind and beside her, laughing uproariously at the OS screen, the light from which spills onto the seats a bit. She's looking down, not smiling, not sad, just...distant.

PANEL FIVE
She emerges from the theater, smiling and waving again.

PANEL SIX
Her limo pulls away from the curb.

WORLD PREMIERE
RAVING MADMEN

PAGE SEVEN

PANEL ONE
Back in her bedroom, night, she's in the bathroom getting ready for bed. The TV is on. It looks like a hospital drama.

PANEL TWO
Same as one; there's a commercial for new improved Flense! She's still in the bathroom, just a corner of her visible.

PANEL THREE
The repeat of the Spider-Man story comes on the TV.

PANEL FOUR
She's out again, this time in her lingerie, watching the story.

PANEL FIVE
Same as panel four.

PAGE EIGHT

PANEL ONE
She's getting into bed. On just the one side.

PANEL TWO
Lights are out. She's in bed. Sleeping on one side.

PANEL THREE
The alarm clock reads 11:30.

PANEL FOUR
On MJ, who is awake.

PANEL FIVE
The alarm clock reads 5:29.

PANEL SIX
On MJ, who is awake and looking at the other, unoccupied pillow. Missing Peter.

ASTOR LIBRARY
FOUNDED BY
JOHN JACOB ASTOR
FOR THE
ADVANCEMENT OF USEFUL KNOWLEDGE
HELP
YOUR
LIBRARY
TODAY

PAGE NINE

FULL PAGE
The New York Public Library, morning.

PAGE TEN

PANEL ONE
Aunt May in the reference area of the library, where they keep the microfiche files for magazine and newspaper archives. She's sitting at one of these microfiche booths.

PANEL TWO
Closer to find her looking at the screen, which is filled with newsprint we can't read, though from the banner we can tell it's the Daily Bugle.

PANEL THREE
Close on the Bugle headline.

TEXT: DAILY BUGLE
SPIDER-MAN: THREAT OR MENACE?

PANEL FOUR
On Aunt May's look of annoyance.

PANEL FIVE
Close on New York Herald headline.

TEXT: THE NEW YORK HERALD
SPIDER-MAN FRIGHTENS RESIDENTS

PANEL SIX
More annoyance from Aunt May

DAILY BUGLE
SPIDER-MAN: THREAT OR MENACE?
EDITORIAL BY J. JONAH JAMESON
New York Herald
SPIDER-MAN FRIGHTENS RESIDENTS

BROOKLYN BANNER
SPIDER-MAN: MISUNDERSTOOD?

PAGE ELEVEN

PANEL ONE
Another headline, this time the Brooklyn Banner:

1 TEXT: BROOKLYN BANNER
SPIDER-MAN, MISUNDERSTOOD?

PANEL TWO
She looks a bit more mollified.

PANEL THREE
A sitting area in the library. May has a notepad in front of her and a Cappuccino from Starhacks. She's thinking.

PANEL FOUR
Same as panel 3.

PANEL FIVE
The cup of coffee is in the trash she's heading across the library.

PAGE TWELVE

PANEL ONE
A panel showing May in front of a typewriter on a table in the library.
She's looking off to —

PANEL TWO
Actually an extension of panel one showing the rest of the table taken up by computers.

PANEL THREE
May is behind one of the terminals, typing (too small to read)

1 TEXT:
TO: SUBSCRIPTIONSEDITOR@NEWYORKHERALD.COM
CC: Because of your

PANEL FOUR
CLOSE on the CRT, which reads —

2 TEXT:
TO: SUBSCRIPTIONEDITOR@THEDAILYBUGLE.COM
CC:

PANEL FIVE
Further down the screen

3 TEXT: Because of your one-sided coverage of Spider-Man I am canceling my subscription to the Bugle.

Because of your
To: subscriptionseditor@thedailybugle.com
Cc:
Because of your one-sided coverage of Spider-Man I am canceling my subscription to the Bugle.

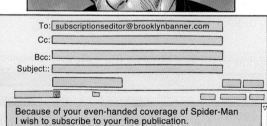

To: subscriptionseditor@newyorkherald.com
Cc:
Bcc:
Subject::
Because of your one-sided coverage of Spider-Man I am canceling my subscription to the Herald.
To: subscriptionseditor@brooklynbanner.com
Cc:
Bcc:
Subject::
Because of your even-handed coverage of Spider-Man I wish to subscribe to your fine publication.

PAGE THIRTEEN

PANEL ONE
On the CRT which reads —

1 TEXT:
TO: SUBSCRIPTIONSEDITOR@NEWYORKHERALD.COM
CC: Because of your one-sided coverage of Spider-Man I am canceling my subscription to the Herald.

PANEL TWO
Looking back to May for a moment then

PANEL THREE
On the CRT which reads —

2 TEXT:
TO: SUBSCRIPTIONSEDITOR@BROOKLYNBANNER.COM
CC: Because of your even-handed coverage of Spider-Man I wish to subscribe to your fine publication.

PANEL FOUR
Aunt May leans back, smiling.

PANEL FIVE
She looks to the CRT booth next to hers.

AGE FOURTEEN

ANEL ONE
side angle of a teenager, looking furtively at he monitor. We see only what looks like a abe, barely dressed, under a website banner eading . . .

BANNER: LIVE NUDE CHEERLEADZERS

ANEL TWO
lay looks at the kid.

ANEL THREE
he kid looks at May with a silent "eep." aught.

ANEL FOUR
he kid, chagrined and unhappy, is now ooking at the image on-screen for a website ntitled . . .

BANNER: PHYSICS THROUGH THE AGES.

ANEL FIVE
lay, smiling, goes back to her typing.

LIVE NUDE CHEERLEADERS
PHYSICS THROUGH THE AGES

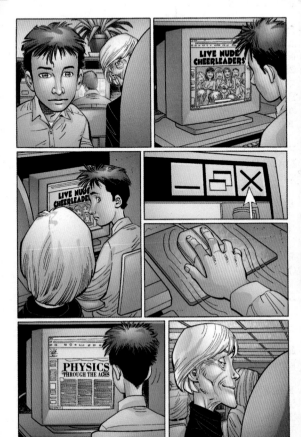

To: The Letterman Show
To: The Tonight Show
To: Larry King
To: Dan Rather
To: Oprah Winfrey
Have you ever considered doing a show about the lives of such super heroes as Spider-Man? I feel they are very misunderstood by the American people. I'm sure that beneath that mask there is a good person, a kind person, a good face, someone who may have been awkward as a child and always has to check the door before he goes out to make sure it's locked, but still a good and kind person who could profit from the exposure your fine program would provide to help set the record straight and see him for the decent, loving, occasionally vegetarian person he is.
Send

PAGE FIFTEEN

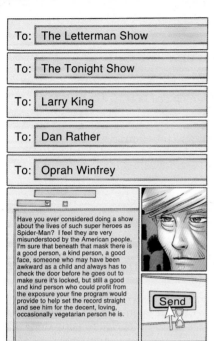

PANELS ONE THROUGH FIVE
Each small panel a CRT screen with a different email address:

1 TEXT: TO THE LETTERMAN SHOW

2 TEXT: TO THE TONIGHT SHOW

3 TEXT: TO LARRY KING

4 TEXT: TO DAN RATHER

5 TEXT: TO OPRAH WINFREY

PANEL SIX
A long horizontal panel just showing the lines on the CRT.

2 TEXT: Have you ever considered doing a show about the lives of such superheroes as Spider-Man? I feel they are very misunderstood by the American people. I'm sure that beneath that mask there is a good person, a kind person, a good face, someone who may have been awkward as a child and always has to check the door before he goes out to make sure it's locked, but still a good and kind person who could profit from the exposure your fine program would provide to help set the record straight and see him for the decent, loving, occasionally vegetarian person he is.

PANEL SEVEN
A small panel as she hits SEND.

PAGE SIXTEEN

PANEL ONE
May's back in the sitting area with another Cappuccino, looking at her notebook.

PANEL TWO
Noting check marks beside some of her to-do items.

DROP OFF LAUNDRY

CANCEL SUBSCRIPTIONS TO PAPERS THAT DON'T LIKE P.

TRY TO IMPROVE P'S IMAGE

PICK UP ZANTAC AND TUCKS

KEEP WORKING TO FORGIVE PETER

PANEL THREE
Closer on May as she looks at –

PANEL FOUR
Closer on the last line:

KEEP WORKING TO FORGIVE P.

PANEL FIVE
Hand touching face, she looks off into the distance.

To do!
1 Drop off laundry
2 Cancel subscriptions to papers that don't like Peter
3 Try to improve Peter's image!
4 Pick up Zantac and Tucks
5 Keep working to forgive Peter
Keep working to forgive Peter

that don't
Try to impr
Pick up Lots of Zant
Keep worki

PAGE SEVENTEEN

PANEL ONE
She's writing in the notebook.

PANEL TWO
She's penciled in LOTS OF between PICK UP and ZANTAC

PANEL THREE
As May exits the library and heads away down the street.

AGE EIGHTEEN

ULL PAGE SPLASH
pider-Man is swinging into a burning building here we see a young woman and her child linging to a broken fire escape.

POLICE
TIMES SQUARE NEW YORK
DOW DROPS

PAGE NINETEEN

PANEL ONE
Spider-Man is carrying the young woman and her child away from the structure.

PANEL TWO
He sets them down on the sidewalk as neighbors come on the run.

PANEL THREE
Spider-Man looks to the building as it collapses and the neighbors move off among themselves or to look on.

PANEL FOUR
Spider-Man starts away, but pauses at the sight of a TV on in the window of an electronics store.

PANEL FIVE
Closer on the TV, revealing Mary Jane at the premiere we saw earlier. Waving, happy.

PAGE TWENTY

PANEL ONE
On Spider-Man's face, unreadable.

PANEL TWO
Tighter still on the screen, where caught in the glare of flashbulbs, MJ looks totally happy.

PANEL THREE
We've pulled back enough to make out Spider-Man's reflection in the glass as he swings away from the store, MJ disappearing into the theater at the same time.

PANEL FOUR
Spider-Man swinging through the night skyline.

PANEL FIVE
Spider-Man entering Peter's apartment through the window, pulling off his mask.

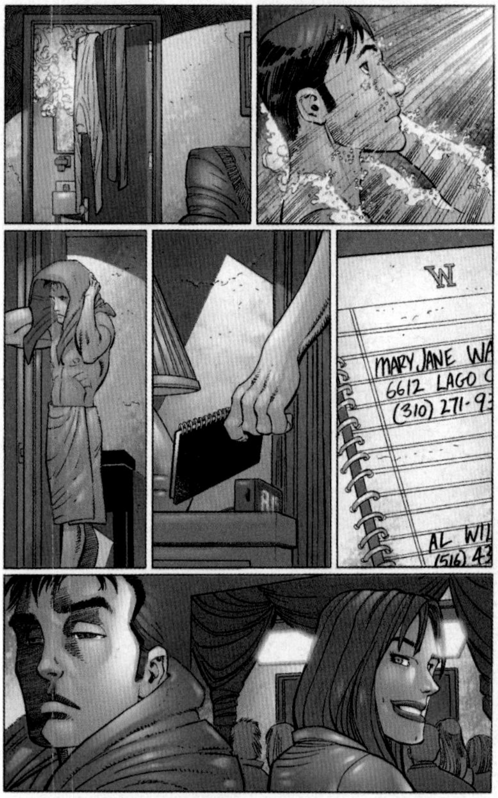

W
MARY JANE WA
6612 LAGO C
(310) 271-9
AL WI
(516) 43

PAGE TWENTY-ONE

PANEL ONE
His costume draped over a chair, steam rises from the bathroom.

PANEL TWO
Close on Peter in the shower, looking distant.

PANEL THREE
He's emerged from the shower, wearing one towel and using another to dry his hair.
PANEL FOUR
He's picked up a personal organizer.

PANEL FIVE
We see part of an entry in the phone number section:

MARY JANE, 310-271-9

PANEL SIX
Close on Peter, considering.

PANEL SEVEN
Flashback to the TV shot of MJ looking happy.

PAGE TWENTY-TWO

PANEL ONE
The organizer is closed now, back on the dresser, as Peter moves off to get dressed.

PANEL TWO
Peter dining across from May at the dinner table, both smiling. It's a sidelong angle, with May and Peter at either end of frame, a photo of MJ on the sideboard between them.

PANEL THREE
MJ, asleep in bed, as we first saw her, a photo of her and Peter visible on one of the dressers.

PANEL FOUR
Aunt May, back supported by several pillows, in bed, glasses on but asleep, a library book on her lap. She fell asleep reading, a one side-table lamp on beside her. The book is THE PSYCHOLOGY OF SUPERHEROES, by Luthor Prang. On one side-table is a photo of her and Uncle Ben, on the other is the same shot of MJ and Peter.

PANEL FIVE
Peter, asleep in his bed, a magazine featuring photos of MJ on a nearby table or dresser. There's something on the dresser beside it.

PANEL SIX
Closer on the magazine, where we see MJ in full display, but part of the Spider-Man mask is covering her.

PANEL SEVEN
Close on the Spider-Man mask, filling the frame, caught in moonlight with cross-hatching from the window frame.

PANEL EIGHT
Just the eyes of the mask, filling frame.
End-

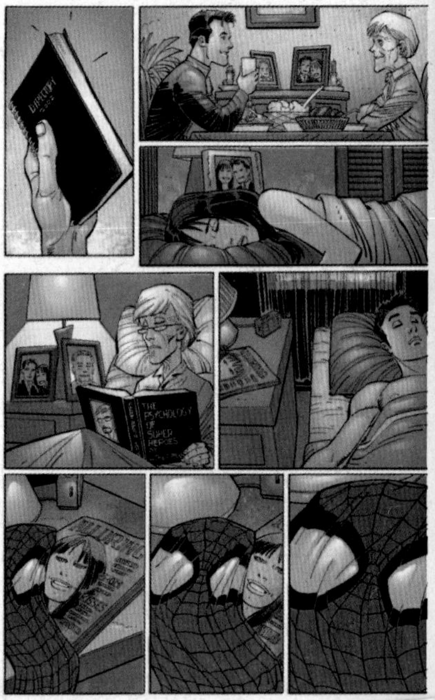

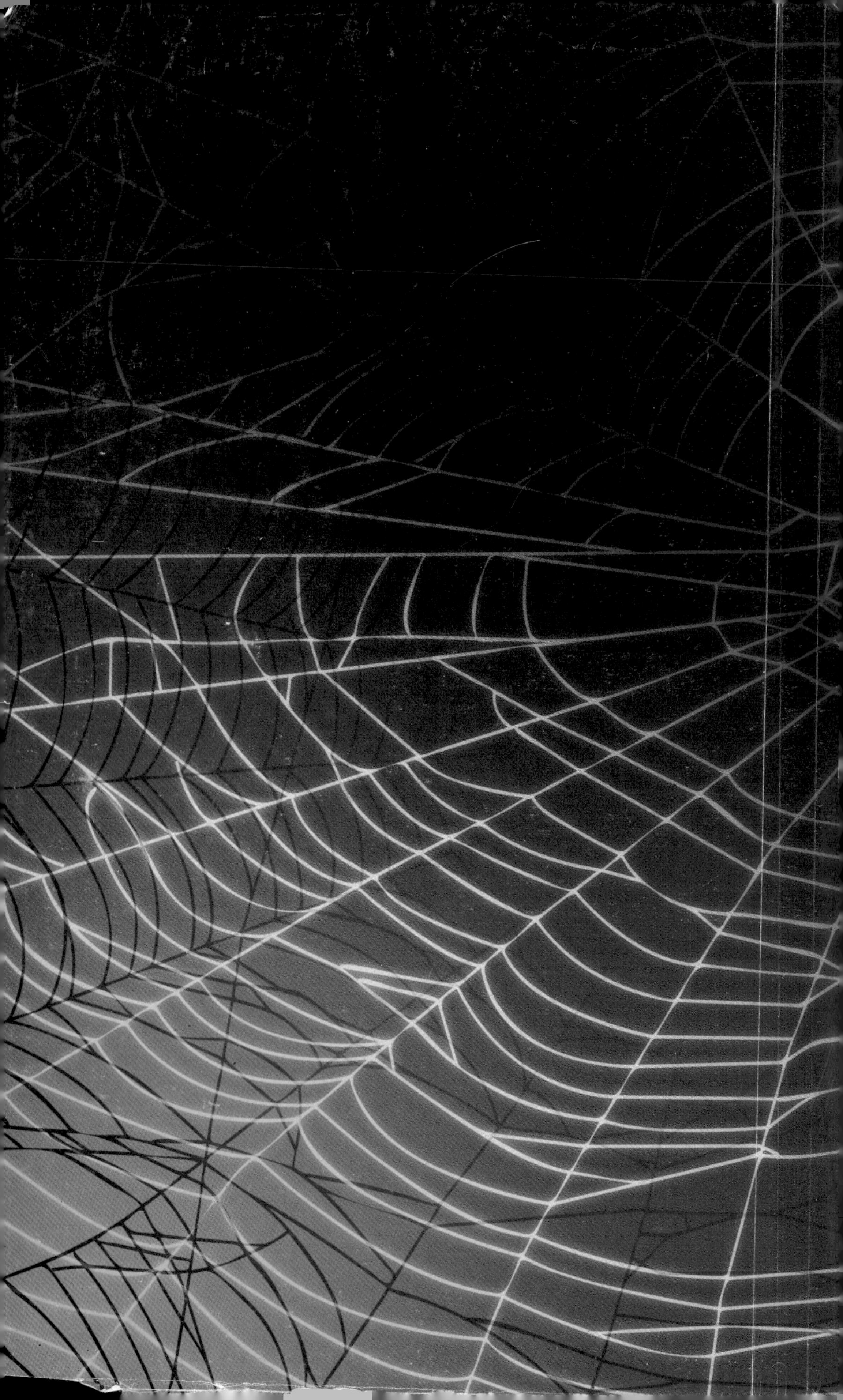